DYING AND GRIEVING

Life Span and Family Perspectives

Second Edition

Alicia Skinner Cook

Colorado State University

Kevin Ann Oltjenbruns

Colorado State University

Harcourt Brace College Publishers

Fort Worth   Philadelphia   San Diego   New York   Orlando   Austin   San Antonio
Toronto   Montreal   London   Sydney   Tokyo

Publisher	Earl McPeek
Acquisitions Editor	Carol Wada
Product Manager	Don Grainger
Production Manager	Linda McMillan
Art Director	Lora Gray

Cover image by Allen Rokach/Center for Nature Photography

ISBN: 0-15-501506-0
Library of Congress Catalog Card Number: 97-77278

Address for orders: Harcourt Brace & Company, 6277 Sea Harbor Drive, Orlando, FL 32887-6777; 1-800-782-4479.

Address for editorial correspondence: Harcourt Brace College Publishers, 301 Commerce Street, Suite 3700, Fort Worth, TX 76102.

Web site address:
http://www.hbcollege.com

Harcourt Brace College Publishers may provide complimentary instructional aids and supplements or supplement packages to those adopters qualified under our adoption policy. Please contact your sales representative for more information. If as an adopter or potential user you receive supplements you do not need, please return them to your sales representative or send them to: Attn: Returns Department, Troy Warehouse, 465 South Lincoln Drive, Troy, MO 63379.

Printed in the United States of America

8 9 0 1 2 3 4 5 6   039   9 8 7 6 5 4 3 2

To my beloved grandmother, Alice Lewis Brown, for
an abundance of treasured memories and for teaching me,
by example, how to nurture others.

—*Alicia Skinner Cook*

To family and friends—Dorothy Henry, Lynn Butler,
Fred Kapp, Jerry Keith, Myrtie Jane Kreutzer,
and Barb Oliver—your lives have left a legacy of joy;
your deaths have taught new insights.

—*Kevin Ann Oltjenbruns*

PREFACE

Death is a highly personal experience. It touches the core of our emotions as human beings. It brings us face-to-face with issues of life and living and leads us to question our values, beliefs, and priorities. Death as an imminent reality, death as the given destiny of all living things, and death as an abstraction all serve to bring critical questions to the forefront and help us define what is important in our lives. Confrontation with death on an emotional, intellectual, or physical level is often a process of growth.

Death is a family event. It occurs within the context of relationships and deep attachments. Families (as well as friends) experience significant transformations when their systems are affected by the loss of one of their members. Understanding this process enables us to more effectively help survivors avoid negative outcomes as they adapt to loss. By building on existing strengths and traditions, the bereaved can use their experiences with death to build closer bonds and enrich their lives.

The larger, societal context of death modifies the way it will be experienced by individuals and families. All societies have developed ways of interpreting and coping with death. Cultural attitudes and beliefs about death affect our personal views, expressions of grief, and rituals surrounding loss. In this second edition, we discuss this material from a perspective that acknowledges the important role of culture and ethnicity in all aspects of dying and grieving. The revised text examines recent developments in the field and identifies issues related to death, dying, and grief that our society will be grappling with in the future. Increased attention is given to sudden death in this new edition, with particular emphasis on homicide and suicide.

This text is firmly grounded in theory, strong in content, and thought provoking. We think that material of this nature must also address the reader's own reactions to the subject matter. We invite you to use this book to examine your own thoughts and feelings regarding various aspects of dying, death, and grief.

UNIQUENESS OF THE TEXT

Death is a natural part of life; individuals typically encounter death and loss as part of the human experience. Developmental theory suggests that the age at which an experience occurs is an important determinant of how it will be understood, adapted to, and resolved. This theory serves as a foundation and organizing framework for the text. An in-depth look at a variety of topics related to dying, death, and grief are provided as they pertain to particular developmental stages.

Individuals do not deal with death in isolation. Rather, they are influenced by the dynamic interactions with others in their family systems and social networks (composed of friends, neighbors, teachers, and others). These are, in turn, affected by larger systems, such as medical establishments, educational institutions, religious groups, human service organizations, legal systems, and the media. This systems approach is an additional unique feature of this text.

"Personal Accounts" follow each chapter. Each is written by an individual who demonstrates personal insights into grief and loss—the kind of knowledge that comes from facing death oneself, suffering the loss of a loved one, or confronting the personal issues of death in a professional role. While originally included as a way to supplement the scholarly material in the text and as a tool to remind students that we are talking about real people in real situations, the voices that are heard in these sections, in some sense, "say it all."

Learning aids are provided throughout the text to facilitate acquisition, understanding, and retention of the material. Chapter summaries and glossaries identify major points and important terms. Lists of suggested readings and related resources provide direction for those wanting to learn more about particular areas. Questions and activities at the end of each chapter provide an opportunity to probe further and ask deeper questions related to the subject matter. They also encourage students to explore their feelings, attitudes, and beliefs regarding a variety of topics and issues related to dying, death, and grief and provide an experiential component to the learning process.

An *instructor's manual* containing true-false, multiple-choice, short answer, and essay test questions is also available. The questions test the student's understanding of the material, while allowing for differences in instructor preferences in evaluation. A variety of other valuable teaching materials are also included in the instructor's manual. Discussion questions, suggestions for journal entries, and case study projects are provided with instructions for effective use. These materials have been pilot-tested in dying, death, and grief courses at Colorado State University and Kansas State University over the past decade and have been modified based on student feedback.

The text and auxiliary materials are appropriate for college and university courses on dying, death, and grief. Written from a multidisciplinary perspective, this text can be used effectively in programs in human development and family studies, psychology, social work, sociology, and other human service fields. Medical schools and nursing schools that emphasize the psychosocial aspects of caregiving will also find the book well suited to their students. The material in the text can be beneficial in other programs, such as pastoral counseling and mortuary science, that must prepare students for dealing with dying and death on an ongoing basis. In addition, professionals currently working in the field of thanatology will find the book to be a valuable resource and useful in staff development.

ACKNOWLEDGMENTS

Many individuals have given time, energy, expertise, and emotional support during the preparation of this manuscript. In addition to providing tangible and needed assistance, their unselfish contributions provided consistent reminders to us of the importance of writing this text. Their enthusiasm and commitment to the project helped sustain us through our years of hard work. Among those who provided invaluable assistance in the preparation of the manuscript were Ashley Harvey, Mindi Higgins, Rosemary Holland, Meiko Iwai, Brad Myers, and Trisha Oberacker. Their willingness to pilot-test materials, give constructive feedback, and ask critical questions has added a special energy to our work. We also thank reviewers involved at various stages of manuscript preparation who have provided the objectivity and expertise needed for refinement and expansion, and we thank the following individuals for their careful reading and helpful comments: David E. Balk, Kansas State University; Eileen Croke, California State University—Long Beach; Richard B. Ellis, Washburn University; Diana K. Larkin, South Puget Sound Community College; Darlene Martin, University of Texas Medical Branch—Galveston; Darlene McCown, University of Rochester; Cynthia Teel, University of Kansas; Patrick S. Williams, University of Houston; Robert Wren, University of Arizona; Paul Zelhart, East Texas State University. We also appreciate the assistance of the editors and staff at Harcourt Brace who patiently worked with us in this process. Further acknowledged are the individuals who have allowed us to include their personal accounts in our text. They have shared some of their most private thoughts and feelings with you. We truly commend their courage.

In closing, each of us as individual authors would like to sincerely thank the other for having made the task of writing this book not only a fulfilling one but an enjoyable one as well. Our friendship and mutual respect has grown as a result of this project. Most importantly, we would also like to sincerely thank our respective spouses, Graham Luckett and Ken Oltjenbruns, for their tremendous contributions to this effort. Their sacrifices, senses of humor, and support have been appreciated more than they know. We hope that they will share in our sense of pride and accomplishment with the completion of this second edition.

Alicia Skinner Cook
Kevin Ann Oltjenbruns

CONTENTS

Chapter 3
GRIEF AND LOSS

Chapter 4
THE BEREAVED FAMILY

Chapter 8
GRIEF AND LOSS DURING ADULTHOOD

PART I

Foundations of a Holistic
Developmental Model

1

Death and Grief in Contemporary Society

In this chapter, we shall look at the changing context of death in our society. Over the past century we have seen significant shifts in the primary causes of death and the settings in which most deaths occur. Further, with the advent of numerous technological advances, many people are living much longer than in past decades. These changes give rise to many bioethical and legal issues as we examine the quality of life in relation to the period of time lived.

CHANGES IN PRIMARY CAUSES OF DEATH

During the early 1900s, the majority of persons in the United States died of communicable diseases such as influenza, tuberculosis, diphtheria, and gastroenteritis. There has been a marked change over time, however, in the relative contribution of these infectious diseases to the mortality rates in this country. In 1900, the category of influenza and pneumonia was the leading cause of death; however, in 1995, it ranked sixth in the United States. Tuberculosis, gastroenteritis, and diphtheria were also primary causes (ranked in the top 10) in 1900; by the late 1960s, however, these three diseases collectively contributed to less than 1% of all deaths in the United States. Other communicable diseases brought under control during the 1900s include what had been common lethal diseases of childhood—whooping cough, scarlet fever, measles, and rheumatic fever. A number of factors contributed to limiting the fatal impact of these diseases:

- widespread immunization has essentially eradicated particular illnesses (such as smallpox);
- availability of better nutrition has minimized susceptibility to certain diseases;
- improved sanitation procedures have decreased the likelihood of rapid spread of many illnesses; and
- increased availability of "wonder drugs" such as penicillin have helped many survive what otherwise would have been a deadly illness.

Table 1.1 shows the leading causes of death in the United States in 1995.

While the devastation of many infectious diseases has been brought under control in most westernized countries, many people in developing countries still die from these diseases. The estimated number of deaths worldwide from leading infectious diseases in 1993 follows: acute respiratory infections under age 5 (4.1 million); tuberculosis (2.7 million); malaria (2.0 million); hepatitis B (900,000); measles (1 million); whooping cough (360,000) (World Health Organization, 1995).

Although we have brought communicable diseases under greater control in the United States, we have seen a significant increase in deaths due to violence. Also, in recent years, there has been an increase in the contribution of chronic degenerative diseases to the mortality rates; these diseases occur primarily in later life and are thought to be related to the aging process. Both of these types

TABLE 1.1

**Ten Leading Causes of Death for the Total
Population in the United States—1995**

RANK ALL AGES	CAUSE OF DEATH	NUMBER	RATE PER 100,000
	All causes	2,312,203	880.0
1	Diseases of heart	738,781	281.2
2	Malignant neoplasms, including neoplasms of lymphatic and hematopoietic tissues	537,969	204.7
3	Cerebrovascular diseases	158,061	60.2
4	Chronic obstructive pulmonary diseases and allied conditions	104,756	39.9
5	Accidents and adverse effects	89,703	34.1
	Motor vehicle accidents	41,786	15.9
	All other accidents and adverse effects	47,916	18.2
6	Pneumonia and influenza	83,528	31.8
7	Diabetes mellitus	59,085	22.5
8	Human immunodeficiency virus infection	42,506	16.2
9	Suicide	30,893	11.8
10	Chronic liver disease and cirrhosis	24,848	9.5
	All other causes (Residual)	442,073	168.2

SOURCE: National Center for Health Statistics (1996). *Monthly Vital Statistics Report.* Washington, DC: U.S. Department of Health and Human Services.

of deaths will be addressed in more detail later in this chapter. To illustrate shifts over time in causality, Table 1.2 identifies the five leading causes of death in 1900, in 1987, and in 1995.

Impact of AIDS

Throughout the entire world, one communicable disease has had devastating consequences during the last two decades due to its rapid spread across populations. What was at one time believed to be an illness limited to people engaging in certain "high-risk behaviors," AIDS is now spreading rapidly through all sectors of society. "A single viral threat had imposed itself on nations at very different levels of economic development; with very different political systems, cultural backgrounds, and attitudes toward sexuality, drug use, and privacy; and with very different conceptions of the role of the state in protecting public health" (Bayer & Kirp, 1992, p. 1). It would be difficult to find individuals who, at this time, do not know either someone who has died of AIDS or someone grieving the loss of a loved one due to this illness.

TABLE 1.2

The Five Leading Causes of Death in the United States—1900, 1987, 1995

CAUSE OF DEATH	RANK AS LEADING CAUSE OF DEATH		
	1900*	1987**	1995***
Influenza and pneumonia	1	5	
Tuberculosis	2		
Gastroenteritis	3		
Diseases of the heart	4	1	1
Vascular lesions affecting central nervous system	5		
All accidents			5
Malignant neoplasms (cancer)		2	2
Cerebrovascular disease		3	3
Chronic obstructive pulmonary diseases		4	4

*SOURCE: National Center for Health Statistics (1983). *Monthly Vital Statistics Report.* Washington, DC: U.S. Department of Health and Human Services.

**SOURCE: National Center for Health Statistics (1987). *Monthly Vital Statistics Report.* Washington, DC: U.S. Department of Health and Human Services.

***SOURCE: Rosenberg, H. M. National Center for Health Statistics (1996). *Births and Deaths: U.S. Monthly Vital Statistics Report, 42*(3). Washington, DC: U.S. Department of Health and Human Services.

While this disease was essentially unknown prior to the early 1980s, AIDS is now pandemic worldwide. The first cases of AIDS were reported by the Centers for Disease Control in the United States in mid-1981 (Bayer & Kirp, 1992); it is now the eighth leading contributor to the death rate in the United States (National Center for Health Statistics, 1995). The World Health Organization has estimated that by the end of 1994, 18 million adults globally were infected with HIV and that by the year 2000, 5 million children will be infected (The World Resources Institute, 1996). Another expected outcome is that 5 to 10 million children worldwide will lose a parent to AIDS by the year 2000 (The NAMES Project, 1997).

By early 1997, the Centers for Disease Control reported that, while AIDS deaths in the United States had fallen from 24,900 in the first half of 1995 to 22,000 in the first half of 1996, there were more people living with the HIV virus than ever before. Researchers believe that the decline might be, at least partially, attributable to the availability of new drugs and the fact that people with AIDS now live longer than they had previously.

There is considerable differential in terms of the geographic regions that have the highest number of HIV infections per year (Mann, Tarantola, & Netter, 1992). This variation is summarized in Figure 1.1.

FIGURE 1.1

Estimate of HIV Infections in Adults by Geographic Region, January, 1992

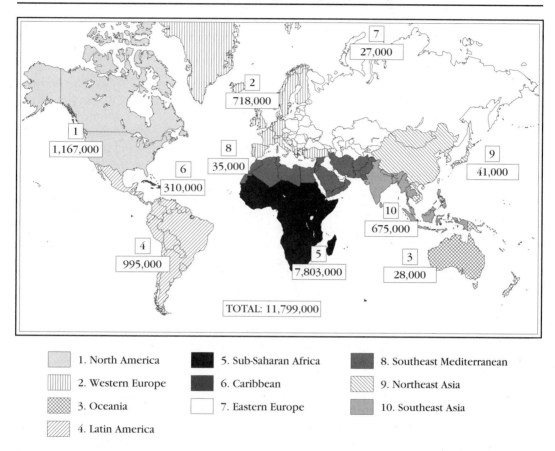

SOURCE: Mann, Tarantola, and Netter (1992).

Issues related to death by AIDS are varied and complicated, and circumstances surrounding these deaths have changed over the past decade. For example, in the United States the HIV virus was once thought to be restricted to intravenous drug users and gay individuals; however, the most rapid growth in the incidence of AIDS has been in the heterosexual population. While the epidemic began primarily with those in the middle-adult age groups, the incidence among individuals between birth and young adulthood is escalating rapidly. There is a growing concern about the number of infants and young children with pediatric AIDS and with the perinatal transmission of AIDS (DiClemente & Peterson, 1994). AIDS is a cause of death in all races, all socioeconomic groups, and for both men and women. Even with the spread of the epidemic, each year brings new hope with regard to medical treatments for AIDS; currently, however, there is no definitive cure.

Increase in Violent Deaths

During various periods of history, the primary cause of death, as noted earlier, has changed. Humankind has demonstrated a long history of violence; war has claimed many lives throughout the millennia. There is a growing trend in the number of people killing individuals in their streets, homes, schools or workplaces. To many, the name "Oklahoma City" now conjures up the pain and anguish caused by the death of 168 people killed by a bomb explosion in a federal office building within that city. Dunblane, Scotland, brings to mind powerful images of 16 kindergartners and their teacher killed by a gunman who then committed suicide. The expression "drive-by shooting" has become common in American news reports in recent years as gang members and others cruise our streets with guns. Worldwide, thousands die each year as family members and acquaintances kill one another. In many countries, homicide has become a significant contributor to the overall death rate. Actual propensity toward violence varies from country to country; but, regardless of the actual number of deaths due to murder or deliberate acts of terrorism, violence has impacted countless individuals of all ages. The potential for violence affects how we feel in our own environments and many people simply no longer feel safe.

Change in the Arena of Death

Prior to the early 1900s, almost all people in the United States died in their own homes. Medical facilities as we know them were essentially nonexistent. If a person was dying, the doctor (when one was available) went to the individual's home. Care depended on unsophisticated implements and utilized relatively few pharmaceutical agents. As medicine has become increasingly dependent on technologies that are essentially nontransportable, the very sick and the dying have moved into hospitals, in order to take advantage of medical advances (e.g., kidney dialysis machines and respirators). Doctors are no longer able to provide the same level of care in an individual's own home. By 1949, 49.5% of all deaths in the United States occurred in an institution. By 1958, that percentage had increased to 60.9. Currently, it is estimated that approximately 85% of deaths in the United States occur in hospitals; frequently these take place within hours of arrival (Vladeck, 1995).

As the arena of death has shifted for the greater part of the population—from home to institution—family members and friends have had fewer opportunities to interact with the dying. There is good reason to believe that this shift made a major contribution to society's discomfort in interacting with the dying and the resultant withdrawal or avoidance patterns.

CURRENT BIOETHICAL AND LEGAL ISSUES

As noted earlier, there has been an increase in the number of people dying of chronic degenerative diseases. Because of advancements in health care, nutrition, and sanitation, individuals are living longer than ever before. These added years, however, do not guarantee optimum quality of life. The elderly are more likely today than in the past to have chronic illnesses or conditions (e.g., the aftereffects of a major stroke) that leave them severely incapacitated. In the past, they would have been much more likely to die a swift, sudden death; today, modern technology allows these elderly individuals to survive for what may be a period of many years. For some of these individuals, the circumstances of their existence can be considered a "living death" (Smith, 1985). Further, Frederick (1994, p. 60) stresses that

> As medical technology advances, the propensity for human life to be extended in the face of incurable, painful, and ultimately terminal diseases increases proportionately. A wasting illness, terminal in a matter of weeks, could potentially be "treatable" in the sense of prolonging the inexorable arrival of death, lengthening the suffering and pain of an individual and his/her family to a period of months or years.

These developments have raised a number of bioethical and legal issues. They have also stimulated vigorous discussion over the belief in a right to die with dignity, the signing of **living wills** or other types of advanced directives that communicate one's wishes regarding the use of extraordinary measures to prolong life, and growing social and legal support for physician-assisted suicide.

Death With Dignity/Quality of Life

Medical technology has increasingly become a double-edged sword. There is no question that improvements in medical care have contributed to a greatly lengthened lifespan for the general population. There comes a time when death would be inevitable were it not for the dependence on life-support mechanisms. With the advent of many technological advances, however, concern arises as to whether we should sustain biological existence without ensuring that the extended life is of a high quality.

Loss of one's humanity to the dictates of modern technology can negate the opportunity to die with dignity.

> We must assure that technology's tremendous benefits do not prolong life at the expense of personhood and individuality. We must give serious attention to the ethical and moral problems associated with the unthinking treatment of people without due consideration to the consequences. We must somehow untie the emotional, legal, and ethical knots that bind us down and keep us from a fresh, vigorous rethinking of the dilemmas of modern medicine and modern dying. We must also reconsider routines, policies, procedures, and attitudes based on matters of mere efficiency and technological convenience and reinstitute those humane and human ceremonies, attitudes, and concerns that permit people to retain their dignity and sense of personal worth even during the process of dying. (Thompson, 1984, p. 229)

Advances in technology and medical care create difficult dilemmas that take on important dimensions as we care for individuals who are dying. Our goal is certainly to encourage "death with dignity." A variety of conditions can contribute to death with dignity—a sense of control, hope, individuality, and self-worth. Compatibility between one's own desires surrounding the process of death and the reality of the situation contributes to a sense of dignity (Martocchio, 1986). If medical technology provides opportunity to extend life but diminishes self-worth, the value and/or appropriateness of this increased technology naturally is questioned. Some choose to forego particular types of care, in order to better insure a sense of dignity. Lester and Leenars (1996) discuss various alternatives in relation to complex medical, ethical, and legal issues. Many of these topics have received much coverage in recent years, in both the popular and professional press:

- **Refusal of life-extending medical treatment,** whereby the patient declines to undergo certain procedures. Most states in the United States support such decisions and they are legalized through various right-to-die laws that protect physicians when they carry out patients' wishes, as expressed in their living wills or other advanced directives.
- **Withdrawal of life-sustaining treatment** for people already regarded as dead, in that they have lost all higher brain function. Significant issues arise in such cases; for example, who should decide and when should the decision be made for treatment to be withdrawn. Legislation supporting durable power of attorney has tried to address these issues.
- **Active euthanasia** means an easy or good death caused by an intervention (e.g., a drug overdose), in contrast to the withdrawal or withholding of treatment.
- **Physician-assisted suicide** refers to physicians helping to provide the means for individuals' to take their own lives. "Assisted suicide is the deliberate and knowing provision of information, the means, and/or help to another person for an act of suicide" (Committee on Physician-Assisted Suicide and Euthanasia, American Association of Suicidology, 1996, p. 9). Although physician-assisted suicide is illegal in the United States, physicians, at times, do assist quietly and privately. In the Netherlands, physician-assisted suicide is openly practiced and the Dutch parliament has passed public-policy guidelines that legalize this process (Battin, 1991; Markson, 1995).

Issues related to these measures are complex and multifaceted. A few of these issues are summarized here to illustrate the many and varied concerns in this arena. Recall that the U.S. government protects the "right to life, liberty and pursuit of happiness." As people struggle with the various medical dilemmas that they face, key issues debated relate to which is the more important legal "right"—the right to life or the right to individual liberty—which, in turn, implies a right to die. This legally oriented discussion is different than that based in religious beliefs. Many individuals' religious perspectives leave little or no room for personal decisions to be made in relation to either active euthanasia or physician-assisted suicide, for they believe that God is the only one to determine the appropriate time for a person to die. Some with strong religious beliefs can and do, however, choose either to refuse or withdraw life-extending treatments.

Medical and hospice personnel who have received training in palliative care measures believe that most dying people can be made more comfortable through various pain management strategies. With diminished pain, many individuals can at some level reengage in activities and relationships that provide an enhanced quality of life. Some individuals who have studied the implications of legalizing physician-assisted suicide are concerned that medical cost containment restrictions of some managed health-care organizations would exert pressure (either real or perceived) to terminate the lives of individuals approaching death.

Advanced Directives / Living Wills

Many in our society are raising questions like the following: Is artificially supported life really "life"? What constitutes "quality of life"? Who defines it? These important ethical issues will continue to be in the forefront of discussions for years to come as we grapple with difficult life and death dilemmas. Many individuals hope to define the type of treatment or measures they would like used in their behalf. For example, numerous individuals have concluded that extraordinary medical measures disallow what they personally define as death with dignity. In the United States, patients have the legal right to refuse treatment. Congress enacted the Patient Self-Determination Act in 1991 in order to protect this right and to establish legal standing for advance directives. This act requires that the patient be informed about living wills and the durable power of attorney for health care. Patients use these documents to inform their doctors about their desires regarding life support as death approaches and regarding the individual they wish to empower to make decisions for them if they become incompetent or unconscious (Phipps, Cooper, & Greenstein, 1993; Vandecreek & Frankowski, 1996).

A significant number of individuals have communicated their desire that measures to prolong their lives not be taken when there is no reasonable expectation of recovery. Many have expressed their wishes by signing a living will (a sample is found in Figure 1.2). Individuals may choose to sign a living will for many reasons, including the following (Bok, 1976):

- to allow an individual to retain some control over what happens at the end of his or her life, even if he or she is then no longer competent to make personal choices or to see that they are carried out;
- to enable individuals to make choices for terminal care while they are still healthy and at a time when there is no doubt of their mental competence; and
- to alleviate some of the guilt and anxiety on the part of relatives and health professionals who will later attempt to determine what type of life-supporting measures are appropriate.

FIGURE 1.2
Example of a Living Will

To my family, my physician, my lawyer, my clergy
To any medical facility in whose care I happen to be
To any individual who may become responsible for my health, welfare or affairs

Death is as much a reality as birth, growth, maturity and old age—it is the one certainty of life. If the time comes when I, _____, can no longer take part in decisions for my own future, let this statement stand as an expression of my wishes while I am still of sound mind.

If the situation should arise in which there is no reasonable expectation of my recovery from physical or mental disability, I request that I be allowed to die and not be kept alive by artificial means or "heroic measure." I do not fear death itself as much as the indignities of deterioration, dependence, and hopeless pain. I therefore ask that medication be mercifully administered to me to alleviate suffering even though this may hasten the moment of death.

This request is made after careful consideration. I hope you who care for me will feel morally bound to follow its mandate. I recognize that this appears to place a heavy responsibility upon you, but it is with the intention of relieving you of such responsibility and of placing it upon myself in accordance with my strong convictions that this statement is made.

Signed _____

Date _____

Witness _____   Witness _____

Copies of this request have have been given to_____

_____

SOURCE: Choice in Dying, 200 Varick Street, New York, NY 10014.

In 1977, California became the first state to pass legislation to protect physicians from legal action if they comply with their patients' desires expressed in a living will. By 1993, only three states in the United States had no statutory provision providing support for some type of living will (Leiter, 1993). While many individuals do sign such a document, many people do not. Vandecreek and Frankowski (1996) summarize a number of reasons why many individuals, even though they may believe in the value of a living will, do not have one:

- they do not know how they would respond to the threat of death until that time comes;
- they do not think of their own impending death very much;

- other concerns in life prevent them from considering how they want their last days managed;
- they believe their doctors would not follow their wishes even if they had signed a living will;
- they believe they might change their minds about how they want their care managed once death approaches; and
- they believe they will live much longer, therefore there is no pressing need to complete a living will.

Physician-Assisted Suicide

In recent years, there has been much public attention given to what is termed *physician-assisted suicide.* Although this has likely been practiced throughout history, it is only in the last decade or so that much public attention has been given and debate fostered. The individual most responsible for bringing the topic of physician-assisted suicide to the forefront of numerous ethical and legal discussions in the United States is Dr. Jack Kevorkian, who, as a retired pathologist, first assisted in the suicide of a woman with Alzheimer's disease. Kevorkian inserted a needle in the patient's arm; she then activated the flow of the drugs that caused her own death. Since that first incident, Kevorkian has played an active role in numerous other suicides and has been brought to trial for a number of them. As of late 1997, he had yet to be convicted.

Another case that received much attention is that of Dr. Timothy Quill, who, in a letter to the *New England Journal of Medicine,* explained his role in helping one of his patients commit suicide. Although he was not present at her death, he had prescribed the barbiturates needed and explained the dosage required to kill herself (Young, 1992). Both of these cases brought much focus to the issue of physician-assisted suicide; they helped to launch a loud and lengthy public discussion.

The debate about physician-assisted suicide has its philosophical roots in the "rational suicide" controversy (discussed in more depth in chapter 9), which centers around whether "suicide is ever a defensible choice, particularly for the terminally ill" (Lester & Leenars, 1996, p. 163). K. A. Marshall (1980) suggested that there are circumstances under which dying is "legitimized." He proposed that death can legitimately be preferred to life when a person

- is unable to be active;
- is unable to be useful;
- becomes a burden on others because of physical or social dependency;
- loses mental abilities; or
- has progressively deteriorating physical health and associated physical discomfort.

J. Werth (1995) found that people with AIDS have a higher suicide rate than members of the general population. Given the difficulties faced by many of these individuals (e.g., cancer, pneumonia, neurological impairment, dementia, social stigma, and isolation), a number in our society believe that individuals with AIDS who choose to commit suicide may be acting in a rational manner. Yet, a question remains: "Does the stigma and isolation faced by many who suffer from AIDS magnify their desire to kill themselves?"

Going beyond those who experience AIDS, many people believe that a variety of individuals act rationally if they choose to commit suicide. For example, some would argue that having any painful and debilitating terminal illness legitimizes the act of suicide (Deluty, 1989). Others, however, strenuously disagree with that conclusion and instead argue that it is the physician's obligation to make these individuals more comfortable by providing relief from both physical and psychological pain (Saunders, 1995). As noted in the *Drake Law Review* (Hoehne, 1993, p. 238),

> The American Medical Association in a Statement of the Council on Ethical and Judicial Affairs has adopted a position in opposition to physician-assisted suicide, stating "for humane reasons, with informed consent, a physician may do what is medically necessary to alleviate severe pain, or *cease or omit* treatment to permit a *terminally* ill patient, whose death is imminent, to die. *However, he should not intentionally cause death.*"

With regard to the dilemma of physicians in such situations, Carson (1979) noted:

> Upon entering their profession, physicians assume a dual obligation: to prolong life and to ease suffering. When these obligations conflict, as they commonly do near the end of a patient's life, physicians must often choose between extending a life while increasing suffering and assuaging suffering at the risk of hastening death by, for example, increasing pain medications to near lethal levels. (p. 365)

In 1990, the National Hospice Organization (NHO) also adopted a resolution against voluntary euthanasia and assisted suicide.

In 1997, the U.S. Supreme Court ruled that there is no constitutional right to assisted suicide. This ruling allows states the right to determine whether that particular locale will ban physician-assisted suicide; many states currently have laws that outlaw one person helping another to commit suicide.

An individual's religious beliefs and personal system of values influence his or her view regarding the legitimacy of preferring death over life in certain circumstances, and criteria used for judging quality of life vary somewhat. Societal and cultural values have a strong influence as well (Kalish, 1985). For example, many North Americans value autonomy, independence, competence, activity, health, and growth. When these are not present, many individuals interpret quality of life as greatly diminished and some would desire to hasten death.

The decisions related to preserving life become more difficult as the definition of "living" becomes more complex. The following are but a few of the bioethical issues that modern society faces today:

- Is it imperative that families take advantage of available technology— technology that may sustain life but does not guarantee its quality?

- Who has the right to determine which is ultimately more important—the quality of life or length of life?
- Who is financially responsible for the extremely high cost of using modern medical interventions?
- Should physicians who assist in suicide be prosecuted in courts of law for their actions?

As medical technologies develop, we must deal with the various dilemmas that often go hand-in-hand with our ever-expanding opportunities.

THE NEXT CENTURY: EMERGING ISSUES

As we enter a new century, technology will occupy center stage as it continues to transform our lives in anticipated and unanticipated ways. These changes will occur in an increasingly diverse social climate, in which different cultural and ethnic groups are impacted in different ways by technological advancements. Professionals in the field of **thanatology** (the study of death, dying, and grief) will be faced with new opportunities as well as ethical dilemmas as they provide quality care to the dying and grieving. Research will need to evolve to enhance our understanding of the increasing complexity of death and grief in contemporary society.

Impact of Technology

While our discussion of technology earlier in this chapter focused on quality of life issues, new technological and scientific advancements go far beyond this focus and have implications for a wide variety of areas related to death, dying, and grief. A few of these are addressed in the following sections.

Medical Diagnosis and Innovative Treatment.   New advances in medicine raise important ethical questions related to appropriate limits of intervention efforts. The following examples raise issues related to the questions "When, and under what conditions (if any) should these procedures be performed?" and "Who should have the responsibility for making the decision?"

- In 1990, a Los Angeles couple purposely conceived a baby to serve as a bone-marrow donor for a 17-year-old sibling who had leukemia.
- After years of research, physicians believe that many incurable conditions, ranging from congenital heart defects to degenerative nerve diseases, can be effectively treated through transplanting organs and tissues from aborted fetuses and anencephalic newborns.
- Organ transplants are becoming increasingly prevalent. With a limited supply from human donors, researchers attempted the first transplant of a baboon heart to a human patient in the mid 1990s.
- Advances in genetic engineering now permit surgeons to perform lifesaving surgeries on fetuses while still in their mothers' wombs.

ORGAN TRANSPLANTS: INCREASING ACCESS

While creating numerous ethical dilemmas, advances in technology have also resulted in advances in life-saving techniques and procedures. For example, over the last few decades, the development of improved surgical techniques and anti-rejection drugs have significantly advanced the science of transplantation and improved survival rates. In the United States, the number of transplants rose from 12,786 in 1988 to 20,109 in 1995. Through the provisions of the Uniform Anatomical Gift Act, first approved in 1968 and revised in 1987, organ donation has been simplified; however, the demand continues to rise faster than the availability of organs. While the overwhelming majority of Americans say they would be willing to make an organ or tissue donation, only a small percentage of the adult population actually carry donor cards (Robbins, 1990).

With the shortage of available organs, who decides which persons will receive them and who pays the associated cost of such expensive procedures? Certain organs may be less accessible to some ethnic minority individuals due to immunological differences between racial groups. However, the number of minority donors has currently risen to its highest level, and they now account for 23% of all donated organs according to the United Network for Organ Sharing (1996). This organization, located in Richmond, Virginia, was congressionally established by the National Organ Transplant Act in 1984 to assist in matching donor organs with potential recipients, to provide for fairness in distribution, and to ensure competence of medical centers where organ transplants are performed.

In an attempt to increase the number of organ donations in the United States, Congress is considering requiring that tax refunds from the Internal Revenue Service be accompanied by a note promoting organ donation and a detachable donor card. The provision was inserted into proposed tax legislation by Senator Bill Frist from Tennessee, a heart and lung surgeon. Because of the thousands who die each year while waiting for a transplant, some are even suggesting that legislation be passed in the United States permitting the removal of cadaver organs unless the deceased carries a "nondonor" card (or another documented form of opposition to the transplant) or if the next of kin objects. This type of "presumed consent" already exists in a number of other countries such as Belgium and Singapore (Roels et al., 1990; Teo, 1991), but little public support for this type of policy exists in the United States.

SOURCE: D. J. Klenow and G. A. Youngs, Jr. (1995). An empirical exploration of selected policy options in organ donation. *Death Studies, 19*(6), 543–557.

Psychosocial Support and Information.   With entry into the twenty-first century, our access to information and communication options has never been greater. Through the use of computer technology, sources of social support have been expanded and the potential for enhanced networking exists (Sofka, 1997).

- On-line discussion groups for those dealing with particular illnesses (such as cancer) give the participants anonymity and provide a supportive group for individuals living in isolated geographical areas with limited services.
- GriefNet was started in 1994 as a free access on-line referral and support network. It provides comprehensive resource listings and a set of electronic mailing lists where subscribers may discuss specific grief- and loss-related topics.

Education and Training.   Instructional innovations have taken place in a wide variety of arenas in an effort to provide more up-to-date, relevant information to practitioners and students.

- Physicians in geographically isolated areas use computer links to major medical centers to aid in the diagnosis of serious illnesses. This innovation diminishes many limitations of geography when it is necessary to access certain diagnostic resources.
- The National Library of Medicine funded the Visible Human Project, in which scientists produce an extensive series of anatomical images that can be stored in computers and distributed over the Internet (Wheeler, 1996). The smallest of details can be manipulated by artists, medical students, and radiologists in an effort to better understand the human body.
- Computer-aided instructional modules (e.g., "Death: A Personal Encounter") are used in nursing programs to develop personal self-awareness related to death and dying (Lambrecht, 1990).
- A variety of organizations and governmental agencies have established homepages on the World Wide Web to provide quick and easy access to information on topics related to death, dying, and grief.

In all of these examples, technological innovations have been applied to meet human needs. Historian Edward Tenner (1996) warns us, however, that technological advances often have both intended and unintended consequences. While providing solutions to specific problems, technology can create new, sometimes unanticipated, concerns.

For example, one on-line chat room included the following interchange:

One evening: Last night my best friend committed suicide. We met at therapy groups and he was the only one who kept me alive. We kept each other alive. Every time suicide crossed my mind he made me understand why I should live, as I did him. But last night he never called me. He never came to my house. He went to the beach and hurled himself into the water. Now I have no one to keep me alive. I feel like it's all my fault . . . My soul is dead . . . now what do I do? —B.

Next evening: I'm very concerned about how you are feeling . . . I can't imagine how you feel, but please tell me, B., please know this, it was not your fault. . . . It sounds like you were a good friend in helping him . . . Please, do whatever you have to, keep yourself moving forward. Talk to anyone who will listen . . . B., I care very much about you, please keep in touch. PLEASE!! . . . Take care and God Bless. —R.

EXAMPLES OF WORLD WIDE WEB SITES RELATED TO DEATH, DYING, AND GRIEF

Mediated Interpersonal Communication

http://rivendell.org
A general discussion list for any topic related to death, dying, bereavement, and other major losses. Sponsored by Rivendell Resources, it is referred to as "grief chat." Individuals simply follow the directions posted at this site to join the chat group.

Expressive Sites

http://www.cnn.com/US/OKC/memorial/
An Internet sympathy card "In memoriam" was created at this site by CNN for victims and survivors of the Oklahoma City bombing.

Narrative Sites

http://www.rights.org/~deathnet/ HELP_AUSTIN.html
This site documents the struggle of Austin Bastable, a Canadian who fought to legalize physician-assisted suicide until his death by assisted suicide on May 6, 1996. Sponsor-

ship of this site by the Right to Die Society of Canada incorporates an advocacy component, sensitizing readers to the legal and policy-oriented issues involved in this individual's experience.

Commemorative Sites

http://www.aidsquilt.org/
The AIDS Memorial Quilt Web site contains examples of quilts that have been dedicated to those individuals who have died from AIDS.

Information and Referral

http://www.nho.org/
National Hospice Organization's Web site.
http://www.aoa.dhhs.gov/naic
National Aging Information Center provides government information on aging.
http://cancernet.nci.nih.gov/
The National Cancer Institute's CancerNet.
http://www.katsden.com/death/index.html
WEBster's Death, Dying, and Grief site—includes a variety of resources related to dying and grieving.

Note: Because of the nature of this medium, Web sites are continuously added, updated, and deleted. Search mechanisms are available for users to access the most current sites related to death, dying, grief, and illness.

SOURCE: Adapted from C. Sofka (1997). Social support "Internetworks," caskets for sale, and much, much more: Thanatology and the information superhighway. *Death Studies, 21*(6), 553–574.

> *Three weeks later:* I am very sorry to inform all of you that my daughter, B., committed suicide last Monday. Her service will be held on (date), so please use that day to mourn her death. —S.

There might be many concerns related to such an anonymous interchange. For example, how does R. feel when discovering that B. has killed herself and what is the impact on R. who had clearly tried to help? What feelings and thoughts arise among those who had entered the chat room but had not engaged in conversation with B. when she was sharing her sense of aloneness after her best friend's death? What impact might this message from B.'s father about her suicide have on others who are considering suicide—others who are not seeking assistance from those around them? Did any who had interacted with B. earlier via this medium feel responsible for the outcome? Those who invented computer technology or designed the Internet could not have possibly considered such outcomes.

As individuals interface with various Web sites, it is important to know that, while many are monitored by professionals, many are not—therefore one has to be cautious about information given or advice shared. It may or may not be accurate or helpful. Further, while communication provided through a chat room can provide a type of informal support, individuals should not forego professional assistance if needed.

Developing a Future Research Agenda

Future research efforts will be intricately linked to technological and social developments as they continue to change and evolve over time. Before we can define a future research agenda, past developments must be considered. As previously discussed, death had become a stranger to most North Americans by the mid-1900s as infant mortality rates declined, the average lifespan increased, and dying individuals were increasingly cared for in institutions (e.g., hospitals, nursing homes) rather than at home. We had in fact become a death-denying society. Largely as a result of her best-selling book *On Death and Dying* in 1969, Dr. Elisabeth Kübler-Ross made a major contribution to weakening the taboo against discussing and acknowledging death. This Swiss-born psychiatrist challenged medical schools, and society as a whole, to begin addressing the needs of the dying and grieving at a time when the topic of death and dying was rarely mentioned in professional training programs.

As an outgrowth of this shifting attitude, and as a result of the work of Kübler-Ross and others, increased numbers of articles addressing death-related issues started appearing in the literature. In a 1974 editorial in the *Journal of American Medical Association* entitled "Dying Is Worked to Death" (Vaisrub, 1974), the author questioned the utility and value of the burgeoning literature on death and noted "we are now witnessing an extraordinary influx of essays, editorials, even books and specialized journals, on the subject of death and dying" (p. 1909). Many, then, referred to this publication phenomenon as a "fad" and a "bandwagon." Fortunately, our society moved toward a greater openness related to dying and grieving; now, more than 30 years later, the trend continues. Thousands of books and scholarly articles have been published on topics related to death, dying, and grief. In fact, much of the information in this text is derived from the theoretical and empirical work done in universities and professional schools during this time frame.

As we enter a new century, it is important to reflect on the current status of thanatological research. What questions still remain unanswered? What topics have received limited attention? What new areas of investigation are emerging?

T. A. Rando (1992) has noted that research in the field has not yet involved sufficient longitudinal study; she also believes that we have put too much focus on certain populations (e.g., widows) and essentially ignored others who may be at risk for complicated mourning. For example, despite the dramatic increase in homicide among youth in the United States, relatively little attention has been given to the survivors of murder victims. Richters (1993) points out in his article "Community Violence and Children's Development: Toward a Research Agenda in the 1990s" that few studies have examined the psychological consequences to individuals and families of living in chronically life-threatening environments. He observes that we are largely "left with little beyond police statistics and newspaper reports" (p. 4) and stresses that there is an urgent need for intensive community-based research.

Increasingly, thanatological research has explored loss in terms of the social and cultural context of survivors. This translates into considerations of family variables, age, and ethnicity of those who participate in bereavement studies. Especially notable, however, is the lack of research on different family structures experiencing loss. As divorce and remarriage rates have increased, families have become increasingly complex; yet most of the family-focused bereavement research has not addressed this complexity in investigations of how families cope with death. Nor have the studies sufficiently accounted for the ways in which cultural variables are intricately linked with factors such as resilience, social support, and acceptance of death.

Several scholars have mentioned the need for bereavement studies of groups with special needs. For example, there has been little effort thus far to understand grief experiences among individuals with developmental disabilities (Harper & Wadsworth, 1993). Demographic changes are producing another understudied group with unique needs—older individuals over the age of 85, the segment of the older population currently experiencing the greatest increase in its numbers. Stroebe, Hansson, and Stroebe (1993) note that these individuals are likely to be frailer than the average widower of today; thus they may have lowered ability to manage finances, maintain social networks, and live independently. Their adult children, if still alive, will be aged themselves and the insights gained from earlier studies of widowhood will not be generalizable in these situations.

As we look toward another decade of thanatological research, Cook and Balk (1995) remind researchers that they must not lose sight of ethical concerns in their quest to better understand the grief process and offer more effective ways to provide supportive services. In a special issue of *Death Studies* on "Ethics and Bereavement Research," these authors and a number of other investigators identified unique aspects of bereavement research (as compared to other social/behavioral research projects) and provided ethical guidelines and considerations for both quantitative and qualitative studies. However, as illustrated in the earlier part of this chapter, many pressing questions in the field cannot be answered by research. These involve complex issues whose answers are based on spiritual beliefs and ethical values, and responses to these issues will vary from person to person and from culture to culture.

Multicultural Environments

All societal changes must be considered in the context of cultural norms and values. Because the United States and Canada have traditionally been predominately white in race and Christian in religion, the training of professional personnel working with the dying and bereaved has been primarily grounded in beliefs regarding life and death, particular rituals, patterns of emotional response, and attitudes reflective of the dominant culture (Irish, 1993). Due to demographic and immigration patterns, the face of many societies has been dramatically altered in the later years of the twentieth century. In particular, the United States truly has become a multicultural and multiethnic society. Societal changes have brought about new challenges as we attempt to understand the many ethnic and cultural variations related to death, dying, and grief. If practitioners are to respond in ways that are helpful to individuals and families, then they must be sensitive to the uniqueness of individuals and range of variations among those they serve.

In today's society, understanding various aspects of diversity is basic to professional competence. This understanding is fostered in professional training programs that recognize the value of multicultural education. Increasingly, leaders in a variety of professional fields are highlighting the importance of developing "cultural competence" as a part of one's array of professional skills and knowledge base (Cook & Dworkin, 1992; London & DeVore, 1988; Parry, 1990; Parry & Ryan, 1995). Yet, according to the American Academy of Nursing's expert panel on Cultural Competence in Nursing Education (1992):

> In the 1990s, slightly less than 25% of the U.S. schools of nursing offer a substantive cross-cultural nursing course in their undergraduate program; only 8% of the master's students have a graduate course on this subject; and less than 2% of nursing students enrolled in doctoral programs in nursing have a full semester focused on cross-cultural nursing. . . . (pp. 32–33)

Much has been written recently on the topic of multicultural education. According to James Banks (1994), "one important characteristic of multicultural education is to help students understand the nation and world from diverse ethnic and cultural perspectives." In the multicultural classroom, students hear numerous voices and varied perspectives (p. 82). Throughout this text, we shall introduce the reader to diverse perspectives as we explore the many issues related to dying and grieving in contemporary society.

THE EFFECTS OF VALUES AND CULTURE ON LIFE-SUPPORT DECISIONS

Issues of life support should always be discussed in a culturally sensitive way. Although professionals are cautioned never to assume that patients and their families may respond in a particular way because of their ethnic backgrounds, understanding the diversity of beliefs around life-and-death issues can help avoid poor communication due to conflicting value systems and life experiences. The following table shows strong ethnic differences in a study conducted with low-income patients in a county health facility in Los Angeles. Participants were given clinical scenarios and asked if they would stop life support in the particular situation described. The responses reflect the different cultural lens through which medical decisions are viewed.

ETHNIC GROUP (N)	PERCENTAGE WHO WOULD STOP LIFE SUPPORT
U.S. born, Anglo (43)	71%
Chinese Americans (17)	65%
Mexican Americans (37)	49%
African Americans (30)	40%
Iranians (25)	24%

Reference Group

Anglo Americans tend to emphasize patient autonomy and self-determination. While a diverse group themselves, their responses generally reflect values of the majority culture in the United States. These values may dominate and bias results of opinion polls and end-of-life decision surveys, thus obscuring important ethnic variations that exist in this country.

Chinese Americans

Chinese philosophy has long included the right to choose death. Each person is seen as part of the whole community, and individual actions must take into consideration the effects on others. When life support is perceived as a burden on others, termination of these measures is likely to be requested. In the teachings of Buddha, the principles of justice and compassion are central. In contemporary society, appropriate distribution of health-care resources is seen as an important aspect of justice, and terminating life support to reduce suffering of the patient and/or family (physically, emotionally, or financially) is seen as an act of compassion. However, there is also some concern that to stop life support is to interfere with a person's *karma*. Suffering may be interpreted as the result of some past deed, with the belief that if one's karma is not resolved in this life, the patient will be forced to suffer again in his or her next life.

(Continued)

(Continued From Previous Page)

Mexican Americans

The majority of Mexican Americans are Catholic and opposed to any action that hastens death. Suffering is seen as part of God's plan, and enduring sickness is a sign of strength. Because there is always hope that the patient may get better, terminating life support can cause much guilt among Mexican American family members. When western medical practices have failed or in cases where they are preferred, a *curandero* (healer) may be contacted. The family is involved in all aspects of decision making for the terminally ill patient. However, in order to avoid rudeness or disrespect, they may not voice direct opposition to a physician's plan of action. As a result, physicians may think they are in agreement with medical recommendations when they are, in fact, strongly opposed.

African Americans

Because of centuries of slavery and racial discrimination, the experiences of African Americans in the United States tend to be dissimilar from all other groups. This history, as well as evidence of continued racism and other concerns with the medical establishment (e.g., less access to primary health care), may lead to fears that life support may be stopped prematurely because of the patient's race. Strong religious convictions combined with the will to survive may contribute to fewer African Americans saying they would terminate life support.

Iranians

Most Iranians are opposed to stopping life support in any situation. In the Islamic tradition, life and death are viewed as controlled by Allah, and the right to die generally is not recognized, even if the person is in considerable pain. Suffering is seen as an opportunity to show courage and faith in Allah. Consequently, continuing life support is viewed as an obligation, not an option. In fact, initiating a discussion of terminating life support may anger a patient or family members. In Iranian culture, female patients may be under the guardianship of male family members who must concur with medical decisions. Family members are expected to be demanding of health care professionals as a way of demonstrating their concern for the patient. It must also be remembered that recent immigrants may have little familiarity with high-tech decisions in the context of contemporary American health care. In rare instances, when a decision to stop life support is made by Iranians, the following customs must be respected: The family should be allowed to stay in the room and recite the Koran so that these are the last words the patient hears; the patient must be positioned so that he or she is facing Mecca at the time of death; and a non-Muslim must always wear gloves when touching the deceased.

SOURCE: J. Klessig (1992). The effect of values and culture on life-support decisions. *The Western Journal of Medicine, 157*(3), 316–321.

SUMMARY

As with many life-related circumstances, issues related to death and dying change somewhat with each new decade. In the past 30 years, much research has been done in the field of thanatology; this chapter suggests directions for a future research agenda. Technology brings to society many changes, anticipated and unanticipated; these changes have numerous positive outcomes but they also have the potential for negative consequences. Technology gives rise to many bioethical and legal questions. While technology may be used to extend the days or years of one's life, it must be balanced with concern for the quality of that life. In order to better ensure that personal desires are followed regarding various medical interventions, many persons either sign a living will or give guidance to families and physicians through other types of advanced directives. Many societies are now embroiled in a debate of whether physician-assisted suicide should be legalized; this debate includes numerous legal, religious, and social dimensions. Further, it is important to understand that all of the societal and technological changes addressed in this chapter must be put into the broader context related to various cultural, religious, ethical, and socioeconomic dimensions.

Personal Account

Vivian Jenkins Nelsen shares a number of memories from her youth—some of them were memories of deaths affecting a nation—the deaths of John F. Kennedy and Martin Luther King. She also shares memories of a more personal nature, those of her brother's death. Nelsen puts these experiences in a social context—shaped, to some degree, by family background, ethnicity, and religion.

One Woman's Interracial Journey
Vivian Jenkins Nelsen

The Assassination of a Young President

The Zapruder film of a young man in a convertible, his head rocked by the shock of a bullet, his life energy spraying on a Texas wind, the young woman crawling across the car's back, played endlessly on television in the weeks that followed

---

SOURCE: D. P. Irish, K. F. Lundquist, and V. J. Nelsen (Eds.), *Ethnic variations in dying, death, and grief: Diversity in universality.* (Washington, DC: Taylor & Francis, 1993), pp. 21-27.

President Kennedy's assassination. I remember the disgust of my favorite college professor at the public's fascination with the Zapruder clip. He quoted the Greek classic describing the death of a king, "Give me a cloth to cover his face."

This public death caused a national outpouring of grief that we shared as a people and that allowed us to talk about death as a shared reality. Death had been something that happened to "other people," the old, the poor, or the sick. Death did not touch the beautiful, the rich, or the chosen. If and when death intruded, we expected those other people, "the bereaved," not to burden us with their grief, but rather to accept their loss with stoicism and quickly return to normal. The young Jackie Kennedy, and later Coretta King, somber in their veiled widow's weeds, saved us from cohabiting their private hells; and for that we were grateful.

We all remember where we were when Jack Kennedy was killed. That day I knew that whites and blacks view death across a great cultural chasm. I was in Kearney, Nebraska, with two other music majors and a professor from our little Lutheran college. We were at the state college, observing a high school music contest in preparation for our careers as teachers. In a small-town grill, we were surprised when the counter clerk shushed us and turned up the radio, which was blasting out the dread-filled news. Our elderly professor, a former military man, retreated to some inner space and left me frightened and uneasy.

My throat constricted and hot tears rose into my eyes. They were unshed, however, as my colleagues calmly went about ordering their food. What was happening? Was it shock? People sometimes go on walking when mortally wounded. What was to happen to us blacks if the shooting of a president means that life goes on as usual?

Black people had suffered many deaths in the civil rights movement. Each new bombing or lynching seemed more savage than the last. This president seemed to be cognizant of our suffering. His standing up to the governor of my home state, Alabama's George Wallace, was a sign that "the times, they are a'changing." Nebraska was the most Republican state in the last election, but surely the shooting of a president merited more than a short pause. My family was Republican, having come out of the South where Dixiecrats were racists and Republicans freed the slaves, but I was deeply disturbed by this turn of events.

I was aware of being observed by white people in the café. I was the only black woman in our college, so I was used to being watched. Living among whites for the first time was a continuing series of revelations. We finished our lunch; the others ate heartily—I picked at my food. When we arrived at the campus auditorium for the choral competitions, a moment of silence was observed as the president's death was announced. I remember looking at the writing above the stage. It was the same as the biblical passage on the front of our Lutheran grade school: "The truth shall make ye free." I wandered blindly from event to event until we left our campus.

There, events and people moved as if the world were normal. No one but I seemed to be grieving. Was I over-reacting? I arrived home by bus, a short 17 miles from campus. My parents and I sat at the dining-room table talking about the amazing responses to this death. Tears shimmered in both their eyes. Mom talked about the kids jumping rope outside her classroom to the disgraceful words, "Kennedy's been shot in his big old head." We watched the unraveling saga on television and mourned together with our all-black community. It was a community calamity. We whispered, "Please God, don't let his murderer be black!"

Childhood Learnings About Death

Although we black folks understood this death in the same way, our ways of grieving were often different, varying from urban to rural, Baptist to Lutheran. As the assistant organist at my father's church, I began playing for funerals when I was 11. Our black Missouri Synod Lutheran Church had occupied the old Danish Lutheran Evangelical Kirke for many decades. As the Danes became more prosperous, they moved to the western suburbs of Omaha, leaving behind them the trappings of a former era. Modern, affluent church-goers had no need of a hand-carved baptismal font or an altar with oil paintings that changed with the church seasons.

We always knew outsiders, black or white, when they attended funerals. They were the people who screamed or cried loudly and were quickly ushered downstairs. My mother used to say that the people who fainted and screamed were the guilty ones. They were guilty of neglecting their loved ones, and the funeral was the place where the mourners would see their guilt masquerading as love. My parents viewed extravagant funerals with great asperity. They understood that poor families who had been coaxed into ordering these lavish displays would soon be hungry and shoeless.

The view of death in our religious community was as an experience to be borne with dignity, solemnity, and something called grace. (For a long time, I thought that this grace had something to do with my Aunt Grace.) Extravagance in emotion, dress, or grieving was merely self-indulgent. I was irritated not only by the funeral practices of our black community but also by the language of dying. "Doesn't he look wonderful? Just like he's sleeping." No, he looks dead. "Mr. Roberts passed last week." Passed from one grade to another? Passed from death to life? Why not, "He died"? Why this shrinking from the truth? Why such care for language? What seemed to me to be a throwback to Victorian civility offered a fascinating view of minority life.

For the person of color in this society, life is full of threats, ever-present and ever-real. Such threats make psychological and physical dents in one's facade that are reminders of everyday ugliness and frailty. The presence of beauty and delicacy in life's most stressful moments can help restore both our human and divine qualities. This need is shown in the careful attention given to dressing the deceased. My mother told us about preparing bodies in Southern rural parishes where morticians were not accessible or affordable. It was the work of churchwomen to bathe, oil, and scent with herbs the loved ones who were kept in the local ice house until the scattered relatives could arrive for the burial. Black people always called each other sister or brother. So "Sister Kizzy," or who-ever was the most gifted hairdresser, performed the final ritual. This last, loving toilet seemed wonderful yet remote to me, viewed through a modern lens.

I remember the family discussion following my questions about the chil-dren's prayer, "Now I lay me down to sleep, I pray the Lord my soul to keep. If I should die before I wake, I pray the Lord my soul to take." It was abundantly clear to me that if you didn't want to die during the night, you just didn't fall asleep. My mother's idea was even better: to simply nix the prayer. Regular sleep times were quickly resumed in the parsonage.

Deaths Experienced in Youth

One funeral of an elderly man who was a faithful parishioner was particularly annoying to me as a young teenager. Why was he buried wearing his glasses? "What is he going to see?" I asked Dad. I don't remember his gentle answer, but I do remember the seemingly endless discussions about how white undertakers never seemed to get a black person's hair or makeup quite right. I resolved then to be cremated and have none of that indecent peeping and chatter. Those prac-tices were for the living, not for the dead, I decided, and they should be promptly abolished. I was to discover, years after, that this decision caused my family great upset. The old Africans in our family believed that all parts of one's body must be present at death to enter heaven. This belief had become part of our religious fabric.

Perhaps the most important learnings about death and dying came during summers at my grandmother's home in rural South Carolina. Being black in the South meant that you were connected to everyone else black, in a palpable way. Being a minority had a special meaning—you belonged. Like Alex Haley's return to Africa, when I arrived as a very small girl, every black adult in that town looked at me and said, "She's a Sims. That must be Francis Sims' grandbaby." My grandmother, Francis Sims, was a very tall, lanky woman whose Indian and African ancestry were evident in both her features and bearing. With quiet solem-nity, I was introduced to her friends and neighbors as "Bea's girl."

Two of my mother's siblings still lived at home: a teacher sister, Aunt Thel, and Uncle James, who owned several small businesses. My young uncles were handsome and always attentive and respectful to me, even as a talkative and opinionated five-year-old. My Uncle Troy was the local black mortician and school principal. Troy was married to a teacher. Since they were childless, I en-joyed an inordinate amount of attention. From these uncles I learned about the physical aspects of dying, clinical descriptions of embalming, postmortems, and lynchings. The white coroner seemingly couldn't face the broken bodies. He sent his assistant, Troy Sims, to retrieve them. I demanded and received detailed, forthright answers to my questions.

I also witnessed this community's response to death as part of the Sacred Hoop. That was the term our Indian relatives used in reference to the life and death cycle. Murders were a disjoining, a forced breaking of the cycle. Death was accepted with a calmness that, to me, bordered on coldness. There were many stories about my African great-grandfather and his Indian wife, known as the "old ones."

Some of the stories are quite funny. They related to my mother and her siblings going to grandpoppa's house every Sunday. My Indian great-grandmother never quite got the hang of cooking food black-style, and she made a white lumpy gravy that everyone ate and nobody dared criticize. The old ones lived several miles from my grandmother's house and the smoke from their chimney was the daily signal that all was well. My grandmother and her mother still used their wood cook stoves even in blistering summer heat. Although my grandmother had a gas stove, she refused to use it. She also disdained the indoor toilet and used the outside privy. She felt that indoor plumbing was a nasty habit.

One Sunday morning, no plume of smoke rose from the old ones' chimney. Troy went to investigate. Grandpoppa had died in his sleep, but great-grandmother steadfastly refused to come into town with her husband's body. When other relatives went to the homestead to comfort her, they discovered that she had turned her face to the wall and died. She was not ill; she had simply willed herself to die. This was explained as "the Indian way." The old ones were so strong and so attached both to each other and the earth that they could choose to live and die together.

While I was on one of these idyllic childhood visits to the South, the news of the death of a young black boy, Emmett Till, sent a chill through every black community, North and South. Thirteen-year-old Emmett had disappeared while visiting his grandmother in Arkansas. By the time I returned North, Emmett was still missing. I remember opening my mother's drawer in her kitchen and finding a *Jet Magazine*. I gazed in wonder at the photo of his crushed face.

This was the era in which the white establishment discouraged the publication of photos of lynching victims for fear that the black community would rise up in riots. Braving the disapproval of the powerful, Johnson publications published the image of Till's battered face. I was mesmerized by his broken face; I was drawn to it day after day. His eyes looked like flowers—like daisies. Till's body was found in a barrel that had been sunk in a river for several weeks. The horrifying story of the torture, mutilation, and murder of this manchild was whispered among us children. Our friends added gory details.

I was afraid of being alone with whites and being spirited off to a terrible death. Even white elevator operators were suspect. The fear changed to rage. I share the rage of the children of Soweto and the West Bank because I, too, raged at the inability of black adults to exact revenge for the death of a child. Perhaps the most important moment in resolving this distressing death came when Emmett Till's mother, a retiring, pretty schoolteacher from some northern city, came to talk at a local church.

The heat was stifling that Sunday afternoon. The only sound was the whisper of paper fans from the local mortuary. Mrs. Till did not weep. She showed no rage, but a deep sadness, strength, and determination. Emmett was an only child. Allegedly, his crime was whistling at a white woman. Mrs. Till told a quiet tale of perfidy, of lies and deception by state, local, and federal authorities. By its very flatness, her voice held us riveted, convinced that things must change—that justice could no longer be blind to the murder of black people, black children.

These monumental public deaths are shapers of private grieving. For many years, we survivors hoped to look and sound as calm as Jackie Kennedy and Coretta King. We had no idea that we would grieve messily for years, in predictable stages. This cross-cultural journey of mine took several unexpected twists in high school when friends my own age died. Frail Rozzie was on the periphery of my circle of friends—a kind, gentle, intelligent girl. When she died of cancer, I asked for and got a full description of an orthodox Jewish funeral from my history teacher. He told me about his mother being wrapped in funeral linens and buried on a rainy day in a European ghetto the day after her death. I was relieved that it didn't rain the week Rozzie died. It seemed at once merciful that her body be buried quickly and unique that professional mourners were there. But I accepted this way of burial as consistent with that of my African and Indian ancestors. I viewed it as different but normal, understandable.

Later that year, the counselor came into the art room and beckoned to me. I knew, instantly, that one of my best friends, Sara, had "made good" on her suicide threats. A beautiful, brilliant, artistic student, Sara had been seriously depressed. This event nearly repeated itself in college with another friend, Betty, whom we managed to get to the hospital in time.

Experiencing Deaths as an Adult

Following college, a young friend and art teacher, Kathy, committed suicide at a boyfriend's house. This time, it was my responsibility to make funeral arrangements, pick the casket, notify the family, deal with the insurance company and employers, manage three minor siblings, and buy the burial plot. I was a young black social worker dealing with an impoverished white rural Catholic family. The family fought at the church over whether Kathy should be buried with a rosary in her hands, although she had converted to Lutheranism many years earlier and the service was taking place at her Lutheran church. The disagreement spilled into the parking lot with various family members making obscene hand gestures at each other from the mortuary limousine. Suddenly, the rigid Victorian code of funeral etiquette practiced by Southern blacks made elegant sense. It enforced civility at this most stressful time.

Not long after this funeral, I attended a Sunday-morning lecture on "Preparing Your Own Funeral." Then I took a seminar on suicide. What an enlightenment it was to discover that anger as well as the sadness of depression can play a role in the decision to end one's life. Not long afterward, I became a founding member of the suicide hotline known as Y.E.S.–N.E.O.N. After hearing a radio lecture on the stages of grief by a then-unknown Swiss physician, Elisabeth Kübler-Ross, I enrolled in a course on death and dying at the university. I was alarmed to hear the professor criticize suicide hotlines as a waste of money. She then said that the surviving family of a suicide should be made to walk behind a cart carrying the body through the streets, as had been the custom in medieval times. The public ridicule and curiosity, she said, would surely curb suicides. I found it necessary to give the professor a taste of that ridicule in class.

The most useful thing I learned from that class was to identify the stages of grief. Knowing them helped me understand my own reactions to the death of my younger brother, James. What they did not prepare me for was the depth and length of feelings. What I also discovered is that different cultural traditions value the stages of grief very differently. For example, the anger and denial stages seemed to come more easily and to stay longer in our family than did the acceptance stage. Part of that has to do with what I consider to be an inadequate theology of death. Our conservative faith has answers for everything, most of them punishing. But I was to find that the rawness of grieving was salved by the old, familiar language, not a brutal rendering of the obvious. I was to perform the age-old last toilet for my brother, a gift to me from all the women in my family. It was a linking of our tradition. This toilet, albeit abbreviated, consisted of restyling James's hair at the white mortuary.

The most painful event surrounding James's death was receiving racial hate-mail with his newspaper obituary notice taped inside. My husband and I resolved not to tell the rest of our family at the time. The letter marked 13 years of harassment from job to job, and house to house, by bigots. Bearing a load of hate for interracial families and adopted children, and invective against Asians, Indians, blacks, Jews, Catholics, this letter, coming when it did, weighed more heavily than the combined effect of all the others. I knew, then, the meaning of the scripture passage that describes the Spirit of God as "groaning in travail" for our world "in sighs too deep for words."

We determined to keep this most destructive of letters and prayed that we could find and stop these deviants. I called a mortician friend who told me that other families had been tortured in the same way. They had been receiving this mail at funeral homes. I knew that I could not come to terms with either my anger or my grief until this group had been found and punished. It took more than three years to find the wealthy individual who had singled me out for this special punishment and to bring him to trial.

And so I continue on my pilgrim way. The hymn writer says, "Let the fiery, cloudy pillar lead me all my journey through."

QUESTIONS AND ACTIVITIES

1. Recall that Vivian Jenkins Nelsen states "The view of death in our religious community was an experience to be borne with dignity, solemnity, and something called grace." Is this true in your personal experience? In a small group, discuss the influence your religion has on your beliefs about death and the rituals you participate in. What exposure have you had to other cultures? Interview students from different cultural or ethnic groups and compare your personal experiences, attitudes, customs, and traditions related to death, dying, and grief.

2. The "baby boomer generation" has vivid memories of the assassinations of John F. Kennedy and Martin Luther King. Can you remember the violent death of some public figure significant in your own life? What are the effects of violence—on individuals and on the greater society?

3. Historically, family members would help prepare the body of the deceased for the funeral. Nelsen shares that she did this for her brother. Would you want to participate in such a ritual? Would your culture be supportive? Why or why not?

4. Talk with someone from your parents' generation and also from your grandparents' generation. Discuss with them the illnesses that would have claimed the lives of people their own ages. Discuss with them changes that have taken place in the medical profession during their lifetimes.

5. Review various news media sources. How often are violent, sudden deaths highlighted? How are they portrayed? How has the increase in violent deaths affected you personally?

6. Discuss with a family member or friend issues related to signing a "living will." Explain why (or why not) you have chosen to sign one. Have you decided to sign a donor card—why or why not? What additional information do you feel you might need before making these personal decisions?

7. If you have access to the Internet, use one of the addresses found in this chapter to see what information is available to you. Print an electronic file that you are interested in; share what you find with another student in class.

8. Identify intended and possible unintended consequences of the new technologies discussed in this chapter. How can one minimize the unintended impacts of interventions? Give an example from history of an inappropriate use of technology.

9. Rank order the following persons in terms of priority you would assign for a liver transplant, and discuss factors you considered in your decisions: a single 54-year-old priest, a middle-aged executive officer in a large corporation who is divorced with two college children, a 62-year-old construction supervisor who is planning early retirement due to a health problem stemming from heavy alcohol use in his twenties, a 26-year-old single mother of three young children. Identify possible arguments for a different ordering of priority. Discuss your thoughts with a peer. Did you come to the same conclusions?

10. In this chapter, several areas of research in thanatology are discussed. List three specific topics in the field that you would like to learn more about. How did these interests develop? How are they related to your own personal experience and/or professional goals?

GLOSSARY

Active euthanasia: an "easy" death caused by an intervention (e.g., a drug overdose), in contrast to the withdrawal or withholding of treatment.

Living will: a type of advanced directive that communicates one's wishes regarding the use of extraordinary measures to prolong life.

Physician-assisted suicide: refers to physicians helping to provide the means for individuals' taking their own lives.

Thanatology: the study of death, dying, and grief.

SUGGESTED READINGS

Aries, P. (1981). *The hour of our death.* New York: Knopf.

This book provides a historical treatment of attitudes toward death in Western culture from earliest Christian times until the present day. It is comprehensive in coverage with interesting illustrations.

Battin, M. P. (1994). *The least worst death: Essays in bioethics on the end of life.* New York: Oxford University Press.

The author examines various social, political, and ethical issues related to the following major themes: withdrawing or withholding treatment, euthanasia, and suicide. Many thought-provoking ideas are raised. As one would expect, given this topic, the reader is left with more questions than answers.

Dane, B. O., & Levine, C. (Eds.). (1994). *AIDS and the new orphans: Coping with death.* Westport, CT: Auburn House.

This edited volume includes discussion of many facets of the AIDS epidemic as it influences the lives of children. Primary focus is on the grief process of those orphaned by this epidemic; two chapters include special emphasis on developmental issues— latency age and adolescence. Variations in terms of issues faced by different ethnic groups are illustrated through the chapters on Latino communities and Black American communities.

Nuland, S. B. (1993). *How we die: Reflections on life's final chapter.* New York: Vantage Books.

Nuland describes the process of dying in a very personal and caring fashion, with a particular focus on physical changes. This is done in the context of concern for an individual's sense of personal dignity. The author focuses on various types of deaths, including cancer, AIDS, accidents, suicide, and homicide.

Wrenn, R. L., Levinson, D., & Papadatou, D. (1996). *Guidelines for the health care provider: End of life decisions.* Tucson, AZ; University of Arizona–College of Medicine– Office of Continuing Medical Education.

This booklet provides straightforward information regarding various facets of advanced preparations and directives, including: living wills, health-care power of attorney, organ and tissue donations, wills, and financial issues. It also includes a listing of helpful resources—journals, organizations, and World Wide Web sites.

RESOURCES

The Hastings Center
Route 9D
Garrison, NY 10524
(914) 424-4040

Choice in Dying
200 Varick Street
New York, NY 10014
(212) 366-5540

United Network for Organ Sharing
P.O. Box 13770
Richmond, VA 23225
1-800-243-6667

REFERENCES

AAN Expert Panel on Culturally Competent Health Care. (1992). *Executive summary, priorities and recommendations, and report.* Washington, DC: Author.

American Association of Suicidology. (1996). Report of the Committee on Physician-Assisted Suicide and Euthanasia.

Banks, J. A. (1994). *An introduction to multicultural education.* Needham Heights, MA: Allyn and Bacon.

Battin, M. P. (1991). Euthanasia: The way we do it, the way they do it. *Journal of Pain and Symptom Management, 6* (5), 298–305.

Bayer, R., & Kirp, D. L. (1992). An epidemic in political and policy perspective. In Kirp & Bayer (Eds.), *AIDS in the industrialized democracies: Passions, politics, and policies.* (pp. 1–6). New Brunswick, NJ: Rutgers University Press.

Bok, S. (1976). Personal directions in the care at the end of life. *The New England Journal of Medicine, 295,* 367–368.

Carson, R. A. (1979). Euthanasia or the right to die. In H. Wass (Ed.), *Dying: Facing the facts* (pp. 360–374). Washington, DC: Hemisphere.

Cook, A. S., & Balk, D. E. (Eds.). (1995). Ethics and bereavement research (special issue). *Death Studies, 19*(2), 103–181.

Cook, A. S., & Dworkin, D. S. (1992). *Helping the bereaved: Therapeutic interventions for children, adolescents, and adults.* New York: Basic.

Deluty, R. (1989). Factors affecting the acceptability of suicide. *Omega, 13,* 127–144.

DiClemente, R. J., & Peterson, J. L. (1994). *Preventing AIDS: Theories and methods of behavioral interventions.* New York: Plenum Press.

Frederick, M. D. (1994). Physician-assisted suicide: A personal right? *Southern University Law Review, 21,* 59–108.

Harper, D. C., & Wadsworth, J. S. (1993). Grief in adults with mental retardation: Preliminary findings. *Research in Developmental Disabilities, 14,* 313–330.

Hoehne, J. L. (1993). Physician responsibility and the right to "death care"; the call for physician-assisted suicide. *Drake Law Review, 42,* 225–253.

Irish, D. (1993). Multiculturalism and the majority population. In D. P. Irish, K. F. Lundquist, & V. J. Nelsen (Eds.), *Ethnic variations in dying, death, and grief: Diversity in universality* (pp. 1–10). Washington, DC: Taylor & Francis.

Kalish, R. A. (1985). *Death, grief, and caring relationships* (2nd ed.). Monterey, CA: Brooks/Cole.

Klessig, J. (1992). The effect of values and culture on life-support decisions. *Western Journal of Medicine, 157*(3), 316–321.

Klenow, D. J., & Youngs, G. A., Jr. (1995). An empirical exploration of selected policy options in organ donation. *Death Studies, 19*(6), 543–557.

Kübler-Ross, E. (1969). *On death and dying.* New York: Macmillan.

Lambrecht, M. E. (1990). The value of computer-assisted instruction in death education. *Loss, Grief, and Care: A Journal of Professional Practice, 4*(1/2), 67–69.

Leiter, R. A. (Ed.). (1993). *National survey of state laws.* Detroit, MI: Gale Research Inc.

Lester, D., & Leenars, A. A. (1996). The ethics of suicide and suicide prevention. *Death Studies, 20*(2), 163–183.

London, H., & Devore, W. (1988). Layers of understanding: Counseling ethnic minority families. *Family Relations, 37,* 310–314.

Mann, J., Tarantola, D. J., & Netter, T. W. (Eds.). (1992). *A global report: AIDS in the world.* Cambridge, MA: Harvard University Press.

Markson, E. W. (1995). To be or not to be: Assisted suicide revisited. *Omega, 31*(3), 221–235.

Marshall, K. A. (1980). When a patient commits suicide. *Suicide and Life-Threatening Behavior, 10*(1), 29–40.

Martocchio, B. C. (1986). Agendas for quality of life. *The Hospice Journal, 2*(1), 11–21.

National Center for Health Statistics (1995). *Monthly Vital Statistics Report.* Washington, DC: U.S. Department of Health and Human Services.

Parry, J. K. (1990). *Social work practice with the terminally ill: The transcultural perspective.* Springfield, IL: Charles C. Thomas.

Parry, J. K., & Ryan, A. S. (Eds.). (1995). *A cross-cultural look at death, dying, and religion.* Chicago: Nelson-Hall.

Phipps, E. J., Cooper, M. R., & Greenstein, S. (1993). The last days of life: A retrospective study of when resuscitation decisions are made. *Family Systems Medicine, 11,* 83–88.

Rando, T. A. (1992). The increasing prevalence of complicated mourning: The onslaught is just beginning. *Omega, 26*(1), 43–59.

Richters, J. E. (1993). Community violence and children's development: Toward a research agenda for the 1990s. *Psychiatry, 56,* 3–6.

Robbins, R. A. (1990). Signing an organ donor card: Psychological factors. *Death Studies, 14,* 219–229.

Roels, L., Vanrenterghem, Y., Waer, M., Gruwez, J., & Michielsen, P. (1990). Effect of a presumed consent law on organ retrieval in Belgium. *Transplantation Proceedings, 22*(4), 2078–2079.

Saunders, C. (1995). A response to Logue's "Where hospice fails—The limits of palliative care." *Omega, 32*(1), 1–5.

Smith, W. J. (1985). *Dying in the human life cycle: Psychological, biomedical, and social perspectives.* New York: Holt, Rinehart, and Winston.

Sofka, C. (1997). Social support "Internetworks," caskets for sale, and much, much more: Thanatology and the information superhighway. *Death Studies, 21*(6), 553-574.

Stroebe, M. S., Hansson, R. O., & Stroebe, W. (1993). Contemporary themes and controversies in bereavement research. In M. S. Stroebe, W. Stroebe, and R. O. Hansson (Eds.), *Handbook of bereavement* (pp. 457-475). Cambridge, MA: Cambridge University Press.

Tenner, E. (1996). *Why things bite back: Technology and the revenge of unintended consequences.* New York: Knopf.

Teo, B. (1991). Organs for transplantation: The Singapore experience. *Hastings Center Report, 21,* 10-13.

The NAMES Project (1997). *Quilt facts: AIDS statistics.* San Francisco, CA: Author.

The World Resources Institute, The United Nations Environment Programme, The United Nations Development Program, & The World Bank (1996). *World resources 1996-97.* New York: Oxford University Press.

Thompson, L. M. (1984). Cultural and institutional restrictions on dying styles in a technological society. *Death Education, 8,* 223-229.

Tucker, K. L. (1995). Physician aid in dying: A human option, a constitutionally protected choice. *Seattle University Law Review, 18,* 495-508.

United Network for Organ Sharing. (1996). *Annual report.* Richmond, VA: UNOS.

Vaisrub, S. (1974). Dying is worked to death (editorial). *Journal of the American Medical Association, 229,* 1909-1910.

Vandecreek, L., & Frankowski, D. (1996). Barriers that predict resistance to completing a living will. *Death Studies, 20,* 73-82.

Vladeck, B. (1995). End-of-life care. *Journal of the American Medical Association. 274*(6), 449.

Werth, J. (1995). Rational suicide reconsidered: AIDS as an impetus for change. *Death Studies, 19*(1), 65-80.

World Health Organization (1995). *The world health report 1995: Bridging the gaps.* Geneva: WHO.

Wheeler, X. (1996). The "visible man": A cadaver in cyberspace. *The Chronicle of Higher Education, 42*(21), A6.

Young, H. H. (1992). Assisted suicide and physician liability. *The Review of Litigation: University of Texas, School of Law, 11,* 623-656.

2

The Dying
Individual

"A dying individual is a living individual." That statement reflects a fundamental premise of this book. Just as healthy people have a variety of needs, so do the dying. Rebok and Hoyer (1979) noted several decades ago that "all deaths involve a complex interplay of cognitive, social, and biological processes" (p. 191). Like healthy individuals, dying individuals are affected by particular developmental trends; therefore their needs, interests, and capabilities vary with each life stage.

A second major premise of this text is that death is a natural part of the life-span. Although life expectancies have been extended significantly in the past century, death cannot be avoided. Even though many people in this country are isolated from the dying process, as a result of the institutionalization (in hospitals or nursing homes) of most dying individuals, we cannot be protected from the deaths of people we love or from the ensuing grief.

A third basic premise is that attitudes, such as respect and empathy, can be as important in helping dying individuals deal with their impending deaths as the functional skills (e.g., giving medication) used in their care. Individuals who are facing death should be treated as whole human beings who deserve our care and concern.

A fourth major premise is that attention must be paid both to the people who are dying and to the social units of which they are a part. The entire family is affected by the death of one of its members. Thus, we need to be concerned not only with the grief responses of individuals but also with the changes in the family system as a whole.

A final premise of this book is the understanding that a holistic approach to meeting the needs of the dying individual and his or her family is valuable to all concerned. It is much too simplistic and unrealistic to assume that the needs of the dying are only physical. Although the decision to pursue curative measures or provide **palliative** (comfort) **care,** together with decisions as to how to provide that care are crucial issues for the dying and their families, many other concerns are also paramount. In addition to physical concerns, emotional, social, psychological, and spiritual concerns must also be recognized as important. Support should be given to the dying in order to meet each of these categories of needs. This approach is known as a **holistic perspective.**

Currently, interdisciplinary teams (physicians, nurses, child-life specialists, social workers, psychologists, ministers, and nutritionists, among others) work together in a variety of health-care settings. Their collaborative efforts emphasize the importance of providing holistic care. Members of the team share insights and information derived from training in their own disciplines and help to create a treatment plan that is more comprehensive and effective than one determined by a single individual.

NEEDS AND CONCERNS OF THE DYING

Before beginning a discussion of the needs and concerns of the dying, it is important to understand that the dying process is unique to each individual.

FIGURE 2.1
Holistic Perspective of the Dying Process

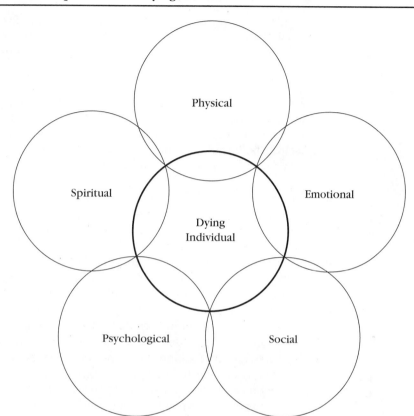

Although we can discuss commonly experienced components of the dying process, it is inappropriate to assume that what is said here is true of every dying person. This section is intended to provide insight, not dictate a "right" way to die. We will examine important issues in the physical, emotional, social, psychological, and spiritual realms (see Figure 2.1).

Physical Needs and Concerns

The realm of human existence that most immediately comes to mind when discussing death is the physical. Although many topics could be examined in this section (including disease entities, treatment modes, and nutritional issues), we shall limit our discussion to two primary areas: pain and body image. These two topics were chosen because they illustrate the close relationship between physical concerns and those of a social, emotional, and psychological nature.

Pain. Pain is the most commonly experienced symptom of terminally ill patients. According to Chapman (1992),

> Patients with persisting intense pain cannot live normal lives. Most suffer a cascade of other symptoms caused largely by the presence of pain itself such as fatigue, difficulty concentrating, insomnia, anorexia, nausea and vomiting. Such insidious problems foster depression and hopelessness and contribute to psychopathology. (p. 16)

In order that the dying may be assured as high a quality of life as possible, many would argue that pain must be controlled in a manner that maintains alertness. Levy (1988) noted that pain control may be based on one of the following basic approaches: modification of the source of the pain, interference with the transmission of the pain to the central nervous system, or altering the perception of the pain.

The **etiology** or cause of the pain must be known before appropriate therapeutic methods can be implemented. In our recent history, the most common treatment modality has been drug therapy. Currently, increasing attention is being given to alternative methods, including biofeedback, hypnosis, relaxation and imagery techniques, and acupuncture, among others. Regardless of the philosophy underlying the control of pain, pain management should be personalized.

Many have argued that it is not sufficient simply to alleviate pain once it is experienced; it is important, if at all possible, to prevent the pain from ever occurring. Alleviation of pain implies that it has been experienced but relieved, while prevention implies that the physical suffering has been avoided altogether. The goal of medication should be such that the dosage is sufficient to cross the pain relief threshold but not of such a quantity or of such a type that the medication causes the patient to become sedated.

Freedom from pain while in a conscious and alert state allows dying individuals to retain control over as much of their lives as possible and to have opportunities to complete their *unfinished business* prior to death. Kübler-Ross (1969) first used this term to refer to the need to draw closure to many facets of one's life. This may include, for example, apologizing for a long-past argument or arranging alternative care for one's surviving children. Not only do the dying need to "finish their business," but so do the grieving. One child, anticipating his mother's death, needed to let her know how much he cared about her:

> When my mom first had that g-tube in I just needed to tell her that I was going to miss her and said I'm going to miss you when you're gone and I know my family didn't want me to do it. But the minute it came out of my mouth I just felt so much better. But if she had died before I said that, I don't think I would have had that feeling. (Horne & Fagan, 1983, p. 16)

Many health practitioners, including proponents of the hospice philosophy (discussed in more detail later in this chapter), believe that medication should be self-administered (Saeger, 1992). Since patients do not need to be dependent on others to administer their drugs, self-regulation allows the dying to retain a sense of control and also minimizes their fear that their pain will be exacerbated if an upcoming dosage is not given in time. If the medication can be self-regulated, the dying can participate in the appropriate modification of the dosage to meet their needs under the guidance of a physician. Although some question the efficacy of a self-administration program, fears that the dying would abuse this opportunity have not been realized. In fact, most patients report a tendency to use fewer drugs when they know the medications are readily available if needed.

Although pain is typically regarded as physical in nature, it also has emotional and psychological components. For some individuals, fear of pain heightens a sense of anxiety which, in turn, magnifies the sensation of pain or other physical stress (Kornell, 1992). Additionally, a type of emotional pain comes from the interpretation of what the pain means or from resulting changes in lifestyle. For example, patients may interpret pain as punishment for some transgression and feel guilty for past acts. Others may experience pain that is so incapacitating that they can no longer walk and, as a result, feel depressed due to a loss of independence. This, in turn, can contribute to a sense of inferiority or shame. In summary, "unrelieved, purposeless chronic pain leads to needless anxiety, depression, and suffering, which in turn can accelerate the natural process of deterioration. The recognition of this concept along with the gradual shedding of inappropriate fears of addiction and tolerance has led to revolutionary ways in which pain is treated . . ." (Johanson, 1993, p. 65).

Body Image.   **Body image** is the internal representation of one's feelings and attitudes toward one's body. In order to create a sense of body image, individuals examine their physical characteristics and use criteria from the cultural milieu to pass judgment on their own physical being. To some degree, the outcome of this process ultimately influences their psychological state.

Body image may change over time as physical maturation progresses and physical skills develop. For example, adolescents must integrate body changes (height, development of primary and secondary sex characteristics, etc.) into the image they already have of themselves. The ultimate outcome of that image in terms of "goodness" or "badness" is closely related to what messages are communicated by the culture in terms of what is attractive, valuable, or even enviable. For example, most North Americans regard a particular range of height, weight, strength, and athletic prowess in males as positive characteristics. Women, on the other hand, are often judged on their facial features and figure.

A terminal illness may affect a previous sense of body image due to such changes as a severe drop in weight or loss of body parts and functions. For example, in a culture that values a female's figure and hair, a woman who has a mastectomy and also loses her hair to the subsequent chemotherapy may have a very difficult time dealing with those losses and convincing herself that others find her attractive or valuable. A woman who has had a hysterectomy must deal with the fact that she will not be able to bear children and needs to reconcile that inability with her definition of womanhood or femininity. A woman who is so weak that she can no longer perform many of the tasks that she was once proud of doing may need to deal with the feeling that her body has betrayed her.

Both physical and psychological support must be given to the dying in order to help them deal with the many changes they experience. A woman who has had a breast removed may be fitted with a prosthesis or a man who has lost his hair after chemotherapy may desire a hair piece. Psychological support can be given by discussing the person's perceptions of these bodily changes and how the individual is feeling about them. Reassurance can also be given, either by words or by physical closeness, that the individual is still attractive. Open communication, together with caring physical contact and comfort, are powerful tools in overcoming potential negative changes in body image.

The body's ability to function normally is referred to as **body integrity.** Dying individuals may face the gradual loss of various body functions. Viney (1984) studied 484 persons who were severely ill and found that a threat to one's body integrity affected an individual's emotional state and was manifest in feelings of sadness, anger, helplessness, and hopelessness. Caregivers should attempt to help the dying individual understand the physical changes and deal with the ensuing emotions.

Emotional Needs and Concerns

Elisabeth Kübler-Ross has challenged professionals and nonprofessionals alike to be sensitive to the needs of the dying. In her classic book entitled *On Death and Dying,* Kübler-Ross (1969) delineated five stages to describe the dying person's progression toward acceptance of his or her impending death. Those stages are summarized here.

1. *Denial:* This is typically the initial reaction to the diagnosis of a terminal illness. It is characterized by the statement "No, not me, it cannot be true." Denial is the initial defense mechanism used to deal with news of impending death, but it is rather quickly replaced by partial acceptance.
2. *Anger:* Feelings of anger, rage, envy, and resentment are experienced as the dying person attempts to answer the question, "Why me?"
3. *Bargaining:* There is an attempt to postpone the inevitable by asking that death be delayed in return for such things as "a life in the service of the church" or similar promises.
4. *Depression:* This stage is marked by two types of depression. The first is *reactive depression,* resulting from losses that are experienced as a part of the illness. For example, a woman may become depressed after the loss of her breast due to a mastectomy. The second type is *preparatory depression,* which anticipates impending losses such as separation from family.
5. *Acceptance:* This stage is marked by "a degree of quiet expectation . . . not a resigned and hopeless 'giving up'" (pp. 112–113). The individual no longer actively struggles to survive.

It is recognized that Kübler-Ross has made a major contribution to the field of thanatology. Concerns have arisen, however, regarding the inappropriate application of her work by others. Many people have treated her theory as if it were a prescription, outlining steps to the "right way to die," rather than as a description of what she regarded to be true after observing hundreds of terminally ill patients. Kübler-Ross herself has argued against persons' attempting to force the dying into a mold based on her theory and, in essence, demanding that they make rapid progress through the first four stages in order to accept their fate. Additionally, Kübler-Ross's theory has been criticized because it does not take into account characteristics inherent in the dying individual (such as sex, age, previous life experiences, ethnicity, coping strategies, or the nature of the illness) or concern itself with such factors as cultural environment or interrelationships with significant others (Kastenbaum, 1981).

The acceptance of the knowledge that one is dying is not necessarily universal, nor is it the culmination of a sequential series of emotional experiences. Rather, dying individuals experience a mix of emotions at any point in time, and those emotions may peak, diminish, and then recur. Shneidman (1978) noted that as he worked with dying individuals, he saw "the wide panoply of human emotions—few in some people, dozens in others—experienced in a variety of orderings, re-orderings, and arrangements" (p. 206). Rather than advocating a stage theory, Pattison (1977) has described three common clinical phases of the dying process. These are depicted in Figure 2.2.

FIGURE 2.2
Phases of the Dying Process

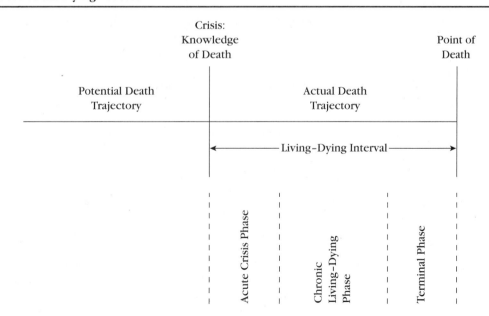

SOURCE: E. M. Pattison (1977).

1. The first phase is the *acute crisis phase*, which is triggered by the crisis of knowing that death is approaching. This phase is marked by great anxiety and sense of threat to one's self.
2. The second phase is the *chronic living–dying phase*. This stage is usually the longest and is typified by a variety of fears, as well as grief for the many losses that are experienced as a part of the dying process.
3. The final phase is known as the *terminal phase* and is characterized by an increased withdrawal into one's self and an increased sense of acceptance of the anticipated death.

Although this framework is helpful in understanding the changing emotional state of the dying, Pattison notes that the insights presented are not necessarily relevant to all dying persons and that it is crucial to respond to each person as an individual. Much has been written about the emotional facets of the dying process. To a great extent, those descriptions primarily deal with what Pattison has described as the chronic living–dying phase. Many of the emotional responses to dying reflect a variety of fears. Others are manifestations of grief in response to the many losses that are a part of the dying process.

Fears.   Dying individuals often experience a wide variety of fears, including fear of pain or suffering, fear of isolation or abandonment, fear of extinction, fear of rejection, fear of the unknown, fear of indignity, and fear of an inability to fulfill one's responsibilities (Callari, 1986). Sometimes fears may clearly be recognized as such and confronted openly; at other times, however, they may not be clearly perceived or openly acknowledged. Instead, these fears may be expressed indirectly. For example, individuals who are afraid of being isolated may not openly acknowledge the fear of isolation but may still find it very difficult to allow visitors to leave. Not only do dying individuals experience a multitude of fears, so do family and friends, who are often afraid of not knowing what to do or say. Survivors may fear a life alone without their loved one and the changes that illness and death precipitate. Health professionals may fear a sense of failure when their patients die. Open communication among all persons in the system allows them to become more sensitive to the presence of fears and to be of mutual support to one another in alleviating their concerns.

Grief.   Grief is a natural response to loss. Although we will examine this reaction in more depth as it relates to survivors in chapter 3, we must also understand that the dying themselves experience grief. The dying grieve in anticipation of the death event itself and the end of life. They also may grieve as a result of the many losses that can be intrinsic to the dying process. Dying persons often respond emotionally to the many physical losses that they might experience (such as loss of prior energy level or loss of hair). Additionally, they are likely to experience many other losses that may not be readily apparent but that elicit deep emotion. For example, dying individuals give up their dreams for the future. They may also lose a sense of control over their health status or body functioning. People who are dying often face a loss of independence and, as a result, a loss of self-esteem, as others insist on performing tasks or making decisions for them. Another loss occurs as the dying become cognizant of family and friends withdrawing from them physically and/or socially. The grief resulting from these many losses is characterized by a multiplicity of thoughts and feelings. Anger, guilt, remorse, anxiety, depression, rebellion, and aggression are among its common manifestations. The dying need an opportunity to express their emotions in a supportive environment. When faced with so many losses, individuals have a right to grieve and a need to know that they are neither weak nor abnormal for doing so.

Positive Emotions.   Although many people assume there are no positive consequences to learning that death is imminent, Mead and Willemsen (1995) would argue otherwise. Crises, such as impending death, allow the dying and their loved ones an opportunity to unlock emotions as they explore other ways of living and deepening human experience. Impending death can serve as an impetus to grow emotionally in the face of adversity, strengthen emotional bonds with others, and develop insights about the world. Mead and Willemsen (1995) reflect on the psychological transformations that dying patients at times experience when given support:

> A shift in attitude and consciousness begins to take place. Frequently these individuals begin to make the most of their lives. They consolidate relationships and discard what is no longer needed in their emotional life. They not only go about completing unfinished business, they begin to live from the essence of life and connect with it . . . Lives are given new meaning by the fact of death. The psyche wants wholeness. Specifically, patients do more of the things they have wanted, but had not allowed themselves to do. Frequently individuals demonstrate a more open willingness to acknowledge their own human pain and suffering as well as their longings, desires, limitations, and choices. (pp. 122-123)

Psychological growth that occurs as one faces death can help counterbalance feelings of depression, anxiety, and fear.

Social Needs and Concerns

In order for the dying to deal effectively with their fears and to come to terms with their own grief, they need to know that others still care about them. As indicated earlier, a primary fear experienced by dying individuals is a fear of loneliness or abandonment (Dupee, 1982). This fear may be exacerbated as others fail to disclose the truth regarding the diagnosis of a terminal illness, refuse to deal openly and honestly with death-related issues and feelings, or physically and emotionally withdraw from dying persons.

Disclosure of Diagnosis.   Although the vast majority of persons say they want to be told if they have a terminal illness, this type of disclosure has not

THE VIEW FROM MY ROOM

Eighteen years ago my assignment for English composition was a one-page essay. It was accepted by my professor only after three drafts and my grouching to the department chairman that I didn't have the time or interest to devote to this subject. Truthfully, I lacked the talent and insight to even begin. I seem to recall a D.

Yet, since school, I've often lain in bed at night in darkness, and thoughts form and flowingly crystallize—usually sharper, more lucid and lyrical than the attached.

I still know nothing about writing. But tonight, "The View From My Room" emerged. It's a gift I can now enjoy just for myself, and perhaps later it will touch someone else who may find it.

It may be too amateurish to share, but still I'm happy not to have the talent of a writer to burden my conscience.

This may be the paper my instructor was trying to get out of me.

(Continued)

always taken place. The majority of studies carried out prior to 1970 found that physicians did not favor telling patients about the severity of their illness (Blumenfield, Levy, & Kaufman, 1978).

There is evidence in more recent years that physicians and medical students are much more likely to disclose directly to a patient that she or he is dying than they have been in the past. Eggerman and Dustin (1985) collected data from 103 medical students and 15 family physicians. In response to the question "What is your feeling about telling a patient that he/she is terminally ill," 93% of the medical students and all of the physicians felt that patients have a right to know the truth about their illness if they request the information. All but 2% of the medical students would tell their own patients. These data reflect a changing trend in sharing with a patient a prognosis of likely death. Health professionals still sometimes hesitate to disclose the truth regarding the diagnosis for a number of reasons: (1) the patient does not want to be told, (2) the patient knows and does not need to be told, or (3) the patient will give up hope if he or she is told. It should be noted that these are perceptions only, not statements of fact.

Many other professionals believe that most persons know they are dying whether or not they are directly told. Dying individuals (Kalish, 1970) gain this insight through

- overheard statements,
- changes in behavior of others toward them,
- changes in the medical care routines,
- changes in physical location of health care,
- self-diagnosis by reading books or charts,
- signals from the body and changes in physical status; and/or
- altered responses by others toward discussing the future.

(Continued From Previous Page)

The View From My Room
Charles Palmisano

As I lie on my bed, gazing out of my window, the act of expressing my thoughts brings a new perspective and appreciation of the beauty beside me.

Straight ahead, to the right, and across the green grass lies a heavily foliaged patch of plant life native to our tightly grouped outpoint. Great, lofty flowers glow with yellows, golds, and rusts against the gray and drab that predominate in this world.

Plants are freely interspersed, their clumps bringing in bright and pale greens of illumination. They are energetic, healthy, life-affirming sights among the fading and aging shade trees. They are matched ideally and joyously to their surroundings.

Ahead of the thicket bloom bouquets of flowers, their colors astonishing. Looking out the window through the rectangular frame brings to mind a classic American painting, yet more vivid and alive, and still peaceful and reassuring.

This is the view from my room.

I'm thankful for being awakened to it.

The Wayland Flowers House is an AIDS residential hospice in Los Angeles. Charles Palmisano was a resident there for 7 months before his death on September 17, 1991. At that time, Paul Hedge, hospice manager, found in Charles's personal belongings an introductory note and essay that had been written by Charles as he approached death.

SOURCE: From *Voices that care: Stories and encouragements for people with AIDS/HIV and those who love them* (pp. 21-22), by N. Hitchens, Ed., 1992. Los Angeles: Lowell House.

As people gather information to confirm their suspicions that they are seriously ill, they are in a state described by Weisman (1972) as **middle knowledge.** "Somewhere between open knowledge of death and its utter repudiation is an area of uncertainty called middle knowledge" (p. 65).

Communication Patterns.   In their classic study entitled *Awareness of Dying,* Glaser and Strauss (1965) examined the communication patterns between dying persons and those interacting with them. They identified four **awareness contexts,** classified by "what each interacting person knows of the patient's defined status, along with his recognition of others' awareness of his own definition" (p. 10):

1. *Closed awareness:* The patient does not know he or she is dying even though medical personnel and family members know it.
2. *Suspected awareness:* The patient does not know but only suspects, with varying degrees of certainty, that he or she is dying. The medical staff and family do know the patient is terminally ill.
3. *Mutual pretense:* The patient, medical personnel, and family know the patient is dying but there is tacit agreement to act as if this were not the case.
4. *Open awareness:* The patient, medical personnel, and family recognize and openly acknowledge that the patient is dying.

DISCLOSURE OF DIAGNOSIS:
CROSS-CULTURAL CONSIDERATIONS

In American culture, truth-telling is considered essential for the patient to cope with the disease, to be in control of the situation, and to plan for the future. It is also essential today in the current legal context in order for the physician to obtain consent for certain treatments. However, attitudes toward disclosure of diagnosis have changed considerably in the United States over the past several decades. In the early 1960s, 90% of U.S. physicians did not inform their patients of this diagnosis of cancer; today at least that many routinely inform patients of their diagnosis. This approach is consistent with the North American values of individualism, autonomy, and self-reliance. Diagnostic information is seen as belonging to the patient, rather than to the family or physician. According to Dr. Rohini Anand, training director of the National MultiCultural Institute in Washington, DC, many Americans also believe that "if the issues are not all laid out, verbally and bluntly, the message won't come across. In other cultures, messages are more context bound, less verbal" (p. 8).

Communication patterns in Japanese culture, for example, are quite different and are often an enigma to Westerners. Japanese communication patterns have the following dominant characteristics: choosing to speak little, communicating without the use of language, indirectness, and awareness of mood (or the appropriate social–emotional atmosphere). The Japanese have many expressions of indirect communication as compared with other cultures, and it is believed that use of direct communication can disturb harmony of the group. In general, Japanese physicians are reluctant to disclose terminal illnesses to their patients, preferring instead to share this information with family members. They do not want to diminish hope and they also reflect a cultural bias toward withholding bad news or *omoiyari*. This term refers to a special form of compassion (the Japanese language has many words that describe varying degrees of empathy and kindness) that implies a deeper level of consideration for the patient. With the growth of the hospice movement in Japan during the 1990s, much debate about the disclosure issue is currently underway and can be expected to continue.

SOURCES: M. Iwai (1996). *Volunteers in the Japanese hospice: Current concerns and future model.* Doctoral dissertation, Colorado State University; L. Paton & M. Wicks (1996). The growth of the hospice movement in Japan. *The American Journal of Hospice and Palliative Care, 13*(4), 26–31; C. Vanchieri (1995). Cultural gaps leave patients angry, doctors confused. *Journal of the National Cancer Institute, 87* (21), 7–8.

Today, even though more patients are directly being told by doctors that they are going to die, interactions with family and friends still often reflect patterns related to Glaser and Strauss's mutual pretense context. These interactions can be characterized as a **conspiracy of silence,** which is a mutual pact to avoid issues of consequence as they relate to the death and to focus only on the mundane (e.g., the weather). This avoidance is not based on malice, but rather

CULTURAL GAPS CAN LEAD TO MISCOMMUNICATION

A Salvadoran woman with advanced cancer was asked through a translator whether she would like chemotherapy to treat her disease, which had recurred despite numerous interventions. The physician felt he had to offer the option, but believed the patient's prognosis was extremely poor regardless of further therapy.

The patient didn't see a choice in the matter. If the doctor offered it, she should take it. When she agreed to the aggressive treatment, other members of the medical team explained to her that the therapy would be too difficult and might make a return trip to her native country impossible. All the while, the interpreter translated only part of what they were saying, because he believed it was too upsetting.

A Navajo patient, on the way to the operating room was told by his surgeon that he might not wake up, that this was the risk of every surgery. For the surgeon, this statement was routine, but the patient heard it as a death sentence and would not consent to surgery. In traditional Navajo culture, the spoken word has the power to shape reality.

During her final days, a Chinese cancer patient was moved to a single hospital room to make her more comfortable and give the family privacy. The family viewed the move as an act of isolation, abandonment.

Overcoming a language barrier is just the first step in meeting the needs of patients from other cultures. Differences in experiences of illness and death and beliefs about the appropriate role of the healers, the patient, and family members go deeper into cultural and religious background. Best intentions may lead to anger, miscommunications, or ignored instructions if the patient's needs and perspective are not determined, or if assumptions are made about a person because of his or her culture.

SOURCE: C. Vanchieri (1995). Cultural gaps leave patients angry, doctors confused. *Journal of the National Cancer Institute, 87* (21), 7–8.

is an attempt to avoid painful or frightening interactions. It is unfortunate, however, that what is done with good intent may actually increase fears or feelings of abandonment. The dying are put into an **emotional quarantine** in which others do not allow them to share their true feelings, but rather force them to participate in formalities and to exchange platitudes (Weisman, 1972).

Many currently used avoidance strategies are similar to those first described by Kastenbaum and Aisenberg (1972):

- *Reassurance:* "You are doing so well now."
- *Denial:* "You don't mean that; you are not going to die."
- *Changing the subject:* "Let's think of something more cheerful."
- *Fatalism:* "We are all going to die someday."

As difficult as it may be for all involved, open communication about the impending death can allow for mutual support, ameliorate fears of loneliness and abandonment, and allow the opportunity to finish business. It is not appropriate, however, to force the dying to participate in a discussion when they are unwilling or unable to do so. The dying should be allowed to determine the focus and set the pace of the dialogue (Evans, Esbenson, & Jaffe, 1981).

Withdrawal.   Charmaz (1980) describes three major contributors to the withdrawal that is frequently experienced by the dying and those in their social environment. First, there may be certain environmental conditions present that make it difficult for previous patterns of interaction to continue. For example, the patient may be in a hospital that is many miles away from family and friends. Circumstances such as these can act as a wedge between the patient and significant others, interfering with regular contact and meaningful support. A second source of isolation is withdrawal by the dying person. This situation may be caused by such factors as discomfort, pain, lapses into unconsciousness, a variety of fears, and so forth. Third, there is often a social avoidance of the dying, which may be the most significant contributor to the dying person's isolation. Society may withdraw because of fear of death, uncertainty as to how to interact with the dying, and/or a feeling that the patient is becoming a burden (see Figure 2.3). **Sociological death** or *social death* are terms used to signify a withdrawal pattern that is of extreme magnitude (Sweeting & Gilhooly, 1992).

Closely related to Charmaz's idea that environmental factors contribute to the withdrawal between the dying and their friends and family is the concept of a *change in a shared reality*. People often base a relationship on shared interests and activities. Once these can no longer be shared, the relationship weakens or terminates. For example, work colleagues may socialize outside of the work environment, but even then the focal point of much conversation is related to the job (tasks, deadlines, other colleagues). When dying persons are forced to leave their jobs, they may then find they have little or nothing in common with certain former coworkers. Thus, a pattern of withdrawal may result. Because the dying must bring closure to more and more facets of their lives, it is only natural that as time passes they would gradually need to terminate certain relationships. There is neither sufficient time nor physical and psychological energy to continue all relationships to the same degree as before the onset of the terminal illness. The "emotional distancing" that results from withdrawal is not founded in ill will, but rather is a common coping mechanism (Evans, Esbenson, & Jaffe, 1981).

Dissynchrony between dying persons and their loved ones, as they struggle to deal with the impending death, may place additional stress on relationships and cause more rapid withdrawal to take place. Christ (1983) explains this dissynchrony as "an unevenness at different points in time in specific cognitive appraisal or affective states" (p. 61). One person in a given relationship, for example, may need to express and discuss feelings while the other may need some emotional distance and therefore refuse to talk.

FIGURE 2.3
Contributors to the Withdrawal Process

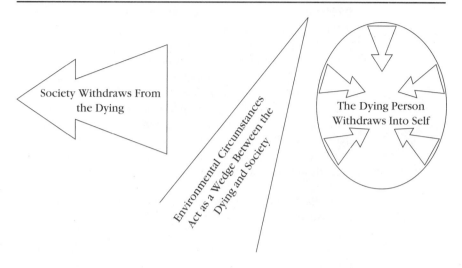

Psychological Needs and Concerns

Psychological needs and concerns of the dying are many and varied. It is difficult, if not impossible, to separate totally psychological issues from those discussed earlier in this chapter. Issues that will be examined in this section are
control and independence, contribution to others, and a review of one's life.

Control and Independence.   Many individuals with life-threatening illnesses have reported that retaining some sense of control in their lives is crucial
to their emotional well-being. Human beings desire this control from a very
young age. For example, a toddler who loudly says "No!" to almost every request
or who refuses all offers of help by a well-meaning adult is, in essence, communicating both a strong desire and a need to be in control of the situation. The
need for control in some aspects of their lives can be crucial to dying individuals in their attempts to retain a positive self-concept, since there is so much that
they can no longer control. For example, individuals who are dying cannot
indefinitely postpone death and continue to live, nor can they prevent others
from emotionally distancing themselves. Also, body functioning may have deteriorated to such a point that they are no longer able to walk, or swallow, or control bladder function.

Since there is so much that the dying cannot control, it is crucial to permit
control where it is possible. For instance, they should be allowed to participate in
decisions regarding their own health care (such as deciding whether to continue
seeking a cure or opt for palliative measures only, providing input regarding

where they prefer to die, or refusing certain medications). In order to make decisions that are personally appropriate, dying individuals need information about their diagnosis and prognosis, available therapies, and other medical options. Information must be presented in clear terminology that is understandable to the patient. Explanations often need to be repeated because of difficulties in assimilating all relevant information at one time.

Closely related to the desire to retain a sense of control is the desire to remain as independent as possible. Dying individuals often prefer to perform tasks for themselves rather than depend on someone else for assistance. This may even be the case when there is a struggle to complete the task. For example, a dying adolescent may prefer to take an hour and a half to bathe and dress himself painstakingly rather than depend on his older brother or parent for help, even though it would take much less time.

Contribution to Others.   Even when given the opportunity to retain as great a degree of control as possible, the dying may still not be capable of doing many things for themselves and may need to depend on others to perform certain tasks. As a result, they may begin to question whether they are a burden to others and whether their lives have any value. In order to counteract a potential sense of worthlessness, caregivers should allow them the opportunity to contribute to the well-being of others. They may choose to do this in a variety of ways, depending to a great extent on such factors as energy level, presence of pain, and time remaining until death. For example, the dying may choose to mend clothes for their children, give directions on the care of the garden, or verbalize part of the family's history so that it may be recorded. All of these types of activities can enhance the dying individual's sense of self-worth.

Review of One's Life.   Most human beings want to know that their lives have been meaningful. The conclusion as to whether this goal has been accomplished is a very personal one; it is related to involvement in various activities, past accomplishments, quality of relationships, and much more. Dying individuals strive to find an answer to the question "Was my life worthwhile?" To help answer this question, they engage in a process of life review. Reminiscing is an important tool in promoting the life review and in breaking out of the conspiracy of silence described earlier. It allows the dying to bring to mind important memories and share them with others. Reminiscing can confirm that others remember the roles they played and value the contributions they made. Although presented here in the context of impending death, the life review process is important in the lives of nonterminally ill persons who are facing death as a natural consequence of age.

Spiritual Needs and Concerns

Many persons' sense of spirituality becomes magnified as death approaches and issues related to meaning, hope, and belief systems are often a primary concern.

Spirituality includes the inspirational and existential aspects of our existence. It facilitates the integration of self into a larger universal scheme (Mauritzen, 1988). The spiritual needs of the dying must be acknowledged as part of a holistic approach to caregiving.

While the modern hospice had its roots in England where the spiritual component was a prominent feature of the service, spirituality has received somewhat less attention in the American hospice experience. However, this important aspect of care has received increased focus in the United States, with the National Hospice Organization holding its first conference on spiritual care in 1991 (Millison, 1995).

Meaning. Many believe that a primary component of our spiritual dimension is a search for meaning—meaning of life and death. Inner peace is promoted when answers to these fundamental questions are found. Doka (1993) identified the following major spiritual needs of dying individuals that relate to our human need for meaningfulness:

- *The need to find meaning in one's life:* The dying often search for the ultimate significance of life—a search that extends beyond the acceptance of death. Existential issues are inevitably faced as one approaches death. The inability to discover or reaffirm meaning can create a deep sense of spiritual pain. Answers do not necessarily have to be found in a religious context. However, religious belief systems give many individuals new purpose in life or help sustain previously developed values.
- *The need to die an appropriate death:* "Appropriate" is defined as being consistent with one's self-identity. In a study in which physicians, nurses, and hospital chaplains were interviewed, "meaning" was found to be one of the three most important factors contributing to an appropriate death— meaning not only in one's past life but in one's remaining life and death as well (Augustine & Kalish, 1975). Dying individuals need an opportunity to interpret their own death within a framework that is congruent with their values and life-style. In many cases, individuals may also be making choices regarding the manner in which they will die. As they make difficult decisions concerning what is appropriate for them, the dying often request spiritual guidance or sanctions from spiritual leaders.
- *The need to transcend death:* A sense of transcendence can come from many avenues. In a religious context, it is often viewed in terms of reassurance of immortality. Transcendence can also be achieved through the knowledge that future generations will follow them or a belief that their deeds will outlive them.

Hope. Spiritual concerns also relate to the concept of hope, which Kübler-Ross (1969) described as a powerful dynamic force throughout the dying process. It reflects a state of mind associated with positive actions.

> One cannot overemphasize the importance of hope. Hope maintains the mo-
> tivation to make active efforts to enhance health, to comply with medical
> management, to strengthen the social support system and thus to live longer.
> (Mead & Willemsen, 1995, p. 124)

Hope, however, is not always related to the expectation of a cure or freedom
from suffering.

> There are those who will find hope in faith and their belief in an afterlife; some
> will look forward to the moment a milestone is reached or a deed is accom-
> plished; there are even some whose hope is centered on maintaining the kind
> of control that will permit them the means to decide the moment of their death,
> or actually to make their own quietus unhindered. Whatever form it may take,
> each of us must find hope in his or her own way. (Nuland, 1993, p. 257)

Sometimes a dying person's source of hope can be as undemanding as the wish
to live until a daughter's graduation or even a holiday that has particular meaning. Regardless of the dying person's nearness to death, hope can still be maintained. Because of this human quality, caregivers can help sustain optimism and
give comfort to the dying as they cope with fear and uncertainty.

Spiritual Beliefs.   Caregivers need to develop insight into the power of
spiritual beliefs in helping many individuals cope with the process of dying. Millison (1988) recommends the following strategies for those working with the
terminally ill:

- Understand that growth in the spiritual realm presents opportunities
  for development and healing that may not be present in other facets of
  one's life.
- Be aware of your own spirituality, whether from a religious or nonreligious origin.
- Do not impose your own spiritual values on dying individuals.
- Be supportive of the patients' sense of spirituality even if you do not personally share a particular belief.

For many, traditional expressions of their faith (e.g., prayer, the sacraments,
and visits from the clergy) give them great comfort. However, Hoy (1983) advises chaplains to "meet people where they are" when assessing the spiritual or
religious needs of the dying; pat formulas cannot be given. Individuals approach
their last days from a wide variety of backgrounds, beliefs, and spiritual experiences and, thus, their needs will vary. Hoy also advises that "the needs of those
who profess no formal religious roots are no less real than those who do" (p. 185).
He urges sensitivity to the ways different individuals may want their needs met
and to whom they may prefer to turn for spiritual support.

Numerous barriers often prevent individuals from meeting their spiritual
needs and exploring related issues. Caregivers and clergy may be intolerant of
patients' belief systems, and they may fail to recognize and respect beliefs that
differ from their own. This attitude can be both confusing and distressful to

individuals anticipating death. Even if caregivers accept the dying person's spiritual orientation, they often feel uncomfortable discussing particular issues (such as the meaning of one's death) because they feel that exploration of these issues may be too painful for the dying person. Other obstacles that can block the expression of deeply held beliefs and the exploration of pressing spiritual questions during this time include limited privacy for discussing concerns, medical procedures that reduce the individual's ability to think clearly and express thoughts, and restricted access to spiritual counselors and religious leaders (Attig, 1983).

In some cases, spiritual concerns cause severe distress. Peteet (1985), in a study of 50 hospital cancer patients, found that over half had concerns involving spiritual issues and about one-third were actively struggling with these problems. While he emphasized that these issues can take different forms in different individuals, Peteet reported that most of the problems identified by patients in his study related to

- loss of religious support (for example, a trusted minister leaves the patient's church),
- pressure to adopt a different religious position (a wife urges her spouse to adopt her religious convictions),
- unusual religious beliefs (a young woman in her final stages of cancer believes that she has been chosen to be a missionary and therefore expects to fully recover),
- conflict between religious views and views of illness (dying individuals may feel unresolved anger toward God and be unable to reconcile their feelings with their religious beliefs, or individuals may feel that their illness is due somehow to their past sins), and
- preoccupation with the meaning of life and illness (an intense focusing on religion and spiritual questions in an attempt to understand what is happening).

In summary, personal philosophies, moral values, and religious belief systems are especially important to individuals facing death, and they need to be acknowledged, respected, and supported by caregivers. Professional caregivers should be aware of the spiritual needs of the dying, as well as the obstacles that prevent them from being met. Staff members who work with the dying also need to be well informed about diverse religious traditions and their importance to particular patients and their families. The spiritual needs of the dying are rooted in their family, religious, and cultural systems (Parry, 1990; Siefken, 1993).

PATIENTS' BILL OF RIGHTS

As concern has grown over providing quality holistic care to dying individuals, many health care facilities have formalized their philosophy by adopting a patients' bill of rights such as the one in Figure 2.4. Additionally, some facilities

FIGURE 2.4
Patients' Bill of Rights

I have the right to be treated as a living human being until I die.

I have the right to maintain a sense of hopefulness, however changing its focus may be.

I have the right to be cared for by those who can maintain a sense of hopefulness, however changing this might be.

I have the right to express my feelings and emotions about my approaching death in my own way.

I have the right to to participate in decisions concerning my care.

I have the right to expect continuing medical and nursing attention even though "cure" goals must be changed to "comfort" goals.

I have the right not to die alone.

I have the right to be free from pain.

I have the right to have my questions answered honestly.

I have the right to have help from and for my family in accepting my death.

I have the right not to be deceived.

I have the right to die in peace and dignity.

I have the right to retain my individuality and not be judged for my decisions which may be contrary to beliefs of others.

I have the right to discuss and enlarge my religious and/or spiritual experiences, whatever these may mean to others.

I have the right to expect that the sanctity of the human body will be respected after death.

I have the right to be cared for by caring, sensitive, knowledgeable people who will attempt to understand my needs and will be able to gain some satisfaction in helping me face my death.

SOURCE: This Bill of Rights was created in 1971 during a workshop on "The Terminally Ill Patient and the Helping Person," in Lansing, Michigan, sponsored by the Southwestern Michigan Inservice Education Council and conducted by Amelia J. Barbus, Associate Professor of Nursing, Wayne State University, Detroit.

have hired personnel to act as advocates for the sick and dying (patient advocates, medical social workers, and child-life specialists, among others). These staff members ensure that patients understand their medical procedures, give them the opportunity to ask questions, and encourage them to participate in decision making.

FIGURE 2.5
Selected Factors Affecting the Dying Process

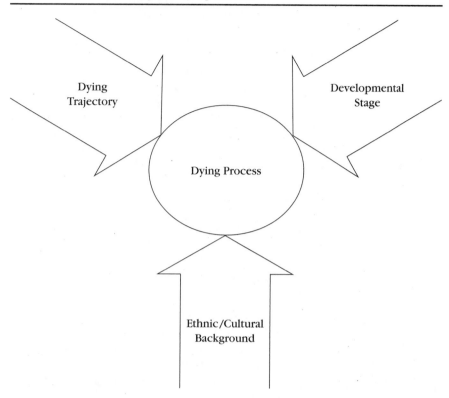

FACTORS AFFECTING THE DYING PROCESS

The needs and concerns discussed earlier in this chapter are common components of the dying process but should not be regarded as universal. Even though
there are many similarities among dying persons, there are many differences as
well. Many factors affect the dying process and contribute to this variability,
including dying trajectories, developmental stages, and ethnic or cultural background (see Figure 2.5).

Dying Trajectories

The certainty or uncertainty that a particular physical condition will end in
death influences the emotional and psychological state of the individual, as does
the time frame within which one is expected to die. Using these dimensions of
certainty and time, Glaser and Strauss (1968) describe four **death trajectories:**

1. *Certain death at a known time:* for example, liver cancer
2. *Certain death at an unknown time:* for example, cystic fibrosis

3. *Uncertain death but at a known time of resolution:* for example, advanced heart disease with outcome dependent on the success of surgery

4. *Uncertain death and unknown time of resolution:* for example, multiple sclerosis

Glaser and Strauss (1968, p. 6) stress that the "dying trajectories are perceived courses of dying rather than actual courses." One may expect to die within a particular time frame, but death may not occur within that time frame. It is the expectation, rather than the fact, that influences the adjustment process of the dying and also others' interaction patterns with them. In addition, Pattison (1978) explains that trajectories with uncertain time frames are ultimately more difficult to deal with than those with certain time frames because of the ambiguity involved.

The four trajectories described by Glaser and Strauss do not appropriately describe all types of deaths. For example, many deaths are sudden and unexpected (such as accidents, suicide, or natural disasters). Because these types of trajectories affect the survivor rather than the deceased, they will be discussed in chapter 3 as they relate to the bereavement process.

Developmental Stages

A study of human developmental processes reveals that individuals' needs and abilities change over time as a result of growth, maturation, and learning. Development is defined as "orderly and sequential changes that occur with the passage of time as an organism moves from conception to death. It includes those processes that are biologically programmed within the organism. It also includes those processes by which the organism is changed or transformed through interaction with the environment" (Vander Zanden, 1985, p. 4). We must realize, then, that there are stage-specific characteristics that influence the dying person's behavior, focus and intensity of fears, desires for particular types of control, ability to understand information about the illness, and particular issues that need to be resolved prior to death.

In order to give insight into the importance of meeting normal developmental needs and of understanding normal developmental characteristics, Erik Erikson's (1963) theory of psychosocial development and Jean Piaget's (1963) theory of cognitive development will be used as a foundation for discussion of developmental issues in subsequent chapters.

Erikson's Theory.   Erikson (1963) hypothesized that an individual normally deals with a series of eight psychosocial stages or crises during the course of his or her lifespan. Each of these stages may potentially be resolved in either a positive or negative direction. The outcome of each crisis is closely tied to the type of environment or social support that is available to an individual facing a particular crisis.

Each of these crises will be discussed in more detail in the upcoming stage-related chapters. They are identified in Table 2.1. Unless specific care is given to

TABLE 2.1
Stages of Development: Erikson's and Piaget's Theories

APPROXIMATE AGE SPAN	ERIKSON'S PSYCHOSOCIAL STAGES	PIAGET'S COGNITIVE STAGES
Infancy	Trust versus mistrust	Sensorimotor stage
Toddlerhood	Autonomy versus shame and doubt	Preoperational stage
Preschool	Initiative versus guilt	Concrete-operational stage
School-age	Industry versus inferiority	Formal-operational stage
Adolescence	Identity versus role confusion	
Young adulthood	Intimacy versus isolation	
Middle adulthood	Generativity versus stagnation	
Late adulthood	Integrity versus despair	

support a positive outcome, factors inherent to the dying process often promote a negative resolution to a particular crisis.

Piaget's Theory.   Piaget (1963) explains that children think in a qualitatively different fashion than do adults. He theorized that their thinking matures over time and progresses through a number of stages (see Table 2.1). To be effective in our communication with dying and grieving children, we must take into account the child's capacity to reason. The relationship of cognitive development to the understanding of death and illness will be described in more detail in upcoming chapters.

Ethnic / Cultural Background

Cultural variables have an effect on dying persons' beliefs about death, their coping strategies, manifestation of feelings, rites, and customs. Variations in practices and beliefs are evident when comparing death systems in different cultures. Gruman (1978) describes a **death system** as "a distinctive network of suppositions, norms, and symbols that are functionally effective in the routinized, communal management of death and dying" (p. 203). These systems may also vary from one subgroup to another within the same country. In their comprehensive study of ethnic groups in the United States, Kalish and Reynolds (1976) found many differences among Anglo-Americans, Black Americans, Japanese Americans, and Mexican Americans. They discovered variations in attitudes, values, expectations, experiences, and customs as evidenced by responses to a series of interview questions. For example, differences were found in how comfortably thoughts and emotions could be shared with others.

Membership in a particular cultural group not only has an impact on attitudes and customs, it can also have an effect on the sensation or expression of pain (Wolff & Langley, 1977). Persons with a strong German heritage, for example, typically do not openly address personal feelings. Some Native American groups regard pain as a sign of weakness and, therefore, socially unacceptable if displayed openly. Older Japanese Americans often try to mask their pain, even if in agony, in order to avoid distressing others (Kalish & Reynolds, 1976).

Bates (1987) presents a biocultural model to explain why the perception of pain varies from culture to culture. Based on an extensive review of the research literature, she theorizes that

> social learning theory is instrumental in the development of meanings for and attitudes towards pain. Learned values and attitudes affect one's memories of prior pain experiences. Each of these is a factor which, according to the gate-control theory, may influence psychophysiological functioning, as well as behavior, when individuals are exposed to potentially painful stimuli. Therefore, it is likely that cultural group experiences influence the psychophysiological processes responsible for pain threshold and perception of pain severity, as well as pain response. (p. 48)

Given the many differences among and within cultural groups, it becomes evident that health professionals, family, and friends must be sensitive to a range of needs, thoughts, and emotions. Assumptions as to how people cope with death and dying cannot be based on either cultural stereotypes or universal statements.

HOSPICE CARE

The word *hospice* originally referred to a way station for weary travelers. More recently, it is the term used for a particular type of care. **Hospice care** is a philosophy of care provided to dying individuals and their families that emphasizes death with dignity. Hospice programs have evolved and spread throughout the world over the last two decades (Iwai, 1996; Sikorska, 1991), adapting to diverse cultural and health-care contexts.

The 1974 creation of Hospice of Connecticut in New Haven, modeled after St. Christopher's Hospice of London, marked the beginning of a rapidly expanding social movement in the United States. Volunteer groups in hundreds of communities engaged in a grassroots movement to humanize the dying process which, over the course of the twentieth century, had become a medical event destined to occur in a hospital rather than a uniquely personal event taking place in one's own home. The passage of the Tax Equity and Fiscal Responsibility Act (TEFRA) in 1982 established the Medicare hospice benefit and the enactment of numerous state statutes. This legislation, prompted by both humane as well as cost-saving considerations, legitimized and mainstreamed the hospice concept in the health care system and promoted a more uniform delivery system. Hospices that are appropriately certified may now receive reimbursement from Medicare, as well as Medicaid. Many private insurance companies also include a hospice benefit.

While hospice care is typically home-based, services may also be delivered in a freestanding structure or in a unit of a long-term care facility. In England, there are even hospice adult day-care programs (Corr & Corr, 1992).

FIRST GERMAN HOSPICES

Inspired by the British hospice movement, several German physicians and theologians in the 1960s began to integrate hospice concepts into their work. It was not until 1971, however, that the wider German public was introduced to the hospice philosophy when a documentary about St. Christopher's hospice was aired on German television. The video entitled "Noch 16 Tage. Eine Sterbeklinik in London" (16 Days Left. A Hospital for the Dying in London) triggered a hot debate between those who wanted similar institutions in Germany and those who opposed them. Some Germans had the misperception that aggressive pain management was equivalent to mercy killing, which they associated with the government-sanctioned euthanasia of Nazi Germany. Despite lack of support from the government and many churches, the first inpatient hospice, similar to the British model, opened at the University hospital of Cologne in 1983. By the early 1990s the hospice movement in Germany had gained official approval from the Evangelical and the Catholic Church of Germany. The number of hospices has increased steadily since that time.

SOURCE: C. Farnon (1996). A personal exploration of the German hospice system. *The American Journal of Hospice and Palliative Care, 13*(14), 32–37.

In most home-based hospice programs, family caregivers are given support by professionals (under the guidance of a hospice medical director). Trained lay volunteers assist by performing daily tasks such as preparing meals or cleaning house, giving backup relief to the primary family caregivers, and providing emotional support for grieving family members. The focus of hospice care is on quality of remaining life, through the provision of palliative (comfort rather than curative) care. Dying persons and their families are offered physical, emotional, social, psychological, and spiritual support. Crucial facets of the hospice philosophy include the belief that dying persons are living persons. As such, hospices strive to maximize the quality of remaining life by meeting the needs of the whole person while allowing the patient and family to retain as much autonomy in their decision making as possible. All hospice programs operate under the following four guiding principles (Rhymes, 1990):

1. The patient and family are the primary unit of care.
2. Care is provided by an interdisciplinary team.
3. Pain and symptom control are paramount.
4. Bereavement follow-up is provided.

The National Hospice Organization (NHO) serves as a regulatory body in the United States to ensure that organizations that call themselves "hospices" follow fundamental guidelines for provision of care (National Hospice Organization, 1987).

This hospice nurse sometimes visits homeless patients, showing his care and concern to those who are ill and dying, regardless of personal circumstances.

Contributors to Success

Many factors have contributed to the rapid acceptance of the hospice philosophy (Ferrell, 1985; Millet, 1983; Paradis, 1985; Tehan, 1982). These are summarized below.

■ *Provision of care either at home or in a homelike inpatient setting ensures a humanizing alternative to the increasing depersonalization that has become a part of a technologically based medical experience.* The focus of hospice care is to provide personal comfort and promote dignity rather than to cure a disease; therefore, the dying individual is regarded as a "person" rather than a "patient." Because the primary caregiver does not have responsibility for a large number of other patients, he or she can spend more time learning how to meet the idiosyncratic needs or desires of the dying individual. For example, a family member who knows the patient well may realize that banana milkshakes have always been a favorite food and, therefore, be able to encourage a much-needed increase in caloric intake by preparing that preferred beverage. In another situation, the primary caregiver may be aware of how very important completion of a quilt is to the dying individual, so that she might give it to her only granddaughter as a wedding gift. Hospice volunteers might then be able to give the assistance necessary to finish the project while letting the dying grandmother do as much of the remaining work on the quilt as she is able to do and wants to do.

■ *Most people derive a great deal of comfort and security from a sense of familiarity. As a result, many individuals prefer to die in their own homes.* There they are surrounded by their own belongings and are accustomed to the sights, smells, and sounds in the environment. Dying individuals can more easily remain in the mainstream of family life by being at home and by spending time in the rooms that are the usual site of daily routines. For example, many families may put a hospital bed in the living room or family room so that conversation and activity may include the patient. This involvement can help counterbalance the common fear of abandonment and isolation.

Although life changes dramatically for a family caring for a dying loved one, all can derive comfort from continuation of daily routines in familiar surroundings. The family can gather, as they have in the past, to watch television, play a game, or look through a photo album. There is a focus on living rather than on dying. One hospice patient's son is quoted as saying: "We're compressing a great deal of life into a very short time. To have as much of the real life available as possible, which the home environment provides, was a paramount consideration" (Leloudis & Pole, 1985, p. 31).

■ *Although dying persons and their family members cannot control the course of the disease itself, they can retain control over many facets of their lives. The hospice philosophy encourages patients and families to determine what is best for themselves.* Once they are given complete information and are made aware of their options, they are the ones who make decisions.

Hospice families, including the dying member, decide what type of support they desire from hospice staff. One family may desire, for example, to have volunteers occasionally come to the home to give spiritual support and also request daily medical attention from a nurse. Another family may ask that a volunteer do the grocery shopping and care for the children for several afternoons a week. Hospice families may choose among various palliative medical treatments, depending on their unique situation. For example, many choose a self-regulated regimen of medication taken orally. If unable to swallow their medication, others would prefer rectal suppositories over shots.

Dying individuals and their families often work together to plan events which will ultimately follow. Will there be a funeral or will there be a memorial service? Will the body be buried or cremated? Who will be the pallbearers? Other decisions revolve around such crucial issues as who will be responsible for the surviving children.

■ *Family members experience a therapeutic outcome from directly contributing to their loved one's care.* Kirschling (1986, p. 124) notes, for example, that the majority of spouses caring for a dying husband or wife cited a number of very important needs, including the need (1) to be with the dying person; (2) to be helpful to the dying person; (3) to receive assurance of the dying person's comfort; (4) to be informed of the dying person's condition; (5) to be informed of the impending death; (6) to ventilate emotions; (7) to gain support from other family members; and (8) to derive acceptance, support, and comfort from health-care professionals. Kirschling also reported that families regarded hospice care as meeting these needs more often than other types of care.

In order to help family members feel more secure in their interactions with the dying, we need to provide education as to how they might perform certain functions. For example, many caregivers need to learn how to help the patient ambulate and how to provide palliative care. Unfortunately, many family members in the past have acquired these skills through trial and error. Hospice staff, however, currently regard that type of education as an important part of their mission.

New Challenges in Hospice Care

Policy Issues.   In the professional literature, few authors have addressed policy issues related to hospice care. A notable exception is the work of Miller and Mike (1995) who have challenged us to examine future terminal care options in context of the health-care reform movement in the United States. In their analysis of federal policy related to hospice care of the terminally ill, these authors have identified a number of contraints:

- The requirement that all care be provided in the home, combined with the need for a primary caregiver, can be problematic for many older persons. Many elderly live alone or with a spouse unable physically to provide care for a terminally ill person.
- There is limited availability of Medicare-certified hospice programs for Medicare beneficiaries that live in rural areas. Because federal guidelines are complex and require hospices to employ many professionals, it has been extremely difficult for very small or rural communities to develop programs that can be Medicare-certified.
- Admission into a Medicare-certified hospice is dependent upon receiving a physician's prognosis of less than 6 months to live. This limitation can exclude individuals who have diseases that are generally terminal but more difficult to predict in terms of duration (e.g., chronic heart and lung problems as well as progressive dementia).
- The funding mechanisms of the Medicare Hospice benefit can pose difficulties for many programs. Reimbursement rates are fixed, and the prospective method of payment can be problematic if patients need extra services or have unexpected complications. A certified hospice, especially those with a low census of patients, runs the risk of spending more than Medicare will reimburse because of this process.

While taking these constraints into consideration, Miller and Mike (1995) argue that we must rethink the goals of terminal care in order to develop policy that is more relevant to actual needs. They charge that the current policy leaves some terminally ill individuals without services.

Issues Related to Patient Characteristics.   While most (71%) patients served by hospice programs have some form of cancer (Strahan, 1994), the number of hospice patients with AIDS is increasing, which poses special challenges for hospice staff (Anderson & MacElveen-Hoehn, 1988). Staff report that working with AIDS patients is more time-consuming and stressful than working with individuals who have other diseases (Baker & Seager, 1991). One reason may be that individuals with a diagnosis of AIDS are typically younger and require a longer duration of hospice care. AIDS patients also have unique physical and psychosocial needs (Kemp & Stepp, 1995), which some hospice staff may be unprepared to provide. One hospice staff member said: "AIDS puts a hospice nurse at risk for burnout because there seems to be no predictable course, and the usual methods and treatments that are helpful for cancer patients often do not work for AIDS" (Buckingham, 1992).

Staff may also be unprepared to serve patients from ethnically diverse groups effectively. While the majority of hospice patients (approximately 80%) are white (Strahan, 1994), persons of color are increasingly recognized as potential consumers of hospice services. In 1995, Infeld, Gordon, and Harper edited a special issue of *The Hospice Journal,* which focused on hospice care and cultural diversity. In this special issue, a number of factors were identified related to low utilization rates of hospice services by ethnic minorities. These include unfamiliarity with hospice services, inability to identify with providers (who were largely middle-class and Caucasian), fear and lack of trust, language barriers, and lack of availability of culturally sensitive services. The "primary caregiver" requirement of most hospices also does not recognize variations in caregiving arrangements among ethnic groups. For example, adherence to the current hospice definition of primary caregiver is restrictive for African American terminally ill patients who may have many people caring for them, with no one relative available all of the time in the same place.

> The nature of the black community's support system, with older generations supporting the younger and greater reliance on nonblood kinship ties, may pose a problem for hospices with a traditional definition of a primary caregiver. What is needed is a redefinition of *which* and *how many* persons can be primary caregivers and an acceptance that the patient may live in multiple locations with nonrelated persons during the course of the illness. (Gordon, 1996, pp. 63–64)

Additional recommendations, in regard to removing barriers, include educating the minority communities about available services, training hospice staff regarding important differences and variations in cultural traditions and beliefs, and actively recruiting hospice staff and volunteers from diverse ethnic groups (Burrs, 1995; Talamantes, Lawler, & Espino, 1995).

SUMMARY

Death is a natural part of the human experience. Dying persons, as living persons, have many needs and concerns that are similar to those of healthy persons. Other needs are unique to the fact that the individuals are dying. Using a holistic perspective, caregivers should give support for physical, emotional, social, psychological, and spiritual needs. Although there are many similarities in the way in which individuals face their own deaths, there is no single "right way" to die. A number of factors affect the dying process, including the expected time frame in which the death will occur, the age and related developmental stage of the dying individual, and his or her cultural background. With the advent of increasingly sophisticated medical technology in health care, there has been a growing awareness that we need to balance that mechanization with human care and concern. Hospice programs have developed and spread rapidly in the context of this heightened awareness. With an emphasis on quality of remaining life, these organizations have brought increased attention to the needs of the dying and to the concept of "death with dignity." Today, hospices face new challenges as they adapt to changes in health care polices and to changes in society at large.

Personal Account

Cecil Neth, a seasoned journalist dying of ALS, writes about coming to terms with his own death. With his characteristic humor and insight, he discusses the hard facts related to his disease and his concern for the impact it will have on his family. In the second part of this personal account, Cecil's wife Jane finishes his story, openly and honestly sharing the difficult decisions made during his last days.

The Courage to Face Death
Cecil Neth

I believe I was, until a few years ago, fairly typical. Thoughts of dying were always thoughts of dying on my own terms.

Death would drift by when the right factors converged. Enough insurance. A secure home. All the children out of school and doing well. It would arrive on

---

SOURCE: From M. Colter and J. Neth (Eds.). (1996). *ALS: A Beginner's Manual.* Red Feather Lakes, CO: Red Mesa Publishing.

my schedule and I, an aging sage, would depart with just the proper measure of patriarchal dignity.

Things are not working out that way.

Nov. 5, 1985, late in the afternoon, Dr. Burk Jubelt, then an associate professor of neurology at the Northwestern University Medical School, told me, as gently as anyone could, that I was dying, ready or not.

I have amyotrophic lateral sclerosis, or ALS, an inexorably terminal neurological disorder.

It is commonly known as Lou Gehrig's disease. Gehrig, an all-star New York Yankees first baseman, gave the disease his name by dying of it twice—once in fact in 1941 and by inference the following year in *Pride of the Yankees,* with an assist from Gary Cooper. ALS was a mystery then, with no known cause and no treatment. It is the same mystery now, more than a century after its identification in France as a singular and specific ailment.

The available knowledge is worth a paragraph.

ALS is a disorder of the anterior horn cells in the spinal cord. The horn cells control muscle movement. ALS wastes the skeletal muscles. Voluntary movements from the neck down are lost. So, often, is the ability to speak and swallow. The heart and other internal organs work. Patients remain in control of eye muscles and bladder and bowel functions. They can hear. The mind is active, retaining what one researcher termed "totally preserved cognitive clarity and psychic energy." The sexual appetite persists—a bit of cosmic mischief amid the ruins.

Everything else is a statistical extrapolation. ALS generally strikes individuals past 40. The annual incidence is a fraction more than one person in each 100,000.

Each patient has a statistical probability of living from three to five years after diagnosis, but that is deceptive. It is impossible to know how long the disease was active before diagnosis. Many patients last less than a year after getting the word. A very few live more than a decade.

And that's that, except for the fact that virtually no one dies of the paralysis that is the final stage of ALS. The weakened body becomes susceptible to common ailments, such as pneumonia—and, I'm beginning to suspect, the mute and wearying frustration of contending with an agile mind in a motionless body.

Sportswriter John Lardner once described a noted shortstop as being not so much big as he was small. That's me: Moderately short. More light than heavy. No room for muscles that ripple. So I was surprised when some did. I was shaving and noticed a rhythmic movement of muscles in my shoulders and upper chest. I took inventory and found a few ripples on my calves and thighs.

The rippling—twitching, actually—is termed fasciculation. It appears in some patients and not in others, but for me it was the first overt symptom of ALS.

Diagnosis, even for the extensively skilled neurologists, is primarily visual. They also tug at the limbs and digits to gauge muscle strength. They employ electromyography—devilish tests with the impact of cold-morning jump-starts—to measure the disease's progress. But diagnosis is mostly by eyeball.

That means that doctors unfamiliar with the disease can easily miss the boat, and do. It means that individuals like me can discover a fasciculation and say, "Oops, too many martinis."

That was my response. I retreated to beer for a week, then reverted. The next symptom was difficulty opening my balcony door with the left hand. I decided I needed more exercise.

Even when my left foot began to drag occasionally and when leg and toe cramps in the night became common, I attributed the difficulties to blips in my lifestyle. I thought only marginally about seeing a doctor.

ALS is, after all, a nearly painless disease without, in most instances, an abrupt deterioration. It strikes mostly older folks like me who don't see anything terribly unusual about a stubborn body part.

And there is no immediate danger from self-deception. ALS is as untreatable in the beginning as at the end. The danger in not attending to symptoms is that they are insidious. They pile up, the muscle loss continues, and injury becomes a constant possibility. My own enlightenment began in the summer of 1985.

When I returned to the *Sun-Times* in 1984 after a teaching hiatus in Colorado, Jane stayed home with the family. She had a job she liked. The kids were in school. Our home had a nice view of the Rockies. I became a commuter husband.

That permitted me to ignore the muscular changes when alone at home in Chicago and to shrug them off amid all the activity when at home in Colorado.

Jane did urge me to see a doctor. I agreed, but procrastinated. I had passed three physicals in the past year, all with perfect numbers. I eventually visited a Chicago internist—who, I learned later, had correctly diagnosed ALS. But I blew off the neurological appointment he had needed for confirmation.

About that time I began to stumble and fall. I could give my body orders, but it didn't always obey.

I fell from a dining chair while reaching for a magazine. I had a cheap folding chaise lounge for watching television. I tumbled several times while getting up from it. I slipped going down the stairs to the street, but didn't fall. I fell once while crossing Lincoln Avenue near my apartment.

Jane arrived in Chicago in July 1985, with our 11-year-old son, Alex. She was concerned with the degree of physical change. I said I would see a doctor again after our trip east.

I fell twice in Maine, once painfully. I discovered I could no longer tie a decent fisherman's knot. The cramps, similar to good, old-fashioned charley horses, regularly woke me up.

Back in Chicago, with Jane and Alex safely in Colorado, I saw Dr. Raymond Curry of the general medicine department of the Northwestern University clinic on East Superior. He arranged a neurological examination that somehow was gummed up. While awaiting another exam, I fell down again.

The date was Oct. 2. I hit the sidewalk adjacent to Welles Park on North Lincoln. I fractured my left cheekbone in three places, spent seven hours in the Passavant emergency room, underwent surgery and connected with Dr. Jubelt, who four weeks after I left the hospital told me why I was no longer nimble.

I couldn't tell Jane with a phone call. I decided to wait until I returned to Colorado for the Thanksgiving holiday.

I needed the time to sort out my own reactions. I needed to discover whether I could be as objective as I wanted to be. I have spent a career in pursuit of objectivity and have found it elusive. But I felt that without a good grip on it, there would be a temptation to lie down and give up.

I drew a mental line in the dirt between self-interest and self-pity and practiced stepping back and forth. I believe I won.

I flew to Colorado and told Jane just before Thanksgiving. I told her I thought that if we kept a sense of the absurd, we could manage. She said that if I could do it, so could she. We are still working at it.

I told the five older children during their Christmas vacation from school. I asked them to keep a sense of humor, but not to giggle when I fell down. I haven't probed, but they seem on the surface to be doing splendidly.

Yet it hasn't been easy for Jane, or the kids, or for me.

For one thing, there is going to be a bottom line. It can't be talked or daydreamed away.

For another, I need so much care that my family has no chance to escape the inevitable.

Because I chose a profession that requires only two fingers and a word processor, I was able to work a full day five days a week for the *Sun-Times*.

Because I had what everyone should have, compassionate bosses, I worked from my Colorado home.

The last months in Chicago were flat-out miserable. Once at work, I was fine. Writing is inherently sedentary. It was the getting to and from work that pained.

My left arm and hand weakened first, then the left leg. The most important loss, except for the instability caused by a wobbly leg, was that of grasping strength.

Dressing for work—and getting undressed at night—became time-consuming labor. Shaving, bathing and brushing my teeth required more time and some new maneuvers.

Once dressed and on the street, there was another challenge, the No. 11 CTA bus. It required a sturdiness of limb that I no longer had and that a newly acquired cane couldn't replace.

Going south in the morning, I could usually persuade the driver not to start the bus until I was seated. Going north in the evening, no way.

I gave up on buses when one driver lurched away from Grand and Michigan, leaving me flat on my back in the aisle like an upended turtle. From then on, it was a cab twice a day between Lincoln and Lawrence and 401 N. Wabash. That smarts.

Meanwhile, of course, I had given up cooking.

From the moment of diagnosis I had chosen to live—to extract whatever measure of life I could from the three to five years the doctor said I would have.

It was dark when I left the doctor's office in the Northwestern University Medical Center. I bought a newspaper for the long bus ride to my neighborhood but didn't read it. I thought instead about Jane and how to tell her. I decided to wait until the next time I flew home. I stopped for a couple of drinks at the usual German restaurant. They went down as smoothly as those of the night before. The walk to the apartment was pleasant. I prepared a substantial meal and ate well. I watched television. I went to bed at the usual time and slept well.

The following day I searched through the phone book and located the Les Turner ALS Foundation. I arranged for some material to be sent to me. I knew little about ALS except that it was fatal.

I still had to go out for groceries, cigarettes and human contact. That meant navigating three flights of stairs, both ways. After a bad fall—and some trouble getting out of the apartment's old-fashioned bathtub—I moved, with the help of a friend, to a ground-floor motel room.

I continued to write daily editorials and had frequent contact with the office. Friends phoned or visited nearly every day. Because it had become difficult to perform even simple tasks, I became inventive. I placed the room's metal straightback chairs inside and outside the bathtub so I could sit down and slide in for a shower. I could slide out to dry although arm problems dictated that most of the drying was by evaporation. In order to dress myself, I spread the requisite amount of clothing on the room's extra bed and sort of slithered into it.

I either sent a motel employee for food or used a cane to walk to the nearby Chinese restaurant. On occasion, when I was feeling unusually fit, I crossed the corner intersection for a coffee shop omelet. On one memorable occasion, a group of friends from the *Sun-Times* picked me up for a night out.

One of the celebrants was *Sun-Times* editor Frank Devine, who, when I told him of my diagnosis, didn't respond with the usual sympathetic platitudes. Instead, he said that I would remain on the payroll and be expected to write editorials regularly from my Colorado home. I was to work out the details with the editorial page editor.

So on Feb. 2, 1986, after a medical checkup and with goodbyes said, and with the help of a friendly cabbie and the O'Hare wheelchair service, I went west to upend my family's routine.

Our home is in a typical Colorado subdivision. In the basement level there is a dandy family room, a dormitory bedroom and a nice bath. When I first arrived home, I worked downstairs. Then, because the stairs were too risky for me, I worked on the main level. Now it has taken on some of the aspects of a nursing home.

I had a walker for short trips, and a wheelchair that became a nearly constant companion. The dining table was moved so that there was room at one end for me to wheel to meals. For relaxation, I had an electrically powered chair that laid me down, then lifted me to a standing position. There was a wheelchair ramp to the back yard. I needed a speaker phone. The list goes on. But mechanical devices are only that.

My day began when Jane helped me out of bed, helped me into clothes and buttoned and zipped them. The day ended when she undid the morning's work and pointed me toward the bed.

She had to serve my food and cut what needed to be cut. She had to wrestle the wheelchair into and out of the car. In a restaurant, she had to open the men's room door and stand by for the call that meant she could open it again to retrieve me. She worried each time that I would fall and that she would have to rush in, devil take the hindmost.

I felt alternately frustrated and guilty because I couldn't manage myself. I went bananas twice, crying and ranting with irrational anger. Once it was because of the difficulty of chasing pieces of salad across the plate.

Jane is always concerned that she is not doing enough, or that she is not doing what she does quickly enough. She worries when she has to leave me alone. But we talk, and we have learned.

This is about Alex.

One approach to dealing with certain death dictates full family involvement. The family supposedly lessens the trauma by becoming its own candid support group.

OK. I told Jane candidly, and the five older kids candidly.

But for months after the rest of the family knew, I stubbornly and wrongly insisted that Alex, the youngest, not be told. I couldn't do it, so I wanted no one else to do it.

I told him the obvious—that I had a muscle disease. He didn't pursue it. I knew he worried about me and there were moments when I wanted to tell him the truth because I wanted to say how much I loved him and to let him hear how deeply it cut to know I wouldn't see him grow up.

It hurt that he trusted me implicitly and that I was deceiving him. But I couldn't face that instant when he would be fully aware and we would be together, alone, with neither of us able to reach out far enough.

So my decision was taken mostly out of cowardice, although not wholly because of it.

At 12, Alex was nine years younger than the next oldest, Marcy. Young sons of older-than-average fathers sometimes have problems, and so do the fathers.

Alex and I haven't because we like the same things. We like reading, early morning birdwatching, fishing through the evening and baseball. That summer was his sixth year in youth baseball. He was not fast but played center field competently and hit .400 for the season.

Like his older siblings, he is just what is wanted when the order for a new child is written.

When I thought in the past of dying on my own terms, Alex set the limits. I needed to see him out of school and grown.

Hal is grown and out of school. Shelley, Caitlin, Cara and Marcy are grown and out of school.

I know them and am happy and satisfied that they have remained friends with each other and that they are intelligent and compassionate adults.

Alex will be that kind of person, too, I am sure. Yet only a freak of nature could permit me to know. There won't be one. I understand what is happening to me and how quickly.

And of all things I confront, he is the toughest because he is so young.

His knowledge makes it better for him. Still, I grieve selfishly because he has to know.

Before ALS, I enjoyed the fundamentals—love, work, food and a thoroughly chilled martini.

The love endures, the others do not.

I stopped going to work on March 2, 1987, the day my last editorial appeared in the *Sun-Times*. (The editorial concerned the famine in Africa and I can't recall a word of it. So much for momentous occasions.)

An argument might be made that I work. I write nearly every day with a computer that I operate by moving my eyebrows. The movement activates a switch attached to a headband.

The process is tiring, so I and those around me occasionally describe it as work. But to a Depression kid whose clothes were sometimes provided by county welfare, work is more than just a tiring activity. Work is having a job and going to it.

My first job was hustling the *Saturday Evening Post* from door to door when I was 8 years old. From then until the onset of ALS, I was never unemployed. Some jobs were better than others—for example, newspapering was better than combat in a B17. But a job is a job.

Earlier, when I began to have trouble getting around with a walker, I had hired some Colorado State University students to push my wheelchair, handle the urinal, clip background articles and perform various other necessary chores.

Two of the most versatile students, both seniors majoring in occupational therapy, were Sharla Peterson, a former nursing home employee from Arizona, and Glen Gargano, who had been a Navy medical corpsman.

There were no typical days, but there was a routine.

Jane, ever cheerful, dressed me each morning then wheeled me to the bathroom. If my internal priorities so dictated, she would lift me onto the toilet. Otherwise, she employed the ever-present, manually installed, completely portable urinal. Mouth care and hair brushing followed. The shave was put off until bedtime.

The next stop was the dining area. Breakfast usually was cold cereal, juice and coffee. Jane fed me—as she had been obliged to do virtually from the first day of my return from Chicago. She brought in the newspapers—*The Rocky Mountain News, Denver Post, Wall Street Journal, USA Today* and *Fort Collins Coloradoan*. The *Chicago Sun-Times* and *Christian Science Monitor* arrived by mail, as did several weekly and monthly news magazines.

Jane's last morning chore—she would never call it that—was to turn the wheelchair so that I faced the patio. I watched the finches until the first student, usually Sharla, arrived. The arrival roughly corresponded with the rumble of Alex's schoolbus.

It was time to get to work.

Jane had converted one of the main-level bedrooms into a combination office and gathering place. In one corner, near the bookcase, was a folding table used exclusively for newspapers, magazines and background files. In another corner, near a window, was a desk that held a speaker phone and the portable computer that had been sent from the *Sun-Times* to replace one that I had rendered senseless. On top of a small bookshelf nearby were the requisite reference books. Across the room, a TV remained tuned to the Cable News Network until after my 1 P.M. deadline.

The room was a comfortable, efficient place to work and it suited my limitations.

The muscles in my arms and hands deteriorated at a slower rate than those in my legs, but the pace was steady. By the start of 1987, I could not navigate the computer keyboard or dial a phone. I could turn the pages of a newspaper by using my forearms and a great deal of body English, but it was an exhausting exercise.

To counter the increasing frustration I began to develop ideas a day or two ahead of time. Newspaper persons are pathologically proud of their ability to produce lovely prose under the most severe time constraints, but ALS had introduced me to the real world.

With Sharla turning the pages and an idea or two tucked away in my head, the morning papers consumed about an hour. After a glance at any newly arrived magazines and calls to gather additional information or insights—or both—it was time for the highlight of the day, the mid-morning, speaker-phone editorial conference.

For most of my waking hours I was accorded too much deference by the students, by visitors, by even my own family. I needed a little abrasion. The editorial conference was a proper forum.

The purpose of such a gathering is to generate an exchange of ideas with the objective of offering readers well-developed statements of the newspaper's position on local, national and international issues.

That occurred. But the ladies and gentlemen of the press are not always ladies and gentlemen. I had to endure a share of the kidding and listen to a share of off-color humor. I loved it.

While it lasted, while I could still perform, I could get, at long-distance rates, what no expensive shrink could give me—a sense of belonging. For a part of each day I wasn't sick.

It couldn't last, of course. My speech got progressively thicker. That made it more and more difficult to dictate my editorials to Sharla and to contribute to the conference. I grew tired more quickly. There were other signs that I should pack it in. So 10 days after I wrote my last editorial, Jane and I and three of our children flew to Chicago for a farewell party. It was a bittersweet pleasure.

Home again, the routine expanded to fill the vacuum. Jane continued to park me where I could watch the birds until the first student arrived. It was early spring and the purple finches, which had come to stay until fall, were tolerating flocks of goldfinches that were migrating from wherever back to the Rockies. The daily fluttering and bickering cried out for a metaphor, but I had become a bystander.

When the student arrived—Sharla now worked only one afternoon a week and Glen only afternoons—we repaired to the office. There we took a leisurely stroll through the newspapers and magazines (most would not be renewed). That done, I'd watch CNN and follow with an old comedy show. (*The Munsters* was a favorite.) Occasionally I watched a soap opera.

Coffee, through a straw, was always at hand. A smoke was close. One of the students straightened a wire coat hanger and attached one end of the left arm of my wheelchair. She fashioned the other end into a cigarette holder that I could reach by turning my head. A nonsmoker, she looked upon the device as Henry Ford might have looked upon the Model T. Instead of holding the filthy weed to my lips, she had only to tap an ashtray against the wire. First the ashes then the butt would fall into the tray, which she could dump in the toilet. She conveyed her message and I had coffee and cigarettes at the ready.

Lunch was a sandwich or leftovers. I longed for a cheese Whopper and fries from Burger King (I still do), but settled for something easy to swallow and easy for the student to feed me. (The standards also precluded another favorite, crunchy peanut butter and jelly.)

Lunch was followed by more TV until Glen arrived. Then it was time to read some Melville.

Shortly after my diagnosis I had settled on three substantial projects to help me through the down time that lay ahead. I promised myself that I would read the Bible from cover to cover, learn something about music and finish reading Herman Melville's novels.

I chose to start with Melville. Glen, already valuable, immediately became irreplaceable. He was the only person in or around the house who could tame the automatic page turner, a loaner from the Muscular Dystrophy Association in Denver.

I still had enough strength to operate the switch that activated the page turning mechanism. I needed only to press a button placed in my lap. When Glen had banished all the glitches and the pages were turning smoothly, Melville's characters had problems. I had none.

Glen also put me down for my afternoon nap. I slept in a small hospital bed—also on loan from the Muscular Dystrophy Association—near the double bed I had shared with Jane. Neither of us had wanted to give up the intimacy but painful muscle spasms in my legs were keeping both of us awake. In the hospital bed my legs could be elevated to ease the stress. The absence of my moans and groans in turn enabled Jane to get some badly needed sleep. We did miss each other's warmth. We still do.

There are not enough superlatives to describe Jane. She does not wring her hands or run in circles. During my first summer in a wheelchair she packed me, Alex, the chair and luggage into our small station wagon for a trip to California. Every pit stop and every motel meant hauling the chair in and out of the car and me in and out of the chair. But we had a great time. We visited our families, saw the sights and made it home without a scar.

Jane made it to Alex's little league games and his school functions with me and the chair. She took the chair and me shopping. We went out for Sunday brunch. We traveled to Santa Fe for Hal's graduation from college.

Despite her demanding job as a junior high school media specialist (librarian plus), she was determined that I have as normal a life as she could give me.

When she arrived home from work and errands, we usually shared a drink— wine for her and gin over ice for me. A common topic of conversation was Alex and his homework. Occasionally Jane would leave after dinner for a book club meeting or school activity. During those occasions, Alex was around to answer the phone. A couple of times during the school year Jane had to attend conferences that required her to be away overnight. When that occurred, Hal or Cara, both of whom lived near the university, spent the night. (Alex loved it!)

Usually, however, Jane was around to feed me, bathe me, shave me and, most important, talk to me.

Jane never avoided complex or sensitive subjects because of my illness. She disagreed with me when she thought it necessary. She saw no reason—and there was none—to revise a healthy relationship because of a random affliction. It is not surprising that she grew furious at those persons, including airline attendants, who believe impaired speech and a lame body are signs of mental retardation.

Jane's effort and common sense could not halt the disease, of course. She could make it more tolerable. She could even keep it at bay for awhile, as I am convinced she did. But eventually it wins.

On June 24, 1987, we tried to celebrate Cara's twenty-third birthday at her favorite Chinese restaurant, but my body didn't want to cooperate. I had felt below par for a couple of days. At the restaurant, I became ill. Even the martini— with straw—went unfinished.

I grew no better as the days passed. Swallowing became progressively more difficult. Meals consisted mostly of a semi-plastic dietary supplement. Constipation was a constant and painful problem. During one bleak night, I forced Jane to wrestle me out of bed for four unsuccessful trips to the portable thundermug she had rented for the bedroom.

On July 2, Jane took me to our family internist. He said I had pneumonia. The following morning, Jane phoned Dr. Steven P. Ringel, an ALS researcher and head of the Muscular Dystrophy Clinic at University Hospital in Denver. He arranged for admission to the hospital the next morning.

The next morning was the Fourth of July. We celebrated with coffee and doughnuts to go. The doughnut was my last solid food.

At the hospital, Dr. Ringel rescued us from the clerks and took us to my room. Jane had to leave because of a tangle of holiday commitments to the rest of the family.

I remember little about the next three days, but the fourth day was memorable because I underwent a tracheostomy. The surgery separated me forever from two of my greatest loves—eating and talking.

The nurses were pleasant and capable but neither they nor the doctors explained the routine I would be following. When the surgeon made his postoperative rounds, accompanied by his gaggle of reverent residents, he simply issued pronouncements, looking and posturing like a gaunt field marshal.

My blunt introduction to postural drainage is a case in point. The procedure is accomplished by sharply tilting the bed or patient—or, ideally both—so gunk can drain from the lungs and be suctioned away. It is not something one should just walk up and do to a semi-claustrophobic and increasingly frustrated and angry older person.

When it happened to me in just that offhand way, I did what I think anyone would do upon finding himself suddenly stuffed head down in a formerly horizontal bed. I fought. It is true that my fighting was limited to arching my back and making what I hoped were terrifying faces, but it got results. The nurse apologized and explained how postural drainage—the phrase was new to me— would help my lungs. I accepted her logic and took my turn apologizing. We became friends.

A similar scenario was followed with percussion—a systematic and informed pummeling of the rib cage to loosen the gunk inside. I fought with the respiration therapist who casually walked up to me and began percussing, and he, too, explained his purpose in common-sense terms. (I could not tolerate the young studs who used my ribs to set the beat for their inner rock 'n' roll. I fought them too, but they won.)

A transfer to Poudre Valley Hospital in Fort Collins brightened my outlook considerably. Jane visited nearly every night. She often brought Alex. The older kids dropped by when their classes and jobs permitted. Former colleagues visited from Chicago. Friends from the university came by frequently. The total experience was both gratifying and humbling.

The room was larger than at University Hospital. It was on the ground floor and afforded a decent view of lawn crews at work. I allowed myself a bit of envy.

Jane learned to read my lips so quickly that we still joke that she reads my mind. (Sobering thought!) She also developed a system of numbered phrases, placed on cards, that enabled nurses to rapidly determine my needs. The cards are still in daily use.

We taught each other to speak fluent alphabet. If I had something to say, I'd stare at Jane intently. She would ask whether my thought began with a consonant. If not, I'd blink and she would recite the vowels. When she reached the correct one, I'd raise my eyebrows. Thus cued by blinks and eyebrows, and years of listening to my speech patterns, she could elicit my thoughts almost as quickly as I could form them.

The period was productive. I spent hours each day listening to KCSU, the university's classical music station. I could and did make satisfying progress with my third long-term project—learning something about music. (A few months later, my stepmother, a wonderful lady known in the family as Grandma Dot, sent me a boxed set of Bible tapes. The Bible became the first of the three projects to be completed.)

Listening, however, whether to music or words about music, was a passive, machine-interposed occupation. It allowed the mind to wander. Mine wandered toward an unfocused depression.

Anything could ignite it—a random thought about Jane or one of the children, a half-remembered childhood incident, an innocent remark by a doctor or nurse. I'd suddenly find myself in tears, knowing that it was pointless and knowing that crying would make me feel worse than had whatever I was crying about. Eventually the tears would stop, a nurse would wipe away the evidence and I could return to concentrating on something more productive.

There was—and is, for the problem occasionally resurfaces—no easily identifiable cause for the depression. Poudre Valley Hospital was a state-of-the-art institution. The staff was first-rate. I did have problems with, and fought with, a few members of the staff, but they were the exceptions. One was a male nurse who specialized in cursory care. Another was the day head nurse, whose battle station was near the door to my room. She disliked classical music and often threatened to perform major surgery on my radio. Skirmishes with both ended in draws. I lost to a petite blonde respiration therapist with a very mean mouth who dredged my lungs for gunk each weekday afternoon. Light or heavy results, she was never satisfied and always told me so with fishwife inflections. My unwavering, silent reply was that I had given my best.

On Oct. 2, 1987, two days less than three months after I had entered University Hospital, Poudre Valley Hospital allowed me to go home.

I had survived six pneumonias during my hospitalization. By contrast, during approximately two and a half years of home care I have had only one pneumonia. That one was a real scorcher, however. I was sick for 20 days and unable to communicate with the nurses for half that. I recall nothing of the entire period except a strange, reminiscent dream. In the dream my 8-year-old self was sitting in the rear seat of what could have been my stepfather's car. He was telling me quietly that I would survive. When I was 8, I was seriously ill with a respiratory problem, but there was no cash for a doctor and our credit was bad. My stepfather borrowed $2 from another oil field worker and bought whiskey. He used part of it to make a strong hot drink for me. I survived both the illness and the whiskey.

I am still wrestling with the meaning of the dream.

At home, Jane had transformed the room I had used as an office into a bedroom for her. She had given me the larger room we had shared. The rearrangement was both selfless and practical. My room was, by necessity, shared with a nurse. It was shared by choice with family, visitors and my air bed.

An air bed is a marvelous contraption with a wooden frame and 22 inflatable gortex cushions covered with a gortex sheet. Air beds were first used for burn patients and later adopted for other long-term patients in order to prevent bed sores.

Air beds do have flaws. Even when they are equipped with an emergency power source, a sudden power failure—because of a storm, for example—will deflate the cushions and allow the bed's occupant to settle slowly downward. It is not an unpleasant trip—I have taken it 38 times—but it is always startling. And, in addition to being playful, air beds are heavy and bulky. When I arrived home from Poudre Valley Hospital, I reclined on the ambulance cot while workmen removed a window so my new air bed could be passed through.

Once the bed was in place with me comfortably on its top, the transition from hospital to home proceeded smoothly. Jane had placed a large bookcase near the bed and facing it. The bit that I could then turn my head permitted me to direct the nurse to the magazine or book that I wanted to read. A tilt-top bedside table from a hospital supply shop had been rigged with rubber bands and clips to hold newspapers and magazines. The nurse turned pages and often read with me. (The reading table was a casualty of our move to a larger home and, for reasons that are unclear, has not been duplicated. More's the pity.)

That first few months at home was a period of extensive, serious reading with the help of the tilting table and a small cookbook rack (Jane's idea), I read widely and steadily.

I read the *Rocky Mountain News* each day and the *Chicago Sun-Times* when it arrived. I had a standing order at the news agency for the Sunday *New York Times* and read it during the week. I read *Business Week* and *Newsweek*. Jane read to me from *Rolling Stone* and the *New Republic*. I read a book about the federal reserve system because the author was—and is—a friend of mine. I read a textbook about music history because for years I had wanted to.

I have always been a willing reader, but not to the exclusion of virtually everything else. Part of the reading fever was conditioned behavior, of course. My newspaper career had ended only a short time before and I was still compulsively trying to stay abreast of developments. But there was another factor. As long as I was engrossed in what someone else had written, I wasn't feeling sorry for myself.

I didn't handle the ALS-imposed leisure efficiently. In addition to hiding behind books, magazines and newspapers, I watched too much television. I also courted depression—and sometimes seduced it—by dwelling on what might have been had ALS not chosen me.

There also was the anger.

Perhaps because of a scattershot childhood, I have always sought to control the pieces of my environment—school, work, play, even marriage (although Jane patiently taught that marriage is a shared opportunity).

ALS defies control and I felt the loss of it more deeply than in either hospital. The loss bred a deep frustration that erupted into frequent bursts of irrational anger. The target of the anger most often was the crew of nurses. They were hired by an agency for their experience and reliability, not their knowledge of ALS. Their job was to execute the orders of my doctor. Any deviation from that routine required consultation. I, however, wanted the nurses to do things my way, even when I didn't know what my way was. When they failed to bow and scrape, I blew up.

As before, I could express anger only feebly. A grimace, an arched back were as good as I could deliver. But the nurses could tell the difference between grateful and furious. A couple of nurses shrugged it off and are still with me. But two left in tears. The turnover and threats to quit prompted a confrontation with the head of the nurse-placement agency.

She walked into my room when Jane was there and delivered a succinct message. I would have to clean up my act or she would not have enough nurses to staff my case. That meant, she said, that I was facing a return trip to the hospital. It was up to me.

I apologized and meant it. The prospect of a prolonged stay in the hospital frightened me. For one thing, it would rapidly drain our resources. More important, it would isolate me from my family. And I was spoiled. I wanted to watch television at night with Jane. I wanted to be home when Alex returned from school. I wanted friends to know that they could drop by on their schedule. I wanted to be near the books and magazines and newspapers and I wanted to listen to music when the mood struck. I wanted, in other words, an ordinary family life. I shudder each time I think of how close I came to spoiling the dream.

Looking back, however, I might once again have given in to anger had it not been for Jane. She insisted that I start writing again.

A computer designed for ALS patients by the Asyst Corporation of Chicago had been sent to me by the Les Turner ALS Foundation of Skokie, Illinois, while I was still writing from home for the *Sun-Times*. I had used it sparingly, however, because I stubbornly resisted learning a new system that seemed to be nothing more than a complicated alarm box. It was much more than that, of course, and three of the graduate students who helped me at home joined Jane in coaxing me to try it. I held out until the revolt of the nurses. At that point Jane decided that I needed something productive to do. She set up the computer and suggested that I use it to write my apology.

She had reasoned correctly that to control both depression and anger I had to reach beyond my room and myself. I needed other people. I needed to reaffirm my commitment to life.

I don't know whether the commitment had wavered or whether the depression and anger had simply obscured it. I believe that the latter was the case but it doesn't matter. What matters is that the commitment emerged strong enough.

And that is that. You already know the rest.

Reaching the End
Jane Neth

Dear Dot,

Brace yourself. What I have to say may appear, at first glance, to be bad news. It isn't.

I have decided to free my family and go with God. Within the next month, give or take a little, I will ask my doctor to give me something that will put me in the deepest sleep of all. He is a gentle man and has not yet said, straight out, he will do it. I suspect that he will.

My decision did not come easily. Jane and I are still very much in love. I get a kick out of the trials and conquests of our kids and grandkids. I still get excited or agitated by the news broadcasts. Jane and I entertained a visitor from Chicago a couple of weeks ago and I had as jolly a time as anyone.

Increasingly, though, the physical and mental demands of just lying here are taking a toll. I can't imagine what a typical day would be like without my computer. It is a godsend! It is my voice—and you know what a Neth is like when he can't talk!

I don't want you to be sad. I want you to think of it as a crossover for just one more old duck who has lost his quack.

With much love,
Cecil

When I read this letter, written by my husband Cecil to his stepmother, I was at a loss—sad, surprised and suddenly aware how tired he had become. His words touched me and helped me to understand. This letter started the process that ended Oct. 1, 1992, when Cecil went off life support.

Once an ALS patient has made the decision to live with the help of machines he or she may face an even more difficult decision later—the decision to discontinue that life support. It is an agonizing decision for the patient and for his or her family.

For about a year, Cecil had been considering how long he wanted to stay on life support. He broached the possibility of disconnecting several times, but each time, I talked him out of it. He said that he wanted to "free" me, but I didn't want to be freed. Even though he had grown increasingly dependent on me, he was my closest companion and I treasured his company. So each time Cecil told me he wanted to die, I urged him to reconsider. The reality is that he was living on borrowed time. Even though we had sued for insurance coverage and won, Cecil and I were very aware of how much money was being spent by all of my colleagues to prolong Cecil's life. His care was an enormous drain on my employer's insurance fund, and we had to acknowledge that this could someday impact another person's ability to receive appropriate care. But as long as he was active and aware, I felt that it was a worthy investment.

Until those last few months, Cecil was mentally alert and went to heroic efforts to maintain that alertness. But he began to have great difficulty remembering important details and making decisions about his life. While he was acutely aware of everything that occurred in his own room, he lost interest in the outside world. Earlier, he could remember information he had heard once; but it got to the point where he had trouble remembering things even after hearing them four or five times. I grew increasingly concerned about his mental acuity, and I worried about him slipping into a place where he would not be able to write or respond to letters as he had always enjoyed doing. I will never love anyone the way I loved Cecil, but I didn't want to see him that way. He became more and more dependent and childlike. These changes were unlike him, and he was unhappy about them; he knew he wasn't thinking as clearly as he always had.

The nurses and I began to think he was purposely shutting down, allowing himself to slow down and let go of life. He was ready to call it quits after years of fighting. Finally, I began to recognize the fatigue he referred to in the letter to his stepmother, Dot. After a year of discussion, I decided I needed to let Cecil make his own decision and I would support it. I finally agreed with Cecil that he should die on his own terms while he was still able to make that decision for himself. This was a gift he really wanted to give me—and it was his last chance to seize control of a life over which he actually had very little control.

I'm 10 years younger than Cecil, and after living with his illness for seven years, I realized it was time we faced the reality of life and death. Although Cecil didn't need to "free" me, I knew that I had put off choices and opportunities in my own life to be by his side. As much as I valued the years Cecil was on life support, more and more, I was thinking about the years remaining in my working life and how much I wanted to apply for an overseas teaching position. While I thought, in theory, that Cecil could have lived without me for a year, in reality I knew that I would never have been able to leave him behind. He was so dependent on me for his happiness that I knew he wouldn't have been able to make it without me there.

All of these thoughts led to my decision, but there is another dimension to this choice that anyone faced with it must bear in mind. To allow a conscious human being to disconnect from the machines that keep him alive can lead to years of guilt and heartache for the survivors. This does not mean the choice is wrong, but all parties must face the decision with their eyes open and with some source of strength and support—whether family, faith, friends or all of the above. I still feel guilty sometimes because I know I could have talked Cecil out of disconnecting. But in truth, I know he made the right choice, and I know I did, too. The guilt exists because I miss him so much, and I keep thinking that I could have had him with me for a few more months.

My family was in complete agreement with Cecil's decision. Actually, a few of our five children felt he should have made his decision years before. They are young, and they couldn't comprehend how he could stand to live as he did. They loved him very much, but they could not understand their strong father being willing to live such a compromised life. And the day-to-day indignity of it angered and depressed them. How could their dad, who had always been a tough-minded, independent person, submit to having his bottom wiped for him by nurses as if he were an infant? They didn't always see the courage it took for him just to wake up every morning. A couple of the young people felt they had lost their dad when he lost his voice in 1987, and they were relieved when they felt he was finally taking control again.

I also think they didn't understand the depth of Cecil's and my relationship. I felt differently about Cecil's years on life support. I didn't feel smothered because he had become so calm and his love was so sincere. It just flowed out of him for me. He wrote me notes every day and had the nurses leave them in my bedroom, telling me he loved me. We talked and watched movies together every night. It helped that I wasn't trapped in our house by his illness. We had plenty of help and support, and I had my full-time job.

Still, his single-mindedness was hard for the kids. He focused almost exclusively on his day-to-day needs and on me, and he didn't keep up with them and their activities.

But Cecil's long struggle was coming to an end. It had been a good fight; we were proud of him. In spite of the indignities he had suffered over the years, he handled ALS in the tough-minded, determined way he handled the rest of his life.

Two doctors and a psychologist each visited our home three times to confirm that Cecil's decision was really his own—that he wasn't being pressured and that he was of sound mind. He was never better. He had the doctors laughing and crying as he told them this was what he wanted. He was making this decision for himself; that was clear.

The nursing staff, who after the first few years had become a strong and supportive crew, supported every decision we made about Cecil's care. In the end, however, there was a little bit of conflict. In spite of the fact that we all loved Cecil, there were different interpretations of the best way to express that love. One of our nurses who had been with Cecil from the beginning believed we hadn't tried enough holistic treatment.

We had set the date for his disconnection, so that our out-of-town children could be there. He changed it once, which was OK because he had some work he wanted to finish. But after I had made flight arrangements for our daughter in California, and the rest of us had arranged for leaves from work, the nurse called me at work and said, "Cecil needs a few more days." Without telling me, she had changed doctors' appointments that were necessary before he could disconnect.

I went home, very upset. I was frazzled. The whole idea of setting a date to die is outrageous to start with, and then to have to keep changing it was just more than I could handle. I got home and sobbed to Cecil that he had to decide whether he was going to do it or not. If he was, he had to set a date and stick with it because I just couldn't take the emotional rollercoaster. It was a moment of honesty. If he wanted the opportunity to say goodbye in a decent way, he had to let the family have some warning. He was calm during this outburst and answered that he hadn't realized he had caused a problem. Often he cried when we discussed life and death issues but this time he was the calm one. I still wonder about that evening. He, of course, knew I had arranged the flight and we had discussed all the plans. I wonder now if this was another instance of fading attention or if he was asking me to talk him out of his decision. I will always agonize over this.

After this confrontation, he decided to stick with the date he had chosen. The day before his death, he wrote to a friend, "I won't describe the mental torment that preceded my decision, but it wasn't easy. It boiled down—for me—to what was best for Jane and the children. Jane will give me an argument, but I win."

Our primary-care physician and the nurse Cecil chose to be present handled the medical details of his death. Early in the morning on Oct. 1, they gave him a shot of morphine to steady his nerves. The kids and I said goodbye and cried with him. Daughter Caite gave him a map to her house, so he would always know where she was. Carrie put him in charge of the weather for her wedding two months away. Hal read a poem. All of us considered it a gift that we could say goodbye to Cecil and he could say goodbye to us. Finally, since the federal election was only a few weeks away and Cecil had always been a political animal, we arranged for him to cast a vote by absentee ballot. This was the last thing he did before they took him off the ventilator.

We watched as the doctor first administered the morphine shot. A short time later, we watched as his ventilator was removed and his body was left to struggle for life on its own. Despite the sedative, Cecil was fully conscious throughout, something that made it particularly difficult for all of us who loved him to watch. As he ran out of air, we saw the struggle in his face, and yet his determination to see it through was clear. His eyes darted around the room at all us of; his mouth was set in a firm, tight line. We almost expected him to cry out. I thought for a few minutes that a miracle would occur and he would breathe on his own, but he didn't. He struggled quietly until the air was gone. I held his hand as he died.

The next day we all went to the mountains and sat at a picnic bench and cried. We will always miss him, but it felt good to give his equipment to others with ALS, and to see his top-notch nursing staff using the skills they acquired with him to help another Fort Collins ALS patient who's just beginning his fight.

We may always feel guilty about letting him pull the plug, but even that's OK. The process of living is a process of making difficult choices, and sometimes those are choices we regret, choices we might handle differently if we had them to do over again. Our years dealing with ALS as a family taught us many things, and perhaps the most important lesson is to appreciate the life that we have in whatever form it takes, and not waste too much time on regret. Cecil would have agreed.

QUESTIONS AND ACTIVITIES

1. What issues did Cecil Neth and his family seem to be facing as they anticipated his impending death? What attitudes, behaviors, or coping mechanisms did Cecil display that are characteristic of the middle years of life?

2. From the information provided in the personal account, what personal attributes did Cecil and Jane Neth have that helped them cope with his disease in its predicted course?

3. Denial is often demonstrated by individuals in the initial stages of many diseases. What purpose does it serve? In what ways may denial be functional? Dysfunctional?

4. Plan a two-hour training session for volunteers working with individuals with life-threatening illnesses. The goal of the session is to enhance the trainees' communication skills while working with these patients. Discuss why listening is such a valuable communication tool. Think of an incident in your own experience after which you wished you had listened more during a particular interaction. What might you have learned if you had listened more attentively? Explore the role of touch in communicating with patients; discuss appropriate and inappropriate use of touching as a therapeutic tool.

5. Why might it be difficult to be honest in our communications with the dying? Are there particular stages of the dying process when it is perhaps more difficult to communicate openly and honestly? Why?

GLOSSARY

Awareness contexts: knowledge each person has regarding a patient's defined status, together with recognition of what others think.

Body image: internal representation of the person's feelings and attitudes toward his or her own body.

Body integrity: the body's ability to function.

Conspiracy of silence: mutual pact to avoid issues of consequence as they relate to death and to focus only on the mundane.

Death system: a distinctive network of suppositions, norms, and symbols that are functionally effective in the routinized, communal management of death and dying.

Death trajectory: course of dying based on certainty of death from a particular cause and expected time of death.

Emotional quarantine: situation in which others do not allow the dying to share their true feelings, but rather force them to participate in formalities and exchange platitudes.

Etiology: cause of a disease.

Holistic perspective: acknowledgment of all aspects of the person (physical, emotional, social, psychological, and spiritual).

Hospice care: a philosophy of care provided to dying individuals and their families that emphasizes death with dignity.

Middle knowledge: uncertainty as to whether one is actually going to die.

Palliative care: palliation, derived from the Greek word for "to lessen or mitigate," is therapy directed toward minimizing symptoms rather than curing the disease.

Sociological death: society's withdrawal, to an extreme degree, from the dying.

SUGGESTED READINGS

Andre, D., Brookman, P., & Livingston, J. (Eds.). (1996). *Hospice: A photographic inquiry.* Boston: Little, Brown and Company.

Photography is used as a medium to communicate the essence of hospice care. The pictures and narrative offer a close and personal view of the hospice philosophy as currently practiced in the United States.

Aries, P. (1981). *The hour of our death.* New York: Knopf.

A historical treatment of attitudes toward death in Western culture from earliest Christian times until the present. Comprehensive in coverage with interesting illustrations.

Byock, I. (1997). *Dying well: The prospect for growth at the end of life.* New York: Riverhead Press.

This book addresses the human potential to grow, as individuals and as members of families, through the process of dying. Written by a hospice physician, actual cases are shared in detail to illustrate the possibilities for "dying well."

Davies, B., Reimer, J. C., Brown, P., & Martens, N. (1995). *Fading away: The experience of transition in families with terminal illness.* Amityville, NY: Baywood.

Based on the findings of a qualitative research project, this book provides a description of the experience of terminal cancer from a family perspective. Quotes by family members are included throughout the text to provide concrete examples of issues faced during a terminal illness. One chapter is devoted to the challenges of conducting research in a palliative care setting.

Doka, K. J. (1993). *Living with life-threatening illness: A guide for patients, their families, and caregivers.* New York: Lexington Books.

The author discusses the challenges of different stages of illness and examines a wide range of coping mechanisms. Emphasis is placed on living with illness, rather than just anticipating its final stage. Clear and practical suggestions are offered to patients, family members, and caregivers.

RESOURCES

Children's Hospice International
2202 Mount Vernon Avenue
Alexandria, VA 22301
(703) 684-0330

National Hospice Organization
1901 North Moore Street
Suite 901
Arlington, Virginia 22209
(703) 243-5900; 1-800-646-6460 (Hospice Bookstore)

REFERENCES

Anderson, H., & MacElveen-Hoehn, P. (1988). Gay client with AIDS: New challenges for hospice. *The Hospice Journal, 4*(2), 37-54.

Attig, T. (1983). Respecting the dying and the bereaved as believers. *Newsletter of the Forum for Death Education and Counseling, 6,* 10-11.

Augustine, M. J., & Kalish, R. A. (1975). Religion, transcendence, and appropriate death. *Journal of Transpersonal Psychology, 7,* 1-13.

Baker, N. T., & Seager, R. D. (1991). A comparison of the psychosocial needs of hospice patients with AIDS and those with other diagnoses. *The Hospice Journal, 7*(1/2), 61-69.

Bates, M. S. (1987). Ethnicity and pain: A biocultural model. *Social Science Medicine, 24*(1), 47-50.

Blumenfield, M., Levy, N. B., & Kaufman, D. (1978). The wish to be informed of a fatal illness. *Omega, 9*(4), 323-326.

Buckingham, R. W. (1992). *Among friends: Hospice care for the person with AIDS.* New York: Prometheus.

Burrs, F. A. (1995). The African American experience: Breaking the barriers to hospice. *The Hospice Journal, 10*(2), 15-18.

Callari, E. S. (1986). *A gentle death: Personal caregiving to the terminally ill.* Greensboro, NC: Tudor.

Chapman, C. R. (1992). The psychology of cancer pain. In J. Kornell (Ed.), *Pain management and care of the terminal patient* (pp. 13-25). Seattle, WA: Washington State Medical Association.

Charmaz, K. (1980). *The social reality of death.* Menlo Park, CA: Addison-Wesley.

Christ, G. H. (1983). A psychosocial assessment framework for cancer patients and their families. *Health and Social Work, 8* (1), 57-64.

Corr, C. A., & Corr, D. M. (1992). Adult hospice day care. *Omega, 16,* 155-172.

Doka, K. J. (1993). *Living with life-threatening illness: A guide for patients, families, and caregivers.* New York: Lexington Books.

Dupee, R. M. (1982). Hospice—Compassionate, comprehensive approach to terminal care. *Postgraduate Medicine, 72*(3), 239-245.

Eggerman, S., & Dustin, D. (1985). Death orientation and communication with the terminally ill. *Omega, 16*(3), 255-265.

Erikson, E. (1963). *Childhood and society* (2nd ed.). New York: Norton.

Evans, M. A., Esbenson, M., & Jaffe, C. (1981). Expect the unexpected when you care for a dying patient. *Nursing, 11,* 55-56.

Farnon, C. (1996). A personal exploration of the German hospice system. *The American Journal of Hospice and Palliative Care, 13*(4), 32-37.

Ferrell, B. R. (1985). Cancer deaths and bereavement outcomes. *The American Journal of Hospice Care, 2*(4), 18–23.

Glaser, B. G., & Strauss, A. L. (1965). *Awareness of dying.* Chicago: Aldine.

Glaser, B. G., & Strauss, A. L. (1968). *Time for dying.* Chicago: Aldine.

Gordon, A. K. (1996). Hospice and minorities: A national study of organizational access and practice. *The Hospice Journal, 11*(1), 49–70.

Gruman, G. J. (1978). Ethics of death and dying: Historical perspective. *Omega, 9*(3), 203–237.

Horne, R., & Fagan, M. (1983). *Summary: Focus group discussions.* Skokie, IL: Les Turner ALS Foundation.

Hoy, T. (1983). Hospice chaplaincy in the caregiving team. In C. A. Corr & D. M. Corr (Eds.), *Hospice care: Principles and practice* (pp. 177–196). New York: Springer.

Infeld, D. L., Gordon, A. K., & Harper, B. C. (Eds.). (1995). Hospice care and cultural diversity. *The Hospice Journal* (special issue), *10*(2), 1–93.

Iwai, M. (1996). *Volunteers in the Japanese hospice: Current concerns and future model.* Doctoral dissertation, Colorado State University.

Johanson, G. (1993). Symptom relief in palliative care. *Caring Magazine, 12*(11), 64–69.

Kalish, R. A. (1970). The onset of the dying process. *Omega, 1,* 57–69.

Kalish, R., & Reynolds, D. (1976). *Death and ethnicity: A psychocultural study.* Los Angeles: University of Southern California Press.

Kastenbaum, R. J. (1981). *Death, society, and human experience* (2nd ed.). St. Louis: C. V. Mosby.

Kastenbaum, R. J., & Aisenberg, R. (1972). *The psychology of death.* New York: Springer.

Kemp, C., & Stepp, L. (1995). Palliative care for patients with acquired immunodeficiency syndrome. *The American Journal of Hospice & Palliative Care, 12*(6), 14–27.

Kirschling, J. M. (1986). The experience of terminal illness on adult family members. *The Hospice Journal, 2*(1),121–138.

Kornell, J. (Ed.). (1992). *Pain management and care of the terminal patient.* Seattle, WA: Washington State Medical Association.

Kübler-Ross, E. (1969). *On death and dying.* New York: Macmillan.

Leloudis, D., & Pole, L. (1985). Reasons for choosing hospice care: How patients and primary caregivers make their selection. *The American Journal of Hospice Care, 2*(6), 30–34.

Levy, M. H. (1988). Pain control research in the terminally ill. *Omega, 18*(4), 265–275.

Mauritzen, J. (1988). Pastoral care for the dying and bereaved. *Death Studies, 12*(2), 111–122.

Mead, S. C. W., & Willemsen, H. W. A. (1995). Crisis of the psyche: Psychotherapeutic considerations on AIDS, loss and hope. In L. Sherr (Ed.), *Grief and AIDS* (pp. 115–127). Chichester, England: John Wiley & Sons.

Miller, P. J., & Mike, P. B. (1995). The Medicare hospice benefit: Ten years of federal policy for the terminally ill. *Death Studies, 19,* 531–542.

Millet, N. (1983). Hospice: A new horizon for social work. In C. A. Corr & D. M. Corr (Eds.), *Hospice care: Principles and practice* (pp. 135–147). New York: Springer.

Millison, M. B. (1988). Spirituality and the caregiver: Developing an underutilized facet of care. *The American Journal of Hospice Care, 5* (2), 37–44.

Millison, M. B. (1995). A review of the research on spiritual care and hospice. *The Hospice Journal, 10*(4), 3–18.

National Hospice Organization (1987). *Meeting the challenge for a special kind of caring: Standards of a hospice program of care recommended by the National Hospice Organization.* Arlington, VA: Author.

Nuland, S. B. (1993). *How we die: Reflections on life's final chapter.* New York: Vantage Books.

Paradis, L. F. (1985). The development of hospice in America: A social movement organizes. In L. F. Paradis (Ed.), *Hospice handbook: A guide for managers and planners* (pp. 3–24). Rockville, MD: Aspen Systems.

Parry, J. K. (Ed.). (1990). *Social work practice with the terminally ill: The transcultural perspective.* Springfield, IL.: Charles C. Thomas.

Pattison, E. M. (1977). *The experience of dying.* Englewood Cliffs, NJ: Prentice-Hall.

Pattison, E. M. (1978). The living-dying process. In C. A. Garfield (Ed.), *Psychosocial care of the dying patient* (pp. 133–168). New York: McGraw-Hill.

Peteet, J. R. (1985). Religious issues presented by cancer patients seen in psychiatric consultation. *Journal of Psychosocial Oncology, 3* (1), 53–66.

Piaget, J. (1963). *The origins of intelligence in children.* New York: International Universities Press.

Rebok, G. W., & Hoyer, W. J. (1979). Clients nearing death: Behavioral treatment perspectives. *Omega, 10*(3), 191–201.

Rhymes, J. (1990). Hospice care in America. *Journal of the American Medical Association, 264,* 369–372.

Saeger, L. (1992). Patient controlled analgesia (PCA) in cancer pain management. In J. Kornell (Ed.), *Pain management and the care of the terminal patient* (pp. 149–153). Seattle, WA: Washington State Medical Association.

Shneidman, E. S. (1978). Some aspects of psychotherapy with dying persons. In C. A. Garfield (Ed.), *Psychosocial care of the dying patient* (pp. 201–218). New York: McGraw-Hill.

Siefken, S. (1993). The Hispanic perspective on death and dying: A combination of respect, empathy, and spirituality. *Journal of Long Term Home Health Care, 12*(2), 26–28.

Sikorska, E. (1991). The hospice movement in Poland. *Death Studies, 15,* 309–316.

Strahan, G. W. (1994). *An overview of home health and hospice care patients: Preliminary data from the 1993 national home and hospice care survey.* U.S. Dept. of Health and Human Services Advance Data, No. 257, 1–12.

Sweeting, H. N., & Gilhooly, M. L. M. (1992). Doctor, am I dead? A review of social death in modern societies. *Omega, 24*(4), 251–269.

Talamantes, M. A., Lawler, W. R., & Espino, D. V. (1995). Hispanic American elders: Caregiving norms surrounding dying and the use of hospice services. *The Hospice Journal, 10*(2), 35–49.

Tehan, C. (1982). Hospice in an existing home care agency. *Family and Community Health, 5*(3), 11–20.

Vander Zanden, J. W. (1985). *Human development* (3d ed.). New York: Knopf.

Viney, L. L. (1984). Loss of life and loss of bodily integrity: Two different sources of threat for people who are ill. *Omega, 15* (3), 207–222.

Weisman, A. D. (1972). *On dying and denying.* New York: Behavioral Publications.

Wolff, B. B., & Langley, S. (1977). Cultural factors and the response to pain. In D. Landy (Ed.), *Culture, disease, and healing: Studies in medical anthropology* (pp. 313–319). New York: Macmillan.

3

Grief and Loss

Individuals grieve after many types of losses. Unfortunately, the grief process is not understood by a large part of society and, as a result, many grieving individuals do not receive the type of support that is most helpful to them.

Although there are differences in the formal definitions of the words *bereavement, grief,* and *mourning,* the words are often used interchangeably.

- **Bereavement** is the state of being that results from a significant loss (e.g., due to death).
- **Grief** refers to the outcome of being bereaved and involves a variety of reactions that constitute the grief response.
- **Mourning** denotes the social prescription for the way in which we are expected to display our grief and often reflects the practices of one's culture (e.g., wearing black or holding a wake).

Although the focus of this text is on loss related to death, it is important to keep in mind that individuals experience grief after many different types of losses, such as

- divorce;
- loss of body function;
- infertility;
- birth of a handicapped child;
- loss of a job;
- relinquishment of a child for adoption;
- imprisonment;
- experience of physical abuse, rape, or incest.

These are only a few examples that illustrate that loss is pervasive in our lives. The grief resulting from these various losses in many ways parallels the emotional reactions triggered by a death. Each type, however, also involves unique factors.

THEORIES OF GRIEF

Many different theoretical perspectives provide insight into the grief process. Like most relatively new fields of scientific study, theories evolve over time. Although some of the earlier paradigms would indicate that there is ultimately a "giving up" of the individual who has died, a newer theoretical orientation suggests that there is an ongoing tie.

Freud's Theory

According to Freudian theory, a major task facing individuals who have experienced the loss of a loved one is to withdraw the libido that was formerly invested in the relationship with the individual who has died. **Libido** refers to the energy of love and pleasure. Freud noted that the withdrawal of the libido is done over an extended period of time and at the expense of a great deal of cathectic energy. **Cathexis** is defined as the investment of psychic energy in, or emotional significance of, an object. To detach the emotional energy that had linked the survivor to the person who has died, Freud (1917) believed that "the memories and hopes which bound the libido to the object are brought up and hyper-cathected, and the detachment of the libido is accomplished. . . . when the work of mourning is completed the ego becomes free and uninhibited again" (p. 154). **Hypercathexis** refers to an extreme amount of psychic energy being invested in an object. Freud indicates that before individuals can let go of a love object, they must first invest all the more energy in thinking about the person who has died. This is reflected by the preoccupation with the deceased that is a normal part of the grief process and is a precursor to the detachment of energy that Freud and his followers believed ultimately took place after the death of a loved one.

Bowlby's Theory

Bowlby's (1980) framework for understanding separation and loss is closely linked to his theory of attachment. Bowlby explains that humans have an instinctive need to form strong attachments to others. Separation, whether through death or other causes, elicits a variety of behaviors (such as clinging, crying, angry outbursts, or protest), indicating that an attachment bond did exist. Although Freud hypothesized that involvement in the grief process necessitated the breaking of emotional ties with the deceased, Bowlby argues that the initial phases of the grief process involve a yearning for the lost person and an effort to reestablish ties. He describes the overall grief experience as progressing through four phases:

1. *Numbing:* This phase involves an inability to truly understand the loss and is reflected in such statements as "I can't believe it," "This isn't happening," or "I am in a dream."
2. *Yearning or searching:* This phase involves the bereaved individual's desire to recover the person who is now gone. Survivors may be preoccupied with the deceased. For example, a glimpse of a stranger may trigger the thought that their loved one is still alive. Memories may become the central focus of the bereaved's thought patterns.
3. *Disorganization or despair:* This phase is marked by despair, depression, and apathy, as the survivors discard old patterns of thinking, feeling, and acting.
4. *Reorganization:* This phase involves many strong emotions. It is a time when survivors must redefine their sense of self and their situation. They must attempt to fill unaccustomed roles and acquire new skills.

Many parallels can be seen between the concepts of hypercathexis and detachment explained by Freud and the phases of yearning/searching and reorganization posited by Bowlby.

Stage Theories

On hearing the news that a loved one has died, an immediate reaction is typically one of a sense of shock, numbness, or denial (Kübler-Ross, 1969). Shortly thereafter, the reality that the death has severed an important bond triggers an acute grief reaction, which gradually subsides as individuals reorganize their lives and accept the death. This process has been described by many authorities as proceeding through a series of stages. Even though authors use slightly different terminologies, their basic structures are quite similar.

Kübler-Ross's (1969) five stages of dying (which have been generalized by many to also describe the grief process) are still commonly identified by authors and researchers. As noted in chapter 2, those stages are denial, anger, bargaining, depression, and acceptance.

Bugen (1979) raised a number of concerns regarding stage theories and made the following arguments:

- Stages portrayed are not necessarily sequential; individuals may experience emotions in an order other than that posed by a particular stage framework and may experience symptoms from more than one stage at a time.
- There are no clear-cut beginning or ending points for particular stages; rather, they blend dynamically.
- Stage theories do not adequately reflect the uniqueness of an individual's grief. Persons may not experience all of the feelings described but may experience many others instead.

CONTINUING BONDS: A NEW PARADIGM

A number of researchers are proposing a new paradigm related to the process and timeline of bereavement that involves the concept of "continuing bonds." Phyllis Silverman and Dennis Klass (1996), together with their colleague Steven Nickman, worked closely with a number of collaborators whose research indicates that, in many instances, the grief process does not end but rather undergoes ongoing adaptation and change. Silverman and Klass (1996) summarize their findings as follows:

> We are suggesting a process of adaptation and change in the postdeath relationship and the construction and reconstruction of new connections. In taking these (research) findings into consideration, our understanding of the

bereavement process shifts. We cannot look at bereavement as a psychological state that ends and from which one recovers. The intensity of feelings may lessen and the mourner become more future—rather than past—oriented; however, a concept of closure, requiring a determination of when the bereavement process ends, does not seem compatible with the model suggested by these findings. We propose that rather than emphasizing letting go, the emphasis should be on negotiating and renegotiating the meaning of the loss over time. While the death is permanent and unchanging, the process is not. (pp. 18-19)

NORMAL GRIEF RESPONSE

Grief is a multifaceted response comprised of a wide variety of physiological reactions, thoughts, emotions, and behaviors.

Manifestations of Grief

Many researchers agree that grief is a "complex, evolving process with multiple dimensions" (Jacobs et al., 1987, p. 41). Looking at grief as a constellation of a wide variety of manifestations that are unique to a given individual in their combination, intensity, and duration provides an alternative to describing grief as a series of stages (Brasted & Callahan, 1984). In the following sections, a variety of somatic, intrapsychic, and behavioral manifestations of grief are briefly described (see Figure 3.1). They will be discussed in more detail throughout the rest of the book in a variety of contexts, including the manner of death (e.g., suicide), age of the bereaved, and type of relationship that was severed. The reactions noted are common components of grief but are not universal. The intensity of any given manifestation is expected to lessen over time if the individual is grieving in a normal rather than a complicated manner. The concept of complicated grief is discussed later in this chapter.

Somatic Manifestations.   **Somatic** manifestations of grief are those that are physical in nature. Lindemann (1944) was one of the first to observe clinically a large number of bereaved individuals. Many of the symptoms described by Lindemann were physical in nature. He noted that somatic distress such as a "feeling of tightness in the throat, choking with a shortness of breath, need for sighing, an empty feeling in the abdomen, and a lack of muscular power" (p. 142) is extremely common.

Other researchers have corroborated Lindemann's findings that grief has a decidedly physical component. In addition to the somatic manifestations identified in Lindemann's classic study, disturbed sleep patterns, loss of strength and energy, change in appetite, and a tendency to be easily fatigued are also reported to be common manifestations of bereavement. Physical symptoms such as headaches, blurred vision, difficulty breathing, abdominal pain, constipation, urinary frequency, and/or dysmenorrhea (i.e., no menstrual cycle) are reported

FIGURE 3.1
Manifestations of Grief

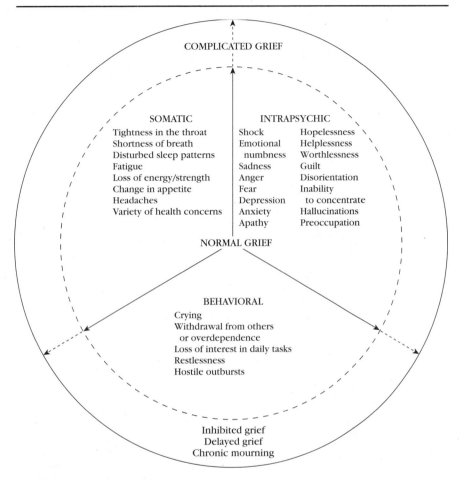

by some bereaved individuals. Further, many who are intensely grieving will seek medical help for a variety of health-related concerns (Warnes, 1985). Parkes (1988) stresses that little is still known about the interaction between the physiological and the psychological interplay of grief reactions, and the research in this area should remain a high priority. For example, although there is a growing body of evidence that bereavement has an effect on the immune functioning of some individuals' bodies, there is still much to learn about this connection (Irwin & Pike, 1993; Kim & Jacobs, 1993).

Intrapsychic Manifestations.   The grief process involves a multiplicity of emotional and psychological reactions to the loss. Researchers have determined that the following **intrapsychic** manifestations are frequent components of grief: shock, emotional numbness, sadness, fear, depression, anger, loneliness, worry, worthlessness, guilt, anxiety, hopelessness, helplessness, discontentment, apathy, and self-pity.

Changes in thought processes are also common intrapsychic manifestations of grief. For example, bereaved individuals have often reported being confused, disoriented, unable to concentrate or attend to detail, and/or unable to make decisions. Another psychological component of grief has been described as being like a "hallucination." In this situation a particular sensory stimulus brings back such a vivid memory that, for a split second, the survivor believes the deceased is still alive. These sensory stimuli may be such things as a car door slamming in front of the house at the time when a widow's husband would normally come home from work or a child walking down the sidewalk wearing a dress very similar to one worn frequently by the parent's dead child.

Some bereaved individuals report that their thoughts are filled with memories of the deceased. They can think of little else other than the events leading up to the death or their previous interactions with the deceased (Lindemann, 1944). In its extreme, preoccupation with the deceased has been described as an **"obsessional review."**

For many individuals, feelings and thought patterns described as normal intrapsychic symptoms of grief are very different in either occurrence or intensity from anything they have experienced previously. As a result, many may question their sanity and may even fear that they are going crazy, or, at the very least, believe "something is wrong with my mind" (Schuchter & Zisook, 1993). It can be helpful to the bereaved to be reassured that, as distressing as these thoughts and emotions are, they are normal manifestations of grief and they will gradually diminish over time.

Behavioral Manifestations.   Common behavioral manifestations include crying, withdrawal from others, overdependence on others, inability to perform daily tasks, restlessness, loss of interest in work or leisure activities, and hostile outbursts. Crying is a behavior that readily comes to mind when thinking of the grief process. It is a natural response for many to the sadness and depression being experienced. There are factors, however, that may encourage or inhibit a crying response (e.g., sex role socialization and/or cultural background of the bereaved). Other behavioral manifestations relate to patterns of interaction with others. Some grieving individuals choose to isolate themselves by withdrawing from persons in their social network. Withdrawal may be related to a variety of beliefs or reactions, such as

- No one cares about me.
- No one can possibly understand the emotional pain I am experiencing.
- Others, too, may die and leave me, so it is wiser not to get involved.
- I am worthless and others will leave me.

THE ANGUISH

The Anguish . . .
is here now . . . choking, physical pain, verging on hysteria, the mind racing, jumping, crying, "No, no, no!"

The Anguish . . .
has slowed down, is taking deep breaths—breathe, breathe. The mind slows, the face relaxes. The tears start again, this time slowly rocking, the violence subsiding.

The Anguish . . .
is sleeping, exhausted, functioning on reserve energy. The body has taken over, calmly, working methodically.

The Anguish . . .
is awakening—a few seconds of nothingness, normalcy, and then, flash! . . . the realization of what occurred yesterday.

The Anguish . . .
is no longer alone, but being shared with others. The pain is spreading out, the grief is paired, together.

The Anguish . . .
smiles today—once, twice. The body still functions methodically. The mind thinks a little of other things today—former things, before.

The Anguish . . .
tasted food today. Talked matter-of-factly today, noticed the outside today—and the sun.

The Anguish . . .
went back to life today—normally. Thought of pain at brief, alone moments. The mind had room for other functions, ideas.

The Anguish . . .
is under the surface—of the past—something thought about in quiet moments . . . alone, in silence.

The Anguish . . .
moves on.

SOURCE: A. Harvey (1996, March/April). The anguish. *Bereavement Magazine*, p. 28.

- My grief is my own private affair.
- I am so exhausted, I have no energy to invest in others.

In contrast, some bereaved individuals become overly dependent on others. This dependence may be an outgrowth of a sense of helplessness that essentially paralyzes them for a period of time and prohibits them from performing tasks or making decisions on their own.

Hostile outbursts may be the result of the anger that is common to grief. This hostility may be aimed at particular individuals such as family members and friends, or it may be aimed at a more diffuse group, such as medical professionals or drunk drivers, whom the bereaved somehow holds responsible for the death. The pent-up emotional energy may be vented through explosive words or actions, such as striking out or throwing objects.

Inability to concentrate on daily tasks and loss of interest in work or leisure activities are indicative of the physical, emotional, and psychological energy expended dealing with the loss itself and reorganizing patterns of living without the deceased. As time passes, survivors may gradually reinvest energy in a wide variety of activities.

Duration and Intensity of Grief

Although there is no absolute agreement as to how long the normal period of bereavement may extend, experts (Marris, 1986) typically agree that it is likely to be significantly longer than the 4 to 6 weeks first stated by Lindemann (1944) as adequate time for recovery. Although the most intense or acute feelings typically begin to diminish within 6 months to 1 or 2 years, many people experience continuing grief-related feelings for a much longer time. This extended time frame is not regarded as abnormal unless there is such intensity after an extended time that the survivors cannot adjust to the loss in a way that allows them to reorganize their lives and function effectively in the real world. **Acute grief** refers to the period in which the death is first recognized cognitively and emotionally. During this phase, the somatic, intrapsychic, and behavioral reactions are most intense. Emotional and physical resources are often drained during this period. Periods of withdrawal are also common; the bereaved may hope to avoid reminders of their recent loss by drawing themselves inward. Zisook and DeVaul (1985) note that "acute mourning may last several months before being gradually replaced by a slow resolution of the grieving, with a return of the feeling of well-being. . . . in this *resolution stage,* the bereaved . . . recognize what the loss has meant to them . . . and begin to shift attention to the world around them. . . . the hallmark of the resolution stage is the ability of the bereaved to recognize that they can . . . reexperience pleasure, and seek the companionship and love of others" (p. 372). Although the grief work continues well beyond the acute stage, the intensity of emotion and constant preoccupation with the loss do gradually lessen.

Certain factors, however, may periodically increase the intensity of the grief reaction even after it has diminished. For example, due to the memories they trigger, certain days of the year often cause the bereaved to experience once again painful emotions and preoccupation with the deceased. These so-called **anniversary reactions** are often precipitated by special days such as wedding anniversaries, birthdays, anniversaries of the date of death, Christmas, Passover, or Thanksgiving. It can be very helpful to the bereaved to have friends and family members recognize the importance of these special days by making a phone call, sending a note, or spending time together.

Feelings of grief may also be intensified by environmental cues such as having one empty chair at the dinner table or seeing the deceased's personal property in various rooms throughout the house. Hearing the deceased's favorite song on the radio, smelling her favorite perfume, or seeing his favorite dessert on a

One year later, a woman grieves the death of a friend killed in the crash of flight TWA 800.

menu may also bring the lost loved one vividly to mind. As time passes and as grief work continues successfully, these reminders of the loved one who has died often no longer precipitate bitter or painful memories, but rather happy or peaceful ones.

GRIEF WORK

Freud (1917) referred to grief as an absorbing process involving the work of confronting one's loss so that there will ultimately be a sense of resolution. Many others have subsequently used the phrase **grief work,** and a number of grief counseling strategies are based on the hypothesis that engaging in grief work is crucial to a positive outcome. As described by Lindemann (1944), grief work involves "emancipation from the bondage to the deceased, readjustment to the environment in which the deceased is missing, and the formation of new relationships" (p. 143). Defined in this way, grief work progresses through a number of steps that involve a change in one's self-concept, aspirations, goals, and relationships with the external world. Using this model, we understand that coping with grief is an experience that is physically, emotionally, and psychologically draining. Grief is an individual's way of regaining balance and of restoring a sense of equilibrium in one's life.

One of the most frequently cited explanations of the progression of activities needed to complete one's grief work is that of Worden (1991), which is based on four fundamental tasks:

1. to accept the reality of the loss;
2. to experience the pain of grief;
3. to adjust to an environment in which the deceased is missing;
4. to emotionally relocate the deceased and move on with life.

The first task, to accept the reality of the loss, demands that the bereaved break through the initial reaction of denial and accept the fact that the loved one has died. Although each individual's experience of grief is unique, the loss of a person to whom one is attached is expected to cause pain. Sometimes the bereaved refuses to feel this pain by cutting off his or her feelings and avoiding painful thoughts or reminders of the deceased. In many circumstances, avoidance of the pain during the time shortly following the death may cause serious repercussions at a later date. The belief that grief work is crucial to adaptation to loss is so fundamental that facilitation of this process currently underlies many programs designed to help bereaved individuals.

Depending on the role the deceased played in their lives, survivors may have a relatively easy or a much more difficult time adjusting to an environment in which the deceased is missing. The bereaved may be forced to develop new skills or find other persons to fulfill some of the lost roles. Worden's description of adjustment to an environment in which the deceased is missing directly parallels Bowlby's fourth phase of reorganization. Worden describes the fourth task of grief work as emotionally relocating the deceased and moving on with one's life. This task involves coming to the understanding that, although one can have important memories of a loved one who has died, the deceased can no longer play a central role in the survivor's daily life. Ultimately survivors "regain an interest in life, feel more hopeful, experience gratification again, and adapt to new roles" (Worden, 1991, p. 19).

DUAL-PROCESS MODEL OF COPING WITH LOSS

Over the past decade, Margaret Stroebe and her colleagues have expanded our understanding of the process of grief work. She and Henk Schut (1995) have developed a dual-process model of coping with loss, which is still being studied empirically. Rather than assuming that ongoing active confrontation with loss is *always* a necessary condition for positive outcome, this model suggests that there are circumstances in which it may be unnecessary and/or inappropriate. These authors stress that there are circumstances in which "repressive, inhibitory or denial strategies" (p. 4) can lead to a positive outcome and that "avoidance of reminders of a deceased person is normal, nonpathological, and even essential at times" (pp. 4–5). Stroebe and Schut (1995) suggest that bereaved individuals typically shift between two different orientations as they cope with their grief:

- **Loss orientation:** involves concentrating on, dealing with, and processing some aspect of the loss experience. Grief work is a key component of this orientation.
- **Restoration orientation:** involves adjustment to numerous changes that have been triggered by the loss. Common aspects of this orientation are solving problems, fulfilling new roles, changing routines, learning new skills, coping with daily challenges. This orientation also involves some periods of time where bereaved individuals "take time off" from their grief. (p. 10)

The dual-process model of coping indicates that most individuals oscillate between these two orientations and that it is necessary to engage in both patterns over time. During the acute phase of grief, more attention is likely spent on the loss orientation. Stroebe and Schut do not propose, however, any particular sequence of phases but rather emphasize ongoing oscillation and flexibility over time.

One major contribution of this dual model of coping is the insight it provides in relation to differential bereavement patterns exhibited by men compared with women, by various cultural groups, and in response to different types of losses. Key facets of the dual-process model of coping with loss are illustrated in Figure 3.2.

FIGURE 3.2
Dual-Process Model of Coping With Loss

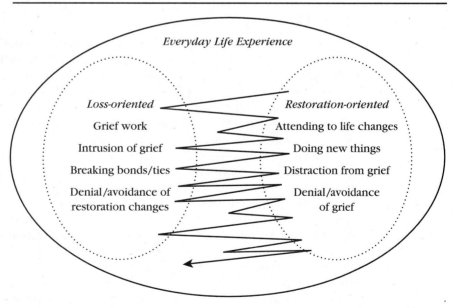

SOURCE: Stroebe and Schut (1995).

Certain groups, although they may shift back and forth over time, often come to healthy resolution of grief with more emphasis on either the loss orientation *or* the restoration orientation. There is evidence, for example, that men typically engage much more heavily in problem-focused coping strategies, whereas women more commonly use emotion-focused strategies. Both men and women, however, can effectively resolve their grief. Stroebe (1992) also reminds us of what seem to be rather extreme differences in cultural norms prescribing ongoing connection with the person who has died. Samoans often recover from their bereavement rapidly and without indication of heightened levels of emotional pain usually involved in a detachment process. Traditional Japanese do not attempt to detach from the deceased but rather develop strategies (e.g., ancestor worship) to keep the deceased accessible through talking to the person who has died or by leaving food for that individual. If one were to adhere strictly to a model grounded solely in the grief work hypothesis, neither of these cultural variations would be expected to result in healthy resolution of the loss. Both cultural groups, however, do typically have positive outcomes.

VARIABLES RELATED TO THE BEREAVED: FACTORS AFFECTING INTENSITY AND DURATION OF GRIEF

The cultural background of bereaved individuals, as well as their gender, age, and personality characteristics, to some extent influence the manifestations of grief and affect the intensity and duration of these manifestations (see Figure 3.3).

Cultural Background

What is typically viewed as an individualized and personal grief response must also be examined within the context of the culture in which one lives. One's cultural heritage helps define prescriptions for what are regarded as appropriate expressions of emotion and appropriate behaviors subsequent to a loss. These prescriptions are part of our early socialization as well as later social dictates. After doing extensive work on death-related systems of many different cultures across the world, Rosenblatt (1993) stresses that there is *great* variation in belief systems, ensuing grief, and mourning rituals.

An individual's grief relates to the personal definition of what has been lost; this is closely related to one's attitudes regarding life (Halporn, 1993). Often, a fundamental part of the meaning of death stems from beliefs handed down from generation to generation or reflects the reality of life in a given society. Japanese Buddhists, for example, view death as one's real birth and bestow a new name on the person at the time of death (Morgan, 1986).

In some societies, individuals are given permission to express their grief openly in public; whereas, in others, the bereaved would be regarded as weak if they exhibited such behaviors. Sometimes the specific form of grief expression

FIGURE 3.3
Variables Affecting Grief Process

FIGURE 3.3
Variables Affecting Grief Process

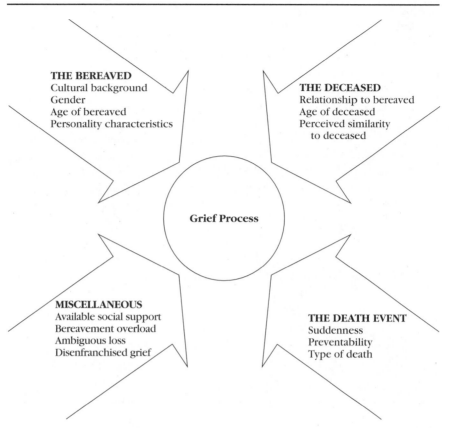

THE BEREAVED
Cultural background
Gender
Age of bereaved
Personality characteristics

THE DECEASED
Relationship to bereaved
Age of deceased
Perceived similarity
    to deceased

Grief Process

MISCELLANEOUS
Available social support
Bereavement overload
Ambiguous loss
Disenfranchised grief

THE DEATH EVENT
Suddenness
Preventability
Type of death

is also dictated by cultural norms. Among the Kapingamarangi in the Federated States of Micronesia, the wake after a death begins with women performing a high-pitched wail, or keening. The keening ceases when the mourners assemble and for the first time following the death, weeping is permitted, but is limited only to soft, intermittent sobs. The wailing stage begins late at night. The wailing is performed as a low, throaty, rhythmic cry and is more like a chant than weeping (Lieber, 1991).

Methods of disposition of the body also vary widely among cultural groups. Funeral rituals are defined by many cultural factors, including ethnicity, religious background, socioeconomic status, and level of technological advancement. Although some groups bury the body in the ground, others leave it exposed to the elements or allow animals to carry it away. Some societies may incinerate the corpse on a wooden frame called a funeral pyre (Barrett, 1993). For example, in

TRADITIONAL JEWISH MOURNING PRACTICES

Rituals vary by cultural and religious groups; to illustrate, we will examine common practices of traditional Jewish families. Mourning rituals play a twofold purpose: honoring the dead and comforting the bereaved. These rituals are clearly defined in the Jewish tradition. During various periods of time following the death, those who are bereaved are encouraged to engage actively in dealing with their grief, and over time, are gradually expected to reengage in normal activity.

Aninut: the period between death and interment. During this time frame, the bereaved are encouraged to spend solitary time reflecting on the loss and they are exempt from the normal demands of religious observance. This is recognized as a period of intense grief.

Shiva: a period of 7 days following the burial. During the first 3 days, visitors are discouraged so that the bereaved might more freely express their loss. During the latter part of this week, visitors readily come to share their concern and support.

Sheloshim: a period of 30 days of mourning during which there is diminished expression of one's grief.

Yahrzeit: the anniversary of the death. It is a time when family gathers to remember the person who has died and to reflect on his or her life.

As the first year after the death progresses, the bereaved gradually reengage in life's normal routines but are expected to forego many sources of entertainment. Self-sacrifice is reflective of the loss that has been experienced.

Kaddish: a prayer recited at the end of the eulogy that affirms both life and an acceptance of the death. The kaddish

(Continued)

Benares, India, there is a particular section of the Ganges River where open cremations of Hindus take place. The bodies, wrapped in cloth, are burned for a number of hours by a fire lit by a family member. The bodies are then carried down the "burning ghats" (concrete or marble slabs on which the pyres are placed) to the bank where the ashes are then committed to the Ganges—considered by Hindus to be the holiest of all rivers. Over the centuries, the ashes of millions have been scattered in the river (Jaffrey, 1995). Many Hindus hope to die in Benares or other holy cities along the Ganges so that they may rinse away their sins prior to death by washing from the river bank or dying in the holy water (Habenstein & Lamers, 1960).

Placement of the remains will also vary by culture and will be influenced by belief systems. Among the Xhosa of South Africa, the deceased are thought to protect the interests of the family. Upon death, the head of the household is therefore buried on his homestead, facing toward the house so that the family will be kept in constant view (Gijana, Louw, & Manganyi, 1989).

(Continued From Previous Page)

prayer is repeated at other defined points following the death; these include the end of the first month after the funeral (*sheloshim*) and the yearly anniversary of the death. The purpose of repeating the kaddish is to ensure ongoing remembrance of the one who has died as well as reaffirming one's faith in God and his justice.

The customs outlined here are reflective of traditional Jewish practices, which have changed and evolved in some multicultural societies as a result of acculturation. Drawing a contrast between traditional and many new practices, Getzel (1995) explains, that in many circumstances today,

. . . the Jewish tradition of having no flowers at memorial services or burial is widely disregarded, and the use of the simple wooden coffin has been displaced . . . ritual prayer and the elaborate mourning customs have been abbreviated or discarded. (p. 27)

Yet, on the other hand, Getzel (1995) also shares:

. . . avoidance of flowers and open caskets have recently been adopted by many non-Jews in an effort to avoid the excesses of the modern funeral, which offend the aesthetic, spiritual, and economic sensibilities of many people. (p. 27)

SOURCES: B. Cytron (1993). To honor the dead and comfort the mourners: Traditions in Judaism. In D. P. Irish, K. F. Lundquist, and V. J. Nelsen (Eds.), *Ethnic variations in dying, death, and grief: Diversity in universality* (pp. 113-124). Washington, DC: Taylor and Francis; G. S. Getzel (1995). Judaism and death: Practice and implications. In J. Parry & A. S. Ryan (Eds.), *A crosscultural look at death, dying, and religion* (pp. 18-31). Chicago: Nelson-Hall Publishers; J. Riemer (Ed.). (1995). *Jewish insights on death and mourning.* New York: Schocken Books; Schindler, R. (1996). Mourning and bereavement among Jewish religious families: A time for reflection and recovery. *Omega, 33*(2), 121-129.

Cultural differences are also found in relation to social support. Raphael and Nunn (1988) note that support is a "complex variable, reflecting aspects of society's interactional patterns and themes. . . . Cultural prescriptions may reinforce behaviors that are helpful or unhelpful" (p. 194). Some cultures have ritualized responses that provide automatic community acknowledgement of a loss and support for the survivors. For example, the entire Tanacross community in Alaska is affected and mobilized by a death. Although their culture values emotional restraint, the Athabasken people who inhabit Tanacross believe that it is society's responsibility to support and attend to grieving individuals so that they are not overcome by sorrow. They accept their responsibility during a 3-day ritual called a "potlatch." The bereaved community marks the separation of the deceased from society and symbolically lets go of him or her through feasting, dancing, singing, oratory, and gift giving. The potlatch is seen as a "phase of reinstallation" in which both hosts and guests reaffirm their relationships through shared sorrow and joy and reknit the bonds of the community (Simeone, 1991).

When we study loss and the ensuing grief, we need to be sensitive to the fact that various ethnic, religious, and cultural groups may have differences along many dimensions: beliefs about death, definitions of what the loss means, rituals related to burial and mourning, and attitudes about the body (Irish, 1993a). Given this diversity of heritages, it is crucial that individuals providing support to bereaved persons who are from cultural backgrounds different from their own understand that what may be out of the realm of "normal" in their own individual experience may be normal and even expected within another person's cultural realm.

Unfortunately, limited information is available regarding variations in patterns of grief among American ethnic groups. To date, there have been few empirical studies examining different ethnic groups in the United States to determine whether there might be variations in the way people personally experience grief or outwardly manifest it. One notable exception is an early study done by Kalish and Reynolds in 1976 and one by Oltjenbruns (in press). In an effort to focus attention on the need for more research in this area, a recent annual meeting of the Association for Death Education and Counseling (ADEC) focused on diversity with the hope that this theme would underscore the importance of this topic. In the future, it is anticipated that our understanding of cultural patterns of bereavement within the United States will be greatly enhanced by increased emphasis in this domain.

In his review of relevant literature, Eisenbruch (1984a, 1984b) raised a variety of questions related to cross-cultural aspects of bereavement that need much more attention from researchers:

- What is the relationship between an individual's private grief and his or her public mourning?
- How widespread and useful are positive factors, such as group support, in facilitating successful resolution of the grieving process?
- How effective are mourning practices of various ethnic groups in preventing complicated outcomes for these groups?

Answers to questions such as these will provide continuing insight regarding cultural influences on grief.

As we learn to interact with and give support to persons of various cultural backgrounds, we must be careful to avoid stereotypes that lead us to inappropriate conclusions about what an individual may be experiencing and may be needing from a support network. Kleinman, Kaplan, and Weiss (1984) caution against stereotyping individuals simply because they are part of a particular cultural or ethnic background. There may be as much variation *within* a cultural group as *among* cultural groups. This can be true for a number of reasons. For example, within a given ethnic group, individuals come from different religions, generations, socioeconomic levels, educational backgrounds, and geographic locales. Each of these factors plays a role in the socialization process that ultimately helps to shape an individual's experience related to a significant loss (Nelsen, 1993; Perry, 1993; Younoszai, 1993; Irish, 1993b). Just as there are many differences among different groups' experience with grief, there are *also many similarities.* It would be just as inappropriate to deny the similarities as it is to deny the differences.

The need to avoid stereotyping can be particularly important in a pluralistic society such as America where, over time, clearly defined cultural expectations have become blurred. First-generation immigrants may face a particularly difficult period of grief in that they may not have brought with them the "traditional resources for carrying out culturally expected bereavement practices" (Kleinman, Kaplan, & Weiss, 1984, p. 206), and, at the same time, it is not personally acceptable or comfortable for them to engage in mainstream mourning practices.

Recognizing the existence of both cultural differences *and* cultural similarities and avoiding stereotypes both within and among cultural groups are important. To better understand the needs of given individuals, we need to seek out information from others in their culture and from the available literature. One of the best resources for developing insights about another's background is to ask bereaved family members and friends to share perspectives from their own cultural heritage.

Gender

Although researchers are attempting to clarify the differences between the grief of females and that of males, we do not yet have definitive answers (Sanders, 1993). Some of the focal points of the gender-related research carried out thus far include the definition of the loss itself, outward manifestations of grief, and access to social support networks. As **thanatologists** (professionals who specialize in the study of death, dying, and grief) continue to research gender differences in response to loss, important questions remain unanswered. For example, are there intrinsic differences in the way men and women react to loss? To what extent are observed differences in the manifestations of grief due to innate differences between men and women and to what extent are they the result of socialization and gender prescriptions? Do differences between the grief reactions of men and women become greater in certain situations? How can we ensure that both men and women get the support they need after a significant loss?

Staudacher (1991) interviewed men who were bereaved by a number of different types of losses over the human life span. Her synthesis of major themes derived from her interviews provides a valuable framework for better understanding some of the reasons differences exist in the way males and females experience grief and come to terms with their loss. Just as individuals among various cultures are socialized differently as to the meaning of death, the expression of grief, the type of support that is appropriate to give and receive, and so on, males and females within a given cultural group are also often socialized differently. For example, in many cultures, males are taught through words, examples, rewards, and punishments that certain things are more or less acceptable to the social group; so, too, are females. This differential socialization can, at least partially, help explain some of the differences between men and women that will be reported in this section.

At risk of being stereotypic (our goal is to be illustrative, not prescriptive), we share the following as examples; they illustrate major themes derived from Staudacher's (1991) interviews with the men with whom she worked. Many of the men believed that they had been taught to be (and were expected to be) in control; confident about their world; courageous even in times of adversity; and able to accomplish tasks, endure stress and pain, and be a provider. In contrast, many of these men felt they were not given permission to cry openly; express fear; feel insecure; or express loneliness, sadness, or depression. These prescriptions are quite different than those given to many women in the same culture and are reflected in behavior. For example, Kalish and Reynolds (1976), who studied Anglo Americans, African Americans, Mexican Americans, and Japanese Americans, found a significant difference in the number of men who said they would attempt to control their emotions in public as compared with women. Men said they would try to control their emotions whereas women said they would let themselves go and cry (both in public and in private).

The men interviewed by Staudacher (1991) reported that social networks seemed to reach out to them differentially, as compared with women. One bereaved father shared:

> There were times I wanted to go around and say, "Hey world. I'm grieving, too. I'm not as strong as you think I am." Who is supported at the funeral? Someone always makes sure the woman is supported. Nobody supports the man. The woman gets all the attention and the man and the children get very little, if any, attention. People say to the children (and me) "Be strong for your mother." (Staudacher, 1991, p. 11)

The information shared in this section thus far has primarily focused on gender differences in the United States. Other cultures also have societal prescriptions in relation to gender-appropriate mourning patterns. Many are quite parallel to those already described, others are not. Lapidus (1996) shares the following when describing traditions of Muslims:

> The male rituals strive for self-control, dignity, restraint, and the worship of God in the face of loss and grief. While the men uphold the rationality of human nature, the women express the passionate side. They gather to loudly lament the loss of a loved one . . . call out the traditional wailing call, cry in a chanted lament, and recite poetry that expresses their anguish, brooding, and despair. . . . they may dance with abandoned grief. (pp. 154–155)

In contrast, for the Lakota Indians,

> Mourning is considered natural, and the unrestrained expression of grief is appropriate and regarded as a good thing for both sexes. Women will typically wail loudly; men will often sing emotional, mournful songs. (Brokenleg & Middleton, 1993, p. 105)

Additional information regarding gender differences and grief will be discussed in upcoming chapters.

Age of the Bereaved

The age of the bereaved is a variable that has an impact on the symptomatology of grief and also on the coping mechanisms available to the individual who is dealing with a loss. Though studies thus far have used different methodologies to determine bereavement outcomes for various age groups, some general trends have been identified. As noted in chapter 2, Piaget's theory of cognitive development and Erikson's theory of psychosocial development are important for understanding the needs of the dying. These theories are also relevant to understanding the variation of grief responses across the life span. Raphael (1980) has noted that developmental conflicts currently being dealt with by the survivor will have an impact on the mourning process. Discussion of these issues, as they relate to particular age groups, will be presented in upcoming chapters.

Young children perceive death somewhat differently than do adults and only gradually learn that death is irreversible and universal, that dead persons are not able to function as living people, and that all individuals will die some day (Speece & Brent, 1984). At this point, however, there is no firm agreement by all researchers as to the age at which the separate components of the concept of death are acquired. A number of research studies focusing on a variety of questions related to concept acquisition are reviewed in chapter 5.

Adults should not assume that because children perceive death differently they do not grieve. They do, in fact, grieve, but manifest their grief somewhat differently. Specific aspects of children's and adolescents' grief are discussed in chapters 5 and 6. A review of the research examining the effect of age on bereavement indicates not only differences between children and adults, but also differences among persons in various stages of adulthood.

Personality Characteristics

The relationship between personality variables and the manifestations of grief and its ultimate resolution has thus far attracted little attention from researchers (Sanders, 1988). A few studies that are available in the professional literature will be highlighted here.

A number of personality characteristics influence the individual's subjective experience of grief. For example, a low tolerance for frustration and anxiety may intensify the chances of a poor outcome of grief or lengthen the bereavement period. Parkes and Brown (1972) explained that poor outcome meant reactions such as acquiring symptoms resembling those suffered by the deceased, extreme self-blame, or overactivity without a goal, among others.

One personality trait related to the premises set forth by learned helplessness theory is that of "locus of control" (Abramson, Seligman, & Teasdale, 1978).

Locus of control refers to the degree to which an individual perceives that an outcome is dependent on his or her own behavior or personal attributes (i.e., internally controlled) or whether the outcome is controlled by an outside force or by chance (i.e., externally controlled).

One hypothesis is that those who measure high on the variable of external control have a more difficult time dealing with a crisis. Stroebe, Stroebe, and Dommittner (1988) found that individuals who were grieving the death of their spouses and had higher external control scores did exhibit higher levels of depression and somatic complaints than those with higher internal control scores. Krause (1986) also found higher levels of depression in individuals who had a higher belief in chance (which parallels a measure of external locus of control).

Individuals at both ends of this personality trait continuum (extremely high internals and extremely high externals) are likely to be particularly vulnerable to the effects of stress. Those with an extreme external orientation do not believe that they have the power to deal with the stressor, and those with an extreme internal orientation are so overcome with a feeling of personal responsibility that they suffer from anxiety and depression when stress is unavoidable.

VARIABLES RELATED TO THE DECEASED: FACTORS AFFECTING INTENSITY AND DURATION OF GRIEF

Relationship of Deceased to Bereaved

The death of a person who held a peripheral role in the survivor's life is likely to trigger a less intense grief reaction than one who held a central role. Bugen (1979) noted that the centrality of the relationship may be determined by either a behavioral commitment or an emotional commitment. A behavioral commitment is related to the role that the deceased played in the bereaved's life and vice versa. For example, if the deceased husband was very dependent on his surviving wife to meet his daily needs, the bereaved widow may feel a great void in her life, not only because of her emotional commitment to her husband, but also because of the many hours in her day that she no longer fills with tasks performed to take care of him. In this case, the death of her husband creates a role loss as well as an object loss. **Object loss** refers to the loss of a loved one. **Role loss** is defined as the loss of one's position or status in society.

When attempting to gain insight regarding the severed relationship and its effect on the grief response, one must look beyond the centrality of the relationship in behavioral terms to the quality of the relationship and its centrality in emotional terms (Rubin, 1985; Wortman & Silver, 1987). The death of someone who was regarded as an intimate, a confidant, and a major source of support has a much greater impact than the death of someone who may have spent much time with the survivor but was never emotionally close (e.g., a person at work who is an acquaintance rather than a close friend).

Age of the Deceased

The age of the person who has died often has an impact on those who are grieving. Many experts believe the most traumatic death to deal with is the death of a child or the parent of a young child. Many individuals react to the death of an aged person as being appropriate because he or she was able to lead a full and long life, but feel that the death of a child is somehow premature or unjustified.

If the person who died was of similar age to the bereaved, the grieving individual often asks questions such as "Why did that person die and not me?" "How much longer do I have to live?" Concerns related to these types of questions have an effect on the bereavement process.

Perceived Similarity to the Deceased

Though relatively little research has been done in this area, there is some indication that if the bereaved perceive themselves to be similar to the deceased, they may experience more grief than those who perceive little similarity. Barnes (1978) has noted that children whose same-sex parent has died often view themselves as particularly vulnerable to death. These children may need special help differentiating themselves from the deceased. Children whose siblings have died may also feel vulnerable because of the perceived similarity due to age.

VARIABLES RELATED TO THE DEATH EVENT: FACTORS AFFECTING INTENSITY AND DURATION OF GRIEF

Suddenness of the Death

The suddenness of the death has been found to be related to the grief experienced by many survivors. Sudden death intensifies the initial shock of the bereaved and, because there was no opportunity to prepare for the loss, all of the grief work must be done after the death (Bowlby, 1980). For example, thousands of individuals die each year due to heart attacks. If there had been no previous indication of heart problems, the survivors must deal with a totally unexpected death.

From the time a life-threatening illness is diagnosed, the dying individual, together with family members and friends, often begins to grieve. They grieve in anticipation of the emotional pain and also for the changes that the death will bring. They grieve the many losses that are a part of the dying process itself. This type of grief is known as **anticipatory grief.** If the death is an expected one, as is the case in death due to a terminal illness, part of the grief work may be done prior to the death. This, then, may serve as a factor in mitigating the intensity and duration of the grief experience once the death has occurred (Lundin, 1984; Sanders, 1989). Additionally, the grief may be somewhat ameliorated by having had the opportunity to say good-bye to the person who is dying and to draw closure on a variety of concerns. There may be fewer regrets and less guilt as a result. If the illness has been a debilitating or a painful one, survivors may even feel a sense of relief when death does come (Chester, Jerardi, & Weger, 1980). Many persons who have an opportunity to engage in anticipatory grief do have less intense reactions and complete their grief work earlier as compared with survivors of a sudden death.

This, however, is not always the case. One exception seems to be related to those situations when the illness is a lengthy one; researchers found a negative impact on many of the survivors who anticipated the death of a loved one for longer than 6 months (Schwab, Chalmers, Conroy, Farris, & Markush, 1975). For example, Sanders (1982) found both qualitative and quantitative differences in the grief response of survivors of short-term chronic deaths (STCD) compared with long-term chronic deaths (LTCD). The LTCD survivors exhibited a greater sense of isolation, rumination, loss of vigor, and loss of emotional control when compared with the STCD survivors. The most debilitating factor was the higher degree of social isolation. Sanders explained this by noting that the care of the individual was so all-encompassing, there was little time or energy to continue previous levels of interaction. As a result, support systems diminished. For short-term illnesses, friends and relatives had not yet drifted away.

The value of anticipatory grief may be diminished in a situation of protracted illness because emotional and physical resources of the bereaved have been taxed to the limit prior to the death. Some hypothesize that survivors who act as primary caregivers for the dying over an extended period must deal not only with the death of a loved one, but also with the loss of this additional role and function.

In addition to the length of an illness serving as a confounding variable when taken into account with the suddenness of a death, there is also evidence that the age of the person who died can be an intervening variable. When an individual is quite elderly, even a "sudden" death is not totally unexpected (Stroebe & Stroebe, 1993).

Many, however, grieve a death that is clearly sudden in nature and, as a result, do not engage in anticipatory grief. Various types of sudden deaths such as homicides, suicides, accidents, or large-scale disasters have often been regarded as traumatic in nature and magnify certain aspects of the grief reaction.

Preventability of the Death

Bugen (1979) has argued that the question of preventability is an important influence on bereavement outcome. He explains that **preventability** is "the general belief that the factors contributing to the death might have been avoided" (p. 36). Whether the accident could have, in fact, been avoided is not really the issue. For example, if the survivor perceives that he or she may have contributed to the death or could have prevented the death, feelings of guilt increase. The belief that someone else is responsible elicits anger toward that person, even if that person is the deceased. Types of death that are generally regarded as preventable are deaths by homicide, suicide, accident, or large-scale disaster.

On occasion, natural deaths are also thought to have been preventable. Some individuals feel that they may have been able to prevent another's death by seeking more timely medical attention. For example, "If only I had taken Dad to the doctor much earlier." The perception of preventability can affect the grief reaction, regardless of whether the death actually could have been prevented. Other deaths that may be regarded as preventable are those that result from an individual's engaging in high-risk behavior. Examples would include a death due to AIDS when the person had been sexually promiscuous or a death due to lung cancer when an individual had smoked two packs of cigarettes a day for years.

Homicide.   Each year, thousands of family members and friends must deal with grief that has been intensified by the nature of the death itself. Due to the violent nature of homicide, the suddenness of the death, a variety of unanswered questions, and a belief that the death was preventable, the grief triggered by murder is often more intense and of longer duration than other types of grief reactions. Problems become magnified by the survivors who also feel stigmatized by the nature of the death. This may interfere with the availability of a sensitive support network to help the bereaved come to terms with their loss. In addition, feelings of frustration or anger at not being allowed to grieve in privacy may be provoked by widespread media coverage.

Survivors of homicide experience somatic symptoms similar to those discussed earlier: insomnia, chest pains, palpitations, and headaches. Many of the intrapsychic and behavioral manifestations of grief precipitated by a murder necessitate additional discussion because they are frequently more intense than for a death due to natural causes. Others are unique to this type of death situation.

Recall that anger is a common component of grief. When a loved one has been murdered, bereaved individuals are likely to initially experience intense anger and rage directed at the murderer. Later, they may exhibit anger at the criminal court system if they deem that justice, as they see it, has not been served (Schmidt, 1986) or if they feel that the system has treated them insensitively. Some even believe that the survivors are twice victimized—first by the murderer and second by the system. Because murder trials often do not even begin for months or years after the crime, resolution of grief is delayed (Sprang, McNeil, & Wright, 1989).

Guilt, too, is a typical component of grief but may be exacerbated if the survivors feel that they could or should have somehow protected the victim. Preoccupation with the deceased and the death event is common to grief resulting from any death, but the preoccupation may be more intense and more painful after a murder. Images that are prevalent both in conscious thoughts and in dreams often focus on "the terror and helplessness of the victim" (Rynearson, 1984, p. 1452). There is great concern regarding the trauma associated with the mode of killing and the suffering endured. Additionally, survivors may experience intrusive thoughts of wanting to kill the murderer as retribution for the crime.

Some behavioral manifestations of grief are unique to bereavement caused by murder. Survivors often experience a pervasive fear that then causes heightened anticipation and protective avoidance of violence as well as hypervigilance and frequent startle reactions. For example, the bereaved may restrict their activities in order to remain in familiar surroundings and to avoid strangers. Many survivors desire to seek retribution and spend many hours providing information to the investigative judicial system or, in some cases, pursuing independent investigations. Some survivors initiate or support legislative action to demand harsher punishment for convicted murderers or to promote gun control. Others may advocate changes in the legal system that would ensure such practices as consistent communication with the family regarding the status of the case. However, a search for retribution should not become a substitution for the necessary grief work and the ultimate acceptance of the death.

Suicide. Like homicide survivors, people who grieve as a result of the suicide of a loved one experience emotions that are somewhat different than those triggered by death due to natural causes. Hauser (1987) explains that there are at least seven reasons why grief following a loved one's suicide may be particularly difficult; so much so that many believe that the survivors who grieve a death by suicide are themselves "victims" and are even referred to as such.

- Death by suicide is often unexpected and typically sudden.
- The death is frequently marked by violence.
- The suicide typically evokes a great deal of guilt among those who knew the deceased.
- The social system within which the suicide occurs is often already highly stressed.
- Mourning rituals are often compromised.
- The suicide may lead to distorted communications among survivors due to the sense of anger involved.
- Some of the social supports commonly extended to others in grief are withdrawn.

Many of these issues raised by Hauser will be discussed in more detail in chapter 9.

Anger and guilt are frequent components of a grief reaction. These emotions, however, are greatly intensified when associated with a suicide. There is often extreme anger at the individual who committed suicide because that person is regarded as having willfully chosen death, which then precipitated the resulting pain, disorganization, and loneliness. Bolton (1986) shares a comment by one father whose daughter committed suicide: "Suicide is not a solitary act. A beloved person thinks that she is killing herself, but she also kills a part of us" (p. 202).

Additionally, survivors are frequently angry at themselves for not having predicted the possibility of the suicide and, thereby, prevented it. They may also be angry for not having helped the deceased to be sufficiently happy or satisfied with life such that suicide would not have even been considered. These survivors often feel at least somewhat responsible for the death and as a result may feel extremely guilty.

The normal preoccupation with the death is often heightened for suicide survivors, as it is for homicide survivors. They may become obsessed with the idea that they could have prevented the death and mentally rehearse the role of rescuer time and time again. Additionally, they engage in an ongoing search for answers to such questions as "What caused the suicide?" or "Could I have prevented it?" Although there are usually no clear-cut answers to such questions, survivors may continue to search for explanations (Dunne & Morrish-Vidners, 1987). Although these survivors may desperately wish they had been able to prevent the suicide, they need help in understanding that they could not ultimately be held responsible for the other person's act.

Family members and friends may also experience a great deal of shame following the suicide. Although the survivors did not commit the actual suicide, they may feel that society is blaming them for the final act of their loved one. Many survivors do report that they feel stigmatized by others. Survivors may also feel shame if they, or others, believe suicide is a criminal act, a sin, or a sign of weakness or instability.

The stigma associated with a suicide often diminishes the availability of support that is crucial to a healthy and timely resolution of grief. Individuals who would normally be helpful during other periods marked by grief often engage in a conspiracy of silence because they feel very awkward and don't know what to say after the suicide. Calhoun, Abernathy, and Selby (1986) studied societal reactions to various types of deaths: suicidal, natural, and accidental. They found that many regarded interacting with survivors of a suicide as an aversive situation and would choose to avoid the family rather than risk saying or doing something that might be deemed inappropriate. In some instances, others may blame the survivor for not having "prevented the death" and choose to withhold comfort. This contributes to an already heavy emotional burden.

Survivors often doubt their own lovableness or sense of self-worth. These doubts can arise as a result of feeling totally rejected by the person who committed suicide. Questions arise regarding the quality of the relationship that had previously existed with the individual who committed suicide. To counteract some of the feelings that are particularly difficult after a suicide (such as shame and guilt), some survivors refuse to believe their loved one deliberately killed himself or herself. Instead, these survivors may insist that the death was caused by an accident.

An important point to keep in mind is that an unsuccessful suicide attempt may also trigger many of the reactions previously discussed. Shame, guilt, blame, and stigma are among the reactions of families and friends whose loved one has attempted suicide (Ginn, Range, & Hailey, 1988).

Accidental Death.   To date, relatively little attention has been paid to the relationship between accidental death and bereavement. Calhoun, Selby, and Abernathy (1984) and Sheshkin and Wallace (1976) contrasted grief due to death by accidental causes to death by suicide and natural causes.

Sheshkin and Wallace discovered that widows whose husbands died by accident were less likely to be blamed for the death and took less of a personal risk when telling others how their spouses had died than did survivors of suicide. Calhoun et al. (1984) found that survivors of accidental deaths could expect more sympathy from others than if the death had been due to either suicide or natural causes. Additionally, participants in this study were asked to rate the amount of difficulty they expected individuals would have in coping with four types of death (murder, suicide, accident, natural causes). They responded that natural causes would be the least difficult, followed by accidents, then suicide and murder. There was no significant difference between suicide and murder but all other pairs did reflect significant differences.

Lord (1987) studied 292 adults who had experienced the death of a family member as a result of an auto accident caused by a drunk driver. Her participants described a number of responses from others that were regarded as unhelpful shortly after the accident: Medical staff often lacked empathy and did not supply adequate information; police were not sensitive to families' needs when notifying them of the accident; the presence of too many people disallowed an opportunity for privacy. Other responses regarded as inappropriate or difficult during the weeks following the accidental death were inappropriate comments regarding money or insurance by people outside the family, lack of responsiveness by the police or district attorney's office, and frustration with the legal system.

Doyle (1980) pointed out a number of factors that are related to the grief of survivors of accidental deaths. These factors include

- the manner in which the survivors were notified of the death;
- the physical condition of the body;
- media coverage of the accident; and
- involvement in lawsuits or insurance negotiations.

Thus, we might expect the following circumstances to have the lowest risk of complicating bereavement:

- compassionate notification of the death;
- minimal disfigurement of the body;
- minimal media coverage that does not focus on the sensational aspects of the accident; and
- absence of need for either litigation or confrontation with insurance companies.

Law enforcement officers or rescue personnel must show compassion when they notify family members that their loved ones have been killed in an accident. Police officers can give psychological support both at the time of notification and later if further investigation of the accident is necessary.

When drivers have been involved in fatal car accidents, "grief may be experienced by the driver for the act he has committed or been involved in"

THE CRASH OF TWA FLIGHT 800

On July 17, 1996, TWA Flight 800 mysteriously crashed into the water off New York's Long Island. All 230 persons on board were killed. A nation watched and waited—for bodies to be recovered, for bodies to be identified, for prayers to be answered. As they waited for information as to what caused the crash, persons throughout the world also struggled to find meaning in such a large-scale disaster. It is likely that definitive answers about causality will never be found; even if they are, the extended delay will have already caused significant pain. As with many sudden deaths, survivors were left to painfully ask questions of "why?" Why the 16 students from the same small community of Montoursville—members of a high school French class who were finally taking their dream trip to Paris? Why the young man who had just proposed to the woman he loved as he left the airport? Why. . . . Why. . . . Why?

(Foeckler, Garrard, Williams, Thomas, & Jones 1978, p. 175), whether or not the driver knew the person who was killed. The drivers studied reported feelings of sadness, guilt, shame, anger, rage, depression, fear, confusion, and anxiety. Some drivers also felt cognitive dissonance when trying to cope with the idea that they (a good person) had killed another (a bad act). These researchers found that the social support of others was considered to be, by far, the most important help received by the drivers. Blame for the accident and the resulting lack of understanding and support were the most negative factors hindering resolution of the crisis.

Chesser (1981) also studied individuals who were coping with accidentally having killed another person. She found that if the survivors knew the person who had died, dealing with the death was even more complicated. They had to deal not only with their feelings of responsibility for the accident, but also with their own feelings of grief.

Large-Scale Disasters.   Often we pick up a newspaper to read of what may be described as a large-scale disaster. Many people simultaneously may lose their lives through natural disasters such as floods, fires, earthquakes, or hurricanes. Further, other large-scale disasters such as plane accidents or acts of terrorism change the lives of many families. There are special circumstances relevant to these types of events. Various disasters bring with them the repercussions common to sudden deaths and raise many questions related to preventability (Chenell & Murphy, 1992). In many circumstances, families are faced with the ambiguity of whether their loved one may be rescued or whether the body will ever be recovered. When bodies are found, they may be severely disfigured. Survivors may be faced with the difficult choice of whether to look at the body or not; one choice may result in great pain by seeing the body so unlike what they would wish to remember. The choice not to look at the body, however, may result in ongoing questioning as to whether the loved one had really died. When bodies are not recovered, questions may linger forever. As with homicides and many accidents, families are often overwhelmed with being the focus of ongoing media attention. Although some may desire the help of the media in searching out answers, others wish to be allowed to grieve privately.

When disasters claim many individuals' lives, those in the community may be faced with multiple losses and run the risk of bereavement overload. How can one cope if one's village has been destroyed and half of its inhabitants are now dead? Further, certain disasters may rob survivors not only of loved ones but also of their homes (e.g., through floods, hurricanes, or earthquakes) or certain resources (e.g., clean running water). When a community is in grief, support for individuals may not be as forthcoming; certain resources (both formal and informal) may simply no longer be available or they may be overtaxed.

ADDITIONAL FACTORS AFFECTING INTENSITY AND DURATION OF GRIEF

Availability of Social Support

The availability of social support from family and friends is an important resource to bereaved individuals and can serve as a helpful mediating variable in promoting a positive outcome to the grief experience. Numerous references to its importance have already been made throughout this chapter. Social support includes the "comfort, assistance, and/or information one receives through formal or informal contacts with individuals or groups" (Vachon & Stylianos, 1988, p. 176). If the support is truly to be helpful, it must be regarded as such by the recipient. Further, what is needed by the bereaved individual may change over time.

Research has shown that many of the widows having a "bad outcome" to their grief have reported that they were not given understanding and support by relatives and friends (Maddison & Walker, 1967). In one study, the widows and widowers who had a poor outcome also expressed a feeling that no one understood or cared about them (Parkes, 1975).

Parkes and Weiss (1983) found that positive resolution to bereavement was correlated to long-term availability of social support. Unfortunately, extended support is often lacking; instead, our society often engages in a conspiracy of silence with the bereaved (similar to the avoidance technique used with the dying).

Although there is strong indication of the value of social support during bereavement, particularly for females, many individuals do not extend continued support to the grieving for many reasons. Often, for example, individuals do not offer help because they simply do not know what to do or say and, as a result, choose to say or do nothing. Unfortunately, this lack of acknowledgment of the death and ensuing grief may be misinterpreted as a lack of caring or concern, rather than avoidance due to discomfort. Additionally, many people in our society do not understand the extended duration of the grief process. Lacking this knowledge, they do not recognize the need to offer support beyond the immediacy of the death (Sprang, McNeil, & Wright, 1993).

Bereavement Overload

A factor that can complicate what would otherwise be a normal grief reaction is related to the number of other losses a person has recently experienced. Some individuals may be faced with a high number of significant losses in a fairly short time. An example is a 45-year-old man whose mother died of cancer and whose son was killed in a motorcycle accident within 6 months. In the following 8 months, he lost his job and was also divorced. Each of these events, in and of itself, might be regarded as a significant loss. The fact that this individual suffered four such losses within the course of 14 months would make him susceptible to what is known as **bereavement overload.** Kastenbaum (1969) first used this term to reflect the situation of elderly persons who, because of their longevity, experience many losses. Bereavement overload indicates that a person is in a physically and/or emotionally weakened state due to a multiplicity of losses that leave little time between them for resolving earlier grief.

Ambiguous Loss

The grief response can be complicated if those who are grieving do not fully understand the true meaning of the loss; in these situations the loss is *ambiguous*. Human beings have the coping capacity to deal with that which is clear to them. When a woman loses her husband to a fatal heart attack, she knows definitively that he is dead. There are some losses, however, that are not so clearly defined.

Physically Present but Psychologically Absent.   A very common example of ambiguous loss relates to those situations when a person is still physically present but is perceived as being psychologically absent (Boss, 1990). The grief of family members cannot be resolved because the final death and loss are yet to occur (Boss, 1990). An example of this type of loss can be seen in families with a member suffering from Alzheimer's disease; this example will be discussed in chapter 8.

Modern medical technology has the capacity to keep a person who is "brain dead" on a respirator for an extended period; with the heart and lungs functioning with such mechanical help it is extremely difficult to accept that one's loved one has gone (Pelletier, 1993). Keyserlingk (1993) gave a powerful example of ambiguous loss in the case of a woman whose husband has been in an irreversible coma for an extended time:

> Grieving will have already begun in the face of real past and present losses, the loss of accessibility to the comatose husband, the loss of her husband's company and comfort, (he is not the person he was), the loss of dreams, of lifestyle, of a future that won't be realized, the progressive debilitation and continuing dependence, the wife being already forced to attend social functions alone, children having to accommodate to a missing father at their big moments. But since he is not dying . . . there can't be the normal facilitating of the grieving process. . . . (p. 33)

Physically Absent but Psychologically Present.   A woman who receives a message that her husband is missing in action during a war or has been taken hostage by criminals does not know whether she is to define his absence as temporary or whether he has, in fact, died. Although he is not physically present, he is very much in the thoughts of his family.

Hostage situations also serve as examples of this type of ambiguous loss. Many families and friends of individuals taken hostage do not know whether they will ever see their loved ones again. In one midwestern town, yellow ribbons were tied around many trees throughout its geographic bounds to serve as a constant reminder of an undefined loss—one of the city's much beloved community members had been taken hostage in Lebanon and, for months on end, there would be no definitive word about his status. For 6 years, each June 9, on the anniversary of his having been captured, townspeople came together to share memories and share their grief—and to express their hope. Finally, their hope was realized and Tom Sutherland returned home.

Most situations of ambiguous loss, however, do not have such a happy ending. It is the uncertainty and unknowing that define the loss as being ambiguous, not the final outcome. The uncertainty of the final outcome, together with the human capacity to hope, even in the most adverse of conditions, can delay individuals becoming engaged in grief work and, to some extent, put their lives on hold. Other examples of losses that may be complicated by this sense of uncertainty or ambiguity are those where no body is found (e.g., a boat has capsized in tumultuous water but the body is never recovered) or those circumstances when, for various reasons, the bereaved do not see the body (e.g., times when the body is very disfigured and family members choose not to view it).

Disenfranchised Grief

Another factor (in addition to the availability of social support, bereavement overload, and ambiguity of certain losses) that contributes to the intensity and duration of grief is known as disenfranchisement. A number of circumstances in our society serve to disenfranchise the griever. Doka (1987, 1989) coined the term **disenfranchised grief** to describe those situations in which the larger society does not socially sanction and/or recognize certain bereaved persons' "right, role, or capacity to grieve" (p. 3). This lack of recognition may stem from various sources (Kamerman, 1993; Rando, 1992). Society may not, for example, recognize certain relationships as being acceptable (e.g., relationships that are homosexual or extramarital in nature) (Klein & Fletcher, 1986). In other situations, persons may assume that a relationship has already been severed and that the death of a given individual would therefore be regarded as insignificant (e.g., death of a divorced marital partner; death of a former in-law). In some circumstances, the larger society may not even understand that a significant loss has, in fact, taken place (e.g., miscarriage, stillbirth, death of a friend or colleague, death of a pet). Some in our society regard certain types of death as carrying an element of stigma (e.g., suicide or death due to AIDS). Many expect the bereaved of such "stigmatized deaths" to suffer in silence. Another contribution to disenfranchisement may be the lesser value that we sometimes place on various groups of people. By diminishing their value as people (e.g., the mentally handicapped or the emotionally disabled), we sometimes diminish their grief (Rando, 1992).

When social networks do not recognize that individuals have a right to grieve, the bereaved's access to support systems that can help them resolve their grief is greatly diminished. In essence, there is an expectation that they live in a "conspiracy of silence." Furthermore, these individuals may experience a great deal of shame or confusion about feeling a sense of loss when others do not believe it is significant. Feelings of guilt, shame, anger, embarrassment, loneliness, and isolation are common to many grief responses. These reactions are typically more extreme in the disenfranchised griever.

POSITIVE OUTCOMES OF GRIEF

Compared with the focus of the literature on manifestations of grief, the factors affecting one's grief process, and the struggle for resolution, little attention has been given to positive outcomes of grief. An expanding body of evidence, however, suggests that growth may result from one's bereavement experience.

Malinak et al. (1979) interviewed 14 adults whose parents had died during the last 2 years. Approximately half of those individuals reported that, even though the death of their parent had been very painful, they realized that they had experienced a beneficial outcome as well. Individuals reported such benefits as "an increased sense of strength and self-reliance, a greater caring for friends and loved ones, and a more general quickening to life and deepening of their appreciation of existence" (p. 1155). Another positive outcome reported was placing value on the present rather than investing so heavily in what the future might bring.

Benoliel (1985) notes that the experience of a significant loss can encourage a search for meaning in one's life. For example, some find meaning in translating their experience into a creative modality such as music, poetry, or artwork. Others find meaning by enhancing relationships with persons around them.

In interviews with 52 adults, ranging in age from 30 to 90, respondents indicated that the majority had experienced the following positive sequelae to the death of a loved one (Calhoun & Tedeschi, 1990):

- the realization that there are people you can count on;
- feelings of increased independence;
- involvement in a greater range of activities than previously engaged in;
- better able to face future crises, more mature, greater ability to understand others;
- more openness when expressing one's own emotions.

Edmonds and Hooker (1992) also found that grief "may serve as an impetus for personal growth" (p. 307). In their study, college students reported a "positive change in life goals" and looked at these in terms of their defined meaning of life. Oltjenbruns (1991) discovered somewhat parallel responses when examining a younger group—93 individuals, ranging in age from 16 to 22. When asked "What positive outcomes, if any, do you feel were the result of your grief experience(s)?" a majority of the group responded that there was

- deeper appreciation of life;
- greater caring for loved ones;
- strengthened emotional bonds with others;
- heightened emotional strength.

Other common answers included increased empathy for others (47%) and better communication skills (28%).

Many of these positive outcomes relate to one's self-perception—for example, as more mature, stronger, more independent. Other outcomes are related to one's social support system—for example, as more caring for others, exhibiting enhanced communication skills, more open in sharing feelings (Calhoun & Tedeschi, 1990).

Even though there is a growing body of evidence that there are positive outcomes to the grief response, those who are giving support *should not* intervene with such comments as "look on the bright side" or "there will be many good things that ultimately come from this crisis." The positive outcomes reported in this section were reported by individuals a number of years after the death of a loved one; therefore, it is likely that personal and social growth that is triggered by a death can only be identified by those who are at some point in the resolution process and *not* in the acute phase of grief. Positive outcomes must be experienced by the person who is grieving. They cannot be defined by external sources who wish them upon the bereaved, for that may frustrate grieving individuals who interpret this response as failure to acknowledge the pain they are experiencing.

HELPING STRATEGIES

Bereaved individuals need an opportunity to express their feelings in a supportive environment. This section includes a brief discussion of strategies that concerned individuals can use to help others who are grieving.

Give Permission to Grieve

In our society, many messages are given that indicate that one should not grieve for more than a very short time. This is partially due to a misunderstanding regarding the duration of a normal grief process and also to the discomfort many people feel in the presence of individuals who are grieving. It can be very helpful, therefore, to communicate to the bereaved that it is normal, healthy, and permissible to grieve (Rando, 1984). Giving permission to grieve can be initiated by such statements as "I know it must be very hard for you right now" or "I miss her, too." Open-ended invitations, such as "If you ever need a shoulder to cry on" or "If you ever need to talk," indicate to grieving individuals that you recognize their right to grieve in addition to indicating your willingness to support them in the process.

Encourage Expression of Grief

As described earlier, the grief process can involve a variety of emotions. If the bereaved are encouraged to identify and express their emotions, they are more likely to become reconciled to their loss instead of inhibiting their grief or prematurely aborting it. The form of expression for grief-related emotions will vary from individual to individual. For example, some may verbalize their feelings to friends, others may write in a journal, and others may release those emotions through physical activity. It is not appropriate or helpful to encourage (or demand) that those who are grieving "Keep a stiff upper lip" or "Look on the bright side." These messages, whether given directly or indirectly, may cause the bereaved additional pain by making them think others do not recognize their loss and the legitimacy of their reactions.

Support Acceptance of All Aspects of the Loss

The bereaved must ultimately come to realize that a loss has occurred and also come to understand what that loss means to them. It can be helpful to the bereaved to talk about the deceased as he or she was during life as well as to discuss the death event itself. Loss is multifaceted. Because the deceased often played a number of roles in the survivor's life, a variety of losses must be recognized and reconciled. For example, a child whose mother or father has died must recognize and deal with such varied role losses as comforter, breadwinner, storyteller, cook, nurse, and teacher, among others. Although other people may contribute to fulfilling these roles, the death of a parent will involve the loss of that individual's contribution to need fulfillment. Each of these various facets can be discussed as the bereaved not only recognizes each loss, but also ultimately accepts each of them.

Listen to the Bereaved

Often people seem to feel that they must have the "right words to say" to the bereaved in order to be helpful and supportive. Experience has taught most counselors and thanatologists, however, that there is no magic formula that will diminish the pain precipitated by the loss. Instead of hoping for magic potions, the bereaved simply seem to want people to show that they care. This can be done by being in close proximity to the bereaved and by being available to listen. Many persons who are grieving indicate a need to share their stories with others. They need to tell and retell anecdotes about the deceased, details of the dying process and death event, and thoughts and feelings related to life without their loved one.

Share Information About the Grief Process

Many individuals who are unaware of the normal manifestations of grief can find some comfort in knowing that their pain is normal and that their experience of such thought-disordered symptoms as disorientation or preoccupation with the deceased does not mean they are "going crazy." Providing information about common facets of grief, then, can be therapeutic. Insights should be shared in such a way that the bereaved can understand that they are not abnormal for experiencing what they do and also that even though their grief may parallel that of others, it is unique to them. Understanding that an individual's grief experience is unique allows the bereaved to understand that there is no "right way to grieve." It also comforts them to know that they are not "bad" if they are not grieving in the same way as others. This knowledge can help alleviate a sense of guilt that may be precipitated by others telling them how they "should" grieve.

Bereaved individuals also need information about the duration of grief. They need to know that the pain does not disappear immediately after the funeral, but, in fact, typically lasts for an extended time. Without this knowledge, many believe that their ongoing grief is abnormal. This is particularly true in a society in which comments such as the following are quite common: "Oh, come on now! Your husband died a month ago! He would not want you to still be so sad!"

Assist in Practical and Concrete Ways

Well-meaning persons often tell the bereaved to let them know if "there is anything I can do for you." People, however, need to be more specific and concrete in their offers to help. Grief can be such a draining experience that the bereaved may have neither the energy nor the insight to determine what others might do for them. Specific offers of assistance such as "I plan to bring a meal over" or "I would like to take the children to the park next week" put much less responsibility on the bereaved and, as a result, may more easily alleviate their burden.

COMPLICATED GRIEF

Background on Complicated Grief

The focus of the chapter thus far has been on normal grief reactions. Although many manifestations associated with grief are regarded as painful and physically taxing, they are most often an indication that grief work is progressing.

Earlier in this chapter, we identified four tasks of mourning that many believe need to be accomplished as a part of one's grief work. If one does not accomplish these tasks, Rando (1992) would argue that the bereaved is attempting essentially to do one of two things:

- to deny, repress, or avoid aspects of the loss, its pain, and the full realization of its implications for the mourner or
- to hold onto, and avoid relinquishing, the lost loved one. . . . These attempts, or some variation thereof, are what cause the complications. . . . (p. 45)

Complicated grief, then, is defined as some compromise, distortion, or failure of one or more of the tasks of mourning, given the amount of time since the death (Rando, 1993).

It is difficult, however, to separate definitively an uncomplicated grief reaction from a complicated one. Rando (1993) stresses that "reactions to loss can only be interpreted within the context of those factors that circumscribe the *particular* loss for the *particular* mourner in the *particular* circumstances in which the loss took place" (p. 12). For example, as discussed earlier, there are particular issues surrounding certain deaths (e.g., suicide, AIDS, homicide, accidents) that may exacerbate certain normal grief reactions and also extend the time needed to accomplish one's grief work.

The demarcation is *not* typically determined by the presence of a constellation of manifestations entirely different from the normal grief response but rather by the intensity or duration of particular symptoms. Demi and Miles (1987) asked 22 experts in thanatology to identify those terms they felt best described grief that "fell outside of the normal range." Descriptors most commonly identified were "pathological, unresolved, self-destructive, dysfunctional, and prolonged" (p. 404). Behaviors, characteristics, or symptoms that were regarded as being outside of the parameters of normal grief were "violence directed toward others, inability to remember or talk about deceased, self-destructive behavior, and loss of contact with reality" (p. 405). Certain factors related to the mourner may increase the risk of unresolved grief; these include

- involvement in a "conflicted" relationship with the person who died (e.g., a child loving a parent who physically abused her);
- previous or current mental health problems;
- perceived lack of social support;
- unresolved losses from the past.

Rando (1992, 1993) argues that there are a number of additional factors converging in modern-day society that increase the likelihood that individuals will experience unresolved grief, as compared with generations past. She explains that there are a number of variables related to the death event that contribute to a somewhat higher incidence of abnormal grief (it is crucial to understand, however, that *none* of these factors associated with the death itself causes abnormal grief reactions to occur). These factors include

- a sudden/unanticipated death, particularly when it is violent or random;
- the cause of death is an extremely lengthy illness;
- the loss of a child;
- the perception of preventability.

All four of these are more prevalent in the United States today, due to such things as gang violence, random fatal shootings, the AIDS epidemic, the increase of suicides, and medical advances that prolong many chronic illnesses.

Examples of Complicated Grief

After the death of a loved one, some individuals may not experience any of the common symptoms of bereavement to any significant degree. Some of these individuals may have truly come to terms with the loss and simply not have experienced any intense grief reaction after the death. Others, however, may be engaged in either an inhibited grief reaction or a delayed grief reaction. Individuals who have **inhibited** their **grief** show a prolonged absence of acknowledged grieving (Bowlby, 1980). These people often pride themselves on their self-control and refuse to allow themselves to feel the emotional pain of the loss. For example, although the normal symptoms do not develop, the grief manifests itself through a variety of physical symptoms such as headaches and chronic indigestion.

Delayed grief, in contrast to inhibited grief, finds direct expression but occurs some time after the death. During the time when people normally grieve and deal with their pain, those with delayed grief have no thoughts or feelings that would indicate a loss has occurred. Subsequently, however, a different loss may trigger a magnified grief reaction that is really tied to an earlier one. For example, a woman who never mourned her mother's death 5 years earlier became emotionally and physically immobilized when her pet cat of 3 months was run over and killed. She admitted that she had loved her parent so much that, at the time of her death, she had simply refused to think about her mother's being gone and would not allow her sorrow to consume her. The sudden death of her cat, however, brought these thoughts and feelings to the surface.

Bowlby (1980) described another variation of the normal grief response, **chronic mourning,** in which the manifestations of grief are unusually intense and last well beyond what is regarded as the normal grief period, which is typically 1 to 3 years (but may often be longer, depending on the circumstances, such as the death of a young child). The bereaved continue in such an intense stage of grief that they cannot plan for the future or reorganize their lives. Aiken (1985) has indicated that one symptom of chronic grief is **mummification** of the deceased. This is a phenomenon whereby the bereaved attempts to leave things just as they were when the deceased was alive. In some cultures, **memorialization** may be regarded as a symptom of complicated grief, however, this is not the case in all. Anglos would usually find the putting of fresh flowers by a deceased child's sports trophies each day for years as a likely sign of not coming to resolution of one's grief. However, other cultural groups such as the Japanese practice ancestor worship each day at an altar within the home itself (Klass, 1996). In Japan, this is a normal and healthy practice.

Survivors who recall only positive characteristics of the deceased are participating in a process called **idealization.** Carried to its extreme, it is destructive. Idealization of the deceased may cause hardship for other people if the survivor continually compares them with the person who has died and finds them sorely lacking. Survivors who continue to idealize the deceased are less likely to invest in other relationships, thinking "perfection" can be attained only once.

Identification with the deceased occurs when the survivor manifests symptoms, problems, or behavioral characteristics that are the same as those of the deceased prior to death. Survivors who have not successfully completed the grieving process may keep "the lost one 'alive' by acquiring the symptoms that the deceased person manifested prior to death or by developing a problem that was a significant part of the character of the deceased person" (Stephenson, 1985, p. 154).

Some idealization of or identification with the deceased may be a part of a normal grief response. Such reactions are only categorized as complicated when they consistently prohibit the survivor's resolution of grief over time. A parent who cannot love a surviving child because the deceased sibling was "perfect" is reacting abnormally. A surviving son who cannot pursue his own greatly preferred vocational choice because he feels he must become an architect like his deceased father is also experiencing an unhealthy grief response.

Funerals provide an opportunity for family and friends to share their grief with one another.

FUNERALS AND OTHER RITUALS

Most societies have rituals that serve as a public acknowledgment that a death has occurred and provide an opportunity for mourning. A **ritual** is a specific behavior or activity that gives symbolic expression to certain feelings or thoughts. They can be repeated or one-time acts. The acknowledgment of death on a formal level can promote acceptance on a more personal level and begin to facilitate the grief process. Rituals often provide powerful therapeutic experiences for both individuals and families and symbolize transition, healing, and continuity. For a ritual to have optimal value, it must have meaning for its participants.

Therapists often prescribe involvement in rituals to aid people in resolving their grief; they need to fit the preferences of the bereaved and should be designed to help people

- accept the reality of the loss;
- express feelings related to the loss; and
- accomplish the tasks of grief work.

As one considers a wide variety of rituals, it is important to remember that certain symbols may involve very different meanings and levels of importance to various cultural groups. The symbolism in various activities is often tied to one's heritage. For example, the type of service, particular dress, and selection of certain music to be played are often reflective of one's cultural roots (Bosley & Cook, 1993). To illustrate, white clothing for many Eastern cultures indicates that a person is in mourning, whereas in many Western cultures black clothing is worn.

Prefuneral Rituals

Although we often regard the funeral or memorial service as the primary death-related ritual, a number of activities take place prior to the funeral that serve as important leave-taking behaviors. These include submitting public notices of the death, viewing the body, selecting a casket and grave marker, and having a prefuneral prayer service (Bolton & Camp, 1987). Each of these activities helps the family to acknowledge personally that the death has occurred. The public notice of the death and prefuneral prayer service provide an opportunity to reach out for support.

Funerals and Memorial Services

Both funerals and memorial services fulfill a number of important functions for the individual, the family, and the larger society (Fulton, 1987; Imber-Black, 1991). Specifically, they

- give recognition that a life has been lived;
- confirm the dignity and worth of human beings;
- provide public recognition that the death has occurred;
- allow the bereaved publicly to express and share the loss;
- facilitate the expression of grief consistent with cultural values;
- provide an immediate supportive network for the bereaved;
- serve as a rite of passage from one status to another for both the deceased and the bereaved; and
- provide an opportunity to reestablish contact with distant relatives and a larger society and promote group cohesion.

Although funerals do serve many important functions, controversy exists surrounding this industry. Many people question the high cost of funeral services in American society and emphasize the vulnerability of family members as they make "consumer" decisions during such an emotionally disruptive time. Some advocate making these decisions in advance of a death to reduce stress during the stage of acute grief.

Individuals and families often participate in private rituals that have special significance (e.g., having a favorite meal in honor of the deceased and leaving an empty place at the head of the table on that particular occasion). In bereavement situations, sometimes the most meaningful rituals are silent, spontaneous, symbolic statements that represent unique feelings related to the deceased. Sealed

Persons from many Latino backgrounds participate in rituals on the Day of the Dead.

letters tucked underneath the casket pillow, a farewell salute, or a single rose placed on the casket are examples (Conley, 1987). A trend has emerged for funerals and memorial services to be more individualized and fit the needs of the bereaved.

Postfuneral Rituals

Acknowledging gifts and cards, sorting and/or disposing of the deceased's personal effects, visiting the grave site, writing letters to inform others of the death, and removing a wedding ring are all types of postfuneral rituals. Exploratory work by Bolton and Camp (1987) suggests that these symbolic acts can facilitate grief work.

Some cultural groups engage in formal rituals on the anniversary of the death (e.g., Jews) and others set aside a special day of the year to gather as a family to pay respects to those who have died. For example, many persons of Mexican heritage participate in various customs on two days each year. November 1st is All Saints' Day, when children who have died are honored. Small altars will be assembled to hold candles, flowers, and food. Toys will be placed nearby for the enjoyment of both the dead and the living children; it is believed that children become more comfortable with death through this play (Pomar, 1987). November 2nd is All Souls' Day, when families pay respect to deceased adults who are believed to make their appearance near dawn. Altars in the home will be adorned with flowers, pictures of the dead, and skeletons made from a sugar paste. Families make an offering to those who have died (typically made of fruit and flowers), light candles around the loved one's grave, and, for a time, think quietly about the one who has died. Later, families often share a picnic among the headstones and interact with friends and neighbors. The value of this type of annual postfuneral ritual includes the normalizing of the death experience and the reassurance that the dead shall not be forgotten but rather will live on in memory.

SUMMARY

Grief is a natural reaction to the experience of loss. This chapter focused specifically on grief reactions related to the death of a loved one. Although each individual's grief is unique, there are many common somatic, behavioral, and intrapsychic manifestations. The intensity and duration of a person's grief reaction is affected by a variety of factors, including variables related to the bereaved individual, to the deceased individual, and to the death event itself. Additional factors include the availability of social support, other recent losses, the ambiguity of the loss, and whether the loss is recognized as significant by others. Although grief involves emotional pain, bereavement also provides an opportunity for individuals to develop in positive ways and offers a new and expanded perspective on the meaning of life.

A number of strategies can effectively be used to help those who are grieving deal with their loss. In some situations, however, survivors do not cope with their loss in ways regarded as normal and healthy but rather exhibit a complicated response. Professional intervention is recommended in these circumstances.

Rituals of many types help facilitate the grief process; they may be either formal or spontaneous acts. Many are prescribed by the bereaved's religious beliefs or cultural heritage.

Personal Account

Jayne Blankenship's husband, Harvey, died of leukemia at the age of 30. They had been together 9½ years. She shares with us her personal experience of grief—her thoughts, her feelings, her reactions. Ms. Blankenship's diary traces her life throughout the seasons of the 3 years after her husband's death. The segment of the book included here reflects grief at 3 months after Harvey's death.

In the Center of the Night: Journey Through Bereavement
Jayne Blankenship

I have little appetite anymore, but find myself eating compulsively, or rather drinking, especially before I leave the house. I'm not actually hungry, but I'm afraid I will be, afraid I won't be able to stand that little extra discomfort for even an hour if I am caught away from food. Repeatedly I open the refrigerator but then can't find anything appetizing. The food is there, but it never appeals. I find myself drinking milk, again and again, to fill the emptiness.

I tried to eat some raisin bran just now before I came upstairs, but it hurts to chew. I have a canker sore under my tongue, which makes me think of the enormous mouth ulcers Harvey had last fall from the drug Cytosar (he called it "the Czar")—or was it Vincristine ("the Count")—and how he couldn't talk. How did he eat? Why can't I remember? Why didn't they feed him intravenously? One day the sores fell off, a couple of hours apart. They were the size of quarters—gray and ugly. That was the day he started peeing blood. Emptying the urinal, I found it and told the nurse but not him. The next day he kicked the thing over, full, and blood spread all over the room and he was frightened and yelled at me for not telling him, and he was right. I was ashamed. But he was carrying so much anxiety that week, having learned he'd entered Blast Crisis, I just couldn't. He recovered though, after Fogle said no one expected he'd ever leave the hospital again. They were all waiting for cerebral hemorrhage because of the dropped platelets. The nurses shook their heads as we left—broad, broad smiles. It didn't surprise me. Our love was there, and his beautiful determination.

Those miraculous recoveries built false hopes, prevented me from recognizing the genuine onset of his dying. Oh, God, if only I could have seen it coming.

SOURCE: From *In the center of the night: Journey through bereavement* (New York: G. P. Putnam's Sons, 1984), pp. 53–60. Reprinted by permission of Canadida Donadio & Associates.

If only I had spent that last night with him. I had stayed over before, in fear, but when it really counted, I was blind. I failed him.

———————————————————

I am trying to get back into the world again, but it is very hard. Even when I wear sunglasses and pull my hair over my cheeks so less of me can be seen, I still feel dangerously exposed. I went back to chorus rehearsals for the first time tonight, but found I couldn't sing. I spent the whole evening fighting back tears, fumbling in my purse for Kleenex. I am grateful to these people—the purity of their voices at the Memorial Service stunned. The loud straight tone, coming suddenly from the balcony behind us, carved away the muscle of our resistance, laying bare the clean white bone of grief. But it is hard to be in public, even with them.

———————————————————

I am deeply troubled that I still cannot envision Harvey's face. Have I perhaps put our life together into a soft cocoon because it is too intense to deal with now? Or have I lost it utterly—will it just get worse? Some days there are tiny windows into it, for a second or two. But in general I have lost my memory. I can't even recall where Jordan and I slept in Kansas City when we went for his burial. It must have been at Harriet's, not Sharlene's, but there's no bed there for Jordan. Did they borrow a crib? I just can't remember. It's blocked. I do remember waking in the night, panicky, short of breath, stagefright waves in my stomach continuous for more than an hour. The light came from the right of the foot of the bed. Couch in Sharlene's den? I remember too, my compulsion to take a bath while the Havra Kadisha people were preparing his body for burial. I wanted to be bathing him by myself, holding him, caring for him. An urgency to soothe, to share, to absorb the pain of it. Or was it guilt? Was it because something in my head said, "If he had only felt more loved, he would have wanted to live, could have beaten the cancer"? Was I washing away my failure to keep him alive? Maybe it was just a means of postponing the finality of his burial. I kept everyone waiting, black limousine running, while I washed.

More and more I notice myself doing things that he would have done even when they are things I'd never do myself. Tennis (if only he could see me learning to play tennis), buying matzoh and gefilte fish, saying Kaddish (the Judaism was his, not mine. Why can't I shake this?), renewing his magazine subscriptions, using his shaving cream, wearing his pajamas and robe at night and his jeans in the day, saying things twice the way he did. Why am I doing this? Is it that I love him so much I want to *be* him? God! Maybe that's why I can't see his face. Because I am turning into him! I am really scared.

It startles me to look at pages I have written, even just grocery lists. I am constantly misspelling words. Freudian slips, substitutions, repeated syllables, phonic spellings everywhere. They shock me, show I'm more undone than even I would judge. And the others—my friends—they infuriate me. Everyone seems to find me perfectly normal and capable. They don't even notice when I forget, mid-sentence, what it was I meant to say.

My inner life is a shambles. Thinking muddled. Loss of structure, of will. Entire psyche rotates, still, around Harvey—only his human force is not here to balance mine. Incessant depletion—strength sucked into a black hole. Directionless floundering. My work is disrupted too—a smaller, but genuine problem. The women's exhibit I put together, focus of eight months' concentration, ended for me with the opening the week before he died, momentum lost once it was framed and hung. The show has moved on now and is creating a stir in the Ætna Building in Hartford, the first place it has visited that is not accustomed to fine-art photography. Half the audience there is outraged by simple nudity (why do they seize on those few images?), and the others are threatened because the same figures aren't centerfold material. Hard to believe. Only a few have responded to the simple humanity in the photographs—women's portrayals of birth, work, friends, aging. I should feel good that it has generated corporate controversy—definitely a plus for the movement—but I am too fragile to feel anything but hurt that they don't admire it as they did in New London or Kingston. I am too tired to defend my efforts, and not really interested anymore.

Grant money for morning child care ended when the show opened, too. The financial aspect is meaningless because Jordan needs me now, not a sitter, but full-time mothering is devastating for me. I cannot complete a single thought. Constant interruptions. Wait. Endure. I hate this feeling. No purpose. Even the disease gave a framework—afternoons and evenings at the hospital, doctors' office visits, trips for immunotherapy, secrecy, driving Harvey to work, drugs, transfusions, seizures, Philip, friendships with nurses, and a constant girding for the unspeakable distant event. Now all I do is "babysit," and I'm incapable even of doing that well. I couldn't be teaching this semester if I had to. I cannot think or organize or care. My arms and legs are leaden. Every simple gesture saps me—getting out of bed, pouring milk on cereal, folding a towel, listening to Jordan, turning the steering wheel, writing a check. Nothing can be accomplished automatically anymore. How many years will this last? Forever? I have no enthusiasm for photographs—my own or others'—for teaching, for anything I know.

I wonder if it would be any different to go through this in a community where I had lived for a long time, where my own genuine deep friends—Sonia, Claire—were close by, and family, and family friends, and former teachers and ministers. Could it make a difference? Could anything soothe a hurt like this?

I am furious! Someone stole our red and purple geometric towels from the laundromat. I left them tossing in a dryer separate from the whites while I went to the hardware store and the market. Then I came home and unloaded the groceries. When I went back to the laundromat, the dryer door was standing open—just one purple washcloth left inside.

I could hardly restrain myself until I got home. I lugged the baskets in together, the full one nested inside the empty, half threw them into the office—clean clothes spilling out onto the rug—and slammed the door behind me. I leaned against it, clenching my teeth and fists and starting to growl. Then I lunged forward onto the stairs up to the kitchen and pounded them as hard and fast as I could with both fists. I kicked out backward, too, like a horse, against the door, not caring if I broke it down.

Those towels were special, damn it! We bought them for our crazy red bathroom in New York, for our first apartment. We always had red and purple anemones in there to match, under the silly framed picture of Mayor Lindsay. Damn! Damn! Damn! Haven't we been victimized enough? My husband died, World! Doesn't that earn us some kind of exemption?

Oh well, it's over now. I bruised the bone in my heel. Can't put any pressure on it. The limp makes me laugh. Sort of.

Today is the 18th of May—the three-month anniversary of Harvey's death. I am obsessed with the fact that I used the last of his shaving cream today. Nine and a half years of red-and-white-striped Barbasol cans—over. That can seemed to keep him closer in time—like the shiva candle, which I kept burning for weeks. As long as it held foam, as long as the candle burned, it couldn't have been very long since he was here. Why did it have to run out on the 18th? The 18th of March and April were hard too. Will this day of the month ever resume a normal face?

A special dream last night, like the early ones.

I am having dinner with friends but interrupt the meal because there's a documentary on TV about how my class at the Ecole Française made films. I am wild with hope to see Harvey, because he was in the last one. The color TV seems to enchant me. I enter into the program physically, like going through the looking glass. Harvey and I find each other in a gleaming snow-covered landscape, a limitless Sahara of snow. No cold, no coats, no trees or features on the drifts. Only the yellow clarity of love. A warm, clinging, wordless embrace—on and on—without a future, without a past. The feel of his neck and back and face and hair in my hands brings a peace beyond anything I have known.

And then I woke up. I was lying on my stomach. The deception slipped away, and the nausea of truth flattened me onto the sheet. To wake up was to be told he had died all over again.

I took a piece of beef out of the refrigerator tonight and set it on the counter. Jordan looked at it and asked, "Is Daddy's body like that now?"

Harvey's life insurance money came today. I stood in the hall with the unopened envelope in my hand. The world would have me be grateful. Do they call a piece of paper a fair trade? A piece of paper for Harvey's warm flesh and smile and compassion and intelligence? Do they call this compensation for his fear and suffering? For suffocating alone at night, drowning in the fluid of his own lungs? For not getting to watch his son grow up? For losing every star and snowflake, leaf and friend on this planet? I tore the end off the envelope and pulled out the check: $20,000. I felt like spitting on it. It could have been twenty million and I would have felt the same. It's as if they consider our not having to worry now about finances some sort of consolation.

I went back into our room, put the check on my dresser, and knelt down to finish sorting through the third drawer of Harvey's bureau—I've been doing one drawer each month. The Social Security doesn't make me angry like this, except that no one let us know about it before he died. He must have worried about what would happen to Jordan and me. The doctors had to have known, the lawyer. Why didn't anyone tell us? I suppose they thought we knew already. The monthly payments are adequate really, not much less than all three of us used to live on after doctor bills. But the insurance money makes me sick.

I couldn't make any more decisions, so I took the one box of things I thought might mean something to Jordan when he is 10 or 12—his father's crepe-soled shoes and favorite tie, his denim jacket, trench coat, Norwegian sweater, wallet—down to the basement and carried the carton of things for the chorus thrift shop out and put them in the back of the car, leaving the rest for another day. Then I pulled a sweater over Jordan's head, put him in his car seat and drove to Westerly and dropped them off.

Now I am home again. The need to cry is acute. Oh, the tears come and my face contorts, but I can't let go or sob. And I need to, I crave the release. It started out all right at the very first, but Jordan got so upset, repeatedly, when he saw me weeping that I developed a kind of inhibition. One day he even threw his blanket over my head. The orgasmic dreams I experienced the first two months are apparently gone now, too. I am a taut coil of grief-tension.

This morning it was raining again, and the grief was pressing out on my skull so hard I was afraid the bone might crack. A sound too violent for others to withstand was going to bellow up out of me. Desperate for privacy, I tried to get a sitter. I called six or eight people, straining to be casual, "I know it sounds silly, but I need to take a walk." No one was free. I began to get frantic. It was hard to get my breath. It felt like I was trapped under water, pinned against something by a crushing current. No, not right—the pressure was *in* me, not outside. Something inside me that used to go to Harvey now had nowhere to go. It built and built and I was afraid that I would fly apart.

Finally I drove Jordan over to some friends—people I've known only a few months—and begged them to watch him for a while. I must have looked deranged. They seemed surprised but said, "Of course, go ahead. Why don't you go to Napatree?" I drove through Westerly too fast, propelled by the yearning to let out of me the ugly sound I felt still building. But when I parked my car and ran, stumbling, up over the dunes to where I couldn't be seen, it wouldn't come. The gray waves were roaring in, ready to cover anything, but nothing came. I couldn't believe it. I just stood there feeling blank.

Disappointed, I headed slowly out toward the point. From time to time, I bent and picked up a translucent pebble. After a while, as I walked, I decided I should keep no more than three—a kind of exercise. So I kept searching and discarding, searching and discarding, for as long as it took to walk out to the point and halfway back, probably an hour—until I had the three most beautiful stones on that long stretch of beach. Then I walked up to where the waves end and stood there. The wind was not as cold as I had thought. I picked one of the stones out of my palm and forced myself to throw it far out into the ocean. "See?" I yelled at the wind, "I can do it. I can play your filthy game." And then I took the second one, "Here! Take it! I can stand it!" and threw it too, defiantly.

But then there was just one left. It was exquisitely hard to let go of that last one. I paced back and forth for a while, clutching for alternatives. Then I went back to the spot in the sand where I had started and simply stood there. The sky was gray, the sea was gray, the beach was gray. I pulled my arm up and did it. As my body came around on the follow-through, doubled over with loss, there appeared at my feet, instantaneously, three extraordinary yellow starfish.

Somewhere deep inside the pain, something shifted. Full of awe, I picked them up—fragile, perfect—and stood with my back to the ocean, absorbing what had happened. With them in front of me, in my hands, I slowly started the long walk back. On the way, I stopped and sat in the damp sand by some big old dock posts. I set the starfish down beside me and leaned sideways against the biggest post and felt the tear-restrainer loosen a little. The wood was cold and smooth against my cheek. It was sunk deep into the earth. It used to hold a pier. I hugged that old post, then, with both my arms, I hugged it and it held me up, and the real crying finally came.

QUESTIONS AND ACTIVITIES

1. Bring to mind the death of a loved one. What was your immediate reaction to the news of his or her death? What were your later thoughts, feelings, actions? How were these similar to or different from those experienced by Ms. Blankenship after her husband's death?

2. The death depicted in this chapter's personal account was the result of natural causes. Have you ever personally experienced the death of a loved one due to a suicide? Murder? Accident? Did your reactions vary with the type of death?

3. Write a condolence letter to a bereaved friend. Use the guidelines set forth by L. Zunin and H. Zunin in their book *The Art of Condolence*, which was recommended as one of the suggested readings for this chapter. Guidelines outlined in that book include acknowledging the loss; expressing your sympathy; noting special qualities of the deceased; recounting a memory about the deceased; recognizing the impact of the loss on the bereaved; offering assistance; and closing with a thoughtful word or phrase.

4. How would you have comforted Ms. Blankenship during the months after her husband's death? Would you have reacted to her differently if the death had been unexpected or if it had been regarded as preventable?

5. Ms. Blankenship shared that her grief was magnified 3 months after her husband's death when she realized that she had just used the last of his shaving cream. Was there some physical object that was particularly difficult for you to give up after a loved one's death? Why was it difficult for you? Was there a particular day when your grief once again intensified? Do you know what made that day more difficult? Did others in your support network understand the significance of that particular day? If so, how did they show their concern for you?

GLOSSARY

Acute grief: grief occurring during the period when somatic, intrapsychic, and behavioral reactions are most intense.

Anniversary reaction: exacerbation of grief precipitated by a special day related to the deceased (such as a birthday).

Anticipatory grief: grief experienced prior to the death of a loved one.

Bereavement: state of being that results from a significant loss.

Bereavement overload: extreme degree of grief triggered by multiple losses in a relatively short time.

Cathexis: investment of psychic energy in an object.

Chronic mourning: grief that is unusually intense and extremely long-lasting (beyond 1 to 3 years).

Complicated grief: a compromise, distortion, or failure of one or more tasks of grief work, given the amount of time since the death.

Disenfranchised grief: situations in which the larger society does not socially sanction and/or recognize certain bereaved persons' right, role, or capacity to grieve.

Delayed grief: relatively extreme grief reaction long after the original loss that person is actually mourning.

Grief: the outcome of being bereaved; a variety of reactions that constitute the grief response.

Grief work: process by which individuals resolve their grief.

Hypercathexis: investment of an extreme amount of psychic energy in an object.

Idealization: distortion of reality regarding deceased; only the positive characteristics are remembered.

Identification: manifestation by a survivor of symptoms, problems, or behaviors similar to those of the deceased.

Inhibited grief: prolonged absence of acknowledged grieving; however, physical symptoms are often manifest.

Intrapsychic: pertaining to the emotions and mind.

Libido: energy of love and pleasure.

Loss orientation: focus is on concentrating on, dealing with, and processing some aspect of the loss experience.

Memorialization: phenomenon where survivor pays homage to the deceased through a particular frequent ritual.

Mourning: social prescription for way in which we are expected to display our grief.

Mummification: phenomenon whereby the bereaved attempts to leave things just as they were when deceased was alive.

Object loss: loss of a loved one.

Obsessional review: extreme preoccupation with the deceased.

Preventability: belief that factors contributing to the death might have been avoided.

Restoration orientation: adjustment to numerous changes triggered by the loss.

Ritual: a specific behavior or activity that gives symbolic expression to certain feelings or thoughts.

Role loss: loss of one's position or status in society.

Somatic: related to the body.

Thanatologists: professionals who specialize in the study of death, dying, and grief.

SUGGESTED READINGS

Cook, A. S., & Dworkin, D. (1992). *Helping the bereaved: Therapeutic interventions for children, adolescents, and adults.* New York: Basic Books.

These authors present specific strategies for therapeutic interventions, tailored to various life stages; ideas for both individual and group intervention are presented. The book is grounded in an understanding of individual differences, together with cultural considerations.

Klass, D., Silverman, P., & Nickman, S. (Eds.). (1996). *Continuing bonds: New understandings of grief.* Washington, DC: Taylor and Francis.

The chapters within this book include broad-based discussions of the resolution of grief within the context of continuing bonds. Numerous types of losses are examined.

Rando, T. A. (1993). *Treatment of complicated mourning.* Champaign, IL: Research Press.

This book provides information about various theoretical perspectives for better understanding complicated loss. Assessment and treatment issues are also discussed; specific clinical problems are examined.

Worden, J. W. (1991). *Grief counseling and grief therapy: A handbook for the mental health practitioner* (2nd ed.). New York: Springer.

This volume describes the role of the mental health professional in helping clients cope with normal and abnormal grief reactions. It includes guidelines for conducting workshops and several sample vignettes for use in role playing.

Zunin, L. M., & Zunin, H. S. (1991). *The art of condolence.* New York: HarperCollins.

The authors provide helpful and specific guidelines as to what to write, say, and do when providing support to others after they have experienced the death of a loved one.

RESOURCES

Mothers Against Drunk Driving (MADD)
511 East John Carpenter Freeway, Suite 700
Irving, TX 75062
(214) 744-6233 or 1-800-438-MADD

National Funeral Directors Association
11121 West Oklahoma Avenue
P.O. Box 27641
Milwaukee, WI 53227
(414) 541-2500

Parents of Murdered Children
100 E. 8th Street, Suite B41
Cincinnati, OH 45202
(513) 721-5683

REFERENCES

Abramson, L. Y., Seligman, M. E., & Teasdale, J. D. (1978). Learned-helplessness in humans: Critique and reformulation. *Journal of Abnormal Psychology, 87,* 49–74.

Aiken, L. R. (1985). *Dying, death, and bereavement.* Rockleigh, NJ: Allyn & Bacon.

Barnes, M. J. (1978). The reactions of children and adolescents to the death of a parent or sibling. In O. J. Sahler (Ed.), *The child and death* (pp. 185–201). St. Louis: Mosby.

Barrett, R. K. (1993). Psychocultural influences on African-American attitudes towards death, dying, and funeral rites. In J. D. Morgan (Ed.), *Personal care in an impersonal world: A multidimensional look at bereavement* (pp. 213–230). Amityville, NY: Baywood.

Benoliel, J. Q. (1985). Loss and adaptation: Circumstances, contingencies, and consequences. *Death Studies, 9,* 217–233.

Bolton, C., & Camp, D. (1987). Funeral rituals and the facilitation of grief work. *Omega, 17*(4), 343–352.

Bolton, I. (1986). Death of a child by suicide. In T. Rando (Ed.), *Parental loss of a child* (pp. 201–212). Champaign, IL: Research Press.

Bosley, G. M., & Cook, A. S. (1993). Therapeutic aspects of funeral ritual: A thematic analysis. *Journal of Family Psychotherapy, 4*(4), 69–83.

Boss, P. (1990). *Family stress management.* Beverly Hills, CA: Sage.

Bowlby, J. (1980). *Attachment and loss (Vol. 3): Loss, sadness, and depression.* New York: Basic Books.

Brasted, W. S., & Callahan, E. J. (1984). Review article: A behavioral analysis of the grief process. *Behavioral Therapy, 15*(5), 529–543.

Brokenleg, M., & Middleton, D. (1993). Native Americans: Adapting, yet retaining. In D. P. Irish, K. F. Lundquist, & V. J. Nelsen (Eds.), *Ethnic variations in dying, death, and grief: Diversity in universality* (pp. 101–113). Washington, DC: Taylor and Francis.

Bugen, L. A. (1979). *Death and dying: Theory/research/practice.* Dubuque, IA: William C. Brown.

Calhoun, L. G., Abernathy, C. B., & Selby, J. W. (1986). The rules of bereavement: Are suicidal deaths different? *Journal of Community Psychology, 14*(2), 213–218.

Calhoun, L. G., Selby, J. W., & Abernathy, C. B. (1984). Suicidal death: Social reactions of bereaved survivors. *The Journal of Psychology, 116*(2), 255–261.

Calhoun, L. G., & Tedeschi, R. G. (1990). Positive aspects of critical life problems: Recollections of grief. *Omega, 20*(4), 265–272.

Chenell, S. L., & Murphy, S. A. (1992). Beliefs of preventability of death among the disaster bereaved. *Western Journal of Nursing Research, 14*(5), 576–594.

Chesser, B. J. (1981). Coping with accidentally killing another person: A case study approach. *Family Relations, 30*(3), 463–473.

Chester, V. A., Jerardi, N. C., & Weger, J. M. (1980). Sudden death/lingering death. In B. A. Orcutt, E. R. Prichard, J. Collard, E. F. Cooper, A. H. Kutscher, & I. B. Seeland (Eds.), *Social work and thanatology.* New York: Arno Press.

Conley, B. H. (1987). Funeral directors as first responders. In E. J. Dunne, J. L. McIntosh, & K. Dunne-Maxim (Eds.), *Suicide and its aftermath: Understanding and counseling the survivors* (pp. 171-181). New York: Norton.

Demi, A. S., & Miles, M. S. (1987). Parameters of normal grief: A Delphi study. *Death Studies, 11*(6), 397-412.

Doka, K. J. (1987). Silent sorrow: Grief and the loss of significant others. *Death Studies, 11*(6), 455-469.

Doka, K. J. (Ed.). (1989). *Disenfranchised grief: Recognizing hidden sorrow.* Lexington, MA: Lexington Books.

Doyle, P. (1980). *Grief counseling and sudden death: A manual and guide.* Springfield, IL: Charles C. Thomas.

Dunne, R. G., & Morrish-Vidners, D. (1987). The psychological and social experience of suicide survivors. *Omega, 18*(3), 175-215.

Edmonds, S., & Hooker, K. (1992). Perceived changes in life meaning following bereavement. *Omega, 25*(4), 307-318.

Eisenbruch, M. (1984a). Cross-cultural aspects of bereavement. I: A conceptual framework for comparative analysis. *Culture, Medicine, and Psychiatry, 3*(3), 283-309.

Eisenbruch, M. (1984b). Cross-cultural aspects of bereavement. II: Ethnic and cultural variations in the development of bereavement practices. *Culture, Medicine, and Psychiatry, 8*(4), 315-347.

Foeckler, M. M., Garrard, F. H., Williams, C. C., Thomas, A. M., & Jones, T. J. (1978). Vehicle drivers and fatal accidents. *Suicide and Life-Threatening Behavior, 8*(3), 174-182.

Freud, S. (1917). Mourning and melancholia. In J. Strachey (Ed.), *The standard edition of the complete psychological works of Sigmund Freud* (Vol. 14, pp. 237-260). London: Hogarth Press, 1957.

Fulton, R. (1987). Death, grief and the funeral. In M. A. Morgan (Ed.), *Bereavement: Helping the survivors* (pp. 123-126). London, Ontario: King's College.

Gijana, E. W. M., Louw, J., & Manganyi, N. C. (1989). Thoughts about death and dying in an African sample. *Omega, 20*(3), 245-258.

Ginn, P. D., Range, L. M., & Hailey, B. J. (1988). Community attitudes toward childhood suicide and attempted suicide. *Journal of Community Psychology, 16*(2), 144-151.

Habenstein, R. W., & Lamers, W. M. (1960). *Funeral customs the world over.* Milwaukee: Bulfin Printers.

Halporn, R. (1993). Asian-Americans in loss and grief. *MADDvocate, 6*(2), 16-17.

Hauser, M. J. (1987). In E. J. Dunne, J. L. McIntosh, & K. Dunne-Maxim (Eds.), *Suicide and its aftermath: Understanding and counseling the survivors* (pp. 57-70). New York: Norton.

Imber-Black, E. (1991). Rituals and the healing process. In F. Walsh & M. McGoldrick (Eds.), *Living beyond loss: Death in the family* (pp. 207-223). New York: Norton.

Irish, D. P. (1993a). Introduction—Multiculturalism and the majority population. In D. P. Irish, K. F. Lundquist, & V. J. Nelsen (Eds.), *Ethnic variations in dying, death, and grief: Diversity in universality* (pp. 1-10). Washington, DC: Taylor and Francis.

Irish, D. P. (1993b). Reflections by professional practitioners. In D. P. Irish, K. F. Lundquist, & V. J. Nelsen (Eds.), *Ethnic variations in dying, death, and grief: Diversity in universality* (pp. 163-179). Washington, DC: Taylor and Francis.

Irwin, M., & Pike, J. (1993). Bereavement, depressive symptoms, and immune functions. In M. S. Stroebe, W. Stroebe, & R. O. Hannson (Eds.), *Handbook of bereavement: Theory, research, and intervention* (pp. 160-171). Cambridge: Cambridge University Press.

Jacobs, S. C., Kosten, T. R., Kasl, S. V., Ostfield, A. M., Berkman, L., & Charpentier, P. (1987). Attachment theory and multiple dimensions of grief. *Omega, 18*(1), 41-52.

Jaffrey, M. (1995). In J. O. Reilly & L. Habegger (Eds.), *Traveler's tales: India.* San Francisco: Travelers Tales Inc.

Kalish, R. A., & Reynolds, D. K. (1976). *Death and ethnicity: A psychocultural study.* Los Angeles: The Ethel Percy Andrus Gerontology Center.

Kamerman, J. (1993). Latent functions of enfranchising the disenfranchised griever. *Death Studies, 17,* 281-287.

Kastenbaum, R. (1969). Death and bereavement in later life. In A. H. Kutscher (Ed.), *Death and bereavement* (pp. 28-54). Springfield, IL: Charles C. Thomas.

Keyserlingk, E. W. (1993). The right to die and the need to grieve. In J. Morgan (Ed.), *Personal care in an impersonal world: A multidimensional look at bereavement* (pp. 31-38). Amityville, NY: Baywood.

Kim, K., & Jacobs, S. (1993). Neuroendocrine changes following bereavement. In M. S. Stroebe, W. Stroebe, & R. O. Hannson (Eds.), *Handbook of bereavement: Theory, research, and intervention* (pp. 143-159). Cambridge: Cambridge University Press.

Klass, D. (1996). Grief in an Eastern culture: Japanese ancestor worship. In D. Klass, P. Silverman, & S. Nickman (Eds.), *Continuing bonds: New understandings of grief* (pp. 59-70). Washington, DC: Taylor and Francis.

Klein, S. J., & Fletcher, W. (1986). Gay grief: An examination of its uniqueness brought to light by the AIDS crisis. *Journal of Psychological Oncology, 4,* 15-25.

Kleinman, A., Kaplan, B., & Weiss, R. (1984). Sociocultural influences. In M. Osterweis, F. Solomon, & M. Green (Eds.), *Bereavement: Reactions, consequences, and care* (pp. 199-212). Washington, DC: National Academy Press.

Krause, N. (1986). Stress and coping: Reconceptualizing the role of locus of control beliefs. *Journal of Gerontology, 41*(5), 617-623.

Kübler-Ross, E. (1969). *On death and dying.* New York: Macmillan.

Lapidus, I. M. (1996). The meaning of death in Islam. In H. M. Spiro, M. G. M. Curnen, & L. P. Wandel (Eds.), *Facing death* (pp. 148-159). New Haven, CT: Yale University Press.

Lieber, M. D. (1991). Cutting your losses: Death and grieving in a Polynesian community. In D. R. Counts & D. A. Counts (Eds.), *Coping with the final tragedy: Cultural variations in dying and grieving* (pp. 169-189). Amityville, NY: Baywood.

Lindemann, E. (1944). Symptomatology and management of acute grief. *American Journal of Psychiatry, 101,* 141-148.

Lord, J. H. (1987). Survivor grief following a drunk-driving crash. *Death Studies, 11*(6), 413-435.

Lundin, T. (1984). Morbidity following sudden and unexpected bereavement. *British Journal of Psychiatry, 144,* 84-88.

Maddison, D., & Walker, W. (1967). Factors affecting the outcome of conjugal bereavement. *British Journal of Psychiatry, 113,* 1057-1067.

Malinak, D. P., Hoyt, M. F., & Patterson, V. (1979). Adults' reactions to the death of a parent: A preliminary study. *American Journal of Psychiatry, 136*(9), 1152-1156.

Marris, P. (1986). *Loss and change* (Rev. ed.). New York: Anchor Books.

Morgan, J. D. (1986). Death, dying, and bereavement in China and Japan: A brief glimpse. *Death Studies, 10,* 265-272.

Nelsen, V. J. (1993). One woman's interracial journey. In D. P. Irish, K. F. Lundquist, & V. J. Nelsen (Eds.), *Ethnic variations in dying, death, and grief: Diversity in universality* (pp. 21-27). Washington, DC: Taylor and Francis.

Oltjenbruns, K. A. (1991). Positive outcomes of adolescents' experience with grief. *Journal of Adolescent Research, 6*(1), 43–53.

Oltjenbruns, K. A. (in press). Ethnicity and the grief response: Mexican American and Anglo college students. *Death Studies.*

Parkes, C. M. (1975). Determinants of outcome following bereavement. *Omega, 6*(4), 303–323.

Parkes, C. M. (1988). Research: Bereavement. *Omega, 18*(4), 365–377.

Parkes, C. M., & Brown, R. J. (1972). Health after bereavement: A controlled study of young Boston widows and widowers. *Psychosomatic Medicine, 34,* 449–461.

Parkes, C. M., & Weiss, R. S. (1983). *Recovery from bereavement.* New York: Basic Books.

Pelletier, M. (1993). Role of organ donation in helping family members with grief. In J. D. Morgan (Ed.), *Personal care in an impersonal world: A multidimensional look at bereavement* (pp. 157–166). Amityville, NY: Baywood.

Perry, H. L. (1993). Mourning and funeral customs of African Americans. In D. P. Irish, K. F. Lundquist, & V. J. Nelsen (Eds.), *Ethnic variations in dying, death, and grief: Diversity in universality* (pp. 51–65). Washington, DC: Taylor and Francis.

Pomar, M. T. (1987). El dia de los muertos: The life of the dead in Mexican folk art. Ft. Worth, TX: The Fort Worth Art Museum.

Rando, T. (1992). The increasing prevalence of complicated mourning: The onslaught is just beginning. *Omega, 26*(1), 43–59.

Rando, T. (1993). *Treatment of complicated mourning.* Champaign, IL: Research Press.

Rando, T. A. (1984). *Grief, dying and death: Clinical interventions for caregivers.* Champaign, IL: Research Press.

Raphael, B. (1980). A psychiatric model for bereavement counseling. In B. M. Schoenberg (Ed.), *Bereavement counseling: A multidisciplinary handbook* (pp. 147–172). Westport, CT: Greenwood Press.

Raphael, B., & Nunn, K. (1988). Counseling the bereaved. *Journal of Social Issues, 44*(3), 191–206.

Rosenblatt, P. C. (1993). Cross-cultural variation in the experience, expression, and understanding of grief. In D. P. Irish, K. F. Lundquist, & V. J. Nelsen (Eds.), *Ethnic variations in dying, death, and grief: Diversity in universality* (pp. 13–19). Washington, DC: Taylor and Francis.

Rubin, S. S. (1985). The resolution of bereavement: A clinical focus on the relationship to the deceased. *Psychotherapy, 22*(2), 231–235.

Rynearson, E. K. (1984). Bereavement after homicide: A descriptive study. *American Journal of Psychiatry, 14*(11), 1452–1454.

Sanders, C. M. (1982). Effects of sudden vs. chronic illness death on bereavement outcome. *Omega, 13*(3), 227–241.

Sanders, C. M. (1988). Risk factors in bereavement outcome. *Journal of Social Issues, 44*(3), 97–111.

Sanders, C. M. (1989). *Grief: The mourning after.* New York: Wiley.

Sanders, C. M. (1993). Risk factors in bereavement outcome. In M. S. Stroebe, W. Stroebe, & R. O. Hannson (Eds.), *Handbook of bereavement: Theory, research, and intervention* (pp. 255–267). Cambridge: Cambridge University Press.

Schmidt, J. D. (1986). Murder of a child. In T. Rando (Ed.), *Parental loss of a child* (pp. 213–220). Champaign, IL: Research Press.

Schuchter, S. R., & Zisook, S. (1993). The course of normal grief. In M. S. Stroebe, W. Stroebe, & R. O. Hannson (Eds.), *Handbook of bereavement: Theory, research, and intervention.* Cambridge: Cambridge University Press.

Schwab, J., Chalmers, J., Conroy, S., Farris, P., & Markush, R. (1975). Studies in grief: A preliminary report. In B. Schoenberg, I. Gerber, A. Wiener, A. Kutscher, D. Peretz, & A. Carr (Eds.), *Bereavement: Its psychosocial aspects* (pp. 78–87). New York: Columbia University Press.

Sheshkin, A., & Wallace, S. (1976). Differing bereavements: Suicide, natural, and accidental. *Omega, 7*(3), 229–242.

Silverman, P., & Klass, D. (1996). Introduction: What's the problem? In D. Klass, P. Silverman, & S. Nickman (Eds.), *Continuing bonds: New understandings of grief* (pp. 3–27). Washington, DC: Taylor and Francis.

Simeone, W. E. (1991). The Northern Athabaskan potlatch: The objectification of grief. In D. R. Counts & D. A. Counts (Eds.), *Coping with the final tragedy: Cultural variation in dying and grieving* (pp. 157–167). Amityville, NY: Baywood.

Speece, M. W., & Brent, S. B. (1984). Children's understanding of death: A review of three components of death concept. *Child Development, 55*(5), 1671–1686.

Sprang, M. V., McNeil, J. S., & Wright, R. (1989). Psychological changes after the murder of a significant other. *Social Casework, 70*(3), 159–164.

Sprang, M. V., McNeil, J. S., & Wright, R. (1993). Grief among surviving family members of homicide victims: A causal approach. *Omega, 26*(2), 145–160.

Staudacher, C. (1991). *Men and grief.* Oakland, CA: New Harbinger Publications.

Stephenson, J. S. (1985). *Death, grief, and mourning: Individual and social realities.* New York: Free Press.

Stroebe, M. S. (1992). Coping with bereavement: A review of the grief work hypothesis. *Omega, 26*(1), 19–42.

Stroebe, M. S., & Schut, H. (1995, June). *The dual-process model of coping with loss.* Paper presented at the meeting of the International Work Group on Death, Dying and Bereavement, St. Catherine's College, Oxford, UK.

Stroebe, W., & Stroebe, M. S. (1993). Determinants of adjustment to bereavement in younger widows and widowers. In M. S. Stroebe, W. Stroebe, & R. O. Hannson (Eds.), *Handbook of bereavement: Theory, research, and intervention* (pp. 208–226). Cambridge: Cambridge University Press.

Stroebe, W., Stroebe, M. S., & Dommittner, G. (1988). Individual and situational differences in recovery from bereavement: A risk group identified. *Journal of Social Issues, 44*(3), 143–158.

Vachon, M., & Stylianos, S. K. (1988). The role of social support in bereavement. *Journal of Social Issues, 44*(3), 175–190.

Warnes, H. (1985). Alexithymia and the grieving process. *Psychiatric Journal, 10,* 41–44.

Worden, J. W. (1991). *Grief counseling and grief therapy: A handbook for the mental health practitioner* (2nd ed.). New York: Springer.

Wortman, C. B., & Silver, R. C. (1987). Coping with irrevocable loss. In G. R. Vandenbos & B. K. Bryant (Eds.), *Cataclysms, crises, and catastrophes: Psychology in action* (pp. 189–235). Washington, DC: American Psychological Association.

Younoszai, B. (1993). Mexican American perspectives related to death. In D. P. Irish, K. F. Lundquist, & V. J. Nelsen (Eds.), *Ethnic variations in dying, death, and grief: Diversity in universality* (pp. 67–78). Washington, DC: Taylor and Francis.

Zisook, S., & DeVaul, R. (1985). Unresolved grief. *American Journal of Psychoanalysis, 45*(4), 370–379.

4

The Bereaved
Family

The experience of loss due to the death of a family member constitutes not only an individual crisis but a family crisis as well. A change in the composition of the family by even a single member has an impact on the dynamics of family interaction. The resultant "grief occurs on multiple levels: an individual level, a family level, and a societal level" (Moos, 1995). In addition to systemic changes after a death, changes in family interaction patterns also occur prior to the death (Cook, 1994; Cook & Dworkin, 1992; Rosen, 1990). As we shift from the discussion of the bereaved individual (chapter 3) to the discussion of the bereaved family, the following illustrates the connection between the two:

> In order to truly understand the nature of grief in families, it is necessary to recognize that both individual and relational factors are operating and that these must be considered simultaneously. Grief within the family, then, consists of the interplay of individual family members grieving in the social and relational context of the family, with each member affecting and being affected by others. (Gilbert, 1996, p. 271)

Family bereavement takes place within a context that is defined by: (Shapiro, 1994; Parry & Thornwall, 1992)

- nature of the death itself;
- role played in the family by the deceased;
- family developmental stage;
- interaction patterns of multiple generations;
- concurrent family stressors;
- resources available to the family;
- cultural beliefs and practices;
- openness of the family system.

Moos (1995) suggests that common manifestations of family grief involve changes in communication patterns, in the structure of the family itself, and in relationships with people outside of the family system.

FAMILY SYSTEMS THEORY

In the 1940s, Ludwig von Bertalanffy, a biologist, first proposed general systems theory to describe all living things. During the past several decades, theorists and practitioners have used **systems theory** (i.e., a framework for studying a group of related elements that interact as a whole) to understand the family. Systems theory includes several basic concepts:

- A system, although consisting of interacting parts, is characterized by wholeness or unity.
- Systems are governed by rules.
- Systems can be described by their degree of openness.

A brief discussion of each of these concepts follows.

Wholeness

A system, although consisting of interacting parts, is characterized by wholeness or unity. To understand the whole, one must understand the parts, the interactions among them, and the relationship between the parts and the environment. Therefore, to understand the family as a system, one must look at individual members of the family, their relationships to each other, and their interactions with others outside the family. Families are composed of smaller units referred to as subsystems. It is useful to understand the subsystems of a family when attempting to understand the family as a functional unit.

Systems are entwined by **boundaries,** which are abstract dividers between or among subsystems that define participation in them. District boundaries can serve to define, protect, and enhance the integrity of individuals, subsystems, and families. Boundaries can change over time and with various situations. The extent of this change will be affected by characteristics of the boundaries (rigid, flexible, diffuse) in each family.

Theoretically, each individual can be thought of as a **subsystem,** which is a smaller structural unit of a family system. There may also be marital, sibling, and parent–child subsystems. Others can be formed by generation, sex, function, or a variety of other factors. In addition, each family has its own particular set of different subsystems. Often referred to as **alliances** or **coalitions,** they are defined by particularly close bonds between certain family members. Members of these coalitions as two or more individuals join together because of common interests or goals (i.e., alliance) or in attempts to keep a balance of power (i.e., coalition) are likely to feel closer to each other, do more activities together, be especially loyal and protective of each other, share opinions and see things the same way in the family, and support one another when disagreements within the family arise.

The death of a family member can have a unique impact on the subsystems of which that individual was a part. All family members may have lost the same person, but not the same relationship. Because alliances within the family have been altered, the family as a whole will be out of balance and will need to reorganize.

Rules

Systems are governed by rules. Both overt and covert **rules** (shared norms and values that govern repetitive patterns of family functioning) help the system to maintain a steady state of dynamic equilibrium or balance, referred to as **homeostasis.** This homeostasis makes the system and the relationships of interacting individuals within the system predictable. The well-known family therapist Virginia Satir used a mobile to illustrate the concept of balance in a family system. When one element of the mobile is removed, the entire system is in a state of imbalance. For a system to change (that is, for a change in homeostasis to occur), rules must be modified so that a new balance can be achieved.

A death results in **disequilibrium** (i.e., a state of imbalance) in the family system and requires a readjustment among surviving family members. Thus, rules must oftentimes be changed following a death to allow the system to meet the needs of the individuals involved and the system as a whole.

In a family, rules govern the **roles** (i.e., expected behavior of family members), division of labor, power structure, and patterns of interaction. Some rules are overtly discussed and agreed upon. Other family rules are not openly discussed but are tacitly acknowledged and followed by family members. For example, it may be an unstated family rule that it is not okay to discuss the impending death of a family member or to show unrestrained emotion.

Open Versus Closed Systems

The terms *open system* and *closed system* refer to the extent to which a family is open or closed to new information and, thus, susceptible to change. An **open family system** is dynamic and open to events and feelings both within and outside the family structure. Information is freely exchanged with others outside the system and between members within the system. In contrast, a **closed family system** tends to be rigid and insensitive. Family members are locked into strictly prescribed patterns with little tolerance for innovation or adaptive change. The open family is sensitive to one another's emotional and physical needs, and regardless of the stress all members experience, they believe they can help one another (Silverman, Weiner, & Ad, 1995).

Open and closed family systems react differently in response to a death. The open family is more likely to recognize the full meaning of the loss; thus, its members may suffer intense emotional responses. After going through a period of disorganization, the family reorganizes in new and effective ways to meet the needs of the individual family members. This result is due, in part, to the fact that family members not only react to the death itself, but also respond to each other's needs by offering nurturance and support. Additionally, they are willing to accept help from others outside of their own system.

In an extremely closed system, the family is more likely to deny the loss, because acceptance necessitates change. Family members are locked into rigid ways of responding to one another, unable to respond appropriately to their current situation. Not only will the family have difficulty responding to the demands of the environment, but it may also be unable to respond to the needs of individual family members. Thus, they may be isolated in their grief. When families fail to respond openly to their loss, individual adaptation may be inhibited. The more closed a family system, the more likely that a death will be met in ways that are maladaptive for the family unit and consequently that it will have negative impacts on family members (Stephenson, 1985). In some situations, family members are even hesitant to share the fact that a member is seriously ill. Certain types of deaths (e.g., AIDS or suicide) are often still stigmatized by society and family members. As a result, some families are more likely to engage in secrets, deny the true cause of death, and withdraw from others for fear that "outsiders" might avoid or condemn them (Lesar, Gerber, & Semmel, 1996; Mayes & Spiegel, 1992; Rosen, 1990).

DEVELOPMENTAL STAGES OF FAMILIES

As with individuals, families move through predictable developmental stages. Although different theorists have proposed slightly different models of family development, Carter and McGoldrick (1989) have identified six stages in the family life cycle:

1. leaving home: single young adults;
2. joining of families through marriage;
3. families with young children;
4. families with adolescents;
5. launching children and moving on;
6. families in later life.

Each stage has particular developmental tasks and changes associated with it, and family roles change significantly upon entry into each new family stage. The resources, needs, and tasks of the family also vary in each stage of development. Although this model is helpful in many instances, differences do exist among families. For example, many couples remain childless throughout marriage; in other instances, extended family forms predominate either because of functionality or because of cultural family values.

Healthy families proceed through each stage relatively smoothly, completing appropriate developmental tasks and modifying patterns of interaction accordingly. Unhealthy families have difficulty and are often unable to complete the developmental tasks associated with particular stages. Consequently, they may get "stuck" in a stage, performing tasks and maintaining patterns of interactions appropriate to that stage but inappropriate for later stages.

The timing of a death in the life cycle of the family is an important variable in the adjustment of the family and of its individual members (Rolland, 1987; Shapiro, 1994). For example, a family that experiences the death of one of its adult members may evolve to a situation in which an adolescent becomes a surrogate parent for younger siblings and a companion for the remaining parent, thus truncating the normal process of separation during this age stage. In many cases, this can present a threat to independence and also delay or prevent the young person from leaving home to start his or her own adult life (Gordon, 1986).

In families that have difficulty accepting loss as a natural part of life, young adults may be unable to separate from their family of origin and venture out on their own as mature individuals. At the same time, family members may not be able to allow the young adults in the family to pull away as part of the normal emancipation process. As a result, the system becomes static and locked into a rigid pattern that is resistant to change. Individuals within this type of system are unable to **individuate** (move toward more autonomous functioning), and thus view themselves as extensions of their families rather than unique, separate individuals. At the extreme are pathologically **enmeshed families** that manifest "total togetherness." These families are composed of family members with little individual autonomy or differentiation (Sieburg, 1985). When a death actually occurs in enmeshed systems, it reconfirms the pain of separation and often leads to further enmeshment.

Family psychopathology often centers around family myths, which serve the same function for families as defense mechanisms do for individuals. **Family myths** consist of beliefs accepted and adhered to by family members that defend against disturbances or changes in existing family relationships. For example, members of enmeshed families may all uphold the myth that "We are only safe if we all stick together and let no one else into our inner circle."

DEATH AS A FAMILY CRISIS

Family stress theory provides a useful model for conceptualizing the family's response to a death. A classic model of family stress developed by Reuben Hill (1949) about 50 years ago serves as a basis for current theoretical work. In this model, a family **crisis** is viewed as arising from a stressor event interacting with both the family's current crisis-meeting resources and their definition or perception of the stressor. The **stressor event** is defined as a life event or occurrence that affects the family unit and produces, or has the opportunity to produce, change in the family system. This change may take place in various areas of family life, such as family goals, patterns of interaction, quality of relationships, roles, values, or boundaries (Lynn-McHale & Smith, 1991). These combined factors all influence the family's vulnerability and, in turn, determine to what degree the family will experience a crisis. A family crisis refers to disruption, disorganization, or incapacity in the family system. A death in a family (a stressor event) usually results in a crisis because of the excessive demands placed on resources and the ability to cope.

Although the early conceptions of family stress focused primarily on pre-crisis variables, McCubbin and Patterson (1983b) have elaborated on Hill's original model to take into account postcrisis variables that influence the family's ability to recover from a crisis (often referred to as the family's **regenerative power**). These additional postcrisis variables include

- the concurrent life stressors and changes that make family adaptation more difficult to achieve;
- the critical psychological and social resources the family seeks out and utilizes when managing crisis situations; and
- the family's interpretation of the crisis experience.

All these factors contribute to the ability to cope and represent the processes the family engages in to achieve satisfactory crisis resolution.

The family's adaptation to a crisis can vary considerably over time and can be viewed on a continuum from maladaptation to bonadaptation. At the negative extreme, **maladaptation** results in the curtailment of individual and family development. At the positive extreme, the outcomes of **bonadaptation** are the enhancement of development in individual members and the enhancement of the family as a unit (McCubbin & Patterson, 1983b).

VARIABLES AFFECTING THE FAMILY'S ABILITY TO COPE

As previously stated, a family's ability to cope with a crisis such as death and recover from it will be determined by other stressors experienced concurrently, the resources of the family, and the family's perception of the event (see Figure 4.1).

FIGURE 4.1
Family Crisis Model: Death as an Example

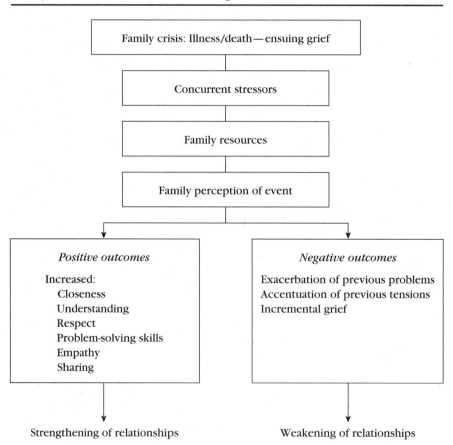

Concurrent Stressors

The ability of the family to cope may be complicated by multiple stressors (Hopmeyer & Werk, 1994). Illness or death within the family does not preclude the possibility of other stressful situations occurring at approximately the same time. Some stressors may be related to the illness or death itself, whereas others may be quite unrelated. Stressors have been categorized by family researchers as

- situational (e.g., war or unemployment);
- normal developmental (e.g., birth of first child or retirement); or
- transitional (e.g., divorce).

Stressors encountered at the same time as the illness or death have a cumulative effect, and thus the family experiences "pile-up." **Pile-up** refers to the accumulation of normative and nonnormative stressors and intrafamily strains (McCubbin & Patterson, 1983a). As the pile-up of stressors continues, the resources of the family become increasingly taxed, and there is an increased risk that family coping will become dysfunctional.

Stressors Related to Illness or Death. The family experiences a variety of stressors that are directly related to the illness or to the death itself. For example, providing care to a person who is seriously ill is physically and emotionally exhausting. As the illness progresses and death approaches, the family is faced with multiple losses: expected loss of life, the loss of a healthy member, and the loss of family life as it had been. Each of these losses is stressful in and of itself and may trigger a grief reaction among individual members. Other frequent stressors include increased time commitments, disruption of routines, lack of time for self and other family members, a sense of social isolation, and financial strain. Additional strains such as interruption of career, housing adaptation, and postponement of planned family activities also precipitate stress (Montgomery, Gonyea, & Hooyman, 1985; Pratt, Schmal, Wright, & Cleland, 1985; Hughes & Lieberman, 1990).

Stressors Not Related to Illness or Death. Holmes and Rahe (1967) identified a number of stressful life events and ranked them in terms of their relative stress factors (see Table 4.1). Many of these factors occur with fair regularity and as such may well occur during the time that a family member is dying. Kalnins, Churchill, and Terry (1980) interacted with 45 families of leukemic children and found that they experienced a variety of concurrent stresses that had no direct relationship to the child's illness. These families experienced stressful events such as the death of another family member or friend, occupational changes, moving, and automobile accidents.

Normal developmental changes also constitute a source of stress. As individuals within the family develop and change over time, each must face new developmental issues and deal with new crises. The family system, too, changes

TABLE 4.1
The Social Readjustment Rating Scale

RANK	LIFE EVENT	MEAN VALUE
1	Death of spouse	100
2	Divorce	73
3	Marital separation	65
4	Jail term	63
5	Death of close family member	63
6	Personal injury or illness	53
7	Marriage	50
8	Fired at work	47
9	Marital reconciliation	45
10	Retirement	45
11	Change in health of family member	44
12	Pregnancy	40
13	Sex difficulties	39
14	Gain of new family member	39
15	Business readjustment	39
16	Change in financial state	38
17	Death of a close friend	37
18	Change to different line of work	36
19	Change in number of arguments with spouse	35
20	Mortgage over $10,000	31
21	Foreclosure of mortgage or loan	30
22	Change in responsibilities at work	29
23	Son or daughter leaving home	29
24	Trouble with in-laws	29
25	Outstanding personal achievement	28
26	Wife begins or stops work	26
27	Beginning or end of school	26
28	Change in living conditions	25
29	Revision of personal habits	24

SOURCE: T. H. Holmes & R. Rahe (1967). The social readjustment rating scale. *Journal of Psychosomatic Research, 11,* p. 216. Copyright 1967 Pergamon Journals, Ltd. Reprinted by permission.

over time and is faced with new challenges, as noted earlier. The birth of a child, for example, is regarded by many to be a crisis in and of itself. Think of how much more difficult the situation becomes if the infant's parents are also caring for another child who is dying of cancer.

Family Resources

Having resources available and being willing to use them can effectively mediate the effects of a family crisis. Resources can include both

- support and strengths within the family; and
- support and services from individuals and organizations outside the family system.

Three features seem to characterize families that are able to respond adequately to stressor events: involvement, integration, and adaptation. **Family involvement** is the commitment that members make to the family and their participation in family life. **Family integration** refers to the ability of family members to work together in order to assist in achieving both group and individual goals and in maintaining psychological equilibrium. **Family adaptation** is the ability of the family and each of its members to change their responses to each other and to the outside world as situations demand (Glasser & Glasser, 1970).

The internal resources of the family, such as integration and adaptability, are crucial to positive family functioning after a crisis. Furthermore, families must also develop or strengthen their ability to seek social support and access community resources external to the family itself. This need for external support was confirmed by Venters (1981) who studied families of children with cystic fibrosis. The life expectancy for individuals with cystic fibrosis is late teens or early twenties. In this study, Venters found that families who had a high level of functioning sought both practical help and emotional support from people both inside and outside the family. Middle functioning families shared their burden extensively within the family structure and minimally outside. Finally, families determined to be low functioning had one or two individuals within the families who were primarily responsible for the care of the sick child and did not request help or support from any external individual or group whatsoever.

Family adjustment to illness and death is also related to a variety of additional factors. These include interpersonal interaction styles, cultural expectations, characteristic modes of dealing with stress, a positive outlook on life, hope, and rules that allow emotional expression and role flexibility (Koch, 1985; Patterson & McCubbin, 1983).

Family's Perception of the Event

Crisis situations may be somewhat neutralized by the cognitive appraisal or the psychological evaluation that is made of them. For example, factors such as religious beliefs affect the family's perception of the crisis (Pratt et al., 1985) and allow individual family members to regard the crisis as a test of their faith or a challenge by which their faith might become stronger. Stinnett, Knorr, DeFrain, and Rowe (1981) found that 56% of the "strong families" in their study indicated that a spiritual or religious belief allowed them to cope more effectively.

Endowing an illness or death with a positive meaning may allow survivors to adjust more easily. In contrast, viewing a death as punishment for past deeds can have a negative influence on the resolution of grief.

At times, the family's perception of the crisis event even alters the feeling of being a family. Family members may perceive the death as "destroying our family" or "the loss of the person who gave life to our family." Bereaved mothers often talk about "not seeming to be a family anymore" after a child's death (Schatz, 1986). These perceptions are important and need to be addressed in any therapeutic intervention.

ADAPTATION OF THE FAMILY UNIT

The Chinese symbol for the word *crisis* is translated to mean "dangerous opportunity." Implicit in this translation is the understanding that the challenges that are precipitated by a death may result in either positive or negative changes for the family. It is unreasonable to expect that a family has a rule to deal with every possible situation. As a result, they may react to a novel or unanticipated situation in a wide variety of ways. Depending on the specific family, the response may be immobilization, breakup, or a marshaling of resources to create a new suitable response to the situation. Crises are not necessarily detrimental to the family. Often new and creative solutions are developed for reacting to situations, such that future crises may actually be dealt with in a more effective manner.

Positive Outcomes

Many families report closer bonds, better understanding and respect for each other's strengths, enhancement of mutual problem-solving skills, greater empathy, and increased sharing following the illness and/or death of a family member. DeFrain and Ernst (1978) studied the effect of sudden infant death syndrome (SIDS) on family survivors. They reported that in cases in which individuals turned to family members for support and that support was granted, family relationships were generally strengthened. Klass (1986) explains that, for some families, a death creates a new bond as members draw together to deal with a shared crisis.

In his study of parents from 100 families with a child who had cystic fibrosis, Venters (1981) found that approximately one-half of the families regarded their crisis as growth producing. Many sought new solutions for dealing with problems and reducing stress.

Negative Outcomes

Not all families experience a positive outcome to the crisis of death. The phrase "dangerous opportunity" implies that there is a risk involved: a risk that the family may not possess the coping strategies to deal with the stress and conflict that may arise after the death of one of its members. Several researchers have found that the death of a family member may produce a variety of negative outcomes. These are highlighted in the next section, which discusses a model of incremental grief.

MODEL OF INCREMENTAL GRIEF

Oftentimes, the crisis of illness or death does not draw family members closer together but rather causes significant discord. A model of incremental grief explains how one loss often triggers another loss. The resultant grief is magnified with each added loss. To simplify the discussion of this model, we shall examine it in terms of the survivors being a husband and wife; however, the model does apply to other surviving relationships (parent–child, sibling–sibling, and friend–friend, among others) and to grief precipitated by losses other than death.

As described in chapter 3, there are many common manifestations of grief; however, each person's grief experience is also unique. Each individual feels the loss in a very personal way, due to the specific relationship that was severed and due to variations in coping strategies. One spouse may be very depressed, guilty, and preoccupied with the death for many, many months after the loss of a child. The other spouse may be deeply saddened by the loss and very angry at the medical profession and other family members for a few months after the death. At a given moment in time, even while in the acute stage of grief, one spouse may feel moderately happy whereas the other is in anguish. This variability of grief-related experiences and time taken for resolution describes the **dissynchrony (or asymmetry) of grief** (Gilbert & Smart, 1992; Lang, Gottlieb, & Amsel, 1996; Rolland, 1994; Schwab, 1992, 1996).

Both during an illness and following the death, family members often use **discrepant coping styles.** For example, some survivors may vent their emotions openly whereas others repress their feelings. Some individuals wish to communicate openly and talk frequently about their grief, whereas others regard their experiences as private and are reticent (Gilbert, 1989, 1996; DeVries, Lana, & Falck, 1994). In studying 27 couples who had experienced either a fetal or an infant death, Gilbert (1989) found that the vast majority of couples experienced what they described as some type of marital conflict at some point during their bereavement; only five couples reported little or no conflict. The researcher believed that "inconsistencies in beliefs and expectations resulting in a perception of incongruent grieving served as the major contributors to most of these conflicts" (Gilbert, 1989, p. 609).

Due to the dissynchrony of grief and discrepant coping styles following the primary loss of death, there is often secondary loss: a loss that is a consequence of death, the primary loss (Rando, 1984). To understand the impact of grief on surviving relationships, we will define the **secondary loss** in this context as a change in the predeath relationship regarded as stressful by the survivors. (Rando uses a broader definition of the term to refer to any loss, either physical or symbolic, that develops as a consequence of the death of a loved one.)

The resultant strain on the relationship is often related to stresses that predated the death. The crisis precipitated by death often exacerbates already existing interpersonal problems or accentuates tensions already present. For example, a husband and wife may never have openly shared their emotions with one another. The death of their child simply makes the ongoing silence in that area all the more noticeable, as well as painful, when one spouse urgently needs to share feelings. In some instances, the stress caused by the death creates new problems for the survivors. For example, after the death of a child, one spouse may physically withdraw from a mate who chooses to deal with his or her grief privately. The rejected spouse may then engage in extramarital relationships, even though that had never been a pattern prior to the child's death. Or, as another example, a parent who had never used alcohol or drugs previously may use them excessively after the death.

If the stress on a surviving relationship is significant, survivors often grieve not only the primary loss of the death but also the significant change from the predeath relationship to the current relationship pattern with another survivor (secondary loss). This grief is termed **secondary grief** (Oltjenbruns, 1996) and emanates from the stressful change in a relationship with another, not from the death itself.

Secondary grief is often characterized by one spouse being angry at the other for not understanding what he or she is experiencing or for not offering support when it is needed. A husband or wife who assumes that all people should grieve the same way may condemn the other, who is grieving differently. One parent may erroneously conclude that the other parent did not love the deceased child because he or she is not grieving openly and, as a result, inappropriately berate their mate for what is perceived to be a lack of attachment to the child who died. There is often a lack of understanding when an expectation of providing mutual support cannot be fulfilled. Grief is such a personally painful and draining experience that bereaved parents sometimes simply cannot reach out to help each other, even when they want to. As illustrated by these characteristics, secondary grief adds to the burden of family members who have experienced the death of a loved one (primary loss), when it results in a significant change in a relationship with another (secondary loss) (see Figure 4.2).

As discussed in chapter 3, individuals need an opportunity to do their own grief work and be given support for venting emotions and sharing thoughts or beliefs. To deal more effectively with secondary grief, counselors, social workers, and others who help families must take a systems perspective, for this grief evolves not only from the individual's personal primary loss but also from the ultimate effect which that loss has had on the relationship with another survivor. In some instances, the secondary grief may permanently alter the relationship, or even terminate it, if appropriate systems-oriented intervention is not provided. For example, Kaplan, Grobstein, and Smith (1976) studied 40 families after the death of a child with leukemia. Serious marital problems were reported by the majority of the families. In addition, many families reported difficulties in parent–child communication. Eighty percent of the families who noted having

FIGURE 4.2
A Model of Incremental Grief

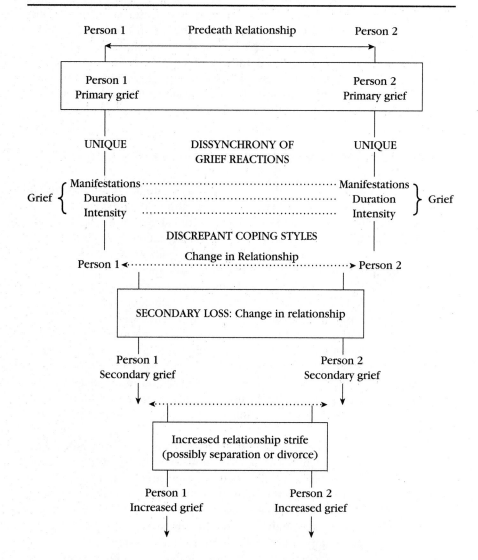

problems believed that these had been precipitated by the illness and subsequent death. Fish (1986) found that 70% of bereaved parents in his study reported significant marital stress related to the loss.

Although consistent data are not available regarding the number of divorces due to the death of a child, many bereaved couples do experience marital difficulty within months after such a death, and divorce for these couples is a possibility if professional help is not obtained. It may well be that the secondary grief phenomenon is a direct contributor to the marital discord. The individual who grieves the following losses—the primary loss (such as the death of a child), the resultant secondary loss (e.g., change in relationship between husband and wife that causes increased stress), and a tertiary loss (ultimately, perhaps divorce)—experiences a shifting in the focus of the grief and also the added grief of multiple losses. This phenomenon is termed **incremental grief** (Oltjenbruns, 1996). Incremental grief is defined as the additive factor of grief due to multiple related losses. The grief resulting from a primary loss may trigger a secondary loss. The grief resulting from the secondary loss may then precipitate yet another loss.

INTERVENTION WITH THE FAMILY SYSTEM

Walsh and McGoldrick (1991) advocate intervention with families following a loss. In their view, the mental health field has failed to appreciate the impact of loss on the family as an interactional system. Because of the complex web of roles and relationships among family members, an individual's coping response has implications for other family members. When effects of a loss on the family system are not addressed, the consequences can, at times, be a legacy of loss.

In some cases, without appropriate intervention, this legacy can be manifest in dysfunctional patterns of interaction and mutual influence among survivors and across generations. If needed, the optimal time for intervention is during the early, acute stage of a crisis. It is during this time that the family is attempting to reorganize and new patterns of interaction are being established. When a terminal illness precedes a death, intervention might begin prior to the actual death, following the confirmation of the diagnosis. **Postvention** is the term that is generally used to refer to assistance offered to survivors following a death. It is at this time in the dying continuum that intervention most often occurs.

If families choose to seek help from a family therapist, they often, at the outset, tie their motivation to a concern other than death. For example, parents may seek professional help because of a parent–child conflict or marital difficulties, without seeing the connection to a previous death. In other cases, the death will not be mentioned because it is a taboo subject for family members. In these situations, the family's "presenting problem" may camouflage the underlying issue of the impact of the death on the family system.

Grebstein (1986) points out that intervention often involves a strong educational component. If families are prepared for the issues they must face, they are more likely to avoid maladaptive coping and poor outcomes. The single most important task for the therapist is to help the family talk openly about the death, its impact on them, and their emotional reactions to it. In this regard, therapists should be sensitive to the uniqueness of each situation. Each family is different, and the therapeutic interventions required may vary considerably; however, intervention with a family system should focus on the tasks described in the following section.

FAMILY TASKS INVOLVED IN COPING

Each individual in the family performs various tasks as he or she comes to terms with the loss. Individual members may communicate with the dying person, grieve for that person both before (if death is anticipated) and after the death, and modify the sense of attachment to the person who has died. Other tasks are relevant to the family system as a whole. Family-oriented tasks include

- maintaining open communication;
- reassigning roles;
- providing support to family members; and
- modifying relationships with external systems.

Maintaining Open Communication

In chapter 2, we stressed that shared communication is crucial if dying individuals are to avoid a sense of isolation, abandonment, or overwhelming fear regarding their impending deaths. Keep in mind there is a difference between "telling" someone something and really being open to shared communication about feelings, as well as basic information (Hughes & Lieberman, 1990). Both the dying individual and the family as a whole typically have a need for closure with one another. This can only occur if there is open communication. Engaging in a conspiracy of silence negates the opportunity for both the dying person and family members to plan for the future, deal with anxieties, and enjoy each other's company. Open communication not only increases the opportunity to interact positively with the dying individual, but also serves as a resource to the family as it strives to regain equilibrium.

> Families with open internal communication systems are more prone to resist the societal taboos surrounding the area of death, and are thus more likely to discuss and make realistic plans for the death of their members. . . . The degree to which it is permissible to express feelings of sadness and loss, as well as the less acceptable reactions of anger, guilt, and relief, seems to play a large role in determining the success of the readjustment period. (Vollman, Ganzert, Picher, & Williams, 1971, p. 104)

If family members do not openly share their thoughts and feelings, the family may be at risk for experiencing negative outcomes. Lack of open communication increases the possibility of guilt, blame, and conflict (Vess, Moreland, & Schwebel, 1985b).

Reassigning Roles

After the death of one of its members, the family must reassign the roles which that person had performed. These roles consist of tasks that may be either instrumental or expressive. **Instrumental tasks** include such activities as serving as primary breadwinner for the family or preparing meals. **Expressive tasks** facilitate the development of a favorable social–emotional climate within the family. They include such activities as promoting affectionate interactions or minimizing conflict.

The number of roles to be reassigned and the centrality of these roles to overall family functioning affect the intensity of the family crisis. "The specific roles depend on the family's stage in the family life cycle, which, in turn, will determine the roles that require reallocation" (Vess, Moreland, & Schwebel, 1985a, p. 2). If the family member who is ill or who has died is a parent/spouse, role reassignment may be all the more difficult than if it were a young child. In this situation, surviving family members are at risk for increased stress and disorganization, because a parent/spouse is likely to have fulfilled a combination of the following roles: financial provider, socializer and caretaker of children, and housekeeper, among others. The surviving parent, then, may attempt to assume too many additional roles, thereby experiencing **role strain.** In other instances, children may attempt to assume roles for which they have inadequate preparation and/or skill. If this is the case, not only do the children suffer, but the roles are likely to be performed inadequately.

Stress due to role reallocation may also be experienced while the dying person is still alive. For example, if family members are involved in providing care to the patient of if they must travel long distances to the hospital, they may experience what seem to be impossible demands on their time. These increased demands result from trying to perform their ongoing old roles, new roles related to the illness, and also some of the patient's former roles that have been reallocated to them.

The opportunity for a positive outcome to the process of role reallocation can be enhanced by a number of factors. Two of these will be briefly discussed here:

- open communication among family members; and
- achievement (as compared to ascription) of roles.

Vess et al. (1985a) studied cancer patients and their families and found that open communication provided an opportunity to negotiate the reallocation of roles, which in turn diminished role strain and role conflict. Without good communication, roles are oftentimes simply reallocated by default, with little attention paid to how they might most effectively be fulfilled.

In discussing assignment of roles, Aldous (1978) differentiates between the ascription of roles and the achievement of roles. She defines **ascribed roles** as those assigned by virtue of some characteristic over which a person has no control, such as gender. For example, a daughter who is expected to perform housekeeping chores after her mother dies, simply because she is a girl, has an ascribed role. **Achieved roles** are acquired by the efforts and skill of the individual. A son or daughter who becomes involved with caring for a younger sibling because he or she has the skills and desire to do so has undertaken an achieved role. The method of assigning roles affects both the performance of the roles and the family environment. "Families who used achieved roles performed their reallocated roles at a higher level than did families who adopted ascribed roles. Specifically, these families were less likely to use a role overload pattern" (Vess et al., 1985a, p. 14).

Providing Support to Family Members

The outcome of a family crisis such as illness or death of a family member is affected by the presence or absence of family support. Support is needed both during the caregiving process (Pratt et al., 1985) and after the death. Stinnett et al. (1981) studied the coping strategies of 66 families who had been identified as "strong families" by persons outside the family unit. When asked who was most helpful in dealing with a crisis, the most common response was family members. A major conclusion of the study was "the primary family unit itself became a major resource in coping with crisis. . . . the strong family has a great deal to contribute to the strength of the individual" (p. 163). However, some family systems do not provide support to one another. Families that do not have good communication skills, respect, or empathy for each other may serve as a liability rather than a resource.

Modifying Relationships With Social Networks

Another task that must be performed by surviving family members is to establish or modify relationships with other social networks. Individuals and families themselves often do not have all the resources that are necessary to deal with a severe crisis and may need to seek additional **social support,** which is defined as "individuals, groups, or institutions that provide assistance of varying degrees and forms to help another individual combat stresses that tax his or her personal resources" (Schilling, Gilchrist, & Schinke, 1985, p. 47). Social support can also be provided to the family system as a whole.

Social networks may be either formal or informal. Informal support networks refer to family members, friends, and neighbors. Formal support networks refer to professionals such as doctors or counselors as well as organizations as hospices and various peer support groups, such as Make Today Count (for cancer patients and their families) or Compassionate Friends (for parents who have lost a child to death).

Both types of support networks can provide instrumental and/or emotional support or provide information regarding other resources. Increasingly, formal networks are being created to help dying individuals and their families. Schwab (1995) found that a formal support group fills an important role for those who have experienced a particularly traumatic loss and may not know anyone in their own networks who has experienced a similar loss.

Although many formal services do exist, one cannot assume that they are necessarily used by all bereaved individuals (Schwab, 1995). Families may choose not to use them for various reasons, including the recognition that they have access to sufficient support from family and friends, the desire to grieve privately, or the belief that their religion provides the support needed to deal with their grief. In other cases, there may be a desire to access services but problems with such things as schedules or availability of transportation disallow participation. Alternatively, some family units simply do not search outward in their time of need and risk depleting their emotional resources as they attempt to deal with crises.

INTERGENERATIONAL ISSUES RELATED TO DEATH

The need for open communication and support extends beyond the boundaries of the nuclear family to extended family members. Issues of grief and loss may even extend through multiple generations (Detmer & Lamberti, 1991). Bowen (1976) theorizes that the effects of major losses in a family can be transmitted to subsequent generations if they are not worked through when they occur. According to Bowen, the death of a family member creates an "emotional shock wave" that is a "network of underground 'after shocks' of serious life events that can occur anywhere in the extended family system in the months or years following serious emotional events in a family" (p. 339). A death in the family has the potential of disrupting the effective equilibrium of the system, which can result in a chronically dysfunctional family. When intervening in such a system, a balance must be maintained between encouraging expression of unresolved grief associated with a death and promoting healthy family interactions so that the family can continue to develop in the future.

Confused and fearful attitudes related to death can interfere with the normal processes of separation and individuation that are a natural part of progressing through the family life cycle. Worden (1991) has emphasized that one important reason for using a family systems approach to intervention is that unresolved grief may not only serve as a key factor in family pathology, but also contribute to dysfunctional relationships across generations. Postponed mourning related to a death in one's family of origin can impede effective coping with emotional loss and/or separation within one's current family. Sometimes, years later, remaining conflicts over loss and abandonment can be projected by adults onto their present-day families. Consequently, normal developmental change can become fearful, anxiety-laden matters.

Shapiro (1994) stresses that "a systemic developmental perspective on the family life cycle crisis of bereavement suggests that the developmental course of all families is inevitably altered by the shattering blow of grief" (p. 278). Recall that this change may in fact be positive; families often draw closer together as they develop enhanced coping and communication strategies—even across generations. The remainder of this chapter addresses a specific type of loss—death of a child—and discusses family systems issues related to parental grief.

EXAMPLE OF FAMILY GRIEF: DEATH OF A CHILD

The death of a child involves both physical and symbolic losses, the true meaning of which varies with the life stage of both parent and child (DeVries, Lana, & Falck, 1994; Hopmeyer & Werk, 1994). Just as the child holds multiple representations for the parents, so too does the child's death hold multiple meanings (Rosenblatt, 1996). There may be a loss of: a sense of security, predictability, and immortality; hopes and dreams; a sense of self as protector; what the child could have become; and the role of parent.

Loss Due to Perinatal Death

Many young parents experience a miscarriage, a stillborn, or the death of a newborn (collectively referred to as **perinatal deaths**).

A growing body of evidence indicates that parents actively grieve after the death of a very young infant, even though the baby lived only a short time. One of the earliest studies was done by Kennell, Slyter, and Klaus (1970), who interviewed 20 women whose children had died between 1 hour and 12 days after birth. Each interview was evaluated for the presence of six signs of mourning: sadness, loss of appetite, inability to sleep, increased irritability, preoccupation with the lost infant, and inability to return to normal activities (p. 345). All the women reported a sense of sadness and preoccupation with thoughts of the baby. The majority also reported irritability, insomnia, and loss of appetite.

A mourning score was given to each woman on the basis of the number of signs present and the duration of the symptoms. In comparing the nine mothers in the "high mourning" group compared with the "low mourning" group, the researchers found high mourning was significantly associated with previous loss of a baby and positive feelings about the pregnancy. The researchers did not find a relationship between the mourning score and the length of the baby's life. Lack of relationship between the grief score and length of the baby's life was confirmed by Peppers and Knapp (1980), who studied 65 women who experienced the death of a child between the 28th week of pregnancy and the 4th week of life. In addition to the six signs of mourning used by Kennell et al. (1970), Peppers and Knapp (1980) also noted feelings of anger, guilt, time confusion, and depression. More recent studies have also confirmed that both mothers and fathers experience grief following perinatal loss (Hughes & Page-Lieberman, 1989; Lasker & Toedter, 1991). There is evidence that mothers grieve more intensely and for longer periods of time than do fathers (Dyregrov & Matthiesen, 1987; Fish, 1986; Thomas & Striegel, 1995), though fathers also experience the pain of the loss. Regardless of any gender differences, both parents need support and fathers often feel that their pain is not recognized during this time. Further, both describe a type of **shadow grief,** a sense of loss that parents feel for the rest of their lives (Peppers & Knapp, 1980).

ABORTION

In contrast to a miscarriage (i.e., a spontaneous abortion), elective abortion is the deliberate termination of a pregnancy. Fogel (1981) estimates that approximately 10% or more women who have had an abortion experience adverse psychological and emotional outcomes. Women who do experience grief explain that it is characterized by sorrow, anger, guilt, or yearning for the lost child.

A number of factors may exacerbate the feelings of grief following an abortion (Harris, 1986; Peppers, 1987):

- Belief that abortion is morally wrong and regret that the decision was made may trigger a grief response.
- Prior emotional disturbance may cause the woman to be more vulnerable to stress.
- Ambivalence about having the abortion often triggers questions later on about the appropriateness of the decision.
- Pressure to have an abortion against one's own wishes may elicit feelings of exploitation, anger, and grief.
- Later timing of the abortion (such as second trimester) contributes to the likelihood of stronger bonding to the baby. The pain experienced by

the woman during this time frame is also typically more intense.

- Abortions performed for medical reasons due to fetal malformation increase feelings of guilt. The parents feel responsible for having created an "imperfect" child and also may feel guilt for choosing to terminate the pregnancy rather than care for the child.
- Lack of support from family and friends may exacerbate negative emotions. Although it is legal in the United States, abortion is often regarded as taboo. Additionally, women may be ashamed or embarrassed and not tell others about the abortion.
- Women may perceive that they are being punished by those who disagree with their decision.

Certainly, not all women experience a grief reaction following an abortion; but for those who do, it can be a very poignant experience. One young author, who had an abortion when she was 17 years old and another two in the decade that followed, writes how, for years, she would track how old the child would have been, had the baby been born, and describes a pain that was very real to her (Kesselman, 1990).

SOURCES: I. Kesselman (1990). Grief and Loss: Issues for abortion. *Omega, 21,* 241–247; L. Peppers (1987). Grief and elective abortion: Breaking the emotional bond. *Omega, 18*(1), 1–12; B. G. Harris (1986). Induced abortion. In T. Rando (Ed.), *Parental loss of a child* (pp. 241–256). Champaign, IL: Research Press.

Miscarriage. **Miscarriage,** sometimes referred to as a spontaneous abortion, is the unwillful termination of a pregnancy prior to the point of viability. Miscarriages may be due to a variety of factors, including improper implantation of the fertilized ovum or abnormality of the embryo. In most instances, there is nothing that can be done to prevent the miscarriage; it is a biological process over which the woman has no control. She did not cause it; she cannot prevent it.

Because miscarriage involves the loss of an unborn child, many have doubted whether a significant loss has truly occurred (Reinharz, 1988) and therefore, have not understood that grief is a likely consequence. In most deaths, families and friends gather to give support to the parents who have lost a child. This is typically not the case following a miscarriage. Not only is social support often lacking, but so are the rituals that symbolize an important transition (Hall, Beresford, & Quinones, 1987). As a result, couples who have experienced a miscarriage often get little attention from others in dealing with their loss (Leff, 1987; Lietar, 1986).

Recent research, however, has provided evidence that most women do grieve after a miscarriage. Although there is anecdotal evidence and strong reason to believe that men also grieve in these situations, there is little research that shows their response to this type of loss.

Lietar (1986) notes that "the amount of grief over a miscarriage will not be determined by the time between conception and aborting, but by the meaning that the pregnancy held for the couple and a number of other factors such as the desire for parenthood, religious training, cultural mores, and the positive value placed on the pregnancy by the couple's social and environmental milieu" (p. 124). A number of factors have been found to be correlated with an increased risk of a complicated bereavement outcome following a pregnancy loss. These include increased pregnancy length, poor mental health prior to the loss, poor social support, and low marital quality (Janssen, Cuisinier, & Hoogduin, 1996).

Miscarriage involves two different losses: the loss of a baby who will never be born and the loss of a dream for what the child would have become. In an interview reported by Borg and Lasker (1981), a woman who had experienced a miscarriage stated:

> By the end of three months of my pregnancy the baby was already going through college in my mind. During that period I had such an active fantasy life; I fell in love with that baby. When I saw the fetus the fantasy became a person and it was more than the death of a fantasy; it was a real baby I lost. (p. 34)

A strong sense of guilt is often evidenced in parents after a miscarriage (Covington & Theut, 1993). Many erroneously feel that they somehow contributed to the termination of the pregnancy through such factors as too much or too little exercise, improper nutrition, continuation or discontinuation of work, or other reasons. Many women feel that they had done something to cause the miscarriage and are worried about subsequent pregnancies. Parents should be given accurate information regarding pregnancy and miscarriage, emphasizing the unlikelihood that they were responsible (Shaw, 1983). Together with the sense of guilt, many couples are burdened by the thought they have failed at what they regard as one of life's normal processes—procreation. They may then assume that their femininity or masculinity is in question.

Stillbirth and Death of a Newborn.   If fetal death occurs after the 28th week of prenatal development, the term **stillbirth** is used rather than the term

GRIEF FOR A STILLBORN DAUGHTER

In the baby section of Foley's in the Cherry Creek mall, there are four racks of white dresses for baby girls.

We had been to all of the other stores with baby sections in the mall that Sunday afternoon and looked at all of the other racks of white dresses for baby girls. We were looking for a white dress for ours. At 9:27 the night before in St. Joseph Hospital, she had been stillborn.

I pulled a white dress with a tiny pink rose stitched on the collar out of the middle of a rack, and when I turned around my wife was standing three racks over and holding up the same dress.

"We found it," my wife said.

The baby was due Oct. 27.

The doctor who delivered her after 16 hours of induced labor said the umbilical cord was around her neck.

We named her Mary.

The week before, I had promised to move the record albums to the basement that weekend. The curtains were supposed to be hung that Wednesday, but we had been told there was a problem with the fabric and they wouldn't be ready until next week. We looked at cribs Thursday night.

When we got home that Sunday afternoon, the book was on the bed where my wife had left it Friday morning, open to the section "I can't detect any movement. Is something wrong?"

(Continued)

miscarriage. **Newborn death** is one that takes place within a few hours or days after birth. Table 4.2 identifies the leading causes of infant deaths in the United States for the years 1980 and 1993.

Society often tends to negate these losses and regard them as unimportant. After all, the parents did not really know the child or so others assume (Hutchins, 1986). Further, family and friends may discount the grief of the parents because they themselves have not had an opportunity to interact with the baby and therefore do not share the parents' anguish (Palmer & Noble, 1986).

An additional factor that complicates grief following a perinatal death is its lack of focus. The families have experienced a significant loss, yet they have few, if any, shared memories that may ultimately sustain families experiencing the death of an older child. Medical personnel and mental health practitioners now recommend that parents be given an opportunity to share what they can with the child in order to facilitate their ensuing grief. Hutchins (1986) explained that families need to say "hello" before they can say "good-bye."

Strategies for helping the brief existence of the baby seem more real include the following:

- Name the child so that he or she is regarded as a person.
- After giving information as to what the baby will look like and feel like, allow parents to hold their child. Time alone with the baby should be provided, if it is desired.

(Continued From Previous Page)

She was 4 pounds, 11 ounces and 21 inches long. She had her mother's mouth.

Even the nurse said she had huge hands and feet. "I would have had to make her practice piano," my wife said.

When we picked out a silver frame for the footprints, the saleswoman asked, "Your first?"

"Yes," I said.

"I could tell," the saleswoman said. "By the second or third, most people just stick the footprints away in a drawer."

The morning of the funeral, I pruned the roses we planted in the spring. It was something to do. It was the only thing I could think of to do, because the lawn had been mowed twice in the same day while we were in the hospital, once by a friend and once by my father.

I cut off a pink rose that had bloomed and faded, and a rosebud that almost was ready to bloom fell to the ground.

All week, friends and family had flown in, called, come over, sent a stack of cards and flowers that covered every flat surface. Almost all of them said there was nothing they could say. Some had gone on to say there must be a reason these things happen.

You can choose to believe that or not, but you can't choose when you will believe it and when you won't.

I picked up the pink rosebud and took it inside the house.

"It's perfect," my wife said.

AUTHOR'S NOTE: *Greg Lopez, author of this column, was killed in an automobile accident in 1996.*
SOURCE: G. Lopez (1994, September 15). A rose for a daughter who won't grow up. *Rocky Mountain News,* p. 4A.

- Provide a concrete memento of the child's existence: a lock of hair, a footprint.
- Share details about the baby's length, weight, hair color.
- Provide information from the autopsy.
- Encourage participation in rituals (funeral or memorial service) which validate that a loss has occurred.

Although each of these strategies has been found to be helpful to many, parents should be given the choice as to what they prefer. Forced participation may cause psychological harm, and Leon (1992) warns practitioners that it is damaging to expect individuals to participate in "choreographed" rituals.

Leff (1987), who is herself a practicing physician, notes that professional caregivers can be of help to parents experiencing a pregnancy loss in the following ways:

- not abandoning the parents who are about to/have just lost their child;
- providing special areas within hospitals where women may deliver fetuses;
- acknowledging the mourning process and its individual variations;
- treating the dead fetus with respect; and

TABLE 4.2
Causes of Infant Death in the United States for 1980 and 1993

CAUSE OF DEATH	NUMBER	
	1980	1993
Total	45,526	33,466
Congenital anomalies	9,220	7,129
Sudden infant death syndrome	5,510	4,669
Respiratory distress syndrome	4,989	1,815
Disorders relating to short gestation and unspecified low birth weight	3,648	4,310
Newborn affected by maternal complications of pregnancy	1,572	1,343
Intrauterine hypoxia and birth asphyxia	1,497	549
Infections specific to the perinatal period	971	772
Accidents and adverse effects	1,166	898
Newborn affected by complications of placenta, cord, and membranes	985	994
Pneumonia and influenza	1,012	530
All other causes	14,956	10,457

SOURCE: U.S. National Center for Health Statistics (1994). *Vital Statistics of the United States,* annual, and *Monthly Vital Statistics Report;* and unpublished data.

- encouraging research on the unique needs of the father, the impact on the marital relationship, and effective interventions for alleviating guilt.

A perinatal death is unique in that it is in such contrast to the joy surrounding an expected birth. The anticipation of one of life's most profoundly happy events is shattered with little or no warning. Individuals who were involved in the positive anticipation withdraw due to the lack of insight or understanding about the resultant grief reaction or discomfort in knowing what to say or do. People who have not yet heard of the death write or call expecting good news, only to find the baby has died.

Sudden Infant Death Syndrome

One of the least understood causes of infant death in the United States is sudden infant death syndrome (SIDS). It is the second highest cause of death of infants between the ages of 1 week and 1 year; 90% of those who die are less than 6 months of age (Willinger, James, & Catz, 1991). Table 4.2 shows that 4,669 children under 1 year of age died of SIDS in 1993 in the United States. Because of the many unique issues faced by survivors, SIDS will be discussed in some detail. Infants, who seemingly are in good health, die suddenly and unexpectedly with little or no struggle. Typically, the infant has been put down to sleep; when the caregiver later checks on the baby, he or she has died. SIDS occurs in families from all racial, cultural, and socioeconomic backgrounds (McClain & Mandell, 1994).

Recent efforts to find the cause of SIDS have resulted in numerous theories; however, no clear-cut answer has yet been discovered. Some of the hypotheses focus on the following variables as either causes or correlates: cardiac imbalance, infection, electrolyte imbalance, allergies, DPT immunizations, abnormal maternal placenta, morphologic abnormalities, position for sleep, and respiratory difficulties (Guntheroth, 1995; Hunt, 1991; Schwartz, Southall, & Valdes-Dapena, 1988; Swoiskin, 1986).

Markusen, Owen, Fulton, and Bendiksen (1978) argue that grief due to SIDS is extremely difficult to resolve. DeFrain and Ernst (1978) collected questionnaire data from 32 parents whose infants died from SIDS. All these parents rated SIDS as the most severe crisis they had ever experienced and reported that it took approximately 16 months to regain the level of personal happiness experienced prior to their infant's death. They noted that it took a somewhat shorter time to return to a fairly smooth level of family functioning. Additional research has helped to articulate common manifestations of grief, including sleep disturbance, shock, disorientation, hostility, anger, guilt, anxiety, and preoccupation (Ostfeld, Ryan, Hiatt, & Hegyi, 1993; Zebal & Woolsey, 1984).

After a SIDS death, many factors contribute to the intensity of the parents' bereavement. Because the death is sudden and unexpected, the parents are unable psychologically to prepare for the loss (May & Breme, 1982). Because the cause of the death is unknown, many parents assume they were responsible and experience intense feelings of guilt. For example, parents often question whether their baby choked to death or suffocated and whether they could have somehow prevented the death. An autopsy often alleviates some of the guilt experienced by parents or blame placed on other caretakers. Although the autopsy does not identify the specific cause of death, it can prove the baby did not choke or suffocate. Sharing the autopsy report can serve as a valuable counseling tool (Kotch & Cohen, 1985).

Parents need support as they mourn the death of their infants. Unfortunately, in some circumstances, persons wrongly blame the parents for the death or even accuse them of child abuse (Chng, 1982). Others negate the loss with the recommendation that the couple try to have another baby as soon as possible. Fortunately, the National SIDS Foundation is involved in attempts to provide support to families dealing with the tragedy of their infants' deaths. The primary goals of the foundation include the following (Williamson, 1986):

- providing services to families and other caregivers;
- educating professionals and community members to better understand the sensitive issues related to SIDS;
- promoting major research efforts related to causation and, ultimately, prevention.

STRESSORS ON PARENTS OF DYING CHILDREN

Many parents of dying children must face a lingering illness and treatment regimen. This experience involves many psychological and physical stresses. Demands related to providing care to the sick child, in addition to other ongoing work and family responsibilities, often claim the majority of each day. Additionally, simply arranging for transportation to and from the hospital or medical center can be difficult (Lynn-McHale & Smith, 1991). Parents have less time to spend with their other children, who then may become hurt or angry and, as a result, add to the stress already being experienced. Diminished time to spend with one's spouse often weakens a familiar support system which, in turn, can exacerbate feelings of distress. Activities that once provided pleasure and relaxation are forgone in order to deal with the additional time constraints, such as traveling to and from the hospital and/or providing care.

Physical exhaustion is common as parents struggle to perform multiple roles, including parent of sick child, parent of healthy child(ren), spouse, worker, and housekeeper, among others. Although it is difficult, if not impossible, to surrender certain roles, parents do welcome short-term respite from particular tasks. Others can be particularly helpful by making specific offers of assistance (to cook a meal, clean house, baby-sit other children, or shop for groceries). Many parents note that they do prefer suggestions of specific ways to help in contrast to a more open-ended offer "If I can do anything, just let me know." This phraseology puts the burden on the parents to determine what needs to be done in relation to the other person's available resources, and, as a result, such offers of help often go unheeded.

Costs of medical treatments not covered by insurance add a great deal of financial stress to many families. Parents may have to work during a period when they want to spend increasing amounts of time with the child who is dying. They feel torn between their commitments and experience feelings of guilt coupled with intense frustration. Medical bills may escalate to a point where families feel their impact for years to come.

PARENTS' GRIEF AFTER DEATH OF A CHILD

Death of one's own child is a catastrophic loss that contradicts the natural order of life. Additionally, the child's death breaks one of the strongest bonds, that of parent and child. Parents may question their fundamental adequacy as adults, because they are so strongly socialized to protect their offspring. Klass (1988) believes that

> the death of a child creates two disequilibria. First, there is a disequilibrium between the self and the social world, for the death of a child radically changes the social environment in which the parent lives. Second, there is a disequilibrium in the inner life of the parent, for the child who died was part of the parent's self. (p. 18)

For years after the death, many parents still experience the pain of their loss and strive to deal with an "empty space" that results from the death (McClowry, Davies, May, Kulenkamp, & Martinson, 1987). Other researchers (Brabant, Forsyth, & McFarlain, 1994) found that parents continue to experience pain from their children's death but nonetheless often regard the deceased child as being "psychologically present." When asked the question "How many children do you have?" bereaved parents face a dilemma. Many bereaved parents share that the answer depends on who is asking. However, answers such as the following are typical:

- I can be open about it. I have three sons, but have lost two.
- We now have two girls, and we lost our five-year-old son three years ago. . . . (Brabant et al., 1994, pp. 200–201)

These responses illustrate the importance of the deceased child in the survivors' definition of family.

Activities that are common throughout various life stages will bring back memories, many painful, although the pain does diminish over time. One woman gives an example of her own mother's long-term reaction to the empty space in her life:

> It will never be the same. Even little things like getting a family portrait. Mother has never wanted to. We get family pictures at weddings but there is a sense still that it's not complete. Despite the fact that Tom, Jim, and I are married and have kids and different things going on, there's still a sense of not everybody being there. (McClowry, Davies, May, Kulenkamp, & Martinson, 1995, pp. 157–158)

Long-term effective coping is related to the level of family support, quality of the parents' marital relationship, effective coping of other family members, lack of additional concurrent stresses, and open communication among family members. As important as support is, parents often report that they get little or no assistance from others after the death of a child or that support is not sustained over a long enough time. Further, many extended family members, friends, and neighbors engage in a conspiracy of silence around the death. One mother shared:

> The neighbors never mention her name or anything; act like nothing happened. They want to talk about their children and all their grandchildren. At first, I wanted to punch them in the face or scratch their eyes out. (Brabant, Forsyth, & McFarlain, 1995, p. 73)

This mother goes on to say that she "feels hostile sometimes, but has learned to forgive . . . they can't know what they haven't experienced."

Bereaved parents often experience intense feelings of guilt. Miles and Demi (1984, 1994) discuss various types of guilt observed in their clinical patients. Although these various types of guilt reactions are quite common, they are not universal.

- *Death causation guilt* involves the belief that the child's death was some-how caused by the parent. Causality may be linked, in the parent's mind, to either acts of omission such as failure to notice early symptoms of the illness or acts of commission, such as giving the child permission to cross the street by himself or herself. These acts may or may not have actually contributed to the death.
- *Relationship guilt* is the sense that the parent has failed in his or her pre-scribed role. The role of parent is based on expectations that he or she will love and protect the child at all times. When a child dies, there are feelings of guilt that the child was not protected. Parents might feel guilty when they recall a past incident in which they became angry at their son or daughter.
- *Moral guilt* is the feeling that the child's death was punishment or retri-bution for some transgression of the parent. Moral guilt may be tied to experiences such as poor church attendance or dishonesty in business transactions.
- *Survival guilt* is the sense that death of one's child is a violation of the natural order of life. Parents are expected to die before their children; when this is not the case, they experience guilt.
- *Grief guilt* is the perceived failure of the survivor to experience the "ap-propriate" emotions or behaviors during their bereavement.
- *Recovery guilt* often occurs as parents begin to resolve their grief and once more begin to enjoy life. They feel guilty that, by not continuing to grieve, they are violating a societal standard and failing to care for their deceased child.

Rando (1983) investigated a variety of factors related to the outcome of grief in parents whose children had died from cancer. Her sample comprised 54 par-ents (27 married couples) whose children had died from 2 months to 3 years previously. Each parent was given a subsequent adjustment score that was ana-lyzed in relationship to a variety of factors, including length of illness, length of time since death, parents' anticipatory grief, parental participation during child's hospitalizations, parental evaluation of the child's treatment, and previous loss experience. Factors that were related to a more positive level of subsequent adjustment included a moderately long length of illness (6 to 18 months), the experience of anticipatory grief, a moderate level of participation in the child's care, and few previous losses.

Both mothers and fathers experience acute grief after the death of a child. Cook (1983) found that both parents were overwhelmed by the intensity of their feelings. Parents do, however, report somewhat different facets of grief. The fathers in Cook's study explained the loss as "something missing." One fa-ther remarked, "There's only three of us. It seems like the biggest problem is having the feeling that the family isn't complete any more. It seems like a void. There isn't enough activity" (p. 48). In contrast, mothers explained the loss in more personal terms and frequently linked the loss to a sense of loneliness, which was rarely described by fathers. Cook interpreted these differences in relation to the type of interaction each parent had previously with the child. Mothers typically described a closer relationship with the child, one that was central to the mother's existence. During their daily routine, they were constantly reminded that the child was no longer a part of their lives. Tasks such as setting one less place at the table for dinner elicited painful memories and evoked a continuing sense of loss.

The men in Cook's (1983) study believed more often than did the women the feeling that they were responsible for managing or controlling other family members' grief. They felt responsible for "lifting the family's spirits" (p. 51), particularly their wives'. Closely related was the feeling the men had that they should grieve in private. Keeping their grief private, however, often acted as a barrier to open communication with their wives.

Oftentimes men exhibit their grief through angry outbursts and irritability, frantic activity, and additional investment in work. These behaviors are sometimes used as avoidance techniques to protect the bereaved father from thinking about the loss. At some point, however, those who may have, at the outset, inhibited their grief must ultimately face it.

Schatz (1986) explains how socialization into the traditional male role in many cultures creates difficult challenges after the death of a child. A man is

- socialized to be strong and to control his emotions, yet we are unsure of the impact that this would have on men's successful grief work;
- taught to protect his family and possessions; however, he was unable to protect his child from death;
- expected to be the problem solver—the person who can fix what is broken but death cannot be avoided; it cannot be fixed;
- socialized to be the family provider, but his grief can impair his on-the-job functioning;
- taught to be self-sufficient, yet he needs others to support him during his grief;
- taught that if he works hard and acts responsibly he can control his own destiny; however, his life and that of his family seem to be out of control due to the death.

Men in our society may need to be given permission to grieve. Although they can be supportive to their families, they need to feel comfortable accepting support from others as well. Sometimes social support is not as readily available for men as it is for women, because many people assume that men are coping and, therefore, do not offer the needed assistance. One bereaved father shared "that it would really hurt him when they would ask 'How is (his wife) doing?' He wondered why they wouldn't include him in the grieving, but added, 'Of course guys can't grieve'" (Brabant et al., 1995, p. 76).

Many strategies can help parents eventually come to terms with the death of a child. Klass (1993) describes a number of ways in which bereaved parents may find solace, including identification of a linking object, drawing on memories that evolve over time, and engaging in religious devotion. A **linking object** is an object or a sensory experience that clearly reminds the parent that, although the child is physically dead, there is validation that the child had lived. This linking object might be a toy, a piece of clothing, or a powerful symbol. One mother's child had searched for sand dollars on the beach as he grew up and shared time with her. She recounts this story after his death:

> . . . I went to Padre Island and one lonely evening I walked the beach alone. . . . It was there I begged Him to show me a sign that E. lives—to "please send me a sand dollar." I knew that it was not the season for sand dollars. Even the local people had told me that they had not seen sand dollars since last summer. But I only wanted just one. . . . Watching the fading sunset and listening to the roar of the waves, darkness began to fall, so I turned to go back when there by my feet, the waves pushed up one lone sand dollar—a small but perfect sand dollar. . . . I cannot begin to tell you the feelings I had. (Klass, 1993, pp. 353–354)

A linking object can give parents the comfort and strength to continue their journey through grief by helping to create an inner representation of the child. Grieving parents also find comfort in their memories; these may be very painful at first in that they remind the bereaved of their loss. Ultimately, however, they bring to mind the fact that a life was lived and happier thoughts of time that was shared. Memories can also bind families and larger communities together, such as when they are shared with one another during funerals or anniversary rituals (Klass, 1993).

Another source of comfort to parents are religious beliefs. Solace derived from religious ties may or may not be based in a particular theological doctrine, although it certainly is for many. Parents' beliefs may provide comfort as they feel that they are cared for by God and that they will later be reunited with their child. For others, the religious base is derived from the parent's sense that the child is now united with a greater power.

GRANDPARENTS AS GRIEVERS

Although individuals usually become grandparents for the first time during middle age, grandparenting is a role that continues into the later years of life. Children and adolescents today are more likely to have grandparents who are living, as more Americans are surviving to reach advanced old age. Many grandparents have a special relationship with one or more of their grandchildren. A strong bond can be created without the friction that is frequently present between parents and children (Wilcoxon, 1986).

The grief experienced by grandparents is usually threefold, as they grieve for their beloved grandchild, for their own son or daughter, and for themselves. Grandparents are more often alone in their grief than any other group and frequently expect themselves to cope well so that they can be more helpful to their adult children and serve as a role model.

Gyulay (1975) describes parents of dying children as being surrounded by concentric circles of disbelief, with the most immediate circle being that of their own parents, the child's grandparents. In this study, it was found that grandparents tended to show more denial and tended to be less accepting of the diagnosis than parents. They are often frustrated that the child's parents may have waited a few days to even call them with the news of the diagnosis.

As the denial subsides, grandparents often feel anger and resentment. The anger can take many forms. Sometimes, grandparents feel angry toward the child's parents for not taking better care of their grandchild or for delaying in telling them news of the child's condition. Additionally, grandparents often feel anger toward God, and they frequently pray that their lives will be taken and the life of the child spared. As the illness progresses and the child's condition worsens, grandparents often become depressed and experience various facets of the normal grief experience.

Grandparents experience a range of emotions in addition to their grief. Although they usually want to help as much as possible, they may be unable to offer much assistance because of poor personal health or other factors such as lack of transportation, limited financial resources, and reduced physical capacities. This situation may be met with feelings of guilt and frustration. When they do offer advice, financial aid, and services such as baby-sitting, their offers are sometimes not accepted by their adult children for a variety of reasons. Some adult children may want to protect their parents from additional stress or see them as having few resources to give. Others may want to provide all the care to the young child themselves and fail to recognize the importance of grandparents' desire to share in that process.

Guilt may be felt by the grandparents for failing to notice the early symptoms of the illness in their grandchild. They assume that, with their greater life experience, they should have detected that something was wrong and done something about it. If allowed to provide care for the child, grandparents may be frightened by some of the child's unfamiliar symptoms and medical needs. Although many older people have cared for the sick and dying in their lifetimes, the context was very different in most cases. Hospitals and modern medicine may threaten their feelings of competency at a time when it is critical for them to show how deeply they care. As a result, they may feel an intense sense of failure as both parents and grandparents.

In some families, conflicts erupt between the elderly and their adult children. Old issues may resurface as a result of the stress family members are currently experiencing. The parents' management of the dying child may be questioned as well. Grandparents sometimes feel that the parents are letting the child do things that may be harmful. Adult children may find they need some distance from their older parents as they try to cope with the harsh reality they are confronting. It may be a particularly difficult situation when genetically transmitted diseases (such as Tay-Sachs) are involved. Members of the older generation may be unable to acknowledge their guilt over the genetic heritage tied to the illness.

SUMMARY

The death of a family member constitutes a family crisis as well as an individual crisis. Family systems react to death in ways that reflect their various characteristics (such as level of openness or existence of particular rules). The timing of the death in the family life cycle also affects the adjustment of the system. Crisis theory provides insight into the family's ability to adapt to the death of one of its members. Concurrent stressors, resources, and family perception of the death all have an impact on recovery patterns. Many families report positive outcomes in that members feel closer to one another after struggling to deal with a shared crisis. In other situations, however, family members indicate that the death precipitated a number of negative outcomes due to the dissynchrony of individuals' grief experiences or discrepant coping styles. As a result, many bereaved may experience a significant level of stress in their surviving relationships.

The process of adjusting involves many important tasks, such as acknowledging the death, allowing mourning to occur, relinquishing the memory of the deceased, and realigning both intrafamilial and extrafamilial roles. To provide an example of the impact of death on the family system and surviving relationships, discussion was included about stresses on parents caring for a dying child and their subsequent grief reactions. Further, it is important to note that the death of a family member in one generation may have an impact on persons for many generations to come.

Personal Account

Pam Landon's son and daughter-in-law were killed in a fire in their apartment building. Her essay entitled "The Longest Day" recounts activities and feelings of that tragic day as well as the impact that the deaths had on the family system that survived.

The Longest Day
Pam Landon

The call. The query. The downy cop.
The wait till those remaining
close in to shield each other's pain.
The helpless disbelief, then certainty
in the charred halls, and the small space

beside the window; a last safety sought.
Time stretched, collapsed and meaningless.
The act of courage, manhood proved.
An absolution in the sunny grove.

What we did not know then and do now know is that longest day in 1983, on which our son Kevin died at age 24, is a day that has no end.

No death of a family member or intimate other ends, even to the next generation, while memory lives. I still experience my mother's forever-painful story of dreaming nightly for years of vainly trying to touch a beloved sister-in-law who died on the day of my birth. My parents died 30 years ago. Often to this day, when I have a marvelously ridiculous encounter or experience a special moment, I think, "I've got to tell Mother about that." Six months after my parents' death, my Aunt Peg wrote me and said what I've found to be true. She said, "Time does not heal; what times does is allow the good memories to come true."

The death of one's child, or one's sibling, at a young age multiplies this ongoing reality because, I think, it is time-warped and not in the natural progression of expectation. You expect to bury your parents and even your spouse, but not your child or your childhood companion. It is shocking. It is not to be believed. It is not expected. You are not prepared, unless, perhaps in wartime or after a long illness. You are not ready. It is not fair. It should have been one of us, not him. It is out of season, and it remains raw and shocking and, most of all, present. Good memories do start to surface, and, after some time elapses, it is not always in the forefront of consciousness. But it is ever present and never loses the raw waves of pain. At least, that is so for his father and me to this present time.

If you live in our area, you may remember the story, which was well covered by the press. It is not uncommon, particularly in major cities. An old house, made over into apartments for the non-Yuppie young and others with either marginal incomes or preference for living "downtown," goes up in flames. It goes up in flames as a result of dried-out wallpaper and inadequate fire systems. It goes up in flames as a result of a drunken party and a small fire started in a wastebasket and human error. You may have seen pictures of the bodies of our son and his wife carried out on stretchers on the 5 o'clock news. We did. We are grateful that they were overcome by smoke and never felt the burning. The smell of the burned-out apartment remains forever in the senses; in the heart, the sorrowful pride for his courage shown in protecting his wife with his body till his death.

It is meaningful to have this opportunity, offered by good colleagues, to think about what this kind of loss meant to our family then, and what it means now, individually and collectively. It was also good to talk with each member about their reactions and thoughts and feelings then and now in a quiet and reflective way, instead of in the passing comments that we seem to have developed over time. Some issues seem to have become clearer to me regarding both our own individual and collective experiences, and how these may relate to other families. This is one reason for the writing. It may repay in part the many kinds of help that others gave to us.

What help do I remember?

The importance of information given. I will never forget Joe, the fire investigator who gave several hours of his time to tell us just what had and had not happened, or the neighbors who told us all they knew of his last hours; I also will never forget, at the opposite end, the official of the well-known disaster program, who when I called at 6:00 in the morning told me I would have to wait until the office opened at 8:30 to find out whether our child was living or dead.

The difference that caring makes: the caring of each of us for each other; of the tears in the eyes of the young policeman who came to the door to tell me what I already knew; of the colleague who became a friend, who came over while I was still in the shower and just "hung out" until my family could get home; of the people who worked with our son and invited us to a restaurant to buy us coffee and tell us what he had meant in their lives; of all the people who came, even out of sickbeds, to the memorial service; of all those who wrote, sent cards, gave contributions. For 2 or 3 weeks, the afternoon mail was a blood transfusion. I used to not go to funerals, not write because I didn't know what to say, not "hang out" because I might be excess baggage. No more. I know what it means. And I will err on the side of presence over absence.

The centrality of sharing: again each of us with each other; the shared experience of the two families which continues, in attenuated form, today; the young son of that family who carefully went through all the burned belongings so we would not have to; the unpressuring and continuing, to the present, offer of Compassionate Friends, the self-help group for parents who have lost children, for the knowledge of whose availability we were grateful, although we did not participate; the others who also lost children and told us how it has been for them; and those who continue to care, knowing there is no set time period for grieving. I wrote to my sister the next April:

> I think the shock and the kind of support you initially get hold you together for
> a while, and then at the time the world expects you to start getting it together
> is when you internally fall apart. At least this seemed so for me. Just when I
> think I'm "on top of it," the waves wash over.

The sharing helps. People experience their humanity in conjunction with other people. Communicating with those who have stood where we stand is for most a major experience in being heard and being understood.

However, if we define our own experience as being the same as that of another, we do individuality of person and family an injustice. Therefore, I'll talk about us as a family: what each person felt individually then and now, how each saw the family then and now, and our speculations as to the why of these feelings and perceptions. I'll offer as thoughts and speculations some reactions I believe may be universal to such an experience and some concepts about how families work that make the universal experience of the death of son and sibling idiosyncratically each family's own.

Our family nucleus is my husband, myself, our oldest son, who was 31 at the time of the death, and a daughter who was 22. Both sets of grandparents had long since died. I was the youngest of a large and very extended family. My husband was the only child of a family no longer in existence. He had two daughters by a previous marriage, one of whom had died 2 years earlier.

At the time of the death, our oldest son had recently remarried and, shortly before the longest day, had returned with his new wife, and we had held the first total family reunion in several years. That reunion was a wonderful and comforting happenstance. I wonder if it was happenstance. I also wonder if the wonderful weekend his father and I had spent with Kevin and his wife in the high country a few weeks before, where much had been talked out and a closer relationship had been established, was also happenstance, or preparation.

Our daughter had come West from Connecticut where she was living with my aunt and going to college. She was driving back East in the very early morning and heard of the fire on the radio and woke me with her phone call. She had heard of a fire in a downtown location and that two people had died. She, not knowing, was sure it was her brother and his wife. I, not knowing, was also sure. His older brother remembers his first reaction as one of "horror, numbness, and inevitability." This reaction I believe must be universal, except where one has a warning, such as after a long illness. Each of us remembers the initial reaction of horror but not of disbelief; in fact, as his father put it, there was a sense of "some way of forcing his own disaster." This may well have been an idiosyncratic factor of our particular family. This son had been an individual with a number of handicapping conditions—physical, intellectual, and emotional—and individually and as a family we had experienced a number of crises centered on him as he grew up. The prescience of disaster may well have been an outcome of this background.

Thus, the nature of the child who is gone is one of the factors that makes each experience different. The fact that our son had overcome multiple difficulties and had succeeded in living independently, completing school, working, and starting his own family and that this had taken a long time and a lot of concentration had different meanings for family members. For his sister, it came as no particular surprise because she had "always considered him her equal and had resented the fact that he got the most attention." For his father, the reaction was not only one of disbelief but also one of anger at the death that cut him off from enjoying his troubled son's coming of age and realizing his potential, anger that this son "was permitted to die as contrasted to someone else. I would much rather it had been me." For his older brother, who had understood and accepted an ongoing responsibility in necessary areas as part of his own future, this death came in sadness but also as a lifting of a burden. "I wish I still had that burden." For me, the loss was heightened by the years of intensive investment, fears, frustrations, and successes.

The nature of immediate and ongoing sorrow was experienced very differently. As his sister said, "What could you expect, we always have to deal with things each in our own way." For his father then and now, "The loss is horrendous. I was devastated. The pain is as sharp as it ever was, seeing a picture, hearing a song, being in a place that has him in it." His sister still waits for him to call with a question for her to answer. "Although our lives were very different, he was the person who shared my childhood and knew me in a way no one ever will. There is a forever void." For his brother, "I can't really talk about the then. Too much remembered pain. The now is remote, pops up at bizarre moments on a quiet evening. Not sure of where or when it will end, but it had to be." For me, the sorrow was all-consuming then, a part of daily living now.

Possibly because of his centrality, guilt did not and does not appear to be a central issue for our particular family. His sister said: "Mostly it was scary. Not much guilt. We fought the last time we were together, but that was normal." His brother expresses more. "I felt guilt for not being there as often as I could have been, not being as much as I should have been." I do not see that as reality. His father does not speak of guilt. And mine are small ones—the fact that the day before he died, I had thought of stopping in to see them and did not because I was running late, and I would call them that evening and I did not. Small regrets, not big guilts. I think the feeling is sadness and ambivalence, not guilt.

All of us were impacted almost immediately by a sense of instantaneous change in the family. Systems theory would say, of course! As his father put it, "His disability tended to pull the family together in our concern for him; everyone shared in the knowledge and the responsibility." His sister said that he had been the "central one—the child still sort of at home, which left us free to do our own thing. He was the force that connected us all and he was gone." Initially, everyone perceived a closeness never experienced before. His father said, "No one really believed a sibling could die." His brother said, "His death forced his sister and me to grow up. . . . Death is a hefty dose of reality, and his death gave all of us a sense of mortality for each of us." His sister talked about that a lot. We all felt the need to communicate a lot more frequently. Both his siblings and I dreamed a lot about him for months. I still do; I don't know whether they do. I worried much more if I had not heard from everybody in a month. I was afraid to be alone, afraid something else would happen. In another part of me, I, like his brother, experienced some relief. We did not have to worry any more. He was all right. We were the ones that were hurting. We found comfort in different people at the time: his sister with an old and valued family friend, my husband with his new daughter-in-law. We are gentler and kinder with each other, and permanently both closer and freer.

Over time, roles have changed. His sister feels more important and more focused on as the only one not married. Has she taken his place as the central force? For his father, the death "clarified relationships with the other children and gave a better understanding of the family unit. Prior to that my understanding of family was intellectual, not emotional, because I never had a family." Our daughter corroborates this and says that he has grown more paternal, and we have become more important to him. For his brother, it has permitted completion of his emancipation and given him permission to concentrate on his own new family, himself and his career, and the birth of his own child. He feels a bit guilty about the relief. So do I.

Over time we have moved from the need for "circling the wagons." His sister said that we have fractured a bit, so that we can deal with his death and our lives each in our own way. "What do you expect, it's the way we always do." His father sees the family as less of a unit than when he was alive and as having permission to make changes and develop in a more normal manner. He predicts that it will pull back more closely in another 10 years when we all have more time and that this is the time to catch up with individual lives on a different level. I sense this, too, and am struggling to adjust to the sense that I am really older. Adjust, yes; accept, I doubt it, anymore than I can truly accept his death. It is as unacceptable as death out of its time is unacceptable. His father, after his initial anger at "being cheated out of seeing him develop and use some of the things I'd been able to give him," is more sanguine than I, for he asks, "Who am I to fight the Higher Power? Apparently it was in His scheme of things that he should die rather than I at this time." His sister talks of his death as almost something animate. "I hate it. I don't understand it. It leaves me with a huge question to which the only answer I have is that fate meant it to be for whatever reason." His brother does not believe there was any reason. I wait to learn it as I have other things over time. I think another universal variable affecting our experience is the nature of our individual spiritual belief systems.

A final factor, in addition to the stage of familial development when the death occurs, that influences and individualizes the experience could be entitled the family rules or messages, or "The Way We See Things." The centrality of this really came home to me in our discussions, along with its intergenerational nature, which I had never seen before. This theme came through from everybody. My husband said: "We had encouraged their disengagement and underwritten their right and necessity of finding their own lives." His sister said: "You taught us to do our thing and lead our own lives." His brother said: "You not only told us to do our thing; you showed us. Mom, you traveled two thousand miles from your family to do your own thing, and you showed us that this was okay." I quietly remember that my husband was the first of his family to leave northern New York, my father the first to come East, and my mother the only child to leave Waterbury for New York City.

There may be a number of other essential elements that make such experiences both the same and different for families. I am left to wonder if our particular family is an essentially disengaged or enmeshed family, or a good bit of both, which I suppose most families are. You who read this are inevitably much better evaluators of that than we who live it. We are not and will never be the same since the death. I think we've grown; whoever said growth occurs without pain? I look at pictures of our family together and separate, laughing, formal, climbing trees, acting as "the littlest angel," and now in graduation garb and holding the next generation. I feel as I do so often the presence of the child who has gone ahead. Perhaps this may have some use. As I look at the picture of the sunlit grove with the two intertwined birches, where our family said our last good-bye to him, I think of the poem the young brother in the other family tucked in my pocket that late afternoon, which perhaps is the right ending for now.

> The Lord walketh
> by my side
> Therefore I am
> Not Alone.
> My Loved Ones lost
> Walketh with the Lord.
> Therefore I am
> Not alone.
> As I walk
> I question not.
> I only live and
> Learn a lot.
> Thanks be to
> My Lord God of Wisdom.

This was the finest of gifts to give. He believed. I also may. Someday.

QUESTIONS AND ACTIVITIES

1. "The Longest Day" describes various family members' reactions to the death of an individual who was killed—a son, a brother. Reactions varied from person to person. Have you seen (or would you expect to see) such variation of grief reactions in your own family? Would your family be apt to have a "dissynchrony of reactions" or utilize "discrepant coping styles"? Would you expect a death of a family member to draw individuals in your family closer together or force them apart? What was the outcome in the Landon family after Kevin's death?

2. Recall the death of a family member and the resulting grief reactions. (If you have not had such a loss, imagine yourself in that situation.) What aspect was the most painful as your family came to terms with the death? What were the secondary losses triggered by the loss? Did relationships among family members change after the death? In positive ways? In negative ways? What was most helpful to your family as you dealt with your loss? What was least helpful?

3. Imagine that someone in your family has died. What roles would need to be reassigned? How would that reassignment most likely take place? Who would be most apt to take on those new roles?

4. Think of someone you know who may have lost a child to death. Go to the public library or local bookstore and review books that focus on the death of a child. Are there any that you feel would have fit that particular situation and would have provided comfort to the parents? Discuss your selections and your reasons for choosing them.

GLOSSARY

Achieved roles: roles acquired by the efforts and skill of the individual.

Alliance: two individuals joining together because of common interests or goals, such as within a family system.

Ascribed roles: roles assigned on the basis of some characteristic over which the person has no control (for example, gender or age).

Bonadaptation: the outcome of a family crisis that results in enhancement of development in individual members and the enhancement of the family as a unit.

Boundaries: abstract dividers experienced between or among systems and subsystems that determine participation in them. Distinct boundaries can serve to define, protect, and enhance the integrity of individuals, subsystems, and families. Boundaries can change over time and with situations. The extent of this change will be affected by characteristics of the boundaries (rigid, flexible, diffuse) in each family.

Closed family systems: families that are self-contained and organized to preserve the status quo and resist change.

Coalition: when two people in a triad join to counteract the power of the third person in an effort to keep the system in balance. For example, if one parent is overpowering, the other parent may form a coalition with a child to balance that power.

Crisis: a life event or occurrence that affects an individual or family and produces, or has the opportunity to produce, change. A crisis produces temporary disequilibrium, resulting in varying degrees of disruption, disorganization, or incapacity. The outcome of a crisis may be either positive or negative.

Discrepant coping styles: differences in the ways that family members cope with a loss.

Disequilibrium: a state of imbalance in a system.

Dissynchrony (or asymmetry) of grief: differences between individuals in their grief experience related to a particular loss and the time needed to resolve the loss.

Enmeshed families: families in which family members have little individual autonomy or differentiation due to diffuse boundaries between individuals and between subsystems.

Expressive tasks: activities that have emotional and social functions and facilitate positive development and interaction among family members.

Family adaptation: ability of the family and each of its members to change their response to each other and to the outside would as situations demand.

Family integration: ability of family members to work together to assist in achieving both group and individual goals and in maintaining family equilibrium.

Family involvement: commitment that members make to the family and their participation in family life.

Family myths: beliefs that are accepted and adhered to by family members that defend against disturbances or changes in existing family relationships.

Homeostasis: a steady state of dynamic equilibrium or balance.

Incremental grief: the additive factor of grief due to multiple related losses.

Individuate: to move toward more autonomous functioning as a part of normal individual development.

Instrumental tasks: activities that contribute to the effective day-to-day functioning of the family.

Linking object: an object or a sensory experience that clearly reminds the bereaved that the deceased loved one had lived.

Maladaptation: the outcome of a family crisis that results in curtailment of individual and family development.

Miscarriage: unwillful termination of a pregnancy prior to the point of viability.

Newborn death: death that takes place within a few hours or days after birth.

Open family systems: families that are open to new information and exchange from the internal and external environment and are, thus, more susceptible to change.

Perinatal death: term referring collectively to miscarriages, stillbirths, and those deaths taking place within a few days after birth.

Pile-up: the accumulation of normative and nonnormative stressors and intrafamily strains.

Postvention: assistance offered to survivors following a death.

Regenerative power: the family's ability to recover from a crisis.

Roles: expected behavior of family members.

Role strain: strain that occurs when a family member assumes too many roles.

Rules: shared norms and values that govern repetitious patterns of family functioning.

Secondary grief: grief associated with a secondary loss (such as change in a predeath relationship with another survivor).

Secondary loss: a loss (such as change in a predeath relationship with another survivor) that is the consequence of a death (primary loss).

Shadow grief: after a death, sense of loss that lasts forever.

Social support: individuals, groups, or institutions that provide assistance of varying degrees and forms to help individuals and families cope with stressful situations.

Stillbirth: a fetal death taking place after the 28th week of prenatal development.

Stressor event: a life event or occurrence that affects the family unit and produces, or has the opportunity to produce, change in the family system.

Subsystems: basic structural units of the family system. These smaller units can be determined by variables such as relationship, generation, sex, age, or function.

Systems theory: a framework for studying a group of related elements that interact as a whole entity.

SUGGESTED READINGS

Finkbeiner, A. K. (1996). *After the death of a child: Living with loss through the years.* New York: Free Press.

The author synthesizes information from the professional literature focusing on grief with the interviews she did of parents who had lost their children to death. She examines the effects of the death on the external world—the marriage relationship, other children, friends, and relatives. She also examines the impact on the internal world of feelings, a sense of meaning, strategies for continuing the connection to the child who died. Finkbeiner elucidates her findings by sharing various case studies.

Klass, D. (1988). *Parental grief: Solace and resolution.* New York: Springer.

This book focuses on the dynamics of parental bereavement and discusses a variety of pertinent topics. Chapters include discussions of the following: an overview of parental grief; striving for social and psychic equilibrium; Compassionate Friends support group; and parents of murdered children.

McGoldrick, M., Giordano, J., & Pearce, J. (1996). *Ethnicity and family therapy* (2nd ed.). New York: Guilford.

This book provides insights about families of various ethnic backgrounds. Although the chapters include many generalizations, the authors give appropriate cautions against making stereotypes or focusing exclusively on differences rather than examining the many similarities among families.

Shapiro, E. R. (1994). *Grief as a family process: A developmental approach to clinical practice.* New York: Guilford.

Dr. Shapiro uses a variety of case examples to help the reader explore a variety of themes, including individual grief in a systemic context; grieving families and their shared development; cultural and social factors in family bereavement; and family development and grief therapy.

RESOURCES

The Compassionate Friends
P.O. Box 3696
Oakbrook, IL 60522
(630) 990-0010

Bereavement Services (an international perinatal bereavement program)
Gunderson Lutheran Medical Center
1910 South Avenue
LaCrosse, WI 54601
(608) 791-4747 or 1-800-362-9567 Ext. 4747

REFERENCES

Aldous, J. (1978). *Family careers: Developmental change in families.* New York: Wiley.

Borg, S., & Lasker, J. (1981). *When pregnancy fails: Families coping with miscarriage, stillbirth, and infant death.* Boston: Beacon Press.

Bowen, M. (1976). Family reaction to death. In P. J. Guerin, Jr. (Ed.), *Family therapy: Theory and practice* (pp. 335–348). New York: Gardner Press.

Brabant, S., Forsyth, C., & McFarlain, G. (1994). Defining the family after the death of a child. *Death Studies, 18,* 197–206.

Brabant, S., Forsyth, C., & McFarlain, G. (1995). Life after the death of a child: Initial and long-term support from others. *Omega, 31*(1), 67–85.

Carter, E. A., & McGoldrick, M. (1989). *The changing family life cycle: A framework for family therapy* (2nd ed.). Boston: Allyn and Bacon.

Chng, C. L. (1982). Sudden infant death syndrome: An inexplicable tragedy for the family. *Family Perspective, 16*(3), 123-128.

Cook, A. S. (1994). Integrating family therapy into grief therapy. *Family Therapy News, 25*(2), 1, 16.

Cook, A. S., & Dworkin, D. S. (1992). *Helping the bereaved: Therapeutic interventions for children, adolescents, and adults.* New York: Basic Books.

Cook, J. A. (1983). A death in the family: Parental bereavement in the first year. *Suicide and Life-Threatening Behavior, 13*(1), 42-61.

Covington, S. N., & Theut, S. K. (1993). Reactions to perinatal loss: A qualitative analysis of the national maternal and infant health survey. *American Journal of Orthopsychiatry, 63*(2), 215-222.

DeFrain, J. D., & Ernst, L. (1978). The psychological effects of sudden infant death syndrome on surviving family members. *Journal of Family Practice, 6*(5), 985-989.

Detmer, C. M., & Lamberti, J. W. (1991). Family grief. *Death Studies, 15,* 363-374.

DeVries, R., Lana, R. D., & Falck, V. T. (1994). Parental bereavement over the life course: A theoretical intersection and empirical review. *Omega, 29*(1), 47-69.

Dyregrov, A., & Matthiesen, S. B. (1987). Similarities and differences in mothers' and fathers' grief following the death of an infant. *Scandinavian Journal of Psychology, 28,* 1-15.

Fish, W. C. (1986). Differences of grief intensity in bereaved parents. In T. A. Rando (Ed.), *Parental loss of a child* (pp. 415-429). Champaign, IL: Research Press.

Fogel, C. I. (1981). Abortion. In C. I. Fogel & N. F. Woods (Eds.), *Health care of women: A nursing perspective* (pp. 524-538). St. Louis, MO: Mosby.

Gilbert, K. R. (1989). Interactive grief and coping in the marital dyad. *Death Studies, 13,* 605-626.

Gilbert, K. R. (1996). "We've had the same loss, why don't we have the same grief?" Loss and differential grief in families. *Death Studies, 20*(3), 269-283.

Gilbert, K. R., & Smart, L. S. (1992). *Coping with infant or fetal loss: The couple's healing process.* New York: Bruner/Mazel.

Glasser, P. H., & Glasser, L. N. (Eds.). (1970). *Families in crisis.* New York: Harper & Row.

Gordon, A. K. (1986). The tattered cloak of immortality. In C. A. Corr & J. N. McNeil (Eds.), *Adolescence and death* (pp. 16-31). New York: Springer.

Grebstein, L. C. (1986). Family therapy after a child's death. In T. A. Rando (Ed.), *Parental loss of a child* (pp. 429-449). Champaign, IL: Research Press.

Guntheroth, W. G. (1995). *Crib death: The sudden infant death syndrome* (3rd ed.). Armonk, NY: Futura.

Gyulay, J. E. (1975). The forgotten grievers. *American Journal of Nursing, 75,* 1476-1479.

Hall, R. C., Beresford, T. P., & Quinones, J. E. (1987). Grief following spontaneous abortion. *Psychiatric Clinics of North America, 10,* 405-420.

Harris, B. G. (1986). Induced abortion. In T. Rando (Ed.), *Parental loss of a child* (pp. 241-256). Champaign, IL: Research Press.

Hill, R. (1949). *Families under stress.* New York: Harper & Row.

Holmes, T. H., & Rahe, R. (1967). Social readjustment rating scale. *Journal of Psychosomatic Research, 11,* 213-218.

Hopmeyer, E., & Werk, A. (1994). A comparative study of family bereavement groups. *Death Studies, 18,* 243-256.

Hughes, C. B., & Page-Lieberman, J. (1989). Fathers experiencing a perinatal loss. *Death Studies, 13,* 537-556.

Hughes, P. M., & Lieberman, S. (1990). Troubled parents: Vulnerability and stress in childhood cancer. *British Journal of Medical Psychology, 63,* 53-64.

Hunt, C. E. (1991). Sudden infant death syndrome: The neurobehavioral perspective. *Journal of Applied Developmental Psychology, 12*(2), 185-188.

Hutchins, S. H. (1986). Stillbirth. In T. Rando (Ed.) *Parental loss of a child* (pp. 129-144). Champaign, IL: Research Press.

Janssen, H. J., Cuisinier, M. C., & Hoogduin, K. A. (1996). A critical review of the concept of pathological grief following pregnancy loss. *Omega, 33*(1), 21-42.

Kalnins, T., Churchill, M. P., & Terry, G. (1980). Concurrent stresses in families with a leukemic child. *Journal of Pediatric Psychology, 5*(1), 81-92.

Kaplan, D., Grobstein, R., & Smith, A. (1976). Predicting the impact of severe illness in families. *Health and Social Work, 1*(3), 71-82.

Kennell, J., Slyter, H., & Klaus, M. (1970). The mourning response of parents to the death of a newborn infant. *New England Journal of Medicine, 283,* 344-349.

Kesselman, I. (1990). Grief and loss: Issues for abortion. *Omega, 21,* 241-247.

Klass, D. (1986). Marriage and divorce among bereaved parents in a self-help group. *Omega, 17*(3), 237-249.

Klass, D. (1988). Achieving social equilibrium. In D. Klass (Ed.), *Parental grief: Solace and resolution.* New York: Springer.

Klass, D. (1993). Solace and immortality: Bereaved parents' continuing bond with their children. *Death Studies, 17,* 343-368.

Koch, A. (1985). "If only it could be me": The families of pediatric cancer patients. *Family Relations, 34*(1), 63-70.

Kotch, J., & Cohen, S. (1985). SIDS counselor's report of own and parents' reactions to reviewing the autopsy report. *Omega, 16*(2), 129-139.

Lang, A., Gottlieb, L. N., Amsel, R. (1996). Predictors of husbands' and wives' grief reactions following infant death: The role of marital intimacy. *Death Studies, 20*(1), 33-57.

Lasker, J. N., & Toedter, L. J. (1991). Acute versus chronic grief: The case of pregnancy loss. *American Journal of Orthopsychiatry, 6*(4), 510-522.

Leff, P. (1987). Here I am, Ma: The emotional impact of pregnancy loss on parents and health-care professionals. *Family Systems Medicine, 5*(1), 105-114.

Leon, I. G. (1992). Perinatal loss: Choreographing grief on the obstetric unit. *American Journal of Orthopsychiatry, 62*(1), 7-8.

Lesar, S., Gerber, M. M., & Semmel, M. I. (1996). HIV infection in children: Family stress, social support and adaptation. *Exceptional Children, 62*(3), 224-236.

Lietar, E. F. (1986). Miscarriage. In T. Rando (Ed.), *Parental loss of a child* (pp. 121-128). Champaign, IL: Research Press.

Lynn-McHale, D. J., & Smith, A. (1991). Comprehensive assessment of families of the critically ill. *Critical Care Nurse, 2*(2), 195-209.

Markusen, E., Owen, G., Fulton, R., & Bendiksen, R. (1978). SIDS: The survivor as victim. *Omega, 8*(4), 277-283.

May, H. J., & Breme, E. J. (1982). SIDS family adjustment to sudden infant death syndrome. *Omega, 13*(1), 59-74.

Mayes, A., & Spiegel, L. (1992). A parental support group in a Pediatric AIDS clinic: Its usefulness and limitations. *Health and Social Work, 17*(3), 183-191.

McClain, M., & Mandell, F. (1994). Sudden infant death syndrome: The nurse counselor's response to bereavement counseling. *Journal of Community Health Nursing, 11*(3) 177–186.

McClowry, S. G., Davies, E. B., May, K. A., Kulenkamp, E. J., & Martinson, I. M. (1987). The empty space phenomenon: The process of grief in the bereaved family. *Death Studies, 11*(5), 361–374.

McClowry, S. G., Davies, E. B., May, K. A., Kulenkamp, E. J., & Martinson, I. M. (1995). In K. Doka (Ed.), *Children mourning: Mourning children* (pp. 149–162). Washington, DC: Hospice Foundation of America.

McCubbin, H., & Patterson, J. (1983a). The family stress process: The double ABCX model of adjustment and adaptation. In H. McCubbin, M. Sussman, & J. Patterson (Eds.), *Social stress and the family: Advances and developments in family stress theory and research* (pp. 7–37). New York: Haworth.

McCubbin, H. I., & Patterson, J. M. (1983b). Family transitions: Adaptation to stress. In H. I. McCubbin & C. R. Figley (Eds.), *Stress and the family: Coping with normative transitions* (Vol. 1; pp. 5–25). New York: Brunner/Mazel.

Miles, A. S., & Demi, M. S. (1984). Toward the development of a theory of bereavement guilt. *Omega, 14,* 299–314.

Miles, A. S., & Demi, M. S. (1994). Bereavement guilt: A conceptual model with applications. In I. Corless, B. Germino, and M. Pittman (Eds.), *Dying, death, and bereavement: Theoretical perspectives and other ways of knowing* (pp. 171–188). Boston: Jones and Bartlett.

Montgomery, R., Gonyea, J., & Hooyman, N. (1985). Caregiving and the experience of subjective and objective burden. *Family Relations, 34*(1), 19–26.

Moos, N. L. (1995). An integrative model of grief. *Death Studies, 19,* 337–364.

Oltjenbruns, K. A. (1996). Death of a friend during adolescence: Issue and impacts. In C. Corr & D. Balk (Eds.), *Handbook of adolescent death and bereavement* (pp. 197–215). New York: Springer.

Ostfeld, B. M., Ryan, T., Hiatt, M., & Hegyi, T. (1993). Maternal grief after sudden death syndrome. *Developmental and Behavioral Pediatrics, 14*(3), 156–162.

Palmer, C. E., & Noble, D. (1986). Premature death: Dilemmas of infant mortality. *Social Casework, 67*(6), 332–339.

Parry, J. K., & Thornwall, J. (1992). Death of a father. *Death Studies, 16,* 173–181.

Patterson, J. M., & McCubbin, H. I. (1983). Chronic illness: Family stress and coping. In C. R. Figley & H. I. McCubbin (Eds.), *Stress and the family: Coping with catastrophe* (Vol. 2; pp. 21–36). New York: Brunner/Mazel.

Peppers, L. (1987). Grief and elective abortion: Breaking the emotional bond. *Omega, 18*(1), 1–12.

Peppers, L., & Knapp, R. J. (1980). Maternal reactions to involuntary fetal/infant death. *Psychiatry, 43,* 155–159.

Pratt, C., Schmal, V., Wright, S., & Cleland, M. (1985). Burden and coping strategies of caregivers to Alzheimer's patients. *Family Relations, 34*(1), 27–33.

Rando, T. A. (1983). An investigation of grief and adaptation in parents whose children have died from cancer. *Journal of Pediatric Psychology, 8,* 3–20.

Rando, T. A. (1984). *Grief, dying, and death: Clinical interventions for caregivers.* Champaign, IL: Research Press.

Reinharz, S. (1988). What's missing in miscarriage? *Journal of Community Psychology, 16*(1), 84–103.

Rolland, J. S. (1987). Chronic illness and the life cycle: A conceptual framework. *Family Process, 26*(20), 203-221.

Rolland, J. S. (1994). In sickness and in health: The impact of illness on couples' relationships. *Journal of Marital and Family Therapy, 20*(4), 327-347.

Rosen, E. J. (1990). *Families facing death: Family dynamics of terminal illness.* New York: Lexington Books.

Rosenblatt, P. (1996). Grief that does not end. In D. Klass, P. Silverman, & S. Nickman (Eds.), *Continuing bonds: New understanding of grief* (pp. 45-58). Washington, DC: Taylor & Francis.

Schatz, B. D. (1986). Grief of mothers. In T. A. Rando (Ed.), *Parental loss of a child* (pp. 303-314). Champaign, IL: Research Press.

Schilling, R. F., Gilchrist, L., & Schinke, S. P. (1985). Coping and social support in families of developmentally disabled children. *Family Relations, 33*(1), 47-54.

Schwab, R. (1992). Effects of a child's death on the marital relationship: A preliminary study. *Death Studies, 16,* 141-154.

Schwab, R. (1995). Bereaved parents and support group participation. *Omega, 32*(1), 49-61.

Schwab, R. (1996). Gender differences in parental grief. *Death Studies, 20*(2), 103-113.

Schwartz, P. J., Southall, D. P., Valdes-Dapena, M. (1988). *The sudden infant death syndrome: Cardiac and respiratory mechanisms and interventions.* New York: New York Academy of Sciences.

Shapiro, E. R. (1994). *Grief as a family process: A developmental approach to clinical practice.* New York: Guilford.

Shaw, C. T. (1983). Grief over fetal loss. *Family Practice Recertification, 5,* 129-145.

Sieburg, E. (1985). *Family communication: An integrated systems approach.* New York: Gardner Press.

Silverman, P. R., Weiner, A., & Ad, N. (1995). Parent-child communication in bereaved Israeli families. *Omega, 31*(4), 275-293.

Stephenson, J. S. (1985). *Death, grief, and mourning: Individual and social realities.* New York: Free Press.

Stinnett, N., Knorr, B., DeFrain, J., & Rowe, G. (1981). How strong families cope with crisis. *Family Perspective, 15*(4), 159-166.

Swoiskin, S. (1986). Sudden infant death: Nursing care for the survivors. *Journal of Pediatric Nursing, 1*(1), 33-39.

Thomas, V., & Striegel, P. (1995). Stress and grief of a perinatal loss: Integrating qualitative and quantitative methods. *Omega, 30*(4), 299-311.

Venters, M. (1981). Familial coping with chronic and severe childhood illness: The case of cystic fibrosis. *Social Science & Medicine, 15,* 289-297.

Vess, J. S., Moreland, J. R., & Schwebel, A. I. (1985a). An empirical assessment of the effects of cancer on family role functioning. *Journal of Psychosocial Oncology, 3*(1), 1-17.

Vess, J. S., Moreland, J. R., & Schwebel, A. I. (1985b). A follow-up study of role functioning and the psychological environment of families of cancer patients. *Journal of Psychosocial Oncology, 3*(2), 1-14.

Vollman, R., Ganzert, A., Picher, L., & Williams, W. (1971). The reactions of family systems to sudden and unexpected death. *Omega, 2,* 101-106.

Walsh, F., & McGoldrick, M. (1991). Loss and the family: A systemic perspective. In

F. Walsh and M. McGoldrick (Eds.), *Living beyond loss: Death in the family* (pp. 1-29). New York: Norton.

Wilcoxon, S. A. (1986). Grandparents and grandchildren: An often neglected relationship between significant others. *Journal of Counseling and Development, 65*(6), 289-290.

Williamson, P. (1986). National Sudden Infant Death Syndrome Foundation. In T. Rando (Ed.), *Parental loss of a child* (pp. 509-512). Champaign, IL: Research Press.

Willinger, M., James, L. S., & Catz, C. (1991). Defining the sudden infant death syndrome (SIDS). *Pediatric Pathology, 11,* 677-684.

Worden, J. W. (1991). *Grief counseling and grief therapy: A handbook for the mental health practitioner* (2nd ed.). New York: Springer.

Zebal, B., & Woolsey, S. (1984). SIDS and the family: The pediatrician's role. *Pediatric Annals, 13,* 237-261.

PART II

Developmental Perspectives
on Dying and Grieving

Overview of the Needs of the Dying: Life Span Issues

General Needs of Dying Persons	General Needs of Dying Children	Stage-Related Needs of the Dying	
Physical • Pain alleviated • Positive body image	Trust	Toddlerhood	• Mastery of skills • Freedom of choice • Opportunities to succeed • Familiar routines • Security
	Minimal separation	Preschool years	• Alleviation of guilt • Clarification of misconceptions • Environment that facilitates exploration
Emotional • Fears allayed • Experience own grief		School-age	• Sense of competency • Acceptance of physical appearance • Development of new interests • Continued school attendance • Continued peer interaction
	Normalization		
Social • Disclosure of diagnosis • Open communication		Adolescence	• Independence and control • Sense of personal identity • Peer interaction • Privacy • Positive body image • Coming to terms with the future
		Young adulthood	• Intimate relationships • Expression of sexuality • Support for choices regarding marriage and children • Realistic support for future goals • Flexibility in work and educational settings
Psychological • Control • Independence • Contribution to others • Life review		Middle adulthood	• Reevaluation of one's life • Continuation of roles • Putting affairs in order • Concern for future of family members
Spiritual • Search for meaning • Hope • Alignment with spiritual beliefs		Late adulthood	• Continued sense of self • Participation in decision making • Reassurance that one's life still has value • Appropriate and adequate health care • Support for personal integrity • Recognition of value of life review

5

Dying and Grieving Children

The next few chapters will examine normal developmental characteristics of individuals across the life span. Insight regarding developmental needs and capabilities will provide the cornerstone for our discussion of the dying process as it relates to individuals of varying ages. Differences in the grief process as it relates to progression through various life stages will also be discussed. These chapters will integrate research findings with an understanding of Piaget's theory of cognitive development and Erikson's theory of psychosocial development. This chapter begins this developmental sequence with a focus on toddlerhood and early childhood and then examines issues related to the school-age years.

COGNITIVE DEVELOPMENT

Background on Piaget's Theory

Piaget believed that we create schemes to deal with the world. **Schemes** are organized patterns of behavior and perception that one constructs to interpret some aspect of one's experience. Piaget sometimes used the term *cognitive structures* as a synonym for schemes. For example, children have one scheme or concept of "cold." It usually means they have a fever, sneeze, sniffle, and will get well soon. The organized activity or strategy for getting over a cold is also regarded as a scheme: taking long naps, drinking lots of orange juice, and other remedies. These schemes are modified over time through one of two processes—either assimilation or accommodation.

Assimilation refers to the process by which new stimuli are incorporated into existing schemes. For example, a 3½-year-old child who regards all illnesses as "colds" is assimilating. That is, any new illness that she encounters that changes her health condition may be interpreted as a "cold," because this is the sickness with which she is familiar. When we have a new experience that does not fit with already existing schemes, we must modify the old scheme to incorporate both old and new information.

Accommodation involves a process by which present schemes are modified or new schemes are created. For example, as this same child gathers more input from the environment regarding her current illness, she determines that she is not sneezing, does not have a sore throat, and is not getting well. Instead, she has spent many days in the hospital, has had a wide variety of medical tests, and has undergone chemotherapy. She then develops a new scheme: one for leukemia. To deal most effectively and comfortably with the world, both children and adults strive for a balance between assimilating and accommodating new information. We take advantage of our past experience while allowing for new cognitive development.

Piaget (1963) studied the maturation of individuals' thought processes over time; the stages of his theory are identified in Table 5.1. He explained that infants are primarily tied to the "here and now" (i.e., they have no concept of the future) and that their processing of the world is dependent on sensory perceptions and

TABLE 5.1

Piagetian Stages and Related Age Spans

APPROXIMATE AGE SPAN	PIAGET'S STAGES OF COGNITIVE DEVELOPMENT
Birth to 2 years	Sensorimotor stage
2 years to 7 years	Preoperational stage
7 years to 11+ years	Concrete operational stage
Adolescence/adulthood	Formal operational stage

motor activities. He thus described infants as being in the **sensorimotor stage** of development for the time span between birth and approximately 2 years of age.

By age 2, toddlers are beginning to use symbols; this capacity is reflected in their ability to use language and engage in imaginative play. Although toddlers and preschoolers do use symbols, they are not able consistently to apply adult logic as we know it. Nor are they able to use what Piaget labels "operations"; therefore, he refers to the time between the ages of 2 and 7 as the **preoperational stage. Operations** refer to the ability to mentally manipulate internal representations of objects. For example, logical operations include mastery of arithmetic equations, categorization into hierarchical relationships, and organized testing of hypotheses.

Characteristics of Preoperational Thought

Preoperational thought is characterized by such factors as

- concreteness,
- centration,
- egocentrism,
- irreversibility,
- animism,
- fantasy, and
- transductive reasoning.

Although Piaget's theory does present a helpful framework for understanding children's cognitive capacity, recent research indicates that he may have underestimated children's understanding of certain concepts at a particular age. The intent of this section on Piaget's theory is simply to provide insight as to how children's thinking differs from adults', rather than to strictly define the thought pattern of a given child at a very specific age.

Concreteness.   Although young children can deal with symbols (e.g., use words to refer to objects, ask questions, and use their imaginations to make believe that a scarf is a carpet in the prince's palace), they cannot develop concepts of things that are abstract. Rather, their thinking is characterized by **concreteness.** They can think only of things that have a counterpart in the physical world; that is, they are unable to deal with abstractions (e.g., they are unable to understand a concept such as "quality of life" because it is abstract). Because children think in concrete, literal terms, their concept of death may be all the more confused if they repeatedly hear adults making comments such as "Put your coat on or you will catch your death (cold)," or "It was so embarrassing, I could have just died."

Centration.   Preoperational children **centrate,** or focus, on a single prominent characteristic of an object to the exclusion of others. These immature thinkers who focus on a single dimension at a time (such as height) do not understand that a medicine dose in a tall narrow glass is equivalent to the same amount of liquid given in a short broad-based glass. Children typically think there is more in the tall glass because they are centrating on the level of the liquid and not the width of the container. As a result, a child may be happier if he or she received a delicious juice in a tall narrow glass and a bitter-tasting medicine in a short broad glass.

Egocentrism.   Piaget's theory stressed the egocentrism of the preoperational child. More current research, however, shows this egocentrism was greatly exaggerated. Nonetheless, there are many times when we see the younger child act in a very egocentric manner. **Egocentrism** refers to the inability to process information from another's viewpoint. Preoperational children assume that what they believe is correct, what they want is desired by everyone, and what is known to them is understood by all. One example of children's egocentric behavior is reflected in their frequent involvement in **dual monologues,** in which both speakers engage in unrelated and separate conversations even though each speaker does pause appropriately to allow the other person to speak. The following brief interaction between 3-year-old Kirsten and 4-year-old Alyce illustrates a dual monologue.

    K: My uncle died last night.

    A: I got slippers at the store yesterday!

    K: My mommy cried.

    A: They're blue with bows on.

    K: She cried and cried and said she had to go to Atlanta.

Irreversibility.   Young children are unable to understand that something may change and then return to (or still be equivalent to) its original state. For example, if a nurse breaks a pill into two halves, the child cannot mentally reverse that operation to understand that the two halves are essentially the same as the original whole pill.

Animism.   Young children's thinking is marked by **animism,** which refers to the belief that inanimate objects are alive. Piaget (1968) noted that animism was marked by the following developmental progression:

1. all objects, animate and inanimate, are alive;
2. everything that moves (such as a car) is alive;
3. objects that move on their own are alive (e.g., the sun);
4. plants and animals are alive.

Fantasy.   Young children are often unable to totally separate reality from fantasy. Children exist in a world filled with much make-believe activity as they engage in imaginative dramatic play. It is difficult, then, to separate desires from outcome. For example, many young children may think that they have caused an illness, injury, or even death because of something they did or felt. A child may feel that his mother died because he got mad at her when she scolded him. The child may feel he himself is very sick because he didn't clean his room.

Transductive Reasoning.   Adults' thinking is characterized by **inductive reasoning,** reasoning from specific examples to a general rule, or **deductive reasoning,** moving from a general rule to a specific case. Preoperational children, however, use **transductive reasoning,** which is based on reasoning from the particular to the particular, or specific to specific. If one situation is like another in one aspect, the child may assume it is similar in other ways as well. For example, young children who learn that they can "catch a cold" may also think that they can "catch a brain tumor." By the same reasoning, healthy young children may fear they are going to die because an older sibling of the same sex has died.

Characteristics of Concrete Operational Thought

According to Piaget's theory of cognitive development, school-age children between the ages of approximately 7 and 11 are commonly capable of thinking at the concrete operational level. Operations allow them to manipulate objects mentally and determine relationships among them. For example, categorizing children by sex and age involves the operation of classification. Determining who has been sick the shortest time and who has been sick the longest involves the operation of seriation. Children in the **concrete operational stage** are "bound by immediate physical reality and cannot transcend the here and now, consequently, during this period, children still have difficulty dealing with remote, future, or hypothetical matters" (Vander Zanden, 1985, p. 294). Although still somewhat limited in its scope, concrete operational thinking is marked by major advances over preoperational thinking. The following descriptors are reflective of the primary shifts in thinking capacity, when comparing concrete operational thought to preoperational thought:

- diminished egocentrism,
- decreased animism, and
- lessened confusion between reality and fantasy.

Also, in contrast to children in the preoperational stage, concrete operational thinkers are able to do the following:

- decenter their focus of attention,
- attend to transformations, and
- master concepts related to conservation.

These cognitive capabilities do not all develop at the same time; rather, they develop gradually and become refined over time. Each will be briefly discussed in this section.

Diminished Egocentrism.   Younger preoperational thinkers often tend to perceive the world from only one viewpoint: their own. Concrete operational children much more clearly and consistently understand that others may think differently from the way they do. Older children, then, care about what their peers think about them. As a result, they put much time and energy into trying to be similar to others in order to avoid becoming outcasts. Children whose bodies have changed due to the ravages of illness often are painfully aware of others' reactions toward them.

Decentration.   Whereas preoperational thinkers focus their attention on one dimension at a time, concrete operational children decenter their attention and consider multiple factors simultaneously. For example, the concrete operational child understands that a friend can be happy and worried at the same time: happy that the leukemia has currently gone into remission but worried that the illness will recur.

Reversibility.   Although preoperational children's thinking is marked by an inability to mentally go back to the initial state (i.e., **irreversibility**), concrete operational thinkers can reverse thought processes. For example, an older child may understand that her father is currently very sick and confined to bed but remembers that he was much healthier at one time and used to participate in many physical activities. Therefore, she is capable of understanding that her father can possibly regain his health.

Conservation.   Concrete operational thinkers are able to understand that certain characteristics of an object do not change (volume, mass, weight), even if other dimensions are transformed; this ability is known as **conservation.** For example, a concrete operational thinker would understand that ½ ounce of medicine is the same whether it is taken from two spoonfuls or one. A preoperational child who has focused on the number of spoonfuls would regard the two as having contained more medicine, even though it still totals ½ ounce.

Transformations.   Concrete operational thinkers are able to perceive intermediate steps (i.e., **transformations**) that lead up to a particular outcome. Younger children perceive only the final state. An older child recalled his sister's illness gradually limiting her attendance at school. She had shifted from full days to half days to two mornings a week. A younger child could only describe the final outcome and could not explain the gradual change.

Related Phenomena.   Although thought has become more logical, school-age children still hold some magical beliefs. Most of us can remember a time when we took great pains to ensure the physical welfare of our mothers—by not stepping on a crack! On our birthdays, we guaranteed our wishes' coming true by refusing to tell our siblings what we had hoped for as we blew out the birthday candles. As twilight fell, we searched for the first star and wished upon it—"Star light, star bright, first star I see tonight. I wish I may, I wish I might."

Because belief in magic is such a normal part of both the preschool years and the school-age years, it is quite common to hear sick children ask the powerful adults in their lives (parents, doctors, nurses) to "fix me" or "make me better," fully believing that they have the power to do so, particularly if the child wishes hard enough that it be accomplished. When adults do not have the power to heal them or make them totally comfortable, some children misinterpret this lack of power as deliberate unwillingness or as a desire to punish them due to some perceived wrongdoing. This phenomenon is termed **psychological causality,** which refers to "the tendency in young children to perceive a psychological motive as the cause" for a phenomenon (Wass, 1991, p. 13). Recall, once again, that many sick children feel guilty, thinking they caused their own illnesses by being bad.

Increased cognitive abilities facilitate the mastery of language, which then allows children to engage in telling jokes and riddles. Many of these have a death-related theme and, in some instances, may be invitations for further discussion of death or grief.

Young Children's Understanding of the Concept of Illness

The previous discussion of cognitive development closely relates to the understanding of the concept of illness and the concept of death. Children in the preoperational stage have a less mature understanding of death and illness than do those in the concrete or formal operational stage. Developmental changes in each of these arenas will now be discussed.

Redpath and Rogers (1984) asked 30 preschoolers a number of questions related to sickness, hospitals, medical personnel, and operations. They found that these preoperational children usually described illness in terms of restriction of activities rather than a change in their bodies. When asked how a person gets sick, they answered "cause you do" or confused a cause with a symptom such as throwing up. They seemed unsure as to why children would go to a hospital and once again confused cause and effect by indicating "people got sick or hurt in a hospital."

CHILDREN'S JOKES RELATED TO DEATH, ILLNESS, MEDICAL PROCEDURES

Death

How do you make a dead man float?
Well, you take a dead man, two scoops of ice cream.

A man wanted to commit suicide. To make sure he did the job, he got a bottle of poison, a rope, a gun, some gasoline and matches. Pouring the gasoline all over his clothing, he climbed a tree and crawled out on a branch overhanging a lake. He hung himself from the limb, drank the poison, set his clothing on fire, and then shot himself. Alas! He missed his head, the bullet hit the rope, he fell into the water, and the water put the flames out. He swallowed so much water that the poison became harmless. Then he had to swim as hard as he could in order to save his life.

There was a young feller named Clyde,
Who fell down a sewer and died.
Now, he had a brother
Who fell down another,
Would you call that double sewer-side?

Illness

How can you tell if a mummy has a cold?
He starts coffin.

Medical Procedures

What is the famous last word in surgery?
Ouch.

What would you call a small wound?
A short cut.

SOURCES: J. Rosenbloom (1976). *Biggest riddle book in the world.* New York: Sterling; J. Rosenbloom (1984). *Laughs, hoots, and giggles: Riddles, jokes, knock-knocks, and put downs.* New York: Sterling.

Children's understanding of illness develops gradually. Bibace and Walsh (1979) reported that preoperational thinkers' explanations of sickness can be categorized as either phenomenism or contagion. A "phenomenistic" response is one that defines illness using a single specific symptom, sensation, or object that the child has associated with the illness. One child in Bibace and Walsh's preoperational group explained, "A heart attack is from the sun" (p. 290). Preoperational children also explained illness in terms of "contagion." When asked how an illness is caused, the children regarded close proximity as related to causality. A child who was asked how people catch colds responded, "other kids." When probed further and queried, "How do other kids give you a cold," the child answered, "You catch it, that's all" (p. 290). These categories of responses (i.e., phenomenism and contagion) reflect normal characteristics of preoperational thought. Bibace and Walsh (1979) explain:

> The child is swayed by the immediacy of some aspects of perceptual experience. The primary characteristics of this stage include: concreteness or preoccupation with external perceptual events; irreversibility, or the inability to construe processes in reverse; egocentrism, or viewing the world from one's

own perspective, centering or focusing on a single aspect or part of experience to the exclusion of the whole; and transductive reasoning, or thinking that proceeds from one particular to another rather than from particular to general or vice versa. (p. 290)

The most common explanations (71%) of preoperational children were categorized as "contagion explanations," while concrete operational thinkers gave markedly different types of responses. Only 17% of the school-agers gave contagion explanations, whereas 75% gave responses that were categorized as "contamination explanations." In these explanations, children were able to articulate the causal link between the source of the illness (e.g., germs) and the illness itself. In contrast to the preoperational child, the concrete operational thinker no longer focuses on a single symptom but rather attempts to integrate multiple symptoms. Concrete, visible bodily processes are discussed. Additionally, "the egocentricity of the earlier stage is less apparent, as the child describes illness as a more general phenomenon ('People get measles,' rather than 'I got measles'; 'Colds come from cold air,' rather than 'A cold is from the wind and I went to the doctor')" (p. 293).

Bibace and Walsh (1979) also noted that concrete operational thinkers' newfound capability of reversing thought processes was apparent in many of their responses. Many children explained that a person who was sick might once again become well. In contrast, younger children do not understand that health and illness are related concepts. Natapoff (1982) reminds us that preoperational children are unable to transform states because they are unable to reverse their thought processes. Therefore, young children do not perceive illness as related to either a previous or future state of health. Furthermore, these children do not understand global aspects of health but rather focus on specific, concrete components such as eating or drinking certain foods (such as carrots, peas, and milk) that they felt were related to health.

Adams-Greenly (1984, p. 6) reports that sometimes children have two different versions of an illness: "the medical version which they can repeat verbatim, and their own private version."

> For example one child (age 6) when asked why he was in the hospital, responded "I have Hodgkins Disease Stage IVB." The interviewer then said "Gee, those are pretty big words! What do they mean?" The child replied "My mother said if I ate too much candy, I'd get sick. So that's what happened, and then they cut me open (splenectomy) and took it all out." (Adams-Greenly, 1984, p. 6)

It is crucial that adults delve deeper than the words themselves to understand the child's true base of knowledge. Without this insight, caregivers' interactions may be less helpful than they could be.

Young Children's Understanding of the Concept of Death

The understanding of the developmental unfolding of a mature concept of death is an area that continues to need much more study. Currently the findings of various research projects are somewhat contradictory. This may relate to a number of different variables that may have some impact on the outcome, including methodological variables such as research design, specific age and developmental stage of subjects, type of object being referred to (i.e., human, animal, plant), and how a particular subconcept of death is defined and measured in a given study. Demographic variables may also have an impact; these include cultural background, religious beliefs, family communication patterns, and exposure to violence through the media (Essa & Murray, 1994). Although some discrepancies are related to children's concept of death, we do know that the concept of death is multidimensional and that some aspects of death seem to be more difficult than others for children to understand.

One question asked by researchers relates to whether the experience of knowing someone personally who has died might accelerate a child's understanding of the concept of death. For example, Mahon (1993) examined whether the death of a sibling in the prior 13 to 17 months affected the development of the children's concept of death. No significant differences were found between a group of 29 bereaved siblings (ages 5 to 12 years) and a comparison group of 29 nonbereaved children who had been matched for race, age, and gender. Although she found no relationship between personal experience with death and concept development, she did find that developmental stage (as related to a Piagetian assessment) was the best predictor of children's understanding of the concept of death.

In this section, we will define frequently studied components of the concept of death and also review, from a developmental perspective, relevant research on children's mastery of these components.

Nonfunctionality.   **Nonfunctionality** refers to the cessation of all life-defining functions (e.g., feeling, moving, breathing, and eating). Nagy (1948) was one of the first to investigate children's concepts of death. She found that the younger children (ages 3 to 5) in her study believed that dead people were capable of some activity, although they regarded dead people as "less alive" than living people. For example, one child in Nagy's study described a dead person as being able to eat and drink but not able to move.

Some children believe that the person who is dead is in a state similar to sleep and can be awakened; euphemisms likening death to sleep can cause much confusion during this stage. Recall that preoperational thinkers are animistic in their thought patterns and often attribute life to inanimate objects; the belief that individuals are able to function, at least in an altered state, is possibly a variation of the child's normal animistic thought. In contrast to the young children in her study (ages 3 to 5) who believed dead people could act and perceive, Nagy (1948) found that the older children (5 to 9) understood that dead persons do not feel, breathe, eat, and so forth.

Irreversibility/Finality.   **Finality** refers to the permanence of the state of death; once a living thing dies, its physical body cannot be made alive again. Koocher (1974) studied 75 children between the ages of 6 and 15 years. Based on performance of particular reasoning tasks, he divided them into three groups: preoperational, concrete, and formal operational thinkers. He found that eight children in his sample responded to the question "How do you make dead things come back to life?" by identifying specific strategies to accomplish that task. One child, for example, explained, "Help them, give them hot food, and keep them healthy so it won't happen again" (p. 408). All the children who answered the question as if you could bring dead persons back to life were preoperational thinkers between ages 6.0 and 7.1 years. Whereas 40% (8 out of 20) of the preoperational children felt that this feat was possible, the older children recognized that death is permanent. One representative answer was "By thinking about them; then they can live in our mind, but you can't really make them come alive again" (p. 408).

Children's cartoons and fairy tales often reinforce the preoperational child's misconceptions regarding the finality of death; although they may be seriously maimed, mangled, and pulverized, many cartoon characters miraculously survive what would certainly be fatal if experienced by a "real" human. Snow White, although seemingly dead, was revived by Prince Charming's kiss.

After hearing a story about how a man was killed by a gun shot, a young girl responded to questions in a fashion clearly reflective of her own personal experience, rather than indicating a mature understanding of the concept of death (Mahon, 1993).

> When asked, "Will Mr. Evans ever be alive again?" one child responded with a question: "How many times was he shot?" She followed this line of questioning with some insistence, explaining "Because my father was shot nine times and he lived." (p. 341)

Universality. **Universality** is the understanding that all human beings will someday die. White, Elsom, and Prawat (1978) used a sample of 170 children from kindergarten through fourth grade to study children's conceptions of death. After hearing a story about a character named Mrs. Wilson who dies at the end, each child was asked questions such as "Do you think that everybody will die someday?" (p. 308). Approximately 62% of the preoperational children ages 2 to 7 answered the question incorrectly by indicating that some people will not die. In contrast, only 38% of those in the concrete operational stage answered this question incorrectly.

Causality. **Causality** refers to those factors that can precipitate death (e.g., cancer, heart attack, car accident). This component was a central focus of Koocher's (1974) interactions with 75 children, ages 6 to 15 years. When asked "What makes things die?" (p. 406), the subsample of preoperational thinkers in the study typically gave very specific responses that seemed to be closely related to their own experiences and, therefore, Koocher concluded, reflected a strong sense of egocentrism, which is common in the preoperational period. Responses included "They eat poison and stuff; pills, you'd better wait till your mom gives them to you." "Yes, you can die if you swallow a dirty bug" (p. 407). The children in the concrete operational stage, however, identified specific weapons or illnesses. One 7-year-old responded, "Knife, arrows, guns, lots of stuff. Do you want me to tell you all of them?" (Interviewer: "As many as you want.") "Hatchets and animals, and fire and explosions too" (p. 407). Although these answers are less egocentric than those given by preschoolers, they are still very concrete as compared to adolescents' responses, which reflect deterioration of life processes or destruction of vital organs.

School-Age Children's Concept of Death

Recall that preschool children do not fully understand the elements of non-functionality, irreversibility, causality, and universality. In their extensive review of studies examining children's understanding of the concept of death, Speece and Brent (1984) concluded that the majority of children at the concrete operational stage have acquired the death-related concepts of nonfunctionality, finality, and universality. Using the idea that the mature concept of death "is defined as a mature understanding of 3 of its key components," (i.e., nonfunctionality, irreversibility, and universality), Speece and Brent (1992, p. 212) researched two key questions:

- At what age do children achieve a mature concept of death?
- What is the pattern of acquisition among the three components? (This examination focused on whether one component is acquired before another [sequential acquisition] or whether two or more are acquired at the same time [concurrent acquisition].)

In relation to the first question, Speece and Brent (1984, 1992), in their early studies, discovered that a majority of children understood the concept of universality by kindergarten. In exploring the second question, they found that a mature concept of universality is mastered prior to either irreversibility or nonfunctionality, indicating sequential acquisition. The concepts of irreversibility and nonfunctionality unfold gradually over time and these two are acquired concurrently. Finally Speece and Brent concluded that most children, by the time they were 10 years of age, had a mature understanding of all three of these concepts of death. In a more recent study, however, with a number of colleagues from China, these researchers found that the developmental progression of the concept of death was not as clear-cut as they had originally thought in either a U.S. or a Chinese sample (Brent, Speece, Lin, Dong, & Yang, 1996). Additional work is needed before we can come to clear conclusions.

TEACHING CHILDREN ABOUT DEATH

There are many opportunities for teaching children about death. Children often share accounts of death with others in their environment—they may explain that a pet died over the weekend or bring a picture of a grandparent who died to share with others during show and tell. They ask many questions of those who are willing to listen and respond. In addition to giving support, parents, teachers, ministers, youth group leaders, and others can effectively use these "teachable moments" to clarify children's understanding of death.

Capitalizing on naturally occurring opportunities to discuss important issues is extremely helpful; often adults do just the opposite as is illustrated in the following anecdote shared by Wass (1991). It is an account of a first grader named Susie a few weeks after her brother died.

> One morning she (Susie) stood before her classmates during "Show and Tell" and told them quietly, "My brother Jamie died." The teacher was totally unprepared, and her response was silence. She pretended she had not heard and motioned to another child to come forward. But Susie was determined and repeated in a louder tone, "My brother Jamie died." Now, all the children had heard, and the teacher could no longer pretend. They looked expectantly at the teacher, then at Susie, then back at the teacher who was petrified. Susie . . . shouted the statement at her teacher who promptly . . . said "We do not shout in this classroom." She then walked Susie out of the classroom. (p. 18)

Although this example focused on the death of a family member, there are likely to be many more opportunities to discuss death in relation to a pet's dying. For example,

> When I was about 9-years-old I came home to find that Penny, my dog, which had looked after me . . . when I was a baby, was no longer at home. I suspected that she had been put down as my mum had removed her basket and tried to remove some blood . . . I asked my mum where she was and all she could say was that she had to go, she was in pain . . . I was so angry . . . what right had they to take her away . . . I began to think it was my fault, maybe I was somehow to blame. Maybe I hadn't fed her properly or taken her out for walks often enough. I felt like this for weeks, until I told my mum how I felt. She told me it wasn't my fault; no one was to blame. She'd had a cancer growth . . . and she was far too old to go through with an operation. (Casdagli & Gobey, 1992, pp. 118-119)

By ignoring opportunities for meaningful discussion, by delaying discussion, or by responding negatively, adults may be sharing any of a number of unintended messages, such as

- death is something to be ignored;
- death is to be feared;
- children should not talk about death or share their grief;
- children cannot expect support as they grieve; or
- children's questions, concerns, and feelings are unimportant.

Exposure to a shared loss (e.g., death of a classmate, media coverage of an event such as a recent plane crash) can create an opportunity for open discussion.

Discussions with children about death must be grounded in developmental principles that include recognition of their need to grieve. Guidelines based on these principles include the following:

- Be open to children's questions and concerns.
- Get clarification from the children regarding what they perceive to be true about a given situation or death in general. It can be helpful to ask children their beliefs and experiences in order to assess a current level of understanding.

    For example, ask questions such as the following:
    - What do you know about how (name) died?
    - Have you ever been to a hospital? A funeral? What was it like for you?

    For example, give children an opportunity to ask you questions. They may include
    - Do dead people suffocate in the ground?
    - When is my brother coming back to play?
    - How much does a funeral cost?
    - Why do people's hair fall out after they get sick?
- Use language that is appropriate to a child's level of understanding and ability to process information.

    For example, with young children
    - speak in concrete terminology;
    - do not use figurative language;
    - do not use euphemisms (e.g., sleeping) to describe death; and
    - use as many examples as possible.

Many adults find it helpful to choose from the many books currently available to help explain important facets of the dying and grieving process. The use of books in this context will be discussed later in this chapter.

CAUSES OF DEATH AMONG CHILDREN

The leading causes of death among children in the United States are found in Table 5.2 (ages 1 to 4) and Table 5.3 (ages 5 to 14).

Accidents are the primary cause of death among children of all ages. Figure 5.1 shows a comparison of the types of fatal accidents most common among children and adolescents. Motor vehicle accidents are responsible for the majority of these accidental deaths, and the probability of death by this means increases with age of the child. Drownings and fires also account for a significant number of accidental deaths of young children each year.

Indicative of the increasing violence in the United States, homicide is the third leading cause of death among the age group from 5 to 14 years and the fourth leading cause of death among the age group from 1 to 4 years. A discussion of homicide can be found in chapter 6.

Many children die from various illnesses—cancer, heart disease, pneumonia, and influenza; even among children, AIDS is now one of the 10 leading causes of death. Cancer takes many forms in children: leukemias are responsible for

TABLE 5.2

Leading Causes of Death: 1 to 4 Age Group, United States, 1995

RANK	CAUSE OF DEATH	NUMBER OF DEATHS	DEATH RATE PER 100,000 POPULATION
	All causes	6,393	40.6
1	Accidents and adverse effects	2,280	14.5
	Motor vehicle accidents	825	5.2
	All other accidents and adverse effects	1,455	9.2
2	Congenital anomalies	695	4.4
3	Malignant neoplasms, including neoplasms of lymphatic and hematopoietic tissues	488	3.1
4	Homicide and legal intervention	452	2.9
5	Diseases of heart	251	1.6
6	Human immunodeficiency virus infection	210	1.3
7	Pneumonia and influenza	156	1.0
8	Certain conditions originating in the perinatal period	87	0.6
9	Septicemia	80	0.5
10	Cerebrovascular diseases	57	0.4
	All other causes (Residual)	1,637	10.4

SOURCE: U.S. National Center for Health Statistics. *Monthly Vital Statistics Report,* 45(11), June 1997.

approximately 30% of cancers of persons under age 16; lymphomas and Hodgkin's disease make up about 12%. According to the National Cancer Institute, the incidence of childhood cancer increased from approximately 12 in 100,000 children in 1980 to 14 in 100,000 in 1990. In 1995, approximately 8,000 new cases were diagnosed in the United States and about 1,600 children died from cancer.

PSYCHOSOCIAL DEVELOPMENT— NEEDS OF DYING CHILDREN

Dying children are living children. Not only do dying children have special needs (i.e., by the very nature of the fact that they are dying), but they also have a need to live life to its fullest given the limitations of their illness. Knowing information about various aspects of normal child development can provide a caregiver with important insights about how to give individual support and create a helping environment that is complementary to the needs, interests, and capabilities of the child. Struggling with a life-threatening illness presents not only a physical crisis but a psychosocial crisis as well (Martinson & Bossert, 1994). We will use Erikson's model to help frame the discussion; a summary of his stages is found in chapter 2.

TABLE 5.3
Leading Causes of Death: 5 to 14 Age Group, United States, 1995

RANK	CAUSE OF DEATH	NUMBER OF DEATHS	DEATH RATE PER 100,000 POPULATION
	All causes	8,596	22.5
1	Accidents and adverse effects	3,544	9.3
	Motor vehicle accidents	2,055	5.4
	All other accidents and adverse effects	1,489	3.9
2	Maligant neoplasms, including neoplasms of lymphatic and hematopoietic tissues	1,026	2.7
3	Homicide and legal intervention	562	1.5
4	Congenital anomalies	449	1.2
5	Suicide	337	0.9
6	Diseases of heart	294	0.8
7	Human immunodeficiency virus infection	189	0.5
8	Chronic obstructive pulmonary diseases and allied conditions	143	0.4
9	Pneumonia and influenza	128	0.3
10	Benign neoplasms, carcinoma in situ, and neoplasms of uncertain behavior and of unspecified nature	105	0.3
	All other causes (Residual)	1,819	4.8

SOURCE: U.S. National Center for Health Statistics. *Monthly Vital Statistics Report,* 45(11), June 1997.

FIGURE 5.1
Comparison of Fatal Accidents Among Children and Adolescents, United States, 1995

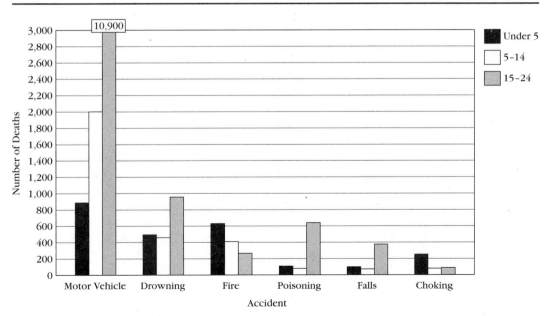

SOURCE: National Safety Council, Accident Facts Deaths Due to Unintentional Injuries, 1995.

POEMS—SELECTIONS FROM "THE ANDREW POEMS"

Wet

Near midnight,
your grandfather came into your room
where Thomas and I had waited.
He said you had been found
and they needed something to cover you,
not for the cold—it was summer,
not for your comfort—too late;
but to wrap the small, wet body
as with a shroud.
I grabbed your bedspread,
gave it to your grandfather.
He left your room
carrying your white spread
draped in his arms
like a child.

I'd rather remember you
wet from your bath.
You would play until chilled and wrinkled.
Then I would wrap

a thick white towel around you.
We loved the patting,
tickling, laughing,
and dusting with powder.
After you wiggled into your pajamas
you would climb on the hamper
to see yourself in the mirror,
comb your wet hair straight back
and ask
if that made you look famous?
With affirmations,
I would carry my legend to his room.

Had I gone outside that night,
no one would have let me bathe you,
wash the mud from your cheeks and legs.
What good to dry and powder you?
You could not come back to your room.
But I wonder,
did the river sweep your wet hair straight
  back
and make you famous?

(Continued)

Toddlerhood: Autonomy Versus Shame and Doubt

Erikson (1963) explains that infants strive to develop a sense of trust rather than
mistrust. Infants need to feel that they are safe in their physical and social environment. Later as they become toddlers, they struggle to become independent
and gain a sense of control over their environment. This is reflected in the crisis of autonomy versus shame and doubt. **Autonomy** implies independence,
whereas **shame** denotes a sense of being bad or worthless, and **doubt** describes
a belief that one is incapable of mastering skills or making appropriate choices.

The term *toddler* conjures up visions of young children who have just
learned to walk and unsteadily, at that. As months pass, toddlers quickly refine
their large motor skills and shortly thereafter learn to climb stairs, run, and so
forth. Mastery of these locomotive skills provides children with much delight,
as well as an opportunity to explore their ever-expanding environment.

During this period, many other skills are also refined. Whereas toddlers have
some difficulty performing tasks that demand highly coordinated fine motor

(Continued From Previous Page)

Communion

On the first anniversary of your death,
I went to the kitchen,
set the table with your Superman place mat
and pulled up your chair.
I made a peanut butter and jelly sandwich,
removed the crust as always
for a special occasion.
I cut it into quarters
and arranged the triangles
on your red plate.
I poured milk in your blue plastic
Crayola crayon mug,
put on its pointed top
with the hole in the tip for a straw.
I had no straws.
I don't buy them anymore.

Sitting next to your place,
I apologized for no straw.
I apologized for your death.
I apologized for not being there.
When I finished,
I wiped my eyes with your napkin,
gave thanks,
ate the bread and drank the milk.

Shelly Wagner's younger son Andrew drowned July 26, 1984, in the river behind her home in Norfolk, VA. Four and a half years later she began writing her poetry. The collection entitled *The Andrew Poems* covered the 8 years following his death. It was awarded the First Book Award by Texas Tech University Press; Wagner had never written poetry before.

SOURCE: S. Wagner. (1994). *The Andrew Poems.* Lubbock, TX: Texas Tech University Press.

movements (such as fastening buttons on a shirt), preschoolers gain great satisfaction from these accomplishments (such as putting Band-Aids on by themselves). With increasing ability to perform certain tasks on their own comes an increased sense of independence.

A child who is encouraged to learn basic self-care skills (to feed or dress him- or herself, for example) in a positive and supportive environment is likely to develop a sense of autonomy. On the other hand, a child who is repeatedly told in a stern voice "Hurry up!" "You're making a mess!" or "You can't do anything right!" is likely to develop a sense of shame and doubt. The same holds true for a child who is rarely allowed to complete a task for him- or herself, for there is an implication, even if it is not verbalized, that the child is incapable of doing it correctly.

To master a sense of autonomy, children must feel that they have a sense of control over their world. Control allows a sense of security, providing comfort in a world that might otherwise seem overwhelming and even frightening. A strong desire for control is frequently reflected in the toddler's use of language. "No!" and "Me do it!" are often repeated words and are certainly indicative of the child's desire, and even insistence, that he or she intends to do something in his or her own way and own time. Freedom of choice—what to eat, what to wear, what to play—can also lead to a sense of control. One hospital lab technician would allow her young patients some control over the procedure of drawing blood by playfully telling them, "You pick it (referring to the finger) and I'll stick it."

Security is derived from knowing what to expect from one's environment. A routine that helps structure the day gives young children a sense of control through knowing what to expect next. Rituals also promote a sense of control. In general terms, a **childhood ritual** is a stereotyped behavior performed to order one's environment. In some cases, rituals of childhood must be followed precisely or the child becomes frightened, hurt, or angry. One of the authors, as a young child, was convinced that a terrible fate would befall individual family members if she did not say, each and every night, "Good night; sleep well; sweet dreams; see you in the morning; don't let the bed bugs bite." This ritual was time consuming in that it needed to be repeated for each individual in the family: mother, father, older brother, two younger sisters, and younger brother. (It was obviously worth the effort: Each of these persons is alive and well today!) Security objects can also offer much comfort to many young children. Certain blankets, dolls, and items of clothing have all been endowed by individual children with the power to dry tears, quiet sobs, and soothe them to sleep.

Circumstances that are often related to the dying process may put toddlers "at risk" for developing a negative resolution to various crises outlined by Erikson. For example, dying toddlers are at risk for developing a sense of shame or doubt rather than a sense of autonomy. This is derived from the fact that they may have little control over their environment. Toddlers who are dying may simply have limited physical capacities compared with healthy children. These limitations, such as diminished stamina, weakness in certain parts of their bodies, and limited range of motion, can have an impact on the ease with which toddlers can master skills that allow them to feel autonomous. Another factor that puts dying toddlers at risk in this stage is the tendency of many parents and medical personnel to show their concern for these children by being overprotective in many situations. Overprotection can deprive these toddlers of opportunities to explore their environment in whatever way they can and do things for themselves. This, in turn, contributes to the potential development of feelings of self-doubt rather than confidence.

Another factor that may have an effect on the outcome of this developmental crisis is related to time. Individuals giving care to a dying toddler may feel pressed for time. They are likely to have numerous other commitments and responsibilities needing their attention and, thus, are often overwhelmed by the sheer magnitude of the task of caring for a dying child. These caregivers, then, may be physically and emotionally exhausted. As a result, they often look for shortcuts in the routine care of sick children. Shortcuts include the caregivers performing tasks or making choices rather than allowing the toddlers themselves to do so. For example, adults who are striving to save time often take responsibility for feeding their children rather than allowing them to feed themselves.

People giving care to dying toddlers must strive to create an environment that allows for the development of a sense of autonomy rather than shame and doubt. Examples of strategies for developing such an environment are as follows:

- Provide opportunities to practice and master those skills that are age appropriate. For example, allow dying toddlers to walk unaided or feed themselves, as best they can, even if it takes longer.
- Allow freedom of choice. This can be done by providing them with a variety of acceptable options. For example, allow children to select the toys they would like to take to the hospital or the pajamas that they would like to wear to bed.
- Help the toddlers succeed at the tasks they do undertake. For example, if they wish to feed themselves, ensure that eating utensils are adapted, if necessary, so that they can be manipulated successfully.
- Try to maintain as many familiar routines as possible within the hospital environment.
- If a routine has to be changed, explain the reasons why and what might be expected (e.g., "You won't get to go to the playroom with your friends today because the nurse is going to give you a shot to make you sleep.").
- Provide an overall sense of security.

Preschool Years: Initiative Versus Guilt

Preschoolers are extremely curious creatures. They ask what seem to adults to be a never-ending series of "Why?" questions. They vigorously explore their environment and seek answers through experimentation. These characteristics and activities set the stage for the psychosocial crisis of the preschooler as described by Erikson (1963) as initiative versus guilt. The positive resolution, **initiative,** involves defining a task and using one's personal resources to accomplish it. This challenge takes place when the child is beginning to develop a conscience. Caregivers must help children develop an understanding of right and wrong without creating an unduly heavy burden of guilt for the shortcomings they often experience as they curiously explore the world around them.

Dying preschoolers, because of their severe illnesses, may be at increased risk for developing a sense of **guilt** rather than a feeling of initiative. Recall that preschoolers are very involved in many imaginative and creative processes. Additionally, they do not fully understand the world around them because of lack of experience and immature intellectual capacities. As a result of these factors, they cannot always separate fantasy from reality. Young children, then, often feel guilty for events that are imagined or that are distorted variations of reality. Dying children may erroneously conclude that they are being punished for some wrongdoing such as fighting with siblings or not putting toys away. Consequently, caregivers must take extra care in addressing these misconceptions.

To develop a sense of initiative, children need to explore their environment, become involved in a variety of creative experiences, and have their curiosity satisfied. These tasks may be difficult due to the physical limitations and also environmental restrictions resulting from preschoolers' illnesses. A number of strategies facilitate dying preschoolers' development of a sense of initiative rather than guilt; examples include:

- Listen to and observe carefully what children are communicating regarding their feelings or knowledge about their illnesses. Many will communicate in direct conversation; others will communicate indirectly through puppets or dolls, paintings, or telling stories about "other" children. Give support for those feelings, provide opportunities to vent or come to terms with their reactions, and clarify misconceptions.
- Reassure dying preschoolers that they did not cause their illnesses, that they are not being punished, and that all that can be done to help them is being done. This should be done in concrete terminology using a variety of many examples.
- Provide an environment that is open to the children's sense of curiosity (e.g., answer their questions in terminology they can understand).

School-Age Years: Industry Versus Inferiority

The crisis of school-age children, as explained by Erikson (1963), is that of industry versus inferiority. During this period, children focus much of their energy on learning new skills, making things, and being productive. If allowed to do these activities successfully and in a way that allows them feelings of pride and competency, school-age children will develop a sense of **industry.** Peers become increasingly important during the school-age years, and children desire to be accepted by their peers and be regarded as an equal, if not a superior, match to others. If they consistently fail, school-agers develop a sense of **inferiority** rather than industry.

The culture of childhood embodies many factors. Berger (1983) explains, "While playing together, children in middle childhood transmit and develop their own subculture . . . complete with language, dress codes, and rules of behavior that adults often do not notice" (p. 334). From age 5 or 6 onward, involvement in school is a focal point of most children's daily activities. They spend many hours a day learning those skills and subjects that our society deems to be valuable. Additionally, children engage in many extracurricular activities (clubs and sports, among others) that provide increased opportunities to develop competencies that give a sense of pride as well as pleasure.

Dying children may be in danger of developing a negative outcome to the psychosocial crisis and a feeling that they are inferior to those around them. They are very capable of making the determination that they are different from their healthy peers. In addition, medical procedures and/or progress of their disease often bring about distinctive changes in their physical appearance. Unless peers are taught to be sensitive, children who look radically different from their peers may feel they are outcasts and develop a sense of inferiority. There are many ways to intervene, however, so that sick children do not feel that they are inferior because of their differences.

Children with life-threatening illnesses typically do not have the same energy levels as their peers and therefore cannot participate in the same variety of activities or perform at the same level of expertise. Oftentimes, dying school-age children are restricted from going to school for part, if not all, of the course of their illness. Separation from the school environment removes them from a typical pattern of interaction with their peers and also makes it more difficult to learn and master skills that are essential to developing a sense of industry.

Numerous strategies are recommended in counteracting a sense of inferiority among dying school-age children. Dying children can be encouraged to develop new interests and skills that they can be proud of and that can be shared with others. For example, suggest they show new magic tricks, photo albums, or baseball card collections to family and friends. Further, many strategies that were noted earlier as being helpful for a younger age group (i.e., toddlers, preschoolers) are also appropriate, if adapted somewhat, for older children. For example, school-age children also have a need for independence and should be given the opportunity to do as many things for themselves as they can.

ADDITIONAL NEEDS OF DYING CHILDREN

Several needs of dying young children have already been discussed as they relate to cognitive and psychosocial development. Additional needs will be examined, together with strategies as to how to help in meeting those needs. These needs include

- trust,
- minimal separation,
- pain management,
- normalization (consistency in activities, continued school attendance, continued peer interaction).

Trust

Many, if not most, terminally ill children seem to know that they are dying. This insight develops even if they are not directly told the truth about the expected outcome of their illness. Children may gain an understanding that they are seriously ill through a variety of cues in their environment (Doka, 1995). They may be hospitalized with little explanation as to what is wrong with them and no reference to when they will get better. Lack of such information, in this situation, may be quite different from other experiences with illness and may suggest to children that something is seriously wrong or else there would be comforting messages to the contrary.

Due to others' tears, withdrawal patterns, hushed voices, or overheard comments, children may suspect that death is approaching. In addition, children may know they are dying by being sensitive to their own symptoms and changes in body functions (Bluebond-Langner, 1978). Although young children who are not dealing with a life-threatening illness may not fully understand the concept of death, as discussed earlier in this chapter, children who are dying "appear to have a precocious understanding of the concepts of death and their personal mortality. This occurs even if the adults have decided not to inform the child of the terminal nature of the illness" (Schonfeld, 1993, p. 273).

Children may share that they are aware of the seriousness of their illness in a variety of ways. For example, Elisabeth Kübler-Ross describes a picture drawn by a young boy who had not been told directly of his impending death. In the drawing, he holds up a stop sign in an attempt to halt the forward movement of a big tank (death) that is approaching. Other children may indicate their awareness by statements such as "I am not going to get old" or "My birthday is going to come without me." Some children directly ask, "Am I going to die?" Sometimes children need to be given a type of "opening statement" from a caring adult so that they know that it is safe to share concerns. For example, an adult might say such things as

- "This must be a time when you are feeling confused or mixed up."
- "This must be a scary time for you."
- "Death is sad for all of us. Let's talk and see if we can help one another."
  (Excell, 1991, p. 88)

Regardless of how children indicate awareness of their approaching death or ask for confirmation of their suspicions, others should give honest answers. Open communication has been found to be beneficial to dying children (Graham-Pole, Wass, Eyberg, & Chu, 1989); it helps to build the essential element of trust. Not only does communication play an important role through the illness process itself, but, if a child survives the illness, the pattern of open communication helps ensure later psychosocial adjustment (Fritz, Williams, & Amylon, 1988).

Information about the illness, treatments, new environments, and other changes should be shared in language that the child can understand. Honesty is an important factor because dishonesty can seriously undermine the foundation of trust in a relationship between the child and parents or medical personnel (Schonfeld, 1993). One of the authors still clearly recalls an incident that occurred when she was 7 years old, during hospitalization for a tonsillectomy. The operation took place a couple of weeks prior to Easter; at one point, the anesthesiologist said, "Count to 10 backwards and you will see the Easter bunny." The author can still recall the anger at waking up without seeing the Easter bunny; and, instead, waking up with an unexpected sore throat! More important, she remembers the distrust that was a direct outcome of that lie.

If trust is undermined, children become increasingly fearful and feel a sense of isolation. Additionally, there is the risk that a child will be told of the illness by someone outside of the family or medical staff: someone who assumed the child already knew about his or her serious illness. Chesler, Paris, and Barbarin (1986) share the following anecdote in which this occurred:

> . . . she knew something was wrong even though we didn't tell her much. A teacher at school one day told the class our daughter had cancer; and she was sitting right there. That was the first she had heard of it. (p. 512)

Evidence suggests that children's fears magnify behaviors such as refusing treatment, agitated crying, and hostile outbursts, particularly in situations they regard to be highly stressful (Broome, 1986). Because a great deal of a dying child's existence is stressful (e.g., ongoing medical exams, various treatment regimens, interactions with strangers), it is crucial that ways be found to minimize their fears.

Withholding information from a dying child is certainly not tied to ill intent. More likely other motivations exist, for example, a desire to protect a child from the knowledge of death (or an uncertain future), or a concern that information will cause the child to "give up" and die more quickly. In an AIDS diagnosis, there is sometimes an unwillingness to admit the parent's own infection and role in passing the disease to the child. Parents may be worried that if they tell the child and the child tells others, the family may be ostracized (Lipson, 1993). Although parents hope that these children will somehow be spared further distress by withholding information, a negative outcome is more typically the case.

Minimal Separation

One of the primary fears of young children is that of separation (Rait & Holland, 1986). Although fear of separation is exhibited in many situations, it is heightened in the hospital setting. Bowlby (1980) described the behavior of hospitalized children and determined that they pass through three stages related to the separation from their primary caregiver. Those stages include the following:

1. Protest marks the initial stage and is characterized by an urgent effort to recover the lost caregiver. The child "will often cry loudly, shake his cot, throw himself about, and look eagerly towards any sight or sound which might prove to be his missing mother" (p. 9).
2. Despair characterizes the second stage as the child's hope for his caregiver's return diminishes. "Ultimately the restless noisy demands cease: he becomes apathetic and withdrawn, a despair broken only perhaps by an intermittent and monotonous wail. He is in a state of unutterable misery" (p. 9).
3. Detachment is the final stage and is characterized by an absence of attachment behavior (such as physically withdrawing, refusing to be held or cuddled) when the child is reunited with the caregiver.

As professionals have become increasingly aware of the need to minimize a dying child's separation from loved ones, particularly parents, we have seen the introduction of a variety of innovations in medical settings. For example, parents are allowed to "room-in" with their children. In some instances, parents actually share the same room; in others, parents stay in another room in the hospital set aside for that purpose. Communities sometimes provide temporary, low-cost housing for out-of-town families seeking medical care. An example of these types of facilities are the Ronald McDonald houses in a number of cities

HOW TO IMPROVE COMMUNICATIONS WITH PARENTS OF DYING CHILDREN

If parents are to be helpful resources to children with serious illness and provide them with the support they need, the parents themselves must clearly understand information regarding the child's situation. Dr. Michael Stevens recommends the following guidelines:

- In early discussions with parents, invite them to include a close friend or relative—they may remember information that the parents themselves may forget.
- If possible, include both parents; there is less chance that one will misinterpret information and this also recognizes the importance of both parents.
- Give the parents a clear description of the illness in language that they will understand.
- Provide sufficient time for the parents to ask questions.
- Give a written summary of the discussion to the parents or tape record the session.
- Since parents are likely to be in shock during the initial discussion(s), repeat information as needed.
- Recommend that the family meet with another family that has a child who has done well with a similar diagnosis.

SOURCE: M. M. Stevens (1994). Improving communication with parents of children with cancer. *The Medical Journal of Australia, 160,* 325–326.

across the United States, supported by the McDonald Corporation and local fund-raising drives.

Opportunities for parents and/or siblings to remain close benefit both the terminally ill children and their families. Children's separation anxiety and parents' ensuing guilt may both be minimized. Additionally, staying in living quarters that are in close proximity to the child reduces travel time and conserves physical energy.

More and more families, with the help of hospice organizations and home health care providers, are choosing to care for dying children in their own homes. Although there are many reasons for this choice, one significant one is that "most children are more comfortable in the home environment as compared to the less familiar and more invasive hospital setting" (Hutter, Farrell, & Meltzer, 1991, p. 197). Another primary reason for caring for a child at home is to minimize the separation of dying children from their families.

Pain Management

Although pain management is clearly a need of individuals of all ages, it is discussed in this chapter because the manner in which children respond to and display pain is affected to some degree by their developmental stage (Bradshaw & Zeanah, 1986; Ross & Ross, 1984).

There are developmental differences in how children communicate that they are in pain and also in how they can cope with discomfort. Because children cannot communicate their feelings or thoughts as clearly and as directly as adults do, caregivers must derive insight from nonverbal cues and provide opportunities for children to express themselves. Nonverbal cues include squirming, rubbing an area, clenching teeth, rigidity, trembling, irritability, and facial cues (Atchison, Guercio, & Monaco, 1986). Young children may physically strike out at the adult who "causes" them pain by performing a particular medical treatment.

Preschool children have language capacity that allows them at least some ability to explain how they feel. Their verbal communication may include comments that it hurts; even so, it may be very difficult for some to accurately describe the type (or intensity) of pain, or localize it (Lutz, 1986).

Preschoolers, who live in the here and now, often do not derive comfort from hearing that the pain will end. The hurt is now and seems as if it will last forever. Preschoolers fear intrusive procedures (Rait & Holland, 1986) and imagine devastating outcomes, such as all their blood running out of the hole in the finger where some blood was drawn. School-age children are able to better understand the cause of the pain and also that it may be time-limited. This age group worries, however, that the pain may limit their involvement in activities with their peers or if they show their pain, peers may think less of them. School-agers, then, may deny that they are in pain, even when they are in distress.

Precautions should be taken to minimize pain and teach children effective strategies for minimizing discomfort (e.g., massaging an area or doing imagery or deep breathing techniques to help one relax). Confidence in one's ability to cope diminishes fear of an anticipated painful event and also increases ability to withstand pain (Ross & Ross, 1984).

Parental attitudes influence the child's unique pain experience. "Parents can do much to console the child, decrease anxiety, and help the child cope with the pain. . . . There can be no better pain medicine than a parent's soothing touch and words of love" (Atchison et al., 1986, p. 403). On the other hand, fears can be magnified by a parent who is overly concerned and highly anxious. This transmission of anxiety is a type of **emotional contagion** and can magnify a child's fears about a painful procedure (Lutz, 1986). In some unfortunate incidents parents can negatively affect a child's anticipation of an event by using a certain procedure as a threat (e.g., "If you don't stop that, I will ask the nurse to give you a shot") or give a child a message about the parent's acceptance of expressing their pain (e.g., "If you keep crying, I will leave").

Some research projects have found gender-related differences connected to the expression of pain. In one particular study, school-age boys said they "felt brave," whereas girls felt "nervous or afraid" (Haley, 1985). These differences would seem to reflect differences in childhood socialization practices.

ONE CHILD'S COPING STRATEGIES

A child with leukemia had developed a variety of coping strategies as he dealt with his illness. His strategies for coping are paralleled with a rationale, as defined by the therapist.

Content of Session	Rationale/Analysis
Tim's tips:	
1. Calm down when the doctor wants to help you.	Belief in power of doctor to take control and cure. Guilt that something you do could jeopardize outcome.
2. Find out what is going to happen and why.	Information seeking in order to master the situation. Knowing what to expect increases feeling of control.
3. Take deep breaths.	Relaxation and distraction aid coping.
4. Get hugs from Mom and Dad.	Need to feel safe; increased dependence on parents; fear of separation and abandonment.
5. Count while the needle is in.	Distraction; active participation to decrease feeling helpless.
6. Think of nice things.	Reaction formation; imagery used for distraction and to minimize negative associations.
7. Think about getting better.	Positive attitude as a way to feel in control and be a partner in cure.
8. It's OK to cry, but never say no!	Appropriate expression of feelings; limit setting on behavior. Doctor and parents are still in control.
9. Drink something or do something else.	Need for nurturance, distraction.
10. When you feel sad, talk to Mom or Dad or someone who is there.	Need for outside support; need for verbalization and expression of feelings.
11. Tell your friends to ignore that you are sick.	Coping with changed identity and need for normalizing childhood experiences and socialization.

SOURCE: N. B. Webb (1991). *Play therapy with children in crisis: A casebook for practitioners.* New York: The Guilford Press, pp. 317–318.

Additionally, cultural background may also affect how a child expresses pain. For example, Hispanic children may feel more comfortable outwardly expressing their pain, whereas Oriental children are typically more stoic (Atchison, et al., 1986). The gender and cultural differences being reported here relate to the expression of pain *not* the actual perception of pain. Further, many within-group (gender or ethnic) differences exist as well.

Normalization

Many changes in the lives of dying children cannot be avoided and often cause stress. It is helpful, therefore, to strive for normalization in other facets of life (Varni, Kata, Colegrove, & Dolgin, 1993). **Normalization** involves a consistency in interactions, activities, and routines that provides a sense of predictability, security, and comfort. To better understand various aspects of this normalization process, one must bring to mind issues raised during earlier discussions of Erikson's stages of autonomy, initiative, and industry. Recall the need to engage in ongoing skill development and enhancement of body integrity.

Consistency in Activities.   Children find comfort in continuing activities that they had enjoyed previously while in good health. These may include playing with siblings, going to day care or to school, and listening to bedtime stories. Involvement in these activities provides a sense of security and also underscores the need to focus on the fact that a dying child is also a living child. Given the understanding of normal physical development, one should ensure, if at all possible, that the child is given opportunity to engage in physical activities appropriate for the child's stage of development.

Many hospitals clearly understand the importance of making children as comfortable as they can and planning activities that are similar to what they would normally be accustomed. Because sharing food in a comfortable atmosphere is a focus of many family interactions, some hospitals encourage all family members to eat together in the playroom. Staff members often put sheets on the tables to serve as tablecloths and create various centerpieces to add color; one program encourages children to engage in a cooking activity with parents, such as preparing a dessert.

Because parents normally discipline their children, they should continue to provide appropriate guidelines and limits for those who are dying. Consistency in expectations and beliefs regarding right and wrong allows a child more easily to predict a parent's reaction and, as a result, engenders to sense of trust and control. Suddenly allowing a child to misbehave (simply because he or she is very ill) can endanger the safety of the child or others, damage property, and cause conflict and much more. Children who repeatedly disobey even after clear guidelines are given may be trying to communicate some symbolic message to others (Bigner, 1998). Parents and other caregivers should attempt to determine a child's motivation for misbehaving in order to deal more effectively with the underlying concerns. For example, a young boy who would repeatedly misbehave in the hospital playroom by throwing toys or being aggressive to other children finally told a staff member, "I want somebody to pay attention to me! My parents never do!"

Children need to be allowed to be children. Even dying children want to engage in play activities, attend school, and interact with peers. Focusing exclusively on either a child's illness or on the child's normal developmental needs can cause despair. We need to acknowledge both the reality of the disease and the need, within limitations prescribed by the disease, to pursue normal activities and interests. Although Levenson and Cooper (1984) made the following statement regarding chronically ill children, it can be generalized to dying children as well:

> As a group, distinctive needs have been identified. To avoid or negate these differences denies many of the realities that shape the child's existence. Conversely, too much focus on differences can be disturbing to the child and exacerbate feelings of alienation and lowered self-esteem. Assurance that they are "like everyone else" can appear as not credible and inaccurate to children daily confronted with their limitations. (p. 448)

Continued School Attendance.   Because school attendance is such a focal point in their lives, most dying school-age children prefer to return to school, if at all possible. Participation in school activities can promote a sense of normality within certain limiting parameters. In addition to continuing their academic development, these children are able to maintain a sense of control and are allowed to continue relationships with teachers and peers (Hobbie & Hollen, 1993).

Levenson and Cooper (1984) identify five major areas of concern regarding the teachers' roles in meeting the needs of children with cancer:

- Communication—Teachers and parents need to share information about the illness with schoolmates so that they feel more comfortable interacting with the child who is sick.
- Organization—Teachers should plan appropriate strategies to promote the child's academic progress prior to and during the reentry period.
- Identification of emotional problems—School staff should be alert to emotional concerns and behavioral changes in order to work cooperatively with parents in facilitating the child's readjustment to school.
- Identification of physical problems—Teachers need to recognize fatigue or other physical changes resulting from the illness or its treatment so that they may appropriately adapt teaching styles, assignments, and instructional equipment.
- Facilitation of the child's involvement in school activities—examples include allowing the child to attend school on a very flexible schedule, sending tutors to the medical facility, and having peers take homework assignments to the child.

Each child should have an individualized education plan (Deasy-Spinetta & Tarr, 1985) that considers the following:

- long-term goals and short-term objectives;
- specialized services needed by the child to function successfully; and
- modification of standards of competency.

Continued Peer Interaction.   School-age children expand their social environment well beyond their family boundaries and pursue opportunities to interact with other children as they play in their neighborhoods and attend school. Peer groups become an important social force during this life stage and serve many different functions. They provide opportunities to develop a variety of interpersonal skills as children communicate with one another, learn to co-operate, assert themselves, and interact in many different ways. Unfortunately, children with life-threatening illness are at risk of developing a sense of isolation, given diminished opportunities to interact with others.

Compared with preschoolers, school-age children have much greater mastery over the use of language. They are able to share information, communicate ideas, and express their desires. Words themselves are imbued with a great deal of power; for example, name-calling can have a dramatic effect on a child's mood. Many childhood fights begin with taunts such as "crybaby" or "fatso." Although some children fight words with words and retort, "sticks and stones may break my bones, but names will never hurt me," other children seem to be emotionally devastated by having been labeled in a negative fashion. A child who has undergone chemotherapy and has lost his or her hair is at great risk of being publicly taunted with "baldy" unless children are told the relevant circumstances. Varni et al. (1993) found that it can be helpful to teach ill children how to interact with their peers and their teachers. In their treatment group, children were taught problem-solving skills, assertiveness, and how to handle teasing and name-calling. Young people receiving this training reported that it was helpful in that they believed they were able to get more assistance from their classmates and their teachers; parents reported that those who had received the training exhibited fewer behavior problems and more school competence as compared with the control group of children who did not have the training. Information and skills training are needed not only by the children who are ill, but also by their peers if they are to be understanding and supportive. One study determined that clearing up misconceptions related to AIDS affected children's reactions to a peer (Maieron, Roberts, & Prentice-Dunn, 1996).

Children derive a sense of belongingness from membership in a peer group, which, in turn, promotes a sense of security and self-confidence. That sense of belonging, however, typically carries with it a definite price. Children must often adhere rigidly to a set of group norms, behaviors, and standards for physical appearance. Individual differences often lead to a child's being ostracized. Kids typically rank members of a group in hierarchical fashion along a variety of dimensions, such as physical attractiveness or athletic capability. Children then use rankings of particular characteristics to make judgments regarding who is to be considered as popular and who is to be rejected. A number of researchers have found a relationship between popularity and social desirability. A child who has experienced many physical changes as the result of a life-threatening illness is at risk for being regarded as "ugly" or "strange" and, therefore, for being rejected from the peer group. Kleck, Richardson, and Ronald (1974) have noted that rejection is all the more difficult for children to deal with if they are unable to change the personal trait causing the isolation.

One fifth-grade class in California so wanted a classmate to feel that he belonged, that they shaved their own heads when the child lost his hair due to chemotherapy treatment for cancer. Although many might question whether this was going "above and beyond" to ensure a sense of belongingness, it certainly illustrates these classmates' caring and their insight that it is difficult to be considered different.

Children who are seriously ill derive comfort from continued peer support. Sick children's psychological adjustment and self-acceptance are influenced by the perceptions and reactions of their peers (Potter & Roberts, 1984). Teaching the dying child how to communicate with peers about his or her illness can facilitate a positive psychological outcome. Weitzman (1984) suggests that parents or teachers discuss with the sick child the variety of possible reactions of peers and even role-play appropriate types of interactions with them. Healthy peers may also have many questions or even anxieties related to their friend's illness. Parents, teachers, and school counselors, among others, can be very helpful by answering questions openly and honestly and by sharing information on an appropriate developmental level.

Sachs (1980) described a situation in which an 8-year-old's classmates visited him whenever they were able. This child with osteogenic sarcoma (a type of bone cancer) had his leg amputated and lost his hair due to chemotherapy treatments. The school counselor became aware that the child's peers were curious about a number of issues and had queried, "'We saw him fall and cut his foot: did that have anything to do with his leg being amputated?' 'Do you get cancer because you fell?' 'Are tumors and amputations contagious?' 'When you remove part of the body does it stop cancer?'" (Sachs, 1980, p. 330). The school counselor and nurse were able to provide much useful information by using visual aids to describe normal and abnormal cell growth, the use of chemotherapy and its side effects, the reason for the amputation, and related matters. Additionally, they showed an artificial limb and demonstrated how it worked.

Although sharing this type of factual information is crucial to a better understanding of a dying child's experience, the discussion should also allow an opportunity for classmates to share feelings. They need to feel comfortable talking about their reactions and gain solace. Anxieties or confusion about such factors as physical differences, mood changes, or uncertain outcomes of the disease may affect continuing peer relationships unless children are given support and guidance regarding how to deal with their concerns.

DYING CHILD'S CONCEPT OF SELF

Myra Bluebond-Langner (1978, 1989) has added much to our understanding of the changes of a child's concept of self as a serious illness progresses. Knowledge that death is approaching is a gradual process and depends on information shared, observations of others, and changing experiences with the illness itself (e.g., experiencing both remissions and relapses). With this multifaceted knowledge base, children must struggle with a changing self-concept. The progression of this change moves from the belief that one is "seriously ill" to the ultimate understanding that one is "terminally ill." Figure 5.2 portrays the parallel between acquisition of information and changes in self-concept.

FIGURE 5.2

Bluebond-Langner's Model of Transitions in the Self-Concepts of Dying Children

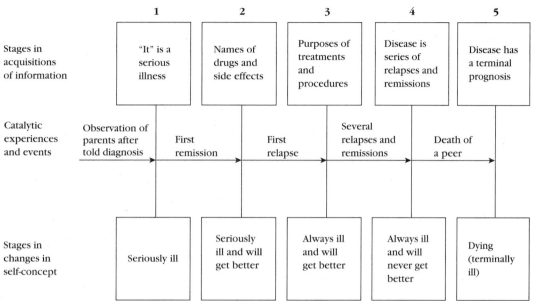

SOURCE: M. Bluebond-Langner (1989). World of dying children and their well siblings. *Death Studies, 13,* 1–16. Reprinted by permission.

CHILD-LIFE PROGRAMS

In an effort to be as helpful as possible in meeting the needs of sick children (of all ages) and their families, many hospitals currently hire staff members called **child-life specialists.** These individuals assume a very important role in preparing the child and family for what is to come. They serve as an emotional support in times of stress and act as an advocate for the entire family. The training of a child-life professional includes an academic background in child growth and development, family systems, facilitation of play activities, and communication skills. An understanding of a child's developmental level provides insights into the age-related needs, capabilities, and interests. This information is crucial if the child-life worker is to be successful in planning interventions that are appropriate for sick children of various ages. The child-life specialist understands that the crisis precipitated by the illness affects the entire family and that care must be taken to meet not only each individual's needs, but also those of the larger family system. Many of the therapeutic interventions discussed later in this chapter are used by child-life specialists in their work, including play therapy and bibliotherapy. A few specific examples as they relate to a hospital setting will be included in this section.

Preparation for Hospitalization

Hospitalization itself, as well as various medical procedures, become all the more frightening if a child does not know what to expect or is confused about the illness itself. Researchers have found that stress that is produced by hospitalization and various medical procedures can be mitigated by appropriate preparation. Opportunities must be given to children both to acquire information and to express their emotions (Bates & Broome, 1986); play can be a powerful tool for accomplishing these goals (see expanded discussion on play therapy later in this chapter). Guided medical play allows professionals to share information about upcoming events with children. Play serves as means for children to explain their perceptions about illness and medical procedures, share their concerns, and vent their emotions (Jesse, 1992).

The following case studies shared by Petrillo and Sanger (1980) illustrate the confusion experienced by many children and the need for clear, honest communication.

> Jenny developed precocious puberty and an insatiable appetite at age four because of a brain tumor. She attributed these symptoms to a little man in her stomach who ate her food and caused her trouble. (p. 70)

> At age five, Audrey required a nephrectomy for treatment of Wilm's tumor. After a five-year remission, she was readmitted with metastatic disease. Her nurse asked the reason for the large surgical scar on her abdomen. She explained, "Parts of my body get rotten." (p. 71)

A child-life worker can prepare the child and other family members using a variety of strategies. For example, a tour of the hospital a week or so before admission allows the child to become more familiar with the physical surroundings. Tours often include the check-in area, the operating area, recovery room, and rooms on the pediatric floor (such as a patient's room and the playroom).

Children also gain comfort by being prepared for various medical procedures that they will encounter. Appropriate information includes such facets as

- aspects of the child's illness;
- the need for a particular procedure;
- information about the procedure itself (e.g., procedural process, body part involved, length of time to perform);
- bodily sensation after completion of procedure; and
- expected outcome (short- and long-term).

Such information needs to be presented in terms that the child can understand. Explanations often become more clear to a child when there is opportunity for active involvement. For example, children who simply hear the terms *stethoscope* or *blood pressure cuff* may have very little comprehension of what they are or how they are used.

Children, however, who are allowed to see and manipulate these devices have a much clearer understanding; they can learn a great deal about an upcoming operation if they are shown a simplified model or picture of the human body. Location of the incision can be identified and an explanation given about the operation itself. Children can be shown how their bodies will change after the surgery and demonstrations of certain procedures can be performed on a doll (such as the application of a real cast).

For example, one hospital uses a doll named Charlie to demonstrate how an IV is inserted in the wrist, with an explanation regarding the rationale for the procedure and how it would feel. Children often stick the doll with a real needle under the supervision of a staff member. The staff member can ask such questions as "Why does the nurse put the needle in your arm?" "What does Charlie have wrong with him?" or "Can you explain how the IV can help Charlie?" Many children often return to the playroom after they have had an IV and ask to play with Charlie again. The children experience a cathartic effect by repeatedly sticking the needle into the doll and once again processing the experience and rationale behind it with a staff member. Books, films, and puppet shows can also be useful in helping to prepare children for upcoming events.

Children acquire preparation through the availability of various props, but the real value comes through the sensitive interaction with a trained individual who can give accurate information and emotional support as the props are being utilized. Opportunity for the child to ask questions and share concerns is crucial.

Emotional Support

By conversing with children and by watching their play, health care professionals can learn a great deal about children's emotional reactions to illness and hospitalization. Although they are by no means the only staff members providing emotional support, child-life specialists do play an important role. Because they are trained in child development, they may have insights that other personnel without this developmental perspective do not have; therefore, during interdisciplinary staffings, they can share important information about emotional concerns and helpful intervention strategies. By the very nature of their professional assignments within the hospital, child-life workers often have more time to spend with children and family members who are struggling with the emotional impact of an illness.

Child-life specialists and other staff members must be prepared to give emotional support for a variety of concerns such as those illustrated by the following anecdote:

> Will, age seven, developed visual disturbances and was hospitalized for diagnostic studies. His parents were so overwhelmed with the realistic possibility of a brain tumor that they could not discuss the illness with him. Will told his nurse that he had figured out he was admitted to have his eyes removed. (Petrillo & Sanger, 1980, p. 72)

Adults need to spend time with hospitalized children to determine their concerns. Children's fears and questions are often manifest in indirect ways at unpredictable times. Additionally, many hospital staff members believe that it is important to spend "nonpainful" time with children between painful medical procedures to help the child learn that it is the procedure that causes pain not the medical professional performing the procedure (Atchison et al., 1986).

Advocacy

Although medical staff are concerned about the well-being of their patients, having others act as advocates in their behalf can still be useful. Policies, procedures, and the physical environment itself should be evaluated on an ongoing basis to ensure compatibility with the primary goal of meeting the needs of patients and families. For many years, hospitals limited the number of hours that parents could spend with their sick child. Through the advocacy work of child-life specialists and others sensitive to the emotional and social needs of young children, those restrictions have been greatly relaxed or even lifted. The policy of limiting visiting hours was found to be detrimental to children who feared separation from parents or who felt they were sick because of something they had done wrong and were being punished by their parents. Recall that separation anxiety and unfounded guilt are common during childhood. It is very beneficial to children and their parents to have persons within the health-related professions serve as advocates: individuals who understand the developmental needs of children and patterns of family interaction.

Child-life specialists and pediatric nurses often serve in this role for young children by stressing the need for normalcy in children's lives. For example, play is an important part of a child's normal existence, and, as a result, large numbers of hospitals have playrooms or games to take to a child's bedside. Staff members also encourage children to bring some of their own toys to the hospital and decorate their rooms; these, too, can help normalize the child's everyday experience.

THE GRIEVING CHILD

Some people may question whether young children grieve as the result of experiencing a significant loss. It is certain that young children do grieve, although they may do so in a somewhat different manner than adults. This section identifies many of the common manifestations of children's grief as well as factors that may intensify that response.

Clinical research has identified a number of common manifestations of grief among children, including

- manifold fears, separation anxiety, fear of abandonment, fear that others close to them will die or they themselves will die, death fantasies;
- guilt due to magical thinking;

A city blocked off an intersection so that children could say good-bye to a friend who was killed a few days earlier when a car struck him.

- learning difficulties, lowered school grades;
- somatic complaints, eating disorders;
- regressive behaviors (e.g., bedwetting, thumbsucking);
- aggressive behavior, temper tantrums, explosive emotions, acting-out behavior, discipline problems;
- inhibited behavior, social withdrawal;
- sadness, crying, despair, depression;
- overdependent behavior, helplessness; and
- sleep disorders.

Similar to grief reactions among adults, those of children are highly variable (Fink, Birenbaum, & Chand, 1994). Elizur and Kaffman (1983) found that bereavement symptoms were more intense in children who had a history of poor impulse control, a tendency to handle frustration with outbursts of anger, a pattern of withdrawal in other relationships, and higher levels of adjustment difficulties. Further, they discovered that, after the death of their husbands, the mothers' mourning patterns were related to their children's in that "where mothers exhibited over-restraint, withholding of emotional expression, and inability to share with the child expressions of grief and memories of the deceased, the children showed signs of considerable emotional distress during the first months" (p. 673). The latter finding confirms our understanding that involvement in a conspiracy of silence minimizes the opportunity to share feelings, magnifies fears, creates misunderstandings and confusion, and contributes to a sense of loneliness.

Although many adults would like to spare children the knowledge that a loved one has died and the subsequent grief, this is simply not possible, nor should it be attempted. Children need the opportunity to say good-bye, to share feelings, and to vent emotions. They also require the same opportunities to accomplish their grief work as do adults. Adults, then, should be prepared to provide support to children who have experienced a loss. Children may interpret a lack of acknowledgment of the death itself or their feelings of grief as insensitivity, meanness, or lack of caring.

Many adults question whether children should be permitted to attend a funeral. It is often helpful to give the children themselves the option as to whether they would like to attend; when the choice is their own, they are less likely to feel angry at someone else for having made a "wrong" decision. Prior to making a decision, children need information regarding various facets of the experience. For example, it is helpful to explain what a casket looks like, whether it is likely to be open or closed, information about the ritual, and the fact that many persons may be distressed, crying, and so on. If children do choose to attend the funeral, they should be allowed the option of not participating in certain aspects of the ritual (e.g., walking by an open casket) that might cause them discomfort. Advantages of attending the funeral include the opportunity to confirm the fact that the death has occurred, to share grief in a larger community, and to feel the support that is offered.

Giving children the choice to attend the funeral is not always possible or reasonable. Based on their usual parenting styles, some parents are simply not likely to provide the option. In other instances, someone else in the family may have such strong feelings against the child's going that it is not wise to give the choice. If the child does not attend the funeral, it is often helpful to encourage participation in some other ritual to say good-bye formally, such as writing a letter to the person who has died.

Although children's experience of bereavement is painful and ongoing, grief does not seem to be as all-consuming as it is for adults. Children can be very sad one minute, but playful and happy the next. Engaging in play may be the child's way of coming to terms with the loss and may provide a much needed catharsis of emotions or allow mastery of a particular concept. In other instances, a child's play may serve a function similar to an adult's preoccupation with work.

Because young children have comparatively short attention spans and are quite easily distracted, adults frequently perceive that children have resolved their grief much sooner than actually is the case. This misconception that children's grief work is completed may cause premature withdrawal of support. As with adults, grief frequently lasts for an extended time, and concern and comfort are needed throughout. Just as there are tasks of mourning for adults who are bereaved, so too are there tasks for bereaved children; these have been defined by Baker, Sedney, and Gross (1992) to include the following:

- understand that someone has died;
- accept and emotionally acknowledge the reality of the loss;
- reevaluate the relationship to the person who is lost;
- face the psychological pain of the loss;
- develop a new sense of personal identity that includes the experience of the loss;
- invest in new emotional relationships without a strong sense of fear of yet another loss;
- maintain an internal relationship with the person who has died;
- return to age-appropriate developmental tasks; and
- cope with periodic resurgence of pain.

To better understand the death from the child's perspective, one must provide opportunities for children to share their thoughts and feelings. As with many aspects of behavior, children will model what they see in adults who are grieving. If they are taught by words or by actions that talking about the person who has died is wrong, children may withdraw and not ask for much needed information and support. If they are taught that crying is a sign of weakness, they may choose to hide their tears rather than seek solace from those around them. "The memory of the death experience and the manner in which the child is treated by adults may last beyond childhood into adulthood" (Dickinson, 1992, p. 169).

Children need accurate information about the death itself and the events that follow (the funeral service, burial, cremation). Children who have misconceptions about these events must be given accurate information in concrete and specific terminology. For example, one can reassure children that the person who has died is not hungry or cold in the casket, does not wish to "get out" of the casket, and so forth. If we are honest with young children, they will still not fully understand the meaning of death, but they will learn that it is acceptable to discuss the death. Further, opportunities to talk can provide a great deal of comfort. Additionally, accurate information can help to alleviate young children's fears, build a sense of trust in others, and serve as the foundation for deeper understanding later on in the child's life, as maturation progresses. Information that is shared must be given at a level appropriate to their cognitive understanding of the event and their developmental level (Schonfeld & Kline, 1994).

Because young children think in concrete terms, rather than in the abstract, and because they tend to understand things in the literal sense, adults must be careful about how they explain circumstances surrounding a death. Adults who tell children that the deceased has "gone on a long trip" may expect to hear responses such as "When is grandpa coming back? Will he bring me a present?"

Many children carry a heavy burden of guilt following the death of another; because they have a difficult time separating fantasy from reality, children may assume they caused the death. One 3½-year-old child was extremely distressed over his older brother's death. The child had told his sibling to "Go away! Get out of here!" when the older brother was teasing him. The next day, the older boy was killed when he fell off the roof of the family's garage. Fortunately, a neighbor finally asked the child why he repeatedly cried, "I am so bad! I wished that he would go away, but I didn't really mean it" during the weeks that followed. His response indicated that he thought he had killed his brother because he had been mad earlier. If the neighbor had not asked the boy to explain how he felt about his brother's death and why he felt he was "so bad," the child might not have been reassured that he was in no way responsible.

As the years pass after the death of a loved one and as children grow and mature in their thinking and emotional processes, they can be faced, once again, with resolving grief-related issues. For example, a 4-year-old girl whose father died in a car accident may not totally resolve her grief in the months or years immediately following the death. As she grows older and her concept of death matures, she will gain deeper understanding of the permanence of death and what it means never again to interact with her father. As she becomes capable of thinking in the abstract, she may philosophically question the meaning of the death. As she becomes an adolescent and searches for her own identity, she grieves her loss anew and wonders how she herself would have been different had her father lived. When she grows into young adulthood status and gives birth to her first child, she mourns another aspect of her much earlier loss—the fact that her own child will never know her father, the baby's grandfather. In summary, it is important to understand that

> Children grieve in stages over many years. They will reprocess the experience at each new stage in their lives, applying new cognitive and emotional insights to try to reach a more satisfying explanation of a significant death. (Schonfeld, 1993, p. 272)

DEATH OF A PARENT

Although many resources are available to those who wish to study the effect of parental death on children, this section will review only a limited number. Berlinsky and Biller (1982) did a thorough review of the related literature available at that time by examining over 200 studies. These authors suggested an organizational model for understanding factors influencing adjustment subsequent to a parent's death.

They note that these factors include the type of death (e.g., sudden or prolonged illness, suicide, homicide, war); parent's age and sex; relationship with the child; the child's preparation for and involvement in the mourning process; and the child's age, sex, personality, and cognitive level. Additionally, family characteristics such as family structure, patterns of adjustment, cultural background, and religiosity must be examined for fuller understanding of the effect of parental death on a child's behavior.

A number of generalizations can be drawn from the work of Berlinsky and Biller (1982) and Ikeman et al. (1987). (Recall that there are always exceptions.)

■ Because mothers and fathers often play different roles and fulfill different needs, loss of a mother would be expected to have a somewhat different

These children's lives will be changed forever as a result of their loss.

outcome than that of a father. Unfortunately, many studies ignore that probability and regard children of deceased parents as a homogeneous group.

■ There are a variety of common reactions to the death. Children typically experience some guilt, believing that something they did do or failed to do led to the death. The children also often regret the nature of their relationship with the deceased parent (wishing they had been closer or kinder, for example). Many children are angry at the deceased parent for having deserted them, particularly because children typically believe that the parent's primary purpose is to take care of them.

■ Children are likely to experience adverse effects if they are not given accurate information about the parent's death. Peers can often repeat exaggerated versions of the death based on conversations with adults. For example, one young child was in anguish thinking her mother had been decapitated in an auto accident. The daughter had seen a great deal of blood on her mother's dress after the accident, and children at school had told her "your mom's head was cut off." Although fatally injured due to severe head wounds, this woman had not been decapitated. Once the daughter was clearly given this truthful information, she was able to continue her grief work successfully.

■ Younger children seem to be more adversely affected by the death of a parent than are older children. It is hypothesized that these findings may be related to the younger child's inability to understand clearly the

PERSONAL SHARING: HELPING CHILDREN HEAL

As my students burst into my room on the first day of school every year, I already feel a bond with them. Maybe I don't yet know which name goes with which face, but I already care deeply about these kids and want to know what's happening in their lives. I want them to know they can talk to me. I want to do for them what no one did for me.

Called to the Office

I remember that October afternoon when I was in 2nd grade. I walked down the polished corridor toward the principal's office, my body tingling with excitement. I'd been called out of my class. Surely that must mean something important and special was going to happen. Maybe I would be the student of the month. My parents would be proud.

As I was about to enter the office, the principal came out to meet me. He suggested we sit in the molded plastic chairs by the school's front door and wait. I was too shy to ask what we were waiting for.

A few minutes passed before a car pulled up in front of the school. Two men got out. I recognized one as our minister and the other as an uncle I saw only once or twice a year. *What are they doing here?* I wondered. *My mom and dad are coming home from their business trip in Florida today. They'll be coming to pick me up soon.*

I slid into the front seat of the car. I saw that my older sisters and my aunt were sitting in the back. There was something scary about the looks on their faces. I said nothing. I sat still, looked straight ahead, and ran my tongue around the inside of my lower lip. After a long time, my uncle spoke.

"Lisa, I have something to tell you. There's been an accident. Your mom and dad's plane crashed into another plane over the ocean. They's only a slim chance that they're alive."

Well, I thought, *my parents are special. Of course they're alive. They're probably on a desert island waiting to be rescued.*

(Continued)

meaning of death, to their greater need for parental supervision, and/or to the lack of accumulated benefits for many of being from an intact family. These hypotheses need to be carefully tested before more definitive statements can be made.

- The family situation is likely to change after the death of a parent; this occurrence, in turn, affects the child's subsequent adjustment. Family circumstances that may be altered include emotional and physical availability of the surviving parent, employment status of the remaining parent, functional roles played by each family member, and possible entry into the family of a parent substitute (a new spouse or a paid caregiver).
- The child's relationship with the surviving parent is typically modified; many children worry about the parent's welfare, fearful that he or she,

(Continued From Previous Page)

But as I looked around me, the somber faces told me my wishful thinking wasn't true. Although I was only 7, I understood the permanence of death. I knew I'd never see my parents again.

No one talked. No one cried. We drove to our house and automatically walked inside.

For the next few days, people I didn't know flowed in and out of our house, bringing foods I didn't like and saying forced, cheery things. I remember the memorial service, all the cards and letters, and adult discussions about "what to do." My aunt gave me and my sisters sleeping pills before we went to bed at night. I just wanted these people to leave us alone.

Silence

I went back to school 3 days later. My teachers didn't mention what had happened, as if not talking about it would make it go away. My mom and dad had vanished from my life, but everyone at school acted as if I'd been out sick with a cold.

When I think about that experience now, ideas of what my teachers could have done to help me flood into my mind. Of course no one could have brought my parents back, but there are things they could have done to ease my pain. A hug would have gone a long way to comfort me. A teacher who took a few minutes to talk with me about my parents' death would have helped. I had so many questions that I needed to have answered and thoughts I needed to share: *Why did the plane crash? Were there sharks in the water? Where were my parents' bodies?* And I wish my teachers would have thought twice about saying, "Have your mom and dad sign your report card" or "Invite your parents to our open-house program." I wasn't the only student who didn't have a mom and dad at home.

I've vowed to try my best to keep these things in mind for my students. I read their records and note who has gone through any type of trauma, such as a death, divorce, or serious illness. I can't always tell if a student is hurting, so I try to let my students know from the very start that they can talk with me about anything. Those discussions aren't easy, but they just might help the student more than I'll ever know.

SOURCE: L. Johnson (1993). Helping children heal. *Learning93,* August, p. 104.

too, may die and leave the child alone. Children may struggle against any separation from the parent, thinking that their presence will ensure the parent's safety. Some children take on extra responsibilities, hoping to spare the parent from additional stress. In some instances, children emotionally withdraw from the parent to protect themselves from another potential loss.

■ The relationship between the surviving parent and the child often becomes strained. Because the surviving parent is dealing with his or her own grief and is also often responsible for roles that had once been performed by the dying/deceased parent, the surviving mother or father may have decreased awareness of the child's needs. Additionally, the surviving parent may be so emotionally drained that there is little energy or attention left to give the child. As a result, the child may experience a double loss: one parent is dying or has died, the other has withdrawn. The child then often becomes angry at the surviving parent whom he or she holds responsible for all of the negative changes in the family's life.

■ In some situations, there may be a positive outcome to the death of a parent. For example, the death of an abusive or emotionally distant parent may have a positive influence on a child's self-concept and emotional adjustment. Even if the death is regarded by the child as a loss, he or she may ultimately become more resourceful as a result of the loss.

Researchers should carefully design controlled studies regarding children's adjustment to parental death. Because factors such as sex of parent, child's age at the time of the death, and suddenness of death have an influence on the outcome, these variables should be taken into consideration when determining the research design (Berlinsky & Biller, 1982).

In their study, Kaffman and Elizur (1979) controlled for the gender of the parent who died (the father) and the type of death (killed suddenly in war). They then compared the adjustment of young children between the ages of 2 and 6 to that of older children between the ages of 6 and 10. The 24 children studied were living on a kibbutz, a type of commune, in Israel. None of the children had been identified as having any unusual problems prior to the death of their fathers in the October 1973 war. Each child's behavior was reported by mothers and teachers over a period of 1 to 6 months after the death. All of the families were middle-class. The survivors did not have to fear financial stress after the death because food, clothing, and lodging were provided by the kibbutz. The similarity of circumstances of the children in this study provided controls not present in most other studies related to parental death.

Children in this study exhibited a variety of grief reactions similar to those noted earlier. Kaffman and Elizur (1979) found that almost all the children in their sample expressed their distress through noticeable behavioral changes and marked increase in the amount and severity of psychological symptoms. The reactive behavioral symptoms included a wide range of problems such as increased aggressiveness, tantrums, augmented dependency, separation anxiety, diverse fears, sleep problems, restlessness, changes in scholastic performance, discipline problems, wandering, daydreaming, eating problems, enuresis, thumbsucking, tics, excessive sibling rivalry, and so on.

Overt sadness, crying, preoccupation with the deceased father, imitation of and identification with the father, searching for a "substitute" father, and striving to remember the father were also common responses. Many children were able to directly relate their feelings of sadness with their father's death. One 6-year-old boy said, "Mommy, I loved Dad and now my heart hurts so much that it goes to my stomach and I can't eat."

The researchers discovered a number of differences between responses of the younger children (2 to 6) and the older children (6 to 10). The memories of younger children typically centered around "shared experiences," such as re-calling times shared with their father, looking at photograph albums, listening to tape recordings of his voice, or holding his personal effects. The older children processed the death at a somewhat different level. In addition to remembering shared experiences, they frequently asked to go to the cemetery or expressed their longing in a new context. One 6-year-old boy made up new words to a pop-ular song: "If I could travel to faraway places, if I could come back home, and see my father, not only my mother, if all our wishes could come true . . ."

Thirteen out of the 24 children talked about their fathers as if they were still alive. Ten of those 13 were preschoolers. They repeatedly made statements about their fathers' expected return, and many thought that their fathers were alive in their photographs. A 4-year-old girl asked her father's photograph, "Daddy dear, why don't you answer me? . . . Where is the war?"

Younger children also differed from the older children in a variety of other symptoms, which these researchers categorized as "behavioral symptoms" in contrast to "grief reactions." Younger children showed a greater increase in problems related to separation from their mothers, excessive demands on adults for assistance, nighttime fears, and rejection of strangers than did the older chil-dren. The older children, however, showed a greater increase in quietness.

It is difficult to conclude with any degree of certainty the long-term effects of parental death on individual children. Many variables influence the outcome, including sex of parent, quality of interaction with family members, age of child, and availability of a surrogate parent. The use of subjects who have sought psy-chological intervention (rather than use of a random sample of bereaved sur-vivors) is a common weakness of research that examines long-term impact of parental death. A clinical sample can give biased results because these individu-als (by nature of their selection) have identifiable adjustment difficulties.

DEATH OF A GRANDPARENT

A significant number of young persons experience the death of a parent, sibling, or friend during their early years; however, the first encounter that most have with death is the death of a grandparent. In some cases, relationships between children and their grandparents are quite close. Without the turmoil of many parent–child interactions, grandparents may represent safety and security for the young family members.

In other situations, the relationship may be more distant; in this case, chil-dren and adolescents may be less likely to experience intense grief at the time of the grandparent's death. However, the death may still serve to remind the young person of the frailty of life and the fact that death is the ultimate destiny of humans.

The grandparent's death may also have a profound impact on the child's parent (the grandparent's own child), which in turn will have consequences for the child. "The child, therefore, responds to the grandparent's death in both personal terms, based on the quality of the lost relationship, and in family systems terms, based on the reactions of other family members to the death" (Webb, 1991, p. 61).

THERAPEUTIC INTERVENTIONS

Intervention by Teachers and Counselors

Teachers and counselors play an important role in facilitating children's coping. Appropriate support is predicated on their understanding the normal grief process and resulting behavior problems. Many grieving children exhibit poor school performance or school phobias. These, too, require sensitivity and understanding. School-age children dread being regarded as different out of fear of feeling inferior. Teachers, therefore, should be sure that their discussions about or interactions with the children do not cause them to be ostracized by classmates.

Many expect that parents and teachers would play a significant role in providing support for bereaved children. However, there is evidence that many who desire to give such assistance feel unprepared to do so (Pratt, Hare, & Wright, 1987). For example, Cullinan (1990) found that only 19% of a group of 192 teachers had ever had any formal death education and 93% believed that they needed such education to be helpful to their students.

Cullinan (1990) suggests that teachers should come to terms with their own feelings of death as part of their preparation to help children who are grieving. Additionally, there are a number of content-based topics that would be helpful, including an understanding of

- children's bereavement patterns, normal manifestations of grief;
- children's cognitive understanding of the concept of death;
- children's common concerns following a death; and
- community resources.

Certainly, parents would also gain from similar educational preparation.

Peer Support Groups

Given the many developmental changes that occur during childhood and adolescence, we shall examine peer support for each of those two life stages. The structure of the groups, activities, and support strategies vary somewhat by age level. (Adolescent groups will be discussed in chapter 6.)

Because peer interaction is such an important part of the culture of childhood, support groups comprised of other children who have experienced similar losses provide an important therapeutic environment (Koch-Hattem, 1986). There are many different types of support groups, hosted by various organizations (e.g., schools, churches, hospices); involvement in such support groups may take place either prior to or after the death, or both. Many group activities involve multiple goals, such as

- allowing children to run, play, laugh, and make noise in order to release pent up energy and feelings;
- meeting other boys and girls who have also had a death in the family. By meeting others like themselves, the children discover that they share similar feelings, that those feelings are normal, and that they are okay for having them.

Although each support group is typically somewhat unique, common themes include (Masterman & Reams, 1988):

- getting to know one another;
- talking about the person who died;
- sharing thoughts and feelings resulting from the death;
- sharing information and feelings about the funeral (memorial service);
- sharing fears about the future;
- sharing information related to death or illness; and
- dealing with misconceptions.

Play Therapy

Play is an important part of young people's lives. It provides an opportunity to master skills, express ideas and feelings, deal with thoughts and emotions, and better understand one's environment. As is true for any child, play can become a valuable therapeutic modality for children who are dying or children who are grieving.

It is often difficult for children, especially younger ones, to articulate their concerns. The medium of play permits them to confront difficult situations on their own terms using a process over which they feel they have some control. For example, children can use dolls or puppets to express their fears and their pain; these toys can ask questions of adults that children are too afraid or too embarrassed to ask directly.

In one instance, a child who was given clay to play with at preschool one day created a body with a grossly enlarged head; shortly thereafter, he began to tear the head apart, saying "My mommy's head is going to explode!" He had overheard a conversation between his father and his aunt regarding the pressure exerted by his mother's brain tumor. After the episode with the clay, this child admitted to being extremely upset by the belief that his mother was going to "explode" and brains would "spill out all over." This young boy had not voiced his fear earlier; it seemed he first needed to communicate it symbolically through the creation of a clay model. Once he had communicated the emotion, his father and teacher were able to provide accurate information regarding his mother's medical situation to help reassure him.

Play activities themselves may be cathartic, allowing children to vent emotions that have long been latent (Segal, 1984) or they may also promote mastery of what children fear. For example, one child whose grandparents were killed in a flash flood repeatedly played with water until he was no longer fearful of approaching the river near his house.

Art Therapy

Children who are dealing with either their own impending deaths or that of another can communicate through various art activities as well. Through their art, children often express their needs, fears, questions, concerns regarding their illness, and even their acceptance of death (McIntyre, 1990; Rollins, 1990; Smith, 1991). Figure 5.3 depicts drawings by a young girl with muscular dystrophy who knows she will be dying soon.

Many facets of doing an art activity can be helpful (Belnick, 1993):
- The creative process can provide an emotional outlet.
- The *content* of the artwork provides important clues to others regarding the child's thoughts and feelings.

FIGURE 5.3
A Dying Child Illustrates Thoughts and Feelings of Her Illness and Death

SOURCE: A. Armstrong-Dailey (1995). *Hospice Journal, 6*(5), 18–20.

FIGURE 5.4
Artwork by Dying Child

SOURCE: The Center for Attitudinal Healing. (1978). *There is a rainbow behind every cloud* (p. 22). Millbrae, CA: Celestial Arts. Reprinted by permission.

■ The *communication* with others about the art piece itself and what it depicts provides opportunity for support (e.g., explain what is meant by the use of a particular color or inclusion of a particular figure, exclusion of a particular person).

Children's art is a tool that allows them to communicate with others symbolically. Sometimes children who rarely, if ever, express emotions verbally will spontaneously share them through their art work (Segal, 1984; Zambelli, Clark, Barile, & deJong, 1988).

Numerous books are currently available that include examples of children's artwork as it relates to concerns of illness, death, and grief. For example, the book entitled *There Is a Rainbow Behind Every Dark Cloud* (Center for Attitudinal Healing, 1978) includes a compilation of pictures drawn by cancer patients between the ages of 8 and 19. Figure 5.4 is one child's response to the request: "Draw a picture of yourself in the hospital." These two drawings are indicative of various concerns and would be good tools to elicit further

FIGURE 5.5
Artwork by Grieving Child

SOURCE: E. L. Levy (1982). *Children are not paper dolls.* Incline Village, NV: The Publisher's Mark. Reprinted by permission.

conversation about such topics as medical procedures, loneliness, being in a strange environment, or feeling overwhelmed by all that goes on in a hospital. The sequel, *Straight From the Siblings: Another Look at the Rainbow* (Center for Attitudinal Healing, 1982) includes drawings portraying the siblings' perspectives of living with a sick brother or sister.

SUGGESTED BOOKS FOR CHILDREN

Children's books offer an excellent avenue for children to better understand their own feelings about illness, death, and grief, while at the same time learning about cultural similiarities and differences.

Alexander, S. (1983). *Nadia the willful.* New York: Alfred A. Knopf. (Middle-Eastern setting; loss of a brother and the need to remember him.)

Bunting, E. (1982) *The happy funeral.* New York: Harper and Row. (Chinese-American; two young girls prepare for their grandfather's funeral.)

Clifton, L. (1983). *Everett Anderson's goodbye.* New York: Henry Holt and Company. (African-American family; grief of a young child after the death of his father.)

Coerr, E. (1977). *Sadako and the thousand paper cranes.* New York: Putnam's. (Japanese; a young girl dying of leukemia is reminded of a beautiful legend by a friend.)

Cork, B. T. (1990). *Going to the hospital.* New York: Derrydale Books. (Anglo; recommended for preschool children having a first hospital experience.)

Goble, P. (1989). *Beyond the ridge.* New York: Aladdin Books. (Native American; beautifully illustrated book for elementary school children focusing on the view of death among the Plains Indian culture.)

Pomerantz, B. (1983). *Bubby, me, and memories.* New York: UAHC Press. (Jewish-American; appropriate for elementary-age children.)

Walker, A. (1988). *To hell with dying.* San Diego, CA: Harcourt Brace. (An African-American college student recounts the life and death of an elderly childhood friend.)

Linn (1982) used artwork as a primary therapeutic modality in working with children whose siblings had died from a variety of causes. Her book *Children Are Not Paper Dolls* includes much of their artwork. The drawing in Figure 5.5, with its accompanying caption, expresses a child's concerns about her brother's death and misgivings about sleeping in the room in which he died. Figure 5.6 illustrates a child's perception of the violence that killed his dad.

Adults who interact with children about their artwork must let the children explain what they have drawn and not come to conclusions without appropriate input. Further, adults must try to understand children's drawings in terms of the cultural milieu. For example, Platt and Persico (1992) explain that Crow (Indian) children

tended to draw outdoor scenes, plants, and animals more readily than pictures of people or houses. In doing so, they seemed to reflect their greater experience with the outdoors, as well as the symbolic value their culture places on many animals and natural events. . . . A nine-year-old girl, separated from her family . . . spent many sessions drawing a bird ". . . all alone above trees, not

FIGURE 5.6

Artwork Depicting a Child's Perception of the Way His Dad Was Murdered as He Was Driving His Delivery Truck

SOURCE: L. Goldman (1996). *Breaking the silence.* Washington, DC: Taylor and Francis. Reprinted by permission.

able to find a nest." Another very withdrawn child first demonstrated feelings of closeness by drawing two horses, instead of the usual one, indicating to the therapist, "and that one's for you. You can ride with me." (pp. 288–289)

Bibliotherapy

Today there are many fiction books written for children and/or adolescents that include death-related content and associated emotional issues. These books allow children as well as adolescents to better understand that death is a natural part of life and that it is normal to feel sad or angry or any of a variety of other emotions. Reading about others who are dealing with similar circumstances and developing insights into their reactions help young people feel less alone in their grief and recognize their own reactions as quite normal. This feeling of normalcy, in and of itself, can provide much comfort. Youngsters who have been unable or unwilling to articulate their own thoughts or feelings may feel more comfortable doing so after reading a story that somewhat parallels their own circumstances.

Adults can use stories to initiate conversations about personal losses experienced by the child or adolescent. After reading a book or hearing a story, young people can explain how their own experience is similar or different to those of the characters in the book. This can provide a way to share thoughts and feelings in a manner that may be less threatening than simply talking about the child's or adolescent's own losses at the outset of a conversation. Further, even those who have not directly experienced a loss can develop a sense of empathy for others through literature (Klingman, 1985).

Storytelling is also a powerful tool for helping one to cope with an environment or a situation that is new or frightening or overwhelming to young people. Adults can tell stories about situations similar to the ones that children are dealing with; through this process, they can normalize feelings or suggest effective coping strategies (Brett, 1992).

SUMMARY

Dying children are living children. Not only do dying children have special needs by the very nature of the fact that they are dying, but they also have a need to live life to its fullest, given the limitations of their illnesses. Knowing information about various aspects of normal child development can provide a caregiver with important insights about how to give individual support and create a helping environment that is complementary to the needs, interests, and capabilities of the child.

As children mature, they refine their physical and cognitive capabilities and struggle to master varying psychosocial tasks. Their ability to comprehend various facets of illness and death matures over time as they move from a more egocentric and concrete interpretation to a more abstract understanding of these concepts. As a result, adults must be careful to explain related issues in a way that is appropriate to a child's level of understanding.

Erikson's theory of psychosocial development illustrates how serious illness puts children "at risk" for developing a negative resolution to developmental crises. Special care must be taken to ensure a positive outcome. Strategies should involve support for normal developmental needs as well as concern for issues specific to having a particular illness.

Normalization of activities and routines such as continued school attendance and continued peer interaction can provide a sense of comfort and continuity. Also, dying children can better retain a sense of control if pain is well managed. Knowledge that children's pain experiences vary somewhat depending on developmental stage, parental attitude, and cultural background can be helpful as one interacts with ill children. Child-life programs provide helpful support to children and families who are dealing with a myriad of issues during a child's hospitalization.

Children who experience the death of a loved one do grieve. Although their grief experience is somewhat different from that of an adult, there are many similarities. A number of therapeutic interventions are helpful to bereaved children, including play therapy, art therapy, and bibliotherapy.

Personal Account

A young woman entered the hospital with the expectation that she would be treated for a serious infection and released within a few weeks. From the time her mother went into the hospital, 3-year-old Ariane began asking a variety of challenging questions. When her mother died unexpectedly, Ariane vented her grief in childlike fashion, showed support for her father as he grieved, and explored the meaning of death from a 3-year-old's perspective.

Conversations With Ariane
Nicholas Putnam

Nearly two years have passed since it happened. The pain in me has eased, and Ariane's questions come less often. The questions are easier to answer now. "Did Mommy like this place?" she asks. The memories and mystery of her passing, however, remain for us both.

My daughter and I lost Nina on January 23, 1978. She was not yet 30 and my daughter was not yet 4. She took with her an unborn child and left us behind in shock and grief. Such tragedies occur often enough, and usually they happen to someone else. When they happen to you, they are true emotional disasters. Adults and school-age children, if they are lucky, go through a period of grief which is both painful and healing. The well of sadness inside me occasionally seems almost dry and then at unexpected moments can fill suddenly and overflow. But what of our little girl? What of Ariane who at three lost the primary source of love, nurturance, identification, and companionship in her life? How can she deal with such a devastating rupture? In fact, she has survived. In small doses she has processed the information, felt the pain, and constructed a new reality for herself. It was an enormous task.

During the month after Nina's death I kept a diary of Ariane's remarks. I am still not sure why I did this. Maybe it was because Nina paid such close attention to all of the little things in Ariane's life. She delighted in Ariane's growth and personality. Perhaps I felt that by writing down Ariane's words I could take some of the sting out of them; I could help myself see these questions as a part of a process, something I could look back on, something "objective." I remember thinking at the time that a record like this could be of some help to others experiencing a similar tragedy. Then again, perhaps I made this diary because it was something I had already begun to do while my wife was still in the hospital. There are many things I did that I continue to do, possibly without reason, but which give me the sense that Nina is still a presence in my life.

It all began in my ninth and final year of training at UCLA. In July, the student years were to have ended, and Nina, Ariane, and I, and the baby she carried, were going to begin the productive middle years of our lives. On November 17, Nina went to the dentist to have a routine oral prophylaxis, to have her teeth cleaned. About three weeks later she began feeling poorly, with vague symptoms including occasional low-grade temperature and fatigue. On Christmas Eve she went to the emergency room at UCLA where an alert intern put together the facts of her recent trip to the dentist and the finding of a heart murmur, a murmur she had never had before. She was admitted to the hospital, and on Christmas Day it was confirmed that she had subacute bacterial endocarditis, an infection of one of the valves of the heart. Apparently the bacteria had traveled from her mouth during the oral prophylaxis and lodged on one of the heart valves, slowly growing there and causing her vague symptoms.

Ariane and I drove to the emergency room as soon as we learned that Nina was to be admitted to the hospital. We had been at a Christmas Eve luncheon, and Ariane knew that her mommy was not feeling well and was seeing a doctor. During the first visit, dressed in her Christmas dress of velvet, lace, and ribbon, she said very little. She appeared relieved when we left the emergency room. The next day was Christmas, and, before being hospitalized, Nina had prepared for Christmas with stockings, tree, and a huge gingerbread house. She had gone about town finding just the things that Ariane wanted. Santa Claus got all the credit, however, and Ariane was eager to get to the hospital as soon as possible to show Nina some of her gifts. That Christmas Day in the hospital, Ariane watched very closely the activities of nurses and doctors. She saw her mother wince and cry for a second as her intravenous medication was begun. Again she saw her mother's tears as she was told that the treatment for this disorder would require four to six weeks of hospitalization, but we all cheered up when we heard that the chances for complete recovery were good, provided she had the proper rest and treatment.

When I first met Nina, ten years ago, she had a little sign in her room from the movie, *Auntie Mame:* "Life is a banquet, and most poor beggars are starving to death." Life was meant to be a celebration. If she had to be in the hospital, we would all make the best of it—with visits, and wheelchair trips around the UCLA campus, card games, dominoes, and puzzles. Ariane was even allowed to try out her new roller skates in the hospital corridors. At least we knew why Nina had felt so tired during the last few weeks. At least now she would get better and go on with the business of life. Ariane began to take an interest in the activities of the doctors and nurses and asked for some IV tubing to start "treatment" on Betty. She and Betty, her doll, were inseparable.

The day after Christmas, Ariane asked an aunt, "Will Mommy die in the hospital?"

Adherence to a routine of daily living is important for children at this age, and so we tried as best we could to continue the routine of life at home. Still Ariane was able to visit Nina three or four times a week. On December 30, she asked me, "Do you know what Betty's thinking? Betty thinks very silly things. . . . Betty thinks doctors put you in the hospital and never let you come home."

"Gee, Betty's silly," I said.

"Betty thinks the doctors stick needles in your arms and your eyes and in your mouth and blood comes out."

"Betty doesn't know very much about what really happens in hospitals, does she?" I asked.

"No, she doesn't."

With her grandmother living in our home and frequent visits with her mother and days spent with friends, Ariane appeared to be adjusting to the new situation surprisingly well. She had a hard time conceptualizing a four-week period, but never asked directly when Nina was coming home.

On January 5, she told me, "Daddy, I'm having a hard time sleeping."

"Why?"

"I'm thinking too much."

"What about?"

"About Mommy."

"What about Mommy?"

"About all the nice things she did for me."

"Yes," I said.

"Daddy, how did she get to the hospital? Did she drive there?"

"She had to go there because was sick. Some germs got into her heart, and the doctors have to give her medicine that will make her all better. She's going to come home in a little while, and she's going to be doing all those nice things again."

"I want she to come home now!"

"She will."

"Mommy is never coming home!" she challenged me.

"Yes, she is."

"No, she isn't."

Clearly, it was hard for her to imagine an end to the separation, and it was hard to separate Ariane and Nina after they had spent a day together in the hospital. But I found consolation in my knowledge that the treatment was going very well, that the complications, for Nina and for the unborn child, were going to be minimal and well within our ability to cope. At the suggestion of Ariane's nursery-school teacher we made a calendar. Nina was to come home in about two-and-a-half weeks and each night we would cross off a day. I moved the day of homecoming back a couple of days so that any last-minute delays would not be disappointing to Ariane.

"I will cross off all the days so she will come home now," Ariane decided one morning.

At last we came to the final week in the hospital. Now we were dealing with numbers that Ariane could understand, six days, four days, three days, only two days left until Mommy comes home. She was to be home on Sunday afternoon, January 22.

Friday morning, the 20th, at 4:45 A.M., the phone rings. The doctor tells me that Nina has had a seizure in the middle of the night and that her condition is serious. He wants me to come to the hospital immediately. At first I am confused as to how this could have happened, but suddenly terrible possibilities flood my mind: a major cerebral artery has burst open, an unexpected result of the endo-carditis, which was virtually cured. I reel out of bed and begin to wail in anguish. Ariane is awakened. She says, "What's wrong? Don't cry, Daddy, everything's go-ing to be okay."

The next four days form a painful blur in my memory. Nina is moved to the neurosurgical intensive-care unit (ICU). My mental state changes from hopeful anticipation of her homecoming to anguish and despair at her rapid deteriora-tion. Close friends gather from around the country and surround me. Ariane vis-its the hospital only once. She takes a quick look into the neurosurgical ICU to see her mother for the last time. Undoubtedly, she notes that some of her worst fears are confirmed. Mommy does have tubes coming from her mouth and head, and her eyes are taped shut. After staring for about twenty seconds from the doorway, she turns her head and asks to leave. She sees me distraught all of the time and in tears much of the time. There is a great influx of adults into her life as friends gather at the house and the hospital.

My mother had taken over her care since my wife had entered the hospital. At first Ariane directed some of her frustrations at her grandmother, whom she called Gigi. However, she also began to form a bond with her and made attempts to understand her new situation. On January 21, she and Gigi ate dinner alone. She played a game she often played with her mother: "Let's pretend we're two people at a restaurant."

"Do you have a daughter, lady?" asks Ariane.

"No, but I have a granddaughter."

"Yes, and her name is Jenny." Ariane continues with her fantasy.

"No, her name is Ariane," replies my mother.

"Does Ariane have a Mommy?"

"Yes, she does, but she's very sick and she's at the hospital."

Nina's chances for recovery dwindled over that long weekend. In a state of shock, I tried to prepare Ariane for what might happen. I told her that Mommy was very sick and that she could die. I told her that if Mommy died she would not be coming home ever again. I told her that we were hoping and praying that this would not happen. I felt that she might not possibly have any idea what I meant. She looked back at me with her big brown eyes, with only the faintest trace of tension showing about her mouth, and said, "Why do you tell me things I already know, Daddy?"

On Monday, January 23rd, at 1:00 P.M., my wife died. A neurologist whom I had known for several years was called to tell me that although her heart was beat-ing, there was no evidence of any life in the brain. Shortly thereafter her heart began to fail and stop, and shortly after that the brief life of the unborn child was stilled. For about 30 minutes I couldn't stand up, and I could barely breathe.

"Jolly" West, the chairman of my department, somehow appeared at my side during this time and explained my body's reaction to me in a way that was rather clinical but quite reassuring at the same time. A state of shock had set in, and I felt completely numb. I felt nothing as I drove myself home. I remember stopping for gas. When I arrived home Ariane was playing with some neighbors.

I told her I had something very important to tell her, and I picked her up and carried her down to a bench overlooking the ocean. I told her that something awful had happened. I told her the worst thing that could ever happen had happened. I began to cry. I told her that Mommy died and that she had gone to heaven. She looked at me for a moment and then she covered her ears, one at a time. She kept looking at me and saying, "Why do you tell me things I know already? Why do you tell me these things, Daddy?" Once again I told her that Mommy had gone to heaven and that we would not be seeing her, but that we would always love her, and that maybe her spirit would always be near us.

"Can we see her spirit, Daddy?"

"No, but we might feel it." I began to sob again.

"Daddy, you're dumb. You're telling me things I already know."

"But I have to tell you these things."

"I'm not going to listen to you. You're dumb."

Friends arrived from all over the country for the services. I became increasingly occupied with the arrangements and with the help and support of friends these normally distressing obligations became increasingly meaningful. At the services, which Ariane attended, our friends and I stood up and talked about the Nina we had known and loved. Ariane ran about the chapel but was not oblivious to the proceedings. She perked up when her name was mentioned and she ran up to me and to Nina's father to kiss us. She involved herself with many of the people who had come to visit and appeared quite cheerful. She knew the services related to her mother, but it soon became clear that death was a complete mystery to her. At the cemetery, a beautiful spot between mountains and sea, she ran about the grounds picking wildflowers and talking to friends. Finally, she settled down on the grass next to the coffin. She said, "This is my bedroom. I'm going to be next to Mommy, and I don't want anyone to disturb me." Then she stood up and began working the handle of the coffin back and forth and said, "Do you see what I'm going? I'm pumping water into their eyes . . . for tears."

Although she appeared more serious than before, most could not detect a major change in her mood. A three-year-old, however, has very little idea of the permanence of death. Her confusion soon became evident. She began to ask, "Where is she?" "I want she here!" "Can I see her?" She looked over my shoulder as I showed some pictures of a recent family gathering to some friends. In these pictures Nina appeared beautiful as ever; radiant. Ariane pointed to her and said, "There's Mommy." But then she added, "Can I see her?"

I replied, "You can see her in the picture."

"No, I can't, she wasn't there. I didn't see her there."

After a week it was time for friends from out of town to leave. She became petulant when they said good-bye. At one point she threw a gift that a friend had given her across the room as he tried to say good-bye to her. Then she hugged him and said, "I don't want anybody to leave this house."

A week later we went out to the desert for a few days. There she developed an earache and woke up from sleep crying and demanding, "I want my Mommy. I want my Mommy!" This was too much for me to bear and I was unable to hold back my own tears. When she noticed my crying, she stopped hers and kissed me. I do know she sensed my suffering.

Despite these episodes during illnesses, her general behavior changed very little. If anything, she appeared more grown up than ever before. There certainly was no regression in her development. She continued going to nursery school and playing with her friends. In the midst of my suffering, I wondered at her ability to go on with life. She saw my crying spells and was comforting, and would say, "You're sad about Mommy." In her own way, however, she tried to grasp what had happened.

I have written down her comments whenever I have had the opportunity to do so. I have not done this because I feel that such comments are in any way typical of three-year-olds dealing with the death of their mother. Children's personalities are as varied as wildflowers. All of us, in our own ways, however, try to make sense of the world around us, and this was true of Ariane during these miserable days.

Ariane's comments about her mother were painful for me to hear, and they may be painful for others to read. But they do provide an opportunity to see how a three-year-old tries to come to terms with the loss of the most important person in her life.

For example, on February 9th she said, "I wish that nobody had taked away Mommy. . . . Only God did. . . . I wish I was magic and could fly up to the sky. I'm going to do magic and bring Mommy here."

Later that same day she ran into a friend in the supermarket. For a while the other little girl followed her around asking, "Did your Mommy die?" Ariane ignored her. Later we heard that that little girl subsequently became quite upset. In fact, many of Ariane's friends whose parents were divorced or separated appeared to take Nina's death with more visible stress than Ariane herself.

The following day she asked, "Does Great-grandma know Mommy's in heaven?"

"Yes."

"You fighted with Mommy, didn't you, and she went to the hospital?"

"When did I fight with her?"

"A long time ago," she said.

"Do you think she died because I fought with her a long time ago?" I asked.

"I don't like arguments, and Mommy shouldn't have goed to the hospital."

"People argue with other people at times, but that doesn't make anyone die. We all get mad at each other sometimes, but getting mad at somebody doesn't make them get sick and die, Ariane. Besides, I wasn't mad at Mommy before she died. Mommy died because she got very, very sick. She got an infection in her blood."

"I don't want to talk about it anymore." And later that day, singing: "Dear God, please make my Mommy come again . . . and everything will be all right . . . and I can just say the magic words and she will come home."

In my anguish I tried to reassure her (and possibly myself) by telling Ariane that Mommy knew how we felt and perhaps her spirit was in the room with us.

Ariane would reply, "I can't wait to go to heaven so she can hold me again."

On February 15th, singing: "Sometimes when I cry Mommy comes right away . . . sometimes when I'm happy, let's not talk about sad, let's be happy every day." And later that day, "I want to sing a song about Mommy: I love my Mommy, Nina. When I was two and had long hair Mommy was here and she took me to the haircutter and they cutted my hair and she did ni-ice things for me and then she went to the hospital and now the end."

We talked about possibly selling Nina's car during dinner one night. Ariane got up abruptly from the table and became quite upset: "You guys don't like my Mommy's car. . . . You're going to sell it. I don't want it selled." I answered her, "I know it makes you mad when we talk about selling the Pinto."

"I'm not mad at Mommy; I'm only mad at God. I want to see her, hug her, and kiss her and give her my picture." The Pinto sits in my driveway to this day.

On my birthday, February 18th, she asked, "God took Mommy to heaven, didn't He?"

"Well," I tried to respond helpfully and yet honestly, "I guess so, she got sick, and I guess it was time for her to die, and God had something to do with it."

"Well then, God can do magic and bring her back."

"God can't do that, nobody can," I groped and hesitated. "You see, God can take her to heaven but nobody comes back from heaven."

"Why not?"

"You'll understand when you grow up." And then I realized immediately that I didn't understand myself, so I added, "I don't know why; Daddy doesn't understand these things. I don't know if anybody understands God or why things happen in life." I continued to grope, "It's terrible that this happened, and we don't always understand God." Somehow I found myself increasingly inclined to use the concepts of heaven and God in dealing with Ariane's questions. This was difficult for me to do, as I had never had a strong belief in an afterlife. However, I was finding some comfort myself in the idea that there is something more to our existence than the short time we spend living on this planet.

In a restaurant one evening she searched through her grandmother's purse. She found a picture of Nina and held on to it, staring at it for quite some time. She said, "I'm going to hold on to this picture and look at it all day and all night and all the time. I'm going to give Mommy my picture." Ariane is an attractive child and, as often happens, a lady in the restaurant waved and winked at her. Ariane responded angrily, shaking her fist at the lady and sticking her tongue out. I scolded her, and she began to cry. It was time to leave, anyway, and I picked her up and carried her out to the car. She kept imploring, "I want my Mommy, I want to see her!" Her tears led to my tears. When she saw me crying, her tears suddenly changed to feigned tears of laughter. She said, "You see, we don't have to be sad all the time." The truth was that we couldn't both be sad at the same time. It was too frightening. When she was feeling okay, she could watch me cry and be comforting. When she needed to cry, it was important for her to feel that I could remain strong. Remarkably, she confined her questions and the open expression about the loss of her mother to a few brief moments each day. For most of the time life went on quite the same as usual.

She began to make an increasing commitment to her relationship with my mother. She gave my mother her own middle name. One night, laughingly, she told me, "Isn't it funny, you have a Mommy and your Daddy died, and I have a Daddy and my Mommy died. It's all together." However, she always included her mother when she talked about her family, saying, "I love a lot of people. I love Betty, Gigi, Mommy, and Daddy," adding several friends and neighbors as well. On our first return to the cemetery late in February, Ariane brought her Big Wheel and rode about on the grounds. She seemed happy to know that this was a special place where we thought about Mommy. She picked wildflowers and placed them in a vase over the plot. I told her that these would be nice flowers for Mommy. She asked, "Can Mommy see the flowers?" I told her that it makes us happy, and perhaps it makes Mommy happy, too, when we put flowers on her grave.

Ariane's experience with grief seemed to be quite different from mine. She dealt with this terrible loss in small increments, a few moments each day, although I imagine that she thought about and still thinks about it a good deal more. On February 23rd, she said:

"I don't like that doggy, Daddy."

"Why?"

"He going to get a gun and kill us, Daddy, and we will go to heaven."

"Oh no," I laughingly reassured her.

"I don't want to go to heaven, and I don't want you to go to heaven or Gigi to go."

"Yes, we all want to live for a long time."

"Yes, I want you and Gigi to stay here so then you can take care of me."

Typically, for a child of three, she was concerned about the possibility of abandonment. A year later she would raise the possibility of something happening to me and then enumerate a number of possible solutions such as, "I could go live with Eric's family." I felt a sense of panic as I contemplated the possibility of her being left completely alone, should something happen to me.

Now, nearly two years later, I realize that I will never "get over" Nina's death: I believe I will eventually get used to it. There seemed to be a life-force in Ariane which helped her through the loss. She was able to live with something she didn't really understand. She made new attachments. She told her grandmother, "I'm lucky to have you." Was she repeating something I had said to her? Or was she beginning to sense the importance of her new relationship with her grandmother? Possibly it was a little of both.

I see Ariane's loss, and my own, and sometimes I see Nina's loss as well. During the month after her death I bought Ariane her first two-wheel bicycle. Watching her pedal the pink Schwinn about and seeing her delight at being able to ride it, brought to mind all of Nina's hopes for her. I felt so down at Nina's not being there that I was almost unable to complete the transaction with the salesman. And yet, I have gotten some comfort from the fact that Ariane has good feelings about her mother despite the loss. Many times she has looked at something in the house and said, "Mommy make that? I only like to look at that . . . reminds me of Mommy!" She asks me, "Did Mommy learn to swim when she was five?" "Did Mommy like to rollerskate?" She appears to have the capacity to identify with the mother she no longer has.

I cannot help my daughter understand something that I don't understand myself. I can't explain it in such a way that everything, or anything, seems logical or fair. As I grieved, and as I still do, I watch Ariane cope. Her confusion was enormous. Although exceedingly cheerful and full of life, one night at dinner, she abruptly turned to me and said:

"Hit me, Daddy!"

"But why should I hit you?"

"Because that's what happened to Mommy. She got hitted."

"I never saw Mommy get hit! No, Ariane, Mommy didn't get hitted. She got very sick, and she died."

"You're wrong, Daddy. You're telling me a lie. She didn't die, she got hitted, and went to heaven."

She looked for answers; from television she must have learned the association between violence (hitting) and death. She looked for psychological explanations for the loss. She wondered, did we get mad at her? Did she get mad at us and go away? But nothing seemed to fit or make sense. Her mother's death remained an enormous mystery. It was no less a mystery to me. And yet, not understanding, Ariane went on living, activated by some vital force within her. She took pleasure in little things and looked forward to the future, noting that she was "almost four, and when I grow up I can be a girl doctor." The presence of that life within her gave me strength and hope.

About a month after Nina died, Ariane asked me, "Daddy, do you miss Mommy?"

"Yes, I miss her very much."

"Do you miss me when I go away to school?"

"Yes I do."

And then realizing that in the past all people we have missed have returned, I added, "Missing Mommy is different, honey, because she can never come back. We can never see her, but we might feel that we're close to her sometimes."

"You're wrong, Daddy, I can see her." And then very softly she went on, "Every night after I'm asleep I see her . . . in a warm . . . cave."

I had no reply for this.

Still more softly, she said, "I stay with her all night until it's morning and I get up."

"That sounds very nice to me," I said. "That must feel very nice."

I learned to trust her capacity to find a pathway through these woods. I could see that she never turned around or slipped back. I could see that she continued to move forward, only occasionally looking back. I could see that she found resting places, warm spots, glimpses into the future, springs of hope.

We made the journey together, and each of us traveled alone. At times the woods were wet with rain, and yet there were periods of sunshine, song, and laughter. Through it all, we kept talking to each other. And we knew we were changed forever.

QUESTIONS AND ACTIVITIES

1. Role-play that you are a teacher in an elementary school. You are to present information to your colleagues so that they may learn how to deal with seriously ill children in the classroom. Summarize six important ideas you would share with your fellow educators; discuss in the context of needs of dying children presented in this chapter.

2. Again, you are a teacher in an elementary classroom. One of your students has died and his/her classmates come to you and say they would like to do something in his/her memory the week following the death. Help them plan a developmentally appropriate activity and explain its importance.

3. Take the role of a school principal. A student has died and you believe that it is important to write each child in that classroom a note after the death. For this assignment, write that letter and share it with a peer and get his/her response. How would that letter be different if you were writing it for first graders, compared with fourth graders?

4. If your community has a children's hospice, interview someone that is involved with its programs. What services does it offer? How does it tailor those services to the developmental needs of children?

5. Think back to your own childhood. Do you remember any conversations you had with classmates or teachers about the subject of death? What was said? Were these conversations helpful? Realistic?

6. If you were the parent of a 5-year-old terminally ill child and were asked directly "Am I going to die?" how would you respond? How would you respond if the child were 10 years old? Explain your answer.

7. Was it "normal" for Ariane to throw a gift across the room and then tell a friend "I don't want anyone to leave this house"? Discuss your response. What is the primary issue dealt with here? Give other examples of this same issue.

8. Summarize various components of the concept of death. Illustrate each of these by giving examples from "Conversations with Ariane."

9. As a child, were you ever protected by your family from such "crisis" situations as death, divorce, alcoholism, and so on? If so, how did they protect you? How did you feel if you were not allowed to communicate openly with others or not allowed to participate in various activities? What do you wish had been done differently?

GLOSSARY

Accommodation: process by which present schemes are modified or new schemes are created.

Animism: belief that inanimate objects are alive.

Assimilation: process by which new stimuli are incorporated into existing schemes.

Autonomy: positive outcome of Erikson's second psychosocial crisis; relates to independence.

Causality: factors that precipitate death.

Centration: act of focusing on a single prominent characteristic of an object to the exclusion of others.

Childhood ritual: a stereotyped behavior performed to order one's environment.

Child-life specialist: professional who serves as an advocate for children and their families in a medical facility.

Concrete operational stage: third of Piaget's cognitive stages, associated with school-age children.

Concreteness: inability to deal with abstractions.

Conservation: understanding that certain characteristics of an object do not change in spite of modifications in its appearance.

Deductive reasoning: ability to think from a general rule to a specific case.

Doubt: negative outcome of Erikson's second psychosocial crisis; relates to a belief that one's self is incapable.

Dual monologue: conversation in which both speakers are talking about distinctly different topics.

Emotional contagion: transmission of an emotion from one person to another.

Egocentrism: inability to process information from another's viewpoint.

Finality: refers to a component of the concept of death; understanding that death is permanent; the understanding that once a living thing dies, its physical body cannot be made alive again.

Guilt: negative outcome of Erikson's third psychosocial crisis; sometimes relates to a distorted belief that one is responsible for certain outcomes, such as someone's death. Apart from the negative resolution of an Eriksonian crisis, guilt is a common manifestation of the grief response.

Inductive reasoning: ability to think from specific examples to a general rule.

Industry: positive resolution of Erikson's school-age crisis. Industry is associated with feelings of pride and competency resulting from successfully learning new skills, making things, and being productive.

Inferiority: negative resolution of Erikson's school-age crisis. Involves feelings of being inferior to those around oneself.

Initiative: positive outcome of Erikson's third psychosocial crisis; relates to a sense of curiosity and creativity.

Irreversibility: refers to cognitive capacity; inability to understand that something may change and then return to its original state. Inability to reverse the transformation mentally.

Nonfunctionality: cessation of all physical processes.

Normalization: consistency in interactions, activities, and routines that provides a sense of predictability, security, and comfort.

Operations: ability to mentally manipulate internal representations of objects.

Preoperational stage: second of Piaget's cognitive stages.

Psychological causality: tendency to perceive psychological motives for a phenomenon.

Schemes: organized patterns of behavior and perception that one constructs to interpret some aspect of one's experience.

Sensorimotor stage: first of Piaget's cognitive stages.

Shame: negative outcome of Erikson's second psychosocial crisis; relates to a sense of being bad or worthless.

Transductive reasoning: thought based on reasoning from one specific instance to another specific instance.

Transformations: ability to perceive intermediate steps that lead to a particular outcome.

Universality: understanding that all humans will someday die.

SUGGESTED READINGS

The following is a list of books for adults wishing to help children and adolescents who are dying or grieving.

Adams, D. W., & Deveau, E. (1995). *Beyond the innocence of childhood* (vol. 3): *Helping children and adolescents cope with death and bereavement.* Amityville, NY: Baywood Publishing.

Doka, K. J. (1995). *Children mourning, mourning children.* Washington, DC: Hospice Foundation of America.

Fitzgerald, H. (1992). *The grieving child: A parent's guide.* New York: Simon and Schuster.

Grollman, E. (1976). *Talking about death: A dialogue between parent and child.* Boston: Beacon Press.

Huntley, T. (1991). *Helping children grieve: When someone they love dies.* Minneapolis, MN: Augsburg.

Jewett, C. (1982). *Helping children cope with separation and loss.* Boston: Harvard Common Press.

Johnson, S. (1987). *After a child dies: Counseling bereaved families.* New York: Springer.

Ward, B. (1989). *Good grief: Exploring feelings, loss and death with under 11's.* Luton, England: White Crescent Press.

Webb, N. B. (1991). *Play therapy with children in crisis: A casebook for practitioners.* New York: Guilford Press.

Wolfelt, A. (1983). *Helping children cope with grief.* Muncie, IN: Accelerated Development.

RESOURCES

Make-A-Wish Foundation
711 East Northern
Phoenix, AZ 85020
(602) 395-9474

Ronald McDonald House
622 West Deming Place
Chicago, Illinois 60614
(773) 348-5322

The Dougy Center
National Center for Grieving Children and Families
3909 S.E. 52nd Avenue
P.O. Box 86852
Portland, OR 97286
(503) 775-5683

REFERENCES

Adams-Greenly, M. (1984). Helping children communicate about serious illness and death. *Journal of Psychosocial Oncology, 2*(2), 61-72.

Atchison, N., Guercio, P., & Monaco, C. (1986). Pain in the pediatric burn patient: Nursing assessment and perception. *Issues in Comprehensive Pediatric Nursing, 9,* 399-409.

Baker, J. E., Sedney, M. A., & Gross, E. (1992). Psychological tasks for bereaved children. *American Journal of Orthopsychiatry, 62,* 105-116.

Bates, T. A., & Broom, M. (1986). Preparation of children for hospitalization and surgery: A review of the literature. *Journal of Pediatric Nursing, 1*(4), 230-239.

Belnick, J. (1993). A crisis model for family art therapy. In D. Linesch (Ed.), *Art therapy with families in crisis* (pp. 23-45). New York: Brunner/Mazel.

Berger, K. S. (1983). *The developing person through the lifespan.* New York: Wadsworth.

Berlinsky, E. B., & Biller, H. B. (1982). *Parental death and psychological development.* Lexington, MA: Lexington Books.

Bibace, R., & Walsh, M. E. (1979). Developmental stages in children's conceptions of illness. In G. C. Stone, F. Cohen, & N. Adler (Eds.), *Health psychology: A handbook* (pp. 285-301). San Francisco: Jossey-Bass.

Bigner, J. J. (1998). *Parent-child relations: An introduction to parenting* (5th ed.). New York: Macmillan.

Bluebond-Langner, M. (1978). *The private worlds of dying children.* Princeton, NJ: Princeton University Press.

Bluebond-Langner, M. (1989). Worlds of dying children and their well siblings. *Death Studies, 13,* 1-16.

Bowlby, J. (1980). *Attachment and loss: Loss, sadness, and depression* (vol. 3). New York: Basic Books.

Bradshaw, C., & Zeanah, P. (1986). Pediatric nurse's assessments of pain in children. *Journal of Pediatric Nursing, 1*(5), 314-321.

Brent, S., Speece, M. W., Lin, C., Dong, Q., & Yang, C. (1996). The development of the concept of death among Chinese and U.S. Children 3-17 years of age: From binary to "fuzzy" concepts? *Omega, 33*(1), 67-83.

Brett, D. (1992). *More Annie Stories: Therapeutic storytelling techniques.* New York: Magination Press-Brunner/Mazel.

Broome, M. E. (1986). The relationship between children's fears and behavior during a painful event. *Children's Health Care, 14*(3), 142-145.

Casdagli, P., Gobey, F. (1992). *Grief: The play, writings and workshops.* London: David Fulton Publishers.

Center for Attitudinal Healing. (1978). *There is a rainbow behind every dark cloud.* Millbrae, CA: Celestial Arts.

Center for Attitudinal Healing. (1982). *Straight from the siblings: Another look at the rainbow.* Millbrae, CA: Celestial Arts.

Chesler, M. A., Paris, J., & Barbarin, O. A. (1986). "Telling" the child with cancer: Parental choices to share information with ill children. *Journal of Pediatric Psychology, 2*(4), 497-516.

Cullinan, A. L. (1990). Teacher's death anxiety, ability to cope with death, and perceived ability to aid bereaved students. *Death Studies, 14,* 147-160.

Deasy-Spinetta, P., & Tarr, D. (1985). Public law 94-142 and the student with cancer: An overview of the legal, organizational, and practical aspects. *Journal of Psychosocial Oncology, 3*(2), 97-105.

Dickinson, G. E. (1992). First childhood death experiences. *Omega, 25*(3), 169-182.

Doka, K. (1995). Talking to children about illness. In K. Doka (Ed.), *Children mourning, mourning children.* Washington, DC: Hospice Foundation of America.

Elizur, E., & Kaffman, M. (1983). Factors influencing the severity of childhood bereavement reactions. *American Journal of Orthopsychiatry, 53*(4), 669-676.

Erikson, E. (1963). *Childhood and society* (2nd ed.). New York: Norton.

Essa, E. L., & Murray, C. I. (1994, May). Young children's understanding and experience with death. *Young Children,* 74-81.

Excell, J. A. (1991). A child's perception of death. In D. Papadatou & C. Papadotos (Eds.), *Children and death* (pp. 87-103). New York: Hemisphere.

Fink, L., Birenbaum, L., & Chand, N. (1994). Two weeks post-death report by parents of siblings' grieving experience. *Journal of Child and Adolescent Psychiatric Nursing, 7*(4), 17-25.

Fritz, G. K., Williams, J. R., & Amylon, M. (1988). After treatment ends: Psychosocial sequelae in pediatric cancer survivors. *American Journal of Orthopsychiatry, 58*(4), 552-561.

Graham-Pole, J., Wass, H. Eyberg, S., & Chu, L. (1989). Communicating with dying children and their siblings: A retrospective analysis. *Death Studies, 13,* 465-483.

Haley, J. (1985). Dealing with children's pain: Learning from personal experience. *American Journal of Hospice Care, 2*(3), 34-40.

Hobbie, W. L., & Hollen, P. J. (1993). Pediatric nurse practitioners specializing with survivors of childhood cancer. *Journal of Pediatric Health Care, 7*(1), 24-30.

Hutter, J. J., Farrell, F. Z., & Meltzer, P. S. (1991). Care of the child dying from cancer: Home vs. hospital. In D. Papadatou & C. Papadatos (Eds.), *Children and death* (pp. 197-207). New York: Hemisphere.

Ikeman, B., Block, R., Avery, J., Niedra, R., Sulman, J., Trentowsky, S., & Yorke, E. (1987). Grief work with children: Access, clinical issues, community advocacy. In M. A. Morgan (Ed.), *Bereavement: Helping the survivors* (pp. 105-119). London, Ontario: King's College.

Jesse, P. (1992). Nurses, children, and play. *Issues in Comprehensive Pediatric Nursing, 15*(4), 261-269.

Kaffman, M., & Elizur, E. (1979). Children's bereavement reactions following death of the father. *International Journal of Family Therapy, 1*(3), 203-229.

Kleck, R., Richardson, S., & Ronald, L. (1974). Physical appearance cues and interpersonal attraction in children. *Child Development, 45,* 305–310.

Klingman, A. (1985). Responding to a bereaved classmate: Comparison of two strategies for death education in the classroom. *Death Studies, 9,* 449–454.

Koch-Hattem, A. (1986). Sibling's experience of pediatric cancer: Interviews with children. *Health and Social Work, 11*(2), 107–117.

Koocher, G. P. (1974). Talking with children about death. *American Journal of Orthopsychiatry, 44*(3), 405–411.

Levenson, P., & Cooper, M. (1984). School health education for the chronically impaired individual. *Journal of School Health, 54*(11), 446–448.

Levy, E. L. (1982). *Children are not paper dolls.* Incline Village, NV: The Publisher's Mark. (Originally published by Harvest Printing, Greeley, CO).

Lipson, M. (1993). What do you say to a child with AIDS? *Hastings Center Report, 23*(2), 6–12.

Lutz, W. (1986). Helping hospitalized children and their parents cope with painful procedures. *Journal of Pediatric Nursing, 1*(1), 24–32.

Mahon, M. M. (1993). Children's concept of death and sibling death from trauma. *Journal of Pediatric Nursing, 8*(5), 335–344.

Maieron, M. J., Roberts, M. C., & Prentice-Dunn, S. (1996). Children's perception of peers with AIDS: Assessing the impact of contagion information, perceived similarity, and illness conceptualization. *Journal of Pediatric Psychology, 21*(3), 321–333.

Martinson, I. M., & Bossert, E. (1994). The psychological status of children with cancer. *Journal of Child and Adolescent Psychiatric Nursing, 7*(2), 16–22.

Masterman, S. H., & Reams, R. (1988). Support groups for bereaved preschool and school-aged children. *American Journal of Orthopsychiatry, 58,* 562–570.

McIntyre, B. B. (1990). Art therapy with bereaved youth. *Journal of Palliative Care, 6*(1), 16–23.

Nagy, M. (1948). The child's theories concerning death. *Journal of Genetic Psychology, 73,* 3–27.

Natapoff, J. N. (1982). A developmental analysis of children's ideas of health. *Health Education Quarterly, 9*(2), 34–45.

Petrillo, M., & Sanger, S. (1980). *Emotional care of hospitalized children: An environmental approach* (2nd ed.). Philadelphia: Lippincott.

Piaget, J. (1963). *The origins of intelligence in children.* New York: International Universities Press.

Piaget, J. (1968). *Six psychological studies* (A. Tenzer, Trans.). New York: Vintage Books.

Platt, L. A., & Persico, V. R. (1992). *Grief in cross-cultural perspective: A casebook.* New York: Garland Publishing.

Potter, P., & Roberts, M. (1984). Children's perception of chronic illness: The roles of disease symptoms, cognitive development, and information. *Journal of Pediatric Psychology, 9*(1), 13–25.

Pratt, C. C., Hare, J., & Wright, C. (1987). Death and dying in early childhood education: Are educators really prepared? *Education, 107,* 279–286.

Rait, D. S., & Holland, J. (1986). Pediatric cancer: Psychosocial issues and approaches. *Mediguide to Oncology, 6*(3), 15.

Redpath, C. C., & Rogers, C. S. (1984). Healthy young children's concepts of hospitals, medical personnel, operations, and illness. *Journal of Pediatric Psychology, 9*(1), 29–39.

Rollins, J. A. (1990). Childhood cancer: Siblings draw and tell. *Pediatric Nursing, 16,* 21–26.

Ross, D. M., & Ross, S. A. (1984). Childhood pain: The school-aged child's viewpoint. *Pain, 20,* 179–191.

Sachs, M. (1980). Helping the child with cancer go back to school. *Journal of School Health, 50*(6), 328–331.

Schonfeld, D. J. (1993). Talking with children about death. *Journal of Pediatric Health Care, 7*(6), 269–274.

Schonfeld, D. J., & Kline, M. (1994). School-based crisis intervention: A role for pediatricians. *Current Problems in Pediatrics, 24,* 48–54.

Segal, R. M. (1984). Helping children express grief through symbolic communications. *Social Casework, 65,* 590–599.

Smith, I. (1991). Preschool children "play" out their grief. *Death Studies, 15,* 169–176.

Speece, M. W., & Brent, S. B. (1984). Children's understanding of death: A review of three components of a death concept. *Child Development, 55,* 1671–1686.

Speece, M. W., & Brent, S. B. (1992). The acquisition of a mature understanding of three components of the concept of death. *Death Studies, 16*(4), 211–229.

Vander Zanden, J. W. (1985). *Human development* (3rd ed.). New York: Knopf.

Varni, J. W., Kata, E. R., Colegrove, R., & Dolgin, M. (1993). The impact of social skills training on the adjustment of children with newly diagnosed cancer. *Journal of Pediatric Psychology, 18*(6), 751–767.

Wass, H. (1991). Helping children cope with death. In D. Papadatou & C. Papadatos (Eds.), *Children and death* (pp. 11–32). New York: Hemisphere.

Webb, N. B. (1991). Death of a grandparent: Family therapy to assist bereavement. In N. B. Webb (Ed.), *Helping bereaved children: A handbook for practitioners* (pp. 61–80). New York: Guilford Press.

Weitzman, M. (1984). School and peer relations. *Pediatric Clinics of North America, 31*(1), 59–69.

White, E., Elsom, B., & Prawat, B. (1978). Children's conceptions of death. *Child Development, 49,* 307–311.

Zambelli, G. C., Clark, E. J., Barile, L., & deJong, A. F. (1988). An interdisciplinary approach to clinical intervention for childhood bereavement. *Death Studies, 12,* 41–50.

6

Death and Grief During Adolescence

Adolescence is a time of many transitions—physical, mental, social, and psychological—a time of moving toward adult status and maturity. During this time, adolescents strive to accomplish many developmental tasks including

- becoming increasingly independent from one's parents and other adults;
- developing a sense of personal identity;
- developing mature relationships with age-mates;
- becoming more aware of and comfortable with bodily changes; and
- strengthening one's own value system. (Balk, 1995; Berndt, 1996; Holmbeck, 1996)

Specific tasks vary somewhat among the three subperiods of adolescence: early, middle, and late (Balk & Corr, 1996). Although the purpose of this chapter is not to provide specifics regarding the substages, per se, it is important to understand that differences do exist. Developmental tasks relate in many ways (both directly and indirectly) to challenges faced by adolescents who are dying and grieving; these ties will be discussed throughout this chapter.

DEATH-RELATED EXPERIENCES OF ADOLESCENTS

Adolescents experience the deaths of others through both direct experience of personal loss and persistent exposure to media sources that highlight violent and sudden deaths. Many young people worry that some day they may be expected to participate in a military conflict or feel threatened by the possibility of falling prey to the random acts of terror that are highlighted in news reports.

In terms of actual numbers of deaths, adolescence is regarded as one of the "healthiest periods of the life span." However, they face many tragedies as age-mates die from what many regard as unnatural deaths. Noppe and Noppe (1996, p. 26) describe it in these words:

> Adolescence ought to be a time to celebrate the richness of biological development. Elements of physical growth and health stand in sharp contrast to considerations of death. Never again will the death rate be lower than it is during the adolescent years, and the causes of death for teenagers are overwhelmingly unnatural, tragic, human-induced aberrations.

The three leading causes of death among young people aged 15 to 24, as noted in Table 6.1, are essentially sudden and traumatic—accidents, homicide, and suicide. Recall the unique issues (discussed in chapter 3) that are faced by those who grieve deaths that are unanticipated and violent.

Table 6.2 summarizes the death rates for three subperiods of the adolescent life stage: ages 10–14, ages 15–19, and ages 20–24. Note that the rate of death rises substantially as the age group gets older. Note, too, that a significant gender difference exists, with males experiencing a much higher death rate than females during all the substages.

TABLE 6.1

Leading Causes of Death: 15 to 24 Age Group, United States, 1995

RANK	CAUSE OF DEATH	NUMBER OF DEATHS	DEATH RATE PER 100,000 POPULATION
	All causes	33,569	93.4
1	Accidents and adverse effects	13,532	37.6
	Motor vehicle accidents	10,354	28.8
	All other accidents and adverse effects	3,179	8.8
2	Homicide and legal intervention	6,827	19.0
3	Suicide	4,789	13.3
4	Malignant neoplasms, including neoplasms of lymphatic and hematopoietic tissues	1,599	4.4
5	Diseases of heart	964	2.7
6	Human immunodeficiency virus infection	643	1.8
7	Congenital anomalies	425	1.2
8	Chronic obstructive pulmonary diseases and allied conditions	220	0.6
9	Pneumonia and influenza	193	0.5
10	Cerebrovascular diseases	166	0.5
	All other causes (Residual)	4,211	11.7

SOURCE: U.S. National Center for Health Statistics. *Monthly Vital Statistics Report, 45*(11), June, 1997.

Not only are there gender differences of death rates in this overall age span, there are also significant racial differences. To illustrate, Table 6.3 compares death rates during adolescence of white males to those of black males. Strong contributors to the higher death rate among black males are the higher incidence of AIDS (Bowler, Sheon, D'Angelo, & Vermund, 1993; DiClemente, 1992) and the higher rate of homicide (Barrett, 1996) among blacks.

ADOLESCENTS AND SUDDEN DEATH

Most adolescents die under tragic and sudden circumstances. In 1995, the primary causes of death for the age span 15–24 were accidents (13,532), homicides (6,827), and suicides (4,789). The most common accidents among this age group are the result of motor vehicle accidents, drownings, and poisonings, as noted earlier in Figure 5.1. Homicides, in the context of societal violence, will be discussed in this section; adolescent suicide will be discussed in chapter 9.

TABLE 6.2

Adolescent Deaths by Substage and Gender, United States, 1995

AGES	NUMBER	RATE PER 100,000 (BOTH SEXES)	MALE RATE	FEMALE RATE
10–14 years	4,454	24.6	30.7	18.2
15–19 years	14,411	84.3	122.4	44.0
20–24 years	20,137	105.7	159.4	50.1

SOURCE: K. D. Kochanek & B. L. Hudson (1994). Advance report of final mortality statistics, 1992. *Monthly Vital Statistics Report, 43*(6), (suppl.).

TABLE 6.3

Comparison of Adolescent Male Death Rates (per 100,000) by Race, United States, 1995

AGES	WHITE MALES	BLACK MALES
10–14 years	28.2	44.9
15–19 years	106.0	218.4
20–24 years	135.4	321.0

SOURCE: K. D. Kochanek & B. L. Hudson (1994). Advance report of final mortality statistics, 1992. *Monthly Vital Statistics Report, 43*(6), (suppl.).

Homicide: The Experience of Adolescents

The Adolescent as Murder Victim.   As noted earlier in Table 6.1, homicide is the second leading cause of death among all those who are 15 to 24 years of age in the United States. Figure 6.1 shows the comparison of homicide rates by age group. Note that homicides increase dramatically in the years past childhood. Barrett (1996) points out that homicides occur at such a high rate among black males and Hispanic males in the United States, that, for them, murder is not only an issue related to criminal justice but also one of public health. Although homicides are more common among the nonwhite, urban poor, there is an increase of homicidal violence among white, suburban, middle-class individuals, as well. The incidence of murders is much higher in the United States than in many other countries of the world, as illustrated in Figure 6.2.

With the number of homicides rising dramatically over recent years, many became concerned that Americans were becoming so sensitized to the statistics reported daily in many large cities that we no longer remembered the individuals who were killed. As a result, numerous attempts have been made to draw attention to the fact that those who are murdered are people, not merely statistics. For example, in the fall of 1996, tens of thousands of pairs of shoes lined the

FIGURE 6.1

Comparison of Homicide Rates Among Various Age Groups

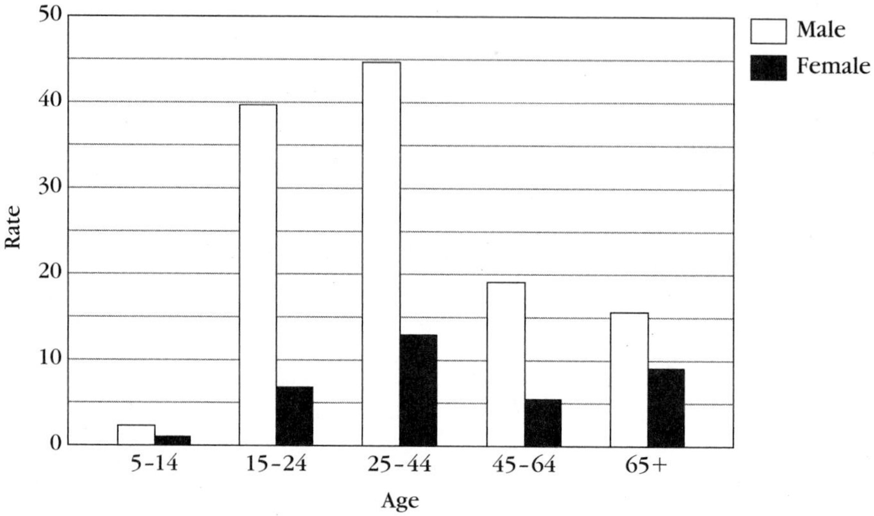

SOURCE: U.S. Bureau of the Census. Statistical Abstract of the United States: 1996 (116th edition). Washington, DC, 1996.

reflecting pool in Washington, DC, as a part of a national protest against violence. The shoes—all sizes, all colors, all styles—were the footwear of many who had been murdered in recent years, symbolizing the everyday life experiences that were now lost to so many. In another attempt to "personalize" the victims, one Chicago newspaper, throughout an entire year, put a closeup picture of any young person murdered in the city on the front page. The picture gallery was comprised of hundreds by the end of the year; the personalization of each individual drew attention to the human lives lost rather than to the escalating numbers.

The Adolescent as Witness to Murder.   Not only do thousands of adolescents become homicide victims each year, but thousands more are victimized by the fact that they witness a murder.

> The witnessing of a . . . murder is always painful, frightening and universally a psychic trauma. At the core of the trauma is the continued intrusion . . . of the central action, when the lethal harm was inflicted (i.e., the plunge of the knife or the blast of a gun). The child undergoes an intense perceptual experience involving all sensory modalities . . . plagued by intrusive memories, unconscious reenactments, startle reactions, recurrent nightmares, fears of repeated trauma, and avoidant or other symptomatic behaviors. (Eth & Pynoos, 1985, p. 174)

In witnessing this act of violence, "survivor-victims" are faced with their own mortality and must deal with the fear that they, too, might be killed without

FIGURE 6.2

Comparison of Homicide Rates Among Numerous Countries

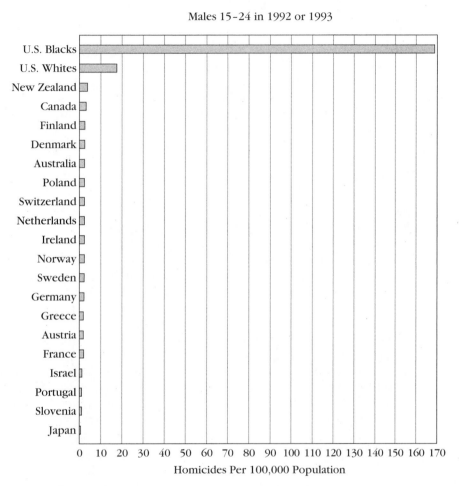

Males 15–24 in 1992 or 1993

Homicides Per 100,000 Population

SOURCE: National Center for Health Statistics. (1996). *Monthly Vital Statistics Report,* vol. 44. World Health Organization.

reason or warning (Sprang & McNeil, 1995). Further, there may be repercussions, even if an individual was not a direct witness to the murder event.

Pynoos et al. (1987) studied 159 children following a fatal sniper attack on their school playground where a classmate and a passerby were killed. These researchers found a relationship between level of posttraumatic stress disorder symptomatology and the location where the child was at the time of the attack in relationship to proximity of the event (e.g., on the playground itself, in the school building, or not at school at that time). Those who were on the playground itself

LIFE AND DEATH IN THE CITY

September 16, 1990—Ever since the death of Brian Watkins, 22, of Provo, Utah, some days ago, I have been thinking about life and death in the city. The city in which Watkins was killed is New York. He and his family, in town for the U.S. Open tennis tournament, were attacked by hoodlums on a subway platform in Manhattan.

As the police tell the story, Brian, his mother, father and others were awaiting a train when the marauders struck. They attacked his father first and took his wallet. They struck Brian's mother; he went to her defense and was stabbed to death.

The attackers, the police say, were on their way to a dance and needed the price of admission to the Roseland Ballroom. Their method of raising money was to rob tourists. This time, the result was also murder.

In Provo the other day, they held Brian's funeral. It was, according to the news accounts, an event of piercing pain: a young tennis star dying, a hero defending his mom from a knife-wielding assailant in the subways of far-off New York City. Above everything else, Brian's family, friends

and neighbors wanted to know why. In the peaceful precincts of Provo, what happened on that subway platform is beyond imagining.

It might come as a surprise to Brian's friends and relatives, but New York's subways have not always been a cesspool of crime. Moreover, the city that now is being called the "rotting apple" once was as humane and civilized a venue as the nation had to offer. It was once no more a haven of crime than were most other cities, even tranquil Provo.

We used to leave our back door open in Brooklyn so that Brownie, our spitz and fox terrier, could go out during the night. Without giving safety a second thought, we rode those same subways and walked the platform where Brian Watkins was killed. New York City in the '50s was a city of gleaming buildings and millions of budding dreams.

How did such a city turn into a nightmare? How did it become a place where Brian Watkins and 20 other people lost their lives on the same Sunday night? Why do its citizens now cower in such fear be-

(Continued)

experienced more severe symptoms than those who were in the school building, who, in turn, experienced more severe symptoms than those who were at home at the time of the attack. Highly exposed children reported intrusive visual images, frightening dreams of the attack, and a sense of life threat. Many children who had not directly viewed the attack still had some level of posttraumatic stress afterwards. For example, "fears of recurrence were not directly related to exposure and their common appearance may be due to what is described as the 'ripple effect' of anxiety or 'symptom contagion,' among groups of children, or between parent and child, following a traumatic event" (Pynoos et al., 1987).

(Continued From Previous Page)

hind locked doors that their mayor pleaded with them to come out and reclaim their streets?

It began to change subtly. I was there, and I saw how New York was transformed from a city of dreams to a place of nightmares. Early in the 1950s, when I was in high school, the word heroin crept into the newspapers. None existed at our school, but we began to read daily of this new menace.

As the drug trade grew, gangs grew. Our gangs in those days were territorial social clubs. The worst that ever happened was an occasional "rumble," a fistfight. As the drug traffic grew, gangs gradually were transformed from clubs to businesses. The businesses became more and more aggressive about marketing their wares.

By the end of the decade of the '50s, a new element had entered the drug equation: guns. Little by little, despite one of the oldest and toughest gun-control laws in the nation, the Sullivan Law, the city was awash in guns. Still, the police had a fighting chance until the mid-'60s.

Social turmoil broke out in New York City in the '60s. Poverty, which had been thought of as temporary, became more visibly a permanent part of the city's scene. The system seemed incapable of responding. The education system collapsed under the burden of politics and poverty. Add to those a growing culture of guns and drugs.

By the end of the '70s, social scientists were predicting that without massive intervention there would be masses of illiterate, untrained youth on the streets. They had no access to effective education, but abundant access to drugs and guns. As the '80s became the '90s, this story was to be repeated to greater or lesser degree across the nation. We had created an underclass, a lawless illiterate lot with zero regard for the common decencies of those more fortunate than they.

Brian Watkins and his family had an encounter with our nation's future. Unless we begin to rechannel the energies and reshape the values of the youth of that underclass, none of us is safe in the subway or any other place. In one ghastly moment, the people of Provo discovered they are indeed connected to the distant disarray of our urban failures.

SOURCE: R. C. Maynard with D. J. Maynard (1995). *Letters to my children.* Kansas City, MO: Andrews and McMeel. Reprinted by permission.

When the young person knows the individual who was killed, he or she will likely experience an interaction between trauma and grief (Nader, 1996); this interaction often results in intensification of many common reactions to loss. Although normal grief often involves a sense of anger, witnessing a murder might trigger a traumatic rage at the perpetrator of the crime. Sprang and McNeil (1995) summarize some of the dimensions of traumatic grief:

- fear of repetition of the trauma; perceived threat of future harm;
- self-doubt or self-directed anger due to a perceived "failure" to protect loved ones;

- anger and resentment at those exempted from the trauma, at the perpetrator, or at others who were not involved;
- morbidity, or an obsession with thoughts of how a loved one felt while dying and concerns about the state and location of the body;
- insecurities and self-loathing at one's vulnerability to harm;
- feeling a loss of control over one's environment; and
- phobic avoidance of trauma-related stimuli; for example, avoiding the scene of the crime or similar places. (p. 60)

This is an area needing much more study; we are only beginning to understand the true complications of a loss triggered by trauma.

One who witnesses a violent crime often feels particularly vulnerable in his or her own environments (Armsworth & Holaday, 1993). Many of our youth question their own safety as they come to terms with the murder of a sibling, a friend, a parent—events that are occurring far too often in U.S. society today.

ADOLESCENTS' UNDERSTANDING OF DEATH

Before we can truly understand what adolescents experience, either as they face their own deaths or grieve the death of another, we must try to understand their thought processes. Significant changes occur in cognitive abilities during adolescence. These cognitive changes have far-reaching effects on the way adolescents view life and death and on the questions and concerns they have about the dying process.

Formal Operational Thought

Cognitive capacity undergoes both quantitative and qualitative change during adolescence. Not only do adolescents acquire more information than do children, but the way they process this information is distinctively different than for younger age groups. Piaget (1972) proposed the stage of formal operations as the last stage in his structural approach to cognitive development, following the earlier sensorimotor, preoperational, and concrete operational stages. According to Piaget, the **formal operational stage** begins at approximately 11 or 12 years of age and continues to develop gradually over a period of several years.

Reasoning processes are altered on entering the formal operations stage of cognitive development; perhaps the most striking characteristic of formal operational thought is its flexibility. On reaching this stage, the adolescent is no longer tied to thinking about the observable. Rather, he or she can reason logically with abstractions that may have no basis in reality; in fact, formal operators seem to enjoy thinking about hypothetical situations. In addition, their approach to problem solving becomes increasingly systematic; possible solutions to a problem are generated and then evaluated. This hypothetical-deductive style of reasoning includes considering hypothetical "if/then" propositions and carrying them to a logical conclusion. With the expanded thought capacities of the adolescent, the way the world is organized is no longer seen as the only way it can be. The ability to think abstractly, hypothetically, and counterfactually allows the adolescent to consider possibilities for change. Anything and everything can become the focus of this type of thinking. Shaffer (1985) captures the essence of formal operational thought in the following statement:

> In sum, formal-operational thinking is rational, systematic, and abstract. The formal operator can now "think about thinking" and operate on ideas as well as tangible objects and events. Piaget believes that these new cognitive abilities are almost certain to have a dramatic impact on the adolescent's feelings, goals, and behaviors, for teenagers are suddenly able to reflect on weighty abstractions such as morality and justice, as well as more personal concerns such as their present and future roles in life, their beliefs and values, and the way things "are" as opposed to the way things "ought to be." Consequently, the adolescent approaching intellectual maturity is apt to become a bit of a philosopher, and his or her preoccupation with thinking and its products is the hallmark of the formal operational period. (p. 355)

Some adolescents and adults never reach the formal operations stage; a certain percentage of adolescents, especially younger ones, may still be rather concrete in their thinking. Possible explanations for this include a limited intellectual capacity or a lack of environmental demands requiring performance at the formal operational level. Shaffer (1985) concluded that the failure of individuals to use formal operational thought is due primarily to lack of experience with formal operations rather than inability to reason at that level.

Cognitive changes reflecting formal operational thinking affect the adolescent's ability to comprehend death and related concepts. Adolescents' increasing ability to use abstract reasoning and to understand symbolism allows them to more fully grasp the meanings of life, death, and time. Abstract concepts such as "eternity," "the purpose of life," and "acceptance of death" can now be considered. Adolescents are capable of considering the interrelationships of several variables (e.g., length of life, quality of life, and effects of medical intervention) rather than focusing on each variable in isolation. Because they can deal cognitively with hypothetical situations, adolescents are able to consider various possibilities when presented with a question such as "What would you do if you knew you were going to die next month?"

Accompanying the development of logical thought is the drive to explore the world of ideas, ideologies, and theories. The newly developed cognitive abilities prompt the adolescent to ponder the meaning of life and death. It is natural for adolescents to consider the limits of life and the meaning of death as they explore the reaches of their own minds.

In comparing questions about death and dying among junior high, high school, and college students, Cook and Oltjenbruns (1982) obtained results that show the strong influence of cognitive development on the individual's specific concerns about death. The differences among those adolescents of various cognitive levels are highlighted in Table 6.4. These investigators concluded that 11-year-olds are seeking different information and asking qualitatively different questions than are older adolescents.

Junior high school students asked questions that focused on concrete events and physical appearance (such as "What do people look like when they die?"). Their questions tended to be fact oriented ("How much does a funeral cost?") and frequently required only a yes/no response ("Is death a bad thing to watch?" "Do some people die happy?" "Do the muscles and stuff still move after the person is dead?"). Most of the questions of the junior high school students indicated that they viewed death as a single event rather than a process. Because of their age, the majority of the junior high school students were still in Piaget's concrete operational stage.

In contrast, the questions of high school juniors showed that they had made a shift to abstract thinking. They appeared more interested in understanding the dynamics of grief, dying, and death than in just obtaining facts and figures. Rather than ask questions that typically started with "what" or "how many," as was true of the junior high school students, the questions of the high school juniors often began with "why" or "how." Many of their questions indicated that they had begun to question their own values and personal philosophies related to life and death. For example, one student asked, "Why treat someone who will die anyway?" Another questioned, "How do people prepare for the end?" The high school juniors no longer viewed death as an event, but rather as a process.

An analysis of the questions asked by college juniors indicated even further cognitive change. Although similar to the high school juniors in many respects, college students demonstrated an increased understanding of the complexity of death-related events. Showing the ability to manipulate more than two categories of variables simultaneously (characteristic of formal operational thinkers), the college students asked questions such as "Does research show that most people fear death, and does this feeling relate to age?" College students also asked questions that challenged widely held ideas about the dying process and questions that showed an unwillingness simply to accept the view of authorities ("Do you think Kübler-Ross's model of the five stages of dying has been used to dehumanize the dying by putting a label on them?"). Other questions showed what Piaget described as the ability to think in relativistic terms, rather than be bound to absolutes. This characteristic of formal operational thought was illustrated in the following questions: "How does the type of death affect family interactions?" "When parents are faced with the death of a child, is their reaction different than that of a child faced with the death of a parent?" This research shows that the cognitive maturation process continues during the adolescence period and influences the ability to comprehend complex concepts, determines the types of questions and concerns adolescents may have about death, and modifies their own experience of the death of a loved one.

Closely related to changes in cognitive development are changes in the manner in which one judges behavior and thinks about moral dilemmas, usually referred to as **moral reasoning** (Piaget, 1932). A key developmental task of adolescence is the acquisition of a set of values and an ethical system that will

TABLE 6.4

Developmental Changes in Questions About Death

JUNIOR HIGH STUDENTS (N = 41)

Questions illustrated concrete thinking, a concern with appearance, and the idea that death is an event, not a process. Many questions required a yes/no or simple factual response.

Do some people die happy?

How many shots do you give a dying person each day?

How much does a funeral cost?

What do people look like when they die?

What do you do with a body right after a person dies?

How many people die?

Does everyone have to die when they get old?

Is death a bad thing to watch?

Do the muscles and stuff still move after the person is dead?

Why does people's hair fall out with chemotherapy?

HIGH SCHOOL JUNIORS (N = 47)

Questions illustrated a shift to abstract thinking, a desire to understand the dynamics of the death and dying process, and an examination of personal values and philosophies.

Will people automatically act differently toward a terminally ill person?

Do the dying have long periods of depression?

How do people prepare for the end?

Why would someone want to be cremated?

Why would someone want to view a body?

What is a dying person's reaction to death?

What is the best way to share grief?

Why treat someone who will die anyway?

Do dying people seem to treasure life more than other people?

COLLEGE JUNIORS (N = 62)

Questions illustrated understanding of interrelated variables and abstract concepts, unwillingness simply to accept all that authorities teach, and relativistic thinking.

Do you believe that people ever reach the "last stage" (so-called) of acceptance? Or do you think resignation or acknowledgment would be a better term?

Do you think that Kübler-Ross's model of the five stages of dying has been used to dehumanize the dying by putting a label on them?

What are some different points of view on life after death and ways to cope with one's own death?

How does the type of death affect family interactions?

Does research show that most people fear death and does this feeling relate to age?

How many people find cremation harder to cope with than what they had previously presumed?

When parents are faced with the death of a child, is their reaction different than that of a child faced with the death of a parent?

How do you go about donating your body to science?

SOURCE: A. S. Cook & K. Oltjenbruns (1982). A cognitive-developmental approach to death education for adolescents, *Family Perspective,* 16, p. 12. Reprinted by permission.

serve as a guide to behavior—in other words, developing one's own personal ideology. The development of a personal ideology is closely related to adolescents' attempts to define themselves and to express who they are as individuals. Each adolescent struggles with developing a coherent value system that includes attitudes toward life and death. Contemporary concerns related to death and dying often involve important ethical issues.

Peers, parents, school, and religion are all important influences as the adolescent develops his or her standards for living. Successful completion of this developmental task is made possible by, among other factors, the adolescent's ability to conceptualize on an abstract level.

Adolescent Egocentrism

Egocentrism is expressed in different ways at each stage of cognitive development. During adolescence, individuals become preoccupied with their own thought processes, leading to limitations on their newly developed cognitive abilities. Elkind (1967) has labeled this phenomenon **adolescent egocentrism.** Because adolescents are preoccupied with their own thinking and thoughts of themselves, combined with a self-consciousness about their physical and sexual changes, they create an **imaginary audience** and believe that they are continually under observation by others. Manaster (1977) describes the concept of imaginary audience as follows:

> The adolescent is said to be anticipating the reactions of the persons around him as if they saw him with his eyes, seeing his strengths, weaknesses, and concerns as he does for himself. And he thinks they are as intensely interested in the minutiae of his appearance and behavior as he is. This tremendous pressure of always being on stage in front of an "imaginary audience" accounts in part for adolescent self-consciousness, overreaction to self-perceived successes and failures, and a need for privacy and seclusion. (p. 47)

Physical changes associated with disease can be especially problematic for younger adolescents, due to this developmental phenomenon.

According to Elkind (1970), individuals ages 15 or 16 and older begin gradually to realize that they are not really standing in the middle of center stage all the time; at this point, then, a more realistic self-concept emerges. Correspondingly, formal operations are becoming better established.

While failing to separate their concerns from those of others, adolescents overdifferentiate their own feelings and see them as new and different, believing that perhaps they have never been experienced so intensely by anyone else. Therefore, they regard themselves as special and unique. This leads to a second aspect of adolescent egocentrism: the **personal fable,** which is the belief the adolescent holds that he or she is a truly one-of-a-kind individual (Elkind, 1970). The exaggerated sense of uniqueness, which often persists into late adolescence, can lead young people to believe that the rules that govern other people's lives somehow do not apply to them. As a result, adolescents act as if they believe that death only happens to others and that it will not happen to them or their family. This belief contributes to adolescents' propensity to participate in a variety of death-defying, dangerous activities and display daredevil behavior.

Although part of the normal adolescent reaction, the view that one is indestructible can also contribute to denial in response to the diagnosis of a terminal illness. Blumberg, Lewis, and Susman (1984) point out that this denial in adolescent cancer patients can be very adaptive. In fact, they have suggested that caregivers encourage adolescents to use some minimal degree of denial as a valid way of adapting to their disease by encouraging adolescents to continue their normal activities. It can be maladaptive, however, if it interferes with adequate medical intervention or results in participation in certain activities against medical advice.

ADOLESCENTS AND LIFE-THREATENING ILLNESS

This section will focus on adolescents dealing with life-threatening illnesses. Although the primary causes of death among adolescents are sudden in nature, many adolescents do face terminal illnesses (e.g., various types of cancer, diseases of the heart, and HIV infection). In fact, illnesses are measurable and significant contributors to the death rate during this life stage.

Of the life-threatening illnesses adolescents may experience, cancer is the most common; overall, it is the fourth highest cause of death among adolescents in the United States. Although adolescents may have any of a variety of cancers (among them Hodgkin's disease and brain tumors), leukemia is the most common type during this age stage. Certain types of cancer are particularly associated with the adolescent years (e.g., tumors of the bone, such as Ewing's sarcoma and osteogenic sarcoma) and are found less frequently in other age groups. Cancer in adolescents is usually treated aggressively with some combination of chemotherapy, radiation therapy, and surgery.

At one time, cancer was almost always fatal, but advances in medical science have resulted in longer **remissions** (disease-free states) and more apparent "cures." Survival rates still vary, however, for different types. In many cases it is logical to view adolescent cancer as a chronic disease with an uncertain outcome, as medical treatment may continue for many years. With medical advances, more young people diagnosed with cancer live longer and fewer die of the disease than in the past. As a result, a greater number of adolescents living today either currently have or have had a malignancy as compared to earlier generations.

AIDS has rapidly become a primary cause of death among adolescents and is currently the sixth ranking cause of death among this group. This is a startling statistic and becomes an even greater concern when we realize that currently the AIDS death rate for teenagers continues to increase markedly (Bowler et al., 1993). Because the incubation period for HIV may be as long as 10 years, many who actually contract the disease during adolescence may not be diagnosed until young adulthood (Millstein, 1990).

Because many adolescents continue to participate in high risk–taking behavior (e.g., sexual activity, intravenous drug usage), the rate of HIV infection is likely to escalate (Bowler et al., 1993). Many health professionals are rightfully worried about the serious implications of this fact; as a result, an increasing number of intervention programs are being implemented to slow the spread of AIDS among youth. Goals of such programs include increasing knowledge of HIV-related issues, changing adolescents' beliefs about themselves and others, enhancing self-efficacy, and decreasing high-risk behaviors (DiClemente, Stewart, Johnson, & Pack, 1996). If these intervention programs are to be successful in reducing the rate of infection, they need to take into account relevant developmental issues such as egocentricity, causal reasoning, feelings of invulnerability as well as various cultural issues (Stanton, Kim, Galbraith, & Parrot, 1996).

Adolescents, like others, experience a great deal of anxiety around being tested for HIV. This anxiety may result in various interpersonal problems, school-related difficulties, shame or guilt over previous high-risk behaviors, and fear of being disgraced or stigmatizing their families. Education is needed to encourage adolescents who are sexually active or who engage in other high-risk activities to seek the test; support should then be made available to those who are told they have tested positive for the HIV virus (DiClemente et al., 1996).

NEEDS OF THE ADOLESCENT WITH A LIFE-THREATENING ILLNESS

The developmental processes of adolescence discussed earlier have implications for the individual's ability to cope with death, dying, and grief. Additionally, adolescents with life-threatening illnesses have special needs related to various developmental tasks; these include the need for

- independence and control,
- strengthening a sense of personal identity,
- peer interaction,
- privacy,
- a positive body image, and
- coming to terms with the future.

These needs must be considered in order to provide optimal care for the adolescent patient. In this section, important changes in physical, cognitive, and psychosocial development will be discussed and related to the needs of young people with life-threatening illnesses.

In working with adolescent patients, the emphasis is often less on returning the person to his or her previous level of functioning and more on fostering development so that it will continue as closely as possible to that of their age-mates (Blumberg et al., 1984). Developmentally, adolescents with life-threatening illnesses are, in many significant ways, very much like healthy adolescents. Although all young people confront the normal stresses and challenges of this stage of life, adolescents with health problems must face the added stresses associated with a particular disease process and related implications in regard to physical and psychosocial functioning. Changes precipitated by illness may be particularly anxiety laden during a life stage already filled with multiple and rapid transitions.

Independence and Control

Ansbacher and Ansbacher (1956), in their book on Alfred Adler, quote his views regarding the centrality of the independence issue for the adolescent:

> For almost every child, adolescence means one thing above all else: he must prove he is no longer a child. . . . Very many of the expressions of adolescence are the outcome of the desire to show independence, equality with adults, and manhood or womanhood. The direction of these expressions will depend on the meaning which the child has attributed to being "grown-up." (p. 439)

Achieving emotional independence from parents and other adults and establishing new and more mature relations with age-mates of both sexes are seen as important developmental tasks of adolescence. These tasks operate in a complementary fashion to help adolescents become emancipated from their parents in preparation for leaving home at the beginning of their adult years. The ultimate goal is to maintain affection for each other and develop interdependence while at the same time breaking the dependency bond remaining from childhood.

Ambivalence (centering around the need to relinquish childhood ties) marks both parental and adolescent attitudes toward the developmental task of achieving emotional independence. Adolescents want to have more control over their lives, yet they are unsure of giving up parental protection. For parents, the development of independence on the part of the adolescent means a corresponding loss of power and influence for themselves. Parents are not sure that their "child" can make it without them, and the adolescent may be unsure as well because he or she is not yet ready to deal with the world in a mature, adultlike manner.

Relationships between terminally ill adolescents and their parents may be especially difficult. Adolescents, particularly younger ones, may vacillate between the desire to be independent from parents and the need to depend on parents for support and protection. The tendency to regress temporarily and become dependent is especially pronounced during high stress periods such as those following diagnosis, relapse, or treatment (such as chemotherapy) (Zeltzer, LeBaron, & Zeltzer, 1984). For example, when adolescents experience side effects from a particular treatment, they may revert to a more childlike state. As soon as the symptoms and side effects subside, they are likely to rebuff parental attention. This dependence–independence cycle can be very confusing for parents. As one parent commented, "When she zigs I zag and we just can't seem to get our zigs and zags synchronized" (Farrell, 1981). Parents may try to show their concern by overprotecting the adolescent at a time when, if the child were healthy, he or she would be learning to let go. In fact, the parents' own sense of loss of control may intensify their concern and caretaking of the adolescent. This attempt on the part of parents to combat their own feelings of helplessness may be viewed negatively by the adolescent. Berman (1980) shares a quote from an 18-year-old patient to illustrate the embarrassment felt in response to the parent's inappropriate attempts to help her:

> My mother thinks I'm two years old again. She hovers over me. When the doctor comes in to talk to me, she talks for me as if I cannot talk. It really bothers me, even though it probably makes her feel better to do these things. (p. 2)

Most adolescents do not want their parents to engage in controlling behaviors; however, they do not want them to disengage totally. For example, adolescents often want parents to participate in such activities as discussions with the doctors (Stevens & Dunsmore, 1996a).

Dependence versus independence is one of the central challenges for adults in dealing with adolescents who have cancer. Diagnosis of particular diseases and the treatments that follow can threaten the young person's sense of control and independence. They tend to perceive more self-control over an illness when the disease is one, such as diabetes, that can be controlled through diet regimens and self-administered medications. In contrast, less control is apparent with diseases such as cancer and renal dysfunction in which treatment and medications are administered in medical settings by professional personnel.

A diagnosis of cancer, for example, can lead to an emotional crisis with concomitant feelings of anxiety, depression, and helplessness. Although loss of control is an issue for all cancer patients, it has a heightened impact on adolescents because of the developmental tasks they are facing. At a time when they should be gaining a strong sense of personal autonomy and mastery over their environment, adolescent patients may find themselves having to cope with a variety of intrusive medical procedures in a hospital setting, procedures that encourage passivity and dependency. When independence is threatened, adolescents' discomfort levels rise. Characteristic behaviors of individuals may become exaggerated. For example, a very sick 16-year-old who has always been direct and outspoken may appear belligerent at times; another adolescent who has always been rather daring may take defiant risks.

In some cases, power struggles that commonly develop between parent and adolescent can jeopardize the patient's physical well-being. Berman (1980) describes a case of a 16-year-old female who refused food as a way of asserting her independence and also testing her mother's concern. This behavior was in response to her mother's focused attention on her food intake and her attempts to "baby" her daughter as she stood over her numerous hours each day. The adolescent was using the only thing she felt was hers—her body—as a means of maintaining control. Once it started, the power struggle escalated to a point where neither mother nor daughter could easily break away from it. This situation was resolved by giving the daughter more legitimate control over various facets of her life, so that she did not have to resort to using her control mechanisms in a maladaptive way.

Despite potential problems that may arise between adolescents and their parents, some patients feel that they can rely on their parents more than anyone else. Those with life-threatening illnesses can feel guilty for being dependent on others and for the extra burden their illness puts on their family. Adolescent patients may be concerned about the cost of their medical treatment, the time the parents have lost from work, and family plans that are spoiled (e.g., missed vacations) due to their illness.

Power struggles can extend beyond the parent–child relationship to the doctor–patient relationship. Lack of involvement in decisions about their treatment and incomplete communications about the nature and progression of their illness can result in lack of cooperation and, in some cases, actually sabotage the treatment plan. Frustrated adolescents, fearing that they are being forced to regress to an earlier developmental stage, may rebel by refusing treatment, breaking hospital rules, or participating in forbidden activities. Actions reflecting noncompliance and lack of cooperation with others may actually be strategies to exert some control over their lives.

One facet of developing a sense of independence during adolescence is not only to become increasingly separated from one's parents, but also to establish a greater control over one's own physical and psychosocial environments. The research of Seligman (1975) and others has shown that the perception of control reduces anxiety and contributes to greater stress tolerance. Their findings suggest that perceiving control, even if one does not necessarily use it or even, in fact, have it, is an important factor in successfully dealing with adverse situations. Maximizing the participation of terminally ill adolescents in their daily lives can have positive effects both from a therapeutic and a developmental perspective. Because control has many dimensions, supporting the adolescent's sense of autonomy and facilitating involvement in certain areas of his or her life can mitigate the negative outcomes arising from lack of control in other areas. By definition, serious illness diminishes control over one's own body and many activities; therefore, attempts need to be made to restore power in other arenas.

Being given choices or opportunities for input regarding their own care should be provided whenever possible for the adolescent patient (e.g., encouraging the teenager to plan his or her own meals according to dietary restrictions) (Stevens & Dunsmore, 1996b). Doing certain tasks, even small ones, by themselves or with minimal assistance can help adolescents experience some level of autonomy even during a period when they may be highly dependent on health care professionals. Although some adolescents seek to deny their illness for a time, most value information about various facets of their disease and prognosis and perceive this as necessary to a sense of control. Access to information is a key resource in allowing one to better solve various problems (Derdiarian, 1987).

Some physical distance from parents and other caregivers can be healthy for the adolescent. During a "well" period, for example, young people often want to return to school. With their own friends, and in their own territory, adolescents may feel safer asserting themselves.

In interviews with parents of adolescent cancer patients, Farrell (1981) found that parents were concerned about their child's degree of involvement in discussions with the health care professionals. Although wanting to protect the child from the implications of their diagnosis, all the parents in the study recognized the need of the teenager to be involved in ongoing decision making with the treatment team. When asked who should be involved in treatment decisions, most adolescents said that physicians, parents, and themselves should all participate jointly (Dunsmore & Quine, 1995).

Sense of Personal Identity

Erikson (1959), in defining his various developmental psychosocial crises, proposed **identity** versus **role confusion** (identity diffusion) as the critical developmental issue to be resolved during adolescence. The adaptive challenge of self-definition and commitment to a role is the major developmental task of this life stage. The many changes that occur during adolescence raise the question of "Who am I?" Perceptions one had earlier about oneself formulated in concrete terms must be reinterpreted in the broader abstractions of formal operational thought. This period of personal definition and reorganization facilitates one's adopting an active role in society and committing to an ideology. Discovering attitudes, ideals, and roles that one will carry into adult life contributes to a more clearly defined sense of self. On the other hand, being unsure of who one is and where one is going leads to a prolonged sense of identity diffusion. An adolescent with a life-threatening illness may have particular difficulty resolving identity issues. An uncertain and often limited future can interfere with positive identity development.

Experimentation is often manifest in the adolescent's search for personal identity. Anyone who has lived with a teenager is familiar with the mood swings, extremism, and strong displays of emotion typical of this age group. Adolescents try out new behaviors and ways of relating to others in order to assess the reaction of others and engage in reality testing. Experimentation is a primary characteristic of adolescence, and everything is a ready target—clothes, hairstyles, attitudes, friendships, and roles. Much of the perceived inconsistency in an adolescent's moods or activities relates to this type of experimentation, as he or she conceives of various potentialities for being and behaving. Also contributing to the apparent inconsistency and lack of maturity in the personality of adolescents is the fact that they are facing a myriad of new situations. As they face these, they simply do not know how to act; they are unsure of what is expected of them and concerned about how well they will perform. Adolescents, therefore, often appear awkward and inconsistent to others as they try out different roles and ways of fulfilling them to find out what comfortably fits and what they will carry with them into adulthood (Manaster, 1977).

The development of "self" emerges out of interaction with others and also out of internal dialogue with one's thoughts and feelings. Identity can be thought of as the "me" in each person. Erikson (1959) viewed identity as including self-esteem, or our feelings about ourselves. A strong and stable identity gives an individual a consistent psychological basis for dealing with the demands of reality.

Adolescents with a life-threatening illness are at risk of a negative resolution of the major psychosocial crisis of this life stage—identity versus role confusion (identity diffusion). They may develop a distorted image of themselves as a result of the disease process and its treatment (due to ongoing and dramatic change in physical appearance, for example). These patients may also have a diffused sense of self due to involvement in the "patient role" or the "dying role." They are often denied the opportunity to experiment with and/or master various roles regarded as normal for this life stage.

Self-expression is a requirement for the development of a strong sense of identity. Self-expression, so valued by the adolescent, is difficult to achieve when parents continue to provide for one's basic needs, when weakness and pain restrict activities, and when the individual is uncertain of his or her skills and abilities. Caregivers in a medical setting need to give special attention to the need of adolescents to express their individuality. Flexible hospital policies and regulations that allow teenagers to wear their own clothes and personalize their rooms (perhaps put their favorite posters on the wall) can be particularly significant and can give the message to young patients that they are unique individuals with special interests, abilities, and traits regardless of their physical condition. Providing recreational activities that encourage self-expression (e.g., painting) can also provide for the sharing of a variety of personal feelings that adolescents may not be able to communicate verbally.

A sense of continuity versus discontinuity is also a key identity issue. Adolescents with serious diseases need help continuing normal, everyday activities as much as possible; they need opportunities to be themselves and to show others who they are. One way of maintaining continuity is by keeping one's identity as a student. Doing this, in whatever capacity is feasible, helps an adolescent maintain a sense of normalcy at a time when he or she may be feeling very different from peers.

Adolescent cancer patients, although feeling that it is important to return to school, understandably have some concerns about it. Some of their hesitations can be alleviated if caregivers plan for their eventual return. Hospitals, schools, and tutors as well as teachers of the homebound can help the young person keep up with class work and thus make the transition back to full-time or part-time student easier. Parents should maintain contact with the school and inform staff of their child's needs in anticipation of his or her reenrollment. Adolescents returning after hospitalization may have some difficulty handling the demands of school because of frequent absenteeism. They may also not feel well enough or have sufficient energy to complete their work or to spend a full day at school. Regardless, there seems to be general agreement that ill adolescents who desire to do so, should return to school as soon as possible to begin reestablishing a somewhat normal lifestyle.

Peer Interaction

One of the most notable social changes during adolescence is the increased importance of peer groups, which serve several important interrelated functions for the adolescent. One important function is the granting of status at a time when the adolescent is striving for self-definition; status is earned through the adolescent's own efforts and interaction with the social environment. Peer relationships provide latitude for young persons to test themselves and try out a variety of roles. In a supportive environment, adolescents often extend the boundaries of self-definition and expand the range of their skills, beliefs, and behaviors. The extent of this expansion is based on reactions and approval of their peers. Toward the end of adolescence, the peer group loses some of its power as a socialization agent; the more confident individuals feel about themselves and their own judgment, the less influence others will have on them.

Peer groups also facilitate the adolescent's quest for independence from parents by often supporting the adolescent as he or she resists adult standards and control. Although emotional bonds to parents are still maintained, the relationship eventually matures as adolescents move toward exercising greater personal autonomy. Identification with a peer group and adherence to its norms assists the adolescent in the transition from emotional dependence on parents to interdependence in a variety of relationships. Age-mates offer support, security, and a feeling of "belonging" as the adolescent negotiates this transition.

Maintaining positive relationships and frequent interaction with peers is critically important to those with life-threatening illnesses. One of the favorite activities of individuals in this age group is to "hang out" with one another away from adult scrutiny. The disease and its treatment can limit opportunities for peer contact and, thus, interfere with the accomplishment of various developmental tasks. When adolescents are separated from their friends, they lose access to valuable emotional support.

Peer involvement becomes more of a struggle with an illness such as AIDS; given the fear and the stigma that often surround those with this illness, many in the social environment withdraw from the person who is ill. A vivid example was the case of Ryan White whose situation drew national attention when it became evident that many in his community were taking definitive actions to keep him out of school and other public settings. These actions severely limited the possibilities that Ryan would have for normal interactions with age-mates.

Although most would agree that an adolescent who is HIV positive has a right to go to school with his peers, it is helpful to teachers and others to know that a particular student does have AIDS. Many parents, however, are fearful of disclosing this diagnosis, given circumstances where in the past some of these young persons and their family members have been discriminated against and/or have been the target of violence. At a time when HIV-positive adolescents and their families need support, they may not receive it and, instead, be the target of negative activities (Sterken, 1995).

In general, adolescents with life-threatening diseases are afraid of being regarded as different from their classmates and of being rejected by them. They are unsure how to respond to others' questions and how to handle teasing. Some impose isolation on themselves and withdraw from peers rather than risk rejection. Physical limitations (such as an amputation that may limit activity) magnify this sense of being different. The individual's perception of his or her social status may be distorted, thus contributing to feelings of inadequacy and incompetence (Blumberg et al., 1984).

Teens who are very ill report that they are bothered more by being stared at or by being avoided by peers than they are by direct questioning about their circumstances. Healthy adolescents, however, may often hesitate to mention the subject of their friend's disease. In a project sponsored by the National Cancer Institute, young cancer patients recommended telling friends the truth about their cancer, its treatment, and its side effects. Another study found that some adolescents felt uncomfortable with their ill friend and worried about saying the wrong thing. Most respondents felt that they acted no differently toward a person because he or she had a life-threatening disease; one-third said they had talked with the person about the illness. Only 14%, however, had visited their friend when he or she was absent from school (Hodges, Graham-Pole, & Fong, 1984). This lack of contact may contribute to strain between sick adolescents and those they regard as friends.

One patient told of the strengthening of a friendship by this type of sharing: "And I prepared one of my better friends. I told her I'm going to come home and probably I'm going to be bald, I'm probably going to look like I'm sicker than a dog. And she said okay, just as long as you're you" (Office of Cancer Communications, 1980). In contrast to this example, however, many patients with life-threatening illnesses lose some of their friends because the situation is more than their peers can handle. Interestingly, peers of adolescents with cancer generally report positive feelings toward the friend who is ill and say they admire the way he or she manages the disease.

Recall that the fear of isolation is common among those with life-threatening illnesses. Peer interaction minimizes feelings of isolation and rejection and can be facilitated in a number of ways. One is by encouraging the visitation of friends both at the hospital and at home, and helping them feel comfortable when they do visit. Visitors provide a vital link to the events external to a world defined by illness and treatment. Activities with friends can have special meaning during the teen years; adolescents may request that their schedule for various treatments be changed to enable them to attend a school function or a sports event. Flexibility on the part of the medical staff is important as long as it does not jeopardize the patient's medical condition.

Inflexible policies, an institutional atmosphere, and a lack of privacy and space can serve to discourage visits from healthy peers. Geographical distance and transportation can also make it difficult for younger adolescents to visit hospitalized friends. Installing a phone by the adolescent's bed or providing equipment for tape-recorded interactions can help the person maintain contact with friends on a regular basis. Increasingly, contact among dying adolescents and their well peers or even with others who are also sick is facilitated by electronic means. Young people can go on-line through the Internet and join chat rooms (Sofka, 1997) where they can communicate about various issues and concerns.

Peers can also promote recovery. In chapter 2, it was emphasized that dying individuals are *living* individuals; adolescents with serious illnesses want to participate in activities and conversations that remind them of life! Age-mates are often the ones who update them on the latest "gossip," music trends, and clothes fashions. Peers who themselves are also sick provide an important contribution of empathetic support and an opportunity to vent feelings and ask questions without being embarrassed. Additionally, other adolescents who have experienced similar diseases, symptoms, and treatments provide important information, insights, and, very often, a sense of reality that others cannot (Carr-Gregg, 1989).

Establishing teen floors in hospitals can foster interaction with peers facing similar challenges. Deep friendships are often formed among adolescent patients; after leaving the hospital, those who had been hospitalized together frequently continue to maintain contact and inquire about each other's condition.

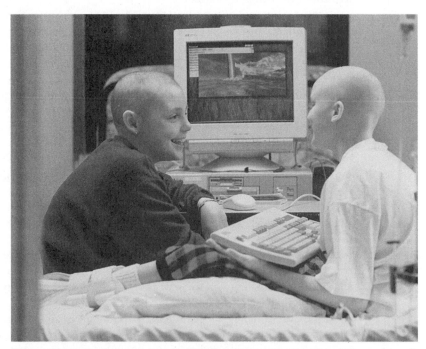

With access to the Internet, terminally ill adolescents can enter chat rooms and share experiences.

Opportunities for group activities in a medical setting are enhanced by the availability of a recreation room containing age-appropriate equipment (e.g., a CD player, computer and/or video games, a pool table). Bringing music and videos from home and sharing them with other hospitalized peers help the adolescent feel more connected to "the real world."

As important as interactions with peers can be, there are times when adolescents do not want companionship. Any person with a life-threatening illness will have some bad days, often precipitated by bad news, pain, or exhaustion. Adolescents may simply want to shut the world out and be left alone at these times; time away from the intrusion of hospital routines can be especially therapeutic. Special areas on the hospital grounds (e.g., outdoor lounges) can be designed with this purpose in mind.

Privacy

Adolescence is often thought to begin with the onset of puberty, a period of rapid physiological change and growth. Hallmarks of this period include the development of primary sexual characteristics associated with sexual maturity. These are often associated with the onset of menstruation for females and the experience of ejaculation and "wet dreams" for boys. Members of both sexes also develop secondary sexual characteristics (e.g., growth of pubic hair) and experience growth spurts. Both males and females experience changes in their genitals. Boys experience vocal changes; girls develop mature breasts. Different parts of the body typically grow at different rates, often resulting in the adolescent's feeling clumsy or unattractive. Many of the physiological changes during puberty seem confusing, frightening, and/or embarrassing to young persons as these changes unfold. Their egocentrism causes them to feel that others are closely focused on them. As a result, most adolescents already feel self-conscious; young persons who are seriously ill are likely to feel all the more so.

This sensitivity needs to be acknowledged and respected by health care professionals. A need for privacy is paramount and can be ensured by such things as avoiding unnecessary exposure of the body, performing physical examinations behind a closed curtain or a closed door, minimizing the number of people present during an exam or treatment process, and entering patients' rooms only after knocking. All of these show respect for the individual and make him or her feel more comfortable in situations that would otherwise diminish a sense of personal dignity.

Mitchell (1980) found that male adolescents' self-consciousness during a physical examination conducted by a female was more related to "what the other guys would think" than to the actual experience. These findings have implications for the way opposite-sex medical staff prepare adolescents for potentially embarrassing medical procedures or hygiene-related processes such as urinary catheterization, pelvic examinations, or sponge baths.

The need for privacy extends into other areas as well. The right to private conversations with friends, siblings, or medical staff is important to the adolescent. If conversations held in confidence are not kept confidential, then the adolescent's trust will be jeopardized. Because of the many issues that they are facing, adolescents may also want some private time away from parents and medical staff. Quiet time for reflecting on one's life experience becomes increasingly important with age. A sense of personal privacy can help to create an environment in which one can begin to process thoughts and feelings about one's potential death and all that means.

Positive Body Image

Physical changes that typically occur during adolescence can be a source of anxiety and concern. One's appearance is very important at this stage, and adolescents may worry, for example, that they are too tall, that their noses are too big, that their teeth are crooked, or that they are generally unattractive. A person's body image relates to several factors, including ideas about how adolescents think they themselves look and how they think others view them or fantasies about how they would like to look. It is also affected somewhat by whether they mature earlier or later than their peers. An adolescent with a positive body image is more likely to develop a positive self-image overall.

Adolescents typically spend considerable time each day grooming, evaluating their physical appearance in the mirror, and trying to become accustomed to their changing bodies. Concern over personal body image is magnified by our society's emphasis on physical appearance. Some adolescents with life-threatening illnesses may enter puberty later than their peers because of growth failure (e.g., those with cystic fibrosis or end-stage renal failure). Consequently, they sometimes look years younger than their chronological age and may be treated more like children than adolescents. This can, in turn, cause much anger and frustration. Such maturational discrepancies can also lead to feelings of being different and social isolation.

Sometimes the side effects of treatment pose an even greater threat to body image than the disease process itself. Outcomes of treatment may include stunted growth, severe weight change, radiation dermatitis, or changes in appearance resulting from amputation and other types of surgery. In a study of adolescents with cancer, the young patients emphasized their need to be informed of side effects in advance. They also felt it would have been useful to talk to someone their own age who had already gone through the treatment in order to be better prepared. Adolescents seem to know what is most important to other adolescents. For example, in discussing the specific effects of chemotherapy, the adolescents did not emphasize nausea and vomiting (although these were common side effects) as much as changes in physical appearance and abilities. Hair loss, cushingoid facies (that is, "moon face"), and the inability to participate in favorite physical activities were mentioned as especially difficult by the adolescents who had undergone chemotherapy. Some of the changes caused embarrassment and threatened young people's self-esteem. No matter how well they felt, the adolescents were constantly reminded of their illnesses by the visible side effects of the treatment (Orr, Hoffmans, & Bennetts, 1984). In fact, many adolescents perceive these changes to be more problematic than the disease itself (Wasserman, Thompson, Wilimas, & Fairclough, 1987).

Adolescents with life-threatening illnesses may also appear preoccupied with their daily grooming routine, because, if it can be avoided, it is important to them not to look different from their peers. Although perhaps appearing excessive to parents, the extra time and energy required for such things as daily hair washing or application of cosmetics may be crucial for the sick adolescent to feel comfortable around others.

Because young persons have such a strong need to develop and maintain a positive body image, caregivers should recognize the importance of this need and provide support and encouragement to the teenager attempting to deal with unpleasant physical changes. For example, **alopecia** (i.e., hair loss) resulting from chemotherapy can be particularly difficult for adolescents to accept. It may affect their perceived physical attractiveness as well as their peer relations. Many patients fear that their hair will not grow back, and consequently need reassurance that it indeed will (if this is, in fact, the case). A wig, scarf, or hat can be used to enhance appearance and make them feel more comfortable until their hair grows. Adolescents are very concerned about what they wear, and they usually have definite preferences; they should be given the opportunity to choose clothes that help them feel good about themselves. Clothes can be selected to minimize the changes in physical appearance caused by weight gain or loss.

Future Orientation

Part of the adolescent's identity relates to his or her plans for the future and the roles he or she wishes to assume upon reaching adulthood. As adolescents mature, they often think of their future in terms of education, career, family, and so on. Planning for career and life goals is difficult when a life-threatening illness occurs. If they know they will not have the opportunity to live as an adult, adolescents with illnesses diagnosed as terminal often feel cheated and angry.

When the dying trajectory is uncertain, a lack of clarity about future possibilities and limitations can leave the adolescent unable to make definite plans (Rando, 1984). In some cases, they may even be reluctant to explore treatment options for fear of having expectations raised, only to have them crushed. In spite of uncertainty about their future (which may vary considerably for different individuals), young persons should be encouraged to make realistic plans. Nannis et al. (1982) suggest that a perception of some control of the future is positively correlated with optimism and participation in activities of daily living.

The adolescent may need some adult assistance and guidance in charting his or her future. For example, if treatment interrupts the adolescent's education, then plans regarding college or employment may have to be altered or delayed. For young people with a certain death trajectory, their "future" may be limited to only a few months. These adolescents need help coping with the fact that they will not have had the opportunity to complete some important life goals.

Not all thoughts about the future are reality-based. Fantasizing about the future is a part of normal adolescent development and should not be considered aberrant in adolescents with life-threatening illnesses. Although some of their fantasies may seem quite unrealistic (e.g., becoming a rock star), these dreams can be important in helping the teenager maintain a positive emotional perspective.

HELPING ADOLESCENTS COPE WITH LIFE-THREATENING ILLNESSES

Adolescents with life-threatening illnesses appear to cope quite well. Research has shown that, in general, chronically ill and terminally ill adolescents seem to have a higher tolerance for stress than do their healthy peers. These findings suggest that adolescents with life-threatening diseases learn to live with their health problems and to cope effectively. In fact, Kellerman, Zeltzer, Ellenberg, Dash, and Rigler (1980) found a negative correlation between anxiety and time since diagnosis, indicating that, with time, increased coping skills are developed and adjustment occurs. Overall, adolescents who face potentially fatal conditions appear to be psychologically healthy, well adjusted, and generally hopeful.

Adolescents may have a resiliency that comes from their views of themselves as immortal (Zeltzer, 1980). For example, viewing death as something in the distant future enables adolescents with cancer to cope better with setbacks during the course of their illness. Examining the effectiveness of experimental drugs after the failure of conventional treatment, Susman, Pizzo, and Poplack (1981) found that adolescent patients displayed an inordinate amount of hope in the remission-inducing potential of the chemotherapy. The majority of adolescents thought they would survive even though the odds were against them.

Honest communication from those around the dying adolescent is crucial if he or she is to develop a realistic perspective of the future and what it may hold. The adolescent cancer patients interviewed by Orr et al. (1984) stated emphatically that they did not want to be given false promises or undergo aggressive therapy if death was inevitable. Honesty was a standard they wanted their health care providers and their parents to practice. Although they considered it vital to maintain hope and consider the possibilities of a cure, they did not believe in deception and readily articulated this belief.

Most want accurate information about their illness, its likely progression, and its outcome. Dunsmore and Quine (1995) studied 51 young individuals, ranging in age from 15 to 24 years, who had various types of life-threatening cancers. They found that almost all felt that they needed additional information on topics such as the chances of the cancer returning, side effects, emotions, long-term effects, reproduction/fertility, need for further treatment, and options for the future. Forty-nine out of the 51 respondents said that they should be informed if they were going to die, their prognosis was poor, or their treatment was not effective. Follow-up comments included: "I have a right to know," "I'm a real person," "It's my body, not the doctor's, not my parents'" (p. 49).

Adolescents use a variety of coping techniques to help them deal with their illnesses. Many adolescents use some level of denial or avoidance for a period of time to ward off anxiety, help support the need to maintain normal functioning, and encourage a more positive self-image.

Other prevalent coping mechanisms of adolescents include overcompensation, intellectualization, and anger. Adolescents in their attempts to deny their illness and appear "normal" may try to overcompensate by outperforming their peers and proving their abilities. Intellectualization, used more by older adolescents than younger ones, can reduce anxiety by repressing emotions while focusing on intellectual aspects of the illness. Activities such as researching the illness and asking detailed questions about the treatment process can reduce their uncertainty as well. Anger regarding the illness and its effects may be channeled in many different directions; often it is displayed in the form of "acting-out" behavior and rebellion against authority figures.

Adolescents also use more mature coping strategies (when compared to those used by younger children), such as altruism (helping others) and humor, which help them maintain a positive attitude. Many adolescents feel that major factors helping them cope with their illness include maintaining a sense of humor, thinking pleasant thoughts, hearing of other patients who are doing well, and having someone to talk to when they are afraid (Zeltzer et al., 1984).

Although a number of studies have been done on the psychosocial outcomes of long-term survivors of adolescent cancer, they are not consistent in their findings. Wasserman et al. (1987) have emphasized the need for such studies because by the year 2000, based on present cure rates, more than 1 in 1,000 people between the ages of 20 and 29 will have survived cancer during their younger years. Further, although the incidence of cancer during childhood is increasing, the mortality rate in that group is declining (Bleyer, 1990).

In their study of individuals who had completed treatment for Hodgkin's disease and had been considered cured for at least 5 years, Wasserman et al. (1987) found high levels of adjustment. Many of the former patients were young adults at the time of the study and were leading essentially normal lives and adjusting to the demands of school, work, and personal relationships. The individuals felt that, because of their experience with cancer, they had an increased appreciation of being alive and an improved outlook on life. For many adolescents who recover from cancer, several beneficial outcomes can be identified. These adolescents often experience feelings of mastery and self-confidence in relation to having conquered the disease. Additionally, they report greater sensitivity and ability to help friends with their problems, increased introspection, the development of strong and helpful coping skills, a tendency to place less emphasis on physical appearance, and a positive self-concept (Fritz & Williams, 1988; Orr et al., 1984).

On the other hand, many who survive cancer at a young age continue to have persistent body image concerns, preoccupation with the disease, and worry about the disease recurring. Consequently, there is often an ongoing preoccupation with bodily functions and characteristics. There is, as well, a sense of fragility or vulnerability (Fritz & Williams, 1988).

Smith, Ostroff, Tan, and Lesko (1991) note:

> Adolescent cancer survivors must assimilate the experience of cancer diagnosis and its treatment into their self-perceptions . . . this impact is quite variable, having both positive and negative valences . . . as confirmed by this study, these young people may have a sense of mastery and achievement that becomes assimilated . . . (yet) alterations in self-perception in this population may also reflect feelings of residual vulnerability as the influence of specific domains in adolescents' lives are explored. (p. 586)

Fritz and Williams (1988) stress that the psychosocial impact of illness and treatment on adolescent survivors of cancer is complex and unpredictable. However, they believe that most are successful in integrating their experiences without causing major distortions in their developmental progress. In their study, Teta et al. (1986) found that survivors whose treatment was brief, who did not have relapses, and whose families were supportive and communicative had the best psychological outcomes.

DEALING WITH LOSS DURING ADOLESCENCE

The lives of many adolescents are marked by significant losses and may include the death of a parent, a sibling, or a friend. Meshot and Leitner (1993) note that

> Facing the death of a close loved one may add considerable upheaval to this time of life characterized by ambivalence, struggle, and confusion. Thus, the bereavement process for adolescents may be different than for children and adults. (p. 288)

Fleming and Adolph (1986) have identified core issues around which adolescents must come to terms with the crisis of bereavement—issues that are fundamental to the experience of being an adolescent. These core issues are based on the following:

- predictability of events,
- self-image,
- sense of belonging,
- fairness/justice, and
- mastery/control.

Just as persons who are dying may find it more difficult to resolve Erikson's psychosocial crises in a positive fashion, bereaved adolescents often find it somewhat more difficult to deal with these primary issues in their lives. Further, the actual manifestations of grief (as seen in various behavioral, cognitive, and affective responses) are linked to the adolescent's current stage of maturation (Balk, 1996). For example, given the strong desire to belong (that is a natural part of this life stage), some adolescents are fearful of seeming to be different from their peers by outwardly showing their grief. As a result, many younger adolescents camouflage their feelings so that those around them do not truly understand the intensity of their reactions to loss (Fleming & Balmer, 1996).

The grief of adolescents is multifaceted, as it is in other life stages, and parallels many reactions described earlier in chapter 3. Common reactions include

- sleep disturbances;
- dysphoric mood, fear, guilt, confusion, anger, sense of powerlessness;
- diminished social competency, loneliness;
- feeling different;
- preoccupation with the death event or the person who died, inability to concentrate, diminished study habits; and
- aggressive behaviors, acting-out behaviors. (Balk, 1983; Davies, 1991; Fanos & Nickerson, 1991; Hogan & Greenfield, 1991; McCown & Davies, 1995; Miller, 1996)

Although most reactions do dissipate over time, some may linger over an extended period (Hogan, Morse, & Tason, 1996). Many of the grief responses noted here will be addressed more specifically as we examine the death of a sibling and the death of a peer.

Self-Concept and Bereavement

A question raised by a number of researchers focuses on whether a relationship exists between an adolescent's experience with grief and his or her self-concept. Earlier research had raised the question as to whether the bereavement process might be a causative factor in negative shifts in adolescents' self-concept; however, this does not always seem to be the case. The relationship seems to be a complicated one and depends on a number of variables (Hogan & Balk, 1990). Although there is no definitive answer as to the actual interaction between the two (i.e., self-concept and bereavement), a number of interesting findings have been reported in relation to this issue.

Hogan and Greenfield (1991) studied 127 adolescents, ages 13 to 18, who had experienced the death of a sibling. Although most of this group showed similar bereavement reactions during the first 18 months following the death, significant differences were apparent beyond 18 months. These researchers found that 18 months or more after the death those young people who had a low self-concept showed significantly more intense grief reactions than did those with a high self-concept. Hogan and Greenfield concluded that there is a strong relationship between lingering bereavement symptomatology and a relatively low self-concept.

Martinson, Davies, and McClowry (1987) studied 29 young persons (ages 8 to 18) following the death of a sibling. Their goal was to examine self-concept a number of years following this significant loss. They compared self-concept scores of the bereaved-sibling group to the scores used to norm the self-concept instrument and found them to be significantly higher. This finding may be further evidence that a crisis such as death can serve as a catalyst for many positive outcomes.

For some, there is a risk that the death of a sibling may contribute to a lowered self-esteem. If, for example, surviving children are always compared to the "special child" who died, they may have difficulty reconciling their own value in comparison to the child who is gone (Adams & Deveau, 1987; Pettle-Michael & Lansdown, 1986). Parents who "overprotect" surviving siblings may have a negative impact on their children's self-esteem in that they find it difficult to display their own independence and prove their own capability.

Coping With Loss

Each individual brings to a crisis situation a wide variety of coping strategies; these vary somewhat by life stage, personality, and previous experiences. It has been argued that adolescents are especially vulnerable to the impact of a crisis and, as a result, their mental health may be at risk. Indeed, bereavement outcomes are often quite complex following a significant loss during adolescence. The crisis of being faced with the death of a loved one may actually strengthen the adolescent's coping abilities *or* it can also leave him or her vulnerable, as new developmental and family issues are faced without the psychosocial capabilities to deal effectively with the situation. Recall earlier discussions of positive and negative outcomes to the grief experience in chapter 3. In some cases, when the grief is either so intense or so long in duration that it becomes disabling, bereaved youth may then need to seek professional counseling (Valentine, 1996). Keep in mind, however, that some adolescents use professional support simply to better understand the grief process and their own feelings, even though they are actively engaged in coming to terms with the death.

Aubrey (1977), in reviewing cases seen at a university counseling center, found that a high incidence of students seeking counseling had experienced a significant earlier loss. Although this information was elicited in clinical interviews, few students initially cited adjustment to the loss as their presenting problem. The loss-related issues that surface during counseling can be quite varied. For example, a young woman may have deep-seated fears of womanhood and sexual activity because of associations formed years earlier when her mother died of breast cancer. Another example would be a young man who is hostile toward his stepfather for trying to take his deceased father's place and anger toward his mother for remarrying rather than "remaining loyal."

On the other hand, when denial of death is reinforced by family and friends and when opportunities for grieving are not provided, adolescents may vent

Peer support can help mediate the experience of loss for adolescents.

their feelings through destructive acts. Unable to express their grief in socially acceptable ways, adolescents may "act out their tears" through delinquent behaviors (Shoor & Speed, 1976). Rosenblatt, Jackson, and Walsh (1972) go so far as to suggest that a great deal of antisocial behavior in our society is the result of anger associated with repressed grief. Acting out may also occur in the form of sexual behavior (Raphael, 1983).

The acting out of grief by the bereaved adolescent can be just a temporary phase or it can become a more permanent pattern. Factors affecting the duration of this behavior include the family's ability to perceive and respond to the adolescent's needs (contributing to the resolution of grief) and the availability of other forms of intervention (Raphael, 1983).

In some circumstances, suicide or consideration of suicide can be an outcome of unresolved loss. For example, in one study of 33 adolescents, thoughts of suicide were reported after the death of a sibling and were associated with feelings of depression and family arguments. Twelve adolescents thought of ending their lives in the few weeks after their sibling died, and nine had considered it several months or years after the death. These adolescents saw suicide as a means of being reunited with their siblings and as a way of escaping their troubles (Balk, 1983).

Although risks have been identified in this section of coping, the majority of adolescents do come to terms with their grief experience. If adolescents are given support from adults and peers, they are often able to cope effectively with the death of a loved one. For example, one effective coping strategy is to engage in socially constructive acts. In one school, following the death of a teacher, students volunteered to help raise money for research to help conquer the disease that caused the death. In another case, following a classmate's death, friends served as peer mentors for younger children as part of a suicide prevention program.

Although more attention needs to be given to the influence of religious beliefs on bereavement outcome, a limited number of researchers have begun to explore this variable (Balk & Hogan, 1995). Many adolescents believe that they were better able to cope with loss (both before and after the death) if they were able to draw strength from a religious belief system (Balk, 1991a; Hogan & De-Santis, 1994, 1996a). Religion does not "anesthetize" adolescents to their grief; yet presence of religious belief seems to have an impact on the presence or intensity of certain manifestations of grief. For example, among one bereaved sibling sample, Balk (1991b) found that those who had stronger religious beliefs were more confused shortly after the death than were those nonreligious subjects in the sample who reported higher levels of numbness, depression, and fear. Further, the nonreligious group ultimately reported higher levels of depression 2 to 3 years following the death.

Sense of Maturity and Bereavement

Despite the many challenges faced as a result of the death of a loved one, many adolescents cope successfully with the pain of loss and continue to lead well-adjusted lives. In addition, the grief experience often has positive consequences, including a sense of maturity, a willingness to deal with responsibility at a young age, an appreciation for life, an ability to cope with adversity, an increased sensitivity to others, an increased resilience and sense of optimism, a sense of faith, and a willingness to help others (Davies, 1991; Hogan & DeSantis, 1996b; Walker, 1993). Parkes (1972) stresses that "the experience of grieving can strengthen and bring maturity to those who have previously been protected from misfortune" (p. 5).

> For many, the death . . . can be a catalyst for growth, maturity, and a new sense of self-awareness. Even for adolescents who struggle with the types of feelings and behaviors described here, the opportunity inherent in crisis can give rise to a stronger sense of self and the value of others. (Tyson-Rawson, 1996a, p. 158)

Many regard a heightened sense of maturity as a final outcome from dealing with crisis. However, Hogan, Morse, and Tason (1996) discovered that "personal growth occurred to some degree across all phases of the bereavement process but was most evident as the survivor is emerging from the acute pain of grief" (p. 58).

One study done by Balk (1990) examined the relationship between grief reactions and various facets of personal maturity. Forty-two adolescents participated in the study; they completed a self-image questionnaire and were also interviewed in relation to their perceptions of personal maturity. Forty of the forty-two participants reported that they believed they were more mature now, following the death of a sibling, than they had been prior to the death. Further, 33 of the subjects considered themselves to be much more mature than other adolescents their own age.

Balk (1991a) suggests that one measure of increased maturity following the death of a family member is an increased importance of religion. "The importance of religion in the lives of bereaved adolescents may signify not only a coping response to grief but also a personal development that interacts with mourning" (p. 3). He further suggests that "coping with grief leads some adolescents to a transformed faith consciousness" (Balk, 1996, p. 381).

DEATH OF A PARENT

The discussion of the death of a parent is relatively brief in this chapter, because many relevant concepts were discussed in chapter 5. Aspects tied more specifically to the adolescent's experience are discussed in this chapter.

Often, because of their more mature age, an adolescent may experience strong familial pressures to assume the role of the deceased parent. If such a role is assumed, it is likely to have negative implications for identity development. This circumstance can lead to a premature and perhaps inappropriate definition of one's self. If the adolescent assumes the role of the deceased, he or she is likely to repress the normal striving for individuation and separation from family. The adolescent survivor may feel tremendous internal struggles as family expectations conflict with developmental imperatives.

Tyson-Rawson (1996b) interacted with 20 young women who had experienced the death of their fathers; of these, 14 regarded their relationship with their father as very close. Daughters emphasized various aspects as having been important in the relationship, including that their fathers had shared in various activities (e.g., sports), provided personal support, and/or attempted to be protective of them along various dimensions. The remaining six participants reported feeling ambivalence or little emotional connection in their relationship.

The majority of the subjects in this study (14 out of 20) reported a "continued attachment" to their deceased fathers. This attachment took different forms that were categorized as either a "welcome presence" or an "intrusive presence." Particularly among those who had had a close relationship prior to their father's death, the daughters reported a welcome ongoing presence in their lives, a feeling that their fathers continued to give support or guidance. A group of four women who reported an ongoing attachment, however, described it in more negative terms. Their lingering connection seemed to be an "intrusive presence" in the form of persistent nightmares, intrusive thoughts, or high levels of anxiety or guilt; they had no sense of having resolved their grief. Tyson-Rawson reports that the common link among these women was that each had reported a sense of "unfinished business" with their fathers. Two had had highly conflictual relationships and had minimal interaction with their fathers as a result; the other two had avoided seeing their fathers during the long illnesses leading to death.

None of the participants in this study said that they had totally "gotten over" their fathers' deaths. Instead, they spoke about having resolved the loss in the sense that they had accepted it as an important part of their personal life histories.

Silverman (1987) also studied college women who had experienced the death of a parent earlier. One of the primary findings was that these women felt that they had grown up in an accelerated fashion. This was due to the need to become more independent and take on various parental roles. In an earlier study done by Balk (1983), similar findings were noted following the death of a sibling in that a number of subjects had noted that the death had made them "grow up fast."

DEATH OF A SIBLING

Prior to examining issues related to bereavement caused by death of a brother or sister, it is important to remember the significant role played by siblings in normal adolescent development.

> Adolescence is a particularly vulnerable time to suffer the loss of a sibling. Both siblings and parents contribute to the adolescent's role and identity consolidation. A drastic change in these relationships resulting from the death of a sibling has the potential to interfere with these important developmental processes. (Hogan & Greenfield, 1991, p. 100)

Predeath

Although siblings have unique needs after the death of a brother or sister, they also have special needs throughout the course of the illness. When one child becomes seriously ill, parents have a diminished amount of time to spend with others in the family. Other children—who are healthy—may become hurt, angry, or jealous when parents are unable to give them the same attention they received earlier (Kinrade, 1985). This can result in a secondary loss as described in chapter 4. Many siblings believe their own personal needs are being neglected and are overwhelmed by many well-meaning individuals who tell them to be strong for their parents.

Koch-Hattem (1986) interviewed 33 siblings of children with cancer (the cancer was currently in remission but the children were still receiving chemotherapy). Twenty-seven of the 33 siblings were older than the patient, and six were younger than their sick brother or sister. A significant number of siblings reported feeling bothered, sad, and scared more frequently after the onset of the illness than they had prior to that time. They also said that the patient seemed to be angry at them more often now that they were ill than they had been previously.

The siblings reported that they dealt with their own varied feelings in many different ways. Some vented feelings by becoming angry or crying; some sought comfort from others. A frequent reaction was one of caring; many well siblings focused their attentions on the child who was sick. A few indicated that they wished they could change places with the patient. One child shared, "Why couldn't it be me instead of him? 'Cause he's so little and so young that I probably could take shots better than he could" (p. 114).

Twenty-two of the 33 siblings expressed fears that their siblings would experience a relapse or death. One 11-year-old sibling said of her 3-year-old sister, "I listen to her sleep, and I worry about her. I'm afraid her tumor will come back" (p. 114).

Koch-Hattem (1986) also asked the siblings in her study what would help them through the course of a brother's or sister's illness. Many noted they would like to learn more about the patient's disease and its treatment, suggesting that parents should keep communication lines open with healthy siblings. For example, if parents hear an adolescent get up to go check on his or her sibling, they might take the opportunity to talk to the child about how the whole family worries at times. Children whose parents allow them to share their own needs and fears make better adjustments than those who are not given this same opportunity (Cole, 1986).

In a study done by Evans, Stevens, Cushway, and Houghton (1992), 44% of the well siblings responded that they did not feel they could speak to their parents about the sibling's illness. Seventy-five percent said they would like to know more, including facts about the illness, what will likely happen to the sibling, and how to answer questions from others about the illness.

Parents should reassure healthy siblings that others in the family are not likely to become seriously ill and answer any questions that arise. After a sibling's death, surviving children may once again feel deprived of the parents' attention, as they struggle to do their own grief work. Lack of family support and lack of open communication can have a long-term impact on bereavement outcome (Martinson & Campos, 1991).

Many grief-related responses actually begin to appear even prior to the sibling's death. These include, for some, "depression, anxiety, fear of failure, sleep disturbance, somatic complaints and social and affective changes" (Martinson & Campos, 1991, p. 55). The type of illness itself may have an impact on grief responses; for example, if one sibling is dying of cystic fibrosis, it is certainly possible that another child in the family is also sick or has already died (because this is a hereditary condition). As a result, another sibling might be fearful that he or she too will die of this disease and have concerns over his or her own safety

(Fanos & Nickerson, 1991). Children whose siblings are dying of AIDS face many unique concerns such as secrecy, stigma, shame, potential and actual discrimination, and the possibility that they may lose a parent to the same illness (Fanos & Wiener, 1994).

Home care for the terminally ill child may have multiple benefits for the siblings (Mulhern, Lauer, & Hoffman, 1983). The family has more time to spend together because the parents spend less time away from home visiting the sick child. Children know that everything possible is being done for their ill brother or sister. Furthermore, siblings may derive satisfaction from helping to care for the dying family member. If home care is not possible, healthy siblings can benefit from liberal hospital visitation policies so that they may spend time as desired with the ill child.

Postdeath

Although the primary focus of this chapter is on adolescents, much of the discussion in this particular section also includes a focus on children. Much of the research done with siblings crosses life stage boundaries; further, discussion of developmental change over time is best done by comparison of the two groups.

Fanos and Nickerson (1991) studied long-term outcomes from the death of a sibling many years earlier from a long-term chronic illness (i.e., cystic fibrosis). Each of the surviving siblings was under age 19 at the time of the death. Common responses reported by this group of surviving siblings included both a global sense of guilt as well as survivor guilt, global anxiety, concern over becoming sick one's self, bodily discomfort, a sense of personal vulnerability, fear of intimacy with others, sleeping difficulties, and excessive concern for others' well-being. These researchers make the point that "The nature and the significance of the sibling bond as it changes over the life cycle has begun only recently to be explored by researchers. For many of the adolescent group, siblings were just beginning to work through competitive relationships and form better relationships. When this process was prematurely cut off a perception of the unfairness of life was fueled" (p. 80). One sibling reported:

> We were just getting to the point that we wouldn't fight as much and we were doing more and more together maybe and I was looking forward to being in school with him. I was going to be a freshman and he'd be a senior in high school. And I was really looking forward to that, because then I felt like he and I would have more in common and I was really looking forward to getting close to him . . . and so I think that when he died I felt kind of ripped off. (Fanos & Nickerson, 1991, p. 80)

Research done with siblings who survive the death of a brother or sister indicates that they often display a variety of behavior problems shortly after the death (McCown & Davies, 1995; Birenbaum, Robinson, Phillips, Stewart, & McCown, 1989; Hutton & Bradley, 1994). Using the standardized Child Behavior Checklist, McCown and Pratt (1985) found that children grieving the death of a sibling displayed significantly more behavior problems in comparison to standardized norms. Problem behaviors included hyperactivity, arguing, excessive talking, running away, nightmares, clinging to adults, and withdrawal. Of the three groups studied (ages 4 to 5, 6 to 11, and 12 to 16), the group comprised of 6- to 11-year-olds showed the greatest disturbance. The authors conclude:

> Several explanations are possible. First, the 6- to 11-year-olds fall within the psychosocial stage described by Erikson as Industry versus Inferiority. The loss of a sibling at this phase may lead to a sense of self-vulnerability and inferiority. A second potential explanation for problems may be related to the 6- to 11-year-olds' death conceptualization. It is between the ages 6 and 11 (about age 9 or 10) that the critical conceptualization of death as universal and personal takes place in the child's understanding. School age children 6 to 11 make a transition from preoperational to concrete operational modes of thinking. They find death bewildering and seek a cause and explanation. For the child in this age group who is making the transition to concrete thought, the event and cause of sibling death may evoke confusion. The increased behavior problems may be a reflection of that confusion and concern. (McCown & Pratt, 1985, p. 333)

Aggressive behavior is fairly common among young persons following the death of a sibling. McCown and Davies (1995) stress that although aggression is often linked to an anger response common among bereaved persons, it may be a strategy to obtain increased attention from parents and others in their social environment.

In addition to behavior disturbances, guilt is one of the most frequent reactions among younger children to a brother's or sister's death. It is often related to hostile thoughts common to sibling rivalry and the belief that such thoughts were responsible for the death. Because surviving children often think that they caused the death, children sometimes conclude that they should not derive pleasure from life anymore. Many surviving siblings (either child or adolescent) feel they should have died with, or instead of, the sibling.

Children often increase their burden of guilt by also assuming they have caused other family members' reactions (such as parental withdrawal or another surviving sibling's behavior problems). After working with 58 children, ages 2 to 4, who had experienced the death of a sibling, Cain, Fast, and Erickson (1964) found that the "guilt was variously handled by each child in accord with his unique personality structure, with reactions including depressive withdrawal, accident-prone behavior, punishment-seeking, constant provocative testing . . . and many forms of acting out" (p. 743).

A conspiracy of silence surrounding the death may alter family communication patterns. Krell and Rabkin (1979) describe this changed communication style as a "conspiracy of guilt." The conspiracy of guilt is often present even though neither parent nor sibling could have done anything to prevent the death. For example, a parent may think, "If only I had checked the brakes on Joni's bike, she would have stopped in time" when, in fact, this may not have been the case. Family members can be "haunted" by questions that are never discussed, therefore never effectively resolved.

Guilt feelings must be explored and, if possible, alleviated. This is true whether the child in no way contributed to the death or was, in fact, instrumental in causing it. Unfortunately, in those cases where a sibling did contribute to the death, it is common for the parents inappropriately to reassure the child that he or she did not cause the death (even when the surviving child knows he or she had), label the death an accident, and/or prevent an open discussion with the child. Cain et al. (1964) found that, in such cases, parents engaged in these avoidance activities for the following reasons:

- Parents felt that talking about the incident would only upset the surviving child more.
- Parents were frightened of magnifying their own intense grief.
- Parents were fearful of rage that they had suppressed in order to protect the surviving child.
- Parents wanted to avoid open assessment of blame so that they might not have to succumb to their own self-accusations and resultant feelings of guilt.

It is helpful to engage in open communication so that each family member may deal with any sense of guilt arising from a belief that he or she contributed to the death. Unfortunately, this often does not occur. Rosen (1985) interacted with 159 individuals between the ages of 15 and 74 who had experienced the death of a sibling prior to the age of 20. Sixty-two percent of the sample reported that they had never discussed the deaths of the sibling with another family member. Twelve percent said they occasionally mentioned the deceased sibling, and 26% participated in extended family discussions.

In the long term, each individual who has experienced the death of a sibling comes to a very personal conclusion about the impact of the death on his or her life. Martinson and Campos (1991) describe three different types of legacies resulting from the illness and death of a brother or sister:

- *A positive legacy*—includes pleasure in time spent with the sibling, in sharing the death experience with others, and in recalling memories of the sibling. This type of legacy is shown in one sibling's statement: "I don't think all the attention she received ever deprived me because she gave me the love I needed in return. . . ."
- *A mixed legacy*—includes belief that family did offer emotional support but did not necessarily identify positive outcomes in their lives from their sibling's illness or death. A mixed legacy is reflected in this response: "My folks always were concerned about my grades. They were always so busy with P. that maybe . . . they could have helped a little bit more. It wasn't their fault. It just happened . . . I don't blame them."
- *A negative legacy*—includes expressions of fear of contact with [the dead] sibling, mixed or negative memories about the sibling, difficulty in discussing the death, perceived lack of support from their family. A negative legacy is reflected in one surviving sibling's statement: "I remember feeling

nobody loved me or cared about me. I was really down . . . when she was dead. Now I will have them (my parents) back and be normal." (p. 59)

Significant numbers of children and adolescents grieve as a result of a sibling dying suddenly rather than dying of a life-threatening illness. Issues discussed earlier in chapter 3 are relevant in understanding issues faced by these bereaved siblings (e.g., not having an opportunity to finish business) (Hutton & Bradley, 1994).

Although the last two decades have seen a great increase in knowledge related to the impact of sibling death, many questions remain unanswered and many methodological concerns exist (Craft, 1993). We need, for example, to do more careful study to gain insight about which children and adolescents are at risk for a negative outcome to a sibling's death and which ones will have a resilient outcome. Although we are beginning to understand the many factors influencing outcomes, more research is needed to clarify their impact. Factors include availability of information about sibling's illness, closeness of the sibling relationship itself, changes in parenting styles, availability of support for well siblings, presence of certain problems prior to the sibling's illness or death, circumstances of the death itself, and coping strategies (Birenbaum et al., 1989; Sahler et al., 1994; Schumacher, 1984).

To better understand siblings' grief reactions, more longitudinal studies are needed. Additionally, research designs involving control groups of nonbereaved siblings for comparisons will add much insight to the long-term effects of sibling death. Further, researchers should continue to become less dependent on parents' perceptions of siblings' bereavement outcomes and put more emphasis on direct assessment of the adolescents themselves (Walker, 1993).

DEATH OF A PEER

Until quite recently, there has been almost no research done regarding the death of a friend (Toray & Oltjenbruns, 1996; Oltjenbruns, 1996). This is certainly unfortunate, given the significant number of children and adolescents who have lost peers to death. For example, in one sample of college students, 36% had experienced the death of a friend during high school (Balk, 1997). Others estimate that up to 87% of all adolescents have experienced the death of a peer during adolescence. Regardless of the statistic, each of the individuals who died left many age-mates behind to grieve.

Given the increasing number of young people dying from suicide, homicide, accidents, AIDS, and drug overdoses, we may expect that young persons will experience the death of a peer with increasing frequency. Much more attention has been paid to the family members of those who have died than to the friends of the deceased. Unfortunately, children and adolescent peers have often been disenfranchised and are often the forgotten grievers (Balk, 1991b).

The death of a friend during adolescence "can be especially profound, due to the fragility of the youthful ego and the intense relationships adolescents have

A mural on a neighborhood street pays tribute to the life—and death—of a friend.

with their friends" (McNeil, Silliman, & Swihart, 1991, p. 133). Other factors contribute to the difficulty of coming to terms with a friend's death during this life stage. For one, adolescents' ability to think in the abstract allows them to face their own personal mortality. Death of an age-mate may then confirm this understanding as they realize—on a truly personalized level—that "I too may someday die." Questions such as "Why her?" and "Why not me?" are natural. If the young person feels that the death may have been prevented, as is often the case (or at least the hope) with a violent death, a sense of guilt may be heightened. Due to a sense of personal fable, bereaved adolescents often feel that the world has somehow let them down. Such thoughts often magnify a grief response. Further, the death of a friend results in a variety of losses, for example, companion, confidant, information resource, and helpmate. Just as with other deaths, each loss must be reconciled (Oltjenbruns, 1996). Given the strength of many friendship relationships, it is not surprising to find that there are more similarities than differences in the grief response following the death of a friend compared to grief following the death of a family member (Lurie, 1993).

The emotional intensity of adolescence adds to the feelings of loss after a death. Recognizing the significance and strength of love relationships during youth and providing opportunities for mourning are critical for the successful resolution of grief in these circumstances.

When the peer who died is known by many in the same group, as is the case when a class member dies, grief may be intensified and normal friendship support systems weakened if appropriate intervention strategies are not developed (McNeil et al., 1991). The outcome is often a secondary loss which results in incremental grief, as discussed in chapter 4.

When the significance of a relationship is not acknowledged, grief may become complicated. During adolescence, boyfriend or girlfriend relationships are common; although these relationships may not ultimately be permanent, they often do involve intense feelings of attachment. No matter how strong the bond between the pair, primary bonds are viewed by society as being with the family of origin; and, therefore, the adolescent's grief for a boyfriend or girlfriend may be ignored or misunderstood. This is even more likely in early adolescence, when couple relationships receive less sanction from the larger society. One young adolescent expressed his pain and lack of support following the death of his girl-friend this way:

> Jenny was my girl. She was special and private, and she was mine. When she died, they wouldn't even let me go to the funeral. I loved her and she loved me . . . and them . . . they knew nothing, nothing, about what it was like for us. They were too old to know. They treated me as though she was theirs and as though I didn't care.
>
> Steve, age 16 (Raphael, 1983, p. 139)

THERAPEUTIC INTERVENTIONS

The availability of support is likely to have an impact on the ultimate outcome of a significant loss. Hogan and DeSantis (1994) have identified a number of sources of support that adolescents themselves indicate were helpful. These include engaging in personal activities to reduce stress and a personal belief system; parental support and a willingness to share memories about the deceased; friends' showing unconditional regard; support groups that helped to normalize the grief process. The latter will be discussed in more depth in the section that follows.

Adolescent Peer Support Groups

Bereaved adolescents often feel their age-mates are better able to understand their needs than are many adults (Gray, 1989). Further, obtaining support from their own peers puts adolescents at less risk of becoming dependent on adults as they seek their own independence (Johnson, 1995) and helps them avoid a sense of isolation following a death (Tedeschi, 1996). Just as there are support groups for children, many adolescents also get involved with such groups. Many themes described in chapter 5 as common to children's groups are similar to those of

SURVIVING THE DEATH OF A BEST FRIEND

Chris and Mike had been best friends since high school. Mike fell asleep while driving his car and was killed in the accident.

I have a crazy fear of telephones; this actually makes no sense at all because my mother told me about Mike's death, face-to-face. Still, every time the phone rings, and I am not expecting a call, I fear the worst; it's like waiting for the other shoe to drop.

I wish the message *had* come over the phone; that would have spared my mother the pain of telling her son that his best friend was dead. Mom (at first) had wanted to drive me to work without telling me the news; she wanted to tell me at the end of my shift instead. But, the moment I opened the door, she broke down and told me about the accident.

I remember dropping to my knees; I cried for what seemed like days, but it was only minutes. My mom consoled me; she did not tell me "It'll be all right," or "He's in a better place." Funny, I never told my mother that I smoked, but I guess she knew. After a couple of cigarettes, the real world broke through the mayhem—my boss called to find out where I was.

I felt confused—no—lost. Like something in the world was drastically wrong; the heavens were out of place. Sure, car accidents happen, they can happen to anyone. No one is immortal, or invincible; and not many people can survive a sixty-five-mile-an-hour roll over, but it just didn't seem real.

I spent a week or so comforting Mike's family; we were pretty close; but that is all I did—no real mourning, no reflection, just consoling. Up 'til the funeral, I only

(Continued)

adolescents' groups. Recall, however, that there are developmental differences in coping strategies, certain manifestations of grief, and cognitive understanding of death.

Orr et al. (1984) recommend using closed groups (membership does not change) instead of open groups (new members can be added at any time) for adolescents. It takes time to develop trust and rapport, and the addition of new members alters group dynamics and affects the quality of interaction. In their 18-month experience with a series of open groups for seriously ill, hospitalized adolescents, Blum and Chang (1981) found that group members had a sense of constantly "beginning over again." Based on observations of a 3-month closed group (for adolescents with cancer), it was found that particularly difficult topics and areas of vulnerability were typically not discussed until after the fourth session, when the psychological comfort level within the group itself had increased (Orr et al., 1984).

Adolescents typically do not like to talk openly about their need for information or confusion about certain aspects of death and its aftermath. A helpful strategy, then, is to use a question box so that participants can write a question

(Continued From Previous Page)

cried when my mother told me what had happened and again when I told my older brother—which I can't explain.

After the funeral, I began experiencing the feelings I would have expected. No family or friends were around; I just looked for answers. I cursed everyone—the survivors of the wreck, God, myself. I felt like I had a huge hole in my body and, no matter what I did, I couldn't fill it. I tried—liquor, food, work, writing—nothing helped. I waited for some sort of higher understanding, some sort of answer to make everything OK, but nothing came. I spent weeks trying to logically figure out what had happened. I considered God's role in the matter, whether it was fate or just pure random error. None of it made sense, and still doesn't. But I have gotten myself to a point where understanding isn't as important as dealing with the issue.

Since the accident, I see certain changes. I no longer think in terms of everything working itself out. I've lost the blind innocence I once had. I have also become extremely independent—no longer asking for or accepting help—even when I need it. I go through life with a more day-to-day perspective; I don't plan too far ahead, because who knows what will happen. I am happy, generally, or am I just content? I don't remember how happy I once was—not the way I was before the accident.

For a while after Mike's death, I held the world in contempt; I hated everything and everyone. I suppose that was natural. But now, maybe something positive has come from this tragedy—I really want to help people, and I really want to make a difference in people's lives. I guess in the long run, if that's what I have taken away from this experience, it is better than nothing.

SOURCE: Chris Jacobson. (1997). Unpublished communication.

anonymously, put it in a box, and have the leader explain the answer to the entire group (Fleming & Balmer, 1991). Not only does the individual asking the question get needed information, but others in the group also gain from the feedback.

Participation in rituals often becomes a focus of group activities. For example, adolescents may play their favorite music as a tribute to the one who died or play a song for their peers in order to express their feelings about the loss. These rituals should be personally meaningful to help them "say goodbye" to the deceased friend. Examples of such rituals include friends coming together to sing a song they wrote especially to commemorate their friend, classmates dedicating the yearbook to the one who died or planting a tree in memory of the deceased in the school yard.

Grief and Death Education

Although the topic of death education is discussed here in the context of adolescence, many of these same recommendations are also generally appropriate for younger children. "Death education is that formal instruction which deals with dying, death, loss, grief and their impact on the individual or on humankind" (Stevenson & Stevenson, 1996, p. 237). It may occur in various settings, for example, at home with one's family, in a church setting, or in schools.

Many opportunities to discuss both death and the ensuing grief exist in the normal curriculum or in relation to ongoing life experiences of students within the school setting. For example, discussions of death might occur in the context of a health and wellness course, and discussions of grief and loss may be appropriate in courses such as psychology, family life education, and sociology, among others. To avoid a conspiracy of silence and to model that it is appropriate to discuss these topics, teachers should consider integrating various facets of grief and death education as are appropriate to the class topic.

When a death occurs among members of the student body, teachers and counselors often provide grief-related information in order to normalize the experience and assist adolescents in understanding their personal reactions to the loss. Further, Stevenson (1995) recommends that schools develop protocols to guide their responses for a variety of occurrences, including informing students of a person's death or even dealing with a school community's grief after a large-scale disaster.

As will be discussed in more detail in chapter 9, numerous schools are developing curricular offerings focusing on suicide. These are designed to facilitate various aspects of prevention and postvention (Deaton & Berkan, 1995).

As various types of death education courses are implemented in schools, Stevenson and Stevenson (1996) provide important guidelines related to the planning efforts:

- The process of planning and implementation should be an open one in which input is requested from students, parents, other teachers, and community members.
- Instructors who teach in this area must be well qualified—both academically and emotionally.
- Death education courses should be offered as electives rather than as requirements.

SUMMARY

Adolescents are not strangers to death. Many have faced the death of a close friend or family member; a number must face their own impending deaths. Adolescents are capable of formal operational thinking; this allows much more flexibility in thought as well as attention to abstract ideas than at earlier stages of thinking. As a result, individuals in this stage are able to understand much more fully the concept of death and related spiritual and ethical issues.

A significant number of young people are victims of homicide. As the United States has become an increasingly violent society, we must become attuned to the needs of the increasing numbers of persons who witness violence and may then experience posttraumatic stress and/or traumatic grief reactions.

Adolescents with life-threatening illnesses face the same developmental tasks as healthy adolescents, but they have special needs associated with their particular illnesses. For example, seriously ill adolescents struggle to maintain a positive body image. This task is a particular challenge, given the normal, rather dramatic, physical maturational changes of adolescence. The need for privacy is closely related to these physical changes, as well as adolescents' sense of ego-centrism. In addition, adolescents struggle to resolve the crisis of identity versus role confusion. As a result, adolescents strive to express their individuality, seek independence and control, and develop more mature relationships with parents and peers. Survivors of life-threatening illnesses during adolescence (and the number is growing significantly with the development of more successful treatments for cancer) report both positive and negative outcomes that ultimately need to be integrated into their self-perceptions.

Adolescents may experience the death of many significant individuals—parents, siblings, friends. Although their grief, in many ways, parallels that of other life stages, there are a number of issues related to adolescents that provide special challenges to resolving their grief. These relate to such normal developmental tasks as the struggle for independence, belongingness, and search for identity. Support can be provided to grieving adolescents through a number of different modalities, including peer support groups and death education programs.

Personal Account

Many adolescents encounter death within the context of a school system. The death of a staff member or of a classmate often triggers intense emotions. This personal account illustrates that adults within the school often share the adolescents' grief, and as a result, predetermined protocols are of great assistance when administrators are faced with this crisis. Such a protocol can help define strategies for providing support to those who are affected by the loss.

When Death Strikes a School
Anonymous

Case One

Thomas Thatcher was the popular principal of a small-town elementary school. He knew every child's name and all the children smiled when they saw him coming.

SOURCE: F. Selder, M. Kachoyeanos, M. J. Baisch, & M. Gissler (Eds.). (1997). *Enduring grief: True stories of personal loss.* Philadelphia: The Charles Press.

His school was like a family. One night after evening prayers with his wife he said that he did not feel well, clutched his chest and fell dead from a massive heart attack. The next day a school full of children had to be told what had happened to a man they all loved.

The next day the schoolchildren were brought together in the auditorium and told what had happened. They sat in small groups with their teachers and shared their emotions. Together they decided that they wanted to do something so that everyone would know what Principal Thatcher had meant to them. With board approval, the school was renamed Thomas Thatcher Memorial School and bears that name today. In regular classes during the next month, the themes of loss and grief were dealt with by discussing current events and children's literature. Names and addresses of local support groups were made available to families and staff, but these appear not to have been utilized. The students in this school displayed no unusual behavior problems as a result of the principal's death.

Contrast this scenario with another school in a nearby district whose officials refused to name an athletic field after an athletic director who was retiring. Even though this man had not died, like the principal at the other school, his departure was a form of loss to the students. This man had guided a generation of students. The officials justified their refusal by saying, "If we start doing this, we may end up making a habit of honoring everyone who has been a part of this district."

Staff members, students and alumni expressed anger at the board's decision and asked what was wrong with showing teachers and students that might indeed make a difference. There was an increase in fighting and vandalism and a lot of absenteeism in the two-month period following the board's decision.

Case Two

Sally was a highly motivated student about to begin her senior year at a local parochial high school. She was described as a bright young woman, a devoted daughter and a good student. Although she did not have many friends at school, she did have a few friends at home. She felt pressure to succeed in high school and was anxious about the approaching year of college applications. During the summer vacation following her junior year, she killed herself by taking an overdose of drugs.

Sally's principal, who held an advanced degree in psychology, ordered the teachers in Sally's school *not* to discuss her death with their students. A school funeral mass, standard procedure for most parochial schools when a student dies, was not said. By foregoing the mass and requesting that teachers keep quiet, the principal desired to avoid the possibility of copy-cat suicides. She also wanted to avoid the "scandal" of suicide. However, every student in the school knew what had happened. Faced with silence by their teachers, they could only conclude one of two things: that their teachers knew how to answer their questions and help them deal with their feelings, but chose not to, or their teachers were helpless to do anything for them and so they dared not try. The first reaction produced anger on the part of many students and the second fostered feelings of helplessness. The students were left to deal with these feelings on their own.

Almost one year later, a staff development day was devoted to teacher concerns. It was not announced in advance that these meetings would have any connection with suicide, but that was their subject. There was a lecture and discussion, after which most teachers remained silent. But after the conference several teachers contacted the lecturer to discuss their concerns about how Sally's death had been dealt with. Because the school had offered nothing and probably even made matters worse by being silent, many teachers and students had attended community support groups for help. They stated that they no longer saw the school as a place where they might receive support in dealing with personal problems. Students at this school were unable to explain their loss of interest in classes or their falling grades. Students did not speak in school about the mounting anxiety they felt as senior year approached and they feared that they might crumble under the pressures they felt had killed Sally.

Case Three

Mr. Joseph, a school principal, had a problem dealing with the topic of death. At the time, two of his former students were hospitalized with life-threatening illnesses. Because both of these students admired him, he asked other faculty members to tell them that he would come to visit them. Though he established several specific times when he said he would go the hospital, he never went and never called. He simply could not deal with the situation. Then one of the students died. Though Mr. Joseph might have been expected to help the school mourn its loss, he informed faculty members that no teacher could be given "official" time to attend the funeral. He said that allowing them the time would be a bad precedent, and because the student had graduated two years earlier and was no longer officially enrolled in the school, it didn't make sense.

Students and teachers had difficulty accepting this position and expressed anger, resentment and confusion. Vandalism (which had been decreasing over the previous year) increased and communication between Mr. Joseph and his staff members suffered. Some teachers reported that they were unable to speak with him. Mr. Joseph offered support to staff members who sought to establish a suicide prevention program in the school (there is often a higher risk of student suicide after the death of a classmate), but did not become personally involved. One year later he sought a position in a different school system.

Mr. Joseph coped with situations he found troubling through denial. He was unwilling to seek counseling, stating that he did not have a problem that needed to be resolved. In his new position he has continued to use denial as his chief means of coping with death-related events. His successor at his former school supported the suicide prevention program that had started during Mr. Joseph's administrative tenure and he expressed a willingness to discuss issues of loss and grief with staff members and students. He also helped staff members initiate peer support groups and took an active role in training student counselors.

He worked with one teacher to develop, implement and publish a protocol for schools to assist students in dealing with a loss.

Use of a Protocol for Schools

It was raining hard when Jim and his friend left the movie theater. Jim's mother was waiting for the boys in her car across the street. Before they crossed the street, Jim looked both ways but did not see the oncoming car. His friend called to him to stop, but it was too late. The car struck and killed him. Jim's mother ran to him and within minutes the town's paramedics arrived. But there was nothing that could be done. Jim's mother, seeing that her son was beyond help, walked over to the teenage driver who had been behind the wheel of the car that had hit her son. She put her arm around the shaking youth and told him that there was nothing he could have done and that it was not his fault.

Later, at the funeral home, a number of parents who decided not to attend, dropped their children off, then returned to pick them up an hour later. Many of these children were facing their first encounter with death and Jim's mother was the only adult who was present to attend to their needs. Although the parents of Jim's friends were expecting their children to go on "as usual," sudden loss is not overcome so easily in children. Successful grief resolution does not happen without some intervention.

A number of resources and programs were available at Jim's school to help students deal with their grief and loss following his death. Along with the boy who had been with Jim when he died, the principal of the middle school visited each classroom on the Monday after the accident to tell the students in person what had happened. He also asked Jim's friend to talk to each class. The principal told the students that it was normal and understandable to be sad about Jim's death, but added that Jim would not want them to stay sad, but to go on with their lives.

The parents' organization had a book passed to each class. Each student was encouraged to write something about Jim, or to put a message in the book for Jim's parents or older sister who was a student in the same school system. One boy wrote that he and Jim had been trading baseball cards and attached the card that he knew Jim needed to complete his set. Others wrote poems or told of times they had shared with Jim. The school board allowed this project, although one board member did say this seemed "very morbid" and that he saw no reason to have the students "dwell" on what had happened.

An outside consultant was brought in to speak to parents of the students at an evening assembly and to address any problems they might have encountered with the responses of their children to Jim's death. During a camping trip that had been planned previously, students were reminded that they could continue to think about Jim if they wished, and that there were people who would be glad to listen to them if they wanted to talk about Jim or about any other issues that Jim's death might have brought up for them. Lists of support groups were supplied to all interested parents and several families attended group sessions or sought individual counseling.

A faculty development conference dealing with student grief reactions in the classroom was planned for late winter for administrators and staff members of all of the schools in the system. The Stevenson-Powers protocol for dealing with a student death was distributed to staff members, and methods of implementing it were discussed. Resource lists of audiovisual materials on the subject were also made available to classroom teachers.

Two weeks after the faculty conference, two more students from the same school system died in unrelated events on the same day. One freshman student died of leukemia (which had been diagnosed only two weeks earlier) and a second student, a high school senior, was killed in a skiing accident. The protocol that had been distributed to staff members was implemented and the school, rather than canceling classes, mobilized staff members to act as a support system for students. The students assumed an active role in planning a memorial service at the high school and the contact people who had already been introduced to the community were again made available to students, families and staff members.

QUESTIONS AND ACTIVITIES

1. Reread Case One in your personal account. Role-play (with a couple of other students) the board meeting discussions that you feel may have taken place prior to the two very different decisions made in regard to naming the athletic fields after beloved administrators. Discuss what might have been a win-win outcome for the second scenario where a board had originally decided "If we start doing this, we may end up making a habit of honoring everyone who has been part of this district." How could such a win-win outcome be facilitated so that the board, the students, alumni, etc. might feel comfortable that a good decision had been made?

2. Given a situation similar to the one described in Case Two in your personal account, discuss how administrators, teachers, and students could be given the support they need (over an extended period of time) to deal with a suicide of someone in their school community. Who should design and then implement appropriate support strategies?

3. Recall our earlier discussion (in chapter 3) of such topics as denial and the conspiracy of silence. How do these concepts relate to Case Three in the personal account for this chapter? What price is often paid when someone engages in these avoidance mechanisms? What hypotheses would you have as to why Mr. Joseph could not get involved with students and teachers in circumstances directly related to death and grief? How could you give Mr. Joseph support so that he would feel more comfortable giving a different type of leadership in this regard?

4. You are the principal of a high school. In that role, you feel it is important to define a protocol for dealing with a death in the school system, prior to its

actually occurring. Briefly outline steps that you would take to communicate about the death with students, teachers, and parents. Who should take responsibility for the communication? What are basic components of that communication effort? What guidelines would you have about who could attend the funeral or memorial service? What long-term grief support activities would you arrange for students? Explain why you think these would be helpful.

5. If you can, access the Internet and "surf" for a resource that you feel would be helpful to an adolescent's family after his/her death. What if he/she had died in an auto accident? Died of cancer? Been murdered? Died of AIDS? Committed suicide?

6. Fleming and Adolph (1986) presented five core issues tied to the thinking, feeling, and behaving of bereaved adolescents: predictability of events, self-image, sense of belonging, fairness/justice, and mastery/control. How are adolescents' attempts to deal with these core issues made more difficult by the experience of bereavement? Based on your understanding of these five core issues, what are the implications for planning intervention strategies for bereaved adolescents?

GLOSSARY

Adolescent egocentrism: preoccupation of adolescents with their own thought processes and their thoughts of themselves.

Alopecia: hair loss (e.g., from chemotherapy).

Formal operational stage: refers to Piaget's fourth stage of cognitive development, beginning in adolescence and continuing through adulthood.

Identity: positive resolution of Erikson's psychosocial crisis associated with adolescence; it implies self-definition and commitment to a role.

Imaginary audience: belief held by adolescents that they are continually under observation by others.

Moral reasoning: process of judging behavior and thinking about moral dilemmas.

Personal fable: feeling, common among adolescents, that one is immune to the bad things that happen to others.

Remission: disease-free state.

Role confusion (Identity diffusion): negative outcome of Erikson's adolescent crisis; individuals having this outcome are unsure of who they are and where they are going.

RESOURCES

Candlelighters Childhood Cancer Foundation
7910 Woodmont Avenue
Suite 460
Bethesda, MD 20814
1-800-366-2223 or (301) 657-8401

National Organization for Victim Assistance
1757 Park Road, NW
Washington, DC 20010
(202) 232-6682

Parents of Murdered Children
National Office
100 East Eighth Street #B-41
Cincinnati, OH 45202
(513) 721-5683

SUGGESTED READINGS

Adams, D. W., & Deveau, E. J. (Eds.). (1995). *Beyond the innocence of childhood (Volume 2): Helping children and adolescents cope with life-threatening illness and dying.* Amityville, NY: Baywood Publishing.

This edited volume consists of 17 chapters that address many different strategies for helping children and adolescents who are dying. Issues such as pain, influences of hospital settings, influence of spirituality, and use of various therapeutic modalities are addressed.

Balk, D. E. (1995). *Adolescent development: Early through late adolescence.* Pacific Grove, CA: Brooks/Cole.

An understanding of the complexity of adolescent bereavement and issues facing the dying adolescent depend on insight of this life stage. The author provides a clear developmental understanding of such topics as cognitive changes and intellectual development, search for identity, and the importance of peers.

Corr, C. A., & Balk, D. E. (Eds.). (1996). *Handbook of adolescent death and bereavement.* New York: Springer.

This collection of articles examines a broad array of issues related to death, dying, and grief during the adolescent years. Topics covered include adolescents' understanding of death; grief following the death of a parent, sibling, or friend; guidelines for providing intervention for dying and grieving adolescents; and issues related to suicide and homicide.

REFERENCES

Adams, D. W., & Deveau, E. J. (1987). When a brother or sister is dying of cancer: The vulnerability of the adolescent sibling. *Death Studies, 11*(4), 279–295.

Ansbacher, H. L., & Ansbacher, R. R. (Eds.). (1956). *The individual psychology of Alfred Adler: A systematic presentation in selections from his writings.* New York: Basic Books.

Armsworth, M., & Holaday, M. (1993). The effects of psychological trauma on children and adolescents. *Journal of Counseling and Development, 72,* 49–56.

Aubrey, R. R. (1977). Adolescents and death. In E. R. Prichard, J. Collard, B. A. Drevitt, A. H. Kutscher, I. Seeland, & N. Lefkowitz (Eds.), *Social work with the dying patient and family* (pp. 131–145). New York: Columbia University Press.

Balk, D. E. (1997). Death, bereavement, and college students: A descriptive analysis. *Mortality, 2,* 207–220.

Balk, D. E. (1983). Adolescents' grief reactions and self-concept perceptions following sibling death: A case study of 33 teenagers. *Journal of Youth and Adolescence, 12,* 137–161.

Balk, D. E. (1990). The self concepts of bereaved adolescents: Sibling death and its aftermath. *Journal of Adolescent Research, 5*(1), 112–132.

Balk, D. E. (1991a). Death and adolescent bereavement. *Journal of Adolescent Research, 6*(1), 7–27.

Balk, D. E. (1991b). Sibling death, adolescent bereavement, and religion. *Death Studies, 15,* 1–20.

Balk, D. E. (1995). *Adolescent development: Early through late adolescence.* New York: Brooks/Cole.

Balk, D. E. (1996). Models for understanding adolescent coping with bereavement. *Death Studies, 20,* 367–387.

Balk, D. E., & Corr, C. A. (1996). Adolescents, developmental tasks, and encounters with death and bereavement. In C. A. Corr & D. E. Balk (Eds.), *Handbook of adolescent death and bereavement* (pp. 3–24). New York: Springer.

Balk, D. E., & Hogan, N. (1995). Religion, spirituality, and bereaved adolescents. In D. W. Adams and E. J. Deveau (Eds.), *Beyond the innocence of childhood: Helping children and adolescents cope with death and bereavement* (pp. 61–88). Amityville, NY: Baywood Publishing.

Barrett, R. K. (1996). Adolescents, homicidal violence, and death. In C. A. Corr & D. E. Balk (Eds.), *Handbook of adolescent death and bereavement* (pp. 42–64). New York: Springer.

Berman, S. J. (1980, September). *Adolescents coping with cancer: The issue of control.* Paper presented at the Annual Meeting of the American Psychological Association, Montreal, Canada.

Berndt, T. J. (1996). Transitions in friendship and friends' influence. In J. A. Graber, J. Brooks-Gunn, & A. C. Petersen (Eds.), *Transitions through adolescence: Interpersonal domains and context* (pp. 57–84). Mahwah, NJ: Lawrence Erlbaum Associates.

Birenbaum, L. K., Robinson, M. A., Phillips, D. S., Stewart, B. J., and McCown, D. E. (1989). The response of children to the dying and death of a sibling. *Omega, 20*(3), 213–228.

Bleyer, W. A. (1990). The impact of childhood cancer on the United States and the world. *Cancer Journal for Clinicians, 40*(6), 355–367.

Blum, R. W., & Chang, P. (1981). A group for adolescents facing chronic and terminal illness. *Journal of Current Adolescent Medicine, 3,* 712.

Blumberg, B. D., Lewis, M. J., & Susman, E. J. (1984). Adolescence: A time of transition. In M. G. Eisenberg, L. C. Sutkin, & M. A. Jansen (Eds.), *Chronic illness and disability through the life span: Effects on self and family* (pp. 133–149). New York: Springer.

Bowler, S., Sheon, A. R., D'Angelo, L. J., & Vermund, S. H. (1993). HIV and AIDS among adolescents in the United States: Increasing risk in the 1990's. *Journal of Adolescence, 15,* 345–371.

Cain, A., Fast, I., & Erickson, M. (1964). Children's disturbed reactions to the death of a sibling. *American Journal of Orthopsychiatry, 34,* 741–745.

Carr-Gregg, M. (1989). CanTeen: The New Zealand teenage cancer patients society—new direction in psychosocial oncology? *New Zealand Medical Journal, 102,* 163–165.

Cole, E. (1986). Anticipatory grief of parents and siblings of children with chronic terminal illness. *Advances in Thanatology, 5*(4), 23–36.

Cook, A. S., & Oltjenbruns, K. A. (1982). A cognitive developmental approach to death education for adolescents. *Family Perspective, 16,* 9–14.

Craft, M. J. (1993). Siblings of hospitalized children: Assessment and intervention. *Journal of Pediatric Nursing, 8*(5), 289–297.

Davies, B. (1991). Long-term outcomes of adolescent sibling bereavement. *Journal of Adolescent Research, 6*(1), 83–96.

Deaton, R. L., & Berkan, W. A. (1995). *Planning and managing death issues in the schools: A handbook.* Westport, CT: Greenwood Press.

Derdiarian, A. (1987). Information needs of recently diagnosed cancer patients. A theoretical framework. *Cancer Nursing, 10,* 107–115.

DiClemente, R. J. (1992). Epidemiology of AIDS, HIV seroprevalence and HIV incidence among adolescents. *Journal of School Health, 62,* 325–330.

DiClemente, R. J., Stewart, K. E., Johnson, M. O., & Pack, R. P. (1996). Adolescence and AIDS: Epidemiology, prevention, and psychological responses. In C. A. Corr & D. E. Balk (Eds.), *Handbook of adolescent death and bereavement* (pp. 85–106). New York: Springer.

Dunsmore, J., & Quine, S. (1995). Information, support, and decision-making needs and preferences of adolescents with cancer: Implications for health professionals. *Journal of Psychosocial Oncology, 13*(4), 39–56.

Elkind, D. (1967). Egocentrism in adolescence. *Child Development, 38,* 1025–1034.

Elkind, D. (1970). *Children and adolescents: Interpretive essays of Jean Piaget.* New York: Oxford University Press.

Erikson, E. H. (1959). Identity and the life cycle. *Psychological Issues, 1,* 50–100.

Eth, S., & Pynoos, R. (Eds.). (1985). *Post-traumatic stress disorder in children.* Washington, DC: American Psychiatric Press.

Evans, C., Stevens, M., Cushway, D., & Houghton, J. (1992). *Child Care, Health, and Development, 18*(4), 229–244.

Fanos, J. H., & Nickerson, B. G. (1991). Long-term effects of sibling death during adolescence. *Journal of Adolescent Research, 6*(1), 70–82.

Fanos, J. H., & Wiener, L. (1994). Tomorrow's survivors: Siblings of human immunodeficiency virus-infected children. *Journal of Developmental and Behavioral Pediatrics, 15*(3), S43–S48.

Farrell, F. A. (1981). *Interviews with five sets of parents of adolescents with cancer.* Unpublished manuscript, University of Arizona, Tucson, AZ.

Fleming, S., & Adolph, R. (1986). Helping bereaved adolescents: Needs and responses. In C. Corr & J. McNeil (Eds.), *Adolescence and death* (pp. 97–118). New York: Springer.

Fleming, S., & Balmer, L. (1991). Group intervention with bereaved children. In D. Papadatou & C. Papadatos (Eds.), *Children and death* (pp. 105–124). New York: Hemisphere.

Fleming, S., & Balmer, L. (1996). Bereavement in adolescence. In C. Corr & D. Balk (Eds.), *Handbook of adolescent death and bereavement* (pp. 139–154). New York: Springer.

Fritz, G., & Williams, J. (1988). Issues of adolescent development for survivors of childhood cancer. *Journal of the American Academy of Child and Adolescent Psychiatry, 27,* 712–715.

Gray, R. E. (1989). Adolescents' perceptions of social support after the death of a parent. *Journal of Psychosocial Oncology, 7,* 127–144.

Hodges, M. H., Graham-Pole, J., & Fong, M. L. (1984). Attitudes, knowledge, and behaviors of school peers of adolescent cancer patients. *Journal of Psychosocial Oncology, 2*(2), 37–45.

Hogan, N., & Balk, D. (1990). Adolescents' reactions to sibling death: Perceptions of mothers, fathers, and teenagers. *Nursing Research, 39*(2), 103–106.

Hogan, N., & DeSantis, L. (1994). Things that help and hinder adolescent sibling bereavement. *Western Journal of Nursing Research, 16*(2), 132–153.

Hogan, N., & DeSantis, L. (1996a). *Adolescent sibling bereavement: Toward a new theory.* In C. Corr & D. Balk (Eds.), *Handbook of adolescent death and bereavement* (pp. 173–195). New York: Springer.

Hogan, N., & DeSantis, L. (1996b). Basic constructs of a theory of adolescent sibling bereavement. In D. Klass, P. Silverman, & S. Nickman (Eds.), *Continuing bonds* (pp. 235–254). Washington, DC: Taylor and Francis.

Hogan, N., & Greenfield, D. (1991). Adolescent symptomatology in a large community sample. *Journal of Adolescent Research, 6*(1), 97–112.

Hogan, N., Morse, J., & Tason, M. (1996). Toward an experiential theory of bereavement. *Omega, 33*(1), 43–65.

Holmbeck, G. N. (1996). A model of family relational transformations during the transition to adolescence: Parent-adolescent conflict and adaptation. In J. A. Graber, J. Brooks-Gunn, & A. C. Petersen (Eds.), *Transitions through adolescence: Interpersonal domains and context* (pp. 167–200). Mahwah, NJ: Lawrence Erlbaum Associates.

Hutton, C. J., & Bradley, B. S. (1994). Effects of sudden infant death on bereaved siblings: A comparative study. *Journal of Child Psychology and Psychiatry, 35*(4), 723–732.

Johnson, C. (1995). Adolescent grief support groups. In D. W. Adams & E. J. Deveau (Eds.), *Beyond the innocence of childhood: Helping children and adolescents cope with death and bereavement* (pp. 229–240). Amityville, NY: Baywood Publishing.

Kellerman, J., Zeltzer, L., Ellenberg, L., Dash, J., & Rigler, D. (1980). Psychological effects of illness in adolescence. I. Anxiety, self-esteem, and perception of control. *Journal of Pediatrics, 97*(1), 126–131.

Kinrade, L. C. (1985). Preventive group intervention with siblings of oncology patients. *Children's Health Care, 14*(2), 110–113.

Kochanek, K. D., & Hudson, B. L. (1994). Advance report of final mortality statistics, 1992. *Monthly Vital Statistics Report, 43*(6), (suppl.).

Koch-Hattem, A. (1986). Siblings' experience with pediatric cancer: Interviews with children. *Health and Social Work, 11*(2), 107–117.

Krell, R., & Rabkin, L. (1979). The effects of death on the surviving child. A family perspective. *Family Process, 18,* 471–477.

Lurie, C. (1993). *The death of friends vs. family members in late adolescence: The role of perceived social support and self-worth.* Unpublished master's thesis, Colorado State University, Fort Collins, CO.

Manaster, G. J. (1977). *Adolescent development and the life tasks.* Boston: Allyn & Bacon.

Martinson, I. M., & Campos, R. (1991). Adolescent bereavement: Long-term responses to a sibling's death from cancer. *Journal of Adolescent Research, 6*(1), 54–69.

Martinson, I. M., Davies, E. B., & McClowry, S. G. (1987). The long-term effects of sibling death on self-concept. *Journal of Pediatric Nursing, 2,* 227–235.

McCown, D., & Davies, B. (1995). Patterns of grief in young children following the death of a sibling. *Death Studies, 19*(1), 41-53.

McCown, D., & Pratt, D. (1985). Impact of sibling death on children's behavior. *Death Studies, 9,* 323-335.

McNeil, J. N., Silliman, B., & Swihart, J. J. (1991). Helping adolescents cope with the death of a peer. *Journal of Adolescent Research, 6*(1), 132-145.

Meshot, C., & Leitner, L. (1993). Adolescent mourning and parental death. *Omega, 26*(4), 287-299.

Miller, M. A. (1996). Re-grief as narrative: The impact of parental death on child and adolescent development. In D. W. Adams & E. J. Deveau (Eds.), *Beyond the innocence of childhood: Helping children and adolescents cope with death and bereavement* (pp. 99-113). Amityville, NY: Baywood Publishing.

Millstein, S. G. (1990). Risk factors for AIDS among adolescents. In W. Gardner, S. G. Millstein, & B. L. Wilcox (Eds.), *Adolescents in the AIDS epidemic* (pp. 3-15). San Francisco: Jossey-Bass.

Mitchell, J. R. (1980). Male adolescents' concern about a physical examination conducted by a female. *Nursing Research, 29,* 165-169.

Mulhern, R. K., Lauer, M. E., & Hoffman, R. G. (1983). Death of a child at home or in the hospital: Subsequent psychological adjustment of the family. *Pediatrics, 71,* 743-747.

Nader, K. O. (1996). Children's exposure to traumatic experiences. In C. Corr & D. Corr (Eds.), *Handbook of childhood death and bereavement* (pp. 201-220). New York: Springer.

Nannis, E. D., Susman, E. J., Strope, B. E., Woodruff, P. J., Hersh, S. P., Levine, A. S., & Pizzo, P. A. (1982). Correlates of control in pediatric cancer patients and their families. *Journal of Pediatric Psychology, 7*(1), 75-84.

Noppe, L. D., & Noppe, I. C. (1996). Ambiguity in adolescent understanding of death. In C. A. Corr & D. E. Balk (Eds.), *Handbook of adolescent death and bereavement* (pp. 25-41). New York: Springer.

Office of Cancer Communications, National Cancer Institute. (1980). Pretest report: Statements on issues of concern to adolescents with cancer. Unpublished report.

Oltjenbruns, K. A. (1996). Death of a friend during adolescence: Issues and impacts. In C. Corr & D. Balk (Eds.), *Handbook of adolescent death and bereavement* (pp. 196-215). New York: Springer.

Orr, D. P., Hoffmans, M. A., & Bennetts, G. (1984). Adolescents with cancer report their psychological needs. *Journal of Psychosocial Oncology, 2*(2), 47-59.

Parkes, C. M. (1972). *Bereavement: Studies of grief in adult life.* New York: International Universities Press.

Pettle-Michael, S. A., & Lansdown, R. G. (1986). Adjustment to the death of a sibling. *Archives of Disease in Childhood, 61,* 278-283.

Piaget, J. (1932). *The moral judgment of the child.* New York: Free Press.

Piaget, J. (1972). Intellectual evolution from adolescence to adulthood. *Human Development, 15,* 1-12.

Pynoos, R., Frederick, C., Nader, K., Arroyo, W., Steinberg, A., Eth, S., Nunez, F., & Fairbanks, L. (1987). Life threat and posttraumatic stress in school-age children. *Archives of General Psychiatry, 44,* 1057-1063.

Rando, T. A. (1984). *Grief, dying, and death: Clinical interventions for caregivers.* Champaign, IL: Research Press.

Raphael, B. (1983). *The anatomy of bereavement.* New York: Basic Books.

Rosen, H. (1985). Prohibition against mourning in childhood sibling loss. *Omega, 15*(4), 307–316.

Rosenblatt, P. C., Jackson, D. A., & Walsh, R. P. (1972). Coping with anger and aggression in mourning. *Omega, 3*(4), 271–284.

Sahler, O. J., Roghmann, K. J., Carpenter, P. J., Mulhern, R. K., Dolgin, M. J., Sargent, J. R., Barbarin, O. A., Copeland, D. R., & Zeltzer, L. K. (1994). Sibling adaptation to childhood cancer collaborative study: Prevalence of sibling distress and definition of adaptation levels. *Journal of Developmental and Behavioral Pediatrics, 15*(5), 353–366.

Schumacher, J. D. (1984). Helping children cope with a sibling's death. In J. C. Hansen & T. T. Frantz (Eds.), *Death and grief in the family* (pp. 83–94). Rockville, MD: Aspen Systems Corporation.

Seligman, M. E. (1975). *Helplessness: On depression, development and death.* San Francisco: W. H. Freeman.

Shaffer, D. R. (1985). *Developmental psychology: Theory, research, and applications.* Monterey, CA: Brooks/Cole.

Shoor, M., & Speed, M. H. (1976). Death, delinquency, and the mourning process. In R. Fulton (Ed.), *Death and identity.* Bowie, MD: Charles Press.

Silverman, P. R. (1987). The impact of prenatal death on college-aged women. *Psychiatric Clinics of North America, 10*(3), 387–404.

Smith, K., Ostroff, J., Tan, C., & Lesko, L. (1991). Alterations in self-perceptions among adolescent cancer survivors. *Cancer Investigation, 9*(5), 581–588.

Sofka, C. (1997). Social support "Internetworks," caskets for sale, and much, much more: Thanatology and the information superhighway. *Death Studies, 21*(6), 553–574.

Sprang, G., & McNeil, J. (1995). *The many faces of bereavement: The nature and treatment of natural, traumatic, and stigmatized grief.* New York: Brunner/Mazel.

Stanton, B., Kim, N., Galbraith, S., & Parrott, M. (1996). Design issues addressed in published evaluations of adolescent HIV-risk reduction interventions: A review. *Journal of Adolescent Health, 18,* 387–396.

Sterken, D. J. (1995). HIV/AIDS in the classroom: Ethical and legal issues surrounding the public education of the HIV-infected child. *Journal of Pediatric Health Care, 9,* 205–210.

Stevens, M. M., & Dunsmore, J. C. (1996a). Adolescents who are living with a life-threatening illness. In C. A. Corr & D. E. Balk (Eds.), *Handbook of adolescent death and bereavement* (pp. 107–135). New York: Springer.

Stevens, M. M., & Dunsmore, J. C. (1996b). Helping adolescents who are coping with a life-threatening illness, along with their siblings, parents, and peers. In C. A. Corr & D. E. Balk (Eds.), *Handbook of adolescent death and bereavement* (pp. 329–353). New York: Springer.

Stevenson, R. G. (1995). The role of the school: Bereaved students and students facing life-threatening illness. In K. Doka (Ed.), *Children mourning and mourning children* (pp. 97–111). Washington, DC: Taylor and Francis.

Stevenson, R. G., & Stevenson, E. P. (1996). Adolescents and education about death, dying, and bereavement. In C. Corr and D. Balk (Eds.), *Handbook of adolescent death and bereavement* (pp. 235–249). New York: Springer.

Susman, E. J., Pizzo, P. A., & Poplack, D. G. (1981). Adolescent cancer: Getting through the aftermath. In P. Ahmed (Ed.), *Living and dying with childhood cancer* (pp. 99–117). New York: Elsevier.

Tedeschi, R. G. (1996). Support groups for adolescents. In C. Corr & D. Balk (Eds.), *Handbook of adolescent death and bereavement* (pp. 293–311). New York: Springer.

Teta, M. J., DelPo, M. C., Kasl, S. V., Meigs, J. W., Myers, M. H., & Mulvhill, B. (1986). Psychosocial consequences of childhood and adolescent cancer survival. *Journal of Chronic Diseases, 39*(9), 751–759.

Toray, T., & Oltjenbruns, K. A. (1996). Building friendships during childhood: Significance of the death of a peer. In C. Corr & D. Corr (Eds.), *Handbook of childhood death and bereavement* (pp. 165–178). New York: Springer.

Tyson-Rawson, K. (1996a). Adolescent responses to the death of a parent. In C. Corr & D. Balk (Eds.), *Handbook of adolescent death and bereavement* (pp. 155–172). New York: Springer.

Tyson-Rawson, K. (1996b). Relationship and heritage: Manifestations of ongoing attachment following father death. In D. Klass, P. Silverman, & S. Nickman (Eds.), *Continuing bonds: New understandings of grief* (pp. 125–145). Washington, DC: Taylor and Francis.

Valentine, L. (1996). Professional interventions to assist adolescents who are coping with death and bereavement. In C. Corr & D. Balk (Eds.), *Handbook of adolescent death and bereavement* (pp. 312–328). New York: Springer.

Walker, C. L. (1993). Sibling bereavement and grief responses. *Journal of Pediatric Nursing, 8*(5), 325–334.

Wasserman, A. L., Thompson, E. I., Wilimas, J. A., & Fairclough, D. L. (1987). The psychological status of survivors of childhood/adolescent Hodgkin's disease. *American Journal of Diseases of Children, 141*(6), 626–631.

Zeltzer, L. K. (1980). The adolescent with cancer. In J. Kellerman (Ed.), *Psychological aspects of childhood cancer.* Springfield, IL: Charles C. Thomas.

Zeltzer, L. K., LeBaron, S., & Zeltzer, P. (1984). The adolescent with cancer. In R. W. Blum (Ed.), *Chronic illness and disabilities in childhood and adolescence* (pp. 375–395). Orlando, FL: Grune & Stratton.

7

Facing Death as an Adult

In this chapter, issues confronting dying adults will be addressed as they relate to developmental concerns. Developmental stages of adulthood are generally divided into three periods: young adulthood, middle age, and late adulthood. Each of these stages involve several developmental themes; each will be discussed and applied to needs of the terminally-ill adult.

YOUNG ADULTHOOD AS A LIFE STAGE

Young adulthood extends throughout one's twenties and thirties. Whereas adolescence involves the crystallization of identity, early adulthood involves the exploration of "still-uncharted depths of that identity" (Schiamberg, 1985). The maximum unfolding of capabilities and opportunities occurs during the early years of adulthood. It is the first time in their lives that individuals can be truly autonomous, making their own decisions and living with the consequences. This developmental stage is one of decision making. Choices about relationships, work, and life-style made at this time help shape and define the remainder of adult life.

For the majority of individuals, young adulthood marks the beginning of many life events and roles—the commitment to a career, the beginning of a marriage, and the initiation into parenthood. Hopes, aspirations, and goals are now beginning to be translated into experience. The high energy level of young adults allows them to live their lives to the fullest. Peak physical strength is achieved in the twenties (Stevens-Long & Commons, 1992), and young adults use their physical strength and stamina as they pursue vigorous, active life-styles. The physical zest of this stage is the antithesis of illness and death.

When a terminal illness does occur, young adults react to the knowledge of their impending death with frustration and disappointment. They feel angry and cheated. They are on the threshold of fulfilling their dreams and aspirations, only to have their lives cruelly interrupted. As compared to any other time in adulthood, the young adult has both more to lose and less to reflect back on. The losses are even more acute because the person will not live to see the promise of relationships fulfilled or experience the future of significant others (such as children). Pattison (1977) has remarked on the tenacity with which young adults hold onto life. They are actively pursuing their goals, and their intensity for life makes them impatient with illness and angry at the threat of death. He further explained that death during young adulthood is "dying with the harness on" (p. 25).

PRIMARY CAUSES OF DEATH DURING YOUNG ADULTHOOD

Because death rates for young adults are generally low, death during this period is often unexpected. Table 7.1 shows the major causes of death for males and

TABLE 7.1

Leading Causes of Death: 25 to 44 Age Group, United States, 1995

		NUMBER OF DEATHS			DEATH RATE PER 100,000 POPULATION		
RANK	CAUSE OF DEATH	TOTAL	MALE	FEMALE	TOTAL	MALE	FEMALE
	All Causes	160,015	111,957	48,058	192.0	269.8	114.8
	Leading Causes of Death:						
1	HIV infection	30,754	25,615	5,139	36.9	61.7	12.3
2	Accidents	27,660	21,096	6,564	33.2	50.8	15.7
3	Cancer	21,985	10,069	11,916	26.4	24.3	28.5
4	Heart disease	17,064	12,268	4,796	20.5	29.6	11.5
5	Suicide	12,759	10,314	2,445	15.3	24.9	5.8
6	Homicide and legal intervention	10,280	7,910	2,370	12.3	19.1	5.7
7	Chronic liver disease and cirrhosis	4,309	3,119	1,190	5.2	7.5	2.8
8	Cerebrovascular diseases	3,492	1,863	1,629	4.2	4.5	3.9
9	Diabetes	2,458	1,421	1,037	2.9	3.4	2.5
10	Pneumonia and influenza	2,102	1,302	800	2.5	3.1	1.9

SOURCE: U.S. National Center for Health Statistics, *Monthly Vital Statistics Report*, 45(11), June 1997.

females (all races combined) between the ages of 25 and 44 during 1995. A large number of deaths for individuals in this life stage are caused by accidents. Although most of the accidents for this age group involve motor vehicles, a significant number are related to participation in a wide range of recreational activities that are potentially dangerous. Young adults tend to be physically active and are often involved in leisure pursuits that test their skills. Some activities such as motorcycle racing and cliff diving, for example, may be viewed as even more exciting because of the element of risk involved.

Disease is also a major contributor to death during young adulthood. HIV infection (which causes AIDS) is now the main cause of death among males between the ages of 25 and 44, and cancer is the leading cause of death among young adult females. Not only are accidents and disease significant contributors to the deaths of young adults, so are suicide and homicide, and suicide and homicide rates for males are about four times higher than for females.

Although gender differences in both the frequency and the cause of death are well illustrated in Table 7.1, important ethnic differences also exist. For example, national statistics show that homicide is the second leading cause of death for African American males between the ages of 25 and 44, whereas HIV infection is the primary cause of death of African American females in this age group (U.S. Center for Health Statistics, 1997).

NEEDS OF YOUNG ADULTS WITH LIFE-THREATENING ILLNESSES

Although death during young adulthood is often sudden, for those who cope with life-threatening illness the knowledge of impending death may be present over many months or years. Young adults have their own developmental concerns, and these must be considered by caregivers attempting to meet the needs of terminally ill individuals in this age group. The following three specific needs of dying young adults will be considered in depth in this section:

- the need to develop intimate relationships,
- the need to express sexuality, and
- the need for realistic support of goals and future plans.

Developing Intimate Relationships

Erikson (1959) identified intimacy versus isolation as the major psychosocial issue to be resolved during the young adult years. **Intimacy** involves the ability to be open, supportive, and close with another person, without fear of losing oneself in the process. The establishment of intimacy with a significant other implies the capacity for mutual empathy, the ability to help meet one another's needs, the acceptance of each other's limitations, and the commitment to care deeply for the other person. An intimate relationship may be sexual or nonsexual, and it can range from a marital bond to a deep friendship or a sibling relationship. Both individuals engaged in intimacy bring their own personal strengths and resources as well as their limitations to the relationship, and both partners are affected by their interpersonal interaction. Prior to adulthood, individuals' identities are too fragile and their egos are too immature to attain the mutuality involved in true intimacy.

Intimacy is the basis for mature love, and the ability to develop close relationships is related to the positive resolution of psychosocial crises of earlier developmental periods. For example, trust is a prerequisite for the development of intimacy, and a sense of identity is also important. Sharing and giving of ourselves is difficult if we do not know who we are as distinct individuals. Failure to develop deep relationships can lead to preoccupation with oneself and superficial interactions with others. Erikson (1959) has used the term **isolation** to describe this outcome.

Stevens-Long and Commons (1992) have emphasized the importance of self-disclosure in the development of intimacy, trust, and understanding with others. The process of self-disclosure is based on reciprocity, and it is critical for the formation and strengthening of close relationships. Little by little, this reciprocal exchange of personal information takes place as the individuals involved feel safe enough to risk self-disclosure. Individuals move slowly in revealing themselves until they feel confident that their sharing of thoughts and feelings will be respected and accepted by the other person. As intimacy is increased, communication is facilitated and feelings are expressed more openly and honestly. Through this process, some of our deepest emotions are shared. The process is disrupted if and when one member does not reciprocate.

Having a close relationship with a significant other has been shown to help adults cope with stressful periods. According to Lowenthal and Weiss (1976), "intimacy is a sine qua non of hope" for many individuals (p. 13). For dying young adults, intimacy with a significant other can be an important avenue for ventilating fears and concerns related to dying and assuaging their feelings of emotional isolation. It can also help them feel valued as unique individuals when the emphasis in the relationship is on who they are in the here and now, rather than on who they might have become.

Different levels of intimacy will be attained with different individuals, depending on the relationship. Self-disclosure of feelings is often overlooked as an important aspect of the professional–patient relationship. Compliance with medical procedures and opportunity to share fears and concerns are intricately tied to quality of relationships between patients and professional caregivers. Professionals who desire to communicate on a less superficial level with their patients must be willing to share something of themselves as individuals separate from their roles. The dying individual will need to communicate with the caregiver as a person as well as a professional.

Following a diagnosis of a serious illness, intimate relationships of the young adult can be threatened. In some situations, close companions may pull away because of their own fears and confusion. For example, they may equate cancer with death and feel they will not be able to cope with the consequences. On the other hand, young adults with life-threatening illnesses may themselves pull away from relationships because they feel they have no future and therefore nothing to offer those close to them. Furthermore, parents and siblings may try to protect the dying young adult from pursuing mature relationships with others for fear he or she will be hurt. Taking emotional risks is part of living, and young adults with life-threatening illnesses have every right to engage in the risks associated with establishing new relationships (Gideon & Taylor, 1981). Mutuality in adult relationships involves giving as well as receiving, and the "giving" component may have special significance for dying young adults as they become the recipients of increased care and attention from family members and health care professionals.

Professional caregivers must be aware of the quality and availability of intimate relationships in the patient's life and be supportive of these relationships. Including a "significant other" in discussions of the illness and its implications can help allay fears and reduce confusion. It may also aid the patient and his or her loved one in making difficult decisions regarding their future together. An open and honest exploration of the issues involved assists young adults in determining what they can offer each other. The relationship may be redefined as the dying individual's condition changes. Sometimes original plans will be changed (e.g., marriage plans may be canceled), but the relationship may still remain as a support and provide intimate companionship for the dying individual.

If the dying individual is hospitalized, the physical setting can have implications for the fulfillment of intimacy needs. Facilities should be designed to facilitate ongoing relationships rather than inadvertently fostering isolation and loneliness. Allowing for privacy and visitation of both family and nonfamily members can be crucial to sustaining emotional support for young adults.

Expressing Sexuality

Sexuality is a natural expression of intimacy in couple relationships, and individuals with life-threatening illnesses share the need to be affectionate and to express themselves in this way. Human sexuality is life affirming and can enable one to feel more like a living individual than a dying individual. Unfortunately, these needs of the dying are often ignored, and they are treated as though they are asexual beings.

Adults are sexual beings regardless of their age, physical status, or stage in life. Expressing ourselves this way contributes to our sense of worth and communicates some of our deepest emotions. Recognizing this, Gideon and Taylor (1981) have proposed a sexual bill of rights for dying persons. They believe that the dying have a right to be sexual in the broadest sense of the term. In their view, sexuality and intercourse are not necessarily the same. Sexuality encompasses a wide range of feelings, attitudes, and behaviors that can be manifest in many ways. If individuals are aware of this, then loss of ability to express themselves through intercourse will be less damaging to the person's identity and self-esteem.

Feeling attractive and positive about oneself physically is an important aspect of sexual identity. Though a positive identity can be facilitated by feeling desirable, many dying individuals fear they will be criticized if they purchase new clothes so close to their anticipated death or spend money to enhance their appearance. Physical appearance is the most visible aspect of one's sexuality, and dying individuals should be given opportunities to engage in activities that promote acceptance of their changing bodies. Gideon and Taylor (1981) also insist that it is the individual's right to maintain control over his or her own body. Some individuals will refuse disfiguring surgeries (despite the recommendations of their physicians) in order to preserve their physical integrity and maintain a positive body image. For example, a breast cancer patient may opt for less radical surgery even though she is told that her risks of recurrence will be greater.

The intimacy and sexual needs of the terminally ill need to be legitimized (MacElveen-Hoehn, 1993). Willingness on the part of caregivers to discuss openly these needs can help in having these needs met. The dying and their partners also need access to counseling and information that will help in accommodating the physical changes occurring in their bodies. Because of taboos in our society surrounding sex and sexuality, both patients and caregivers find it difficult to bring up the subject. Spouses may also fail to bring up sexual issues because they sense the professional's discomfort with the topic. Unfortunately, this situation can have devastating consequences, as can be seen in the following example:

> One young woman, Mary, came home from the hospital after a series of cancer treatments with only a few months to live. Her husband, Tom, took a leave of absence from his job to care for her, with the assistance of a local hospice, during her remaining time. Mary wanted to be physically intimate with her husband in order to reaffirm their relationship and to have the comfort and reassurance of being held and loved. Sexual issues were not discussed with her physician, and Tom incorrectly assumed that intercourse would be too physically taxing and painful for Mary and that it might worsen her condition, and thus, hasten her death. Tom even started sleeping on a cot rather than in their bed so that Mary would be more comfortable. Mary did not share her feelings and assumed that Tom should know that she wanted him to be physically close, as she always had. When Tom failed to respond in familiar ways, she interpreted his withdrawal as rejection. As the months passed, Mary felt more and more distanced from Tom because of these misunderstandings regarding her needs for sexual intimacy.

To avoid this situation, couples need to be aware of each other's fears and concerns. This awareness can be encouraged by sensitive professionals with training in sexuality and medicine. Open communication between partners should be encouraged to facilitate the mutual meeting of their needs.

Changes in body function affecting sexuality often occur as a result of the patient's disease and related medical treatment. Some examples are as follows:

- Radiation therapy to the vaginal area may leave it drier and less elastic, requiring the use of lubricants for pleasurable intercourse.
- Drug therapy such as the use of some tranquilizers can reduce sexual interest and inhibit ejaculation.
- Some diseases and their treatments can result in impotence (e.g., estrogen treatment given to males for prostate cancer), whereas others result in sterility but not necessarily impotence (such as removal of the testes).
- Impotence and other sexual problems can be caused by general ill health.
- Fatigue and chronic pain often accompany terminal illnesses and can result in a general lack of interest in intercourse. Patients with chronic pain often report a decrease in the frequency and quality of their sexual activity.

Changes such as these can surprise, frighten, and sometimes demoralize couples and result in a drastic reduction in sexual activity, although such reduction is unnecessary. When medical personnel openly discuss anticipated changes and effects on sexuality, couples can be helped to understand what is happening and adjust or adapt their sexual practices accordingly. If not prepared for these side effects, the individual may attribute these changes to his or her own inadequacies and thus experience a great deal of anxiety. Lack of confidence in one's ability to perform can lead to a poor self-image, which can further contribute to impaired sexual functioning (Gideon & Taylor, 1981).

Many times couples need specific suggestions about sexual practices. For example, one couple felt awkward until they learned that the husband's colostomy bag could be placed in such a way as to permit holding and cuddling each other comfortably. For other couples, new positions for intercourse or different ways of releasing sexual tension need to be explored (Gideon & Taylor, 1981).

Institutional settings, such as hospitals, can sometimes interfere with a partner's ability to share physical displays of affection. Privacy is essential for couples to show their love and support in an intimate way, and hospitals provide few opportunities for private moments. Having a loved one sleep next to them can provide tremendous comfort to some dying individuals. To accommodate these intimacy needs, hospital rules and regulations must be relaxed and hospital staff should maintain nonjudgmental and accepting attitudes.

Receiving Realistic Support for Goals and Future Plans

Young adulthood is a time of dreams and aspirations, and individuals in this age group often feel shortchanged when faced with a life-threatening illness. They need help in evaluating their futures and deciding on appropriate goals for the time they have remaining. Future plans for young adults often involve marriage, children, and career goals. The particular disease, the prognosis and associated dying trajectory, the individual's personality and coping style, and available social supports all contribute to the definition of what is "realistic" and "appropriate." Young adults need to talk about the future and the implications for themselves and their loved ones.

Marriage.   The decision of whether or not to marry should be determined by the individuals involved. Couples may decide they want to go through a formal ceremony to publicly show their commitment to each other despite a very negative prognosis for the terminally ill partner. The realities of the illness should be made clear to each individual, but whatever the couple's decision, it should be supported by friends and family. Sometimes the pair will not want to plan a future together as a married couple. The individual with the disease may be concerned about the possibility of a recurrence and the burden it would place on the spouse if they were married. The healthy individual may feel he or she does not have the personal strength to cope with the uncertainty of the disease process and the probability of widowhood at an early age. In these situations, couples can benefit from timely therapeutic intervention. Marriage therapists can work with the two individuals, both together and separately, to help clarify each person's feelings and facilitate understanding of the partner's fears and concerns. The outcome of therapy will vary for each couple; some will recommit to the relationship and resume their plans for marriage, whereas others will decide that marriage is not the best option for them. Whatever the outcome, the integrity of the relationship can often be preserved and any negative consequences for the two individuals can be avoided. Guilt, martyrdom, and fear of hurting the other person are inappropriate motivations for marriage. Individuals with life-threatening illnesses, if they do marry, deserve a relationship based on love and trust rather than sympathy.

If the dying individual is already married, he or she may want to discuss the spouse's future. The survivor's happiness and satisfaction in a future marital relationship may be very important to the dying person. The dying partner may feel a strong desire to discuss remarriage and be supportive of the spouse. Common reactions of the spouse often include statements such as "That's in the future—we have a long time together yet" or "That's silly, you know I could never be married to anyone but you." For some individuals, the mention of their remarriage suggests betrayal, and assistance may be needed to redefine what future relationships will mean after the death of their spouse. A vow never to remarry can cause emotional problems years later when that spouse meets someone with whom he or she wants to share his or her life. An honest sharing of feelings is appropriate whenever the subject is mentioned. The future is important to the dying young adult, and it should not be a taboo subject to which communication is closed by "pat" responses. Although the discussion may be painful because it involves acknowledging the reality of one individual's eventual death, each person can benefit from this type of sharing with his or her marital partner. Both will have unique concerns about the future, and partners should listen to each other rather than assume that they know the other's agenda of issues.

Children.   Some couples want to have a child together even after receiving a terminal diagnosis for one of the partners. Gideon and Taylor (1981) have asserted that dying individuals have the right to bear or father children within the confines of full understanding between the two parents.

Sometimes couples will view children as an important and lasting manifestation of their love for each other. Although knowing that their time is limited, they may wish to have children as a way of having a part of themselves survive death. Other motivations for having children at this time can include demonstrating one's masculinity or femininity, wanting the opportunity to experience the parental role, enhancing one's feelings of competence or achievement, exerting some control over one's life, providing an avenue for the expression of nurturance, and tapping into the universal life–death cycle through the creation of another human being.

A woman's decision regarding whether to have a baby usually involves medical considerations. Being pregnant can preclude many types of medical treatments for women with life-threatening diseases because of the potential danger to the fetus. Also, the hormonal and other bodily changes that occur during pregnancy can exacerbate the illness and associated symptoms.

Sterility is a side effect of some medical treatments. Wasserman, Thompson, Wilimas, and Fairclough (1987) have suggested that male patients be encouraged to bank their sperm prior to receiving cancer treatment because reproductive capacity can be negatively affected by both chemotherapy and radiation treatments, although this is not inevitable. New developments in the field of infertility (such as artificial insemination and *in vitro* fertilization) create an increasing number of options for men and women who survive cancer and want to be parents. If the treated partner is not sterile, a couple may wonder about the effects of the cancer therapy on the children they might have. Such concerns are not easily answered because the long-term effects of cancer therapy are not fully known.

Decisions regarding childbearing should be made only after an in-depth exploration of the implications. Discussion of issues regarding single parenting, the probability of a future marriage with another partner, and medical issues for both the unborn child and the terminally ill adult are necessary for responsible decision making. Concerns regarding children also involve financial matters. Dying individuals who have children will want to know that their children's needs will be met. Many young adults have limited savings and assets and have devoted little time to planning for financial security. Having a clear picture of how their family will be supported and cared for following their death can be reassuring and can help give them more peace of mind. After receiving full and complete information and weighing their options, some couples decide to go ahead and have children despite their limited time together as a family.

Career.   Work and education are other issues that are paramount in the lives of young adults. Occupations and vocations help define a significant aspect of one's "self" and contribute to feelings of competence. According to Stevens-Long and Commons (1992), "an occupation provides an important social and personal anchor, a stronghold of identity. It is impossible to understand adult life without understanding the role of work" (p. 201).

Young adults with a life-threatening illness may choose to continue in their student or work roles for as long as possible. For some individuals, finishing a university degree or a work project will be very important. In a school environment, academic advisors can be helpful in clarifying what goals are realistic, given the person's diagnosis. They can also serve as advocates and help the student avoid some obstacles by providing accurate information and effectively communicating with various offices on campus when appropriate.

In a work environment, employers can be supportive of work-related goals by maintaining a "place" at the work setting for the individual (office or desk) and providing extra assistance (clerical help, modified equipment, and so forth) as it is needed. Work policies that allow part-time employment, flexible hours, telecommuting, and "at-home" work can be critical for terminally ill employees who wish to be productive as long as they are physically able. Even though friends and family members may feel the individual should "slow down and enjoy the last remaining months," the wishes of the dying individual should be respected. When dying individuals are no longer able to work, they may find it reassuring to review work accomplishments and the contributions they have made in this sphere of their lives.

Young adults who survive a life-threatening illness may also have work-related concerns. In a study of long-term survivors of Hodgkin's disease, Wasserman and her colleagues (1987) found that this group identified job discrimination as a major problem. To avoid potential prejudice, some of the individuals in the study said that they do not mention that they have had cancer on their job applications. They felt this action was justified because they were considered cured and previous health problems would not adversely affect their present work performance. Some subjects still had strong feelings about career opportunities that were closed to them because of their past experience with cancer. For example, young adults who were excluded from military service felt that this had a negative impact on their lives (e.g., by depriving them of the opportunity to use the GI Bill to help further their education).

Employers are often concerned that hiring a former cancer patient will adversely affect their insurance program. The young adults in the Wasserman et al. (1987) study cited earlier frequently mentioned the problems they had obtaining health and life insurance. Although almost two-thirds of the sample had some form of health insurance coverage, it was usually through a group plan associated with their own jobs or through coverage provided through their spouse's or parents' place of employment. Even among the individuals who were covered by a group insurance plan, some still encountered difficulties. One person's policy excluded all cancer-related problems; another man was unable to accept a better position because he would have lost his coverage. Without the group option, however, health insurance for these former cancer patients was either expensive or unobtainable. In addition, less than one-third of the sample had life insurance, and some of their policies contained a cancer exclusion clause.

MIDDLE ADULTHOOD AS A LIFE STAGE

Middle adulthood includes the forties, fifties, and the early sixties. These years are often referred to as the "prime of life." It is a time of achievement. At this point, individuals have accumulated a broad range of personal, social, and work skills; they are usually at the peak of their vocational development. By midlife, the quest for the adolescent dream has been replaced by the protection of gains (Schiamberg, 1985). Competencies, skills, relationships, and lifestyles that have been developed are maintained and nurtured.

As with previous life stages, new challenges are encountered and new perspectives are also gained during the middle years. In midlife "the impetuous drive of youth mellows to the steady pull of maturity. A growing sense of the surety and familiarity of oneself, one's marriage, one's spouse leads toward a possible appreciation of the more subtle and muted rewards of life" (Pattison, 1977, p. 25). Butler and Lewis (1982) attribute this increased appreciation of life to the restructuring and reformulation of concepts of time, self, and death that occur during middle age.

Some individuals experience a midlife crisis when confronted with the fact that life is not filled with unlimited time. Stephenson (1985) has described the midlife crisis as a form of anticipatory grief—grief over loss of youth, opportunities, endless life. This crisis is often prompted by developmental events that signal that persons are getting older (e.g., the event of the last child leaving home; changes in physical appearance associated with aging, such as graying hair; or menopause marking the end of childbearing ability in women). By mourning these losses, the individual can better accept his or her own aging process and the transition to another life stage. Coming to terms with midlife allows individuals to more fully value and appreciate their lives.

PRIMARY CAUSES OF DEATH DURING MIDDLE ADULTHOOD

By the beginning of the middle years of life, death due to disease increases significantly. Specific primary causes vary somewhat for males and females. Table 7.2 shows that for middle-aged males, heart disease is the leading cause of death, followed by cancer. The order is reversed for females, whose primary cause of death in the middle years is cancer.

The most common types of cancer are also different for males and females. Breast cancer is responsible for most malignancies in women, whereas prostate cancer is the most prevalent type of cancer found among the male population.

TABLE 7.2

Leading Causes of Death: 45 to 64 Age Group, United States, 1995

RANK	CAUSE OF DEATH	NUMBER OF DEATHS			DEATH RATE PER 100,000 POPULATION		
		TOTAL	MALE	FEMALE	TOTAL	MALE	FEMALE
	All Causes	378,512	233,212	145,300	725.0	924.5	538.5
	Leading Causes of Death:						
1	Cancer	132,084	70,077	62,007	253.0	277.8	229.8
2	Heart disease	102,738	72,337	30,401	196.8	286.8	112.7
3	Accidents	16,004	11,429	4,575	30.7	45.3	17.0
4	Cerebrovascular diseases	15,208	8,365	6,843	29.1	33.2	25.4
5	Chronic obstructive pulmonary disease	12,744	6,673	6,071	24.4	26.5	22.5
6	Diabetes	12,184	6,462	5,722	23.3	25.6	21.2
7	Chronic liver disease and cirrhosis	10,603	7,557	3,046	20.3	30.0	11.3
8	HIV infection	10,499	9,119	1,380	20.1	36.1	5.1
9	Suicide	7,336	5,679	1,657	14.1	22.5	6.1
10	Pneumonia and influenza	5,537	3,400	2,137	10.6	13.5	7.9

SOURCE: U.S. National Center for Health Statistics, *Monthly Vital Statistics Report,* 45(11), June 1997.

Lung cancer, however, is the leading cause of cancer deaths in both groups (American Cancer Society, 1997). Figure 7.1 shows the current rates of cancer incidence and cancer deaths by site for both sexes.

Cancer type and survival is also affected by ethnicity in the United States (see Figure 7.2). For example, cancer incidence is generally higher for blacks, especially males, compared with whites and most other ethnic groups (American Cancer Society, 1997). Although Figure 7.2 shows the incidence of cancer among American Indians as much lower than those for white or black Americans, it should be emphasized that considerable variation exists within each of these categories. For example, the remarkably lower incidence of lung cancer among Southwestern Indians (6.3% per 100,000 compared with 51.8% for

FIGURE 7.1
Leading Sites of New Cancer Cases and Deaths—1997 Estimates*

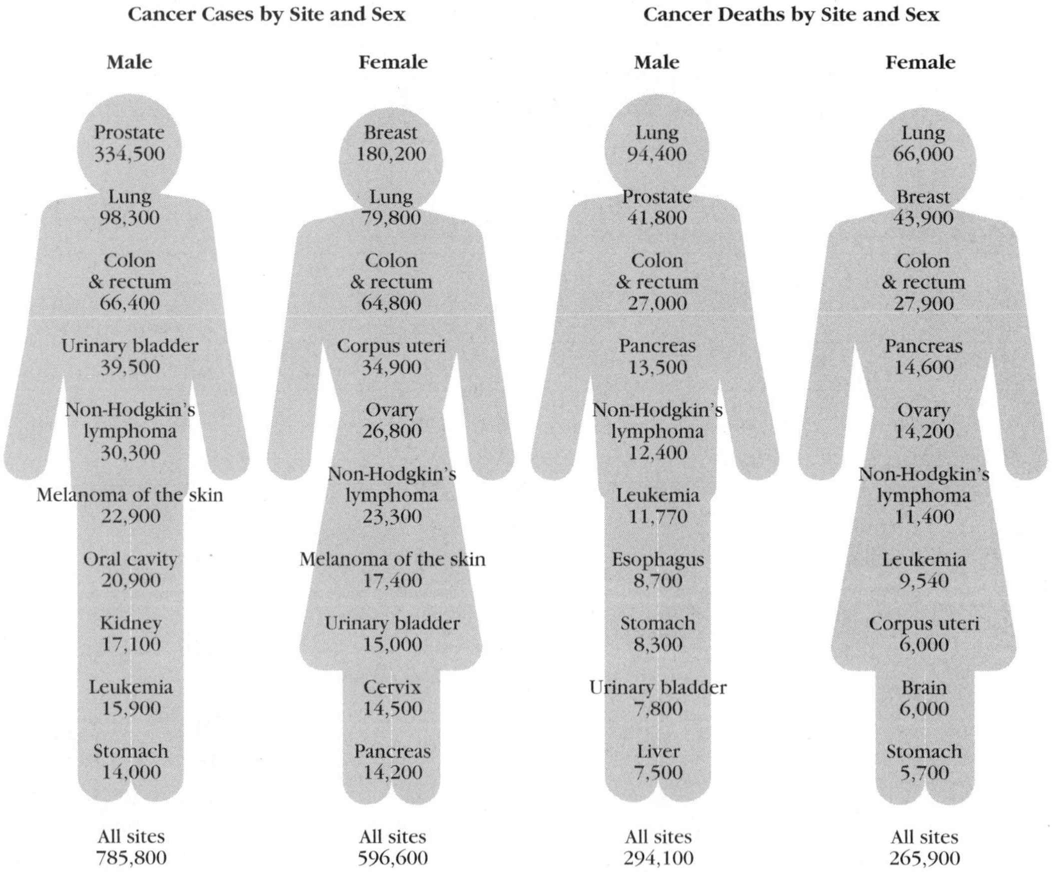

Cancer Cases by Site and Sex		Cancer Deaths by Site and Sex	
Male	**Female**	**Male**	**Female**
Prostate 334,500	Breast 180,200	Lung 94,400	Lung 66,000
Lung 98,300	Lung 79,800	Prostate 41,800	Breast 43,900
Colon & rectum 66,400	Colon & rectum 64,800	Colon & rectum 27,000	Colon & rectum 27,900
Urinary bladder 39,500	Corpus uteri 34,900	Pancreas 13,500	Pancreas 14,600
Non-Hodgkin's lymphoma 30,300	Ovary 26,800	Non-Hodgkin's lymphoma 12,400	Ovary 14,200
Melanoma of the skin 22,900	Non-Hodgkin's lymphoma 23,300	Leukemia 11,770	Non-Hodgkin's lymphoma 11,400
Oral cavity 20,900	Melanoma of the skin 17,400	Esophagus 8,700	Leukemia 9,540
Kidney 17,100	Urinary bladder 15,000	Stomach 8,300	Corpus uteri 6,000
Leukemia 15,900	Cervix 14,500	Urinary bladder 7,800	Brain 6,000
Stomach 14,000	Pancreas 14,200	Liver 7,500	Stomach 5,700
All sites 785,800	All sites 596,600	All sites 294,100	All sites 265,900

*Excluding basal and squamous cell skin cancer and in situ carcinomas except bladder.
SOURCE: American Cancer Society Surveillance Research, 1997. ©1997, American Cancer Society, Inc.

whites and 69.8% for blacks) results from their low levels of smoking. Other Native American populations in which smoking is more common, such as those in Oklahoma and the Northwest, have higher lung cancer rates (American Cancer Society, 1991).

It is hoped that studying ethnic variations in disease rates will lead to more effective strategies for prevention and treatment:

> Because cancer risk is strongly associated with lifestyle and behavior, differences in cancer rates between ethnic and cultural groups can provide clues about factors involved in the development of cancer such as dietary patterns, alcohol use, and sexual and reproductive behaviors. Screening behaviors also vary between racial and ethnic groups. Cultural values and belief systems can

FIGURE 7.2

Cancer Incidence Rates* for All Sites Combined by Race, Ethnicity, and Sex, U.S., 1988–1992

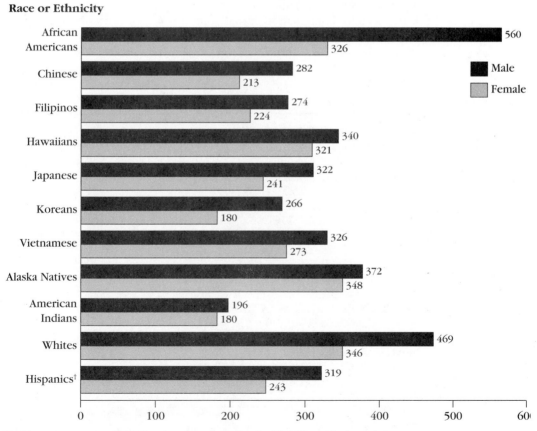

Race or Ethnicity

*Incidence rates are per 100,000 and are age-adjusted to the 1970 US standard population.
†Persons of Hispanic origin may be of any race.
SOURCE: NCI Surveillance, Epidemiology, and End Results Program, 1996. ©1997, American Cancer Society, Inc.

affect attitudes about seeking medical care or following guidelines. Factors such as lack of health insurance or transportation can impede access to care, and lead to late diagnosis and poor survival. (American Cancer Society, 1996, p. 20)

Cancer rates also vary considerably by country. For example, Figure 7.3 shows the incidence of breast cancer in a variety of different countries. Note that the incidence in the United States is more than five times higher than it is in Japan. Researchers suspect that the high-fat diet common in the United States and many other Western nations contributes to differential breast cancer rates. Currently, researchers are attempting to better understand the effects of diet and lifestyle on a variety of different diseases such as cancer.

NEEDS OF THE DYING AT MIDLIFE

The needs of the dying at midlife relate to the responsibility they have for others as well as increased self-reflection, and include the following:

- the need for reevaluation of one's life,
- the need for continuation of roles, and
- the need to put affairs in order.

FIGURE 7.3
Incidence of Breast Cancer by Country

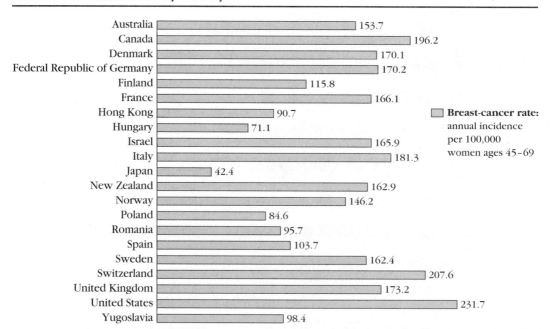

Country	Breast-cancer rate: annual incidence per 100,000 women ages 45–69
Australia	153.7
Canada	196.2
Denmark	170.1
Federal Republic of Germany	170.2
Finland	115.8
France	166.1
Hong Kong	90.7
Hungary	71.1
Israel	165.9
Italy	181.3
Japan	42.4
New Zealand	162.9
Norway	146.2
Poland	84.6
Romania	95.7
Spain	103.7
Sweden	162.4
Switzerland	207.6
United Kingdom	173.2
United States	231.7
Yugoslavia	98.4

SOURCE: Prentice, R. L., Kakar, F., Hursting, S., Sheppard, L., Klein, R, & Kushi, L. H. (1988). Aspects of the rationale for the women's health trial. *Journal of the National Cancer Institute, 80* (11), 802–814.

Reevaluating One's Life

Although reevaluation can occur during any life stage, this process has a special quality during middle adulthood. According to Schiamberg (1985), the primary concern of the middle-aged person can be viewed as that of the proverbial man who wondered aloud if his glass was half empty or half full. Individuals at midlife are faced with limited future choices while also being acutely aware of the influence of past decisions and events on their lives. Midlife is, therefore, a period of questioning. Questions such as "What is the meaning of my life?" and "Should I continue in the same direction?" are commonly asked by individuals at this time. This type of life evaluation has been referred to as **stock-taking** (Butler & Lewis, 1982). Individuals take stock of their lives with full awareness that what they find is and will continue to be their life unless they make some changes soon. This questioning is a normal and natural part of midlife, as individuals become increasingly conscious of their own mortality.

Stock-taking occurs in terms of one's relationships, career, achievements, values, and other commitments made earlier in life. The outcomes of this reevaluation take several directions. Following the assessment of previous choices, individuals may recommit themselves to the path previously chosen or they may seek major life changes. The decision to pursue new directions or relationships at this stage are reflected in midlife career changes and the high rate of divorce during the middle years. Regardless of the outcome, the individual must come to grips with his or her actual achievements in relation to the hopes and aspirations of young adulthood.

For the individual facing death in the middle years, reevaluation of one's life will be accelerated and compressed into the remaining time the individual has left. The individual may appear quiet and introspective to others while engaging in this process. One outcome of this stock-taking is typically the need to mourn losses: goals never attained, aspirations never reached, and deeds never done. Impending death will raise issues and remind the individual of all he or she will be leaving behind.

Continuing Roles

Much of an individual's identity is derived from his or her adult roles. In the early years of adulthood, self-perceptions help determine what roles are chosen. The enactment of these roles and the addition of others, as one moves through midlife, affect one's sense of self. As a result, adult identity becomes more complex and differentiated.

Through one's roles, individuals are able to make lasting and significant contributions. Erikson (1968) has identified the central issue of midlife as generativity versus stagnation. **Generativity** is reflected in a deep concern for the next generation and a desire to contribute to the future. Generativity is achieved through the channeling of one's energy and creativity in a direction that will produce lasting and worthwhile results—a legacy for the future. Failure to develop a generative lifestyle in midlife will result in self-indulgence and **stagnation** (Erikson, 1968).

Individuals facing death at midlife may ask themselves: Have I made a significant contribution to the next generation? Have I been a productive and creative member of society? The dying individual must be supported in maintaining his or her adult roles whenever possible. Too often, the dying person is seen only as "ill" and "dying" and is not given opportunities to function as a parent, spouse, mentor, or friend. Giving advice to a younger colleague, helping to complete plans for reorganization of their company, and providing emotional support to family members are examples of important goals of the middle-aged person coping with a life-threatening illness. By continuing to participate in life and ongoing relationships, individuals will be more likely to resolve the generativity versus stagnation conflict positively and to feel they are leaving behind a legacy after their death. They will also face death with a strong sense of personal identity and a better understanding of the purpose of their lives.

Putting Affairs in Order

Middle age is the life stage in which individuals typically have the greatest responsibilities. Leadership positions in work settings and community organizations are typically held by those in their middle years. This may also be a time of heightened psychological pressures and financial demands as support is provided for other family members. Adolescent children may still be in college or establishing themselves as young adults. In addition, the parents of middle-aged individuals are aging and may begin to need more assistance and attention from their adult children than ever before.

For the terminally ill individual at midlife, responsibilities and obligations to others are of the utmost importance. Faced with impending death, the middle-aged person is often less concerned about death per se and more concerned about his or her responsibilities and obligations to loved ones that may go unmet after death. Therapeutic intervention will often involve helping the person plan for those who will be left behind: spouse, children, aging parents, and employees, among others. The person usually wants to carry out his or her duties to whatever degree possible through making appropriate arrangements and plans prior to death (Pattison, 1977; Rando, 1984).

LATE ADULTHOOD AS A LIFE STAGE

Death is most often associated with the later years of life. In the United States, more than two-thirds of deaths occur among individuals who have passed their 65th birthday. The average life expectancy of Americans is currently 75.9 years, with women on the average living approximately 7 years longer than men, and whites living approximately 6 years longer than blacks (U.S. Bureau of the Census, 1993).

Despite the high frequency of deaths occurring during the later years of life, most older individuals lead healthy, active lives. As individuals age, however, a greater likelihood exists that they will experience deteriorating health and disabling conditions. Many gerontologists (professionals who study the process of aging, or **gerontology**) have found it useful to distinguish between the "young-old" (65 to 74 age group) and the "oldest-old" (those 85 years of age and older), due to the large differences between these two age groups (Riekse & Holstege, 1996). Unfortunately, much of the research on the elderly has failed to differentiate findings based on this classification (Morgan, 1995).

The prevalence of death in the later years is related to a number of developmental themes of late adulthood. Erikson (1950) has postulated "ego integrity versus despair" (the last of his eight stages) as the critical developmental issue for the aged. Resolving this issue positively involves acceptance of one's personal experiences. According to Erikson, the achievement of inner balance and harmony is directly linked to coming to terms with one's past and the successful resolution of earlier developmental tasks. When **ego integrity** predominates, it is often accompanied by the wisdom that has typically been associated with the later years of life (Erikson & Erikson, 1981). Resolution of this issue in terms of **despair** occurs when the elderly view their lives as poorly spent and feel that it is too late to compensate for unfortunate choices made earlier. For these individuals, death will often come too soon.

Reminiscence in the elderly is part of a normal, healthy process brought about by the approach of death. Robert Butler (1963) was the first to use the term **life review** to describe this process of surveying and reflecting on one's past. During reminiscence, past experiences are spontaneously brought to consciousness for review and possible reinterpretation and reintegration. Reconsideration of the past often results in revised or expanded meanings and the resolution of old conflicts. Such reorganization of past experience may give new and significant meanings to one's life, thus helping to prepare for death.

Consistent with Butler's observation are empirical findings related to shifts in intrapsychic personality dimensions as individuals age. Neugarten (1977) has reported an increase in introspection and self-reflection during the second half of life. Referred to as **interiority,** this tendency appears to be even more pronounced in late adulthood.

Although other age groups may also reminisce and engage in introspection, Butler and Lewis (1982) point out that the intensity of these mental activities is most striking in the later years. During this period, a reassessment of life occurs as the elderly realize that their personal myth of invulnerability and immortality can no longer be maintained. As individuals advance in age, they begin to accept that they too will die and are less afraid of this eventuality.

Kalish (1985) has offered three possible explanations for the diminished fear of death found among older persons. First, older persons may accept death more easily because they have been able to live a full life span. Second, the elderly may be socialized to accept their own deaths through repeated experiences with the deaths of others. The third possible explanation is that the elderly may perceive the costs of giving up life to be lower because they view their lives as having less value than the lives of younger persons.

PRIMARY CAUSES OF DEATH DURING LATE ADULTHOOD

Gender differences in leading causes of death decrease with age. Among both men and women over 65 years of age, heart disease is the leading cause of death, followed by cancer and strokes (see Table 7.3). Other diseases and conditions responsible for a significant number of deaths in the last years of life include chronic lung disease, pneumonia, and influenza.

Ethnic differences in health conditions also exist that may lead to death. For example, both blacks and Hispanics tend to have high rates of hypertension, and Native Americans are 10 times more likely than whites to develop diabetes (American Association of Retired Persons [AARP], 1993). Mutchler and Burr (1991), however, conclude from their research that blacks and whites have similar health patterns when socioeconomic differences are taken into account.

TABLE 7.3
Leading Causes of Death: 65 and Over Age Group, United States, 1995

RANK	CAUSE OF DEATH	NUMBER OF DEATHS			DEATH RATE PER 100,000 POPULATION		
		TOTAL	MALE	FEMALE	TOTAL	MALE	FEMALE
	All Causes	1,694,326	776,232	918,094	5,052.8	5,670.6	4,626.6
	Leading Causes of Death:						
1	Heart disease	615,426	276,756	338,670	1,835.3	2,021.8	1,706.7
2	Cancer	381,142	199,536	181,606	1,136.6	1,457.7	915.2
3	Cerebrovascular diseases	138,762	51,030	87,732	413.8	372.8	442.1
4	Chronic obstructive pulmonary disease	88,478	46,425	42,053	263.9	339.1	211.9
5	Pneumonia and influenza	74,297	32,557	41,740	221.6	237.8	210.3
6	Diabetes	44,452	18,144	26,308	132.6	132.5	132.6
7	Accidents	29,099	14,399	14,700	86.8	105.2	74.1
8	Alzheimer's disease	20,230	6,837	13,393	60.3	49.9	67.5
9	Nephritis, nephrotic syndrome, and nephrosis	20,182	9,421	10,761	60.2	68.8	54.2
10	Septicemia	16,899	6,764	10,135	50.4	49.4	51.1

SOURCE: U.S. National Center for Health Statistics, *Monthly Vital Statistics Report, 45*(11), June 1997.

Socioeconomic factors such as education and economic resources appear to be critical factors in health status, affecting health practices and health care access. These authors also point out that other differences among ethnic groups such as life-style, diet, and stress associated with racism and various forms of discrimination cannot be overlooked as influences on health. The effects of life-long patterns tend to accumulate with age and affect patterns of illness and death.

The changes in the body that are associated with aging tend to be gradual. As one ages, systems of the body become less efficient and less well integrated. Much variability exists, however, among individuals in the rate of physical aging. The changes that occur in the body over time are cumulative. As individuals age, the progressive effects of years of poor dietary habits and sedentary life-styles can take their toll and affect the normal aging process. Also, a lifetime of exposure to cigarette smoking or polluted air can sometimes produce the first signs of health impairment in old age when systems begin to wear down. It is difficult at times to distinguish between changes associated with "normal aging" and physiological changes resulting from particular dietary and life-style practices prevalent in our culture.

Many elderly individuals function well physically in the absence of demands on their physiological systems. However, the aged body is vulnerable and becomes more so with time. It can no longer deal as effectively with physiological stress. As the effectiveness of the immune system decreases, the individual becomes more susceptible to disease, both degenerative diseases associated with aging and infectious diseases (Hooyman & Kiyak, 1996).

The deterioration of the cardiovascular system in particular is associated with age. As cells age, the overall efficiency of the system is reduced. Eventually, the system wears out because cells of the heart, arteries, veins, and capillaries cannot divide and reproduce. Rates of coronary artery disease are very high in the United States and other highly industrialized nations. With this disease, the amount of blood supplied to the heart is deficient because of blood vessel constriction. In atherosclerosis, arteries are occluded (obstructed), which forces the heart to work harder to force blood through them. Strokes can occur when blood flow is restricted to the brain, usually resulting in either disability or death.

Due to advances in health-related technology as discussed in chapter 1, many older individuals tend to survive longer with major health problems. When in the past they would have died, modern medical interventions often extend their lives for many years. Nursing homes and other long-term care institutions have been developed as an option of care for older individuals in these circumstances. Although only 5% of the elderly are residents of long-term care institutions at any one time, this percentage increases dramatically with age, ranging from 1% of persons 65–74 years of age living in nursing homes to 24% for persons 85 and above (AARP, 1995). Consequently, long-term care institutions are increasingly a place of final residence for a substantial number of elderly.

HEART DISEASE: THE LEADING CAUSE OF DEATH FOR AMERICANS

He awoke at 7 A.M. with pain in his chest. The sort of pain that might cause panic if one were not a doctor, as he was, and did not know, as he knew, that it was heartburn.

He went into the kitchen to get some Coke, whose secret syrups often relieve heartburn. The refrigerator door seemed heavy, and he noted that he was having trouble unscrewing the bottle cap. Finally, he wrenched it off, cursing the defective cap. He poured some liquid, took a sip. The pain did not go away. Another sip; still no relief.

Now he grew more attentive. He stood motionless, observing symptoms. His breath was coming hard. He felt faint. He was sweating, though the August morning was still cool. He put his fingers to his pulse. It was rapid and weak. A powerful burning sensation was beginning to spread through his chest, radiating upward into his throat. Into his arm? No. But the pain was getting worse. Now it was crushing—"*crushing*," just as it is always described. And worse even than the pain was the sensation of losing all power, a terrifying seepage of strength. He could feel the entire degenerative process accelerating. He was growing fainter, faster. The pulse was growing weaker, faster. He was sweating much more profusely now—a heavy, clammy sweat. He felt that the life juices were draining from his body. He felt that he was about to die. (Lear, 1980, p. 11)

Cardiovascular diseases are responsible for nearly one-half of all deaths in the United States. Of the cardiovascular diseases, myocardial infarction (commonly called heart attack) is the most prevalent (American Heart Association, 1997). Death from a heart attack is typically sudden, with little warning, and the majority of heart attacks occur outside a medical setting. Many victims who do not survive die within a few hours after their first symptoms appear. Initially, individuals may tend to attribute their chest pain to some other problem (e.g., severe indigestion) and thus delay seeking assistance. Because of the nature of myocardial infarction, it can be viewed as usually having an uncertain outcome and an uncertain time of death. The trajectory can change if the cardiovascular system becomes severely damaged or diseased. Medical interventions, such as surgery and heart transplants, can also alter the death trajectory.

SOURCES: M. W. Lear (1980). *Heartsounds.* New York: Simon & Schuster. American Heart Association. (1997). *Heart and Stroke statistical update.* Dallas, TX: Author.

NEEDS OF THE DYING ELDERLY

The dying elderly, like other age groups, have unique needs that are linked to their particular developmental stage. Four specific needs of elderly people with life-threatening illnesses are as follows:

- maintaining a sense of self,
- participating in decisions regarding their lives,
- being reassured that their lives still have value, and
- receiving appropriate and adequate health care services.

Maintaining a Sense of Self

According to Tobin (1985), one of the primary developmental tasks of late adulthood is the maintenance and enhancement of the individual's sense of self. Preserving their identities as unique individuals is essential in order for the elderly to end their lives with a sense of integrity. Ego integrity can be facilitated through the life review process, as the elderly reminisce about the roles they played, the relationships they had, and their own particular life circumstances. To reexamine their lives through their memories can reaffirm their identity in old age and validate who they are and have been in life. Reminiscing can also strengthen emotional bonds between individuals and promote family cohesiveness as significant aspects of family history are shared. With additional information about elderly persons from stories of their past, professional caregivers also have the opportunity to relate to older persons as individuals rather than as "patients," "nursing home residents," or "senior citizens."

To aid the elderly in maintaining their sense of self, Verwoerdt (1985) has suggested adjusting the environment to the person rather than adjusting the person to the environment. For example, when individuals are placed in institutional settings, a dramatic change in their behavior can oftentimes be observed. Removed from familiar surroundings and faces and placed in a strange environment, the elderly may feel that they have been separated from most of what has made their lives meaningful. Thus, they may become disoriented and withdrawn. Institutions such as nursing homes can recognize each person's individuality and uniqueness by taking individual differences into account. Ways of doing this include allowing the nursing home residents to furnish their rooms with personal furniture and decorate their rooms with important photographs and mementos, and encouraging contact with people and participation in events outside the nursing home. Additionally, directors of activity programs should inquire about each person's interests and past activities and incorporate them into the program instead of simply offering a standard slate of recreational events. Residents are often capable of using some of their skills and abilities in the nursing home setting. By emphasizing the remaining abilities of the elderly rather than their disabilities, feelings of self-esteem and worth are enhanced.

The self-identity of the dying elderly also can be maintained when they give significant others tangible personal items that are important to them. Many individuals see their valued possessions as extensions of themselves. Giving a treasured keepsake to a loved one who will value it can be a reminder of one's enduring significance to others.

Participating in Decisions Regarding One's Life

Dowd (1980), using the perspective of social exchange theory, has stated that the problems of the aged in 20th-century industrial societies have been primarily due to the decreasing power of the elderly. He argues that, because of practices such as retirement, the elderly are more likely to be economically and socially dependent than other adults. As a consequence, they gradually lose personal power as their opportunities to offer and exchange services decrease. Thus, they are placed in a position in which compliance with the wishes of others may be their only remaining option.

Like all adults, older individuals have a right to maintain as much control over their lives as possible. Unfortunately, this right is often disregarded as the individual's age. When the deteriorating physical condition of older adults necessitates a change in their living situation, they are often excluded from discussions about plans for their future. Well-meaning family members and professionals may want to spare the elderly from the difficult choices to be made, when in fact they may be making the situation more painful and frightening by excluding them.

Most older individuals value their independence and express concern over being dependent on their children. Many times families of the elderly are not fully aware of housing options or community support services that could allow their aged parent to retain some degree of independence while obtaining needed care. Out of concern for their parent's safety, adult children often insist that they move in with them. If this situation is not feasible or fails to work, a nursing home placement is often considered.

Commenting on nursing home environments, Solomon (1982) suggests that moving into a long-term care facility can lead to learned helplessness. Life in this setting can threaten the elderly person's remaining feelings of mastery and control as he or she is socialized into the institutional routine. In this environment, many of the decisions and responsibilities of the older person (including what to eat and when to sleep) are taken away, and patients are labeled as sick and helpless regardless of their actual condition. Even the best-run institutions seem to limit the residents' option to exercise choices.

A feeling of loss of control over aspects of their own lives can contribute to feelings of depression, physical decline, and premature death in the institutionalized aged. Maizler, Solomon, and Almquist (1983) have used the term **psychogenic mortality** to refer to a syndrome in which a patient's psychological condition triggers physical reactions that lead ultimately to death. A somewhat conscious decision seems to be made by the person after appraising his or her life situation and concluding that it is not worth living. This "giving up" of self results in a state of hopelessness and helplessness, affecting physical functioning.

Butler and Lewis (1982) have observed that much of the authoritarianism in institutions is designed to meet the needs of providers rather than the consumers of services. Patients in nursing homes and hospitals often are not aware that they have rights as well. These rights, mandated by the federal government, include the right to

- obtain complete and current information from their physician regarding their diagnosis, treatment, and prognosis, in terms that they can understand;
- give informed consent before any procedure or treatment is begun and to be given information on alternatives;

- refuse treatment to the extent permitted by law; and
- refuse to participate in experimental research.

Long-term care residents maintain their rights as citizens and can legally voice grievances and recommend changes in policies and services. Yet even if residents are aware of their rights, they may remain silent for fear of retaliation.

Intervention programs, however, do seem to be effective. When residents of long-term care facilities are allowed to take responsibility for some aspects of their lives, positive outcomes result. In studies that have introduced choices (such as having several entrées available for a meal instead of one) and responsibilities (planning social events for the facility, for example), the investigators have consistently found residents to be happier and more active as a result of the intervention (Banziger & Roush, 1983).

Retaining a sense of control in our lives appears to be critical for positive mental health. The elderly need avenues for the expression of their competence and remaining independence. They also need opportunities to participate in the decisions that will affect them. The extent to which they are capable of utilizing these opportunities will vary widely, depending on their current mental and physical condition.

Being Reassured That One's Life Still Has Value

Social gerontologists have used the term **ageism** to refer to discrimination against the elderly solely on the basis of their age. In our youth-oriented society, this negative bias exists against older individuals in virtually every area of their lives. The old are viewed in stereotypical ways that do not fit the majority of individuals in the over-65 age group. Conceptions of the elderly as unproductive, dependent, and incompetent result in low social value being attached to this segment of our population. These attitudes can also influence attitudes of older persons toward themselves. In addition to loss of their work role, sensory impairment, and decline of other functions, ageism can be a potent force in the lives of the elderly.

Sense of worth and value can be even more of an issue for older persons who are terminally ill. They may fear that their social death will precede their physical death. This fear may be validated if they observe professional staff avoiding them and visits from family decrease. For many people, aging is associated with death, and contact with the elderly evokes fears and anxieties about both of these processes in themselves. Baltz and Turner (1977) found that effective versus ineffective nursing home aides could be differentiated on the basis of their attitudes toward illness and death. Those with negative attitudes toward illness and death were more likely to have difficulty relating to the residents and have a higher turnover rate. Baltz and Turner recommended that these attitudes be considered when employing aides, as a means of improving the quality of life in nursing homes.

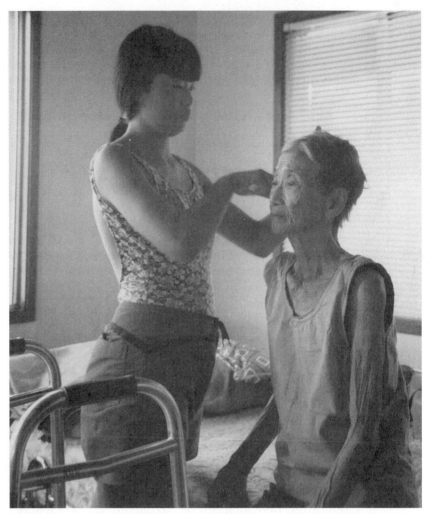

The elderly need to feel their lives are valued and that they are important to others, especially family members.

The feelings of family members may also interfere with positive interaction with their elderly relatives. The importance of providing support and guidance to families of institutionalized elderly cannot be overemphasized. As more opportunities for satisfactory patterns of interaction are established, family visits can be associated with satisfaction and pleasure rather than obligation, guilt, and frustration.

Messages of value can also be communicated by actions that give older persons a "living" rather than a "dying" status. Providing the individual with new glasses, dental work, physical therapy, and other aides and services can serve as important symbols of their social value. These acts also imply that the elderly have "a future," however short it might be.

The elderly need to feel that their lives are valued and that they are still important to other people. Conveying a sense of their continued value and significance as human beings can greatly influence the remaining quality of their lives. If they feel more connected to life than to death, they will maintain their will to live. Professional caregivers should recognize this need as a major psychosocial issue in their treatment of the dying elderly.

Receiving Appropriate and Adequate Health Care Services

Older individuals are entitled to receive quality health care and appropriate services. **Geriatrics** is the field of medicine that focuses on care of the elderly. Few physicians have been attracted to this area because, unfortunately, it is not seen as having the status or professional challenge of other specialties. In testimony before the U.S. Congress in 1992, Dr. Robert Butler, professor and chair of the geriatrics department of the Mount Sinai School of Medicine, pointed to a major shortage of geriatricians in practice as well as faculty with this specialty in medical schools to adequately train new health care professionals in this field. Of the 126 medical schools in the United States, only 13 required courses or clinical experience in geriatrics or aging (U.S. House of Representatives Select Committee on Aging, 1992).

Perhaps of even more concern is the evidence of age bias among the medical profession. Intrieri, Kelly, Brown, and Castilla (1993) concluded from their literature review that "medical personnel often hold a biased and negative view of the old, are not well versed in normal changes that occur with age, and show little desire to treat older persons" (p. 374). In a study representing seven specialties, a random sample of private practice physicians were asked to record the amount of time they spent with each patient over several typical office days. When the results were examined by age of the patients, the investigators found that the physicians spent considerably less time with individuals in the over-65 age group than they did with patients in the other age groups. This finding held true for office, hospital, and nursing home visits (Kane, Solomon, Beck, Keeler, & Kane, 1981). These results are the opposite of what one would expect, because individuals over the age of 65 are the heaviest consumers of medical services in this country (AARP, 1995).

Lack of knowledge about the aging process among physicians can lead to misdiagnoses and inadequate treatment plans in some cases. Early symptoms may be simply dismissed and attributed to "just aches and pains that go along with being old." Delay in treating many life-threatening diseases can be fatal. The changing demography with increased numbers of elderly worldwide may well stimulate changes in the training and subsequently the attitudes of physicians toward providing medical treatment for the aged.

Despite these predicted shifts in attitudes and training priorities, older Americans as a group may continue to be at risk of receiving less than adequate health care due to economic factors. Medicare, a national health insurance program designed for the elderly in the United States, was created by Congress in 1965 as part of the amendments to the Social Security law. Financed through the Social Security tax, the passage of Medicare was seen as a major breakthrough toward providing adequate health care for older Americans. It was designed to provide coverage related to episodes of acute illness. A separate program, Medicaid, provides health care for the indigent of all ages. Although the Medicare program is limited in scope, its budget has continued to grow, due in large part to the increased number of aged individuals in our society. Measures to curb this growth have resulted in a system referred to as the **prospective-payment system (PPS).** Under this system, hospitals are paid a predetermined amount for a patient's treatment. This amount is determined by the **diagnostically related group (DRG)** in which the particular treatment is classified. If the patient's bill is less than the DRG amount, the hospital keeps the balance; if it is more, the hospital must absorb the difference (Hooyan & Kiyak, 1996). This system can potentially have a negative effect on the elderly if they are discharged from hospitals prematurely or when complicated cases are avoided by physicians for economic reasons.

Furthermore, Medicare fails to provide many needed services. Due to these gaps in coverage (including hearing aids, dental care, preventive services, and long-term nursing home care, among other services), many older persons purchase supplemental private insurance policies. Unfortunately, many people tend to purchase policies that duplicate Medicare coverage rather than supplement it. Oftentimes, elderly individuals do not realize the limitations of their coverage until they are in a critical health crisis. Despite the existence of Medicare, Medicaid, and private insurance options, the elderly pay about one-fourth of their health bills themselves, and annual medical expenditures for elderly Americans currently total $162 million, four times the cost of medical care for younger persons (AARP, 1995). As health care costs continue to soar in this country and the income of the elderly remains fixed, individuals in this age group are in jeopardy of receiving inadequate and insufficient health care services. Concerns also continue to be raised regarding the increasing proportion of health care provided through managed care organizations and the potential consequences of restricted services and access.

LOSSES ASSOCIATED WITH ILLNESS

The psychological realities of coping with a life-threatening illness are directly related to aspects of one's particular disease. Rolland (1991) has emphasized that illnesses have different characteristics, and illness type and phase will provide a "timeline of potential nodal points of loss, including disability and death."

According to Rolland (1987), the experience of illness will be influenced by a variety of factors, including

- onset (acute, gradual);
- course (progressive, constant, or relapsing/episodic);
- outcome (nonfatal, possibly fatal, fatal); and
- level of incapacitation.

Each particular disease also has its own constellation of symptoms and treatment options. In this section, three different life-threatening illnesses of high prevalence (AIDS, cancer, and Alzheimer's disease) are discussed as they relate to unique disease-specific aspects of loss.

Young Adults With AIDS

As indicated earlier in this chapter, more and more young adults are dying of AIDS. Due to the nature of AIDS, some rather unique circumstances complicate the grief process and make coming to terms with the illness more difficult. Individuals with this disease cope with a variety of loss issues, including those related to loss of health and well-being. Of great concern is the fact that the shame and stigma associated with AIDS may cause those with the disease to hide their initial symptoms, delay being testing for the HIV virus, or deny their diagnosis (Sherr, 1995). As a result, they are unlikely to receive timely and appropriate medical care. They may continue practicing unsafe sexual activities, thus putting others at risk of contracting the virus.

Unfortunately, however, when the diagnosis of AIDS is known by others, negative repercussions often follow. Friends may withdraw due to fear of the disease. As a consequence, individuals with AIDS may find their social network constricted and thus experience feelings of isolation and alienation. Furthermore, individuals may encounter ambivalent, or even rejecting, medical staff.

In some settings, individuals with AIDS have been fired from their jobs because of the extreme fear among some employers. The U.S. courts, however, have ruled in favor of AIDS patients' rights to continue their employment. One such patient, Michael Collen, shared that "AIDS patients suffer in two basic ways: We suffer from a life-threatening illness, and we suffer from the stigma attached from being diagnosed with AIDS" (Siegal & Siegal, 1983, p. 183).

Self-condemnation and guilt can result if the disease was transmitted through promiscuous sexual behavior or drug use. Anger is typically present when the person is infected through assumed safe sexual practices (e.g., sexual relations with a spouse unknown to be HIV positive) or medical procedures (e.g., a blood transfusion). A normal grief reaction commonly involves such feelings, but they are exacerbated by this particular illness. Other common grief reactions include fear, shock, panic, and denial. The diagnosis of AIDS may heighten those responses unless patients are provided with accurate information and sensitive psychological support (Kelly & Raphael, 1993). Group counseling sessions have

AIDS IN RURAL AREAS

From 1991 to 1995, the incidence of AIDS in rural communities in the United States rose by 80 percent, outpacing the growth in both large and smaller urban areas. Yet still many rural residents live with the myth that AIDS is an "urban disease." To address this misperception, the Rural Center for AIDS/STD Prevention was established at Indiana University in 1994 with initial funds from the U.S. Department of Agriculture. As the demographics of the AIDS epidemic change, the need for education about this disease (especially among young people) becomes critical for rural residents. In addition to educational efforts across the United States, the Center plans a study of the financial impact of AIDS and other sexually transmitted diseases on rural communities. Sparsely populated, rural areas are often the poorest; thus the impact of AIDS and its expensive treatments can be much greater than in urban centers.

SOURCE: J. McMillan, (1996). Preventing AIDS in rural America. *The Chronicle of Higher Education, XLIII* (12), A10.

become an important therapeutic mode for people with AIDS, because other patients can share their fears and provide factual information, social support, and physical comfort. This type of support can be crucial, as many AIDS patients report diminished contact with their former network of friends (Donlou, Wolcott, Gottlieb, & Landsverk, 1985).

If not married, young adults often return to a parental home as their illness progresses. At times, especially when the caregiving parent lives at a distance, this geographic relocation separates the person from remaining peer support structures and may further alter the amount and type of social support available (Bor, Miller, & Goldman, 1993).

Caregiving issues of AIDS patients are becoming increasingly complicated as this illness becomes more prevalent. While adults with AIDS are coping with their own illness, they may at the same time be dealing with the threatened loss of a partner or family member who has contracted the same disease. Of increased concern are the number of families in which multiple cases of AIDS are present. As HIV infection continues to rise among young women of childbearing age, so too does the infection rate in infants. In fact, young parents often receive their own diagnosis at the same time they learn that their child also has AIDS (Rolland, 1991). Reflective of this increasing occurrence, the terms *HIV+ families* and *AIDS orphans* are now appearing in the professional literature (Dane & Levine, 1994; O'Donnell, 1996).

Cancer at Midlife

Often appearing at midlife, a diagnosis of cancer presents the individual with a series of challenges. The issues associated with the disease change over time and vary by prognosis. The intensity of treatments, adverse side effects, and associated complications are often worse than the initial symptoms of the disease itself (Koocher, 1986). Readily visible disfigurement from the disease or its treatment can lead to a devastating loss of self-esteem and to reclusive behavior. Some of the physical changes are temporary (hair loss as a result of chemotherapy, for example), whereas others are permanent and require long-term adjustment.

The impact of loss of a body part or function depends, in part, on a person's self-concept. The more secure individuals are in their relationships with others and in their own sense of worth, the more capable they will be of adjusting to the loss and maintaining a positive self-image. However, adjustment to physical disfigurement is always a challenge in a society that places a premium on physical appearance and offers constant reminders of the cultural ideal of physical attractiveness. Moller (1990) uses a patient's own words to describe the feelings associated with changes in physical appearance after cancer treatment:

> I feel very self-conscious about losing my hair. Really, I'm scared to start a relationship with anybody. I gained a lot of weight on my first chemotherapy, and that didn't help my image any. . . . I used to have a lot of confidence and be pretty outgoing. Now I feel shy and ugly . . . trying not to be noticed too much. I sort of withdraw and don't really like to go out too often. . . . To a certain extent, I feel so much less adequate than before. I'm so very self-conscious, I feel like I don't know how to communicate anymore. You know, make conversation, small talk . . . So I avoid people very often. (p. 77)

Attitudes of significant others toward the patient's body change will also affect the individual's attitude. For example, if a husband reacts negatively after his wife's surgery, it will affect her adjustment. Breast cancer patients, in particular, may feel that they have been mutilated; they often fear losing their "wholeness" and "femininity" as a result of losing a breast (Stolar, 1982). A partner may refrain from close physical contact for fear that he may hurt his spouse at the surgery site or possibly remind her of changes in her body. Support from loved ones and reassurance of one's desirability are extremely important.

Anderson and Jochimsen (1985) have observed that difficulty with sexual functioning is highest for cancer patients whose disease is located at a sexual body site. Two groups that are particularly at risk are women with breast cancer or gynecological cancer (that is, cancer of cervix, endometrium, or ovary). When changes in sexual behaviors occur, it is important to understand their origins in order to offer appropriate intervention.

Fears of recurrence are also often strongest immediately after treatment. For some individuals, this fear will persist for years or it may be reactivated at followup visits by new symptoms that may be unrelated to the cancer, and by events or environmental cues that remind them of their vulnerability and their experience with cancer. If treatment is unsuccessful or the disease reappears, the issues the individual faces are markedly altered. Although hope may continue for an extended remission or for remaining periods of comfortable and productive life, the patient's experience will be very different from that of a survivor in complete remission. As adults experience the impact of the cancer on

SURVIVING CANCER ACROSS A LIFETIME
JANET TREVER

I have the dubious honor of thus far being a 50-year cancer survivor. The first was a terminal neuroblastoma behind my right eye at age five, then a mastectomy at age 35, and most recently a salivary gland cancer at 48. All were primary cancers and unrelated, yet it is clear to me now that my body "does this" and future genetic research into cancer repressor genes will probably show why.

Like in the opening lines of *A Tale of Two Cities,* I've known the best of times and the worst of times. I learned over the years to treasure and transform life, whenever possible. Since high school years I've designed, sewn, and worn hundreds of

matching eye patches as a result of my eye loss; they reframe the frightening and unnatural appearance of the immovable artificial eye & lid implant of my childhood into interest in my uniqueness and appreciation for my creativity. In college, my sorority sisters asked to borrow my fanciest patches with the agreement that they would each tell me about their adventures while wearing them.

Music, theater, and movies often have a direct line to my inner self and distract me from surgical or treatment pain and the accompanying gnawing fears about the future. Whenever I have been a hospital patient, I have had music playing around

(Continued)

their bodies as well as on their careers and personal relationships, feelings of helplessness are often accentuated.

Fortunately, much progress has been made in detecting and treating many types of cancer. Of patients diagnosed with cancer in 1997, 4 out of every 10 can be expected to be alive 5 years later. This 5-year survival rate, however, varies considerably by type of cancer and stage of detection; for example, it is only 14% for lung cancer compared to 87% for prostate cancer (all stages combined) (American Cancer Society, 1997).

Alzheimer's Disease and the Elderly

As discussed earlier in this chapter, physical changes are inevitable as individuals grow older, and these changes may be perceived as states of loss or threats of loss. In certain age-related diseases that are not a part of normal aging, symptoms such as memory loss, personality change, and diminished intellectual capacities are present. Because of these changes, few first-person accounts are available to help us understand how these losses are experienced by the older person. We do know however that many families face an ambiguous loss, as described in chapter 3.

An ambiguous loss occurs when a person is still physically present but is perceived as being psychologically absent (Boss, 1991). The grief of family members

(Continued From Previous Page)

the clock in my room. One hospitalization did not offer the option of a private room for the days of postsurgical recovery, so a friend loaned me a little flat speaker that goes under the bed pillow and attaches to a cassette tape player. Even when semiconscious, I could hear comforting classics, hauntingly beautiful chants, or affirmative lyrics without disturbing anyone else. It is wonderful to drift in and out of consciousness on the wings of music.

I love to look forward to a future event: a trip, a celebration, an invitation, even if it seems impossible as I lie flat in bed with brain swelling. I will crawl over to the dresser to pull out clothes for packing, just to somehow make the future plans more concrete.

After 2 very rough years of recovering from heavy neutron radiation I got a sheltie puppy—an affirmation of ongoing life force and loving energy, a plan to stick around for a while, and a guarantee of lots of positive touch to counteract my overload of painful medical touch.

I feel justified in living when I leave things better than I found them, leave behind footprints in the sand that will help someone else. I volunteer for the Yul Brynner Head and Neck Cancer Foundation, the Cancer Wellness Center in Illinois, for local hospital staff training, and for numerous requests for speaking. Against all odds, I've had a rich, unique, incredible life including a marriage, having children, working with many world famous innovators and role models; it seems crucial to find a way to give back.

cannot be resolved because the final death and loss are yet to occur. Alzheimer's disease is an example of this type of loss. In the early stages of the disease, individuals seem forgetful and have difficulty remembering recent events (e.g., that they made a phone call or turned off the stove). As the disease progresses, persons become more confused and their judgment becomes increasingly impaired. Slowly, their behaviors become more and more inappropriate and their personalities appear altered. In addition, language becomes limited; Alzheimer's patients may have difficulty communicating their thoughts. Before death occurs, individuals with Alzheimer's disease move into an almost infantile state and need assistance with eating, dressing, and personal hygiene (Belsky, 1984).

In Alzheimer's disease, as with other types of **dementia,** the person that loved ones once knew is dying a little at a time, and "only fragments of familiar behaviors and personality remain as sorrowful reminders to the family of what has been lost" (Kapust, 1982, p. 79). Watching these changes can be extremely painful, and family members often feel a sense of helplessness and outrage. Toynbee (1968) has commented that an assault by nature on human dignity occurs when the death of the human spirit precedes the death of its body. This process has been described as "dual dying" as the individual initially continues to have physical health while experiencing dramatic intellectual and social decline (Jones & Martinson, 1992).

THE COMPUTERLINK PROJECT: A WAY TO HELP CAREGIVERS

Spouses and adult children face a myriad of challenges as they care for loved ones diagnosed with dementia. Funded by a grant from the National Institutes on Aging, the ComputerLink Project provides family caregivers of Alzheimer's patients with information and support at home via computer terminals and phone lines. By using this electronic medium to connect with other caregivers in similar situations and to access a variety of information sources, family members feel they are better able to make informed decisions about plans of care. Technologically based interventions have high potential for timely and convenient contact with caregivers, offering many of the benefits of support groups and other more traditional service programs. Following is an example of an on-line "conversation" among participants in the ComputerLink Project.

From: Dorothy   Subject: Idle time

My husband is in the middle stages of the disease and I would like some suggestions on how to occupy his time other than walking. When he doesn't have anything to do, he seems to want to nap during the day.

From e.k.   Subject: Re: Idle time

Dorothy, I also have a problem with my wife who likes to walk and gets bored! She loves to rearrange her drawers in her dresser! I fix and she rearranges them, it

(Continued)

Kapust (1982) has described living with dementia as "an ongoing funeral" for the healthy spouse and other family members. She points out that although the family grieves for the losses, no formalized rituals exist to help them through this time. Lezak (1978) also supports this view: "The spouse cannot mourn decently. Although he lost his mate as surely and permanently as if by death, since the familiar body remains, society neither recognizes the spouse's grief, nor provides the support and comfort that surrounds those bereaved by death" (p. 593).

Diseases such as Alzheimer's that tend to occur during the later stages of life prompt reactions among family and friends that can make interactions and extended care very difficult. The family's grief is often accompanied by feelings of helplessness. The family can do nothing to alter the situation, but they must cope with the changes that occur and observe the continued deterioration until death comes.

SUMMARY

Intimacy versus isolation is the psychosocial crisis of young adulthood. Dying persons of this age span strive to become emotionally close to others—a task that is especially difficult because limited time raises questions as to whether

(Continued From Previous Page)

gives her something to do! They always seem to want to be occupied and want to help but is hard for her! Do your best on this subject.

From: SB   Subject: Re: Idle time

Hi, this is Sue (login SB). I noticed a reply to Idle Time. Idle time is a real tough one. My mother-in-law is in day care 5 days a week which helps during the day. She is in middle stages. She always wants to be doing something when she is home. I have a real hard time trying to figure things for her to do. She loves to go shopping. I try doing that a few times during the week or I take her for a ride. I have children's books we try reading. I have her read and sort playing cards. These are a few things that I do. I take her for walks, she does dishes

(they generally have to be done again, but it is something for her to do). It sounds like I have found a few things to occupy her time but believe me it is not enough. The weekends are the worst. Are there things for them to do without you (or I should say me) having to be right with them? That is the problem!! There are things to do, but I have to be with her to do them and I can't get anything done of my own.

Has anyone out there found something for our loved ones to do on their own? I spend 2 to 5 hours a day entertaining her and sometimes it is a drain. My mother-in-law once she sees me is pretty much attached to me, looking to me to occupy her time.

SOURCE: P. F. Brennan & S. M. Moore, (1994). Networks for home care support: The ComputerLink project. *Caring Magazine,* August, 64–70.

one should marry, have children, and make other interpersonal commitments. Investment of time in a career or in additional education involve other important decisions as these young adults seek fulfillment of aspirations.

Middle-aged persons typically take stock of their lives and then face the decision whether to recommit themselves to choices made earlier or make changes. Many individuals at midlife desire to leave a legacy and be remembered as someone who made a contribution to their family or to the larger society. Dying individuals at this age are often less concerned about death per se and more concerned about their responsibilities and obligations to others that they fear may go unmet after they die.

Individuals in their later years attempt to come to terms with their past through the process of life review. If a person concludes that his or her life has been well spent, ego integrity is the predominant outcome, as compared to despair. Elderly patients need to participate in decisions regarding their lives and thereby retain a sense of independence and control. In a youth-oriented society, family members and health care professionals need to reassure older persons that their lives still have value, because the elderly sometimes fear that they will die a "social death" prior to their actual physical death. For the elderly to receive quality health care, health care professionals need a better understanding of the aging process and awareness of the negative effects of ageism.

Oftentimes, the elderly experience grief related to the accumulation of physical changes that occur with age. Body image may be altered due to such common age-related changes as reduced muscle strength, sensory loss, and changes in appearance. The extent of these losses and the reactions to them vary considerably from individual to individual. Over time, these losses tend to accumulate and threaten one's identity, independence, and self-esteem. For some older persons, these changes involve disability, chronic health problems, and restricted mobility. These losses lead the elderly and their families to make many psychological adjustments and adaptations. By recognizing and mourning each loss, individuals and their families can begin to come to terms with aging and the approach of death, thereby helping to retain the integrity of the remaining life of the elderly.

The issues that adults and their families face as they cope with life-threatening illness will depend on unique aspects of their particular disease process related to onset, course, outcome, and level of incapacitation. An individual's illness type and phase will to a large extent define specific loss issues that will be faced prior to death. Predeath losses associated with disease can include loss of social support, impaired body functioning, physical disfigurement, and a change in personality and cognitive abilities.

Personal Account

Using a letter format, the author shares her emotional reactions to her second experience with breast cancer and the threats it posed to her sense of self. She also emphasizes the potential for personal growth and self-awareness that often accompany a health crisis.

Excerpt From Love, Judy
Judy Hart

Dear Reader,

Recently my oncologist asked if I'd talk with a patient who was going through a rough patch emotionally. It was my conversations with her that reminded me of an important issue. A diagnosis of cancer brings a jumble of fears, including fear of dying, loss of body parts or disfiguration, pain, upheaval in work, lifestyle, finances, and perhaps relationships. These are no small fears, but you may experience another fear that could be harder to define, and may be playing into other fears—namely the fear of losing yourself, your self-identity or self-esteem.

SOURCE: J. Hart (1993). *Love, Judy: Letters of hope and healing for women with breast cancer.* Berkeley, CA: Conari Press.

Some women know they have this fear. Others may not have identified it and may benefit from having it brought into the light. Perhaps there are patients for whom it plays little or no part, but I bet it's woven in, however subtly, for almost everyone.

Words are inadequate to define our sense of self, because it is made up of more than we can articulate. I see it as the core of each person. It's what makes each of us feel: *This is who I am; this is what makes me a worthwhile person; this is at the very center of the meaning of my life.* We can probably list some of the elements that make up our sense of self. It may include roles such as mother or partner, and self-images such as "sexy" or "in control," and it is even more informative if we define just what a role or self-image consists of personally. One person's "sexy" or "good mother" differs from another's and may be more or less affected by cancer. But unquestionably, cancer takes an especially hard toll on us if it threatens those things we identify as essential to who we are. So what aspects of this whole blooming business threaten *your* sense of self?

The most obvious cluster might be in the area of sexuality and feminine identity. Breast cancer treatment may affect sexual pleasure, appearance, and relationship with sex partners. All of us breast cancer patients have to grapple with these issues, but how deeply will vary. Depending on the nature of the cancer and treatment, they may be temporary discomforts or changes for life.

The negative impact of my first breast cancer on my sexuality and appearance was minor and short term. My breast was tender and hypersensitive if knocked against for some time, my lumpectomy scar was unnoticeable, my radiation suntan diminished with time, and I looked normal when dressed. I even enjoyed heightened pleasure in the nipple for about a year after radiation. However, my second cancer changed my life forever. The double mastectomy felt like a significant loss to my sexuality. On the plus side were my long, committed relationship with my husband and the fact that I was clear about sacrificing my breasts to save my life.

As a person who lives a high-on-comfort, low-on-fashion life, I never investigated wearing prostheses. I experienced a spell of mild self-consciousness about my flat chest, but now it is as totally me as were large breasts previously. If I had lost the benefit of breasts, then I was going to revel in the freedom from the discomfort of harnessing bras—certainly not replace them with another nuisance! After the amount of medical intrusion into my body, I had no desire to do reconstruction surgery. Though I never said it in so many words, there's no way of knowing what life span is ahead of me, and I wanted to get back to physical well-being as soon as possible and enjoy it for as long as possible. My choices were made before questions arose about the safety of breast implants, so that was not a consideration. Although I miss the appearance, and, more importantly, the pleasure of breasts, and occasionally still feel the sting of my losses, my sense of self was not impaired. This is an example of what might potentially be the greatest threat to self-identity turning out not to be so. For another woman, it might cause a greater threat to self-identity. How your sexual partner feels about and deals with it and how openly you can talk about it will also be factors. But loss is loss. If we encounter whatever the losses are, I think ultimately we'll find the self intact. (I see *encounter* as a series of small, not necessarily, recognizable steps. Your reading and musing about this may be part of your encounter.)

Threat to self, especially to sexual self-image, might even be a determining factor in choice of treatment. This is particularly true if mastectomy is recommended. The woman my oncologist put in touch with me told me she had said to him, "If you save my life, but lose me, the person, you haven't done me any favors." She was relieved that her concern was received as an important factor in how they should proceed—and I give a big thumbs-up to my doctor for his responsiveness to her as a whole person.

The issue of fear of loss of self may not be fully understood or valued by family, friends, and even some doctors. They all want you to get well, and their anxiety is often best alleviated by knowing that you're "doing all the right things" and "have a wonderful attitude." They may not be aware that this could put pressure on you. Some of your divergences from these models of perfection may be connected to fear of loss of self. The more you can identify which things threaten your sense of self, the more you will be able to make your choices consciously, explain your needs to others, and when necessary, protect yourself from well-meaning people who pressure you.

What about loss of hair? It can not only alter our sense of femininity, but so changes our face that it can make us feel not like ourselves. Wearing a wig made me feel framed by something alien and artificial as well as physically uncomfortable. In contrast, my colorful, goofy hats suited my sense of self and allowed its playful aspect to shine. Wigs may be less of a problem for women who wear them purely for style or for whom time spent on hairdos and makeup is an integral part of their day. I found I would have been more threatened if my hair hadn't grown back than I was by the loss of breasts. I never would have guessed that in advance. Perhaps we are more adaptable than we realize; I was called on to say only a temporary good-bye to my hair, but I had to deal with the permanent loss of my breasts.

Does the intrusion of cancer on your work, your professional life, and your creative life also affect your sense of self? For me, the diagnosis of cancer interrupting the book I was writing was a major threat to my sense of self. Although that book got stashed, and I didn't encounter my grief about it until two years later when looking to see if parts of it could be incorporated into this book, writing the cancer letters kept my identity as a writer.

Which other aspects of your situation threaten your sense of self? Losing accustomed independence and self-sufficiency? Being forever peered at and poked in a partially undressed state? Let's face it: Heads of state and corporate power-houses do not do business in hospital gowns. Even if you do not feel the need to dress for success, the hospital gown does not clothe your self-image!

Your sense of self could also be threatened by distressed or angry feelings popping out when and where you'd rather they didn't. You may attach a lot to feeling in control. Cancer sure gets in the way of that! What about the phrases "having cancer," "being sick," and "being a cancer patient"? You may identify yourself as a healthy person who doesn't fuss and complain, and suddenly you may feel like a fusser and complainer.

You may think of things that are particular to you that you can't imagine anyone else understanding, not even another person with breast cancer. Be sure to name and honor those things too. When you've covered the easily named things that feel important to your sense of self, you might ask if that covers it or if there is something you haven't yet gotten hold of. You might open up to further discovery by spending time with some sense you have of yourself that you may not yet have words to describe. Slop around on the paper with messy prose or scribbled drawings or ask a good, non-interfering listener to let you explore the question aloud. Try taking a moment to listen inside your body and see if anything comes into awareness, and then see if you can describe what it is, or just be with the feeling. I recall touching a deep sense of myself when doing impromptu expressive movement in my living room. What came was something like: I'm here inside myself, right at my own center, whole and free, in the midst of all this cancer treatment whirligig.

*   *   *

Although I see the self as ongoing through our lives, different facets may be important at different times. We may feel more grounded in the self and more "like ourselves" in some stages of life than in others. You may also want to include an assessment of how grounded or off balance your sense of self feels.

How hard cancer, or any crisis, hits emotionally is greatly affected by where we are in life when it strikes, and where we are in relation to self and our deepest personal meanings. What stage of life are/were you in at the time of diagnosis and treatment, and what defines you in this period?

Are you in middle age, perhaps dealing with aging parents, teenagers' problems, or other major demands? Are you experiencing the empty nest or/and midlife crisis, trying to figure out where to go from here, perhaps feeling that you've lost a familiar sense of self and not yet forged a new one? Are you in a bumpy place in your primary relationship or in your work? Are you in full rush in a career that needs you to give your all? Are you just starting a new relationship? Have you left an old relationship without a new one yet on the horizon, but are hoping for one? Have you daughters whose cancer risk is higher now, or who are developing breasts just as you are having breast disease? Are you among the now-younger generation of women getting breast cancer in their thirties and early forties, occasionally even in their twenties? Are treatments bringing on an early menopause? Are you pregnant? Have you a new baby or young children? Have you just gotten a lot of stuff behind you and were ready to embark or just embarked on something new? Are you grappling with problems of aging? Does cancer come on top of other health problems? Are you grieving for the death of a spouse or someone else important? Have you just moved to a new house, living arrangement, or community? Or is this a time that is fairly stable? There's no such thing as a good time to get cancer, but timing and some conditions in your life can certainly add to or ease the burden.

As you contemplate the phase of your life in which cancer struck, allow yourself to step back and see what your timing and circumstances look like. What are the particular meanings for you? Do they threaten your self-identity? Acknowledge whatever is nasty in your situation. "No wonder I'm having a rough time," you might say. "As if it's not bad enough to have cancer, it's coming at this time when. . . ."

As you look at those things which make the particular moment difficult, you might also see if there are aspects of your life and sense of self that offer support. For instance, I had gone through menopause about a year before my diagnosis, so I not only didn't have to deal with the physiological and emotional effects of chemo-induced menopause, but also had largely ridden out the bumpiest issues of aging and self connected to that passage.

You may also want to consider what aspects of your self are alive and well in spite of crisis. Are there things you thought would threaten you deeply and turned out not to? Are you finding some new strength and shift of meaning as you take on this challenge?

During my first cancer I worked on my timidity about telephoning doctors to ask something I forgot when I was there. I realized the distance I had traveled on this issue when, a few months ago, a pain in my arm suddenly triggered cancer fears. My rational self thought it highly unlikely and that my anxiety was piggybacking on other anxieties. Even though I had a regular checkup in ten days, I telephoned to talk to someone rather than live with unnecessary fear.

Give yourself credit when you see such a change in your behavior. And remember that whenever you make a conscious choice of small daring, it yields the benefit of personal growth that outlasts the crisis. The very things that threaten your sense of self may well be the cause not of loss of self, but rather of deepening of self.

Although your view of yourself may get shaken up, you may also discover that your self-identity goes deeper than the things you thought it depended on. I believe that whatever you face and whatever you bring to your encounter will enrich and strengthen the very self you may fear to lose.

Here's to your self: the one you have already developed, are enriching, and will come to know better because of your experience.

Love, Judy

QUESTIONS AND ACTIVITIES

1. In Judy's letter, she talks about her sense of "self." In what ways was Judy's sense of self strengthened and enhanced by her experience with cancer? Identify characteristics of your own sense of self and consider how your self-image might be affected by a major illness. In what ways do you think personality affects coping style and how was this demonstrated in the personal account?

2. Select three potentially life-threatening diseases not mentioned in this chapter. Compare and contrast them using the factors identified in Rolland's model (onset, course, outcome, and level of incapacitation). In what ways would these factors influence the subjective experience of each illness and how might this vary by individual?

3. Rank order the following in terms of your definition of "a good death." Identify the underlying values associated with your rankings, and discuss these with a classmate.
   a. Amelia, age 87, at home after 15 years of feeling more or less "useless" due to chronic health impairments.
   b. Fernando, age 42, suddenly of a heart attack while at work.
   c. Carl, age 57, after 4 weeks in the hospital, having experienced much pain but having the opportunity to say goodbye to family members and close friends.
   d. Lupe, age 27, in an automobile accident that left her husband and two young children uninjured.
   e. Ian, age 72, in a nursing home 6 months after his wife died.

4. Interview several adults of varying ages and inquire about their attitudes toward quality-of-life issues. Do they appear to have strong opinions about how they want to spend their final days? Are the issues different for them than they were for their parents a generation ago? How has the context of death changed?

GLOSSARY

Ageism: discrimination against the elderly solely on the basis of their age.

Dementia: progressive mental deterioration due to organic disease of the brain; typically, impairment of memory is one of the earliest signs.

Despair: the negative resolution of Erikson's late adulthood stage. The elderly view their lives as poorly spent and feel that it is too late to compensate for unfortunate choices made earlier in life.

Diagnostically related groups (DRG): diagnostic group in which a particular treatment is classified in order to determine the amount of a payment under a prospective-payment system.

Ego integrity: the positive resolution of Erikson's late adulthood stage. It results in positive acceptance of one's own life experiences.

Generativity: the positive resolution of Erikson's middle adulthood stage. A deep concern for the next generation and a desire to contribute to the future by channeling one's energy and creativity in a direction that will produce lasting and worthwhile results.

Geriatrics: the field of medicine that focuses on the care of the elderly.

Gerontology: the study of the psychological, sociological, and biological aspects of the aging process.

Interiority: the introspection and self-reflection observed among the elderly.

Intimacy: the positive outcome of Erikson's young adulthood crisis. Intimacy involves the ability to experience an open, supportive, and close relationship with another person, without fear of losing oneself in the process. The positive resolution of Erikson's middle adulthood stage.

Isolation: the negative outcome of Erikson's young adulthood crisis. Isolation is the inability to develop intimate relationships, which leads to preoccupation with oneself and superficial relationships with others.

Life review: process of surveying and reflecting on one's past through reminiscence.

Prospective-payment system (PPS): a system by which a predetermined amount is paid by Medicare for a patient's medical treatment.

Psychogenic mortality: a syndrome in which a person's psychological condition triggers physical effects that lead ultimately to death.

Stagnation: the negative resolution of Erikson's middle adulthood stage which results in focusing inward on oneself rather than contributing to others.

Stock-taking: the questioning and life evaluation that occurs at midlife as individuals become increasingly aware of their own mortality.

SUGGESTED READINGS

Harpham, W. S. (1994). *After cancer: A guide to your new life.* New York: W. W. Norton.

Written by a physician who was herself diagnosed with lymphoma, this book focuses on recovery from cancer. Physical aftereffects of treatment as well as emotional and practical issues of survivorship are covered.

Jecker, N. S. (Ed.). (1991). *Aging and ethics: Philosophical problems in gerontology.* Clifton, NJ: Humana Press.

Bioethical issues as they relate to an aging society are considered by leading scholars in the field. Included are discussions of a just distribution of medical resources between generations, responsible medical decision making, and health care goals for older Americans. Two competing fears of elderly persons who are dying are also covered: abandonment and lack of care on the one hand, and excessive treatment and painful extension of their lives on the other.

McCarthy, D. E. (1995). AIDS and its effect on a business partnership: Crisis intervention and follow-up. *Clinical Social Work Journal, 23*(2), 173–183.

A case study is used to address a variety of psychodynamic, social, economic, and systemic factors that influence the success or failure of a small business in which one partner has AIDS. The brief intervention strategies employed by the consultant deals with the effects of the illness on the working relationship.

Underwood, M. R. (1995). *Diary of a death professional.* Hartford, CT: Association for Death Education and Counseling.

A professional in the field of thanatology for over 20 years, Mirrless Underwood shares her own experience of coping with cancer and interacting with the American medical system. Entries from her personal journal are intertwined with anecdotes from her career as a death educator and counselor.

Yeo, G., & Gallagher-Thompson, D. (Eds.). (1996). *Ethnicity and the dementias.* Washington, DC: Taylor & Francis.

This edited volume discusses variations in dementia characteristics among ethnic groups in the United States, assessment of cognitive status among different ethnic populations, and the role of families in providing support to an impaired relative. Cultural dynamics are discussed in terms of service delivery, policy issues, and future research.

RESOURCES

AIDS Action Council
1875 Connecticut Avenue, N.W.
Suite 700
Washington, DC 20009
(202) 986-1300

Alzheimer's Disease and Related Disorders Association
919 N. Michigan Avenue
Suite 1000
Chicago, IL 60611
(312) 335-8700

American Cancer Society
(CanSurmount, Reach to Recovery, I Can Cope)
1599 Clifton, N.E.
Atlanta, GA 30329-4251
(404) 320-3333

American Heart Association
7272 Greenville Avenue
Dallas, TX 75231-4596
(214) 373-6300

National Stroke Association
96 Inverness Drive, East
Suite I
Englewood, CO 80112
(303) 649-9299

REFERENCES

American Association of Retired Persons. (1993). *A portrait of older minorities.* Washington, DC: Author.

American Association of Retired Persons. (1995). *A profile of older Americans.* Washington, DC: Author.

American Cancer Society. (1991). *Cancer facts and figures for minority Americans—1991.* Atlanta, GA: Author.

American Cancer Society. (1996). *Cancer facts and figures—1996.* Atlanta, GA: Author.

American Cancer Society. (1997). *Cancer facts and figures—1997.* Atlanta, GA: Author.

American Heart Association. (1997). *1997 Heart and stroke statistical update.* Dallas, TX: Author.

Anderson, B. L., & Jochimsen, P. R. (1985). Sexual functioning among breast cancer, gynecologic cancer, and healthy women. *Journal of Consulting and Clinical Psychology, 53*(1), 25–32.

Baltz, T. M., & Turner, J. G. (1977). Development and analysis of a nursing home screening device. *The Gerontologist, 17,* 66–69.

Banziger, G., & Roush, S. (1983). Nursing homes for the birds: A control-relevant intervention with bird feeders. *The Gerontologist, 23,* 527–531.

Belsky, J. K. (1984). *The psychology of aging: Theory, research, and practice.* Monterey, CA: Brooks/Cole.

Bor, R., Miller, R., & Goldman, E. (1993). HIV/AIDS and the family: A review of research in the first decade. *Journal of Family Therapy, 15,* 187–204.

Boss, P. (1991). Ambiguous loss. In F. Walsh & M. McGoldrick (Eds.), *Living beyond loss* (pp. 164–175). New York: Norton.

Butler, R., & Lewis, M. (1982). *Aging and mental health* (2nd ed.). St. Louis, MO: Mosby.

Butler, R. N. (1963). The life review: An interpretation of reminiscence in the aged. *Psychiatry, 26,* 65–76.

Dane, B. O., & Levine, C. (1994). *AIDS and the new orphans.* Westport, CT: Auburn House.

Donlou, J., Wolcott, D., Gottlieb, M., & Landsverk, J. (1985). Psychosocial aspects of AIDS and AIDS-related complex: A pilot study. *Journal of Psychosocial Oncology, 3*(2), 39–55.

Dowd, J. (1980). *Stratification among the aged: An analysis of power and dependence.* Monterey, CA: Brooks/Cole.

Erikson, E. H. (1950). *Childhood and society.* New York: Norton.

Erikson, E. H. (1959). Identity and the life cycle: Selected papers. *Psychological Issues,* Monograph No. 1.

Erikson, E. H. (1968). Generativity and ego integrity. In B. L. Neugarten (Ed.), *Middle age and aging* (pp. 85–87). Chicago: University of Chicago Press.

Erikson, E. H., & Erikson, J. M. (1981). On generativity and identity: From a conversation with Erik and Joan Erikson. *Harvard Educational Review, 51,* 249–269.

Gideon, M. D., & Taylor, P. B. (1981). A sexual bill of rights for dying persons. *Death Education, 4,* 303–314.

Hooyan, N., & Kiyak, H. A. (1996). *Social gerontology: A multidisciplinary perspective* (4th ed.). Needham Heights, MA: Simon & Schuster.

Intrieri, R. C., Kelly, J. A., Brown, M. M., & Castilla, C. (1993). Improving medical students' attitudes toward and skills with the elderly. *The Gerontologist, 33*(3), 373–378.

Jones, P. S., & Martinson, I. M. (1992). The experience of bereavement in caregivers of family members with Alzheimer's disease. *IMAGE: Journal of Nursing Scholarship, 24*(3), 172–176.

Kalish, R. A. (1985). Death and dying in a social context. In R. H. Binstock & E. Shanas (Eds.), *Handbook of aging and the social sciences* (2nd ed.; pp. 149–170). New York: Van Nostrand.

Kane, R. L., Solomon, D. H., Beck, J. C., Keeler, E., & Kane, R. A. (1981). *Geriatrics in the United States: Manpower projections and training considerations.* Lexington, MA: D. C. Heath.

Kapust, L. R. (1982). Living with dementia: The ongoing funeral. *Social Work in Health Care, 7*(4), 79–91.

Kelly, B., & Raphael, B. (1993). AIDS: Coping with ongoing terminal illness. In J. P. Wilson & B. Raphael (Eds.), *International handbook of traumatic stress syndromes* (pp. 517-525). New York: Plenum Press.

Koocher, G. P. (1986). Coping with a death from cancer. *Journal of Consulting and Clinical Psychology, 54*(5), 623-631.

Lear, M. W. (1980). *Heartsounds.* New York: Simon & Schuster.

Lezak, M. D. (1978). Living with characterologically altered brain injured patients. *Journal of Clinical Psychiatry, 39,* 592-598.

Lowenthal, M. F., & Weiss, L. (1976). Intimacy and crisis in adulthood. *Counseling Psychologist, 6*(1), 10-15.

MacElveen-Hoehn, P. (1993). Sexual responses to the stimulus of death. In J. D. Morgan (Ed.), *Personal care in an impersonal world: A multidimensional look at bereavement* (pp. 95-119). Amityville, NY: Baywood.

Maizler, J. S., Solomon, J. R., & Almquist, E. (1983). Psychogenic mortality syndrome: Choosing to die by the institutionalized elderly. *Death Education, 6,* 353-364.

Moller, D. W. (1990). *On death with dignity: The human impact of technological dying.* Amityville, NY: Baywood.

Morgan, J. D. (1995). Living our dying and our grieving: Historical and cultural attitudes. In H. Wass & R. A. Neimeyer (Ed.), *Dying: Facing the facts* (3rd ed.; pp. 25-45). Washington, DC: Taylor & Francis.

Mutchler, J. E., & Burr, J. A. (1991). Racial differences in health and health care service utilization in later life: The effect of socioeconomic status. *Journal of Health and Social Behavior, 32,* 342-356.

Neugarten, B. L. (1977). Personality and aging. In J. E. Birren & K. W. Schaie (Eds.), *Handbook of the psychology of aging* (pp. 626-649). New York: Van Nostrand.

O'Donnell, M. (1996). *HIV/AIDS: Loss, grief, challenge, and hope.* Washington, DC: Taylor & Francis.

Pattison, E. M. (1977). *The experience of dying.* Englewood Cliffs, NJ: Prentice-Hall.

Rando, T. A. (1984). *Grief, dying, and death: Clinical interventions for caregivers.* Champaign, IL: Research Press.

Riekse, R. J., & Holstege, H. (1996). *Growing old in America.* New York: McGraw-Hill.

Rolland, J. S. (1987). Chronic illness and the life cycle: A conceptual framework. *Family Process, 26,* 203-221.

Rolland, J. S. (1991). Helping families with anticipatory loss. In F. Walsh & M. McGoldrick (Eds.), *Living beyond loss* (pp. 144-163). New York: Norton.

Schiamberg, L. B. (1985). *Human development* (2nd ed.). New York: Macmillan.

Sherr, L. (1995). The experience of grief: Psychologic aspects of grief in AIDS and HIV infection. In L. Sherr (Ed.), *Grief and AIDS* (pp. 1-27). New York: Wiley.

Siegal, F. P., & Siegal, M. (1983). *AIDS: The medical mystery.* New York: Grove Press.

Solomon, K. (1982). Social antecedents of learned helplessness in the health care setting. *The Gerontologist, 22,* 282-287.

Stephenson, J. S. (1985). *Death, grief, and mourning: Individual and social realities.* New York: Free Press.

Stevens-Long, J., & Commons, M. L. (1992). *Adult life* (4th ed.). Mountain View, CA: Mayfield.

Stolar, G. E. (1982). Coping with mastectomy: Issues for social work. *Health and Social Work, 7*(1), 26-34.

Tobin, S. (1985). Psychodynamic treatment of the family and the institutionalized individual. In N. Miller & G. D. Cohen (Eds.), *Psychodynamic research perspectives on development, psychopathology, and treatment in later life.* New York: International Universities Press.

Toynbee, A. (1968). *Man's concern with death.* New York: McGraw-Hill.

U.S. Bureau of the Census. (1993). *Statistical abstracts of the United States, 1993.* Washington, DC: U.S. Government Printing Office.

U.S. Center for Health Statistics. (1997). Washington, DC: U.S. Government Printing Office.

U.S. House of Representatives Select Subcommittee on Aging. (1992). *Geriatricians and the senior boom: Precarious present, uncertain future.* Washington, DC: U.S. Government Printing Office.

Verwoerdt, A. (1985). Individual psychopathology in senile dementia. In N. Miller & G. D. Cohen (Eds.), *Psychodynamic research perspectives on development, psychopathology, and treatment in later life.* New York: International Universities Press.

Wasserman, A. L., Thompson, E. I., Wilimas, J. A., & Fairclough, D. L. (1987). The psychological status of survivors of childhood/adolescent Hodgkin's disease. *American Journal of Diseases of Children, 141*(6), 626–631.

8

Grief and Loss During Adulthood

Most individuals experience loss at some time during their adult years. Some of these losses are untimely, as in the death of a child, whereas others can be anticipated and are part of the normal course of events as we age. Nonetheless, each has its own set of related issues and adjustments. In this chapter, major losses of adulthood and their ramifications will be discussed, as well as interventions available to adults to help them cope.

WIDOWHOOD

Loss of a spouse (referred to as **conjugal loss**) is a common occurrence during the later years of life. Because marital partners rarely die at the same time, either a husband or a wife eventually must face the loss of this primary relationship. The remaining spouse is typically a female as shown in Table 8.1. Among persons over the age of 75 in the United States, 64.9% of females are widowed as compared with 21.6% of males in this age category (U.S. Bureau of the Census, 1996). Both the longer life span of women and the tendency to marry men older than themselves contribute to these differential rates. Due to their lower numbers, considerably less research has been done on widowers than on widows.

Loss of a spouse at any time during the adult years involves a variety of adjustments. Emotional responses, role loss, social adjustments, and financial issues must all be faced (see Figure 8.1).

Emotional Adjustment

Emotional adjustment is perhaps the most difficult aspect of widowhood. Loss of a spouse involves loss of a primary relationship. Depending on the length of the marriage, many couples have shared their youths, had children together, and supported each other during many life transitions and family crises. They have

TABLE 8.1

Percentage of Widowed Individuals, Classified by Sex and Age Level, 1995

AGE	MEN	WOMEN
35–44 years	0.4	1.3
45–54 years	1.0	4.2
55–64 years	2.8	12.9
65–74 years	8.6	33.1
Over 75 years	21.6	64.9

SOURCE: U.S. Bureau of the Census (1996). *Statistical Abstract of the United States: 1996* (116th ed.). Washington, DC: U.S. Government Printing Office.

FIGURE 8.1
Major Aspects of Adjustment to Widowhood

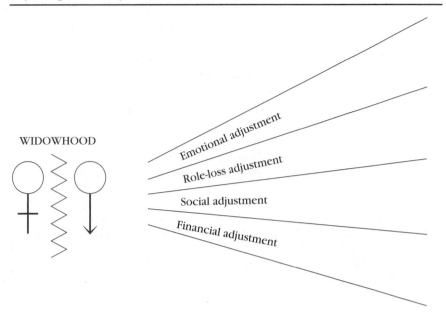

been friends, companions, and sexual partners. Loss of this "significant other" can have a profound emotional impact. Loss of a husband or wife is, in fact, ranked as one of the most stressful of all potential life changes on life event scales (Holmes & Rahe, 1967; see Table 4.1 in chapter 4).

When examining the grief process and the subsequent adjustment, age appears to be a particularly salient factor. Developmental stage of the griever, length of the relationship, and length of life remaining can significantly alter the way in which one copes with a loss.

Older women often engage in mental rehearsals of their own potential widowhood as they watch friends and relatives lose loved ones. Thus, they have the opportunity to make plans in the event they should survive their spouses. For the young married person, loss of a spouse is usually unanticipated and few, if any, preparations have been made for this eventuality. The grief response of widows and widowers often involves a feeling of being abandoned or deserted. When conjugal loss occurs during the early years of marriage, the remaining spouse often has concerns about being left as a single parent. The thought of raising children alone can be frightening for some.

Anger and guilt may also be strong components of the grief experienced in conjugal bereavement. Anger is often present if the bereaved feels that the deceased's death was induced or hastened by failure to seek medical care, lack of compliance with the physician's advice, or continuation of self-destructive

---

MEN SPEAK OF GRIEF

When someone you love dies, and you're not expecting it, you don't lose her all at once; you lose her in pieces over a long time—the way the mail stops coming, and the scent fades from the pillows and even from the clothes in her closet and drawers. Gradually you accumulate the parts of her that are gone. Just when the day comes—when there's a particular missing part that overwhelms you with the feeling that she's gone forever—there comes another day, and another specifically missing part.

John Irving
A Prayer for Owen Meany

Her absence is like the sky, spread over everything. . . .

I have no photograph of her that's any good. I cannot even see her face distinctly in my imagination. Yet the odd face of some stranger seen in a crowd this morning may come before me in vivid perfection the moment I close my eyes tonight. No doubt, the explanation is simple enough. We have seen the faces of those we know best so variously, from so many angles, in so many lights, with so many expressions—waking, sleeping, laughing, crying, eating, talking, thinking—that all the impressions crowd in our memory together and cancel out in a mere blur.

C. S. Lewis
A Grief Observed

SOURCES: John Irving, *A Prayer for Owen Meany;* C. S. Lewis, *A Grief Observed.*

---

habits. Failure to prepare for the family's financial well-being in the event of death can also be a source of anger. Expressions of anger toward the deceased can be shocking to some who are attempting to provide comfort to the bereaved. The outcome of bereavement tends to be more negative when the bereaved feel they do not have a supportive environment in which to share the full range of emotions they are experiencing. Friends are generally considered supportive if, in addition to accepting the widow's feelings, they also allow the bereaved to discuss her past life, relationship with her husband, and events surrounding his death. An excessive focus by friends on the present and future while ignoring the past is often viewed by recently widowed individuals as unhelpful (Stylianos & Vachon, 1993).

Moss and Moss (1984) have argued that the elderly widow(er) after many years of marriage continues to maintain a deep attachment to the deceased. They emphasize that this emotional tie persists through the grieving period and that it is potentially a significant and permanent theme in the elderly person's life. Rather than viewing this persistent tie to the deceased as pathological and nonadaptive, Moss and Moss see it as normal, having been formed out of many years of being together. It also has the potential for enhancing the widow(er)'s identity and sense of well-being. By remaining affected by the memory of the deceased, continuity is maintained by integrating the past with the present. This view is consistent with the "continuing bonds" paradigm of grief introduced in chapter 3 (Klass, Silverman, & Nickman, 1996).

The memory of the deceased spouse appears to be a welcome one for the elderly, and it can serve as an emotional resource. Many elderly often report feeling "the caring presence" of their spouse years after the death. When making decisions, they frequently continue to consider what the husband or wife would think or do in a similar situation, thus continuing to influence the widow(er)'s behavior (Moss & Moss, 1984). Many times, photographs will be used to create a sense of presence. If widow(er)s enter a nursing home and are restricted to bringing only a few personal possessions, treasured pictures of the deceased spouse or the couple together are often included.

Moss and Moss (1984) point out that our society supports this persistent tie among the elderly widowed. Family and friends continue to recognize the older widow(er)'s link to the deceased spouse, as indicated by such phrases as "Mr. Hill's widow." Women tend to keep their deceased husband's name (e.g., Mrs. Ray Wong), and therefore they have daily reminders of their identity as the wife of their spouse. The home of the elderly also serves to support the ongoing emotional bond between the couple, serving as a constant reminder of the love and caring involved in the marital relationship and evoking a sense of continued care and security.

Role Loss and Related Adjustments

Widowhood is a very disorganizing experience. In addition to a personal loss, the individual often faces a major role loss as well. Reorganization of social roles is required whenever responsibilities are removed or added, or when the relative importance of existing roles is altered. The degree of disorganization depends on the degree to which the deceased was an integral part of the mate's life and self-concept, as well as the status of widow(er)s in the particular culture involved (Lopata, 1993). The degree of change experienced following the death of a spouse varies widely in different societies. In modern Western societies such as the United States, the degree of change resulting from death of a spouse is usually significant. The widowed individual often has to assume family roles left by the deceased. In the context of the nuclear family, much interdependence typically exists among family members. If gender roles were well defined in their marriage, the widowed individual needs to assume many unfamiliar tasks, often without the requisite knowledge and skills (Morgan, 1994). In marriages in which responsibilities have been jointly shared rather than assigned by gender, the transition may be smoother. However, most individuals widowed early in life experience role overload as they assume the sole responsibility for rearing children and the financial and emotional demands associated with parenting.

Not only are additional responsibilities assumed after a spouse dies, but a major role is lost as well. Unless remarriage occurs, the individual is no longer a "wife" or a "husband." This loss can be particularly devastating if the person has

CROSS-CULTURAL DIFFERENCES IN WIDOWHOOD: STATUS AND SUPPORT ISSUES

Israel

The economic and financial status of widows in Israel depends on the cause of the husband's death. The loss of status after death of a husband is greater for the "civilian" widow than for the war widow. The war widows are the most privileged, receiving financial aid and a variety of other services from the government. (Included in this category are all deaths connected to the security of the country, whether in military service or as a result of hostilities against the civilian population.) Consequently, war widows generally report that they are not worried with financial or bureaucratic problems. The following statement made by a member of Knesset Yalin-Mor reflects the national feeling of debt to the deceased and their families: "We are not granting (war widows) charity . . . we have to pay them ransom for our own lives . . . it is because of them that we have a free and independent homeland."

Reasonable pensions are also received by widows whose husbands died in work-related accidents. However, the majority of widows have lost a spouse due to illness or natural causes and receive only minimal support from social security.

India

In traditional Indian society, *suttee* (the act of bereaved wives throwing themselves on their deceased husband's burning funeral pyre) was practiced by higher caste Hindu widows as a form of sacrificial death. Today, widows from higher castes are still strongly discouraged (in some cases forbidden by custom) to remarry, but the practice of remarriage is fairly common among the lower caste. (No remarriage restrictions are placed on men who are widowed.) While widowhood diminishes a woman's status (e.g., she can no longer attend certain religious ceremonies), she still retains her power with the household. Upon marriage,

(Continued)

derived much of his or her life satisfaction from it. As children grow up and leave home during the parents' middle years, the marital relationship becomes even more important. For a woman who has invested most of her "self" in being a wife, the death of a husband can result in a major identity crisis. Accustomed to deriving much of her status and identity from her husband, she must now redefine who she is in the absence of that relationship. This personal struggle can be very difficult and confusing. Women who previously have had stable images of themselves and their purpose in life often have these images shattered by the experience of widowhood.

For other individuals, the loss of the spouse is not as traumatic. For some, the marital role is viewed as one among a complex of many in which they are involved. For example, young women today may be committed to multiple roles,

(Continued From Previous Page)

a young wife typically enters a patrilineal joint family system in which she has a very low status. Her status increases with the birth of children, and her highest status is reached when her sons marry, after which she can delegate day-to-day chores to her daughters-in-law. After widowhood, older women continue to live in this extended family in which they are accorded respect. Of course, this arrangement is based on having male children. If one does not, one's security and support is in jeopardy; daughters, once married, have no financial responsibility for their own parents.

Western Nigeria

A married Yoruba woman in Western Nigeria has no rights of inheritance to her husbands' estate. In fact, the woman herself is regarded as her husband's property and is inherited by a relative of her late husband. (If a widow does not wish to be inherited, her only option to free herself from this obligation is to refund the dowry paid at the time of the marriage.) Widow inheritance is one of the ways that widows have been cared for in traditional Yoruba culture, and it has usually been in the woman's best interest to remain in her late husband's home where she has access to a support system and land. She is encouraged to remarry within the family (usually the brother-in-law or another eligible male in the family). In contemporary society, however, the role of Nigerian women is changing. Some are now highly educated and employed, yet their legal rights after spousal death are still very limited. As a result, any emotional support a widow may have received from in-laws is often eroded by conflicts over inheritance issues, exacerbating her grief. Despite changing conditions in husband-wife relationships, government policies do not exist that recognize joint acquisition of property of couples during marriage (Adamolekun, 1995).

SOURCES: K. Adamolekun (1995). In-laws behavior as a social factor in subsequent temporary upsurges of grief (STUG) in Western Nigeria. *Omega, 31*(1), 23–34; H. Z. Lopata (Ed.). (1987). *Widows: The Middle East, Asia, and the Pacific.* Durham, NC: Duke University Press.

expanding their views of themselves as they enter nontraditional work arenas. Males are also more actively engaged in parenting activities than in past generations. If these current trends continue, the transition to widowhood may be made somewhat easier, reducing the degree of change precipitated by the loss and increasing the continuity available to the individual.

Social Adjustment

Loneliness is a major problem of both widows and widowers, and it is often seen as their single greatest concern (Clark, Siviski, & Weiner, 1986). Upon the death of a spouse, individuals lose a companion as well as a significant source of emotional support. In addition, other relationships are often altered. Oster-weis, Solomon, and Green (1984) have referred to widowhood as a time of "so-cial marginality" for many. As a result of the couple orientation in American society, those who do not have a partner may feel like a "fifth wheel" in many social situations.

Having an "available" male or female in social groups can be very threaten-ing. Individuals sometimes fear that their spouses may become attracted to the unattached person. Also, the presence of a widow(er) in the group reminds others of their own vulnerability and that of their spouse. The avoidance of death in American society sometimes extends to those who have been widowed as well. These factors operate to prevent, in many cases, the widowed from re-maining integrated in their former social networks.

Widowers in particular are often socially isolated and lonely after the death of their wives. In many marriages, the wife assumes the role of maintaining so-cial and kinship ties and organizing social events. Upon her death, social contact for the husband is often sharply reduced. Furthermore, widowers are less likely than widows to have close, intimate friendships that could serve as a buffer against loneliness and isolation (Campbell & Silverman, 1996). Also, widowers are less likely to have friends who have lost a spouse because of the lower fre-quency of widowhood among males.

In general, widows are more likely than widowers to report a larger number of people in their current social group and more positive feelings toward these individuals (Farberow, Gallagher-Thompson, Gilewski, & Thompson, 1992). The impact of spousal loss on a woman's friendship patterns is largely determined by the number of her friends who have been widowed previously. Being the first in one's social group to experience the death of a husband is especially difficult and is more likely to be the case for younger women. If many of her friends have been widowed, a newly bereaved individual may find more support and under-standing for her situation.

The younger the widow or widower, the greater the chances of remarriage. Widowers are more likely to remarry than widows (and do so sooner) regardless of age, contributing to the differential marriage status of older males compared to females (see Figure 8.2). It may be difficult for both widowed males and fe-males to meet single persons in their age group, and dating can seem very awk-ward after many years of marriage. Remarriage is easier for older males than for older females following death of a spouse due to the higher ratio of females in their age group. Further, there are social sanctions against women marrying men younger than themselves.

Although many widowed males remarry, those who do not have an in-creased risk of their own dying, particularly during the months immediately fol-lowing the death. This association between bereavement and mortality risk has been shown across a wide range of cultures, historical periods, and socio-economic groups. The death of a spouse clearly has profound effects on the sur-vivor, and the toll it takes on health (both directly and indirectly) seems to be greater for men (Stroebe & Stroebe, 1993).

FIGURE 8.2

Marital Status of Persons Age 65 and Over, United States, 1995

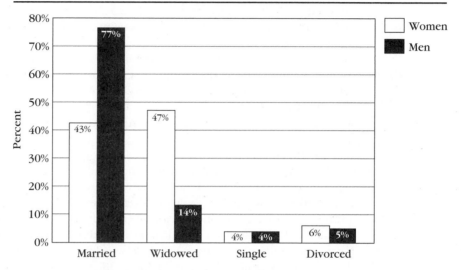

SOURCE: U.S. Bureau of the Census (1996). *Statistical Abstract of the United States: 1996* (116th edition). Washington, DC. U.S. Government Printing Office.

Adolescent or adult children may interfere with the possibility of their widowed parent's remarriage by objecting to their deceased mother or father being "replaced" and not accepting the surviving parent's desire to seek adult companionship. The tendency of the bereaved spouse to idealize the deceased can also interfere with developing new relationships. Lopata (1979) first used the term **husband sanctification** to refer to the tendency of bereaved widows to overly idealize their deceased husbands. (This concept can also apply to males who have been widowed.) The women in Lopata's study described their late husbands as unusually good fathers, husbands, and men in general. Some even said that the deceased had no faults. When this idealization is exaggerated, few living males will be able to compete with the perfection attributed to the widow's former husband.

Financial Adjustment

A major aspect of adjustment to widowhood relates to financial issues. Dealing with these issues at a time of great emotional pain can be overwhelming to both widows and widowers; however, financial stresses usually increase after losing a spouse. The high medical bills often associated with a long, extended illness must be paid. Understanding and taking action related to insurance benefits, burial policies, and other financial and legal concerns is also necessary, but can be frustrating and require a great deal of time and energy. The less experience one has had in this area, the more stressful it will likely be. Acquiring financial knowledge can be an important way to help a spouse prepare for widowhood, and gaining experience in financial decision making can lower the anxieties associated with these tasks.

Unfortunately, financial issues pertinent to widowhood are too often ignored by many couples. Discussing topics such as wills can be threatening because it forces them to think of the possibility of separation through death—a thought that is anxiety-provoking for many. Adults usually expect that they will have many years left to live and, therefore, feel no rush to put their affairs in order. As a result, widows in particular often find themselves with inadequate resources, which can necessitate a change in life-style.

The death of a spouse dramatically increases the risk of a drop in economic well-being for women, but tends to have little or no effect on men. Widows, compared with widowers, are more likely to enter poverty after spousal loss and to experience a large income decline (Burkhauser, Butler, & Holden, 1991). Bound (1991) found that a woman's financial resources decreased by 18% following the death of a husband, and widows on the average live 18.5 years after their husband's deaths. King (1985) poignantly states:

> It is a cruel irony that women, who generally have fewer economic resources at their disposal at earlier stages of their lives, are the ones who must live longer on relatively less and less. The aging of the population makes the "feminization" of poverty a pervasive reality. (p. 63)

Because financial status is usually lowered after death of a husband, many widows are forced to seek employment (if they are not already employed). Unfortunately, they are often ill-equipped to enter the labor market. Many have invested themselves in the roles of wife and mother to the exclusion of a career role. After 30 years or more with little or no work experience outside the home, most widows have difficulty finding suitable employment and many must settle for unskilled, low-paying positions. The financial plight of widows may be much improved in the future as increasing numbers of women obtain higher levels of education, enter professional fields, and combine occupational roles with family roles. Longer and higher-earning work careers are generally shields against poverty in old age. However, in American society women still tend to earn less than men even when they have equivalent positions or levels of training. Furthermore, considerable variability exists among ethnic groups, with widows from ethnic minority groups being more at risk for poverty. For example, only 15% of African American women and 7% of Hispanic women (compared to 22% of all American women over 65) receive any retirement pension income (Campbell & Chauncey, 1994).

Most current information on the experience of widows is based on data from older women who have had traditional marriages and assumed traditional roles. As today's younger women age and experience widowhood, their adjustments may be quite different. Compared with elderly women of today, they will have acquired more formal education, have identified more strongly with a work role, and have higher earning potential. They will also have more experience with financial matters.

Interventions for the Widowed

During the past decade or so, numerous programs and services for widow(er)s have been shown to be beneficial in terms of providing support, reassurance, education, and information. These groups have taken a variety of different forms.

SUPPORT GROUPS FOR MEXICAN AMERICAN WIDOWS

Similar to the mutual support groups like Widow-to-Widow, which have been highly successful with middle-class Anglo Americans, a six-month pilot intervention program in Arizona was designed specifically to be sensitive to the cultural needs of Mexican American women. This culture includes a deep sense of privacy and personal pride; a social structure in which family roles are clearly demarcated; mourning customs which restrict the widow to her home except for essential errands and church; and social interactions limited to family. The women targeted for participation spoke little or no English, had little experience in discussing intimate matters with strangers, and were unaccustomed to mental health therapy. The facilitators were bilingual Mexican American women, with the necessary education and experience to conduct the groups. Time and place of support group meetings, greeting and leaving behaviors, traditional snacks, and use of space were planned to fit the culture and needs of the participants. (For example, the meetings were held in a fa-miliar neighborhood center of a Mexican American *barrio* which did not require transportation.) Evaluation upon completion of the program showed higher levels of life satisfaction, less anxiety and depression, and fewer somatic and emotional symptoms among participants as compared to a control group not participating in the support groups. The members of the support group described themselves in more positive terms and reported an improved sense of self. These findings contradict the common assumption that intervention outside the natural support system is unnecessary for Mexican American women adjusting to widowhood. These individuals have often not accessed existing community services due to language barriers and cultural constraints. An outgrowth of this project is the development of a peer network of widows chosen from the intervention program. With the goal of reaching out to the wider Hispanic community these women have named their network "*Apoyando Viudas Hispanas*/ Helping Hispanic Widows."

SOURCE: M. Kay, J. Guernsey De Zapien, C. A. Wilson, & M. Yoder (1993). Evaluating treatment efficacy by triangulation. *Social Science Medicine, 36*(12), 1545–1554.

Self-help groups are a popular approach to aid the widowed, and they have gained wide acceptance in the United States. Self-help groups are composed of persons who share a common condition, situation, heritage, symptom, or experience. They emphasize self-reliance and generally offer a face-to-face or phone-to-phone fellowship network. Self-help groups emphasize the power of members to assist one another rather than depend on the help of professionals. As a result, individuals can gain a sense of community and feel that they are helping themselves as well as others (Lieberman, 1993).

In a 2–year investigation of postbereavement adaptation, Vachon and her associates (1980) studied widows who were paired with other widows for emotional support and practical assistance. These investigators found that women participating in the program followed the same course of adaptation as those who did not; however, the adaptation of those in the intervention group was accelerated. Lund, Dimond, and Juretich (1985) discovered that a sizable number of older widowed adults have interest in participating in bereavement self-help groups. They emphasized that interest in participating does not necessarily imply lack of social support in the person's life. In fact, a significant number of potential participants report having very strong support networks. These individuals were coping well but they were interested in additional psychosocial benefits from this type of intervention.

The Widowed Persons Service (WPS), sponsored by the American Association of Retired Persons (AARP), is based on the concept of mutual help and peer support. This outreach program builds on the pioneering work of Phyllis Silverman (1986, 1987) at Harvard University Medical School in the late 1960s. Her original Widow-to-Widow program focused on bereaved wives in general, rather than only those individuals identified as high risk or in definite need of intervention. In this program, widows themselves became support persons for the recently widowed. They provided emotional support, served as role models, and acted as bridge persons in the transition from wife to widow. Because of her own experience, a widow has special empathy for others who have experienced loss of a spouse. She is therefore more likely to accept the distress of the bereaved over an extended period of time. In addition, her services are often more likely to be accepted than those of a professional because less stigma is generally attached.

Silverman conceptualized widowhood as a major life transition, extending over a number of years and requiring major changes in self-concept, roles, and tasks. This process of adjustment can lead to "dramatic growth" or "quiet reorientation." Many widow(er)s do not seek services until several years following the deaths of their spouses, reinforcing the notion that it is not only the recently bereaved who can benefit from support.

In addition to peer-support efforts, therapy groups can be especially helpful for widow(er)s considered to be at risk for a poor recovery. A group of Canadian researchers found that recovery after loss of a spouse was related to availability of social support, situational variables, and personality. Vachon and her colleagues (1982) found that the widows who were the most distressed

2 years after the death of their husbands had (1) fewer social supports, (2) greater health problems, (3) greater financial stress, (4) lower emotional stability, and (5) higher anxiety. In general, the effect of personality on adjustment to widowhood has been understudied, but it appears to play a major role. Positive self-esteem and personal competencies in particular have been shown to be related to desirable long-term bereavement outcomes (Lund, Castera, & Dimond, 1993).

The marital tie itself also appears to be an important predictor of recovery after bereavement. Parkes and Weiss (1983) have associated poor recoveries with conflictual marriages in which the survivor had very ambivalent feelings, rather than mostly loving or nonloving feelings. The bereaved spouses in this category showed less emotion immediately after the death but displayed more problems than other widows when they were interviewed approximately 1 year later. Strong feelings of anger and guilt were also linked to poor long-term outcomes. Research is needed to determine particular treatment needs of widowed individuals at risk for adjustment difficulties.

Overall, results of studies on intervention after the death of a spouse have been encouraging. As new programs are introduced and evaluated, more information will be available regarding appropriate models of service delivery, precautions to take when designing and implementing programs, and critical factors to consider for timely intervention.

Loss of a Former Spouse: Grief After Divorce

Feelings associated with widowhood can also apply to other situations. Several authors have compared the loss of spouse through divorce to loss due to death (Kitson, Lopata, Holmes, & Meyering, 1980; Raphael, 1983). The losses (e.g., emotional, social, financial) experienced appear to be somewhat similar in both circumstances. In divorce, however, the adjustment process may be complicated by feelings of failure and rejection. Also, because the former spouse is still alive, resolution may be difficult because of the possibility of being reunited. For some individuals, the element of choice may be a critical variable in adjustment. If both partners decide that a divorce is in their best interests, the grief associated with the ending of the spousal relationship may be minimized. However, if disagreement exists, guilt may be a predominant emotion experienced by the initiator of the divorce, whereas anger is keenly felt by the partner resisting the divorce. The circumstances surrounding any particular situation must always be considered when examining the effects on the individuals involved. As high divorce rates continue, mental health professionals need to be cognizant of the grief associated with marital dissolution. Three main tasks of divorced individuals are to

- resolve feelings related to the loss;
- redefine their relationship to their former spouse; and
- adjust to a life in which the former partner is no longer a significant part.

Ex-spouses have had a significant relationship together, oftentimes for many years. This relationship combined with the divorce is likely to engender strong, but perhaps ambivalent, feelings. In some situations, one partner may still be in love with his or her former spouse; in others, the adults have established new relationships yet remain friends. Although some couples are emotionally distant following their divorce and rarely interact, contact continues on some level for many individuals, especially those who have had children together. However, individuals outside of the relationship assume the bond to have been effectively ended with the divorce.

What happens if death of a former spouse occurs before grief associated with the divorce has been resolved? Unfortunately, little is known about the impact of death in this type of situation. Grief studies have tended to focus on survivors who have had identifiable and recognized role relationships to the deceased, such as the spouse and children, while other significant relationships have been ignored (Doka, 1986). Doka points out that lack of a socially recognized and sanctioned relationship may in fact disenfranchise the bereaved (as previously discussed in chapter 3). In other words, a person's grief may not be recognized or supported by others even though he or she is experiencing a typical grief reaction. The very nature of these relationships may complicate grief, because traditional sources of support are either limited or lacking.

Ambivalent relationships, concurrent crises, and previous losses can negatively influence the course of grief (Raphael, 1983). These conditions are often found in situations in which divorce precedes death. In an exploratory study, Doka (1986) interviewed adults who had experienced the death of the former spouse and found that the degree of loss experienced by the surviving ex-spouse varied. Half of the individuals in Doka's (1986) study described the impact of the death as minimal and felt emotionally uninvolved. One woman said that she felt as if a distant relative or remote friend had died. For the remainder of the sample, strong affective responses were evident. This reaction was especially strong when the loss associated with the divorce had not been fully resolved prior to the death. One respondent described her reactions "as normal and poignant as any widow." Feelings of guilt and regret were prevalent among several of the survivors. As one woman expressed it, "I felt devastated—I never really stopped loving him. I felt guilty—guilty about the divorce, the death. Maybe he would still be alive if I hadn't thrown him out" (p. 444). The ambiguity of the ex-spouse's role made it especially difficult if he or she visited the former spouse at the hospital or attended the funeral. The ex-spouse often felt uncomfortable and out of place. One woman described her visit to her former husband in the hospital in the following way: "I visited but I saw him and his new wife and his new friends and I felt very ill at ease. I didn't know what to say or how to act. They didn't either" (p. 446).

Difficulties at the funeral of an ex-spouse may be quite varied and range from questions of seating (e.g., should the ex-spouse sit with her children in the section reserved for his family?) to emotional reactions to the eulogy (e.g., a minister focusing on the present marriage of 4 years duration without mentioning the previous marriage of 25 years triggers feelings of jealousy and anger). Some ex-spouses anticipate difficulties associated with going to the funeral and choose not to attend. By doing so, they are denied the therapeutic benefit of rituals related to death and public mourning.

Often, social support is lacking. Many note that friends do not know what to say or how to respond to their needs during bereavement. If the survivor is now remarried, it is sometimes difficult to share their grief with the new spouse. As one woman stated, "Whenever I mention Stan (the late ex-spouse) my John stiffens" (Doka, 1986, p. 446). Relationships with former in-laws may be tense and nonsupportive. In some instances, in-laws blame the death on the ex-spouse (e.g., in-laws assuming that a heart attack was caused by the stress of the divorce).

Grieving ex-spouses may feel a lack of support in other spheres as well. Because the deceased is no longer "a family member," the ex-spouse may not be given time off from work or other special considerations, even though he or she is grieving intensely. Some persons who would like to seek comfort from a church may refrain from doing so if their religion does not sanction divorce.

LOSS OF AN ADULT CHILD

The death of a child is traumatic for parents, regardless of the age of the child. Numerous studies have examined grief related to the death of young children, but relatively few researchers have focused on the death of adult children. Sadly, society is often not supportive of older parents' losses. Many assume that the spouse and the children of the deceased are the ones who most need care and, thus, overlook the pain of the parents (DeVries, Lana, & Falck, 1994). The loss of an adult child is compounded by grief resulting from the many normative losses likely to be experienced during this life stage (e.g., the parents' own retirement or diminished health) and may magnify the sense of loss.

As more people live to advanced old age, it is increasingly probable that one of their children will die before they do. A survey of a national sample of elderly found that 1 out of every 10 older individuals who have had children experienced the death of at least one of them when the parent was age 60 or older (Moss, Lesher, & Moss, 1986).

When a child of any age dies, the death disrupts the anticipated order of the generational cycle.

> Parents who have experienced decades of the natural rhythm of life, of the orderliness of family development, report feeling that their world view has been violated, that life has become chaotic and unpredictable. There is a profound existential sense of insecurity which emerges when the rational order of things has gone awry. (Moss et al., 1986, p. 213)

In the case of the death of adult children, aged parents question why their lives have been spared when their offspring are taken in their prime.

For some frail elderly, well-meaning relatives may withhold specific details surrounding the death or not inform them of their child's illness or death at all in an attempt to protect them from the pain of grief. Brubaker (1985) illustrates this in the following example:

> An elderly woman is a resident of a long-term care facility when her daughter becomes ill with cancer. The family makes the decision not to tell the mother about her daughter's illness out of concern that this will upset her. Also, the family believes that it is likely that the mother will die before the daughter. When the daughter dies, the family again decides to "spare" the mother by hiding this information. The mother frequently questions family visitors and nursing home staff about why the daughter no longer visits. She is anxious about her daughter's well-being and becomes concerned that she has offended the daughter in some way. Although she is not aware of the daughter's death, she does mourn for loss of a relationship with her daughter. (pp. 39–40)

Grief resolution among elderly parents may be especially difficult for the following reasons:

- They may have fewer options for reinvesting in other relationships following the loss.
- They have fewer diversions such as employment to provide temporary relief from their emotional pain.
- Health problems and transportation difficulties may prevent them from participating in grief groups.
- They may have less support for their grief because of a dwindling support network and because society is more likely to view the deceased's spouse and children as the primary grievers.
- The elderly parents may have little involvement in rituals that can help in the resolution of grief (e.g., planning the funeral or sorting through personal items belonging to the deceased), as the spouse of the deceased will usually assume this responsibility.
- The elderly are more likely to have medication prescribed for their emotional distress, which can interfere with grief work.
- They may have limited strength and endurance to help them cope with the intensity of the loss. (Rando, 1986)

Grief can be compounded if the surviving parents experience distancing from other family members after a death. In addition to the loss of a son or daughter and what that loss symbolizes, the elderly parent may also lose contact with grandchildren and in-laws, especially if remarriage of the adult child's spouse occurs. Watching someone take over their deceased child's role in the family can be especially difficult for older parents. Further, grandparents often fear that their grandchildren will forget their child (the deceased parent) (Rando, 1986).

Death of an adult child may result in additional crises. For example, the risk of institutionalization of the surviving elderly parent may increase since adult offspring are often caregivers for their older parents, and their absence may minimize the availability of assistance. Thus, death of an adult child may increase the need for formal services for the surviving parent (Moss et al. 1986).

The bond between elderly parents and their adult children is unique. The older parent who loses a child generally views the relationship from a life-long developmental perspective, and the image of the child spans a long time frame from childhood through adulthood and is tied to the survivor's history as a parent (Moss et al., 1986). The death of an adult child can threaten the elderly's sense of continuity and generativity, which is important to successful aging. If the deceased adult child was seen as "the one to carry on the family name" or was the primary person responsible for operating the family business, the elderly parent may feel that the future of the family is at stake as well (Rando, 1986).

LOSS OF AN OLDER PARENT

Losing one's parents during one's own midlife is viewed as a normative event. In fact, it is the most common type of bereavement during the middle adult years. As individuals age, their parents age also and death is inevitable. By age 54, half of all adult children have lost both parents (Umberson & Chen, 1994). The death of a parent can affect us deeply. It is a significant life event that can elicit a variety of complicated emotions, while serving as a catalyst for self-development. Despite the frequency of this type of loss at midlife, most research on the effect of parental death has focused on young children or adolescents as survivors.

When comparing adult responses to the death of a child, a spouse, and an older parent, Sanders (1980) found that death of a child produced the most difficult and prolonged grief. Death of an elderly parent was typically anticipated because of the individual's age and/or physical condition and usually resulted in less severe grief reactions in general than did death of a spouse or child. As Moss and Moss (1983) have observed, adult children are somewhat braced for the death of their aged parents. Also, loss of a parent at this stage in life is generally less disruptive in terms of their everyday lives and requires fewer adjustments. Survivors are usually able to meet family and job commitments despite their recent loss.

Although loss of an older parent may not be as devastating as other types of loss, it is a very painful event and has its own unique adjustments and associated issues. In part, the parent for whom the adult is grieving is the parent from one's childhood years; therefore, the loss of a parent may have many meanings for surviving adult offspring. It may mean the loss of that "perfect," unconditional love experienced during childhood, a loss of security and support, or a giving-up of the "child" within themselves because their parent is no longer present. Accepting the death means acknowledging that one's family of origin is, in part, irreplaceably lost (Moss & Moss, 1983). One study found that, for many, death of a mother was more difficult than death of a father, possibly because of the mother's earlier status as the nurturing caregiver (Horowitz et al., 1984). Rather than reflecting differences in parental relationships, the findings may simply be suggesting that death of a second parent is more difficult than the death of the first (since women typically outlive men). When the mother dies, adult children may mourn the loss of having "parents" in addition to mourning that specific loss. Adults who have experienced the loss of both parents are more likely to describe a sense of "orphanhood," which often leads to a new sense of alone-ness (Scharlach & Fredriksen, 1993).

Adult children may react with ambivalence to the death of an aged parent. A sense of relief may be experienced by some if the death occurs after a long, extended illness. Other surviving adult children may feel guilty for resenting the strains of caregiving. Even while grieving the loss, they may ultimately feel good about the circumstances under which the death took place (e.g., a quick death with little pain). Due to common gender differences in caregiving responsi-bilities, adult daughters in particular often feel a renewed sense of freedom and time for self.

The actual nature and intensity of the grief response are influenced by the history of the particular parent–child relationship. In unhealthy family systems, death of a parent may indicate an end to destructive family ties, an opportunity to be free of parent expectations, or a chance to be truly independent as an adult (Moss & Moss, 1983). In these situations, grieving can be complicated by the mixed reactions the death brings and the symbolic significance of the death. Of-tentimes, parent–child relationship difficulties are not simply resolved by the death of the parent. Repercussions can include an enduring influence on the individual's identity, feelings of self-worth, and patterns of relating to others, which are not easily altered. Therapeutic intervention may be needed for the individual to be able to redefine himself or herself in the absence of a strong parental figure and overcome negative familial influences.

Few close relationships are free of conflict. Even in healthy families, an adult child may harbor unresolved feelings regarding an earlier event involving his or her parent. Following a parental death, these events are tied to the memory of the deceased. As the adult child matures and faces the ongoing challenges of adulthood, he or she may begin to view the situation from the parent's per-spective and substitute forgiveness and understanding for blame. In some cases, this reinterpretation of a significant aspect of the parent–child relationship can be important in the resolution of grief.

In addition to emotional reactions related to the personal loss, the death of an older parent also brings the adult child face-to-face with death and his or her own finiteness:

> The loss of parent represents the removal of a buffer against death. As long as the parent was alive the child could feel protected, since the parent by the rational

order of things was expected to die first. Without this buffer, there is a strong reminder that the child is now the older generation and cannot easily deny his or her mortality. (Moss & Moss, 1983, p. 72)

The surviving adult children are given a "developmental push" into their next stage of maturity as the oldest generation in the family. As a result, they often feel that they must assume responsibility for other family members, take over operation of a family business, and/or begin to view themselves as the patriarch or matriarch of the extended family. This developmental transition can lead the surviving adult child to a renewed commitment to care for others, the establishment of a stronger sense of identity, and a deeper understanding of life and its cycles—themes consistent with adult development during midlife (Douglas, 1990; Osterweis et al., 1984).

Scharlach and Fredriksen (1993) found that loss of a parent during midlife often resulted in a greater sense of personal maturity. The 83 bereaved adults they interviewed spoke of feeling more autonomy, more self-directed, and more responsibility for themselves and others. Their increased awareness of death seemed to lead to a reevaluation of personal priorities, in some cases resulting in significant changes in career plans and personal relationships. Robbins (1990) also found evidence of significant personal transformations occurring among many middle-aged women experiencing loss of a mother. In some cases, death of a parent results in new psychological and financial freedom that permits more personal flexibility and choice.

PEER DEATH AND MULTIPLE LOSS

Emotional ties that can exist outside family relationships are often not acknowledged by society, particularly in the case of friends (Fowlkes, 1990). The term *friend* is often applied to a range of emotional connections—from the most casual to the most intense—and the generic use of the term often contributes to the lack of recognition of the important role that friends frequently play in adult life. The following sections discuss peer death in the context of multiple loss using three quite varied examples: war, AIDS, and normal aging.

War Trauma and Loss

Military troops are largely composed of young adults. In fact, many nations routinely prepare their young men, and at times their young women, to participate in the defense of their homelands. Young adults, however, are likely to have had limited experience with death and loss prior to their military service. War always involves death and killing; participation in combat requires taking the lives of other human beings and fighting for one's own survival. In war, conventional rules and moral sanctions regarding killing do not apply. Taking someone else's life is often not only necessary but also considered heroic, whereas the same action under other circumstances would be considered murder.

Hendin and Haas (1984) charge that society has been slow to recognize the personal price that combat soldiers pay in service to their country. According to these authors: "Only since World War II have we begun to realize that killing, sustained exposure to the possibility of sudden death, and witnessing the violent deaths of friends have lasting traumatic consequences for a high percentage of combat soldiers" (p. 6). They also point out the tendency of American civilians to view postwar difficulties as weaknesses because of their idealized image of soldiers as heroes.

Most soldiers who return from conflict have experienced a variety of significant losses. All have lost their innocence and youth, and most have lost peers on the battlefield and with them important friendships and attachments that grew out of surviving together in a combat zone. Still others are injured and have lost body parts and/or functions, a permanent and visible reminder of their war experience (Parson, 1986).

Post-Traumatic Stress Disorder.   For many war veterans, the emotional scars remain. The aftereffects exhibited by a significant number of veterans constitute a syndrome identified as **post-traumatic stress disorder (PTSD)** (American Psychiatric Association, 1994). PTSD is a condition resulting from exposure to a traumatic event and often characterized by nightmares, loss of control over behavior, emotional numbing, withdrawal, hyperalertness, and recurrent and intrusive recollections of the trauma. In addition to war, other **traumatic stress** situations that may produce symptoms of PTSD include other deliberate human-caused experiences (e.g., bombings, death camps), natural disasters (floods, earthquakes), accidental disasters (plane crashes, auto accidents), witnessing a violent crime (murder), and violent personal assaults (rapes). Pearce, Schauer, Garfield, Ohlde, and Patterson (1985) found that the first category, deliberate disasters such as war, produced the most severe PTSD symptoms.

When PTSD symptoms have been analyzed for veterans, four major components have been evident:

- depression,
- residual guilt or grief,
- reexperiencing the trauma, and
- detachment and anger. (Silver & Iacono, 1984)

Of special interest are the grief-related components of PTSD. Veterans often feel guilt, shame, and remorse about what they did while in combat. They also grieve over the losses that they themselves experienced as a result of the war. In addition, they frequently report feeling **survivor guilt** (i.e., guilt over having survived when many others, especially friends, have died). In extreme situations, survivor guilt can induce feelings of needing to "pay one's dues" for surviving.

This attitude can be manifest in ways that can have destructive and negative consequences (such as starting fights, engaging in behaviors that elicit rejection from family members and friends, or getting involved in a high number of accidents). These individuals feel that they do not deserve to be alive and enjoying life.

Which individuals are more likely to develop PTSD? Do predisposing factors place certain individuals at greater risk? Foy and Card (1987) found that combat exposure was related to PTSD symptomatology although premilitary adjustment was not. An earlier study also found that childhood and preservice experiences did not play a major role in the development of post-traumatic stress disorders (Solkoff, Gray, & Keill, 1986). These investigators found, however, that veterans diagnosed with PTSD, as compared with veterans who were not, more frequently sustained injuries in the war and had more death-related experiences. They were more personally involved in killing and were also in combat for a longer time. More of their friends were killed, and they reported feeling more guilt over surviving. The group of veterans who had symptoms of PTSD also had fewer contacts with other veterans after they were discharged.

Many visit the Vietnam Memorial in Washington, DC, to honor those who died and to share their own grief.

THE WALL

Concrete symbols of remembrance of those who have died can bring comfort to the bereaved and serve as a focal point for shared grief (Cook & Dworkin, 1992). The following passage, written by Vietnam veteran Jim O'Meara, illustrates the poignancy of the Vietnam Memorial in Washington, DC, for many of those who survived the Vietnam War:

> There isn't anything else like it. It's a black, polished granite cliff, formed into a shallow "V," that has the names of the missing and dead from the Vietnam War inscribed on it in white letters. 57,939 of them. It's technically a "Memorial," but that doesn't begin to cover what it means. "Monument" isn't right either. Most of the Veterans who went there for the dedication called it, simply, "The Wall."
>
> At first, I was skeptical. For me, Vietnam was thirteen years ago, buried somewhere back in my mind. I hadn't heard much about the memorial, and I was leery of bringing up old feelings, of waking up at night, sweating, with the smell of dry, red central highlands dust mixed with hot canvas in my nostrils and the heat of helicopter blades in my ears, or dealing with the deep, bitter emotions, the feeling of betrayal at the reception I'd received when I got back. Like most of the other Vietnam veterans, I never spoke about it. I heard the rumor that the State of Wyoming was paying for air fare to fly some guys to Washington, DC, for the dedication. No, I told myself, don't get involved. But it wouldn't go away. I told my wife about it.
>
> "You're going, of course," she said.
>
> "Can we afford it?" I asked.
>
> "Does that make any difference? You were there, you should go."
>
> On Friday, I went to see the Wall. I went alone, when not so many people would be there. I thought it might be a heavy time for me. From the subway station, it's about a mile down a grassy mall, past the Washington Monument and along a pond, to where the memorial was supposed to be. I'd heard about it, but I wasn't sure what it

(Continued)

Healing the Emotional Wounds. Figley and Salison (1980) have emphasized the value for veterans of contact with their peers from the war: "Those who share the injuries are major sources of reassurance, strength, encouragement, guidance, and counsel" (p. 139). According to Tick (1985), combat veterans often need therapeutic grief intervention because they are in a state of **psychic numbness,** which helps keep strong emotional feelings at a distance. In combat situations, psychic numbing may be necessary for survival and effective functioning. Outside of a combat situation and over an extended period, it can lead to alienation from one's own feelings. One veteran described his emotional numbness this way: "I couldn't feel anything. I didn't want to feel anything. Feeling is too painful. I think I killed myself inside to help me forget" (Parson, 1986, p. 15). For veterans who experience psychic numbness for a

(Continued From Previous Page)

would actually look like. As I got closer, I saw some guys sitting around in small groups or walking alone, wearing old fatigue uniforms or parts of them. I didn't know what to expect. Lots of anxiety.

I walked over a small rise, and saw it. It looked small and black. I felt a little disappointment, it wasn't tall and grand. It was even below ground level. I was looking into the shallow V. From where I was, you couldn't tell its size. I started walking toward the apex.

As I walked closer, down the long slope toward the bottom of the apex, the polished black granite arms tapered off on either side. I was about ten feet from the Wall when the impact of the thing hit me. From ten feet higher than my head, stretching out of sight on either side, were the names of 57,939 people. The dead and the missing from Vietnam. I was slammed with the enormity of it all, the weight of those people who were not here, who had died because they had been asked, or sent, to do a job their nation wanted done. Emotions washed across me, and my eyes filled with tears. I moved away and sat alone on the grass.

Time passed, an hour or so I guess, and I picked up a brochure that said how to find the year and the month you were looking for. I went back to the Wall and found the names I had come to see. I said to myself the things I had to say. I read a little further and found some names I hadn't expected to find. I thought they'd made it home. I sat on the grass, then, for a very long time.

Later, I watched a couple, obviously tourists, start at one end and walk toward the apex, chatting and looking around. About three-quarters of the way down, I saw it hit them, too. They suddenly knew what it was and what it meant. In the last analysis, this is what Vietnam was all about, 57,939 people listed on the Wall and millions of veterans who, in their minds somewhere, sat on the grass abandoned and alone, betrayed by the nation they'd fought for.

If the Wall could do that, I thought, it's doing all that could be asked of it.

prolonged period, the grieving process is often incomplete, distorted, chronic, or frozen.

This alienation from feelings can create a powerful obstacle in interpersonal relationships as well, especially those typically characterized by emotional closeness. For example, spouses often feel that they, too, are victims of the war. The development of secondary stress responses in significant others results from their need to make sense of their partners' traumatic experiences and their efforts to maintain a stable and workable relationship. Relationships with children likewise may be affected if a parent is emotionally inaccessible and unable to show intimacy. In addition, children may experience adverse reactions resulting from the long-term separation from the parent during the combat period (Figley & Kleber, 1995).

In support groups, veterans' wives often describe their husbands as emotionally distant and unable to express and share their feelings. Some of these problems are exacerbated by policies such as the one during the Vietnam War of flying combatants home quickly after their tour of duty was finished. Soldiers were often back home with their families within 36 hours from the time they were processed out of Vietnam. As one veteran said, "One day I was out in the bush, killing . . . , seeing buddies get killed, covered in mud, trying to sleep at night with the threat of ambush by the VC and two days later I was trying to talk to my family at the dinner table. I couldn't tell them what I had been through. They couldn't have understood it" (Brende & Parson, 1985, p. 73). This type of situation was especially difficult because many of these men had fantasized about coming home, and they were not prepared for the adjustments that they and their families would face upon their return.

Various therapy approaches are often used to improve communication among family members. Increased communication can aid the veteran in successfully working through the trauma of the war and also increase spousal satisfaction with the marital relationship, thus affecting other relationships in the family as well. Peer support groups can also provide a forum for sharing and addressing adjustment difficulties. As individuals do their own grief work and confront their losses, their relationships with others may be strengthened.

AIDS in the Gay Community

Given the rapid spread of AIDS through all segments of our population, peer loss as a result of AIDS is certainly not limited to the homosexual population. However, this group has had a unique and painful experience with the disease. By the mid-1980s in San Francisco's Castro district, the early epicenter of the AIDS epidemic in the United States, it was hard to remember a "time before the illness." HIV and AIDS had changed individuals and the gay community in profound ways (Small, 1993). Leon McKusick, a psychotherapist, observed at that time that the gay community had been going through the stages "that individuals are said to go through when faced by a life-threatening disease: denial, rage, bargaining, and acceptance" (Fitzgerald, 1986, pp. 113–114).

Schwartzberg (1992) has questioned whether traditional models and theories of grief can adequately address AIDS-related bereavement of gay men given the scope, severity, and complexity of grief in these circumstances. Because the number of deaths among the male homosexual community has been so staggering, members of this community have typically experienced multiple losses with little intervening time to mourn any single loss effectively. The term **survivor syndrome** has been applied to HIV-negative gay men coping with the AIDS crisis (Martin & Garcia, 1989). Previously used to describe a constellation of psychological reactions experienced by war survivors, this syndrome includes the following manifestations:

THE NAMES PROJECT:
FACTS ABOUT THE AIDS MEMORIAL QUILT

Number of Panels: 43,077 containing 78,656 names (represents 22% of all U.S. AIDS deaths) as of September 1997.

Each panel is 3 × 6 feet, and all panels displayed together would cover over 18 acres. Its increasing size reflects the reality of the disease and its impact.

Names You Might Recognize: Arthur Ashe, tennis player; Tina Chow, clothing designer; Perry Ellis, fashion designer; Allison Gertz, AIDS activist; Rock Hudson, actor; Stewart McKinley, U.S. congressman; Freddie "Mercury" Bulsara, lead singer of rock group "Queen"; Rudolf Nureyev, ballet dancer; Max Robinson, ABC News anchor; Dr. Tom Waddell, Olympic athlete.

Most of the panels, however, are dedicated to ordinary individuals who have died of AIDS and represent much diversity in terms of gender, age, sexual orientation, manner in which the disease was contracted, ethnicity, or country of origin. Panels have been contributed from 40 different countries outside the United States, which illustrates the worldwide attention this project has received. Panels have also been created to honor parents and children from the same family who have died of AIDS. Because of the dynamic nature of this project, new panels are continually submitted.

Examples of Materials Used in the Quilt: Buttons, champagne glasses, corduroy, cowboy boots, cremation ashes, first-place ribbons, flags, beer cans, human hair, jeans, jewelry, lace, love letters, Mardi Gras masks, merit badges, needlepoint, paintings, photographs, quartz crystals, sequins, silk flowers, stuffed animals, ties, wedding rings.

The range of panel designs, as well as materials used in construction, vary as widely as the makers' skills and the individual lives the panels represent. The panels are reminiscent of Victorian mourning quilts, which incorporated clothing of the deceased and stitched together symbols and text. In contrast to this earlier female tradition, the AIDS Quilt contains panels created by both men and women (as well as children) to preserve the memory of loved ones, to raise public awareness about the AIDS epidemic and HIV prevention, and to encourage support for people living with AIDS.

You are invited to view panels from the NAMES AIDS Quilt Project at the following Web site: http://www.aidsquilt.org

SOURCES: The NAMES Project Foundation Quilt Facts, September 12, 1997; Hawkins (1996).

- survivor guilt,
- death anxiety, and
- psychic numbing.

Gay men who are HIV negative often experience one or more of these manifestations as a result of witnessing the illness and death of many members of their community and possibly having engaged in the same sexual behavior that led to HIV infection in others while their own lives were spared. Some even report feeling "out of synch" with the gay community because so many of their friends are HIV positive (Dilley & Moon, 1994).

Those who grieve the death of an AIDS patient not only experience the common somatic, behavioral, and intrapsychic symptoms of grief, but also face societal stigma, rejection, and a sense of isolation (Richmond & Ross, 1995). In the early 1980s, AIDS was thought to be primarily a disease of homosexuals (and was even called the "gay plague"). This fact caused those who suffered from this syndrome to be shunned by a social structure that condemned that population's life-style. Families who have never admitted to others that a son or brother is gay may be particularly unwilling to do so when AIDS is diagnosed. Through their denial, they often sacrifice the support that at least some friends or family members would like to give. Lovers of persons with AIDS also may be rejected by those who do not accept their homosexuality. As a result, a lover may not even be recognized as one who legitimately should be allowed to participate actively in the care of the AIDS patient and later in the funeral (Doka, 1989). Survivors

The AIDS Memorial Quilt is displayed on the Capitol Mall in Washington, DC. Smaller exhibits have also been held in schools, shopping malls, museums, places of worship, hospitals, and corporate offices.

Women in Zambia work on a panel. In many nations worldwide, the concept of the AIDS Memorial Quilt has been adapted by people to fit their own cultures.

of AIDS victims—lovers, family members, and friends—are also frequently ostracized by the larger society and even members of the medical community. Some still fear that AIDS may be caused by casual contact, even though medical evidence indicates otherwise. Nonetheless, bereaved survivors (regardless of how the deceased contracted the illness—blood transfusion, drug usage, sexual activity) may be socially isolated due to fear that they may also carry the virus and spread it to others (Biller & Rice, 1990).

Added to the stress of rejection, stigmatization, and isolation, survivors must also deal with their own fears about the illness. Whether they, in fact, do carry the virus, they must deal with that possibility. "AIDS tests" actually test for the presence of antibodies to the virus, not the AIDS virus itself, and therefore do not yield conclusive results for a period of months immediately after transmission may have occurred. Further, a positive result on an AIDS test does not necessarily mean the individual will develop the symptoms of AIDS. Also, years can elapse between the time of infection and the first symptoms (Mills & Masur, 1990). Mental health professionals have found extreme stress in a group they label the "**worried well**"—individuals who do not have AIDS at present but fear they will develop it. Even those who do not test positive on the antibody test may report feeling that their own lives are in jeopardy, and may suffer from depression and health-related anxiety (Galea, Lewis, & Baker, 1988). Results of a 7-year longitudinal study of psychological distress among gay men suggest that concern over one's own health status may be replacing grief relating to AIDS losses as the primary determinant of psychological stress among gay men (Martin & Dean, 1993). As Sullivan (1990) has observed, death has become less of an event and more of a psychological environment for gay men today.

It is imperative that we deal with the issues that currently prevent AIDS patients and survivors alike from receiving the human support given to others who are dying or grieving. Although any loss is emotionally difficult, multiple losses can put individuals at greater risk and complicate the healing process.

Thoughts and feelings related to grief can be expressed metaphorically through the design and creation of objects that commemorate the deceased. The panels in the Memorial AIDS Quilt Project serve this purpose for many. The idea for this project originated in 1985 when gay activist Cleve Jones decided to do something to counter the anonymity of those dying from AIDS. At an annual march in San Francisco, he asked participants to make placards bearing the names of someone they knew who had died of AIDS, which they hung on the façade of a federal building. The dramatic visual effect reminded Jones of a patchwork quilt handed down in his family and used to comfort the ill. In February 1987, Jones made the first panel of what was to become the NAMES Project AIDS Memorial Quilt. The project was formally organized on June 21, 1987, and, since that time, thousands of panels have been publicly displayed. The quilt has become a public metaphor for a shared national tragedy, as well as a powerful way for survivors to share their grief and commemorate the life of individuals who have died of AIDS (Hawkins, 1996).

Friend Loss Among the Elderly

Each year, approximately 13% of the elderly experience loss of close relationships, including friends, through disability or death (Morgan, 1994). Strong social networks among the elderly are associated with psychological adjustment, life satisfaction, and well-being. These social relationships can serve as a buffer against the challenges associated with increased age and help older persons to maintain positive self-regard and optimism under the most difficult of circumstances (Stevens-Long & Commons, 1992). This experience of frequent loss in one's social network, although a normative event in the later stages of life, can result in significant and ongoing bereavement overload. These losses of significant relationships typically occur in a broader context of loss during late adulthood, which can also involve loss of health, physical abilities, status, role, and financial security.

Friends are an important component of the social network of the elderly, but their role in the lives of older persons has been understudied. Roberto and Stanis (1994) report that maintenance of close friendships appears to have a stronger, more positive influence on older adults' sense of well-being than their relationships with family members. Particularly after loss of a spouse, older individuals tend to rely on their friends for increased social support and companionship. In one of the few studies of bereavement patterns of adults losing a close friend to death, the investigators found grief responses that paralleled those reported after the death of a close family member (Sklar & Hartley, 1990). Unfortunately, the significance of friendship losses among adults are not generally recognized.

In their study, which focused on reactions of older women to the death of a close friend, Roberto and Stanis (1994) found that loneliness was often a critical aspect of the loss. When asked what they missed most about their close friendships, the most common responses of the older bereaved "friend-survivors" were "doing things and just being together" (43%) and "talking and sharing" (33%). The investigators point out that this type of loss is likely to have a greater impact among the elderly who already have a shrinking social network, due to advancing age or widowhood. However, many of the older women in the Roberto and Stanis study appeared to compensate partly for their loss by becoming closer to their remaining friends. A quarter of the sample also reported developing new relationships. Intervention efforts at the community level should involve providing more opportunities for older citizens to socialize and expand their existing network of peers.

PET LOSS

Many people view pets as important in their lives, and recent studies have substantiated the strength of the bond between humans and animals. Pets not only

The human-animal bond can be very strong and satisfy basic human needs for love and companionship.

can contribute to one's quality of life, but also appear to satisfy basic human needs for love and companionship. The majority of pet owners report receiving more companionship from their animals than from neighbors and friends. In fact, many say their pets are as important to them as family members and relatives (Sussman, 1985). Although the death of a pet is often the first exposure to death for many children, it may also be a significant cause for grieving for some older individuals.

Lagoni, Butler, and Hetts (1994) in their book *The Human-Animal Bond and Grief* emphasize that pets can be an avenue for the expression of affection, nurturance, and competence at all stages of the human life span. For older persons, these functions of pet ownership may be especially important. As an age group experiencing a variety of losses, the elderly often experience diminished self-esteem, threatened images of self-identity, and exclusion from meaningful social participation as an accompaniment to these losses. Pets can serve special needs in the lives of the elderly by relieving loneliness, giving a sense of usefulness and purpose, and contributing to a sense of continuity and structure. Older pet owners continue to feel loved and valued by their animals despite other losses in their lives—changes in their appearance, income level, and physical abilities. Pets can also have symbolic value for individuals in the later stages of life. For example, following the death of a spouse, a family pet may be associated with feelings surrounding earlier family relationships and therefore serve as a link with the past (Ryder, 1985).

The death of a pet tends to elicit the normal range of responses associated with grief; however, others tend not to acknowledge the significance of the loss. The human-animal bond is discounted by comments such as "It was only a dog. You can get another one." For the elderly, a pet dying may mean much more than simply the loss of a valued relationship. The event can also represent the end of an era, a social and emotional void, and the beginning of the unknown. When this loss occurs to persons having few remaining friends and family, their reasons for living may be challenged (Cowles, 1985; Shirley & Mercier, 1983).

Loss of a companion animal by the elderly is often not due to an actual death but rather life circumstances. For instance, older individuals may be forced to give up their pets if they move into senior citizen housing programs or nursing homes. Even if remaining in their own homes, they may develop physical problems that are incompatible with pet ownership. Reduced and fixed income may also make it difficult to provide an animal's needs, especially during times of illness. A single pet surgery or treatment can easily cost as much as the total monthly income of many older individuals. When older persons are no longer able to care for their pets, they are sometimes placed with a relative or friend so that the owner still has some contact with them. When older, sick animals are involved, **euthanizing** the pet (the act of causing death painlessly so as to end suffering) may be the only alternative left. Depending on the circumstances surrounding the loss, the grief experienced by the pet owner may involve a great deal of anger and guilt (Lagoni et al., 1994).

Recognizing the needs of individuals in anticipation of or following a loss, the Veterinary Teaching Hospital at Colorado State University has established a resource program, referred to as CHANGES, for individuals dealing with grief-related issues pertaining to their pets. In addition to offering counseling and support, the staff gives guidance on how to explain the death of a pet to children, assists owners in making decisions about euthanasia, and makes appropriate referrals for those individuals needing further assistance. Involving professionals from a variety of disciplines, this program also provides instruction and training for veterinary students on the human-animal bond, the experience of grief, and their role in the grief-related situations they will encounter in the practice of their profession.

INTERVENTIONS FOR BEREAVED ADULTS

In this chapter, we have mentioned the importance of support groups and various forms of therapy as often useful in coping with loss. Chapter 3 also emphasizes the critical role of social support for the bereaved. Individuals themselves frequently engage in activities that promote their own healing. These activities are often expressive and may involve art, music, or literature. The following section offers further understanding of why these types of activities (using literature as an example) are often therapeutic.

Writing During Bereavement

Writing during bereavement can be therapeutic for many individuals. According to Lattanzi and Hale (1984):

> Writing can be a helpful and healing experience for grieving persons. It has not been fully explored or understood as a coping response in relation to the grief process. Just as people are changed by the experience of grief, the experience of expressing their grief can also change them. Shakespeare wisely advised us to "give grief words." It is generally acknowledged that the expression of grief can soften the impact and contribute to the management of the experience. (p. 45)

These authors point out that throughout time, people have described some of their deepest thoughts and feelings through their writings. An examination of some of the best-known literature throughout the centuries will reveal an abundance of books, plays, and poetry that convey themes of grief and loss. Lattanzi and Hale (1984) emphasize that writing will not be therapeutic for all persons or in all situations, but they feel that in many instances it can facilitate positive outcomes. "By tapping one's creative energy, writing can be not only a way for the bereaved to address their despair, but also a means of instilling hope through exploring the meaning of the experience" (p. 52).

Individuals may choose to put their grief into words for varying reasons. Writing, especially for professional writers and journalists who have experienced a profound loss, may be a natural way to express their pain. It can also be a way to immortalize the deceased or the writer's relationship with the deceased. Grieving individuals may also feel a sense of responsibility to share their experience with a larger audience in an attempt to educate or enlighten others. Many personal accounts of bereavement have been published in books and popular magazines. The authors of these works often express the hope that others will find comfort, or in some way benefit, from their literary contribution. Through this process, the death is seen as having some positive outcomes.

In addition to published materials, individuals often find solace in more personal forms of written expression, such as diaries and journals. At times, recording thoughts and feelings can be a vehicle for stating that which cannot comfortably be said aloud. If writings are shared with significant others, they can often be an avenue for increased communication and emotional support. The process itself can also provide valuable insights and perspectives. As time passes, a review of earlier writings can help the bereaved recognize the personal changes they have experienced and the healing that has occurred.

Bibliotherapy

Adult bereaved survivors can also benefit and derive meaning from reading literature written by others. Individuals who are grieving often request written materials to help them better understand the grief process. Reading an account of another person's bereavement can sometimes reassure them that their grief is normal and that they, too, can cope.

The therapeutic use of literature is referred to as **bibliotherapy** (previously discussed in the context of childhood grief). Through bibliotherapy, persons can often identify with the circumstances they are reading about, leading to catharsis and insight about their own particular situation. A range of feelings and reactions are validated as they read detailed narratives of the healing process. The personal accounts included in this textbook are excellent examples of grief literature that can benefit others. Although the process of writing is typically therapeutic for the author, the benefits extend to many who have the opportunity to read and learn from their work.

SUMMARY

Loss is part of adult life, occurring with increased frequency as individuals age. Death of a spouse, for example, especially among women, is a common occurrence during late adulthood. Widowed individuals at any age face a variety of emotional, social, financial, and role adjustments. Death of a former spouse may also cause grief, even if the couple had been divorced for some time prior to the death. This is particularly true if the grief triggered by the divorce itself has not been resolved.

Loss of one's parents is the most common type of bereavement during the middle adult years. Reaction to this loss is complex and involves facing one's own mortality, accepting that one's family of origin is irreplaceably lost, and feeling the weight of responsibility for younger generations.

As more individuals live to advanced old age, the probability increases that they will experience the death of an adult child. Although the adult child may also be elderly, the death of one's offspring is difficult at any age. During the later years of life, death of a child is also often associated with loss of a major source of social support.

Peer loss during the adult years has received little attention. Some situations and life stages involve multiple peer loss: combat situations during times of war, the male homosexual community with its high incidence of AIDS, and the normal loss of peers with advanced age. Each of these circumstances also involves multiple additional losses and unique issues that can challenge one's ability to cope (e.g., survivor guilt among war veterans, the social stigma associated with AIDS, and the dwindling social networks of the elderly).

Many older persons have pets who fulfill special needs in their lives and give them a sense of usefulness and purpose. When their companion animals die, their owners frequently experience grief; however, the intensity of their feelings is often not acknowledged by others.

Various approaches to intervention for adult survivors have been developed. Support groups, in particular, have been used to help groups such as widows, war veterans, parents of deceased children, and others cope with the unique circumstances of their loss. Writing during bereavement can be meaningful for many grievers, and some bereaved individuals share their writings with others through published accounts of their experience with loss. The readers of these works often find inspiration from learning how others have coped during painful circumstances similar to their own.

Personal Account

A decade after the Challenger space shuttle disaster, the father of Gregory Jarvis, one of the crew members, reflects on his son's life and death as well as his own continuing feelings of loss and sadness.

Father of Challenger Crew Member Still Struggling With Anguish
Marcia Dunn

They were entertaining friends and relatives when the phone rang that January night. It was Greg calling to say hello—his father and stepmother hadn't heard from him in a while—and to tell them tomorrow appeared to be The Day.

After months of being bumped from flight to flight and enduring multiple launch delays, Greg Jarvis felt sure he finally would be heading into space aboard the shuttle Challenger.

The call lasted only a few minutes. The other astronauts were waiting to use the phone at the Kennedy Space Center, and Greg had to be brief. He waited until he was ready to hang up, and then he said it: "I love you, Dad."

He had never told his father that before.

Right then and there, in front of his wife and their out-of-town company, Bruce Jarvis, normally unemotional, broke down in tears. "I love you, son," he replied. He had never said that before, not in all of Greg's 41 years.

That was their last conversation, their very last words to one another. An omen, Bruce Jarvis now feels.

On Jan. 28, 1986, at 11:39 a.m. EST, Gregory Bruce Jarvis and his six Challenger crewmates died in a fireball in the sky.

Years later, his father is still heartsick and bitter about the decision by NASA and booster maker Morton Thiokol Inc. to launch Challenger that cold fateful morning, despite engineers' warnings about the now-infamous O-rings. He no longer dwells on it, though, and is trying to make amends for his son's lost life, and their lost relationship.

At age 78, he figures it's now or never.

This is his story.

It's a sunny Orlando morning and, as usual, Bruce Jarvis is prowling his neighborhood and nearby shopping-mall parking lots in search of Challenger license plates.

He used to go by foot, striding up and down the endless rows of cars and leaving blue thank-you cards on the driver's-side windows of vehicles with

SOURCE: From Marcia Dunn, "Father of Challenger Crew Member Still Struggling With Anguish," The Associated Press.

the commemorative plates. Nowadays, Jarvis has trouble walking, so he bikes. Even though he's slower and doesn't get out as much—"I just don't have the health"—he won't stop. He can't.

He's always on the lookout for the fundraising plates, even when he goes down to the lake on the edge of his condominium complex at daybreak to feed the ducks.

"I got so that I could spot one of these things a half-mile away," he boasts.

Jarvis never leaves the house without a pocket full of the business-size cards, even though there seem to be fewer and fewer Challenger plates around these days.

The cards are signed by both Jarvis and his wife of 20 years, Ellen. They read: "On behalf of Greg Jarvis and the crew, Bruce and Ellen Jarvis thank you for purchasing a Challenger plate. Your continued renewal is appreciated."

Jarvis has been cursed on occasion and left standing in engine exhaust; the drivers thought he was peddling something. But for the most part, motorists are touched and grateful.

He figures he and his wife, also 78, have handed out about 5,000 cards since the first Challenger license plates were issued to Florida residents a year after the accident. (The couple got the first two; his bears Greg's birth date.) The commemorative plates have raised $16 million for the Astronauts Memorial Foundation at the Kennedy Space Center, paying for a huge granite monument bearing the names of the 16 Americans who have died so far in the line of space duty, and a space education center.

It is Jarvis' passion and mission in what's left of his life. He and his wife see it as a way to keep the memory of the Challenger Seven—especially that of Greg—burning bright.

Of the seven crew members, he is, perhaps, the one most overlooked, the one most easily forgotten.

There was Christa McAuliffe, the schoolteacher from Concord, N.H., who was going to use Challenger as an orbital classroom. Schoolchildren everywhere tuned in to watch her soar; their joy quickly turned into anguish.

CHALLENGER'S CREW

It was as diverse a space shuttle crew as ever—male, female, white, black, Asian-American, Christian, Jewish. A look at the seven:

- Ellison Onizuka: Air Force lieutenant colonel from Kealakekua, Kona, Hawaii, and first Asian-American in space. Age 39. Married. Two children, now 22 and 28. Second shuttle flight.
- Michael Smith, pilot: Navy captain and former combat pilot from Beaufort, NC. Age 40. Married. Three children, now 20, 26 and 29. First shuttle flight.
- Christa McAuliffe: Schoolteacher in Concord, N.H., and first private citizen chosen to fly in space. Age 37. Married. Two children, now 18 and 21. First shuttle flight.

- Francis "Dick" Scobee, commander. Former Air Force and combat pilot from Cle Elum, Wash. Age 46. Married. Two children, now 33 and 36. Second shuttle flight.
- Gregory Jarvis: Hughes Aircraft Co. engineer in Los Angeles. Age 41. Married. No children. First shuttle flight.
- Ronald McNair: Physicist from Lake City, SC and second black person in space. Age 35. Married. Two children, now 13 and 15. Karate instructor, jazz saxophonist. Second shuttle flight.
- Judith Resnik: Electrical engineer from Akron, Ohio, and second American woman in space. Age 36. Divorced. No children. Jewish. Classical pianist. Second shuttle flight.

There were commander Francis "Dick" Scobee and pilot Michael Smith; Judith Resnik, the second American woman in space; Ronald McNair, the second black person in space; and Ellison Onizuka, the first Asian-American in space.

And there was Greg, a Hughes Aircraft Co. engineer who had been bumped from Discovery by a senator and from Columbia by a congressman. He was going to conduct fluid experiments in orbit. He designed and managed satellites but was not a professional astronaut.

"This is my one chance," Greg had said.

Neither Bruce nor Ellen Jarvis was concerned about his safety. After all, NASA's winged space planes had been flying since 1981. Shuttle flight had become almost routine, in fact, and was generating less public interest.

For Greg, though, this was "the ultimate trip."

It lasted 73 seconds.

Challenger ruptured 8.9 miles above the Atlantic Ocean while traveling at 1,460 mph, or nearly twice the speed of sound. The pressure seals, or O-rings, in a critical joint of the right solid-fuel rocket booster had given way in the cold—it was 36 degrees at launch time—and failed to contain the combustible rocket gases.

It was like a blowtorch, fast and furious, creating a hole in the external fuel tank, which collapsed. At the same time, the tip of the leaking booster rotated and crashed into the upper part of the external tank, the final blow.

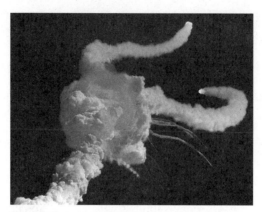

*The Challenger exploded suddenly over the
Atlantic Ocean as the world watched in shock
and disbelief.*

Bruce and Ellen Jarvis watched in disbelief from the launch site as chunks of shuttle rained onto Earth. "Obviously a major malfunction," Mission Control reported amid the confusion.

The couple were hustled away by NASA officials, along with the other astronauts' families. Jarvis, then 68, required medical attention; his wife feared he had gone into shock.

Greg Jarvis' remains were the last ones found, three long months after the accident. His widow, Marcia, scattered his ashes into the Pacific Ocean, off the Southern California coast where the two had lived—they had no children—and cut off contact with her in-laws.

For Bruce Jarvis, peace, such as it was, lay in the Astronauts Memorial Foundation, created shortly after the accident, and in the thank-you cards.

"Greg would appreciate what we're doing, what they're doing, what we're helping them do, much more than anything else I can think of," he says.

It helps Bruce and Ellen feel closer to Greg—and maybe, just maybe, Jarvis says, it makes up for all the time he should have, and could have, spent with his son over the years.

"I wish I'd had more time for all of them," he says of his three sons. "But now that I've got the time . . ." His voice trails off.

He explains it another day:

The Jarvis family wasn't particularly close while Greg and his two younger brothers were growing up in Mohawk, N.Y. Like his father before him, Bruce Jarvis was too busy running the family pharmacy to dote on his children. So it was only natural that after Greg left for the State University of New York at Buffalo, he returned home less and less, especially after he married Marcia and his parents divorced.

Bruce Jarvis' subsequent marriage to Ellen, who encouraged him to be a more expressive father, gradually improved the relationship between father and son. Greg kept his father abreast of his growing number of achievements in the satellite world, first with the Air Force and then with Hughes Aircraft in Los Angeles, as well as all his outdoor adventures with Marcia—100-mile bike rides, white-water rafting, cross-country skiing.

Gregg's selection as a space shuttle payload specialist in 1984 was, for father and son, a professional pinnacle. His phone call to his father the night of Jan. 26 or 27, 1986—Bruce and Ellen Jarvis disagree which night it was—surpassed that, at least in the eyes of the father.

"Oh, God, I was ecstatic," Jarvis recalls.

But in one horrific instant, all the dreams-come-true and dreams-to-be were snuffed out.

A commission appointed by President Reagan blamed the accident on a frightening number of mistakes rooted in history—a faulty rocket-joint design, unrelenting pressure to meet the demands of an accelerating flight schedule, a silent safety program, poor communications, slack management.

The findings rocked NASA and forced changes. Even unwitting members of the launch team were ashamed and felt guilty.

Some still do.

"There are some who today are not totally over the Challenger event," says shuttle operations director Bob Sieck, who was in the launch control center that fateful morning. "Nobody who was a member of the team will forget it."

Especially heart-rending for Jarvis was—and still is—not knowing precisely when his son died. He suspects Greg was alive when the crew cabin slammed into the Atlantic and was possibly aware of what was happening.

"I'll never forgive them," Jarvis says of Morton Thiokol.

Like other relatives of the Challenger crew, Jarvis sued. He received an undisclosed sum from Morton Thiokol, enough, he says, to live comfortably.

No matter how much it still hurts, Bruce and Ellen Jarvis go to every Challenger memorial to which they're invited. They feel obliged.

"It can be devastating, really," he says. "You cry at every one."

They have no idea how many ceremonies they have attended around the country over the past decade, or how many times they have made the hour-long drive to the Kennedy Space Center for Challenger tributes. The Astronauts Memorial Foundation plans a low-key ceremony next Sunday; Jarvis will be there.

"He's the kind of guy who will go anyplace, anytime, to spread the gospel of the foundation," says foundation President Jim DeSantis. "He's been a key player in all of this, never wavered, always been supportive."

But finally, mercifully, life has become calmer for the Jarvises. There are fewer ceremonies, fewer people telling them where they were when Challenger exploded and how very sorry they are, and fewer tears.

Last January, they sent piles of newspaper clippings, cards, letters and other mementos to the Weller Library in Mohawk, population 2,986, for a permanent display dedicated to hometown hero Greg.

Still, plenty remains.

Framed photographs of Greg, the entire crew, even the aftermath of the explosion adorn the Jarvises' living-room walls (seven birds are shown flying out of the plumes of smoke). Tables and shelves hold plaques, other commemorative gifts and snapshots of the couple at various memorials.

Carefully packed away in the bedroom are a seldom-worn man's white cardigan sweater and a gold-colored golf ball, cherished presents from Greg, as well as snapshots of the bundled-up couple on launch morning and of the rising shuttle. There's also a copy of the letter the Jarvises wrote to Greg right before the flight, telling him how proud they were and how he should take their love with him into space.

"Time helps," Jarvis says. "But, unfortunately, it doesn't seem like it was 10 years ago."

"It doesn't," his wife agrees, barely audible.

"Here we are still living," she goes on, "and all these people had such dreams and that vision and had so much to contribute. It's just not in sequence. It should be the other way around."

Shuttles have flown 49 times since the Challenger accident, each time with Jarvis at home holding his breath. The score so far is 73 successes, one failure. NASA estimates the odds of a disaster at about one in 100 missions. This is NASA's best guess.

For many reasons, those odds included, Jarvis will never go back for a launch. Ever. But he has changed his mind, mellowed if you will, on another emotional matter.

He wants to reconcile with his daughter-in-law, who still lives in California.

"I don't want to be dead before I've made amends," he says. So he'll try. After 10 years, he says, it's time to live and let live.

QUESTIONS AND ACTIVITIES

1. Where were you when you heard about the Challenger disaster? If you can, recall your reactions and those of others close to you. What do you remember about the ways teachers, the news media, and government officials responded to this national tragedy?

2. How do the mass media portray death? What ethical issues arise when reporters interview the bereaved? Should guidelines be developed for coverage of death-related issues on television and other forms of mass media? If so, who should set them and what should they be? What are the dangers of this type of action?

3. Individuals can grieve over the loss of someone they did not know personally, but learned about through media coverage. Identify a recent death that may have affected you this way. What were your reactions as the person's story unfolded in the media?

4. In what ways are civilians affected when a military conflict occurs in their homeland? Use a recent international event covered in the news to illustrate your points. Can you think of places in the world that are virtual war

zones due to ongoing conflict and unrest, even though a war has not been declared?

5. Use the Internet to access Web site http://www.aidsquilt.org and view samples of panels in the AIDS quilt. What common themes are present? In what ways are cultural traditions, symbols, and images reflected?

GLOSSARY

Bibliotherapy: the therapeutic use of literature.

Conjugal: pertaining to a marital relationship.

Euthanizing: the act of causing death painlessly so as to end suffering.

Husband sanctification: the tendency of bereaved widows to overly idealize their deceased husbands.

Post-traumatic stress disorder: a persistent condition resulting from exposure to a traumatic event.

Psychic numbness: intellectual awareness of death and suffering, concurrent with emotional desensitization that may be necessary for survival and effective functioning.

Traumatic stress: a situation or event that is generally outside the range of normal human experience and therefore would evoke significant symptoms of stress in almost anyone.

Self-help groups: intervention groups composed of members with similar experiences that emphasize mutual support.

Survivor guilt: guilt over having survived when others have died.

Survivor syndrome: constellation of psychological reactions, which include survivor guilt, death anxiety, and psychic numbing.

Worried well: individuals who do not have AIDS at present but who fear they will develop the disease.

SUGGESTED READINGS

Campbell, S., & Silverman, P. R. (1996). *Widower: When men are left alone.* Amityville, NY: Baywood.

Through firsthand accounts of widowers, the authors explore and analyze the grief process experienced by men. A variety of loss situations are presented that offer insight into different ways of successfully coping with loss of a spouse.

Hughes, M. (1995). *Bereavement and support: Healing in a group environment.* Washington, DC: Taylor & Francis.

Concrete suggestions are given on how to establish and facilitate both structured and unstructured bereavement support groups. Unique needs of special populations (e.g., children, grievers of homicide deaths, victims of community disasters) are also addressed.

Seliger, M., & Kahn, L. (1996). *When they came to take my father: Voices of the Holocaust.* New York: Arcade Publishing.

First-person accounts of the Holocaust experience and the loss of loved ones accompany intimate photographs that attest to survivorship and the strength of spirit. This powerful collection of words and images gives us a close look at grief associated with traumatic and large-scale death.

Sherr, L. (Ed.). (1995). *Grief and AIDS.* Chichester, England: Wiley.

Based on current knowledge and clinical practice, this book provides a detailed look at contemporary issues related to AIDS and HIV infection and implications for counseling. The focus is on the unique issues and needs of those dying or bereaved from the disease. Deaths of a parent, child, and partner by AIDS are addressed in separate chapters.

RESOURCES

CHANGES (Grief education and support program)
Veterinary Teaching Hospital
Colorado State University
300 West Drake
Fort Collins, CO 80523
(970) 491-7101

International Association for Traumatic Stress Studies
60 Revere Drive, Suite 500
Northbrook, IL 60062
(847) 480-9028

Tragedy Assistance Program for Survivors, Inc. (TAPS)
807 G Street, Suite 250
Anchorage, AK 99501
(907) 272-TAPS or 1-800-959-TAPS

Widowed Persons Service
AARP/American Association of Retired Persons
601 E Street, N.W.
Washington, DC 20049
(202) 434-2260

Department of Veteran's Administration Affairs
810 Vermont Avenue, N.W.
Washington, DC 20420
(202) 273-5400 or 1-800-827-1000

REFERENCES

American Psychiatric Association. (1994). *Diagnostic and statistical manual of mental disorders* (4th ed.). Washington, DC: Author.

Biller, R., & Rice, S. (1990). Experiencing multiple loss of persons with AIDS: Grief and bereavement issues. *Health and Social Work, 15*(4), 283-290.

Bound, J. (1991). Poverty dynamics in widowhood. *Journal of Gerontology, 46*(3), S115–S124.

Brende, J. O., & Parson, E. R. (1985). *Vietnam veterans: The road to recovery.* New York: Plenum Press.

Brubaker, E. (1985). Older parents' reactions to the death of adult children: Implications for practice. *Journal of Gerontological Social Work, 9*(1), 35–48.

Burkhauser, R. V., Butler, J. S., & Holden, K. C. (1991). How the death of a spouse affects economic well-being after retirement: A hazard model approach. *Social Science Quarterly, 72*(3), 504–519.

Campbell, G., & Chauncey, C. T. (1994). Money matters: The economics of aging for women. In P. B. Doress-Worters & D. L. Siegal (Eds.), *The new ourselves, growing older: Women aging with knowledge and power* (pp. 187–203). New York: Simon & Schuster.

Campbell, S., & Silverman, P. R. (1996). *Widower: When men are left alone.* Amityville, NY: Baywood.

Clark, P. G., Siviski, R. W., & Weiner, R. (1986). Coping strategies of widowers in the first year. *Family Relations, 35*(3), 425–430.

Cook, A. S., & Dworkin, D. S. (1992). *Helping the bereaved: Therapeutic interventions for children, adolescents, and adults.* New York: Basic Books.

Cowles, K. V. (1985). The death of a pet: Human responses to the breaking of a bond. *Marriage and Family Review, 8,* 135–148.

DeVries, R., Lana, R. D., & Falck, V. T. (1994). Parental bereavement over the life course: A theoretical intersection and empirical review. *Omega, 29*(1), 47–69.

Dilley, J., & Moon, T. (1994). Supporting uninfected gay and bisexual men. *Focus: A guide to AIDS research and counseling, 8*(6), 1–4.

Doka, K. (1986). Loss upon loss: The impact of death after divorce. *Death Studies, 10*(5), 441–449.

Doka, K. (Ed.). (1989). *Disenfranchised grief: Recognizing hidden sorrow.* Lexington, MA: Lexington Books.

Douglas, J. D. (1990). Patterns of change following parent death in midlife adults. *Omega, 22*(2), 123–137.

Farberow, N. L., Gallagher-Thompson, D., Gilewski, M., & Thompson, L. (1992). The role of social supports in the bereavement process of surviving spouses of suicide and natural deaths. *Suicide and Life-Threatening Behavior, 22*(1), 107–124.

Figley, C. R., & Kleber, R. J. (1995). Beyond the "victim": Secondary traumatic stress. In R. J. Kleber, C. R. Figley, & B. P. R. Gersons (Eds.), *Beyond trauma: Cultural and societal dynamics* (pp. 75–98). New York: Plenum Press.

Figley, C., & Salison, S. (1980). Treating Vietnam veterans as survivors. *Evaluation and Change: Services for Survivors* [Special issue], 135–141.

Fitzgerald, F. (1986). *Cities on a hill.* New York: Simon & Schuster.

Fowlkes, M. R. (1990). The social regulation of grief. *Sociological Forum, 5*(4), 635–652.

Foy, D. W., & Card, J. J. (1987). Combat-related post-traumatic stress disorder etiology: Replicated findings in a national sample of Vietnam-era men. *Journal of Clinical Psychology, 43*(1), 28–31.

Galea, R. P., Lewis, B. F., & Baker, L. A. (1988). Voluntary testing for HIV antibodies. *Journal of the National Association of Social Workers, 33*(3), 265–268.

Hawkins, P. S. (1996). *Ars Memoriandi:* The NAMES Project AIDS quilt. In H. M. Sprio, M. G. McCrea Curnen, & L. P. Wandel (Eds.), *Facing death: Where culture, religion, and medicine meet* (pp. 166–179). New Haven, CT: Yale University Press.

Hendin, H., & Haas, A. P. (1984). *Wounds of war: The psychological aftermath of combat in Vietnam.* New York: Basic Books.

Holmes, T. H., & Rahe, R. (1967). Social readjustment rating scale. *Journal of Psychosomatic Research, 11,* 213–218.

Horowitz, M. J., Weiss, D. S., Kaltreider, N., Krupnick, J., Marmar, C., Wilner, N., & DeWitt, K. (1984). Reactions to the death of a parent. *Journal of Nervous and Mental Disease, 172*(7), 383–392.

King, G. B. (1985). Social security and the changing role of women. In U.S. Senate, Special Committee on Aging, *Fifty years of social security: Past achievements and future challenges* (pp. 60–72). Washington, DC: U.S. Government Printing Office.

Kitson, G. C., Lopata, H., Holmes, W., & Meyering, S. (1980). Divorcees and widows: Similarities and differences. *American Journal of Orthopsychiatry, 50*(2), 291–301.

Klass, D., Silverman, P. R., & Nickman, S. L. (Eds.). (1996). *Continuing bonds: New understandings of grief.* Washington, DC: Taylor & Francis.

Lagoni, L., Butler, C., & Hetts, S. (1994). *The human-animal bond and grief.* Philadelphia: Saunders.

Lattanzi, M., & Hale, M. E. (1984). Giving grief words: Writing during bereavement. *Omega, 15*(1), 45–52.

Lieberman, M. A. (1993). Bereavement self-help groups: A review of conceptual and methodological issues. In M. S. Stroebe, W. Stroebe, & R. O. Hansson (Eds.), *Handbook of bereavement* (pp. 411–426). New York: Cambridge University Press.

Lopata, H. Z. (1979). Widowhood and husband sanctification. In L. A. Bugen (Ed.), *Death and dying: Theory/research/practice* (pp. 205–211). Dubuque, IA: William C. Bown.

Lopata, H. Z. (1993). The support systems of American urban widows. In M. S. Stroebe, W. Stroebe, & R. O. Hansson (Eds.), *Handbook of bereavement* (pp. 381–396). New York: Cambridge University Press.

Lund, D. A., Caserta, M. S., & Dimond, M. F. (1993). The course of spousal bereavement in later life. In M. S. Stroebe, W. Stroebe, R. O. Hansson (Eds.), *Handbook of bereavement* (pp. 240–254). New York: Cambridge University Press.

Lund, D. A., Dimond, M., & Juretich, M. (1985). Bereavement support groups for the elderly: Characteristics of potential participants. *Death Studies, 9,* 309–321.

Martin, J. I., & Dean, L. (1993). Effects of AIDS-related bereavement and HIV-related illness on psychological distress among gay men: A 7-year longitudinal study, 1985–1991. *Journal of Consulting and Clinical Psychology, 61*(1), 94–103.

Martin, J. L., & Garcia, M. (1989). The impact of AIDS on a gay community: Changes in sexual behavior, substance abuse, and mental health. *American Journal of Community Psychology, 17*(3), 269–293.

Mills, J., & Masur, H. (1990). AIDS-related infections. *Scientific American, 263* (2), 50–57.

Morgan, J. P., Jr. (1994). Bereavement in older adults. *Journal of Mental Health Counseling, 16*(3), 318–326.

Moss, M. S., Lesher, E. L., & Moss, S. Z. (1986). Impact of the death of an adult child on elderly parents: Some observations. *Omega, 17*(3), 209–218.

Moss, M. S., & Moss, S. Z. (1983). The impact of parental loss on middle-aged children. *Omega, 14*(1), 65–75.

Moss, M. S., & Moss, S. Z. (1984). Some aspects of the elderly widow(er)'s persistent tie with the deceased spouse. *Omega, 15*(3), 195–206.

Osterweis, M., Solomon, F., & Green, M. (Eds.). (1984). *Bereavement: Reactions, consequences, and care.* Washington, DC: National Academy Press.

Parkes, C. M., & Weiss, R. S. (1983). *Recovery from bereavement.* New York: Basic Books.

Parson, E. R. (1986). Life after death: Vietnam veterans' struggle for meaning and recovery. *Death Studies, 10,* 11-26.

Pearce, K. A., Schauer, A. H., Garfield, N. J., Ohlde, C. O., & Patterson, T. W. (1985). A study of post-traumatic stress disorder in Vietnam veterans. *Journal of Clinical Psychology, 41*(1), 9-14.

Raphael, B. (1983). *The anatomy of bereavement.* New York: Basic Books.

Rando, T. A. (1986). Death of the adult child. In T. A. Rando (Ed.), *Parental loss of a child* (pp. 221-238). Champaign, IL: Research Press.

Richmond, B. J., & Ross, M. W. (1995). Death of a partner: Responses to AIDS-related bereavement. In L. Sherr (Ed.), *Grief and AIDS* (pp. 161-179). Chichester, England: Wiley.

Robbins, M. (1990). *Midlife women and death of a mother.* New York: Peter Lang.

Roberto, K. A., & Stanis, P. I. (1994). Reactions of older women to the death of their close friends. *Omega, 29*(1), 17-27.

Ryder, E. L. (1985). Pets and the elderly: A social work perspective. *Veterinary Clinics of North America: Small Animal Practice, 15*(2), 333-343.

Sanders, C. M. (1980). A comparison of adult bereavement in the death of a spouse, child, and parent. *Omega, 10*(4), 303-322.

Scharlach, A. E., & Fredriksen, K. I. (1993). Reactions to the death of a parent during midlife. *Omega, 27*(4), 307-319.

Schwartzberg, S. S. (1992). AIDS-related bereavement among gay men: The inadequacy of current theories of grief. *Psychotherapy, 29,* 422-429.

Shirley, V., & Mercier, J. (1983). Bereavement of older persons. *The Gerontologist, 23,* 276.

Silver, S. M., & Iacono, C. U. (1984). Factor analytic support for the DSM-III's post-traumatic stress disorder for Vietnam veterans. *Journal of Clinical Psychology, 40*(1), 5-14.

Silverman, P. R. (1986). *Widow-to-widow.* New York: Springer.

Silverman, P. R. (1987). Widowhood as the next stage in the life course. In H. Z. Lopata (Ed.), *Widows: North America (Vol. 2)* (pp. 171-190). Durham, NC: Duke University Press.

Sklar, F., & Hartley, S. (1990). Close friends as survivors: Bereavement patterns in a "hidden" population. *Omega, 21,* 103-112.

Small, N. (1993). HIV/AIDS: Lessons for policy and practice. In D. Clark (Ed.), *The future of palliative care* (pp. 80-97). Philadelphia: Open University Press.

Solkoff, N., Gray, P., & Keill, S. (1986). Which Vietnam veterans develop post-traumatic disorders? *Journal of Clinical Psychology, 42*(5), 687-698.

Stevens-Long, J., & Commons, M. L. (1992). *Adult life* (4th ed.). Mountain View, CA: Mayfield Publishing.

Stroebe, M. S., & Strobe, W. (1993). The mortality of bereavement: A review. In M. S. Stroebe, W. Stroebe, & R. O. Hansson (Eds.), *Handbook of bereavement* (pp. 175-195). New York: Cambridge University Press.

Stylianos, S. K., & Vachon, M. L. S. (1993). The role of social support in bereavement. In M. S. Stroebe, W. Stroebe, & R. O. Hansson (Eds.), *Handbook of bereavement* (pp. 397-410). New York: Cambridge University Press.

Sullivan, A. (1990). Gay life, gay death. *The New Republic,* December 17, 19-25.

Sussman, M. B. (1985). Pet/human bonding: Applications, conceptual and research issues. *Marriage and Family Review, 8,* 1-4.

Tick, E. (1985). Vietnam grief: Psychotherapeutic and psychohistorical implications. In E. M. Stern (Ed.), *Psychotherapy and the grieving patient* (pp. 101–115). New York: Haworth Press.

U.S. Bureau of the Census. (1996). *Statistical Abstract of the United States: 1996* (116th edition). Washington, DC: U. S. Government Printing Office.

Umberson, D., & Chen, M. D. (1994). Effects of a parent's death on adult children: Relationship salience and reaction to loss. *American Sociological Review, 59,* 152–168.

Vachon, M. L. S., Sheldon, A. R., Lancee, W. J., Lyall, W. A. L., Rogers, J., & Freeman, S. J. J. (1980). A controlled study of self-help intervention for widows. *American Journal of Psychiatry, 137,* 1380–1384.

Vachon, M. L. S., Sheldon, A. R., Lancee, W. J., Lyall, W. A. L., Rogers, S., & Freeman, S. J. J. (1982). Correlates of enduring distress patterns following bereavement: Social network, life situation, and personality. *Psychological Medicine, 12,* 783–788.

9

Suicide

Dear Mom, Dad, and everyone else,

I'm sorry for what I've done, but I loved you all and I always will, for eternity. Please, please, please don't blame it on yourselves. It was all my fault and not yours or anyone else's. If I didn't do this now, I would have done it later anyway. We all die some day, I just died sooner.

Love,
John

When left, suicide notes like the one above (Berman, 1986, p. 151) offer few reasons for the self-inflicted death. Suicide is a complex behavior with multiple determinants. No easy answers are found when family and friends ask "Why?" with regard to the self-destructive acts of their loved ones.

Suicide is typically an act of desperation by a person who believes that his or her only remaining option is self-destruction. This inability to consider alternative ways of dealing with a difficult situation is referred to as **tunnel vision.** The inability to perceive available options or solutions is affected by emotional depression, which is prevalent among many who attempt or complete suicide. Depression often involves feelings of helplessness and hopelessness. Consequently, suicidal individuals often feel that nothing they can do will make a difference. These kinds of thoughts occur when individuals are unable to mobilize their resources, view themselves as powerless, anticipate that their situation will not improve, and can see no way other than suicide to escape their emotional pain (Fairchild, 1986).

Recognizing that multiple factors contribute to suicidal acts, Stillion and McDowell (1996) have identified a number of common factors across age groups in a model they developed to describe suicide trajectories (see Figure 9.1). This model includes biological, psychological, cognitive, and environmental risk factors that can lead to suicidal ideation, possibly resulting in suicidal behavior. This behavior is often marked by ambivalence and frequently (although not always) preceded by a triggering event as well as warning signs. While there are many commonalities, these researchers emphasize that each age stage has unique risk factors, warning signs, and triggering events that must be taken into consideration when assessing suicide risk, providing appropriate intervention, and attempting to understand self-destructive behaviors.

Although there usually is no single cause of a suicide, loved ones struggle to find and comprehend reasons for the death. Professionals involved with the death are also left with many questions. Years ago, Shneidman (1969) introduced the **psychological autopsy** procedure, recognizing the need for a process of examination following a suicide (see Table 9.1). The focus of this formal review, used by many mental health facilities and other organizations, is on establishing events and other factors that preceded the suicide to identify causal and contributing factors. It should be held several weeks or months following the suicide, after the initial shock has subsided and feelings have been addressed. At this time, professionals can often benefit from a closer examination of the death and a discussion of preventive steps that could have been taken in a particular case.

FIGURE 9.1

The Suicide Trajectory: Life-Cycle Commonalities

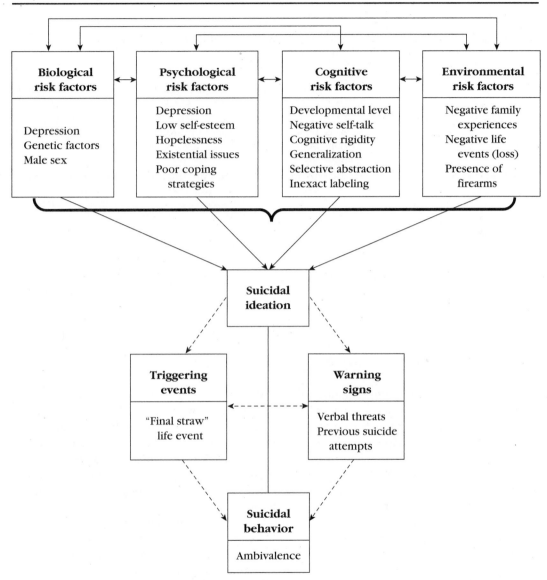

SOURCE: J. M. Stillion & E. E. McDowell (1996). *Suicide across the life span* (2nd ed.). Washington, DC: Taylor & Francis, pp. 21, 23. Reprinted by permission.

TABLE 9.1

Contents of the Psychological Autopsy

CATEGORIES	DESCRIPTIONS
Identification	Name, age, sex, marital status, residence, religious practices, employment status
Details of death	Cause, method, time, place, rating of lethality
Personal history	Medical history, psychiatric history, family history (medical illnesses, psychiatric illnesses, death, other suicides)
Personality and behavioral profile	Personality, lifestyle, typical reaction to stress, nature of interpersonal relationships, attitudes toward death (accidents, suicide, and homicide), extent of use of drugs and alcohol and their possible role in the death
Precipitating events	Circumstances immediately preceding death, changes in routine prior to death (habits, hobbies, sexual behavior, eating, work, etc.), incidence of positive influences in life (e.g., success, satisfaction, enjoyment, plans for the future), crises during past 5 years
Assessment of intentionality Reaction of informant to the death Comments	

SOURCE: J. M. Stillion & E. E. McDowell (1996). *Suicide across the life span* (2nd ed.). Washington, DC: Taylor & Francis, p. 230.

INCIDENCE OF SUICIDE

World Health Organization suicide statistics for both men and women in selected countries appear in Figure 9.2 and show considerable variation. (Official suicide mortality data are not available for most African countries and many Middle Eastern countries.) Suicide rates are, in most cases, much higher for males than for females, regardless of the cultural context. Exceptions include China (which currently only reports data on 10% of its population) and Papua New Guinea (which has a high incidence of wife battering, possibly contributing to the higher suicide rates among women).

No consistent association however has been found among the variables of age, gender, culture, and suicide mortality. In the United States, suicide mortality rates peak at midlife for women and in late life for men. In some other countries, this gender pattern is reversed (e.g., Scotland). A common pattern in many cultures is an increase in suicide rates with increased age for both men and women (e.g., Italy) (Canetto & Lester, 1995).

Meaningful comparisons among nations are often difficult because important contextual information (e.g., occupation, socioeconomic status) and demographic variables (e.g., ethnicity) are often not available. A more serious limitation is the lack of standardized and internationally accepted criteria for the determination of suicide mortality. Classification of a death as a suicide by

FIGURE 9.2

Age-Adjusted Suicide Rates per 100,000 Population for Men and Women for Selected Member Nations of the World Health Organization, 1990 and 1991

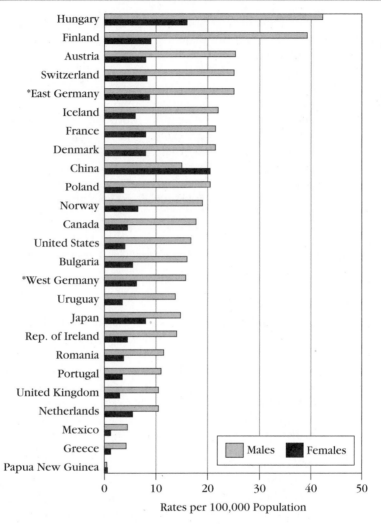

*Data obtained prior to reunification.
SOURCE: World Health Organization (1990, 1991).

coroners and medical examiners is influenced by cultural beliefs and social consequences of self-inflicted death. Although it is generally accepted that the official rates underestimate the true prevalence, this underestimate is likely to be higher for females than for males. Women's suicidal deaths are particularly susceptible to underreporting because they tend to use methods, such as poisons

HISTORICAL AND CULTURAL PERSPECTIVES ON SUICIDE

Attitudes toward self-inflicted death can only be understood within the particular historical and cultural context in which it occurs. All societies have developed a position toward suicide ranging from acceptance to prohibition, and the meanings attached to suicide have changed significantly over time. In ancient Greece, suicide was considered an acceptable option under certain situations, such as extraordinary sorrow or intolerable disgrace. The Buddhist tradition in China and Japan included the image of the "Great Death" and contributed to certain ritualized suicides considered as honorable (e.g., acts of *hari-kiri* committed by *samurai* warriors to avoid capture). One of the strongest cultural traditions regarding suicide is the Judeo-Christian view of suicide as sinful. Within this tradition, certain sanctions have been levied against those who take their own lives (e.g., denial of burial in a hallowed place, excommunication) (Kastenbaum, 1995; Sprang & McNeil, 1995).

SOURCES: R. J. Kastenbaum (1995). *Death, society, and human experience* (5th ed.). Boston, MA: Allyn & Bacon; G. Sprang & J. McNeil (1995). *The many faces of bereavement.* New York: Brunner/Mazel.

and medically prescribed drugs, that are more likely to lead to misclassification (Canetto & Lester, 1995).

Methods used also vary by cultural context. Firearms are the most common method used in the United States, especially for males. Only about 10% of Chinese Americans use this method; they are much more likely to hang themselves when attempting to end their lives. Also in European countries, firearms are much less likely to be used in suicides and there is much in-country variation based on ethnic group. For example, among Indian immigrants residing in England and Wales, committing suicide by setting oneself on fire is common, particularly among women (Canetto & Lester, 1995; Lester, 1994).

Figure 9.3 shows suicide rates by age, race, and gender in the United States. Of particular concern are suicide rates among the elderly and among adolescents; the highest suicide rate in America is among white elderly males, and the adolescent suicide rate has been escalating at an alarming rate for the past several decades. To illustrate the unique aspects of various life stages in regard to suicide, the following sections will focus on these two age groups.

DEVELOPMENTAL ISSUES

Suicide Among the Elderly

Although suicide threats are relatively uncommon among the elderly, they should be taken very seriously when they do occur. While there is only one suicide completion for every 100 to 200 attempts among those between 15 and

FIGURE 9.3

Suicide Rate by Age, Race, and Sex, 1993

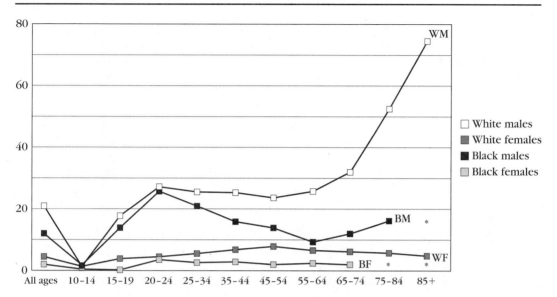

*Base figure too small to meet statistical standards of reliability.

SOURCE: U.S. National Center for Health Statistics, *Monthly Vital Statistics Report* (1993); and unpublished data.

24 years of age, there is one suicide completion for every four attempts among persons over 65 (American Association of Suicidology, 1996).

As shown in Figure 9.3, the suicide rate of elderly white males (65-74 years of age) in the United States is about 3 times that of black males, almost 5 times that of white females, and almost 16 times that of black females in the same age group. The reasons for these gender and ethnic differences in suicide rates among the elderly are not clear, but researchers do have several hypotheses. One common hypothesis is that retirement has a role in the suicides of elderly males. Retirement is a major life transition that involves leaving the workforce when one may still be competent and capable of working. It is also often associated with a change of routine, reduction in social network, and perceived lack of economic contribution to one's family and/or society. As a result, the elderly may feel unproductive and devalued following retirement. For many, it can symbolize a lowering of social status and income and may occur concurrently with a decline in physical and mental health. In addition, older men may have difficulty adjusting to a domestic role involving work in the home, given the traditional gender roles within this particular age cohort. Older white females and ethnic minority males and females who leave the workforce may not be affected as much by these losses because many have had to adjust to dependency and lower status all of their lives. In contrast, white males are generally more accustomed to having power and influence and, thus, have the greatest adaptation to make after retirement (Stenback, 1980).

CASE STUDY: ELDERLY SUICIDE

W. D. Henshaw killed himself on his 81st birthday. He carefully spread a newly purchased tarpaulin on the concrete floor of his garage, lay down on it and shot himself in the head. The terse suicide note he left said simply, "It's time."

W. D. was a self-made man. He often bragged to his children and grandchildren that he had come from a small dirt farm in the South, worked his way through college, and worked hard all his life. He had risen to a position of responsibility in an agricultural wholesale business by age 32. He had then resigned and started his own wholesale business. Working night and day, he was personally responsible for the success of his business. It was at that time in his life that he developed the habit of working from 5:30 A.M. until 7.30 P.M., a habit that lasted his entire life.

W. D. married at age 36. His wife was from a wealthy family, and her wealth provided even more security for the business. Although Mrs. Henshaw was 34 when they married, they had two children. The Henshaws appeared to have a stable if unexciting marriage. However, Mrs. Henshaw developed breast cancer at age 52 and died within six months. W. D. never remarried, devoting himself instead almost totally to his business.

W. D. bragged often about his reputation for hard work and honesty. As he grew older, his son and daughter tried to get him to slow down, to develop hobbies, to take vacations. They had little success.

(Continued)

Canetto (1992, 1995) has challenged traditional explanations of gender differences in suicide rates, emphasizing that more attention needs to be given to the reasons for the lower rates of older women. She provides evidence that women in general are more likely to engage in help-seeking behavior, which offers more opportunity for intervention prior to a suicide. She also suggests that gender differences in coping may account for the differential suicide risk. Specifically, women have been shown to be more flexible in their coping strategies. They tend to be more adaptable and willing to compromise as a result of their socialization and developmental experiences, which typically involve many role changes. They also appear more willing to adopt more passive means of coping, in contrast to males who are encouraged to be assertive and "in control."

Depression is one of the main factors associated with the risk of suicide among both male and female elderly. The individual may experience hopelessness and despair with the onset of a physical illness or after the death of a spouse. Some individuals express a sense of worthlessness as they grow older and fail to see purpose and meaning in their lives. Signs of depression in the elderly are often disregarded and erroneously attributed to "natural manifestations of old age" (e.g., "He's just an old crank who likes to be left alone."). As a consequence, social interactions decline and the person's depressive state escalates (Richman, 1993).

(Continued From Previous Page)

When W. D. turned 70, his son tried to talk him into retiring. The two men argued violently, and W. D. stayed on the job, although he did cut back his customary workday from 14 hours to 10.

In spite of his iron determination, W. D. found himself napping during the day, sometimes even in important meetings. He also complained to his daughter that he had constant indigestion and that food had lost its taste. At age 78, he agreed to have his hearing tested and was fitted with a hearing aid. In general, however, his health remained good until he began to have a series of small strokes at age 79. Between hospitalizations and as his health permitted he continued to go to the office but was aware that it was running well without

him and that he could no longer remember many of the details of the business. He had a long talk with his son, admitting his growing confusion and weakness. W. D. officially resigned from the presidency of his company. He spent several months putting his affairs in order. In an uncharacteristic gesture, he invited his family and the executives of his company to a cookout on his 81st birthday. His children commented after the party that they had been impressed with W. D.'s renewed energy. His daughter had felt that it was a sure sign of physical improvement, while his son felt it was caused by removal of the stress of the job. After the party, W. D. straightened the house, piled the dishes neatly in the sink, and wrote his two-word note.

SOURCE: J. M. Stillion & E. E. McDowell (1996). *Suicide across the life span* (2nd ed.). Washington, DC: Taylor & Francis, pp. 188–189.

Youth Suicide

Although suicide rates of youth are not as high as those of the elderly overall, the incidence among this age group has increased at a rapid rate; and this appears to be an international trend (Stillion & McDowell, 1996). As a result, this cause of death has received considerable attention from the media, from school personnel, and from mental health professionals. The upward trend of youth suicides began in the United States in the 1960s and accelerated in the 1970s (see Figure 9.4). Over the last three decades, the largest increases have occurred among males (especially African Americans) in the 15–19 age group as shown in Table 9.2.

Adolescents from other ethnic minority populations also appear to be at greater risk. Unlike the general population, Native Americans show a peak suicide rate occurring in the teens and twenties rather than during late adulthood. It must be noted, however, that tribal differences are quite large. For example, lower suicide rates exist among the Navajo who have maintained a strong cultural identity and tribal values, whereas the Apache have rates much higher than the national average and also have relatively higher rates of alcoholism, substance abuse, and unemployment, as well as greater access to firearms (Garland & Zigler, 1993; McIntosh, 1993).

FIGURE 9.4

U.S. Suicide Rates 1932–1992 for the Nation and for Those Aged 15 to 24

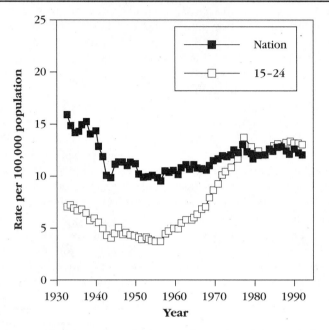

SOURCE: Generated by John L. McIntosh, Ph.D., professor of psychology, Indiana University South Bend, based on annual data published by the National Center for Health Statistics.

Of major concern overall is the fact that 1 out of every 1,000 American adolescents attempts suicide, and many more at least consider it (Walker & Mehr, 1983). These figures are even more alarming when one considers the fact that unsuccessful attempts to end one's life are often not reported and many actual suicides are recorded as accidents. The available statistics, therefore, may significantly underestimate the extent of this problem.

Boldt (1982) concluded that youth of today are more accepting of self-inflicted death than their parents' generation. When compared with adults, high school seniors in his study viewed suicide in terms that were less judgmental of the individual and less stigmatizing. They were less inclined to think of suicide in religious or moral terms and placed greater emphasis on an individual's right to choose to die. These more accepting attitudes of contemporary youth may influence the likelihood of suicidal behavior due to greater tolerance and diminished fear of ending one's life.

Because of their struggle with identity issues, imitation and modeling of the behavior of others is common. For example, adolescents are especially likely to copy mannerisms, clothes, and actions of their peers and popular public figures such as rock stars. Modeling may extend to suicidal behavior as well. For example,

TABLE 9.2

Adolescent Suicide Rates per 100,000 Population for 1970, 1980, & 1990 by Age, Sex, and Race

AGE	WHITE MALES				BLACK MALES			
	1970	1980	1990	% CHANGE	1970	1980	1990	% CHANGE
15–19	9.4	15.0	19.3	+105	4.7	5.6	11.5	+145
20–24	19.3	27.8	26.8	+39	18.7	20.0	19.0	+2

AGE	WHITE FEMALES				BLACK FEMALES			
	1970	1980	1990	% CHANGE	1970	1980	1990	% CHANGE
15–19	2.9	3.3	4.0	+38	2.9	1.6	1.9	−34
20–24	5.7	5.9	4.4	−23	4.9	3.1	2.6	−47

SOURCE: U.S. Bureau of the Census. (1992). *Statistical Abstract of the United States* (112th. ed.). Washington, DC: U.S. Government Printing Office, p. 90.

adolescents are more likely than most other age groups to participate in the "**copy cat suicide**" phenomenon in which several suicides of a similar nature (often in terms of method, location, date) occur following a single highly publicized suicide. They are also more vulnerable than other age groups to **cluster suicides** in which individuals with similar demographic characteristics who live in the same geographical area commit suicide within a relatively short time span (Stillion & McDowell, 1996).

> Plano, Texas, was a booming Dallas suburb that had everything: wealth, beautiful homes, good schools. A Texas magazine proclaimed it the "perfect city," though most Americans would never hear of Plano until 1983—the year that six of its children died by their own hands. The string of teen suicides that started in February would continue into the following spring. By May 1984, eight high school students would be dead, and a new phrase, "suicide clusters," would enter the national vocabulary. . . . (*The News & Observer,* November 21, 1993, p. 1)

SUICIDE PREVENTION, INTERVENTION, AND POSTVENTION

Attempts to reduce the incidence of suicide require efforts in the areas of prevention, intervention, and postvention. **Prevention** refers to actions taken to avoid a stressful or harmful situation, whereas **intervention** includes therapeutic efforts to reduce the intensity and negative effects of a crisis or difficult situation. **Postvention** involves dealing with the aftermath of a traumatic event and minimizing the impact (Valente & Saunders, 1987). The context of these efforts may vary, but it is essential that school systems and communities take responsible action.

SUICIDE AND THE MEDIA RESPONSE

The possible effect of media coverage on behavior such as copycat suicides is a matter of concern. The power of the media is also acknowledged in terms of educating the public about warning signs, thus aiding the suicide prevention effort (Centers for Disease Control, 1992). Although suicide is usually deemed a newsworthy event, the amount or type of coverage is related to factors such as notoriety and age of the person, whether the death occurred in public, and if other recent suicides have occurred in the community. In the print media, news of one suicide may appear as a banner headline, whereas another is discreetly placed in the obituary section. In general, as knowledge of mental health issues has increased, so has the social sensitivity of reporters; however, much variation still exists. Particular angles taken by reporters in news coverage of a suicide can be detrimental to survivors, especially those that add to the stigma of this type of death or portray the deceased in negative terms (Dunne-Maxim, 1987). The perspective of a family member in response to this situation is provided in the following account:

> I first became aware of the media's power to affect the outcome of grief following a suicide in 1972, when my 16-year-old brother killed himself. He threw himself into the path of a commuter train one early winter evening. He carried no identification with him and so it was not until the next after-

(Continued)

Suicide in the Schools

To prevent suicides, Maris (1985) suggests that we give young people an optimism for the world they live in and its future:

> Any suicide is a waste. Young suicides are particularly tragic, since many have really never lived. To help people live, we have to restore a sense of hope about the goodness, purpose, pleasure, and viability of life itself. (p. 108)

Prevention.   Specific programs that increase the self-esteem, decision-making abilities, and coping skills of adolescents have an important role in suicide prevention. Individuals with poor self-concepts and few problem-solving skills are at risk for mental health problems. Impulsivity and few alternative strategies for coping can turn suicidal thoughts into suicidal behaviors (Berman, 1986). Many skills can be taught through developmental counseling in the schools. **Developmental counseling** attempts to prevent potential crises from occurring by initiating contact with students before they have a need to see a counselor. Counselors work with students in small groups to help them become more aware of themselves, how they interact with their environment, and how they may effectively cope with the various tasks involved in growing up. At times, counselors may come into classrooms and use group discussions, formal

(Continued From Previous Page)

noon that his body was identified by our family. Because he had chosen to end his life in a very public manner, the story of his death was carried by the local newspaper.

The newspaper account stated that the Long Island train conductor saw the boy "dive" in front of the moving train. Our family was horrified by this description, since it sounded as though my brother had been on an LSD trip (this was the early 1970s). The only information the public had was the fact of the death as it had been reported in the newspaper. That did not represent a true picture of the Tim we wanted the world to know. We went to see if we could include some of Tim's accomplishments in an obituary. The editor of *Newsday,* a Long Is-

land newspaper, decided to write a feature article on Tim based on what we told him. The public disclosure of his accomplishments was a very significant factor in my grief resolution. It read:

He never missed a year on the honor roll. He was editor of the Junior High yearbook and produced his own anti-war film that was presented at the Rockville Center Library. He received awards for playing the cello and had recently been mountain climbing with the Boy Scouts in Switzerland. He was brilliant and sensitive and the question will always remain with those who loved him—Why did he die?

(Dunne-Maxim, 1987, p. 47)

SOURCE: K. Dunne-Maxim (1987). Survivors and the media: Pitfalls and potential. In E. J. Dunne, J. L. McIntosh, & K. Dunne-Maxim (Eds.), *Suicide and its aftermath: Understanding and counseling the survivors* (pp. 45–56). New York: W. W. Norton.

presentations, and structured activities to assist students in addressing personal issues.

In addition to programs aimed at meeting general affective needs of students, many schools and communities have also developed programs specifically aimed at preventing adolescent suicides. A primary objective of these programs is to educate teachers, parents, and adolescents about the warning signs of suicide (Peck, Farberow, & Litman, 1985). Early identification allows the opportunity for prevention. School personnel have a critical role in suicide prevention because they interact with most of the youth in our society (Ross, 1985). Teachers in particular often play an important role by detecting distress signals from suicidal children and adolescents. As teachers become better informed, many more deaths may be avoided. Appropriate referrals by teachers to counselors and other mental health professionals need to occur before the crisis of suicide is imminent.

Peers can also be taught to identify warning signs and make appropriate referrals. When surveying high school students, Kalafat and Elias (1992) found that nearly a third had talked to a peer who was considering committing suicide. Teenagers often share their concerns with each other rather than approaching an adult, underscoring the need for programs that teach students how to respond

HOW SHOULD YOU RESPOND?

What to Do

Listen. A frank and honest discussion is the important first step toward suicide prevention. It is critical for a suicidal person to be able to talk about why he or she wants to die. Discuss his or her feelings of suicide openly and frankly. Ask questions about how she or he feels and about the reasons for those feelings.

Be honest. Admit to being frightened or uncomfortable by the suicidal thought or actions, if that is the case. Offer to try to understand the situation if the individual will describe his or her thoughts and feelings about it.

Access. Find out if there is a specific plan. Is there a gun at home? Where is it? Are pills collected? What are they?

The more specific the plan, the more likely it is to be implemented.

Be supportive. Let the young person know the concern of the helper and the school. Break through the sense of isolation and stay close. Assure the person that suicidal impulses are temporary, and problems can be solved in spite of how bad things are now.

Take charge. Emphasize that help is at hand, and waste no time in finding it.

Get help. Do not try to handle the problem alone. Seek professional help immediately. Encourage the person to seek help through the family physician, a suicide prevention center, a crisis intervention center, a mental health clinic, or a clergy member. If the person refuses,

(Continued)

effectively in these situations. To encourage peer participation in suicide prevention activities, many youth suicide prevention programs have been initiated in which adolescents themselves take an active role. For example, community suicide prevention centers in various locations have collaborated with school personnel in training students as peer counselors. Training, supervising, and supporting the adolescents who choose to participate are critical elements in the success of these programs (Berman, 1986; Valente & Saunders, 1987).

There are a number of signs to watch for among teenagers that may indicate the existence of significant problems and possibly high suicide potential. These signs include the following:

- self-destructive tendencies, such as carelessness or accident-prone behavior;
- exaggerated or extended apathy, inactivity, or boredom;
- academic decline;
- involvement in substance abuse (drugs, alcohol);
- tearfulness and depressed feelings;
- decrease in verbal activity and withdrawal from peers and previously enjoyed activities;

(Continued From Previous Page)

explain the situation to reliable family members, or call a suicide prevention center or other sources of help yourself.

Make a contract. Get a commitment, preferably in writing, that she or he will not attempt suicide.

Vital Questions

Have your problems been getting you down so much lately that you've been thinking of harming yourself?

How would you harm yourself?

Do you have the means available?

Have you ever attempted suicide?

What has been keeping you alive so far?

What is your hurry? Why do it now?

What do you think the odds are that you will kill yourself?

What do you think that the future holds in store for you?

What Not to Do

Do not assume the situation will cure itself.

Do not leave the person alone if the situation is lethal.

Do not act shocked at what the suicidal person tells you.

Do not challenge or dare the person to commit suicide.

Do not argue or debate moral issues with the suicidal person.

Do not be sworn to secrecy about the suicide attempt.

SOURCE: R. L. Deaton & W. A. Berkan (1995). *Planning and managing death issues in the schools.* Westport, CT: Greenwood Press, pp. 79–80.

- recent hostile behavior or an increase in interpersonal conflict;
- decrease in ability to tolerate frustration;
- truancy from school and running away from home; and
- physiological and behavioral indicators such as loss of appetite, excessive eating, or sleep disturbance (Balk, 1995; Deaton & Berkan, 1995; Goldman, 1996).

All these behaviors may be indicative of depression, which is manifested in a variety of ways among teenagers. Although depression is often associated with suicide, it is often difficult to identify in adolescents because of the natural mood swings experienced by those in this age group (Martin & Dixon, 1986).

Intervention.   Well-trained specialists are needed for intervention once an adolescent has been identified as suicidal. Many school systems today have mental health professionals on staff who can provide counseling and consultation. Appropriate and timely intervention involves helping the adolescent who is at risk to see viable alternatives to his or her situation and to develop coping skills and resources. It is important to recognize, however, that individuals who have attempted suicide are likely to try again. Four out of five people who kill

SCHOOL RESPONSIBILITY GUIDE
FOLLOWING A SUDDEN DEATH

Principal	Crisis Response Team	Teachers	Guidance Counselors
■ Receive notification of death	■ Initiate phone tree	■ Read announcement	■ Run Crisis Centers
■ Verify information	■ Notify family liaison	■ Modify classes	■ Talk with students
■ Notify Superintendent	■ Call outside consultants	■ Talk with students	■ Clarify misinformation
■ Notify Crisis Response Team, call meeting	■ Contact community resource people	■ Clarify misinformation	■ Encourage students to express feelings
■ Notify media liaison	■ Contact student leaders	■ Schedule activities to encourage expression of feelings	■ Express own feelings
■ Schedule special staff meeting	■ Open Crisis Centers	■ Express own feelings	■ Give grief information
■ Hire substitute teachers	■ Distribute literature	■ Give grief information	■ Show no judgment of grief
■ Write announcement to be read in classes	■ Notify librarian to put grief books on reserve	■ Show no judgment of grief	■ Give priority to referrals
■ Write phone inquiry statement	■ Attend faculty meetings	■ Schedule activities to encourage remembering deceased	■ Support students
■ Attend special staff meetings	■ Plan community meeting	■ Make referrals when necessary	■ Use support resources for self
■ Make announcement to school		■ Support students	■ Make referrals to psychologist, M.D.
■ Write and send letter to parents		■ Use support resources for self	■ Contact parents if necessary
■ Notify other principals		■ Send condolence note to family	■ Attend funeral if desired
■ Grant release time for funeral attendance		■ Have in-school and outside resources talk with classes	
■ Send condolence note to family		■ Attend funeral if desired	
■ Attend funeral if desired			

(Continued)

(Continued From Previous Page)

School Psychologist/ Social Worker

- Be primary referral
- Provide in-school treatment of students
- Provide staff counseling and education
- Complete student assessments
- Make referrals to physician or community agency
- Contact parents
- Attend funeral if desired

School Nurse

- Care for physical needs
- Allow students to express emotions
- Provide comfortable location
- Make assessment of students
- Make referrals
- Attend funeral if desired

Physician

- See students
- Make assignments
- Make referrals
- Contact parents
- Attend funeral if desired

Family Liaison

- Contact family
- Offer help
- Obtain needed information
- Inform of school procedures
- Help gather personal items of deceased student
- Attend funeral if desired
- Keep in contact with family after the funeral

Media Liaison

- Be primary person to talk to media
- Notify media you are contact person
- Keep media out of school
- Attend funeral if desired

Support Staff

- Listen to students if approached
- Take students to Crisis Center
- Make referrals
- Attend funeral if desired

Librarian

- Put appropriate reading and A/V material on reserve
- Listen to students if approached
- Take students to Crisis Center
- Make referrals
- Attend funeral if desired

Students

- Talk with faculty and staff
- Express feelings
- Use support network
- Send condolence notes to family
- Participate in remembrance activity planning
- Attend funeral if desired

SOURCE: R. L. Klicker (1990). *A student dies, a school mourns . . . Are you prepared?* Buffalo, NY: Thanos Institute, pp. 41–42.

themselves have made previous attempts (Martin & Dixon, 1986). Fairchild (1986) emphasizes that frequent counseling contact with suicidal students is necessary. Even though the immediate threat of suicide may seem to have passed, the 2 or 3 months after the attempt are considered critical. During this period, some students again attempt to end their lives after apparent improvement in mood (Morgan, 1981). Many times, the adolescent's issues are inseparable from family issues, and intervention at the family level is needed (Walker & Mehr, 1983). Depending on the circumstances, the adolescent and family should be referred for professional consultation.

Postvention.   Unfortunately, many suicide programs tend to deemphasize bereavement and fail to have a postvention component to address the after-effects of a suicide on a school population. Although no definitive research exists that indicates how often adolescent suicide is related to bereavement, the literature suggests that the experience of loss, especially when accompanied by depression and feelings of alienation, can lead to suicidal thoughts (Richman, 1986).

After a suicide, classmates, friends, and school staff need a forum for sharing their grief. Special events, student assemblies, and individual consultations can all provide mechanisms for meeting needs of individual survivors. In situations in which peer counselors had interacted with the victim, they may have feelings of failure and guilt because they were not able to prevent the suicide. Special attention needs to be given to these adolescents as well as to teachers or adult counselors who may have similar feelings. Grief and associated reactions of school personnel often go unrecognized, because their role is seen as providing support to surviving students. Provisions need to be made as these individuals cope with their sense of loss by attending the funeral, taking time off from work, and reducing their involvement in extracurricular events. Hiring substitute teachers as well as using the services of mental health services can relieve school personnel of the full responsibility of dealing with ongoing activities while responding to a crisis (Rowling, 1995).

Young people, especially adolescents, are highly vulnerable to the influence of others. When a suicide occurs in a school, subsequent suicide attempts or completions by others may follow. The first suicide possibly serves as a model and gives permission to others considering suicide. Berman (1986) suggests that it is important to address the phenomenon of **contagion** through various interventions and preventive programming efforts. Some adults have been reluctant to discuss suicide because they fear that talking about it will encourage suicidal behavior in young people. Ross (1985) however insists that silence following a suicide should be avoided because it deters important discussions that could help prevent other suicides and that could also help many adolescents deal with grief.

It is imperative to remember the crucial role of parents in prevention, intervention, and postvention. In a survey of high school students, the majority identified parents as their primary source of information on death and dying.

School personnel need to keep parents informed of death-related events that may affect their children, actions taken by school personnel to respond to these situations, and resources available to better equip them to meet their children's needs (Glass, 1990).

We will continue to see innovative programs develop as schools and communities grapple with the problems associated with adolescent suicide. Several state legislatures in the United States have already mandated suicide prevention programs in high schools (Leenaars & Wenckstern, 1991). A corresponding decrease in the frequency with which young people take their lives will hopefully occur as the effectiveness of these programs improve.

SAMPLE LETTER TO PARENTS

Following some deaths, the principal communicates with parents by mail and/or public forums. A sample letter to be used following a student suicide is given below. A similar letter may be needed after a homicide death or tragic accident.

Dear Parents:

The _____ school community has been saddened by the suicide death of one of our students, _____ .

I want to let you know what steps we are taking to assist our grieving students. (*Describe what actions are being taken.*)

You can expect that your child will be affected in some way by this tragedy even if he or she did not know this student well. I encourage you to talk to your child about what happened. Discussing thoughts and feelings about death is important to the resolution of grief. You will not "put ideas into your child's head" by talking about suicide. We all need to reinforce, however, that such actions are foolish and that there is help for any problem. Encourage your child to talk to you or some other adult when life stresses become overwhelming. If you are concerned about your child, please contact _____ (staff person) at _____ (phone number) .

I have enclosed an information sheet that may help you understand and respond to your child's feelings. (*Enclose information about helpful responses, how students this age react to death, and warning signs of depression or at-risk behaviors.*)

A meeting for concerned parents will be held _____ . (*If a meeting is planned, give the details.*)

If you have any questions concerning this incident or the actions we are taking, please call my office. You are an important part of our school community and your child's life.

Sincerely,

_____ , Principal

Enclosures

SOURCE: M. D. Oates (1993). *Death in the school community: A handbook for counselors, teachers, and administrators.* Alexandria, VA: American Counseling Association, p. 122.

Suicide Prevention in the Community

Most major American cities have suicide prevention centers, which typically consist of 24-hour telephone service for crisis counseling, with some centers supplemented by walk-in clinics. These services can be a lifeline for many, because suicidal persons often do not really want to die, but do not want to continue living in their current state of despair. As an indication of this ambivalence, individuals contemplating suicide often communicate their need for help. Approximately three out of four people who eventually kill themselves have given some earlier clues to friends, family, or other significant people in their lives. These communications of intent can be verbal (e.g., "If things don't get better, you'll be reading about me in the paper") or behavioral (e.g., giving away valued possessions). Because of the popular myth that people who talk about suicide don't actually commit it, these warning signs are often ignored (Kastenbaum, 1995). More subtle clues also may not be attended to because they go unrecognized or undetected.

Older individuals considering suicide are less likely than younger people to ask for help; therefore the possibilities for intervention with this older age group may be fewer. The low rate at which suicidal elderly seek psychological help may be affected by the bias of many mental health workers against the elderly, rather than indicating lack of interest in these services by older individuals. In discussing the prevalence of ageism in the mental health field, Butler and Lewis (1982) have stated that professionals are often pessimistic about the opportunities for positive outcomes with older clients. They are also less likely to use psychotherapy as a method of treatment, and they are more likely to prescribe medication. Aging may be equated with inevitable decline, and health care providers may fail to recognize that late adulthood can be a very satisfying and rewarding period of one's life. Furthermore, they may consider it futile to invest maximum effort in a person with a limited life expectancy. All of these factors contribute to fewer and oftentimes poorer quality of services for older adults, despite the fact that emotional problems in this age group can be effectively treated.

The elderly oftentimes seek familiar sources of assistance, particularly professionals with whom they have already established relationships. Approximately 75% of the elderly who take their own lives visit a primary care physician sometime during the month before their suicide (American Association of Suicidology, 1996). Blazer (1982), however, reports that most physicians are poor in predicting the imminent suicide of patients they are treating. Some individuals may deliberately cause their own deaths by indirect means such as starving themselves, refusing to take prescribed medication, or delaying medical or surgical treatment. Health care providers should give serious consideration to behaviors that might indicate self-destructive tendencies (Butler & Lewis, 1982).

Clergy are in a unique position to collaborate with mental health professionals in helping suicidal persons. A Gallup poll found that the elderly are more willing to turn to their clergy than to their medical doctor or a mental health

OPPORTUNITIES TO INTERVENE: A CASE EXAMPLE

On June 11, 1987 my husband left for work at his usual hour. He said "Good-bye, I've always loved you and I love you." To the children he said "Be good to your mom." These comments to the children were very unusual.

I tried to reach him by phone at 10:00 A.M. and he hadn't reported for work. There was something terribly wrong.

After waiting for him to return from work and not knowing what had happened, I called a friend to help me decide what to do. I then called the police and explained the situation. Their reply was he was over twenty-one years old and he could go anywhere he wanted. However, they took his car description and license number just in case they heard something.

My husband was parked outside the police station, across the street from their lot. Later I found out an acquaintance of ours noticed him parked there the morning he left for work.

The night passed and I was panicking more and more. The next morning Dr. Dalke was contacted to help me cope with my fears. I was to see him the next day. As my friend and I drove to Dr. Dalke's office

I noticed my husband's car parked outside the police station. All I could see was his shoulder behind the steering wheel. My friend used her automatic door locks and would not let me out of the car. We went into the police parking lot. As I cried, the officer went to his car and found him dead. He had shot himself in the mouth. I found out later he was in his car dead since the previous night. He left a note saying he could not live with his anxiety anymore and we would be better off without him.

The children had been with my friend's husband. All they knew was their dad had not come home from work. When I returned to my house after being at the police station, the children were brought back to find out their father had committed suicide.

After he died, I found out he had tried to talk to a priest at a church near the police station and that he had made eye contact with one of the police officers, while walking around his car. The priest was busy and the police officer did not know that he needed help. My husband spent two days trying to decide whether to live or die.

SOURCE: D. Dalke (1994). Therapy-assisted growth after parental suicide: From a personal and professional perspective. *Omega, 29*(2), p. 115.

specialist when a friend is contemplating suicide (Gallup Organization, 1992). Likewise, they may seek religious counsel when they themselves are in need. Pastors and rabbis often stay in close contact with members of their congregation, holding regular services and at times making home visits. Clergy play an especially vital role in rural or small community settings in which churches and synagogues often substitute as a community counseling resource (Weaver & Koenig, 1996). Unfortunately, clergy are often inadequately prepared to recognize the suicide potential in those who seek their assistance. Interfaith educational material is now available that acknowledges the role of religious communities and their leaders in responding to the threat of suicide; hopefully, it will be increasingly used in training programs for clergy (Clark, 1993).

Education and training (for the lay public and for professionals) are crucial aspects of any successful suicide prevention program, and these efforts should include information regarding

- myths about suicide and suicidal behavior;
- identification of at-risk individuals;
- recognition of warning signs;
- assessment of lethality at time of suicide threat;
- availability and existence of community resources;
- variety of suicidal behaviors that may be exhibited, including both direct and indirect self-destructive behaviors;
- range of problems associated with suicide survivorship, with the possibility of the bereaved attempting to end their lives; and
- normal aging and the unique concerns of the elderly (McIntosh, 1995).

Cultural factors should also be examined in relation to high suicide rates among older individuals. The United States has been described by some as a society that devalues its older people, is unresponsive to their needs, and strips away much of the meaning from their lives by encouraging their disengagement from major life roles (through retirement, in particular). If this is the case, then prevention efforts also need to focus on changing societal attitudes, policies, and practices that decrease the options of older Americans. Although many elderly will still have physical limitations and health concerns, these by themselves do not usually prompt individuals to end their lives.

A number of **suicidologists** (professionals who specialize in the study of suicide) emphasize the need to plan for the next generation of older persons. Based on the large numbers of baby boomers who will be entering late adulthood, it is predicted that the numbers of elderly suicides will be even higher in the future. Primary prevention efforts must begin now to meet the needs of the increasing numbers of elderly and to improve the quality of life for this age group (McIntosh, 1992).

THE AFTERMATH OF SUICIDE

Grief of Family Members

Each suicide leaves behind loved ones who must cope not only with the death, but also with the fact that it was self-inflicted. Several of the unique aspects of grief following suicide were previously discussed in chapter 3. Because it is typically a sudden death, loved ones do not have the opportunity to say goodbye. In addition, the components of guilt and anger tend to be particularly strong, because the question of preventability is almost always an issue. The trauma associated with this type of death is exacerbated if family members witness the suicide or discover the body. Intrusive images of a violent death haunt survivors as they grieve.

Because of the stigma of death by suicide and the taboos associated with it, survivors often feel a sense of shame, embarrassment, and rejection. As a consequence, funeral rituals may be restricted to immediate family members or eliminated altogether, depriving the bereaved of a valuable avenue of comfort and support (Hauser, 1987). The social support received after a suicide, however, is generally less than with other types of death. Friends and colleagues may feel awkward in these circumstances and avoid interactions with those closest to the deceased. Thus, survivors may feel abandoned at a time when they are most vulnerable and in need of support (Stillion, 1996).

Parents of children who have committed suicide face special difficulties during their period of mourning. They often have heightened fears that their other children may also commit suicide and may become overly concerned when they discipline or punish their children, wondering if this will trigger suicide by them as well. Existing fears are magnified as they question their own capabilities of being effective parents.

Developmental issues are also intertwined with loss of a loved one through suicide. For example, a parent's self-inflicted death can negatively affect children's sense of self-esteem if they view themselves as "not worth hanging around for." This perceived rejection may pose a serious threat to identity development. Identification with a father or mother may also assume a pathological, destructive quality when the parent commits suicide. Under extreme circumstances, the process of overidentification with the deceased can lead to suicide attempts by the griever. The strength of this identification can clearly be seen when the bereaved child chooses the anniversary of the parent's death, the same method, and/or the same location to attempt his or her suicide.

In addition to consequences for individual survivors, suicide can also have dramatic effects on the dynamics of ongoing family relationships. At times, adult family members do not openly acknowledge that a death was due to suicide. This "secrecy" interferes with open communication among family members and can result in anger and resentment when the cause of death is discovered at a later time. Dalke (1994) recommends avoiding giving children false information they will have to "unlearn" later. He also believes that telling the truth about suicide conveys a message—"We can deal with important things in an honest way"—to surviving family members. Such messages spill over into other aspects of family life and childrearing, setting the stage for effective coping and the development of trusting relationships.

A daughter recalls how she found out, at age 14, the cause of her father's death, which occurred when she was a toddler:

> I was told that my father had a heart attack . . . . My stepsister and I were fighting . . . and I said, you know you wouldn't treat me like this if my father was

> here and she said "Your father thought so much of you that he hung himself . . ." and I was so shocked, like someone had just thrown me against the wall. I said "Don't tell Mama I know . . ." I didn't want anyone to know I knew. I was embarrassed, I was ashamed. (Demi & Howell, 1991, p. 353)

Some families develop secret codes to avoid directly confronting the issues of suicide and keep others outside the family from knowing. One man, now with children of his own, described how his family handled this "secret":

> Even though we never talked about the suicide part we talked about it indirectly a lot . . . My father would refer to "when I was 6" or "back before the kids," and that was a code for the old days, before my mother's suicide. (Demi & Howell, 1991, p. 353)

In other situations, there is a conspiracy of silence, not only about the death, but also about the individual who died, as a way of trying to avoid the pain of the event. For example, one young man resented his mother because she would never permit his father's name to be mentioned after his dad committed suicide. The son grew up with few memories of his father and no opportunity to clarify who his dad was as a person through normal conversations with other family members. The only legacy he retained was the manner in which his father had died and the ramifications for his surviving family. After completing college, the son spent a summer locating former friends of his father. Through these efforts, he was able to expand his perception of his dad and balance his negative memories through the recollections of others who had known him during happier times.

Shared reminiscence has been shown in a variety of grief circumstances to provide social support, facilitation of grief work, and an avenue to building relationships with the living and the deceased (Rosenblatt & Elde, 1990). Yet sharing feelings of loss can be very difficult for some survivors, as illustrated in the following poignant statement by a father whose son took his own life:

> Trying to talk about Mitch's suicide, even ten years later, still brings many thoughts to mind regarding all of my feelings . . . then and now. The feelings are so personal, so private, so utterly my own, that the thought of sharing them with another is still difficult today.

In chapter 4, the idea of intergenerational issues related to grief was introduced, with the premise that unresolved issues of loss and abandonment from the distant past can impede present-day family functioning. Losses have the potential to affect both family relationships and the individual development of family members, particularly with regard to the normal developmental processes of separation and individuation.

To adequately assess family dynamics and identify sources of difficulty, therapeutic tools are often needed to gain an intergenerational perspective. Used in a variety of circumstances, a **genogram** is a structured family history in which the therapist diagrams information about the family, their relationships, and important family events (McGoldrick & Gerson, 1985). Through this process, the family's experience with death, as well as other significant life events, can be determined. This technique can be particularly useful when a suicide is part of the family's history, because this type of death is often a "taboo" subject and off-limits for discussion.

The genogram, in addition to discovering important clinical information from the past, can also have therapeutic benefits as families are given permission to discuss their previous losses (Grebstein, 1986). The assessment of a family should also include current level of functioning, family strengths and vulnerabilities, resources, and sources of support.

Figure 9.5 illustrates a genogram depicting a family in which separation and loss are recurring themes. The 28–year-old son, Lenny, was referred for therapy following a long history of psychosomatic illness. He was unemployed and living with his mother, Anna. A probe into the family's history revealed that Lenny's father had committed suicide 10 years earlier and that his twin brother had died at birth. As events in earlier generations were explored, additional loss issues surfaced. Anna's father (Thomas) had deserted the family when she was 9, leaving her mother (Rosa) alone to raise five children. Anna's grandfather (Lorenzo) had also died at an early age. Through discussion of these events with the therapist, it became evident that Anna had developed an unhealthy dependence on Lenny, which was interfering with his normal transition to adulthood and independent living. She so feared another loss that she attempted to control his behavior and prevent his leaving by making guilt-inducing statements related to his father's suicide. Lenny wanted to make up for all of his mother's pain and to "save" the reputation of the men in the family by standing by his mother no matter what the costs. His personal sacrifice was enormous and, without intervention, Lenny's health problems may have resulted in his own early death—despite his pledge never to leave his mother.

Families with unresolved intergenerational issues related to loss, especially when suicide is involved, can benefit from family therapy. This type of intervention can assist families in identifying and addressing the source of their pain and help them develop healthier ways of interacting. As a consequence, more normative individual and family development can occur.

Reactions of Mental Health Workers

Mental health professionals work on a regular basis with individuals who are depressed, and at times suicidal. Regardless of the quality of care provided, a client may attempt or complete a suicide while seeing a therapist. In fact, it is estimated that more than 15 to 20% of psychotherapists from different disciplines have experienced a patient's suicide (Valente, 1994).

One of the most potentially shattering emotional experiences a psychotherapist can have is the death of a client by suicide (Millen & Roll, 1985). This experience can precipitate both a personal and professional crisis. Although the research in this area is sparse, the available literature indicates that mental

FIGURE 9.5
A Genogram

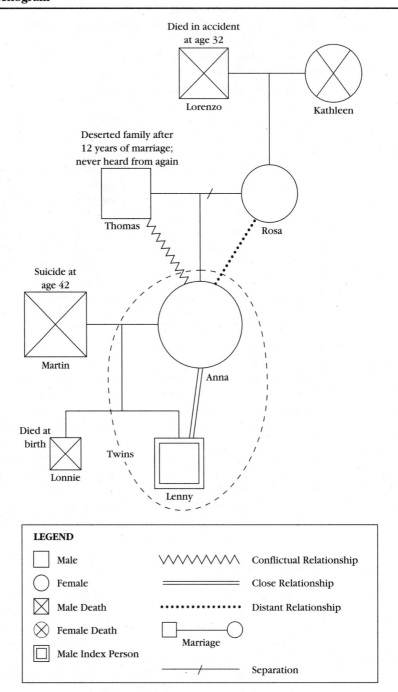

Died in accident
at age 32

Lorenzo

Kathleen

Deserted family after
12 years of marriage;
never heard from again

Thomas

Rosa

Suicide at
age 42

Martin

Anna

Died at
birth

Twins

Lonnie

Lenny

LEGEND

☐ Male	\/\/\/\/\/\ Conflictual Relationship	
◯ Female	═══════ Close Relationship	
⊠ Male Death	•••••••••••• Distant Relationship	
⊗ Female Death	☐—◯ Marriage	
▣ Male Index Person	——/—— Separation	

health professionals are vulnerable to grief reactions similar to those of friends and family members of the suicide victim. This vulnerability is related to the length of time the therapist has interacted with the suicide victim and the intensity of the professional-patient relationship.

On learning of a client's suicide, psychotherapists commonly express disbelief. At times, this reaction may be demonstrated by requesting additional verification of the death (e.g., asking to see the coroner's report). Anger is also a common component of the therapist's grief—directed toward the suicide victim (i.e., the client) for having "betrayed" the therapist, the family for not having been more watchful, and oneself for not having prevented the suicide from occurring. These professionals often experience guilt and question what they could have done differently ("Should the last session have been longer and more focused?" "Why didn't I call her that day?"). Thus, one's feelings of professional competence are threatened. Negative feelings can be heightened if grieving families displace their own anger and guilt onto the therapist and blame him or her for the death (Sanders, 1984).

Therapists who experience a suicide of a client need emotional support, time to reflect, and relief from high-stress tasks. Unfortunately mental health professionals, like families of suicide victims, commonly feel isolated in their grief. Outlets for discussing the suicide are limited for professionals because of ethical issues surrounding confidentiality. Their work context (whether private practice, crisis center, inpatient facility, or outpatient facility) can make a difference regarding the support available to them (Jones, 1987). A private practice setting can be the most isolating for therapists, whereas available support is likely to be greater for therapists employed in community agencies, hospitals, or psychiatric facilities. A positive and nonjudgmental staff response can do much toward enhancing the therapist's ability to deal with a suicide. The opportunity for discussion in a supportive atmosphere can help therapists sort through feelings of inadequacy and failure. Although sharing the details of the incident with respected colleagues (in a confidential manner) is often therapeutic, this type of interaction may be avoided because of feelings of the therapist's own shame and embarrassment.

Jones (1987) recommends the establishment of ongoing support groups for grieving therapists. Following the suicide of one of his patients, he organized such a group. Of the therapists who attended, their patients' suicides had occurred from a few days to 20 years prior to their involvement in the support group. Many participants commented that this was the first time they had been given an opportunity to "talk it out."

In addition to providing an opportunity to explore feelings related to the suicide, support groups can help therapists deal with numerous professional concerns. Jones (1987) has reported that the experience of a patient suicide can affect professional attitudes and practices in a variety of ways. Some therapists become more conservative in the management of other patients who are potentially suicidal; and, in some cases, this conservatism results in inappropriate hospitalization. Other therapists refuse referrals of patients who are identified as high risk in order to avoid suffering another loss by suicide. Many question their worth as therapists or the value of therapy itself and, consequently, consider leaving their profession. For those who are able to work through these issues, positive outcomes include paying greater attention to suicidal behaviors, attempts, and gestures. Goldstein and Buongiorno (1984) found that therapists who experienced the suicide of clients engaged in more explicit questioning and exploration of suicidal thoughts and feelings during therapy sessions than they had done previously.

Resolution of a client's suicide, with all of its ramifications, can take many months or even longer. For resolution to be facilitated, therapists need to acknowledge their own grief. They must also remind themselves that suicides will occur despite the best treatment. On resolution of this experience, the therapist often crosses a threshold in terms of professional maturation. Sanders (1984) describes the significance of the experience this way:

> The first patient suicide, at least, becomes an initiation rite, an undesired challenge, which not only humbles one but also becomes a transforming and maturing experience. The therapist not only faces a significant object loss with all the accompanying grief reactions of anger, guilt, and sadness, but also suffers a chink in his or her professional armor as well. Some of the magical expectations of therapeutic omnipotence must be relinquished. At the same time, however, a deeper sensitivity is realized, a keener compassion to patient suffering. (p. 30)

RATIONAL SUICIDE

When discussing the prevention of suicide, one must ask the following question: Do individuals have a right to determine the time and circumstances of their deaths? This question has been the focus of much debate between proponents and opponents of **rational suicide.** As previously presented in chapter 1, the practice of physician-assisted suicide as a form of rational suicide has taken centerstage in recent debates, but the concept and scope of this discussion is much broader.

Rational suicide, according to its advocates, has the following characteristics: (1) the mental processes leading to the individual's decision to commit suicide are unimpaired by psychological illness or severe emotional distress, and (2) the motivation for the decision would be understandable to the majority of the members of the person's community or social group (Siegel & Tuckel, 1984). Illness-related suicide is increasingly seen as acceptable under certain circumstances; nearly 50% of Americans believe that a person has the right to end his or her own life if that individual has an incurable disease (Siegel, 1988). In a study of American college students, respondents were much more likely to say that a suicide was justified if a person had AIDS or cancer than if the person suffered from schizophrenia or depression (Ingram & Ellis, 1995).

Advocates of the right-to-suicide position argue that everyone should have the right to end his or her life. In their view, suicide may be strongly in one's self-interest. The individual, they argue, is the best judge of what is in his or her best interest and that decision should be strictly left up to that person because it can reflect one's fundamental values. For some, it is important to end their lives with their physical and intellectual abilities intact, prior to reaching a stage of debilitation and dependence (Moody, 1984).

On the other side of the debate is the sanctity-of-life argument that maintains that suicide should never be permitted under any circumstances. Human life is seen as sacred and it is to be protected at all costs. Proponents of this view believe that there are no legitimate grounds for killing oneself or others. According to this view, the choice of death over life is not a decision that belongs to human beings (Moody, 1984).

A second argument against rational suicide is based on the view that suicide is indicative of mental illness or emotional disturbance. Questioning the validity of the concept of rational suicide, Siegel and Tuckel (1984) point out that one of the inherent problems in trying to legitimize rational suicide is the exclusive focus on thought processes when the urge to commit suicide "usually originates in the realm of feelings and emotions and not in the domain of evaluative reasoning in which the individual can objectively assess his or her situation" (p. 267). This view is common in the mental health field and is closely linked with the philosophy of suicide prevention programs. These programs are based on the premise that life is a good thing and that it is better to live than to die. The state of mind leading to suicide is viewed as temporary; many people change their minds about living when a suicide attempt has been interrupted and help is then offered.

Personal values are inextricably linked to the issue of rational suicide. The potential impact of prejudice and discrimination against certain groups in society can also contribute to our view toward the acceptability of suicide. Ableism, ageism, racism, and sexism, as well as AIDS phobia, may all play a part in the types of suicide a particular society finds "acceptable" under certain conditions (Werth, 1996). If suicide were to become an accepted option, this might intensify pressure on particular groups, such as the elderly and the terminally ill, to end their lives. The option to commit suicide might easily be converted into an obligation to take one's own life (Siegel & Tuckel, 1984).

SUMMARY

Suicide rates vary significantly by gender, culture, age, and ethnicity. In the United States, the highest rate is found among elderly white males. Although lower in comparison, rates for American youth are of concern because of their rapid escalation over the past several decades. Survivors of a suicide are left with many questions about the death and its preventability. They also often experience guilt and shame because of the stigma associated with this type of death. Like friends and family members, mental health professionals who provided services to the deceased, but failed to prevent the suicide, will also experience a range of emotional reactions as well as self-doubt. The issue of suicide must be addressed at the individual, family, and societal level. Schools and communities have important roles to play in terms of prevention, intervention, and postvention.

Many current issues related to suicide are historically unprecedented. First, never before has medical technology made it possible for individuals with severe chronic diseases and disabilities to survive for extended periods of time. Second, individuals have never lived to such advanced old age after losing so many of their traditional roles. Third, the current public discussion of suicide as an acceptable alternative in certain circumstances and the ensuing coverage by the mass media are unparalleled. As these trends continue, new questions regarding the right to end one's life will emerge. Quality-of-life issues will become more complex, and many ethical questions will need to be addressed.

Personal Account

Eight years after the death of her mother by suicide, Natalie recalls the horror of learning that her mother jumped off an 18-story building. In this essay, she shares her reactions in the weeks, months, and years following the death as she and her sister attempted to come to terms with the way in which their mother chose to die.

Natalie: Dreams of Catching Her

My mother killed herself on one of the coldest days of the year, during a period of subzero temperatures. It was not just winter; it was like hell. I mean, it was unbelievably cold. She went out in the middle of the night and jumped off an eighteen-story building. The violent aspect of her death is something I can barely keep in my consciousness for more than a second at a time.

For the longest time, I obsessed about her being cold. I guess you attach yourself to these stupid little things. The thought of her being out in the cold just drove me crazy. I found her boots in the car, and I got very freaked. What was she wearing? Did she go out barefoot? I asked the police what they'd found

---

SOURCE: From V. Alexander (1991). *Words I never thought to speak* (pp. 21–30, 180–188). New York: Lexington Books.

on her feet. I wanted to know what she was wearing, and basically the coroner's report was a list of every bone in her body being broken. They said, "There's nothing left of what she was wearing. It was all shredded." That was one of the things I obsessed about—her shoes and whether she was cold.

I went through garbage pails, looking, trying to put together pieces of paper that she had torn apart, so I could figure out what was going on. It was just pure hell going through that, having your world fall out and trying to put the pieces together, trying to figure out what could have happened.

I had been visiting her that week, and I thought, "How could I have not known? How could I have not figured it out?" She had hidden everything. She had gone to the point of trying to rent an apartment so that she could jump out of it. Later, we found all these ads that she'd clipped. And in fact, she'd put a deposit down on an apartment. I don't know whether it was so that she could get inside the building and see what it was like and how she could do this. It was like a James Bond thing. My mother was a schoolteacher who never did anything; I don't think she ever had a traffic violation. Yet she had worked out this elaborate scheme. She had made all these calls about apartments and had gone through the process of putting a security deposit on one of them. She had rented a car and hidden it somewhere, because it was nowhere near the house. She must have parked it far away.

The night my mother killed herself, my sister got a phone call, at around 4 A.M. My sister said she heard a kind of whispering sound at the other end. At the time, she thought it was a crank call. Afterward, we were pretty sure it was my mother, that she wanted to hear my sister's voice. She may have been in a psychotic state by that point, or she was just trying to keep my sister on the phone so that she could hear her voice before . . . It's hard to imagine someone being that tortured. It's not hard to imagine, it's hard to let in that she could have been that tortured. And that was always the hardest thing for me with my mother: she was in a lot of pain, and I just couldn't do anything to help her. I tried. I feel that most of my growing up had to do with realizing that I couldn't. And it just rips me apart, because it's so sad.

My mother and I had seen the movie *Elephant Man* the night that she killed herself. It's about a person who was so physically deformed he felt he had no place in the world and was totally a misfit. At the end of the movie, he lies down to sleep, which because of his deformity essentially kills him. I was holding my mother's hand in the movie theater, and when that happened, I squeezed her hand. I don't know what was going on, whether she thought I knew she was going to do it, and she felt that was my way of saying it's okay. I was just feeling that I knew how alone and awful she felt.

It blew me away that that's what we saw that night. I think maybe if we had seen something else, if we hadn't seen that movie, maybe she could have changed her mind at the last minute. People have gone over this with me a million times. She had planned this—she had rented a car, looked for apartments. She had been doing this for weeks. It's not something she thought of that night. But I just think, how could we have seen *that* movie *that* night? It was one of the saddest movies I've ever seen in my life. And to me it encapsulates that experience, the whole time. My mother's deformity was totally internal—it was her experience of herself—but I don't think she felt any less of an elephant person.

Sometime late that night she drove to the apartment building in the rented car. She went up to the roof and jumped. I can't imagine what she was thinking as she looked over. She left her purse and a stepladder. There must have been a ledge, and she needed the stepladder to get over it. I don't know whether she brought the ladder with her or found one when she got there, whether she got there and all of a sudden realized she couldn't do it without a stepladder—I don't know.

She left a note in her purse saying that the person to contact was my sister's boyfriend. She made sure that neither my sister nor I would be contacted by the police, that we would be told by someone else. She didn't want either of us to be alone when we found out, and I think the way she thought it out was by starting it off with the first contact not being either of us but my sister's boyfriend. Then he would tell my sister, and my sister would tell me. I think she chose not to be in the house so that neither of us would find her body. I don't think she thought that we'd still have to identify her body.

The next morning I woke up and noticed that the front door was ajar. I didn't understand that. I never could understand why she didn't close the door after she left. She didn't have any keys on her, and I guess my fantasy was that she wanted to get back in the house. That was my wish, somehow, that she was allowing herself to get back in.

Her bedroom door was also slightly ajar, and it looked like she was in bed. My mother was an early riser, and it was unusual for me to get up before her, but I figured she was sleeping late. Finally, it was about 10 A.M., and I thought it was really odd, so I opened her door, and I realized that the bed was stuffed with pillows. I think at that point I knew something was terribly wrong, but my denial kicked in. I started looking around for her. I called my sister, who said to call her back in an hour if I hadn't heard from my mother. Her car was still there, and I couldn't imagine where she'd gone. That was the thing that really threw me off: her car was there. It never occurred to me that she had rented a car.

I started driving around, thinking maybe she had walked somewhere. Maybe she'd gone crazy, and she had just all of a sudden done some lunatic thing. Not that my mother had ever done anything like that, but I was thinking of these possibilities more than thinking that she could have done something like kill herself. But I know that was in the back of my head, because eventually I drove over to my aunt's house. My aunt had died six weeks earlier. I looked in the window. I was terrified, because I thought I'd see my mother lying there, dead. That's where I thought she would have gone. I thought of death and my aunt and her going back to my aunt. And she had gone back to my aunt, in a sense; she'd killed herself. There are times when I get into otherworldly kinds of thoughts . . . that somehow my mother was with everybody she had always wanted to be with all these years and had been separated from through death: my father and her father and mother and my aunt.

We didn't realize that she'd rented a car until we got a call from the rental place a few days later. We ended up having to go to the building where she'd jumped, because we had to find the car and return it. That was awful. My sister and I were both terrified to go there. It was as though we thought we'd see her lying there, although by that time we had buried her. But I had to get out and look. A newspaper story had said something about a broken tree limb, and I wanted to see which tree was broken.

For the longest time, whenever I passed a tall building, I'd start counting—one, two, three—trying to figure out whether it was as tall as the building my mother had jumped from. Most of them were not eighteen stories. I'd count the stories, and it would be fourteen, and I'd think, "Bigger than that?" I'd seen the actual building, but it was just this unconscious thing where I'd pass a building and start counting stories.

Another thing I got very stuck on was my mother's letter to my sister and me, which she'd left in her purse. At the police station, after we'd identified her, they wouldn't give us the letter. I guess they wanted to keep it because there had to be some kind of investigation to make it official that it was suicide. Someone could have pushed her, I suppose, which of course entered my mind. You know, it's so unbelievable that a lot of unbelievable thoughts come into your mind. Suicide seemed as bizarre as the idea that she might have been having an affair with some person and he pushed her. What's more bizarre? They're all bizarre!

At first, the police were only going to let us read the letter. They wanted us to leave without it, but I would not leave. I said, "This is all I have left." They'd seen the body of my mother, which was in a bag essentially, and that they could even imagine keeping that letter from us seemed like more of an injury than we should have to bear. They finally gave us a copy.

I wanted the letter read at the funeral. That was the other part—not wanting to hide that it was a suicide. My uncle asked me what I wanted to say to people, and I said, "What do you mean? I'm not ashamed. That's what she did, and that's who my mother is, and I'm not ashamed of it."

The funeral, in a way, is a blur to me. There were so many people there, and I was fixated on wanting the letter read and not hiding the suicide. My sister and I had gone back to the temple we had belonged to when we were kids and asked the rabbi there to do the ceremony. The only thing I insisted on was that the letter be read. Other than that, I said, "Do a funeral." The rabbi did read the letter, but he left off the last line, which was, "I can't go on."

One thing that was really bizarre was that the rabbi's name was the same as my mother's maiden name. There was a way that I attached myself to these kinds of things and drew great comfort from them. I felt they were signs of something.

It was amazing how many things like that happened. When we sold my mother's house, the lawyer representing the bank was the same lawyer who had been there when my mother and father had bought the house thirty years before! He had done the closings for the developer. The same person who'd sat with my mother and father thirty years before, when they'd bought the house, sat with me and my sister when we sold it. And my mother killed herself after making the last payment on that house. The last payment had been made, the house was finally hers, and she killed herself.

I was very attached to that house. After my mother died, I felt that I needed to soak it up as much as I could before it was gone, because I knew that part of my life had been irrevocably changed and taken away from me. I felt comfort in the house. I wanted to be close to my mother. I wanted somehow to get whatever it was that she was trying to say. I was desperate for answers, desperate to know, desperate to feel connected to her.

I don't think I could have made it without my sister. We had different ways of coping and different ways of wanting to deal with the situations that arose, but we had always been very tight, and through the initial period after my mother's death, we were incredibly close. We went through a rough time shortly after that, which I think had to do with the anger that was bouncing off the walls at that point. Just the basic stress of what we were dealing with could make any two people go at each other. But also my mother was removed as a buffer between us. In some ways, we'd been able to put a lot of the tension in our relationship—the competitiveness or whatever—onto my mother, and now we were left with each other. We were dealing with this trauma together, and we desperately needed each other, yet sometimes we drove each other up the wall.

My sister and I have very different styles. I'm more of a talker, more of an emoter. This is all relative. When I'm in a group of people, I realize that I'm pretty shy, but my view of myself is so shaped by how I was in my family. In that microcosm of the world, I was the emoter and my sister was the quiet one.

We were like Siamese twins for the first twenty-four hours after my mother died, and for the next two weeks we were like Siamese twins attached by a string. The first night we didn't let each other out of sight. The thought of losing each other, even if only by sight, was unbearable, so we stayed together.

Someone had told me, at some point, that spirits don't leave the earth for twenty-four hours. I said to my sister, "We've got to talk to her, because if she's still around, it's our only chance to clean up our act with her." We cried and we laughed and we half-jokingly tried to talk to her. We were trying to reach her or reach ourselves or something. Basically, I think we wanted forgiveness from her. And what we were probably saying was that we forgave her, that we loved her and wanted her to be at peace, finally. But I think we were also terrified that she was around and would grab us up. It's a wish and a fear at the same time. It's the wish to have the person still be there and the denial that the person is gone. The fear is that what's happened is horrific; it's murder. When people kill themselves, there's violence. Will they come and get you? Will they take you with them? To me, that's part of the stuff of survivors—being scared that we'll kill ourselves, too.

I had many dreams about my mother. They were all nightmares to me. Often, they were dreams of me trying to catch her. I had awful dreams, so awful that I couldn't stand them. But I'd also been terrified after my father's death, when I was a child. I remember being scared to take showers. So in a way it's not only the suicide aspect; it's the death itself that's scary. Death is such a hard thing to comprehend. When someone dies, it brings death closer to you, so you fear you'll be taken. Maybe the fear comes from beginning to deal with your own mortality.

After my father's death, when I was so scared of ghosts, my mother said to me, "If your father did come back, you know he would never hurt you, because he loved you very much." She didn't say, "There's no such thing as ghosts." She said, "Your father's ghost would never hurt you." That helped me when my mother died, because I believe in my heart that she truly loved me and didn't want to hurt me. There are ways that she did things that were hurtful to me but never intentionally, always almost against her will. So I think that I let her statement come back to me and comfort me.

Other than finding out about the suicide itself, closing out my mother's house was the hardest thing I ever had to do. It was the house that I had grown up in. It had every piece of that life in it, and it was also the only place that I had known my father. So letting go of that house was really saying that I didn't have any parents anymore and that I didn't have a family, in a sense. There was no way that I could ever again feel like a child in this world. I was an adult, like it or not, for the rest of my life. I had no cushion. I was really dealing with the rock bottom of it, the realization of how completely and drastically my life had been altered, how it would never be the same, and how my parents were never to be in my life alive.

And then there was the whole issue of possessions, the classic who's going to get what. God help me, I never thought I'd get into that, never in a million years! I was from the nonmaterial era—you know, give me a sleeping bag and an orange, and I'll survive. And here we were, my sister and I, fighting over my father's desk, the only thing that we knew was my father's possession in the house. We both wanted it, and we each felt the other wasn't willing to make compromises. I know this is how she felt, and I felt the same way. In the end, I said, "You can have the desk," because I felt that my dead father's desk was not as important as my living sister. I'm sure she would not see it as generously as that, because she thought I got everything else! And I felt that I gave her the only thing I really cared about. We were each in our own camp. When I look back on it now, I think I felt that I wasn't getting what I wanted. I didn't want this whole situation, and the fact that I didn't get the desk was just part of the picture—things were not going my way. And maybe I allowed those feelings to surface around the possessions. At the time, some of those things stayed with me and became important.

My sister and I healed over a period of time; it took a while. We were really angry but not disconnected; we never gave up on each other. This was the first time in our lives that we were really angry with each other, other than when we were children. But there was always such unconditional love and support between us.

I was so devastated and needy when my mother died. I was like a dry sponge; any little bit of moisture I made into more than it was. If someone said anything nice to me, I could take that small amount of support and stretch it into a much bigger thing, because I was just needing so much at that point.

I contacted my mother's former therapist, and the things that she said that were comforting to me I held on to and really milked for all they were worth. [I felt as though] my mother had somehow said, "You're not okay enough for me even to stay alive for." When her therapist saw me afterward, she didn't say, "You're the daughter? You're the cause of this. You were terrible!" She still treated me like an okay person. And for my mother's therapist to be doing that meant that maybe I didn't have to think I was as awful as I could have thought I was.

As much as I was struggling internally with all these things, to the external world I was coping remarkably well. People were just amazed that I seemed to be handling it so well emotionally. Plus I was dealing with the police, the funeral arrangements, lawyers, and closing the house. And in all my dealings, I think I was coming across as appropriately sad. No extremes—I wasn't falling apart, and I wasn't pretending that it hadn't happened. I was the perfect bereaved survivor. That people perceived me this way helped me feel that I could keep on keeping on.

I did allow myself to depend on people in a way I hadn't ever before. The first day I sat by the phone and called up all the friends I felt fairly close to. My way of dealing with the shock, the unbelievableness of it, was to tell each person. I didn't want other people to make the phone calls for me, because if I did it twenty times, maybe I'd start believing what I was saying. Each time it was a relief to me. Each time, if I could allow myself to break down while telling people what had happened, it gave me an enormous amount of comfort. And people's responses to me were incredibly genuine and wonderful. I didn't feel stigmatized at all.

I think the thing that healed me the most was that I was able to talk to people about what had happened. I told people the gory details. I would go through, step by step, what happened. And all of that was necessary for me to repeat and repeat and repeat. This is what happened, then I did this, and then this is what happened. Telling people how she killed herself became enormously important to me. Each time I would tell someone how, in my mind I would imagine it, and the horror of it would somehow be worked out for me. I could imagine this horrible thing, and I didn't feel so alone. I brought people with me so that I didn't have to go through imagining it alone.

I worried that people would eventually tire of hearing about it, that I would wear out my welcome. Mostly, that didn't happen. But after about six months to a year, they needed to have it behind me. It wasn't uniform, and I wouldn't say it was all the time, but even with people I think are very sensitive, there was a real aversion to staying with it for that long. They didn't have to stay with it, and I could understand that they wouldn't want to. I had to stay with it, because it wasn't gone yet. I remember saying to one friend, "I'm worried that you'll think there's something wrong with me because I'm still so upset." And she said, "Oh, no, I don't think that. If you were still like this in a year, then I would worry about you." I made a mental note of that, and I said to myself, "Okay, in a year I'll never say another word about it to this person." There was a certain amount of tolerance beyond which people could not deal with the magnitude of the loss that I had experienced. Their wanting it to be over was their way of containing the horror of it for themselves. That's the way I came to understand it. At a certain point, they really reached a limit.

I was always in a race against time. I was trying desperately to make sure that I could push everything back in and get it all back together in the time frame that I thought people expected of me. I had the sense that there wouldn't be someone who could listen long enough and hard enough to what I had to say for me to feel that I had really been heard, to the end.

It ends up being easier to talk about my mother and her history than about my experience of her suicide, because it is so painful to talk about how it actually felt to go through that experience. There are times when I feel it was like an out-of-body experience. I can hardly go back to it, because I think it's almost unbearable to touch. I'm sure there's a part of me that just doesn't want to. I put my whole life back together; I put myself back together. And as much as it's okay to feel the pain of it all or to think about it—and I do at times—you have to distance yourself in a certain way to be able to go on.

I felt incredibly angry at my mother immediately after she died. I thought, "How could she do this to me?" But then, at a certain point, I felt an even deeper anger that it really was cruel what she did to me. I don't think she did it to me purposely—"I'm going to make you suffer"—but her action had an irrevocable impact on my life that was cruel. For someone who supposedly loved me as she said she did, and I think she did in her way, she shouldn't have done it.

It feels better at this point not to be so angry. It feels better to know that after all that happened in my relationship with her, I loved her and I love her, and I would rather have had her here than not here. As much as I'd rather have her alive, it's also in part a relief not to have her alive. It's taken me a while to feel comfortable saying that.

It really upsets me now if there's something that isn't right between me and somebody else. I know that relationships can't always be problem-free, but I sometimes think, "If I never see this person again, is this the way I want it left?" It's taken a lot of willpower to allow myself to go through the downside in a relationship and not try to rush it, just stay with it rather than try to make it all better. It takes a lot on my part to realize that most people don't die the way my mother did. I don't have to worry every time I say good-bye to someone that I'll never see that person again.

My mother's suicide made me think about what it means to be a mother. I decided that if I chose to become a mother, I would be making a decision never to kill myself. It was very clear in my mind that I could not decide to be a parent if I could not make that commitment. However bad it might get for me, I could never do that to a child, even an adult child.

It's always felt very heavy for me to think about becoming a parent, and I'm sure that was partly because of my family life and having lost my father and then the experience with my mother. I think that's why I postponed having a child as long as I did. It's a huge commitment, a commitment to life. In the end, that's the commitment I wanted to make anyway, but I had to think it through.

After my son was born, I went back to the house I'd grown up in. I loved that house. It contained the memories of my whole life. We had moved there when I was a year old. It was the only home I had ever known. My father and my grandmother died there. It was my roots, everything. I wanted my son to know where I'd grown up.

Going back to that house was sad; it felt like a completion. We walked around the neighborhood and ran into some neighbors I'd known. I'd grown up with their kids, and they'd known my father. We had lemonade with them in their backyard. They were very sweet. There's a way in which I long for people who knew my life as it was when my family was intact. If there's anyone who knew me as a regular person, a regular kid, it says something—I mean, it makes me feel that something was normal. There's some documentation of things before they fell apart, which to me started when my father died.

Part of the experience after suicide is the loss of control. As much as you might have thought about empowering yourself and making your life work—all those terms from the '70s and '80s—you get to know how little control you have over certain things, and that's just the way it is. I feel jaded when I think of the innocence I've lost that I envy in other people. It's this hard-earned knowledge about life that I feel people get angry at me for sometimes. It's not that I think you have to crawl in a hole because life is awful. It's a comprehension of certain realities that you just don't comprehend until you really come up against it. Until you bump your nose right up against it, you just don't *know*! I guess it's hard to know and then be able to regain the positive and allow yourself to have your dreams.

It's another one of those balances. How do you acknowledge your powerlessness in the world and then feel powerful? Before my mother's suicide, I used to feel that I could do anything. I was young and energetic and into political movements, marching for this and marching for that—all things that I think were very important and that I still believe in. But I had a narrow vision of the world and myself in the world. My mother's suicide made my vision of the world open up. I got to see how big the world actually is and how much of it I don't understand. I used to feel that I understood a lot more than I do now. It's the old cliché that as you get older, you know less and less, but when you're young, you think you know everything. I had the whole world wrapped up at twenty-five; I had all the answers! You know—innocence is bliss. Yet when I think back on it, I don't know how blissful it really was. I have a certain contentment now that I never had back then. I see things more realistically. It's interesting to think of having less anguish now, after my mother's suicide, than before.

When people ask me about my parents, I say that they're both dead, and I don't have any trouble saying how my mother died. There might be circumstances in which I wouldn't tell, but if they're people I like and I'm getting to know, I want them to know who I am and what my life has been. There was a time when it felt pressing to tell people about my mother's suicide. I almost couldn't be with someone unless that person knew. Now it really surprises me to think that in the group of people I've met more recently, there are some who didn't know for a long time. I didn't have to tell them. I could be with these people and feel that they actually knew me without my having to say, "There is something terribly important that you should know about me."

QUESTIONS AND ACTIVITIES

1. In the Personal Account, describe Natalie's needs as she coped with her mother's suicide. In what ways were others supportive or nonsupportive? How did the "legacy of suicide" continue to affect her life and her interactions with others?

2. Should suicides be routinely reported in the media? Under what circumstances might this practice be harmful or helpful to the bereaved family members? In what ways might it be beneficial to the general public? What ethical issues are involved in decisions to provide media coverage of suicides and what guidelines should be followed?

3. What suicide prevention, intervention, and postvention programs are available in your community? If possible, interview a staff member involved in one of these programs and inquire about services offered, clientele served, and program evaluation findings.

4. Gather statistics on suicide for your city and state. How do community statistics compare with national averages in terms of incidence, average age, gender distribution, methods used? If differences exist, what possible contributing factors can you identify?

5. Genograms can be useful in examining family loss history, regardless of the cause of death. Talk with your parents and/or grandparents. Construct a genogram that traces your family's loss experiences and includes at least three generations. What new information or insights did you gain through this exercise? Has a death in an earlier generation affected current relationships in your family? In what ways?

6. What is your view of rational suicide? Do you ever think that suicide is ever justified? Under what conditions?

7. Do you know anyone personally who has taken his or her own life? What were your own reactions upon hearing of the death? What was your understanding of factors contributing to the death? How did the professionals involved (e.g., police, physician, funeral director) respond? What was done well and what could they have done differently?

GLOSSARY

Cluster suicides: a phenomenon in which individuals with similar demographic characteristics who live in the same geographical area commit suicide within a relatively short time frame.

Contagion theory: belief that talking about suicide will encourage suicidal behavior.

Copy cat suicides: a phenomenon in which several suicides of a similar nature (often in terms of method, location, and/or date) occur following a single highly publicized suicide.

Developmental counseling: attempts to prevent potential crises by helping students become more aware of themselves, how they interact with their environment, and how to cope effectively with the various tasks involved in growing up.

Genogram: a structured family history in which information is diagramed about the family, their relationships, and important family events.

Intervention: therapeutic efforts to reduce the intensity and negative effects of a crisis or difficult situation.

Postvention: actions taken to deal with the aftermath of a traumatic event and to minimize the impact.

Prevention: actions taken to avoid a stressful or harmful situation.

Psychological autopsy: a formal review focusing on establishing events and other factors that preceded a suicide in order to identify causal and contributing factors.

Rational suicide: a much debated concept related to an individual's conscious and presumably rational decision to end his or her life.

Suicidologists: professionals who specialize in the study of suicide.

Tunnel vision: inability to consider alternative ways of dealing with a crisis.

SUGGESTED READINGS

Canetto, S. S., & Lester, D. (Eds.). (1995). *Women and suicidal behavior.* New York: Springer.

Experts on suicidology from both the United States and Canada have contributed chapters to this important volume that challenges some of the assumptions about suicidal behavior found in the current professional literature. An emphasis is placed on the role of social and cultural factors, including social class, social support, gender socialization, and cultural norms.

Leenaars, A. A., & Wenckstern, S. (Eds.). (1991). *Suicide prevention in the schools.* New York: Hemisphere.

A comprehensive approach to suicide prevention in the school setting, this book includes useful information for both elementary and secondary school personnel. Case examples from both the United States and Canada are included that illustrate specific suicide prevention approaches and programs.

McIntosh, J. L., Santos, J. F., Hubbard, R. W., & Overholser, J. C. (Eds.). (1994). *Elder suicide: Research, theory, and treatment.* Washington, DC: American Psychological Association.

Contributors to this volume summarize and critique the latest research in the field. Factors associated with elderly suicide are examined and discussed in the context of relevant theory. Treatment options and effectiveness of clinical interventions are reviewed.

Range, L. M., & Knott, E. C. (1997). Twenty suicide assessment instruments: Evaluation and recommendations. *Death Studies, 21*(1), 25-58.

The authors describe and critically review a broad range of suicide assessment instruments that vary in length as well as age group for which they were designed. Specific information on psychometric properties, strengths, weaknesses, and appropriate applications are provided.

Stillion, J. M., & McDowell, E. E. (1996). *Suicide across the life span* (2nd ed.). Washington, DC: Taylor & Francis.

Developmental themes are interwoven throughout the text as a broad range of issues related to suicide are examined using a trajectory model. The authors utilize an interdisciplinary approach and provide historical perspectives. Of particular interest is the emphasis on cohort effects for different age groups.

RESOURCES

American Association of Suicidology
4201 Connecticut Avenue, NW, Suite 310
Washington, DC 20008
(202) 237-2280

American Foundation of Suicide Prevention
120 Wall Street, 22nd Floor
New York, NY 10005
(212) 363-3500 or 1-888-333-AFSP

Suicide Awareness/Voices of Education (SA/VE)
7317 Cahill Road
Minneapolis, MN 55439
(612) 946-7998

Suicide Information and Education Centre
Suite 201, 1615 Tenth Avenue, S.W.
Calgary, Alberta
Canada T3C OJ7
(403) 245-3900

REFERENCES

American Association of Suicidology. (1996). *Elderly suicide fact sheet.* Washington, DC: Author.

Balk, D. E. (1995). *Adolescent development: Early through late adolescence.* Pacific Grove, CA: Brooks/Cole.

Berman, A. L. (1986). Helping suicidal adolescents: Needs and responses. In C. A. Corr & J. N. McNeil (Eds.), *Adolescence and death* (pp. 151-166). New York: Springer.

Blazer, D. (1982). *Depression in late life.* St. Louis, MO: C. V. Mosby.

Boldt, M. (1982). Normative evaluations of suicide and death: A cross-generational study. *Omega, 13*(2), 145-157.

Butler, R. N., & Lewis, M. (1982). *Aging and mental health* (2nd ed.). St. Louis, MO: C. V. Mosby.

Canetto, S. S. (1992). Gender and suicide in the elderly. *Suicide and Life-Threatening Behavior, 22* (1), 80-97.

Canetto, S. S. (1995). Elderly women and suicidal behavior. In S. S. Canetto & D. Lester (Eds.), *Women and suicidal behavior* (pp. 215-233). New York: Springer.

Canetto, S. S., & Lester, D. (1995). Gender and the primary prevention of suicide mortality. *Suicide and Life-Threatening Behavior, 25*(1), 58-69.

Centers for Disease Control. (1992). *Youth suicide prevention programs: A resource guide.* Atlanta: Author.

Clark, D. C. (1993). *Clergy response to suicidal persons and their family members: An interfaith resource book for clergy and congregations.* Chicago: Exploration Press.

Dalke, D. (1994). Therapy-assisted growth after parental suicide: From a personal and professional perspective. *Omega, 29*(2), 113-151.

Deaton, R. L., & Berkan, W. A. (1995). *Planning and managing death issues in the schools.* Westport, CT: Greenwood Press.

Demi, A. S., & Howell, C. (1991). Hiding and healing: Resolving the suicide of a parent or sibling. *Archives of Psychiatric Nursing, 5*(6), 350-356.

Dunne-Maxim, K. (1987). Survivors and the media: Pitfalls and potential. In E. J. Dunne, J. L. McIntosh, & K. Dunne-Maxim (Eds.), *Suicide and its aftermath: Understanding and counseling the survivors* (pp. 45-56). New York: W. W. Norton.

Fairchild, T. N. (1986). Suicide prevention. In T. N. Fairchild (Ed.), *Crisis intervention strategies for school-based helpers* (pp. 321-369). Springfield, IL: Charles C. Thomas.

Gallup Organization. (1992). *Attitude and incidence of suicide among elderly.* Princeton, NJ: Author.

Garland, A. F., & Zigler, E. (1993). Adolescent suicide prevention: Current research and policy implications. *American Psychologist, 48*(2), 169-182.

Glass, J. C., Jr. (1990). Death, loss, and grief in high school students. *The High School Journal,* Feb./March, 154-160.

Goldman, L. (1996). *Breaking the silence: A guide to help children with complicated grief—suicide, homicide, AIDS, violence, and abuse.* Washington, DC: Accelerated Development.

Goldstein, L. S., & Buongiorno, P. A. (1984). Psychotherapists as suicide survivors. *American Journal of Psychotherapy, 38,* 392-398.

Grebstein, L. C. (1986). Family therapy after a child's death. In T. A. Rando (Ed.), *Parental loss of a child* (pp. 429-449). Champaign, IL: Research Press.

Hauser, M. J. (1987). Special aspects of grief after a suicide. In E. J. Dunn, J. L. McIntosh, & K. Dunne-Maxim (Eds.), *Suicide and its aftermath: Understanding and counseling the survivors* (pp. 57-70). New York: W. W. Norton.

Ingram, E., & Ellis, J. B. (1995). Situational analysis of attitudes toward suicide behavior. *Death Studies, 19*(3), 269-275.

Jones, F. A., Jr. (1987). Therapists as survivors of client suicide. In E. J. Dunne, J. L. McIntosh, & K. Dunne-Maxim (Eds.), *Suicide and its aftermath: Understanding and counseling the survivors* (pp. 126-141). New York: W. W. Norton.

Kalafat, J., & Elias, M. (1992). Adolescents' experience with and response to suicidal peers. *Suicide and Life-Threatening Behavior, 22*(3), 315-321.

Kastenbaum, R. J. (1995). *Death, society, and human experience* (5th ed.). Boston, MA: Allyn & Bacon.

Leenaars, A., & Wenckstern, S. (1991). *Suicide prevention in the schools.* New York: Hemisphere.

Lester, D. (1993). Differences in the epidemiology of suicide. *Omega, 31,* 90-93.

Maris, R. (1985). The adolescent suicide problem. *Suicide and Life-Threatening Behavior, 15*(2), 91-109.

Martin, N. K., & Dixon, P. N. (1986). Adolescent suicide: Myths, recognition, and evaluation. *The School Counselor, 33*(4), 265-271.

McGoldrick, M., & Gerson, R. (1985). *Genograms in family assessment.* New York: W. W. Norton.

McIntosh, J. L. (1992). Older adults: The next suicide epidemic? *Suicide and Life-Threatening Behavior, 22*(3), 322-332.

McIntosh, J. L. (1993). Suicide: Native-American. In R. Kastenbaum & B. K. Kastenbaum (Eds.), *The encyclopedia of death* (pp. 238-239). Phoenix, AZ: Oryx.

McIntosh, J. L. (1995). Suicide prevention in the elderly (age 65-99). In M. M. Silverman & R. W. Maris (Eds.), *Suicide prevention: Toward the year 2000* (pp. 180-192). New York: Guilford Press.

Millen, L., & Roll, S. (1985). A case study in failure: On doing everything right in suicide prevention. *Death Studies, 9*(6), 483-492.

Moody, H. R. (1984). Can suicide on grounds of old age be ethically justified? In M. Tallmer, E. R. Prichard, A. H. Kutscher, R. DeBellis, M. S. Hale, & I. K. Goldberg (Eds.), *The life-threatened elderly* (pp. 64-92). New York: Columbia University Press.

Morgan, L. B. (1981). The counselor's role in suicide prevention. *The Personnel and Guidance Journal, 59,* 284-286.

Peck, M. L., Farberow, N. L., & Litman, R. E. (Eds.) (1985). *Youth suicide.* New York: Springer.

Richman, J. (1986). *Family therapy for suicidal people.* New York: Springer.

Richman, J. (1993). *Preventing elderly suicide: Overcoming personal despair, professional neglect, and social bias.* New York: Springer.

Rosenblatt, P., & Elde, C. (1990). Shared reminiscence about a deceased parent: Implications for grief education and grief counseling. *Family Relations, 39,* 206-210.

Ross, C. P. (1985). Teaching children the facts of life and death: Suicide prevention in the schools. In M. L. Peck, N. L. Farberow, & R. E. Litman (Eds.), *Youth suicide* (pp. 147-169). New York: Springer.

Rowling, L. (1995). The disenfranchised grief of teachers. *Omega, 31*(4), 317-329.

Sanders, C. M. (1984). Therapists, too, need to grieve. *Death Education, 8* (Suppl.—Suicide: Practical, developmental, and speculative issues), 27-35.

Shneidman, E. (1969). Suicide, lethality, and the psychological autopsy. *International Psychiatry Clinics, 6,* 225-250.

Siegel, K. (1988). Rational suicide. In S. Lesse (Ed.), *What we know about suicide behavior and how to treat it* (pp. 85-102). Northvale, NJ: Jason Aronson.

Siegel, K., & Tuckel, P. (1984). Rational suicide and the terminally ill cancer patient. *Omega, 15*(3), 263-269.

Sprang, G., & McNeil, J. (1995). *The many faces of bereavement.* New York: Brunner/Mazel.

Stenback, A. (1980). Depression and suicidal behavior in old age. In J. E. Birren & R. B. Sloane (Eds.), *Handbook of mental health and aging* (pp. 616-652). Englewood Cliffs, NJ: Prentice-Hall.

Stillion, J. M. (1996). Survivors of suicide. In K. J. Doka (Ed.), *Living with grief after sudden loss* (pp. 41–71). Bristol, PA: Taylor & Francis.

Stillion, J. M., & McDowell, E. E. (1996). *Suicide across the life span: Premature exits* (2nd ed.). Washington, DC: Taylor & Francis.

Valente, S. M. (1994). Psychotherapist reactions to the suicide of a patient. *American Journal of Orthopsychiatry, 64*(4), 614–621.

Valente, S. M., & Saunders, J. M. (1987). High school suicide prevention programs. *Pediatric Nursing, 13*(2), 108–112.

Walker, B. A., & Mehr, M. (1983). Adolescent suicide—a family crisis: A model for effective intervention by family therapists. *Adolescence, 18*, 285–292.

Weaver, A. J., & Koenig, H. G. (1996). Elderly suicide, mental health professionals, and the clergy: A need for clinical collaboration, training, and research. *Death Studies, 20*, 495–508.

Werth, J. L., Jr. (1996). *Rational suicide? Implications for mental health professionals.* Washington, DC: Taylor & Francis.

PART III

Implications for Caregivers

10

Issues for Professional Caregivers

Throughout this text we have examined the needs of individuals and families touched by death and bereavement. In this final chapter, the focus of our attention is on professional caregivers—the individuals who play a critical role in meeting the needs of the dying and their families. In their efforts to help others, caregivers often fail to address their own needs and concerns. What are the effects of working in situations that involve grief and loss on a regular basis? What coping mechanisms do physicians, nurses, clergy, social workers, therapists, and other professionals use to maintain both the quality of patient care and their own emotional well-being? How can training programs and institutional support be improved to prepare future professionals for the death- and grief-related situations they will face and for avoiding the consequences of "burnout"? This chapter will explore answers to these questions and consider the unique emotional demands of working in professions in which loss is a common element.

CONCERNS OF PROFESSIONALS

Individuals planning to work in the physical and mental health care fields often have concerns about their ability to work effectively with the dying and their families. Others have questions about the occupational hazards of this work in terms of personal stress (Benoliel, 1988). Until recently, little has been written to help individuals address these concerns and to assist them in coping with the personal aspects of their professions.

Personal Grief Reactions

Grief is a common reaction of professionals to the suffering, loss, and death of patients. For example, Hinds and her colleagues (1994) report that the professional literature provides consistent evidence of the strong emotional attachment that nurses have to their patients and the grief that they feel when they begin to anticipate or actually experience a patient's death. Working in a professional role does not protect individuals from the emotional impact of death-related experiences. Although the grief reactions of professional caregivers are similar to those of patients and families discussed in earlier chapters, they are usually of less intensity and shorter duration. While all situations involving death can have a potential effect on human service professionals, the situational context in which care is provided and the type of death both appear to have a strong influence on the reactions of caregivers.

Variables Affecting Grief Reactions.   Age of the patient is a particularly important variable affecting the grief response of professionals. Grief reactions among health care workers are especially pronounced following the death of an infant or child as, for example, in the case of sudden infant death syndrome

(SIDS). Although SIDS usually strikes in the home, such a death can also occur in a variety of other settings. After a particular SIDS death at the Minneapolis Children's Health Center, a follow-up study focused on the effects of the death on the hospital team involved in the infant's care. In nearly all of their reactions, the nursing staff mirrored the questions and concerns of families who have lost a child to SIDS. All expressed shock and disbelief on discovering or learning about the death. Feelings of guilt were strongly related to the amount of responsibility each nurse had for the infant. The nurse who was the primary caregiver engaged in exhaustive self-questioning of her actions, similar to "the kind of haunted and tormented thinking that families go through" (Friedman, Franciosi, & Drake, 1979, p. 539). Staff members expressed apprehension about adequate staffing and began checking more frequently on sleeping children. Affect disturbance was more pronounced and of longer duration in the staff member who had spent the most time with the SIDS victim. She was initially fearful of handling other infants and reported frequent crying, appetite problems, and bad dreams associated with the death. All of the staff were eager to go over the autopsy findings with the staff pathologist, and they had questions about whether they could have predicted or prevented the death of the infant. The information and reassurance provided through the group's discussion of the autopsy report was important in helping the staff cope with their feelings associated with this crisis. Recovery from this incident was also related to support from other staff members and from the infant's physician. This case illustrates the need for timely intervention and the importance of allowing each professional involved with the patient an opportunity to express his or her feelings and receive support following this type of death (Friedman et al., 1979). At the Massachusetts SIDS Center, training for nurses who provide support to bereaved families includes a component that addresses the impact on the professional and the development of strategies for coping with their own stress (McClain & Mandell, 1994).

Part of the trauma associated with SIDS is due to its sudden and unexpected occurrence in an assumed "well" population. The age of the patient, however, also influences the grief reactions of staff members in medical care settings in which all patients are gravely or seriously ill. For example, the death of a child on an intensive care unit (ICU) typically elicits a different response from staff members than does the death of an older person. When a dying child is on the unit, nurses make concerned comments more frequently and attend to the young patient with extra diligence as compared to older patients. When the child dies, the staff is more likely to feel guilty and question what else they could have done for the child. In contrast, the usual concern over the death of a geriatric patient relates more to issues of pain control and death with dignity, and staff members are more likely to accept an injured elderly person's statement about being ready to die than they would a similar statement from a younger person. Furthermore, death of an older person is often met with comments such as "He has had a good life" or "She has lived 84 years" (Swanson & Swanson, 1977).

Although grief appears to be generally less intense in response to the death of an older patient, grief reactions are still prevalent for those working with this age group. Lerea and LiMauro (1982) asked nurses and nurses' aides from a general hospital and three geriatric centers if they had ever grieved in response to a patient's physical or emotional condition. In each setting, the majority of staff reported having experienced grief reactions. Mourning was reported by 98% of the nursing staff at the 500–bed general hospital. (In this type of facility, positive results are often anticipated as a result of medical intervention; therefore, the staff are often not prepared for the death or deterioration of a patient.) The incidence of bereavement reported by staff at the geriatric centers was lower (63%), presumably because of the higher expectation of patient loss in this setting and the greater willingness to accept death in an older population. The most common psychological reactions for staff in both the general hospital and the geriatric centers included thinking and talking about the patient (92%) and feelings of helplessness (84%). Fatigue was the physical response most frequently recalled (55%). However, the full range of grief reactions, as typically reported by the bereaved, were observed in this sample of professionals (see Table 10.1). More than 1 month following the grief-related incident, psychological and physical grief reactions were still present for 50% of the general hospital

TABLE 10.1

Percentage of Health Care Workers Experiencing Physical and Psychological Grief Reactions

PHYSICAL	%	PSYCHOLOGICAL	%
Fatigue	55	Thinking or talking about the patient	92
Headache	44	Feelings of helplessness	84
Sighing respiration	42	Crying or despondency	53
Insomnia	41	Disbelief or shock	51
Loss of appetite or overeating	40	Difficulty concentrating	51
Dry mouth	35	Anger toward others	50
Restless or lethargic	34	Anxiety	47
Numbness	31	Irritability	43
Nausea or acid stomach	31	Guilt	37
Excessive perspiration	30	Withdrawal or feelings of aloneness	37
Constipation or diarrhea	16	Difficulty remembering	29
Dizziness	15	Apathy	22
Shortness of breath	13	Indecisiveness	20
Sexual difficulties	11	Tardiness or absenteeism	15

SOURCE: From E. L. Learea & B. F. LiMauro (1982). Grief among healthcare workers: A comparative study, *Journal of Gerontology, 37,* 5, p. 606. Copyright © 1982 The Gerontological Society of America. Reprinted by permission.

staff and 38% of the geriatric staff. No differences were found between the grief reactions of nurses and nurses' aides.

In addition to the age of the patient, a number of other variables such as degree of emotional attachment can also affect the intensity and type of grief reactions experienced by professional caregivers. For example, Hinds and her colleagues (1990) reported the death of a favorite patient as the most stressful and emotionally painful experience for oncology nurses. In contrast, ICU nurses often react to patients treated for drug overdoses and self-inflicted injuries with feelings of irritation, anger, and resentment because these cases take time away from other patients. Degree of consciousness of the patient also seems to have an effect on the caregiver's grief response. ICU nurses show less grief following the death of someone who enters the unit in a comatose state because the person's nonalert state prevents much emotional involvement on the part of the staff. One of the most difficult patients for the ICU nurse to care for is the individual who enters the unit in an alert state and then deteriorates. The longer the patient is on the unit in an alert state and able to communicate, the stronger the staff response will be. When it is apparent that the individual is dying, the attending nurse will often show signs of mild depression. "The nurse appears sad, works with less speed and zeal, and appears less interested in her job" (Swanson & Swanson, 1977, p. 246). At this point, the nurse often tends to withdraw emotionally from the patient and to show greater interest and concern for the monitors and the "busy work" involved in caring for the patient. Often when a death appears imminent, the ICU nurse, in order to avoid involvement with the actual death, will work hard to keep the patient alive so that he or she will not die on that shift but on someone else's.

Bennett and Kelaher (1993) report that medical staff issues of grief are further complicated by circumstances within their own lives. For example, physicians who identified themselves as gay were more likely than their heterosexual counterparts to experience increased anxiety, overwork, stress, and fear of death when working with AIDS patients. Overidentification with patients, perceptions of their own possible "at-risk" status, and overcommitment resulting in excessive work are possible explanations of these findings.

Professional caregivers are typically more affected by patients and families that are at the same stage of the individual and family life cycle as themselves, especially when untimely illnesses and death are involved (Rolland, 1994). Such life cycle synchronicities can promote high levels of empathy as well as personal reactions of emotional distancing or overinvolvement. Working with the dying and grieving may evoke intense personal feelings and arouse pervasive fears. Understanding patients' needs requires insight into one's own issues surrounding death (Cook & Dworkin, 1992). Thus, individuals who work with the dying and bereaved continually confront their own mortality and that of their loved ones. Previous losses are reawakened, and future losses are anticipated.

Vulnerabilities of Professional Caregivers.   As professional caregivers increasingly attempt to respond to the psychosocial needs of the dying, stronger attachments to the patient will be made, leaving the caregiver even more vulnerable to experiencing grief. Attachments can be accentuated in the absence of strong family support for the dying. This support may be lacking due to disrupted family systems, distance among family members created by social or geographic mobility, disengagement of family members from the dying individual, and the tendency of individuals today to die in institutions. These sociological trends are contributing to the development of a role for the caregiver as a **surrogate griever** (one who grieves in the place of family members). Diseases that often carry stigma, such as AIDS, can also contribute to the surrogate role of the health care provider, especially when traditional sources of support are not available. As one nurse expressed it,

> When they develop AIDS, all they experience is rejection until they encounter us, and we become the support for them, we become the family for them. . . .
> (Bennett, 1992)

In some medical and mental health specialties death is encountered infrequently, although no specialty is "death-free." In other specialties, caregivers work with the dying on a regular basis and run the risk of **bereavement overload.** This term, introduced earlier in the text, refers to the situation in which a griever must deal with several deaths in close succession and does not have the time to cope with the first death before he or she is confronted with another. If this accumulated grief is not resolved, the caregiver can be vulnerable to the same range of complicated grief reactions as any other griever. In addition to multiple losses, several other factors can interfere with adequately processing and working through grief. Factors most relevant to the caregiver role include unresolved guilt concerning the care of the patient, social negation of the loss (the impact on the caregiver is not acknowledged by others), and the assumption that one has to be "strong" because of a given occupation or professional role.

Grief reactions of professionals are complex and reflect losses on a number of levels. Although grief among medical workers is usually associated with the debilitating illness or death of a patient, other types of loss are frequently encountered as a consequence of working with dying patients. For example, loss of the caregiver's idealized role expectations may precipitate a separate but related grief reaction. Medical and nursing schools usually have a strong orientation toward curing patients; this perspective emphasizes technical skills geared toward treating disease and saving lives. For many medical professionals, losing a patient is interpreted as defeat. In fact, our idealization of medical workers often involves an image of omnipotence; they are seen as capable of saving us from "the enemy"—death. To work with dying patients means to confront one's limitations as a professional caregiver and to encounter the universal truths of life and death as part of the human experience.

Although research shows general patterns of grief responses for professionals in a variety of situations, there are wide variations among individuals. People react to death in unique ways based on their own coping styles, personalities, and experiences with loss.

Work-Related Stress

Job stress can affect an individual's health, personality, and job performance. During the past decade, the topic of job-related stress has received a great deal of attention, and the term **burnout** has become a familiar word. Burnout is a syndrome of mental and physical exhaustion, low morale, cynicism, and despair that occurs frequently among individuals who do "people work." Burnout involves a progressive loss of idealism, energy, and purpose, and anyone can experience it, regardless of age, discipline, or degree of formal training (Maslach, 1982).

What are the consequences of burnout? Related research shows the outcomes to be serious for clients/patients, agencies, professional staff members, and their families. Burnout can lead to deterioration in the quality of services and has been shown to be an important factor in job turnover and absenteeism. Further, it is correlated with several indices of personal stress, including illness, increased use of alcohol and drugs, and psychological problems. Professionals who describe themselves as "burned out" also report higher levels of marital and family conflict (Pines, Aronson, & Kafry, 1981). In their review of the literature, Riordan and Saltzer (1992) found that caregivers who work with the dying experience stressors that are unique to their specialty as well as many that are common to other health care workers. Health care professionals specializing in the care of AIDS patients, for example, report that watching the incidence of the disease increase in such a short time has been very stressful (Bennett, 1995).

Stress Due to Professional Roles.   Differences in roles and the attitudes that sometimes accompany them can contribute to stress among health care workers. In their study of 1,800 intensive care nurses, Claus and Bailey (1980) found that interpersonal conflict—with physicians, supervisors, and other staff nurses—was the most commonly reported source of stress.

Physicians carry the burden of ultimate responsibility for their patients. Although physicians have the primary role in treatment decisions, nurses perform many of the diagnostic and treatment procedures. Therefore, nurses spend a relatively large amount of time with patients and may be the ones who have to face the anger and dissatisfaction of families with regard to the patient's treatment regimen. Moreover, families may find it difficult to confront or criticize physicians directly because of their high status in the medical establishment. On intensive care units, the rotation of attending physicians with their varying treatment approaches can make the role of the nurse even more difficult.

Other professionals can also be affected by the status hierarchy in the health care field. Child-life workers and recreational therapists often see aspects of the patient that go undetected by nurses and physicians. If their input is not respected and they are not seen as having a legitimate role on the health care team, these individuals may become frustrated as they attempt to share these insights.

Stress in Intensive Care Units.   Burnout can be better understood if one considers the nature of specific stressors involved in a given work environment. For example, nurses and their coworkers in certain medical settings are more likely to face multiple stressors and demands than those in other settings. Staff members working in intensive care units, emergency rooms, coronary care units, and oncology wards seem to be especially vulnerable to stress due to the tremendous pressure under which they work, the high level of performance that is expected on a daily basis, and the unrealistic expectations of patients and families.

An examination of the work environment in an intensive care unit (ICU) illustrates the extraordinary stressors that many professional caregivers face on a regular basis (Small, Engler, & Rushton, 1991). The ICU is different from other areas of the hospital in that the physical environment itself contains a massive array of potentially stressful sensory stimuli. Flashing lights and beeping and buzzing monitors of the sophisticated ICU equipment are in constant motion. Gurgling suction pumps and whooshing respirators provide other background sounds. Although habituation to these stimuli occurs with time, their ever-continuing presence can still contribute to stress. The human environment in the ICU includes desperately ill or injured human beings connected to the machinery; many are between life and death. Working in the ICU involves seeing disfigurement and hearing human sounds associated with discomfort and pain. These sights and sounds present a strong element of surrealism. Hay and Oken (1977) have pointed out that the ICU environment

> directly challenges the definition of being human, one's most fundamental sense of ego integrity, for nurse as well as patient. Though consciously the nurse quickly learns to accept this surrealism, she is unremittingly exposed to these multiple threats to the stability of her body boundaries, her sense of self, and her feelings of humanity and reality. (p. 383)

The workload of the ICU staff is also unique. Vital signs must be monitored at 15-minute intervals (sometimes more often). Tracheas must be suctioned, intravenous infusions changed, respirators checked, EKG monitors interpreted, and so on, and so on, and every step must be charted. Every procedure is potentially lifesaving; any error may be life threatening. Subtle changes in the patient's condition may be of critical significance. As part of the daily routine, the ICU nurse faces the ever-present possibility of confronting death. A patient's death is a significant loss. The intense and intimate contact promotes emotional attachment of ICU nurses to their patients, especially those that are conscious and verbal. Even if the patient lives, they do not leave the unit "well." The ICU patients who are "successes" are usually still seriously ill and are transferred to another unit in the hospital.

Working on an intensive care unit requires great vigilance and stamina. An ICU patient's life can depend on the care received during this critical period in the illness or injury. The quality of care is a function of both the professional skills and the psychological state of the caregivers. If staff stress and anxiety are excessive, it can reduce efficiency and the ability to make decisions. The outcomes can be fatal for the patient and also greatly threaten the physical and emotional well-being of the caregiver.

Stress in Hospices.   Increasingly, medical care is provided outside a hospital context through programs such as hospices that provide alternative models of care. In home-based hospice programs, caregivers do not have the opportunity to maintain a familiar work environment. They are constantly having to adjust to new settings as they work with different families in their own homes. Furthermore, caregivers may experience a form of culture shock as they shift from working in an acute care environment to a palliative care setting in which their roles, responsibilities, and orientation are different. In contrast to traditional medical care settings, quality of life is of paramount importance, rather than prolongation of life. Caregivers in hospices are expected to have greater skill in addressing psychosocial issues than is typically the case in acute care hospitals (Rando, 1984). These aspects of hospice care, combined with the hospice philosophy, can result in some unique stresses for staff members such as the following (Gray-Toft & Anderson, 1986; McNamara, Waddell, & Colvin, 1995; Paradis, 1987):

- difficulty accepting the fact that the patients' physical and psychological symptoms cannot always be controlled;
- disappointment if expectations for patients to die a "good death"—however this may be defined—are not met;
- anger at being subjected to perceived higher-than-standard performance expectations and exposed to considerable scrutiny;
- difficulty deciding where to draw limits on involvement with patients and their families, particularly during off-duty hours.

Yancik (1984) examined three hospices in which 93 professional staff members were asked, "What are the three most stressful events you experienced professionally as a hospice worker in the last three months?" The subjects described 242 situations, which were then categorized. Approximately half of the stressful situations related to issues of staff support. The most prevalent concerns in this category centered around conflicts with other staff members, administrative problems, and work and emotional overload. One staff member commented: "We have an ongoing problem of providing support to each other and ourselves. We have needs that are not always heard or responded to, but the expectation is to continue to offer good work to others" (Yancik, 1984, p. 25).

The second category, which accounted for slightly more than 37% of the incidents, emphasized concern for patients and families as a source of stress. At times, feelings of sorrow or loss were especially strong with regard to a particular patient. In other circumstances, staff members felt frustrated in their attempts to support the patient and family. For example, family members were sometimes already physically and emotionally exhausted from coping with the illness by the time the patient entered the hospice program. Interestingly, management of the disease process was only a minor source of stress for most hospice staff workers. The specific situations mentioned in this category revealed feelings of helplessness and vulnerability associated with the limitations of medical intervention.

Yancik (1984) also found that the types and frequencies of stresses varied with each hospice facility, particularly in the area of staff support. This finding has important implications for hospice programs and shows that an organization can effectively intervene to reduce staff members' stress.

In another study of hospice nurses, Moser and Krikorian (1982) examined satisfactions as well as stresses. Their findings concerning stresses were similar to those obtained by Yancik (1984). When the nurses were asked what gave them satisfaction in their work, working conditions were cited in only about 30% of the responses, whereas the satisfaction derived from working with patients and families accounted for over half of the reported incidents. Although potentially a source of significant stress, direct interactions with patients and their families can also be the most meaningful and satisfying aspect of hospice work.

Although hospice work involves a variety of potential sources of stress, Vachon (1986) found that hospice workers in fact have fewer manifestations and

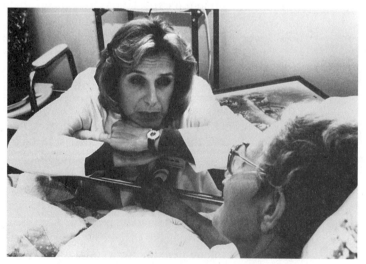

Most hospice staff find their direct interactions with patients to be the most meaningful and satisfying aspect of their work.

reports of stress than do health care workers in other settings, such as emergency centers or intensive care units. Reasons for this finding were attributed to the hospice emphasis on philosophy of care, team support, and team building.

Stress and Trauma Work.   Work-related stress must also be considered for mental health professionals. Figley (1995) has used the term **compassion fatigue** to refer to a type of secondary victimization in which "professionals who listen to clients' stories of fear, pain, and suffering may feel similar fear, pain, and suffering because they care." He points out that often the most effective therapists—those who have the greatest capacity for feeling and expressing empathy for those with whom they work—are the most vulnerable to this mirroring or contagion effect. In Cerney's (1995) view,

> This affront to the sense of self experienced by therapists of trauma victims can be so overwhelming that despite their best efforts, therapists begin to exhibit the same characteristics as their patients—that is, they experience a change in their interaction with the world, themselves, and their family. They may begin to have intrusive thoughts, nightmares, and generalized anxiety. They themselves need assistance in coping with their trauma. (p. 137)

Figley's work and that of other researchers suggest that therapists treating post-traumatic stress disorder with grief components are at risk with regard to secondary trauma. The potential of compassion fatigue warrants discussion in professional training programs, combined with suggestions for "self-caring" in order to avoid negative consequences associated with this possible occupational hazard. For practicing therapists, avoiding overexposure to traumatic situations (in terms of frequency and duration) and paying close attention to one's personal reactions can be important tools to prevent this particular type of burnout.

Similar concepts can be extended to other occupational groups (e.g., rescue workers, firefighters, police officers) who are typically on the frontline when large-scale traumatic events occur. Those handling bodies after violent deaths report the following to be particularly stressful:

- sensory stimulation and overload (e.g., mutilated bodies, strong odors, tactile experiences),
- the shock of unexpected events associated with the dead (e.g., the massive number of casualties in a large-scale disaster),
- identification or emotional involvement with the dead (either by knowing the victim personally or through seeing the deceased's family on television), and
- handling children's bodies (Ursano & McCarroll, 1990).

Other events that are most likely to cause traumatic loss reactions in rescue workers include those that

- are human-caused,
- are life-threatening to the worker,

Rescue workers report high levels of stress associated with handling bodies after violent deaths, especially those of children.

- violate the worker's sense of how the world is or should be,
- have high media coverage, and
- relate directly to the worker's life (e.g., involves death of a coworker or family member, familiarity with event scene, or in some way parallel the worker's life).

Reactions may surface immediately at the scene of the incident, within 24 to 72 hours, days or even weeks later (Dick, 1996). Reactions for some are severe and may include alcohol or other substance abuse, memory loss or cognitive confusion, difficulties in interpersonal relationships, and intrusive and avoidant imagery (Gibbs, Drummond, & Lachenmeyer, 1993).

COPING MECHANISMS

Stress arises out of transactions between individuals and given milieus. The meanings attached to potentially stressful events depend on the particular individual participating in the event. Individual differences in perceptions, interpretations, and coping capacities can make the difference between those who suffer deeply and are immobilized and those who are challenged and grow.

Individual Strategies

Professionals have a responsibility to care for themselves as well as for their patients. They must replenish themselves if they are to continue to be effective in

"HEROES" HAVE NEEDS TOO

Listed below are coping strategies for rescue workers that can be implemented before, during, and after the traumatic events. Although individuals involved in rescue efforts often emerge as "heroes" in the eye of the public, their own needs and reactions following a disaster are often not recognized. Establishing and implementing procedures and practices designed to minimize worker stress in these situations can help reduce mental health difficulties related to trauma (McCarroll, Ursano, Wright, & Fullerton, 1993).

Stressors and Coping Strategies

PERIOD	STRESSOR	STRATEGY
Before	Anticipation (inexperienced workers)	Practice drills Prebriefing Information on tasks required
	Anticipation (experienced workers)	Social and professional support Information on tasks required
During	Multiple sensory stimuli from bodies	Avoidance strategies: masking odors, wearing gloves, averting gaze
	Handling victims' personal effects	Increase emotional distance
	Dissatisfaction with own performance	Breaks, sleep, food
	Strong personal feelings (inexperienced workers)	Pairing with more experienced workers
After	Need for a transitional event	Information postevent briefing
	Strong personal feelings	Support from family and work unit
	Fatigue	Rest and time off work

The acknowledgment and expression of grief by leaders (i.e., commanders, supervisors) in a public forum, referred to as "grief leadership," has also been shown to be valuable for group and community recovery (Ingraham, 1988). Leaders also can play an important role after a crisis event by recognizing the efforts of individuals involved. Commendations and other types of acknowledgments facilitate the recovery process and reinforce a sense of pride. Ceremonies following disasters mark an end to the event and show participants that their work was appreciated and its difficulty recognized (McCarroll, Ursano, Fullerton, & Wright, 1992).

SOURCES: L. I. Ingraham (1988, October). Grief leadership in work groups. Paper presented at the Fourth Annual Conference on Military Medicine, Uniformed Services University of the Health Sciences, Bethesda, MD. J. E. McCarroll, R. J. Ursano, C. S. Fullerton, & K. M. Wright (1992). Community consultation following a major air disaster. *Journal of Community Psychology, 20,* 271–275. J. E. McCarroll, R. J. Ursano, C. S. Fullerton, & K. M. Wright (1993). Handling bodies after violent death: Strategies for coping. *American Journal of Orthopsychiatry, 63*(2), 209–214.

giving of themselves to others. Unlimited giving without replenishment leads to burnout. Part of nurturing oneself includes learning to cope with the stresses and strains of one's work. To survive and grow as they work with the dying, caregivers need to assume some responsibility for reducing their own stress levels.

According to Pearlin and Schooler (1978), individuals cope in three basic ways:

- by cognitively controlling the meaning of the experience, which neutralizes its stressful character;
- by managing to accommodate the stressor after it has arisen; and
- by modifying or eliminating stressful situations.

To cope by any of these means, specific coping strategies must be employed as discussed below.

Perception of the Experience. Stress lies to a great extent in our perceptions of life events, rather than in the events themselves. The ways in which we define our work and our professional roles will determine whether we view our work as frustrating or fulfilling. A great deal of stress arises from belief systems that are unrealistic and problematic (Sutterley, 1982). Distress occurs when incongruency exists between our visions and ideals and the realities of our work situation.

Bugen (1980) views the internal resources of the caregiver to be an important dimension of managing stress. **Internal resources** are "those abilities, attitudes, values, beliefs or techniques that help people handle difficult moments or periods of time" (p. 246). Bugen refers to the importance of giving up idealistic and perfectionistic goals. It is also important for the caregiver to differentiate between the process and the outcome of caregiving. One can invest in the process of helping a patient without expecting to cure that individual. Caregivers will not always be able to save lives, but they will be able to make the process of dying easier and to help individuals achieve a higher quality of life during their remaining time.

Some professional caregivers' expectations for patients are related to their own needs. According to Lattanzi (1983), training programs for those who work with the terminally ill should encourage an increased awareness of the needs of others as well as an increased knowledge of one's own self. She urges caregivers to examine their motivations for working with the dying and to gain insight into how their motivations can affect their interactions with patients and families. Insight into their own needs, vulnerabilities, and expectations can allow professional and volunteer caregivers to separate their own issues from those of their patients.

Although the term **codependent** has been used primarily to describe certain dysfunctional relationships and families, Wolfelt (1991) believes that it can apply to caregivers at times as well, especially those who confuse caregiving with caretaking. A caregiver who consistently puts the needs of patients/clients before his or her own may have fallen into a pattern of codependency. Warning signs include

- thinking of oneself as indispensable to patients/clients,
- constantly worrying about patients/clients even when away from work,
- neglecting one's own personal relationships, and
- demonstrating a tendency to overcommit.

These behaviors are often indicative of unresolved grief issues that the caregiver is indirectly trying to work out by providing care to dying or bereaved persons. They can also be related to a need to raise one's self-esteem, which has become linked in an unhealthy fashion to "helping others."

Management of Stress.   Some degree of work-related stress is unavoidable. Only when it becomes excessive and unmanageable does it have detrimental effects. Part of learning to cope with adult life includes acquiring healthy ways to handle the daily hassles that we encounter. Learning to cope with a demanding occupation requires a recognition of one's stress level and a concerted effort to regulate it. Self-regulation of stress can involve a variety of approaches; for example, regular physical exercise helps to discharge tension and increase physical stamina and fitness. A high level of physical wellness, developed through proper nutrition and exercise, can combat the potentially detrimental effects of stress on the body. For individuals who are experiencing excessive muscle tension, biofeedback and relaxation training can be useful in lowering physiological arousal levels. No technique will work, however, unless the individual incorporates the skills into his or her daily life (Sutterley, 1982).

Marshall and Kasman (1980) recommend a "decompression" routine after work to serve as a transition between work and private time. This routine needs to include an activity that is enjoyable and relaxing for the person (e.g., running, walking, listening to music). This type of activity can facilitate a shift from the role of "caregiver" with its accompanying pressures and concerns to the multiple roles involved in one's personal life. By releasing mental and physical tensions accumulated during the day and achieving a state of relaxation, more quality time outside of work can be experienced and enjoyed.

Taking time off for rest and relaxation can also be important. Allowing time for oneself can help to sustain vitality and a high level of caring on a long-term basis. Too often, caregivers have difficulty setting limits and feel guilty for thinking of themselves instead of their patients. However, failure to attend to their own physical and mental health needs can lead to burnout and the inability to provide quality care to others.

The ability of a caregiver to adapt to the stresses of work is also related to the availability of an effective support system. Having an available source of emotional support has been shown to be an important moderator of stress. **Support networks** can be formal (e.g., the relationship with a counselor in the client role) or informal (e.g., a family member, personal friend, neighbor), and the type of support offered can take several distinct forms. Support systems offer emotional support through empathic listening and genuine caring or material support in the form of tangible goods and service (such as covering a weekend shift for a coworker when he or she has had a particularly difficult week).

TABLE 10.2
Indicators of Burnout

HEALTH INDICATORS	EXCESSIVE BEHAVIOR INDICATORS	EMOTIONAL ADJUSTMENT INDICATORS	RELATIONSHIP INDICATORS	ATTITUDE INDICATORS
Fatigue and chronic exhaustion	Increased consumption of caffeine, tobacco, alcohol, over-the-counter medications, psychoactive prescription drugs, illicit drugs	Emotional distancing	Isolation from or over-bonding with other staff	Grandiosity
Frequent and prolonged colds		Paranoia	Responding to clients in mechanical manner	Boredom
Headaches		Depression: loss of meaning, loss of hope		Cynicism
Sleep disturbances: insomnia, nightmares, excessive sleeping	High-risk-taking behavior: auto/cycle accidents, falls, "high-risk" hobbies, general proneness to accidents and injuries, gambling, extreme mood and behavioral changes	Decreased emotional control	Increased isolation from clients	Sick humor—aimed particularly at clients
Ulcers		Martyrdom	Increased expressions of anger and/or mistrust	Distrust of management, supervisors, peers
Gastrointestinal disorders		Fear of "going crazy"		Air of righteousness
Sudden losses or gains in weight		Increased amount of time daydreaming/fantasizing	Increased interpersonal conflicts with other staff	Hypercritical attitude toward institution and/or peers
Flare-ups of preexisting medical disorders: diabetes, high blood pressure, asthma, etc.	Increased propensity for violent and aggressive behavior	Constant feelings of being "trapped"	Increased problems in marital and other interpersonal relationships away from work, including relationships with one's children	Expressions of hopelessness, powerlessness, meaninglessness
		Nervous ticks		
Injuries from high-risk behavior	Over- and undereating	Undefined fears		VALUE INDICATORS
	Hyperactivity	Inability to concentrate	Social isolation: over-involvement with clients, using clients to meet personal and social needs	Sudden and often dramatic changes in values and beliefs
Muscular pain, particularly in lower back and neck		Intellectualization		
		Increased anger		
Increased premenstrual tension		Increased tension		
Missed menstrual cycles				

SOURCE: J. F. X. Carroll & W. L. White (1982). Theory building: Integrating individual and environmental factors within an ecological framework. In W. S. Paine (Ed.), *Job stress and burnout: Research, theory, and intervention* (p. 44). Beverly Hills, CA: Sage Publications.

Support is also given by providing needed information and perspectives. For example, information about the anger experienced by many dying patients helps health care providers reinterpret uncomfortable interactions they may have had and better understand that angry feelings are not necessarily in response to something the caregiver has done wrong.

Modification or Elimination of the Stressor.   The most drastic step in coping with work-related stress is changing jobs, work settings, or professions. Although this may sometimes be the best course of action, it can often be avoided by monitoring stress levels and intervening before they become excessive and lead to burnout. A variety of personal indicators that can be useful in this process are listed in Table 10.2.

Individuals experiencing stress often perceive that they have far less control over their work situations than they actually do. By working with one's supervisors and peers, one can often alter some aspects of the work environment that contribute to stress and implement programs and policies that will increase job satisfaction. Pines et al. (1981) recommend the following four intervention strategies:

- being aware of the problem,
- taking responsibility for doing something about the source of stress,
- achieving some degree of cognitive clarity about the situation, and
- developing new tools for coping.

Monitoring personal reactions to stress is an ongoing process. Burnout can be cyclic and repeat itself many times in the same particular job situation. Having successfully intervened in the burnout cycle does not make one immune to work-related stress in the future.

Agency and Institutional Support

Pattison (1977) was the first to use the term **death saturation** to refer to the limits of personal tolerance for death-related work. He emphasized that we can only work for so long with so much personal investment and intensity before we reach our limits. Our bodies get fatigued and need sleep in order to function well. Likewise, human spirits also get exhausted. Individuals must recognize their personal saturation points and give themselves opportunities for reprieve and reconstitution. Organizations can also avoid death saturation and burnout among their caregivers by reducing stressful working conditions, giving group support, and providing ongoing educational opportunities.

Reducing Stressful Working Conditions.   Many organizations have experimented with a variety of work patterns aimed at reducing staff stress. Some hospices and hospitals have found that a 4-day workweek with an occasional night or weekend on duty improved staff attitude and level of efficiency. Other facilities have used part-time staff and a "day-away" system to provide needed relief and to prevent staff exhaustion. Careful monitoring of caseloads and the demands of each individual case can also be beneficial. Time off after deaths that are particularly difficult (such as death of a child) can be particularly critical.

Job rotation can be another solution. Occasionally assigning nurses to other units in the hospital gives them a chance to see more patients who are responding well to treatment. In hospice situations, volunteers can also benefit by participating in varying responsibilities. In addition to working directly with patients and families, hospices usually also need volunteers to work in the administrative office, answer telephones, give community presentations, publish newsletters, and participate in a variety of training and educational programs. Alternating time among these various roles can help individuals revitalize between cases.

The physical setting also influences stress levels and needs to be carefully planned. Over 20 years ago, Hay and Oken (1977) proposed a circular pattern design for intensive care units in which patients occupy "spokes of a wheel" separated by dividers. Glass enclosures can reduce the sensory bombardment of the ICU and be a barrier to contagion while still allowing patients to be in view of a central "hub" nursing station. A physical setting that allows for some staff privacy helps reduce the stress of working in a unit in which the behavior of caregivers is so open to scrutiny. Staff members need some privacy to work out possible disagreements among themselves and to openly express their emotions away from patients and family members.

The social climate is a critical factor in both exacerbating and alleviating stress. It has frequently been observed that caregivers often use humor to reduce the emotional impact of their work. Joking, laughing, even singing can sometimes be observed in critical care settings. It usually occurs in small groups and is usually brief. Although appropriate humor can be therapeutic for caregivers and reduce tension, relatives of critically ill patients may have difficulty understanding this response.

Giving Group Support.   Support in the workplace can be critical in coping with work-related stresses by providing a forum for open discussion (Plante & Bouchard, 1995). Although emotional support is often available from family members and friends, those individuals may lack true insight regarding the caregiver's specific concerns. Sometimes, significant others simply get tired of hearing about their loved one's "death work."

In the neonatal intensive care unit at Children's National Medical Center in Washington, DC, a formal program of staff support has been introduced. This program includes unit-based memorial services to remember infants and children that have died and to give critical care nurses the opportunity to mourn the loss of their patients (Small et al., 1991). Organized support groups composed of coworkers who meet regularly can serve several different purposes. First, they provide an outlet for the expression of feelings. Feelings are not only heard by others but validated by them as well. Staff members discover that they are not alone in experiencing the stress and grief associated with terminal patient care. In addition, individuals can learn useful coping strategies from other group participants. Younger, less experienced group members can model other professionals who have been able to cope with their job demands, achieve job satisfaction, and manage their stress effectively. An added benefit of this type of support is the group cohesion that it promotes. This cohesion can lead to better working relationships and less staff conflict.

Providing Ongoing Educational Opportunities.   Organizations, institutions, and agencies can also support their staff members by providing relevant educational and training opportunities. There is constant need for individuals working with the critically and terminally ill to be aware of new information and to upgrade their skills. Continued learning is not only necessary for quality patient care, but also has been shown to be a stress reducer. Regular in-service sessions can guard against stagnation, enhance job satisfaction, and increase caregivers' feelings of competence in dealing with patient issues. Through an organized educational program, staff members can work together to question past approaches and consider new avenues in view of recent research developments.

PROFESSIONAL TRAINING PROGRAMS

Preparing Professionals to Cope With Death, Dying, and Grief

Evidence suggests that efforts in death education in the United States are not sufficient to meet the needs of medical professionals working with dying and grieving individuals. Of 600 physicians surveyed, 78% felt that medical schools should put more emphasis on training medical personnel to communicate effectively with terminally ill patients and their families (Dickinson, 1988). Another study found that although 91% of 1,501 practicing physicians, nurses, pharmacists, dentists, and veterinarians agreed that communication skills are important, over a third (36%) gave their schools a poor rating in this area (Richardson, 1992).

The lack of adequate preparation to meet the needs of the dying and their families is not limited to the United States. Over half of 800 Canadian physicians, residents, and medical students sampled have said that they did not feel their skills were adequate to meet the psychosocial needs of their terminally ill patients (Perez, Gosselin, & Gagnon, 1980). Another study in England found that 77% of the medical students surveyed expressed apprehension about interacting with dying patients, and communication was identified as their greatest concern in this area (Field & Howell, 1986).

Historically, death education has not been a significant component of professional training programs, despite evidence showing that health care professionals who are taught concepts about terminally ill patients and families in medical school have more positive attitudes toward working in this area (Durand, Dickinson, Sumner, & Lancaster, 1990). Medical school faculty have frequently argued that there is not enough time in the curriculum to include instruction on dying and grieving.

PALLIATIVE CARE AS A MEDICAL SPECIALTY IN BRITAIN

Medical students in Britain now have the option of specializing in care of the dying. One of the most exciting developments in British medicine has been the official recognition of palliative medicine as a medical specialty with its own training program. Those who enter the program must already have a medical degree and have completed their general professional training. For physicians in the U.K. selecting palliative care as a career, four additional years of training are required which include work in an approved hospice or palliative care unit and experience in areas such as pain control, psychiatry, oncology, and AIDS. They also receive training in management, teaching and public speaking, and counseling in recognition of the wide array of skills needed in the field of palliative care. Thus far, there seems to be no shortage of U.K. physicians interested in this specialty. While this training program is a major step in providing improved care to terminally ill patients, it does not address the thanatological education needed by physicians in other specialties. Regardless of field, most health care workers encounter and interact with dying and grieving persons in the practice of their professions.

SOURCE: D. Doyle (1991). Palliative care education and training in the United Kingdom: A review. *Death Studies, 15,* 95–103.

Nonetheless, Dickinson, Sumner, and Frederick (1992) report that 96% of medical schools, 95% of nursing schools, 62% of pharmacy schools, and over 70% of social work programs in the United States offer at least some death education in their curricula. However, the amount of content offered is limited; the vast majority of professional schools still continue to offer death education as a minicourse or through occasional lectures. In 1990, only 18 out of 107 American medical schools surveyed had a full-term course in death and dying (Mermann, Gunn, & Dickinson, 1991).

In addition to limited formal death education, the direct exposure that medical students have to death in their training tends to distort their views toward it:

> Medical school curricula do not offer the perspective that death is the ultimate, inevitable outcome of being alive, and that the acceptance of the finality of physical existence is a vital part of the wise use of medical knowledge and skills. Most medical students encounter death in their training in emergency situations: observing cardiopulmonary resuscitation in a cardiac arrest, dealing with severe gunshot wounds and injuries sustained in automobile accidents in an emergency room where the urgent demands of the trauma leave little opportunity to consider the patients. These are the common experiences that imprint the images of death in medical students. They seldom have the opportunity to see death as the natural, peaceful ending of long illness or old age, and

they are not required to observe a nonacute death in order to become familiar with the dying process and the role of death in our lives. (Seeland, 1988, pp. 127-128)

A number of medical schools have used innovative approaches to enhance the training of health care professionals. Dr. Sandra Bertman, a faculty member at the University of Massachusetts Medical Center, has become an international leader in promoting the use of humanities, literature, and the arts in death education. In her writing and teaching, she points out that these resources have been relatively untapped by death educators and clinicians: "The backbone of science is logic and experiment: that of art, intuition and insight. The arts uncover realities that lie outside the quantifiable or statistically measureable. They invite us into the world of dying persons in a manner different from but no less penetrating than scientific analysis" (1991, p. 6). Images from the visual and literary arts can stimulate insight, dialogue, solace, and resolution by acquainting us with the universal language of human suffering and therefore connecting us to the experience of others.

Professionals outside the medical arena who are called on to offer emotional support to dying and grieving individuals also receive little preparation for this role. When members of the American Association for Marriage and Family Therapy were questioned about their training and experience in death, dying, and grief, 97% felt that training in this area was important for a therapist and only 24% were satisfied with the amount of death education they received in their professional training programs. The majority of therapists in the sample had counseled dying persons and had worked with grieving families. These therapists expressed the need for additional training to increase their expertise in working with grief and loss issues (Stephenson, 1981).

Comfort levels involved in working with death and grief situations must also be taken into account. Kirchberg and Neimeyer (1991) asked 81 beginning counselors to rate their degree of comfort in working with 15 counseling scenarios, 5 of which involved death or loss (e.g., terminal illness, suicidal client, parental grief) and 10 of which concerned other issues (e.g., rape, marital conflict, child behavior problems, physical abuse, alcoholism). Counselors rated situations involving death and dying as substantially more uncomfortable than other presenting problems, strongly suggesting the need for death education that addresses personal reactions as well as skill development.

Although studies show that experience and training in death and loss are associated with increased comfort levels with dying and grieving clients (Terry, Bivens, & Neimeyer, 1996), it is important to recognize additional specialized needs within the broader field of thanatology training. For example, as professionals are faced with an increased number of AIDS-related cases, many do not feel adequately trained to meet the needs of this particular group of patients. Findings from a large survey of urban social workers suggest that lack of adequate training combined with misconceptions about the disease can impede empathetic and competent service delivery. In this survey, 90% of the respondents desired training in clinical issues related to AIDS (psychosocial issues, individual and group support, work with families), whereas only 12% of these social workers had received this type of specialized training. When participants in this study were asked to identify their greatest difficulty working with HIV-infected clients, "forming relationships with young people who are dying" was the response most frequently given (Gillman, 1991).

Positive developments in thanatology currently include postdegree training opportunities in death, dying, and grief for individuals who feel their own training has been inadequate, incomplete, or is outdated. Organizations such as the Association for Death Education and Counseling (ADEC) have established certificate programs for counselors and educators who work in this area. ADEC's certification program is based on standards set by leading authorities in the field and has involved input from professionals in a wide variety of disciplines (Zinner, 1992).

Professional training programs in the mental and physical health care fields can play an important role in preparing individuals to cope with the unique demands of working with the dying and their families. This preparation includes the acquisition of a range of professional skills, a base of knowledge, and an examination of one's own feelings and attitudes.

The most successful death education efforts seem to be those that integrate intellectual content with the opportunity to explore feelings and attitudes. Although formal training on how to help dying individuals and grieving families has increased, little training is designed to help professionals deal with their own personal feelings of loss, grief, and self-doubt (Neimeyer, Behnke, & Reiss, 1983). Nurses trained in sophisticated techniques of medical care are sometimes no better equipped than aides in coping with their own emotional responses to illness and death. At times, educational institutions may actually teach health care providers to disassociate their feelings and emotions from intellectual concerns by placing emphasis on the technical (rather than the human) aspects of medicine and focusing on the disease instead of the whole person.

Caregivers must face their own feelings about death in order to help a person facing death more effectively and comfortably. As humans, professionals have significant emotional needs that they must cope with to ensure successful intervention with dying and grieving individuals. Unless these needs are acknowledged, the helping relationship may be jeopardized. Emotions, particularly anxiety, can affect professional perceptions, diagnoses, and even treatment of patients. Death anxiety can lead to avoidance of dying persons as well as inability to engage in direct, honest communication. Death anxiety can even cause the professional to project his or her feelings onto the patient. After listening to a patient with acute leukemia speak in a death and dying seminar, psychology graduate students who reported high levels of anxiety during the presentation tended to view the individual as more denying, more angry, less accepting, and less hopeful than did students with low anxiety levels. Although the same person was observed by all the students simultaneously, perceptions varied as a result of the observer's own emotional responses (Bugen, 1980).

CONFRONTING DEATH IN A MEDICAL SCHOOL ANATOMY LABORATORY

I glanced about the room. No other body seemed to have a tag on it. No one was looking my way. As if it were forbidden, I surreptitiously untied the tag (from his big toe) and slipped it into my pocket. I felt I had been entrusted with Ingmar Wollenstrum's identity. I was the last person ever to know his name . . . Throughout the year as I sat dissecting him, I tried not to imagine Ingmar's life, but I pictured him strong and vital, looking at the sun from the deck of a ship, hauling in a rope, feeling the spray of the ocean. I memorized the exposed tendons of his hand and wondered what barroom brawls it had been in, what women it had caressed. I wondered how Ingmar had died, and where. Had someone been with him? . . . We masked our emotions and curbed our imaginations in favor of scientific interest. It was a sink-or-swim introduction to shutting off our feelings. (Sharkey, 1982, p. 32)

A medical student's first "patient" is usually a dead one, encountered in the anatomy laboratory as a human cadaver. Unfortunately few programs discuss with students the impact of the cadaver experience on their own feelings, leading them to perhaps question their emotional reactions and to feel that it is wrong to feel anxious or uncomfortable. William (1992) believes that student attitudes are influenced by the tacit "don't discuss" rule encountered in medical school, and concludes that medical students carry forward into the physician-patient relationship the communication patterns first developed in medical faculty-student relationships. To confront the emotional experience of dealing with cadavers and concerns about violating the body of another person, some medical schools have developed memorial services which are held at the conclusion of the class. These services, in which gratitude is a common theme, are often organized by the medical students and attended by students, faculty, and donor families. At one school, the ceremony includes a short walk to a cemetery near the medical school where the cremated remains of the cadavers are buried. The stone marking their burial plot reads "They gave in death for those in life" (Schotzinger & Best, 1987).

Preparing Professionals for Multidisciplinary Work

In this chapter, we have discussed personal reactions of professionals and their need for support from peers as they face the stresses of working with the dying. However, individuals working together on multidisciplinary teams often have difficulty providing support to each other. The **multidisciplinary approach** involves more than a variety of professionals (physicians, nurses, clergy, psychologists, social workers, child-life specialists, and occupational therapists, among others) providing care. It includes the belief that a team approach with professionals from several disciplines working together can provide integrated

optimum care for patients. The process of working together implies cooperation, communication, and common goals.

In reality, professionals typically have little experience in working as part of
a multidisciplinary team. Most individuals become part of a team after having
been socialized into their respective professions during their many years of
training. Professional socialization refers not only to the cognitive aspects of education in which skills and knowledge are acquired but also to the acquisition
of attitudes, feelings, and values. Each specialist speaks a different jargon, has
a unique orientation, and possesses a distinct set of professional skills. When
these differences are great they can interfere with clear communication and
group cohesion.

Teamwork also involves exposure to the critiques of others, and the close
scrutiny of other group members forces you to examine your own behavior and
your ability to give and receive feedback. Working as part of a cohesive unit will
bring you face-to-face with both your strengths and your weaknesses:

> Being a team member means looking at yourself—your needs for power and
> control, your difficulties with sharing or collaborating, and a host of other per-
> sonal issues related to team functioning. This forced self-awareness can be pain-
> ful, but it can also be an opportunity for personal growth if you approach
> yourself and the members of your team with an attitude of openness, flexibil-
> ity, and respect. (Larson, 1993, p. 202)

Training programs can be instrumental in preparing students to assume occupational roles in which they interact with other professionals. Mutual respect
and understanding are critical for individuals to function as a team. These can
perhaps be developed through increased interaction as part of the critical socialization that occurs before students assume their professional roles. The
inclusion of courses in formal training programs (e.g., medical and nursing
schools, counseling programs) that involve faculty and students from several disciplines can have positive outcomes if accompanied by faculty commitment to
multidisciplinary exchange and cooperation.

If individuals can get beyond the battleground of disciplinary turf issues,
they can learn to nurture each other and provide collegial support. If not, they
fail not only themselves and their colleagues, but also their patients. The more
they are able to work through their own personal and professional issues, the
better quality of care they will be able to provide for dying individuals and their
families. With this goal comes the rewards and satisfactions of defining one's
work in terms of integrity, meaning, and value.

CARING FOR THE DYING: AN OPPORTUNITY FOR GROWTH

Despite the grief and stress they often experience, many professionals spend
their lives working with the dying and bereaved and find innumerable rewards
and satisfactions. We have much to learn from these individuals and families. In

the process of providing our services, we can enlarge our personal capacities as we learn to cope with our own concerns and anxieties:

> Exploring the realm of death and grief promotes an awareness of a more complex sense of reality than many of us are readily able to embrace. This reality involves the dynamic tension between one's unlimited possibilities for growth and one's ultimate finiteness. Reconciliation of these two forces means accepting life as a mandate to pursue your potential and expand your capacity as a human being. (Cook & Dworkin, 1992, p. 173)

When an individual's psychological equilibrium is disrupted, the adaptational process that follows can lead to a new reality within the person, involving new insights and perceptions. As professionals work with the dying and their families, they often find that their coping skills are increased, their support systems are strengthened and expanded, and their priorities are reordered. Working with the dying can teach us much about life and living. Elisabeth Kübler-Ross, who has worked with many terminally ill individuals, has often spoken about the enriching aspects of this experience. In her book *Death: The final stage of growth* (1975), she has said: "Facing death means facing the ultimate question of the meaning of life. If we really want to live we must have the courage to recognize that life is ultimately very short, and that everything we do counts" (p. 126).

SUMMARY

Professional caregivers can experience many stresses as a result of ongoing interactions with the dying and the bereaved. Grief is a common reaction, although its intensity depends on a number of factors, including patient variables and other losses experienced by the caregiver. Job-related stresses should be closely examined to determine possible solutions for avoiding or diminishing the risk of staff burnout. Both individual staff members and supervisors need to be aware of warning signals and develop appropriate coping mechanisms as well as methods of prevention.

During the last decade, more and more professions have realized the importance of training their students in theory and application of knowledge related to death, dying, and grief. Many professional curricula now include at least some focus on these topics. Others are in the process of developing courses in these areas. Evidence suggests, however, that present efforts in death education are still not sufficient.

Many disciplines have developed over time in response to various needs of individuals and families. In our complex world, a team of professionals from various backgrounds is often needed to give clients optimal holistic care. To help different disciplines work together effectively, a multidisciplinary perspective must be introduced and demonstrated in professional training programs. Despite the stresses experienced, individuals from many fields can derive satisfaction from working with the dying and the grieving as personal skills and insights are developed that enrich all facets of their lives.

Personal Account

> *Dr. Selwyn candidly shares his personal reactions to the loss of AIDS patients over time. In doing so, he reflects on the connections between the loss experiences in his professional career and the personal losses suffered early in his life.*

Before Their Time: A Clinician's Reflections on Death and AIDS
Peter A. Selwyn

This brief essay has a much more personal tone than the scientific papers that I have written about AIDS, because I have come to understand that it is precisely through one's own relationship with death and loss that a physician can be most helpful to patients who are facing AIDS and other life-threatening illnesses.

I graduated from medical school in June 1981, the same month and year that the first cases of AIDS were reported by the Centers for Disease Control (CDC). In a brief description that appeared in the *Morbidity and Mortality Weekly Report,* the CDC reported several clusters of cases of Pneumocystis carinii pneumonia and Kaposi's sarcoma in young homosexual men in New York and California. It was not evident to the CDC at the time, and certainly not to me as I went forward from my medical school graduation, that this new disease, later to be called AIDS, would become the leading cause of death for young adult men in the United States by the end of the decade. It was even less evident to me, with my belief that I had acquired in medical school the knowledge to serve as the foundation for my medical practice, that this disease, which was not known when I began my training, would soon become the major focus of my work as a physician.

I began my medical training at the end of the historical period that John Arras, my former colleague at Montefiore Medical Center in the Bronx, used to refer to as the postwar "Pax Antibiotica." Infectious diseases had become apparent vestiges of the prescientific past, and the ability of medicine and technology to conquer disease—in the true military sense of the word—seemed limitless. When death occurred, it happened either to the very old or, less commonly, to the very young. AIDS profoundly changed all this.

Source: P. A. Selwyn (1996). Before their time: A clinician's reflections on death and AIDS. In H. M. Spiro, M. G. McCrea Curnen, & L. P. Wandel (Eds.), *Facing death: Where culture, religion, and medicine meet* (pp. 33–37). New Haven, CT: Yale University Press.

In 1984, when the first wave of the AIDS epidemic was just beginning to overwhelm the vulnerable population of drug injectors in the South Bronx, I took a position as the medical director of Montefiore's drug abuse treatment program there. It felt as if we were witnessing the arrival of the plague, as tens and ultimately hundreds of patients became critically ill and quickly died from this disease whose course we could do very little to affect. Unlike the few of my earlier patients who had died of other causes, these hundreds of patients were virtually all in their early thirties, almost all of them within five years of my own age. They also included many women, some of whom I attended during pregnancy and the birth of their children. These young families seemed to represent some sort of terrible anomaly in the usual patterns of the life cycle, an anomaly in which death seemed to have crowded out life and cruelly and painfully destroyed the family, often over generations. These events were particularly compelling to me since the pregnancies of my wife and the birth of our two children occurred during those same years. I would sometimes share stories with the women about my wife's pregnancies, the birth and early development of our children, and then watch helplessly as these same women became ill and died, sometimes preceded by their infants. For the uninfected children, orphans of the epidemic, we began to see a steady stream of grandparents, themselves often weathered by life and their own struggles, coming forward to care for them after having watched their own children die of AIDS.

Surrounded unexpectedly by so much suffering and death, I was for a time oddly unaffected by it emotionally. I felt a strong need to be doing this type of work, although I could not have articulated what this need was about, and I found a great satisfaction in being with my patients. On a certain level, however, something was missing for me. After working in this environment for several years, one day I attended a concert at the Cathedral of Saint John the Divine in New York, near Columbia University. As I was leaving the church after the concert, I noticed an area along one of the side walls where many candles were burning on a small table, in front of a plain white scroll. On the scroll, in calligraphy, were the simple words, "In Memory of Those Who Have Died of AIDS." I stopped and stared at these words, and suddenly began to cry for all of the patients I had lost, whose faces I could see through the flickering light of the candles. I realized then that this work was about me and my life in ways that before then I could not have understood.

Elisabeth Kübler-Ross, who has been one of my most important teachers, has said, "You never cry for anyone else, you only cry for yourself." After my experience in the cathedral, I came to understand the meaning of this simple phrase. My own father died suddenly at the age of thirty-five when I was eighteen months old, either in an accident, or, more likely, by suicide. Because of the unusual circumstances of his death, this event and even the memory of his life quickly became family secrets that I was not permitted to discuss, so in effect I experienced a double loss. It was not until over thirty years later, when I was confronted with all the deaths of these young men and women, whom I could do little more to save than I could have saved my father, that I began to realize how I had never come to terms with this first and primal loss. This realization became a gift for me as I then began the work of grieving both for my father, which I had never done, and for all of my patients who had died. After going through this process, I found that I became better able to be with my patients in their pain, to support them without feeling the blind compulsion to rescue them from something from which there was no rescue, and to stay with them as they approached death without feeling that I had somehow betrayed their trust.

I have learned that the greatest gift that I can give to patients is to allow the awareness of my own pain and loss to deepen my solidarity with them as they face their illness and death. I am now convinced that it is the physician's fear of death, and his or her own unexpressed grief, that are the biggest impediments to true empathy, and result instead in pity, despair, revulsion, and the kind of numbing detachment that finds refuge in technological interventions and narrow medicalization.

I do not wish to indulge in the romanticization of death, nor in imagery of the nobility of dying young. I cannot sit and listen to a young father, as he bargains with God to be allowed to live long enough to dance with his eight-year-old daughter at her wedding, without feeling the crushing sense of injustice that permeates this disease. Indeed, it has been very gratifying to me, and a great relief as a clinician, to experience the dramatic advances in the medical care of people with AIDS over the past decade. These advocates have affected the clinical course of HIV infection in profound ways, and helped to convert a fulminant and rapidly fatal illness into a more chronic and treatable, albeit incurable, disease.

Nevertheless, I can recall with a kind of wistfulness the simple and unencumbered nature of my relationships with patients at an earlier time in the AIDS epidemic. Before our current therapies even existed, we coexisted with patients in the grim but complete knowledge that all that physicians could do was to be there, to bear witness, support, comfort, and accompany patients through their illness. What enabled, or even entitled, us to do this was simply our commitment not to abandon the patient and our experience in traveling this road with others before. I believe that this fundamental connectedness with the patient best characterizes the history of the physician-patient relationship over the centuries, until powerful forces over the past decades fragmented and distorted it, often in the name of specialization, expertise, or increasing technical sophistication. At times it has been disturbing to observe how the rapid introduction of medical interventions for AIDS—which, thankfully, have increased in number and complexity in recent years—has resulted in some ways in the tendency to over-medicalize the disease and lose sight of the important fundamental dynamics of life and death that still ultimately define it. I can only hope that the advent of the therapeutic era for AIDS, while eagerly awaited, does not have as a consequence the loss of empathy and the doctor's willingness simply to *be* with the patient, when instead one can find solace or distraction in pharmacological protocols and technological tinkering.

It has always seemed ironic to me how those who are confronted with dying are much more aware of living, and, in some cases, able to live in a much more immediate and intense way than those whose daily lives are dulled by the unconscious assumption that time is unlimited. Many patients have told me that having AIDS has allowed them, required them, to dispense with all of the superficial distractions and wasted energy that take up so much of our attention, and has led them to focus on what was truly important in their lives. One patient said to me, "AIDS is kind of like life, just speeded up." This anecdote describes well the accelerated process in which, over a period of weeks to months, people with AIDS may have to confront issues in the life cycle that normally would have taken years to decades: the deaths of peers and family, the loss of physical and sexual functioning, deterioration in cognition and memory, and the effects of aging on one's bodily appearance. Another patient once remarked, with a little bitterness but also some satisfaction, that AIDS had taught him who his friends really were. I remember yet another patient, a thirty-six-year-old late-stage AIDS patient, who had been using intravenous drugs for over twenty years and for the first time in his life had been able to stop. Confronting death had enabled him to undergo a spiritual conversion, stop using drugs, and reconcile with his family. Shortly before he died, he told me that he was thankful that he had finally learned what it was like to live in the world and experience life without being addicted to drugs, and was only sorry that he had to die in order to do so.

Ultimately, for both patients and physicians, AIDS is about letting go. Only through a process of letting go of fear and blame, and through an acceptance of our own vulnerability and powerlessness, can we become truly powerful. Only in this way can we, as the great labor organizer Mother Jones put it, "mourn the dead and fight like hell for the living," and go beyond the artificial distinctions between physician and patient to get on with the process of living and dying that all of us have to confront. Elisabeth Kübler-Ross has said, "Nobody gets out of this life alive." I think the avoidance of this reality often impedes physicians' ability to be effective in truly caring for their patients.

I often recall my last conversation with a patient in her early thirties whom I will call Maria. She had been ill for several years and seemed to be lingering on well past the point that anyone thought she would survive. She had a six-year-old daughter, whom I will call Lisa, who was being cared for by her aunt because Maria was already too weak to care for her. The aunt had agreed to raise the child after Maria's death, which helped relieve Maria's concerns but made her feel guilty that she was leaving her only child. In fact, it became clear that this was the only reason she had survived as long as she had. She felt that she needed to die, but couldn't. She was also saddened because Lisa was angry with her at times for not being able to play with her and not being there to put her to bed at night. Finally, when I asked Maria what she was most afraid of, she said that she was afraid that by dying she would be betraying her little girl, that this would somehow be a sign to the child that she didn't truly love her. After we talked about it, she came to realize that these two things were totally separate; she had to die, but nothing could ever take away the bond between her and her daughter. I encouraged Maria to talk to Lisa about this and to let her know that she would always love her and always be with her in her heart, no matter what happened. The next day Maria spent the whole day with her child, and said everything that she needed to say. Two days later, she died, peacefully, at home.

For me, the thirty-nine-year-old physician, with the eighteen-month-old boy inside who had never had that last conversation with his father, nothing could have been more gratifying.

QUESTIONS AND ACTIVITIES

1. As you read Dr. Peter Selwyn's reflections on his work with AIDS patients, what feelings and thoughts did you have? In what ways can you apply the concepts presented in this chapter to his experiences?

2. For the following professions, describe a death or grief situation commonly encountered: clergy (priests, rabbis, ministers), funeral home directors, coroners, military medical personnel in combat zones, and veterinarians. Identify several stresses that are unique to each profession. Interview individuals from one or more of these groups and inquire about strategies they have used to cope with the personal demands of their jobs.

3. How might the life stage of the professional affect his or her response to particular types of death? What developmental issues of young adulthood, middle age, or late adulthood might be relevant?

4. Examine your own potential for working with dying and/or grieving individuals. What characteristics and life experiences do you have that would enhance your ability to work with these populations? What traits and personal concerns might interfere with your effectiveness? Consider your motivations for doing this type of work and write a brief essay delineating your thoughts.

5. Explore your own susceptibility to burnout. What are your expectations regarding your future work? How do you currently handle stresses in your life? Prepare an inventory of your internal resources, support systems, and lifestyle patterns as you contemplate your future plans.

6. How much realistic and reliable information do you have regarding your career field? Conduct an interview with a professional currently doing the type of work you would like to do. Inquire about the rewards and satisfactions of the job as well as the stresses and frustrations. What does the individual do on a day-to-day basis? In what ways does he or she work with professionals from other fields? What training and experience does one need to be considered for similar positions?

GLOSSARY

Bereavement overload: occurs when a griever must deal with several deaths (or other losses) in close succession, without time to cope with the first death before being confronted with another.

Burnout: a syndrome of mental and physical exhaustion, low morale, cynicism, and despair related to job stress.

Codependent caregivers: caregivers who overcommit and consistently put needs of patients/clients before their own, thus neglecting their own personal relationships.

Compassion fatigue: a secondary traumatic stress reaction among therapists who work with traumatized clients.

Death saturation: the limits of personal tolerance for death-related work.

Internal resources: abilities, attitudes, values, beliefs, or techniques that help individuals handle difficult moments or periods of time.

Multidisciplinary approach: involves professionals from a variety of disciplines working together as a team to provide integrated optimum care for patients.

Support networks: individuals, groups, or organizations that offer emotional or material support.

Surrogate griever: one who grieves in the place of family members.

SUGGESTED READINGS

Bertman, S. L. (1991). *Facing death: Images, insights, and interventions.* New York: Hemisphere.

An educational process is described in which visual and literary images of illness and death are used to elicit personal feelings and reactions to dying and grief. The book is rich with concrete examples of artistic works that can be used in death education, as well as guidelines for their use. Responses of diverse audiences are included to show the value of the arts as evocative tools for people of all ages and backgrounds.

Givelber, F., & Simon, B. (1981). A death in the life of a therapist and its impact on the therapy. *Psychiatry, 44,* 141–149.

The authors discuss the work-related problems and opportunities that arise when therapists experience the death of a close family member. Givelber and Simon discuss how interactions with patients may be affected and how intended and unintended outcomes can occur as a result of telling patients about the loss.

Hilfiker, D. (1985). *Healing the wounds: A physician looks at his work.* New York: Pantheon Books.

Dr. Hilfiker gives an honest and moving account of his personal experiences as a physician. This book provides insight into the extraordinary pressures involved in practicing modern medicine.

Knott, J. E., Ribar, M. C., Duson, B. M., & King, M. R. (1989). *Thanatopics: Activities and exercises for confronting death.* Lexington, MA: Lexington Books.

A variety of structured exercises and organized discussion activities are presented that assist with examining one's feelings and attitudes toward death. Each activity includes a statement of the purpose, time, and materials required; specific procedures for leading the exercises; and suggestions for debriefing of participants.

Larson, D. G. (1993). *The helper's journey.* Champaign, IL: Research Press.

This book focuses on the challenges of working with grieving, seriously ill, or dying persons for both professionals and volunteers. The author identifies practical skills and ideas for more successful caregiving, increased personal growth, and effective stress management.

RESOURCES

Association for Death Education and Counseling
638 Prospect Avenue
Hartford, CT 06105-4295
(860) 586-7503

REFERENCES

Bennett, L. (1992). The experience of nurses working with hospitalized AIDS patients. *Australian Journal of Social Issues, 27,* 125-143.

Bennett, L. (1995). AIDS health care: Staff stress, loss and bereavement. In L. Sherr (Ed.), *Grief and AIDS* (pp. 87-102). Chichester, England: Wiley.

Bennett, L., & Kelaher, M. (1993). Variables contributing to experiences of grief in HIV/AIDS health care professionals. *Journal of Community Psychology, 21,* 210-217.

Benoliel, J. Q. (1988). Health care providers and dying patients: Critical issues in terminal care. *Omega, 18*(4), 341-363.

Bertman, S. L. (1991). *Facing death: Images, insights, and interventions.* New York: Hemisphere.

Bugen, L. A. (1980). Emotions: Their presence and impact upon the helping role. In E. S. Shneidman (Ed.), *Death: Current perspectives* (2nd ed., pp. 241-251). Palo Alto, CA: Mayfield.

Cerney, M. S. (1995). Treating the "heroic" treaters. In C. R. Figley (Ed.), *Compassion fatigue* (pp. 131-149). New York: Brunner/Mazel.

Claus, K. E., & Bailey, J. T. (Eds.). (1980). *Living with stress and promoting well-being: A handbook for nurses.* St. Louis: C. V. Mosby.

Cook, A. S., & Dworkin, D. S. (1992). *Helping the bereaved: Therapeutic interventions for children, adolescents, and adults.* New York: Basic Books.

Dick, L. C. (1996). Impact on law enforcement and EMS personnel. In K. J. Doka (Ed.), *Living with grief after sudden loss* (pp. 173-184). Washington, DC: Hospice Foundation of America.

Dickinson, G. E. (1988). Death education for physicians. *Journal of Medical Education, 63,* 412.

Dickinson, G. E., Sumner, E. D., & Frederick, L. M. (1992). Death education in selected health professions. *Death Studies, 16,* 281-289.

Doyle, D. (1991). Palliative care education and training in the United Kingdom: A review. *Death Studies, 15,* 95-103.

Durand, R. P., Dickinson, G. E., Sumner, E. D., & Lancaster, C. J. (1990). Family physicians' attitudes toward death and the terminally ill patient. *Family Practice Research Journal, 9,* 123-129.

Field, D., & Howell, K. (1986). Medical students' self-reported worries about aspects about death and dying. *Death Studies, 10,* 147-154.

Figley, C. R. (1995). *Compassion fatigue.* New York: Brunner/Mazel.

Friedman, G. R., Franciosi, R. A., & Drake, R. M. (1979). The effects of observed sudden infant death syndrome (SIDS) on hospital staff. *Pediatrics, 64,* 538-540.

Gibbs, M. S., Drummond, J., & Lachenmeyer, J. R. (1993). Effects of disasters on emergency workers: A review, with implications for training and postdisaster interventions. In R. D. Allen (Ed.), *Handbook of post-disaster interventions* (pp. 189–212). Corte Madera, CA: Select Press.

Gillman, R. (1991). From resistances to rewards: Social workers' experiences and attitudes toward AIDS. *Families in Society: The Journal of Contemporary Human Services, 72*(10), 593–601.

Gray-Toft, P. A., & Anderson, J. G. (1986). Sources of stress in nursing terminal patients in a hospice. *Omega, 17*(1), 27–39.

Hay, D., & Oken, D. (1977). The psychological stresses of intensive care unit nursing. In R. H. Moos (Ed.), *Coping with physical illness* (pp. 381–396). New York: Plenum Press.

Hinds, P., Fairclough, D., Dobos, C., Greer, R., Herring, P., Mayhall, J., Arheart, K., Day, L., & McAulay, L. (1990). Development and testing of the stressor scale for pediatric oncology nurses. *Cancer Nursing, 13,* 354–360.

Hinds, P. S., Puckett, P., Donohoe, M., Milligan, M., Payne, K., Phipps, S., Davis, S., & Martin, G. A. (1994). The impact of a grief workshop for pediatric oncology nurses on their grief and perceived stress. *Journal of Pediatric Nursing, 9*(6), 388–397.

Ingraham, L. I. (1988, October). *Grief leadership in work groups.* Paper presented at the Fourth Annual Conference on Military Medicine, Uniformed Services University of the Health Sciences, Bethesda, MD.

Kirchberg, M., & Neimeyer, R. A. (1991). Reactions of beginning counselors to situations involving death and dying. *Death Studies, 15,* 603–610.

Kübler-Ross, E. (1975). Death as part of my own personal experience. In E. Kübler-Ross (Ed.), *Death: The final stage of growth* (pp. 119–126). Englewood Cliffs, NJ: Prentice-Hall.

Larson, D. G. (1993). *The helper's journey.* Champaign, IL: Research Press.

Lattanzi, M. E. (1983). Learning and caring: Education and training concerns. In C. A. Corr & D. M. Corr (Eds.), *Hospice care: Principles and practice* (pp. 223–236). New York: Springer.

Lerea, E. L., & LiMauro, B. F. (1982). Grief among healthcare workers: A comparative study. *Journal of Gerontology, 37*(5), 604–608.

Marshall, R. E., & Kasman, C. (1980). Burnout in the neonatal intensive care unit. *Pediatrics, 65*(6), 1161–1165.

Maslach, C. (1982). *Burnout: The cost of caring.* Englewood Cliffs, NJ: Prentice-Hall.

McCarroll, J. E., Ursano, R. J., Fullerton, C. S., & Wright, K. M. (1992). Community consultation following a major air disaster. *Journal of Community Psychology, 20,* 271–275.

McCarroll, J. E., Ursano, R. J., Wright, K. M., & Fullerton, C. S. (1993). Handling bodies after violent death: Strategies for coping. *American Journal of Orthopsychiatry, 63*(2), 209–214.

McClain, M., & Mandell, F. (1994). Sudden infant death syndrome: The nurse counselor's response to bereavement counseling. *Journal of Community Health Nursing, 11*(3), 177–186.

McNamara, B., Waddell, C., & Colvin, M. (1995). Threats to the good death: The cultural context of stress and coping among hospice nurses. *Sociology of Health and Illness, 17*(2), 222–244.

Mermann, A. C., Gunn, D. B., & Dickinson, G. E. (1991). Learning to care for the dying: A survey of medical schools and a model course. *Academic Medicine, 66,* 35–38.

Moser, D. H., & Krikorian, D. A. (1982). *Nursing Leadership, 5*(4), 9–17.

Neimeyer, G. J., Behnke, M., & Reiss, J. (1983). Constructs and coping: Physicians' responses to patient death. *Death Education, 7,* 245–264.

Paradis, L. F. (Ed.). (1987). Stress and burnout among providers caring for the terminally ill and their families. *The Hospice Journal* (special issue) *3*, 1–276.

Pattison, E. M. (1977). *The experience of dying.* Englewood Cliffs, NJ: Prentice-Hall.

Pearlin, L. I., & Schooler, C. (1978). The structure of coping. *Journal of Health and Social Behavior, 19*, 2–21.

Perez, E. L., Gosselin, J. Y., & Gagnon, A. (1980). Education on death and dying: A survey of Canadian medical schools. *Journal of Medical Education, 55*, 788–789.

Pines, A. M., Aronson, E., & Kafry, D. (1981). *Burnout: From tedium to personal growth.* New York: Free Press.

Plante, A., & Bouchard, L. (1995). Occupational stress, burnout, and professional support in nurses working with dying patients. *Omega, 32*(2), 93–109.

Rando, T. A. (1984). *Grief, dying, and death: Clinical interventions for caregivers.* Champaign, IL: Research Press.

Richardson, W. C. (1992). Educating leaders who can resolve the health-care crisis. *The Chronicle of Higher Education,* June 1, B-1.

Riordan, R. J., & Saltzer, S. K. (1992). Burnout prevention among health care providers working with the terminally ill: A literature review. *Omega, 25*(1), 17–24.

Rolland, J. (1994). Working with illness: Clinicians' personal and interface issues. *Family Systems Medicine, 12*(2), 149–169.

Schotzinger, K., & Best, E. (1987). Closure and the cadaver experience: A memorial service for deeded bodies. *Omega, 18*, 217–227.

Seeland, I. B. (1988). Death: A natural process. In R. DeBellis, E. R. Marcus, A. H. Kutscher, S. C. Klagsbrun, I. B. Seeland, & D. W. Preven (Eds.), *Thanatology curriculum—Medicine* (pp. 127–132). New York: Haworth.

Sharkey, F. (1982). *A parting gift.* New York: St. Martin's Press.

Small, M., Engler, A. J., & Rushton, C. H. (1991). Saying goodbye in the intensive care unit: Helping caregivers grieve. *Pediatric Nursing, 17*(1), 103–105.

Stephenson, J. S. (1981). The family therapist and death: A profile. *Family Relations, 30*, 459–462.

Sutterley, D. C. (1982). Stress and health: A survey of self-regulation modalities. In D. C. Donnelly & G. F. Donnelly (Eds.), *Coping with stress: A nursing perspective* (pp. 173–194). Rockville, MD: Aspen Systems.

Swanson, T. R., & Swanson, M. J. (1977). Acute uncertainty: The intensive care unit. In E. M. Pattison (Ed.), *The experience of dying* (pp. 245–251). Englewood Cliffs, NJ: Prentice-Hall.

Terry, M. L., Bivens, A. J., & Neimeyer, R. A. (1996). Comfort and empathy of experienced counselors in client situations involving death and loss. *Omega, 32*(4), 269–285.

Ursano, R. J., & McCarroll, J. E. (1990). The nature of a traumatic stressor: Handling dead bodies. *Journal of Nervous and Mental Disease, 178*, 396–398.

Vachon, M. L. S. (1986). Myths and realities in palliative/hospice care. *The Hospice Journal, 2*(1), 63–79.

William, J. L. (1992). Don't discuss it: Reconciling illness, dying, and death in a medical school anatomy laboratory. *Family Systems Medicine, 10*, 65–78.

Wolfelt, A. D. (1991). Exploring the topic of codependency in bereavement caregiving. *Forum Newsletter, Association for Death Education and Counseling, 15*(6), 7–8.

Yancik, R. (1984). Sources of work stress for hospice staff. *Journal of Psychosocial Oncology, 2*(1), 21–31.

Zinner, E. S. (1992). Setting standards: Certification efforts and considerations in the field of death and dying. *Death Studies, 16*, 67–77.

PHOTO CREDITS

SUBJECT INDEX

Author Index